Brassroots Democracy

Benjamin Barson

BRASSROOTS DEMOCRACY

Maroon Ecologies
and the Jazz Commons

Wesleyan University Press   Middletown, Connecticut

Wesleyan University Press
Middletown CT 06459
www.wesleyan.edu/wespress
© 2024 Benjamin Barson
All rights reserved
Manufactured in the United States of America
Designed by Mindy Basinger Hill / Typeset in Minion Pro

Library of Congress Cataloging-in-Publication Data

Names: Barson, Benjamin, author.

Title: Brassroots democracy : maroon ecologies and the jazz commons / Benjamin Barson.

Description: [First.] | Middletown, Connecticut : Wesleyan University Press, 2024. | Series: Music/culture | Includes bibliographical references and index. | Summary: "The author delivers new understandings of jazz history through a fine-grained social history of African American musicians, from the Civil War until the onset of Jim Crow, placing New Orleans in a global context and exploring Black Atlantic critiques of slavery, racism, and capitalism" —Provided by publisher.

Identifiers: LCCN 2024000523 (print) | LCCN 2024000524 (ebook) | ISBN 9780819501127 (cloth) | ISBN 9780819501141 (trade paperback) | ISBN 9780819501134 (ebook)

Subjects: LCSH: African Americans—Music—History and criticism. | African American musicians—Social conditions. | Jazz—Louisiana—New Orleans—To 1921—History and criticism. | Brass bands—Louisiana—New Orleans—History. | Desdunes, Rodolphe Lucien. | Desdunes, Daniel, approximately 1870–1929. | Civil rights movements—United States—History—19th century. | Haitians—United States.

Classification: LCC ML3479 .B39 2024 (print) | LCC ML3479 (ebook) | DDC 780.89/96073076335—dc23/eng/20240326

LC record available at https://lccn.loc.gov/2024000523
LC ebook record available at https://lccn.loc.gov/2024000524

5   4   3   2   1

The Publisher gratefully acknowledges the AMS 75 PAYS Fund of the American Musicological Society, supported in part by the National Endowment for the Humanities and the Andrew W. Mellon Foundation.

Author and publisher gratefully acknowledge the support of the Roland Jackson Memorial Grant of the American Musicological Society.

FOR GIZELXANATH RODRÍGUEZ

CONTENTS

Acknowledgments ix

INTRODUCTION A Long Song from Haiti 1

ONE The Common Wind's Second Gale:
The Desdunes Family 35

TWO Mamie Desdunes in the Neo-Plantation:
Legacies of Black Feminism among Storyville's Blues People 81

THREE La Frontera Sónica: Mexican Revolutions in Borderlands Jazz 118

FOUR Sowing Freedom: Abolitionist Agroecology in Afro-Louisiana 170

FIVE Black Reconstruction and Brassroots Democracy:
Sonic Assembly in the Post–Civil War South 211

SIX Black Unions and the Blues:
Dockworkers' Activism and New Orleans Jazz 238

CONCLUSION Telegrams from the Spiritual Plane 273

Notes 283

Bibliography 331

Index 391

ACKNOWLEDGMENTS

Acknowledgments can mean many things. It is hard to know where, with whom, or how to begin. I want to start by expressing my deep gratitude to my musical mentors who welcomed me into their world and shared with me information that is truly sacred. These include the late Fred Ho, Geri Allen, Salim Washington, Nicole Mitchell, and Radam Schwartz. Your generosity of spirit has deepened my understanding of the artistry, culture, and heritage of this music.

This book is the product of fourteen years of thinking, research, music making, and activism, and it is a pleasure, at long last, to thank all those who inspired it in print. Matt Sakakeeny gave me detailed feedback on a number of drafts, and my gratitude to him will probably never be sufficient. Bruce Boyd Raeburn helped in significant ways. Sherrie Tucker's support—and the whole team at Wesleyan, including Suzanna Tamminen—has been indispensable. Thank you to the anonymous peer reviewers for your supportive and honest feedback, and to Ann Brash and Natalie Jones for your patient, thorough, and herculean editorial assistance. George Lipsitz provided invaluable feedback on an early draft and helped me check myself. Lynn Abbott at the Hogan Jazz Archive answered innumerable inquires and his encyclopedic knowledge was essential. The historian Mary Gehman's detailed history on New Orleans's free people of color and their journeys to Mexico has been revelatory, and I thank her for her generosity. Marcus Rediker, who reminded me that any history where working people cannot recognize themselves is not good history, has been a cornerstone mentor and unyielding source of ideas and inspiration. This project would not exist without Michael Heller, who read more drafts than I would like to count. Thank you to Fumi Okiji, Cisco Bradley, and Max Homen for sharing then-unpublished work. José Castañeda, Charles Kinzer, and Dan Vernhettes all shared their research with me generously. John K. Bardes and Mimi Sheller both read early versions of this work and expanded my thinking considerably. Marleen Julien and Henry Stoll assisted with vital and complex translations of Haitian Creole. Dr. Mark A. Johnson shared invaluable research and feedback, as did Cisco Bradley and Mark Lomanno. Rebecca Barrett-Fox has been a dedicated collaborator and co-conspirator on this project, and a patient editor. An essential reader was Chris Batterman Cháirez, whose commitment to this work was unwavering. Robin D. G. Kelley's reservoir of comraderly support buoyed my ship. Mark Roudané deserves a special thank you for reading a draft and living the legacy of his ancestor. The wisdom and embodied knowledge of percussionist Irán Farías Saínz of Santiago de Cuba has been essential. A deep and resonant thank you goes out to Laurent Dubois, Tejasvi Nagaraja, Erin O'Keefe, Carla Nappi, Zoltan Vaci, Varshini Narayanan, Andrew Brown, Emma Campbell, Eli Namay, Jason Chang, Alexis Dudden, Peter Rachleff, Jeffrey O. G. Ogbar, Jesse Olsavsky, Olivia Bloechl, Christina Heatherton, Michele Reid-Vazquez, Michell Chresfield, Diane Fujino, Steven Moon, Woody Steinken, Danielle Maggio, Lee Caplan, Zack Furness, Luke Leavitt, Devan Carpenter, and all others who provided crucial feedback.

I received support from the Africana Studies and Research Center and the Society for the Humanities at Cornell University, the Humanities Center at the University of Pittsburgh, the Tinker Foundation, the Opportunity Fund, and Tulane University's Global South Fellowship. The Fulbright-Garcia Robles provided support that grounded my scholarship in Mexico. So, too, has the IIC-Museo de UABC and the professors there, especially Lorenia Urbalejo, Areli Veloz, David Bautista Toledo, Christian Fernandez, and its dedicated librarian María Luisa Rivera. Thank you to Patricia García and Oscar Xavier Martínez, both doing amazing work in Oaxaca at the intersections of music, jazz, and indigeneity.

To my parents, Michael and Jean, who have never lost interest in hearing of, and grounding, my journeys into the unknown. To my grandma Beverly, who has given me so much, and my aunts Sherry and Shauna, who have been so supportive. To my *suegros*, Jesus and Rosa, for their engaged interest in a subject even when its contours are not yet clear. To my brothers, Dan and Adam, for their spirit and reminding me of the importance of community and joy. To my big sister, Florence Houn.

To my comrades in music and the movement, especially Nejma Nefertiti, Iván Martínez, Quincy Saul, Kanya D'Almeida, Mario Luna, Margaret Cerullo, Dana Ventriglia and Lee Grice, Nathy Carrillo, Magdalena Gómez and Jim Lescault, Peggy Choy, Ruth Margraff, Charlotte Hill O'Neal, Azize Aslan, Adam Cooper-Terán, Kempis Songster, Daro Behroozi, Deb and Saed Engel-DiMauro, DeeDee Halleck, Joel Kovel, Divad Durant, and Abraham Mwaura. I hope this book can animate our freedom dreams.

This volume demanded unwavering faith and it is dedicated to my partner and wife, Gizelxanath Rodríguez, as you have been that beacon. Te quiero.

Brassroots Democracy

INTRODUCTION
A Long Song from Haiti

> The blues has grown, but the country has not
> The blues remembers everything the country forgot.
> *Gil Scott-Heron, "Bicentennial Blues"*

> In all living things is seed.
> *Nicole Mitchell and Lisa E. Harris, "Biotic Seed"*

In writing this book, I have been haunted by images of "White Leaguers" and Ku Klux Klan members attacking meetings of freedpeople in the post–Civil War US South. Haunted not by phantoms but because, as Karl Marx wrote, "the tradition of all dead generations weighs like a nightmare on the brains of the living," and present-day white nationalism rhymes all too strongly with the nineteenth-century paramilitary movements that inform this study of Louisianan jazz history.[1] Extrajudicial executions of Black Americans, like those of George Floyd and Breonna Taylor, starkly reveal that the specter of plantation hierarchy still orders American society.[2] Today, from professional athletes to jazz musicians, Black cultural workers have increasingly defined their work as a site of political struggle, reenvisioned, in the words of Shona Jackson, as a space where "resistance is a kind of Black becoming."[3] Black music has historically borne witness to the cruelty of white racial violence and created a space for transcendence. Terence Blanchard, writing about Marvin Gaye's "What's Going On," attests: "Many people listen to the groove and the melody of this song, without really hearing the words. . . . Many well-meaning people have heard only the melody of our plight, without knowing what the song means for us."

> Sure, they can hum it back with the same phrasing, can mimic all the inflections in Marvin's voice, enough to make themselves and us think they know

the song as well as we do. They can groove to the beat the same way we would, can know the exact timing of each phrase, to the point where it seems they must get it. But when it comes to the words, it's like we're singing in two different languages. The pain we sing of is a lingering, never-going-away pain. For the well-intentioned co-conspirator, it's a temporary pinprick—just enough discomfort to provide a false sense of assimilation and understanding.[4]

For Blanchard, protest is something beyond language; it is an affect that animates musical decisions, a grammar of interaction within and against the white supremacist reality. Processing and challenging oppression is as fundamental to Black music as notes and chords. It is an immanent key that resonates through musical expression across era and locale, an imperative resulting from a "never-going-away pain." Yet this very music often produces a near-sacred sense of joy, whose affirmation of life transforms its practitioners and its audience. As New Orleans activist and author Kalamu ya Salaam explains, "Even in the midst of grieving over the death of a loved one, a family member, we dance our defiance and celebrate the joy of life."[5] The composite of lament and celebration reflects a broader cultural strategy that traces back at least to the post–Civil War era. In Southern cities, in a sea of antagonist whites and a nascent Ku Klux Klan, African Americans unveiled daily displays of unique fashion, dance, and manners of speech, channeling what Tera Hunter calls "the joy of freedom."[6]

Within writings about jazz, these associations with Black music and Black social memory have a long, contested history. Jazz musicians themselves, however, have long theorized their work as political. In his autobiography, New Orleans clarinetist Sidney Bechet depicted his grandfather Omar as a maroon who had withstood beatings, torture, and the separation of his loved ones by his so-called master. Likely speaking in metaphor—Omar Bechet was a free person of color who worked as a shoemaker—Bechet nonetheless tapped into a transatlantic maroon historiography to situate anti-Black violence as foundational to modernity. Not unlike Blanchard, Bechet did so to think through an alternative history of, and a specific impetus for, jazz: "No one had to explain notes or rhythm or feeling to him. All the things that was happening to him outside, they had to get there to be measured—there inside him where the music was."[7]

These connections are contested not only because of their content but because of their context. The ideological stakes of jazz are high precisely because the music's ability to "measure" this pain has the potential to demystify the centrality of Black exploitation to wealth stockpiles within the United States and the foundation of capitalism at large. The late saxophonist-composer Fred Ho considered jazz to be "the revolutionary music of the twentieth century—not just for America, but for the planet as well. It is the music that embodies and expresses the contradiction of the century."⁸ Building on this insight, it can be posited that this contradiction mirrors the interplay of emancipatory joy and historic pain: African Americans in the aftermath of the Civil War developed an expansive notion of freedom rooted in a cooperative ideal, yet plantation capitalism contorted their labor and their bodies against those same freedom dreams. The sociomusical engagements called for by Ho and Blanchard unmask the unprocessed participation in Black suffering, oppression, and exploitation that lie at the heart of this country's wealth. *Brassroots Democracy* engages these histories by providing a fine-grained, empirically based investigation of Black working-class Louisianans and their counter-plantation Afro-Caribbean comrades. What arises most powerfully in the stories that follow are the alternative visions of freedom and social relations produced by Louisiana's Black musicians themselves.

BRASSROOTS DEMOCRACY'S BIRTH IN NEW ORLEANS

New Orleans and Black Louisiana prefigured a radical, democratic tradition that confronted plantation capitalism, white nationalism, and patriarchy in meaningful and sometimes breathtaking ways. New Orleans's preeminence as a center for Black activism, a bellwether for civil rights legislation, and home of a powerful mixed-race union movement helped make it a Black musical mecca and the "birthplace" of jazz. Not surprisingly, these spheres orbited in shared harmony. Music was not only politics by other means; it was produced by the same historical circumstances and creative resistance that made Louisiana's post–Civil War political environment so explosive.

The connection between music and politics was not merely aesthetic or metaphorical but concrete and material. Connections between the grassroots and what I call the *brassroots*—community-led brass bands, populated by plantation laborers, urban activists, and Union army veterans that became an expression of Black cultural and political power in the postwar years—made New Orleans a crucible of radicalism. Even before the Fourteenth Amendment granted Black male suffrage in 1866, community-led bands accompanied Black activists and recently emancipated people at mass meetings in New Orleans that numbered in the thousands. In these spaces, Black candidates were nominated to run for office even though it was not yet possible; Black voters were registered to rolls even though they could not yet vote; communally harvested lands were protected, parceled, and negotiated without legal claim; and common pools of resources, managed through credit unions, were generated and shared.⁹ Whether at Economy Hall, the Mechanics' Institute, or the parades in the streets of New Orleans, these spaces—alternatives to capitalism called *the commons*—effectively created a parallel state and civil society to the white apartheid regime still in power despite the abolition of slavery. These activists fulfilled an essential criterion for a successful revolutionary movement whose major task, as Eqbal Ahmad notes, is "not to outfight but to outadminister the government."[10]

The connections were not incidental. In 1867, the Black-owned *New Orleans Tribune* described a truly "new and glorious era in our history" ushered in by a parade with some "fifteen thousand Chinese lanterns," "banners and flags flying to the breeze," and "drums, fifes, and brass bands [that] were heard from all sides." These were political spaces as much as musical and celebratory ones, and slogans were borne, and born, on these streets: "Eight Hours a Day's Work," "No Contract System," "Free Press," "We Know Our Friends," and "Free School Open for All" adorned banners.[11] New forms of political speech reflected the broad, multiclass character of parishioners. Their sophisticated political lexicon, diverse geographic backgrounds, and revulsion to the postwar contract system—which reproduced slavery-like social relations on former plantations—became expressed in a participatory public art form.[12] This democratic revolution in Louisiana—what W. E. B. Du Bois named "Black Reconstruction," emphasizing its leadership in the Black working class[13]—fused with a distinctive brass band performance culture, giving rise to a new aural space where activists could "rehearse identities, stances, and social relations not yet permissible in politics."[14] I call this simultaneous and syncretic expansion of public and musical spheres *brassroots democracy*, and its utopian soundscape is the compass guiding this book's journey. *Brassroots Democracy: Maroon Ecologies and the Jazz Commons* traces the Black Atlantic struggles that informed this practice of music-as-world-making, from the Haitian Revolution through Reconstruction to the jazz revolution, highlighting the modalities by which the New Orleans brass bands expressed the venerable connection between celebration, abolition, and a sociosonic commons. This unique jazz commons reverberated through what I delineate, echoing Justin Hosbey and J. T. Roane, as maroon ecologies—nurtured in the sanctuaries of swamps and forests, of mountains and at sea, "where the enslaved formed a fleeting Black commons, [and] whereby they used their unique knowledge of the landscapes and waterscapes to extend a fugitive and transient freedom."[15] These maroon ecologies, the improvised socialities of plantation refugees that fostered Afro-Indigenous alliance, were vibrant cradles of cultural creation, and not only due to their elusive and multinational characteristics. Édouard Glissant reminds us how "historical marronage intensified over time to exert a creative marronage, whose numerous forms of expression began to form the basis for a continuity."

Glissant points beyond metaphor. An 1837 police report, uncovered by historian John Bardes, depicts a raid on a musical ceremony in the back swamps outside of New Orleans. Sixty-one enslaved and free Black people were arrested. Many instruments were confiscated—"clarinets," "trombones," and "drums."[16] In brass band performance, the subaltern voices of the plantation Americas echoed a polyphonic reminder of unity, an arpeggiated chain of resistance and refusal. From Bechet's allegory to Glissant's theorization, from this arrest report to the 1867 parades: the jazz commons were not merely a product of maroon ecologies; they also nurtured and expanded them, even when the land practices that informed their rebel epistemologies were suppressed or destroyed.

Brassroots democracy thus opens a window into the breadth and depth of brass band improvisation—its links to this commoning practice. Although the thick, textured polyphony of New Orleans's collective improvisation tradition did not cohere until the turn of the twentieth century, other improvisational traditions were documented during the Haitian Revolution, observed among Afro-Louisianan militias, and developed in relation to the needs of African American freedpeople in the postwar arena.[17] In each of these contexts, improvisation encouraged new generations to make anew the wisdom of old. According to Sidney Bechet, the culture of post–Civil War plantation migrants in New Orleans brought with them new songs transformed by abolition:

> It was years they'd been singing that ["Go Down Moses"]. And suddenly there was a different way of singing it. You could feel a new way of happiness in the lines. All that waiting, all that time when that song was far-off music, suffering music; and all at once it was there, it had arrived. It was joy music now. It was Free Day . . . Emancipation. And New Orleans just bust wide open. A real time was had. They heard the music, and the music told them about it. They heard that music from bands marching up and down the streets and they knew what music it was. . . . That music, it wasn't spirituals or blues or ragtime, but everything all at once, each one putting something over on the other. . . . Some of those people didn't even know what Emancipation was; they just know there was a hell of a parade going on, a whole lot of laughing and singing, a whole lot of music being happier than the music had ever been before.[18]

Bechet's account relates more to an imaginary of the moment than a historical account, as the evolution of brass band improvisation unfolded over several decades. Nonetheless, Civil War diaries and newspapers corroborate that Black celebration was a powerful catalyst for the emergence of new intercultural expression, and music often accompanied the moment of jubilee and the Reconstruction organizing that followed.[19] In Alexandria, for instance, one conservative newspaper complained that "long before day light [sic]" whites were awoken by "the steady tramp of the dark column of the 'Radical Republican Clubs'" whose Black activists, "the well-dressed, ragged, bare-footed all," were united in "marching to the music of the . . . promised land."[20]

Bechet, then, evocatively describes the way brass bands developed a new mode of musical production over the *longue durée* of Reconstruction into Jim Crow: proactively remixing liberatory lineages by performing "everything at once." *Brassroots Democracy* will explore just what that "everything" entailed.[21] Hybrid musical forms converged with rural Louisianan migrants, a long-established cadre of Creole of color activists with connections to Haiti, and a Black Civil War sonic culture. Brass bands eventually became the preferred vehicle for a new, jubilant interculture. New Orleans was home to deeply rooted patterns of Afro-Atlantic creolization, and this cultural elasticity proved useful to cohere the cross-class and multilingual social revolution that erupted in the city and its environs. Projecting an infectious optimism, brass bands facilitated a new imaginary wherein rural and urban freedpeople enacted and defended an emergent social order through organized displays of enthusiasm, solidarity, and social commentary. Afro-Louisianan cultural workers thus tapped into the creative celebration of the present in a manner both intersubjective and: multisensorial, with a militant fidelity to their space and moment.[22] They demonstrated that their answer to the Black suffering provoked by plantation slavery was a synchronized joy that nurtured the roots of their community's collective militancy. This was, in the words of James H. Cone, a "unity music": it united "the joy and suffering, the love and the hate, the hope and the despair of black people; and it moves the people toward the direction of total liberation . . . affirm[ing] that black being is only possible in a communal context."[23]

Brassroots Democracy illuminates how the political philosophies, communal epistemologies, and improvisations of Reconstruction and early jazz were derived from these disparate traditions. While focusing on African American sonic practices as both archives of anti-Black violence and joyful repositories generative of democratic cultural norms, this book also explores the varied Black Atlantic cultures in Louisiana. Following authors including Rebecca Scott, Shannon Dawdy, and Thomas Fiehrer, I situate New Orleans as intimately connected to a larger Caribbean world, not only by the economies of enslavement but also by patterns of cultural exchange.[24] The music united joy with communal militancy as well as the varied sectors of Afro-Louisianans with distinct family origins—which ranged from Haiti and Cuba to Virginia and Mississippi, from the maroon communities of Louisiana's cypress swamps to Black refugee communities in the Mexican borderlands.

A wave of insightful scholarship, such as that advanced by Gerald Horne, Matt Sakakeeny, Dalton Anthony Jones, Sherrie Tucker, and Charles Hersch, has brought a critical lens to racial and class politics in the era of early jazz.²⁵ When read in dialogue with the scholarship that details the evolution of Jim Crow racial apartheid in New Orleans by scholars like Rebecca Scott and Clyde Woods, this work paints a nuanced portrait of the early twentieth century in the city, in which transnational identities and grassroots mobilizations are intertwined within the structural forces of white supremacy and New South capitalism.²⁶

Yet, despite the considerable number of critical studies that explore this period, discourses surrounding Black radical traditions and jazz tend to bypass this era, thereby misleadingly suggesting that an explicit racial politics begins with bebop and continues on in specific communities understood as avant-garde or militant. Historically, this understanding of the early jazz era as supposedly apolitical originates from the contentious culture wars that surrounded bebop's emergence. One facet of this was the "moldy fig" Dixieland revival led by white critics and historians, which projected a sanitized, nonmilitant depiction of genuine African American cultural practices rooted in a selective misrepresentation of the era. A broad swath of contemporary jazz studies continues their legacy, and resists acknowledging the explicit political resistance practiced by jazz communities before the bebop era. The Martinican philosopher Frantz Fanon vividly critiqued this historical imagination, but in doing so he also reproduced certain aspects of it. "It is the colonialists who become the defenders of the native style.... In their eyes jazz should only be the despairing, broken-down nostalgia of an old Negro who is trapped between five glasses of whiskey," he wrote about the white promoters of early jazz. "It is not utopian to suppose that in fifty years' time the type of jazz howl hiccupped by a poor misfortunate Negro will be upheld only by the whites who believe in it as an expression of negritude, and who are faithful to this arrested image."²⁷

Fanon's critique holds striking resonance even today, as the broader image of New Orleans early jazz remains confined to these narrow views, overshadowing the militant spirit and activism of the musicians of that period. Our task, now, is to unshackle this rich musical heritage from the arrested images that have confined it for far too long, rediscovering and celebrating the bold sociomusical framework crafted by the Black and Afro-Creole musicians who fostered a thriving brassroots democracy in turn-of-the-century New Orleans.

In order to break the power of this myth, this book follows Fumi Okiji's study of jazz's "heterophonic chorus in revolution," in which she encourages jazz historians to expand their sense of "both the loci of jazz work and the kinds of interaction that take place there."²⁸ Answering both Okiji's call and the vibrant transnational networks of New Orleans's Black Atlantic musicians, this book "follows the people" (and not only their music).[29] I do this through dissonant readings of state archives—police records, WPA interviews, Freedmen's Bureau reports, plantation invoices—as well as those generated by a Black counterpublic, including Black newspapers, SAPC meeting notes, and musicians' interviews—in order to trace the varied ideologies and soundscapes that animated brassroots democracy's freedom dreams. One takeaway is that musicians were hybrid actors with a variety of commitments to Black social life; the line demarcating longshoreman, volunteer firefighter, civil rights activist, and cornetist was thin or nonexistent. Clarinetist Willie Parker was involved in the union movement; James Humphrey and Kid Ory were urban farmers; Louis Tio was born in a an Afro-Creole agricultural commune in Mexico; Joe Oliver, Louis Armstrong, and George Lewis worked on the docks.[30] Understanding these experiences as tied to the development of early jazz is crucial to hear the worlds the music created. Pianist Vijay Iyer notes that jazz's "story dwells not just in one solo at a time, but also in a single note, and equally in an entire lifetime of improvisations . . . the story is revealed not as a simple linear narrative, but as a fractured, exploded one."[31] By sounding their freedom dreams, dreams that encapsulated a transnational flow of overlapping emancipatory narratives, the joy music described by Sidney Bechet prefigured a counter-plantation revolution throughout Louisiana and the South at large. While Reconstruction was ultimately repressed, its abolitionist imaginaries nonetheless threaded through the "birth" of early jazz. Its lexicon of rhythms, expressions of meter and groove, interplay of form and freedom, and genre of truth-telling to power connected the age of revolution in the Caribbean to Afro-Louisiana.

BRASSROOTS DEMOCRACY'S CONCEPTION IN THE CARIBBEAN AND HAITI

I came to Haitian music through New Orleans.
Leyla McCalla[32]

Nineteenth-century Louisiana's link to Caribbean markets and migration patterns was structured by its integration into a regional sugar plantation system, which required massive outlays of capital and a sophisticated industrial infrastructure that led to unimaginable violence and a high rate of mortality for enslaved people.[33] Sugar-producing regions shared planters, enslaved people, specific patterns of work and overwork, as well as a trans-Caribbean revolutionary culture marked by antislavery and anti-imperialist ideas.

A chance recording in Tulane University's Hogan Jazz Archive helps reveal the scale and scope of this trans-Caribbean infrastructure of feeling in Louisiana. In 1958, Alice Zeno (1864–1960), the mother of clarinetist George Lewis, was interviewed by jazz historian Bill Russell. Hopeful that Zeno would speak of her Senegambian ancestry, Russell prods her to sing a "song from Africa." When Zeno finally shares a song learned from her grandmother, she sung not in Senegambian Wolof but in Haitian Creole:

All Haitians, for more than eleven years
Have suffered the greatest misery
Food was expensive, there was no money
Hunger had already killed a lot of mothers.

During Sabbath
Finally, let's bless the Lord,
They made Faustin leave by the order of Renard

God in the sky, to end to the injustice
Of these men, filled with crime and malice
Who wanted the victorious general
Geffrard to arrive to put an end to our sorrows

Down with the Cross of Honor
Down with the Governor
He took down the Crown of Iron,
Without having anyone killed.[34]

When asked what the song was about, Zeno explained, "Well, it was when they had the revolution in Haiti . . . and they had President Geffrard, and he had to help them out, because they were starving, starving, the mothers were starving."[35] Fabre Geffrard was president of Haiti from 1859 until 1867, suggesting the song circulated in Louisiana during the Civil War and Reconstruction eras. The song's description of a bloodless transfer of power stood in stark contrast to the carnage of the Civil War.[36] Yet its story of political change was intelligible to Alice Zeno's grandmother and her peers, not to mention its blend of French and Haitian Creole. Such correlations provoke intriguing questions, ones unfortunately overlooked by Zeno's interviewers. Why were Haitian songs about contemporary events circulating in New Orleans in the 1860s? How did Afro-Louisianans, at the forefront of battles for suffrage, soil, and self-determination,

FIGURE 0.1 Photo of Alice Zeno and George Lewis, date unknown. From the William Carter Papers, Courtesy of the Department of Special Collections, Stanford University, MSS 2083.

interpret these Haitian Creole melodies that portrayed social movements across the Caribbean?

Delving into the intertwined histories of Haiti and Louisiana reveals a rich mosaic of deep-seated connections informed by war and plantation production. Thousands of migrants—forced and voluntary, enslaved and enslavers, free whites and free people of color—fled the armies of Louverture, Napoleon, and Dessalines in Saint-Domingue/Haiti from 1791 to 1810. Many moved to Santiago de Cuba before settling in Louisiana. Estimates of the total number of migrants range from ten to twenty-five thousand.[37] Their cultural influence is difficult to overstate. The capital Port-au-Prince's population at the time of the Haitian Revolution rivaled that of Boston or Baltimore at around twenty-five thousand souls. Its inhabitants were at the center of a dynamic and violent global economy in which sugar and coffee harvested with slave labor funded lavish spending in the arts, fashion, and a variety of consumer goods.[38] In contrast, the French founded Louisiana with the aim of imposing a government-controlled trade system and curbing smuggling with the Spanish colonies. Its location on multiple frontiers required a dependence on privateers and French convicts, and it developed a reputation for "disorder."³⁹ New Orleans's period of Spanish rule (1763–1803) resulted in renewed economic development, and its manumission laws and dependence on Black military service prompted the ninefold growth of free people of color between 1771 and 1791 alone.⁴⁰ Yet by 1800 New Orleans's population was still only eight thousand.⁴¹ The Haitian Revolution changed this.⁴² By the end of the Saint-Dominguean emigration wave in 1811, the Crescent City's population had exploded to twenty-four thousand, and the majority of the new migrants from what was now named "Haiti" were African or African descended.⁴³

Numerical data alone might mask the qualitative shift. Emigrants brought both technical know-how and experiences of a vibrant urbanity. Judges, plantation managers, artists, and revolutionaries helped make New Orleans the new heart of a global struggle between the plantation and the counter-plantation. In 1795, Antoine Morin, a chemist from Saint-Domingue, developed the granulation method that revolutionized Louisiana's sugar economy, allowing for nearly year-long production. It transformed New Orleans into a prominent sugar exporter and spurred the growth of its market for enslaved peoples, which soon became the largest in the United States.⁴⁴ Then, in 1811, Charles Deslondes, possibly an enslaved migrant from Saint-Domingue, burned the cane fields that Morin's work enabled in the largest slave revolt in United States history. Traumatized planters remembered this "German Coast uprising" by drumming, singing, and marching that evoked the insurgent militaries of the Haitian Revolution.⁴⁵

Deslondes and several of his followers were brutally executed, and verifying his Saint-Domingue lineage may forever remain an elusive task. Yet it is undeniable that the enslaved individuals forcibly brought by enslavers fleeing the Haitian Revolution fundamentally altered the cultures of both plantation and urban Louisiana. Forced migrants from Saint-Domingue contributed to 25 percent of the growth in the Orleans Territory's enslaved population, which rose from 22,701 to over 34,000 between 1806 and 1810.⁴⁶ Around seventy-five years later, St. Charles the Baptist Parish, the same ground where Deslondes's German Coast uprising began, would also nurture the talent of the influential early jazz trombonist Kid Ory. Narratives of the rebellion persisted as oral literature among the enslaved and their descendants, resonating through the annals of history into Ory's childhood.⁴⁷

While the Louisiana sugar country was both made and unmade by these Saint-Domingue/Haitian migrants, New Orleans's Black arts scene was similarly transfigured. Saint-Domingue immigrants almost immediately founded the South's most renowned opera company upon arrival, which became well attended by both free and enslaved peoples of African descent.⁴⁸ Among the Saint-Domingue diaspora were influential free Black artists, including the sculptor Alexander Nelder.[49] Afro-Creole writer Victor Séjour was born in New Orleans but his father was from Haiti, who sent his son to Paris to prevent his potential imprisonment for publishing abolitionist literature.[50] Séjour's 1837 masterpiece, "Le Mulâtre" (The Mulatto), was set in revolutionary Saint-Domingue and vividly narrated the harsh physical and mental aspects of slavery, including the sexual exploitation of enslaved individuals. The work employed techniques that anticipated pre–Civil War slave narratives and abolitionist novels and was one of the first published short stories by a person of African descent.[51] Both white and Afro-Creole musicians from Saint-Domingue became prominent instructors, and enslaved Saint-Domingue migrants were reported to be influential musicians among other enslaved peoples throughout the Caribbean.[52]

Migrant planters thus unwittingly imported not only the violent modernity of the sugar plantation to Louisiana but also the counter-plantation expressive culture of its enslaved workforce. While the counter-plantation most clearly refers to a land practice that rejected monocrop agriculture and industrialized overwork, the Haitian economist Jean Casimir poetically defines the counter-plantation as both physical and metaphysical. The will of the Haitian revolutionaries, Casimir writes, was propelled by a "sovereign universe that preceded slavery," one which the enslaved "kept reproducing by taking shelter from colonialism or zombification in a world situated beyond capitalism."[53] *Brassroots Democracy* traces how the music inspired by the Haitian diaspora in Louisiana propelled this sovereign universe through an embodied ethics of cocreation that defied the designs of plantation capitalism.

While situated in New Orleans, the questions that this book raises in dialogue with Alice Zeno's "Song from Haiti" are inspired by the collective project of understanding "how the Haitian Revolution reshaped [the] cultures and imaginations" of the Atlantic world.[54] Through a sustained study of the Haitian Revolution's musical legacies, this manuscript builds on the valuable scholarship of the "Haitian turn" in history and Black studies.[55] This collective project is one that, as of this writing, has yet to be systematically realized in dialogue with the musical cultures of Black and Afro-Creole New Orleans—an urgent project to which this book endeavors to make a contribution.

BRASSROOTS DEMOCRACY'S COMMON WIND LEGACIES

For decades, scholars have analyzed the politics of the colonial archive and its role in constructing a white supremacist episteme.[56] Despite, or rather because of, the distortions of enslaved people's lives inherent within it, the slavery archive is a contested site of knowledge production where one can hear valuable glimpses of agency, perhaps most evident in accounts of cultural production. As Laurent Dubois writes, "Afro-Atlantic music . . . offers us a fascinating and vital archive through which to tell alternative histories that may allow us to speak back to, and perhaps even bypass, the 'Colonial Library.'"[57] *Brassroots Democracy* prioritizes how those held in bondage understood their own musical experiences, but archives generated by colonists are also interrogated with "against-the-grain" readings, listened to with what Johari Jabir calls "postcolonial ears," "a listening hermeneutics that accounts for the sonic work in black music as an aural epistemology."[58] Just as music illuminates history from below, it is also true that situating Atlantic geographies of violence and brutality, resistance and revolution, is essential to hearing the aural episteme that produced the music. Historical contextualization is not only necessary but necessarily a political-ethical act that can locate Black Atlantic music as part of a counter-plantation practice against the plantation and its archive. It is one narration of many "counterhistories of slavery" that Saidiya Hartman describes as contributing to "a history of the present," that is, "the incomplete project of freedom."[59]

With this in mind, it is important to underscore that the Saint-Domingue exodus to Louisiana is but one context in which Zeno's song was sung by her great-grandmother. These migrants do not explain how this melancholy melody, dating to the 1860s, island-hopped its way to New Orleans. Nor does this migratory wave fully encapsulate the vast and intricate network of exchanges through which a transnational counter-plantation episteme cohered. Exploring a parallel historical process may shed light on the channels through which this tune and others like it were circulated. Zeno's song was a kind of sequel to a repertoire of revolutionary songs that circulated throughout the Black Caribbean and Louisiana following the Haitian Revolution. Throughout the late eighteenth and nineteenth centuries, a network of underground communication distributed news from the "masterless" Caribbean—such as maroons, privateers, and urban free Black people—throughout America's slave societies. Information exchange between enslaved people was a matter that perplexed enslavers, who complained of the "unknown mode of conveying intelligence amongst Negroes." The historian Julius Scott has identified this "transatlantic news pipeline" among "free coloreds . . . [who] tested the limits of their masterless status." He coined this regional network of communication as "the common wind" which connected Afro-American communities across the Atlantic world to a shared knowledge of, and will to, struggle.[60]

The vocal repertoire of Alice Zeno points to a means by which the common wind was consummated: Afro-Atlantic song, one of the "unknown modes" of disseminating news whose meanings were often out of reach of masters. In 1806, revolutionary Haitians affiliated with Haitian Emperor Jean-Jacques Dessalines organized a slave revolt in Martinique whose insurgents were heard singing "Vive Dessalines!"[61] Ten years later in Jamaica, a chorus sung by enslaved Africans signaled another uprising: "What negro for to do? Take force with force!" The conspiracy had involved two hundred fifty enslaved peoples and included, according to an overseer, "one black ascertained to have stolen over into the island from St. Domingo [Haiti]" with a leadership role. Simultaneously, a new heel-drumming technique first documented in Haiti was popularized by enslaved Jamaican musicians.[62] The Dutch colony of Curaçao, which housed unruly enslaved prisoners from Saint-Domingue, Cuba, Jamaica, and Brazil in the late eighteenth century, was home to a one-thousand-strong rebellion in 1795. It was co-led by an enslaved Curaçaoan man, Tula, and a Haitian prisoner, Louis Mercier. Mercier, along with other imprisoned Saint-Domingue rebels, had shared news of the revolution's success. Tula changed his name to Rigaud during the revolt to invoke the Haitian General of the same name. The uprising was defeated after one month, and its leaders were executed, but their names were immortalized in the song "Rebeldia Na Bandabou," an insurgent anthem still performed by Afro-Curaçaoan *Tambú* artists today.[63]

From Puerto Rico to Venezuela, revolutionary songs that celebrated the "Negro Toussaint" alarmed colonial officials, who paranoically supervised Africans in bondage while expanding plantation production.[64] Crucial to this panorama is how songs and lyrics—as well as new instruments, playing techniques, and conceptions of rhythm and feel—crossed borders. *Brassroots Democracy* contextualizes these links between antislavery agitation and intercultural improvisation throughout the diaspora to explore how aesthetic innovation was an expression of historical self-awareness.[65]

With what velocity, and through which vessels, did the common wind reach the ears of Black communities in the United States? For Black Americans, free and enslaved, Haiti was a powerful symbol of Black liberation both in the antebellum period and during Reconstruction. Free Black communities in the United States emigrated to Haiti throughout the first half of the nineteenth century, and many refugees who escaped with the Underground Railroad—such as the couple Thomas and Isabella Harrison—moved to Haiti where they were joined by other survivors of exodus across the Americas.[66] The abolitionist imagination attached to the Haitian Revolution was enunciated by Frederick Douglass for his entire adult life. Having marooned himself to liberty some ten years earlier, Douglass wrote in his newspaper *The North Star* in 1848 that Haiti was the "original . . . emancipator of the nineteenth century"; in 1893 he continued: "We should not forget that the freedom you and I enjoy today is largely due to the brave stand taken by the black sons of Haiti ninety years ago ... they struck for the freedom of every black man in the world."[67] In this forty-five-year span, the Haitian Revolution and its inspired aural culture laid the groundwork for a cultural revolution in New Orleans and beyond.

Haitian culture loomed large in Louisiana, and a hidden archive of "popular song" enunciated its freedom dreams. A genre of adapted ephemera, its lyrics, melodies, and rhythms spread knowledge of the Haitian Revolution in the Crescent City. Writing in 1981, the historian Eugene Genovese recorded how "the slaves in Louisiana were heard singing revolutionary songs first heard in the early days of the revolution in Saint-Domingue,"[68] but scholars have not yet systematically tended to the musical elements Genovese saw as evidence of Afro-Atlantic revolutionary inspiration.[69] One telling example is that of an 1810 "wanted" poster for a Haitian-born fugitive named Pierre who had escaped from his Charleston enslaver to the Crescent City. The ad, purchased by the enslaver seeking to reclaim Pierre's body, described him as barber who carried "a Tambarine [sic] unstrung in his hand and a razer, from which it is presumed he plays on it." Pierre had learned how to drum in Saint-Domingue, manifesting an Afro-Atlantic performative culture on the loose in antebellum New Orleans.[70]

These maroon ecologies of song, rumor, and embodied freedom produced temporary refuge for performers, and inspiration for listeners, as the culture of the common wind took root. Much like the music of brassroots democracy some generations later, this music had a dialectic relationship with the spaces that gave it shelter. Pierre's occupation as a New Orleans barber is an important detail, for as don Simón Rodríguez observed in Caracas in 1794, barbershops became revolutionary schools where Black and mulatto youth were educated by "improvised teachers" who taught their students how to "read and comb hair, write and shave" at the same time.[71] These improvised teachers also improvised a dynamic curriculum rooted in principles of popular education. Here musician-artisan-refugees such as Pierre found an audience and purpose to share songs from Haiti within the context of a growing abolitionist underground. Memoirs produced by Black barbers mention how stories of the Haitian Revolution, Mexico's abolition of slavery, and the Underground Railroad were all discussed or sung alongside guitars and other instruments.[72] "Revolutionary songs performed in an overcrowded barbershop," writes Cristina Soriano in her study of Afro-Venezuelan anti-colonial activists, "were far more important than any French or American revolutionary text."[73] The imbrication of barber shops with the radical possibility promised by the Haitian Revolution—W. E. B. Du Bois's father, Alfred, was a barber from Haiti—connected style and substance, aesthetics and ethics, and these semi-autonomous spaces continued to have a lasting impact on Black life in New Orleans through the jazz age.[74] As Donald Marquis notes, barbershops were important incubators of New Orleans's Black vernacular culture through the 1890s, as spaces where young jazz musicians like Buddy Bolden could seek out both musical knowledge and performance opportunities.[75] All these encounters, informed by the Haitian Revolution and the democratic, interdisciplinary culture it contributed to, became inscribed on the improvisatory moment—the musical unmaking and remaking of the world.[76]

It may seem odd that an enslaved person would escape to the slave market of the Deep South instead of points North. But Pierre was one of many maroons who traveled through the Crescent City. Fugitive enslaved peoples often interacted with the urban enslaved as the latter could sell their services on their Sundays off, a practice known as "self-rent."[77] Pierre and other maroons took advantage of this system, evidenced by an 1810 law that to sought to "prevent Negroes . . . from hiring themselves, when they are runaways." These interactions provoked considerable fear from enslavers. In 1804, a petition to city council complained that "fugitive slaves are gathered around the city, which makes our own slaves receivers of their stolen goods, that our slaves provide them with food and ammunition."[78] Refugees fleeing enslavement indeed created improvised homes at the peripheries of plantations, a phenomenon Sylviane Diouf has identified as "borderland maroons."[79] But at least until 1852 it seems that much of urban New Orleans was a borderland between freedom and enslavement. In 1834, a man named Alexis managed to escape from the plantation where he was enslaved in Iberville Parish, Louisiana, finding his way to New Orleans. For four years, he shared a home with Marie Rose Hudson, a free woman of color. Eventually he was located and taken captive.[80]

Barber shops were one site where musical cultures and maroon ecologies weaved one another in a harmonic fashion. But perhaps more central, and more visible to enslaver regimes, were the taverns that hosted dances for hundreds of free and unfree people of color. Reaching a critical mass at the end of the eighteenth century, Louisiana's Spanish colonial government took note; one official complained that balls of wine merchant Bernado Coquet were "the place where the majority of slaves in this city gather," while a white Louisianan complained that the enslaved "prolong[ed] their dances and games long after sunset."[81] Tambourinists like Pierre would have been welcome. The transmission of revolutionary fervor through dance and music was a deep-seated fear of the Spanish, who suppressed the French contradanza, banned "La Marseillaise," and censured other radical songs in Louisiana in 1793, explicitly citing their role in Jacobin and Black incitement.[82]

To make matters more complicated, officials' ability to counter the presence

> 50 Dollars Reward
>
> WIL be given to any person for apprehending a mulatto fellow named PIERRE, (tho' he may have changed his name) Creole of the Cape; about 5 feet one inch high, French measure; between 25 and 30 years of age; much pitted with the small pox, in consequence of which his beard is in spots: his face is thin and the nose a little turned up. He was seen last Sunday with a Tambarine unstrung in his hand and a part of razors, from which it is presumed he plays on it, and also may be a barber, having been, when a boy, at a barbers shop in Charleston, where I purchased him. I understand he was a drummer at the Cape after he had ran away from me. When he was seen last Sunday he wore a large white flapped hat, a whitish coatee with blue stripes, of the stuff the French call calendelit, a pair of Nankeen pantaloons and Boots. The above reward will be paid on delivering him to the subscriber, who forwarns all masters of vessels and others from harboring or carrying him out of this city.
>
> Claud Guillaud,
> July 20.   81 Ann Street.

> AVIS.
>
> PAYON, arrivant de St. Jago de Cuba, enseigne à jouer de la Clarinette & de la Flûte; il a l'honneur d'offrir ses services aux personnes qui désireraient apprendre à jouer de ces instrumens. Il ose se flatter que sa manière d'enseigner & son exactitude rempliront l'attente des personnes, qui l'honoreront de leur confiance.
>
> 3 Juillet.

FIGURE 0.2 *Left*: A bounty offered for a fugitive enslaved person, a drummer named Pierre, published in *Courier de la Louisiane*, July 23, 1810. *Right*: An ad for a musical instructor, recently arrived from Santiago de Cuba, likely earlier from Saint-Domingue/Haiti, offering flute and clarinet lessons, published in the *Moniteur de la Louisiana*, July 5, 1809. These two items reflect distinct musical literacies shared by the Saint-Domingue exodus. The first ad is discussed in Johnson, *Slavery's Metropolis*, 24–27. The second ad was previously published in Johnson, *Fear of French Negroes*, 133.

of either maroons or enslaved mobilities was hamstrung by the city's economic dependence on free Black workers. During almost the entire United States antebellum era, this bustling Louisiana port encountered a recurring challenge as it grappled with a chronic shortage of skilled artisans and steamboat workers due to yellow fever and other diseases.[83] According to newspaper stories from the 1850s, out of the sixty thousand sailors and steamboat workers who arrived in New Orleans each year, a substantial number, possibly hundreds, were free African Americans.[84] Until 1852, New Orleans's three separate administrative districts competed with each other to increase their share of the city's maritime trade, and police officers were instructed not to seize out-of-state Black seaman. This security lapse encouraged the growth of an emancipatory network extending from the docks to taverns: one enslaver wrote in an 1850 runaway slave ad that Austin Fox, an enslaved stevedore, had escaped his grasp, and that he "played the fiddle and was to be found about cabarets."[85] It was thus relatively strategic for maroons like Pierre to make base in the maritime city, as they could blend in with both urban enslaved people and transient Black seamen as they shared information and affective kinship through musical performance.

A Black maritime presence also propelled the improvisatory musical cultures that crisscrossed rural Louisiana, as not only New Orleans but also its plantation hinterland was connected by water. Sugar plantations required access to riverways to transport their goods and nurture their extractive crop. "Every planter," wrote George W. Cable in 1886, "had his boat and skilled crew of black oarsmen. The throb of their song measured the sweep of the oars."[86] Documented songs on these boats included a French Creole song that celebrated escape by sea. Titled by George W. Cable as a "Song of Defiance," this song took aim at "General Florido," possibly a reference to Louisiana's eighteenth-century attorney general, François Fleuriau, who persecuted "undesirables" and "runaway slave units" with a special task force in colonial Louisiana.[87] In defiance of Flueriau and his predecessors, the song declared, "O general Florido! . . . There is a schooner out at sea. It's true they cannot catch me!"[88] Just as early ragtime was influenced by Afro-Caribbean cultural currents through its connection to the Mississippi River, so, too, were the politics and sound libraries of enslaved and free people a generation earlier.[89] In 1841, the New Orleans press panicked over free Afro-Jamaicans who manned Mississippi River steamboats. One overseer in Bayou Sara claimed to overhear enslaved people planning a celebration of the British abolition of slavery. Dancing and musicking were quickly banned.[90] The aural culture shared by Black seamen broke the plantation's blockage and impressed upon enslaved peoples that maritime fugitivity was a meaningful avenue to freedom. Even more fundamentally, these songs also reminded them that there was a movement ready to welcome them if they could find a way out—musicians created the affect of community through a single militant stanza.[91]

This songbook of the common wind passed from lips and ears to legs and feet. Griot-bards, moving through plantation sugar mills, steamboats, and Black barbershops, bore the imprint of a massive improvisation complex marked as much by marronage and political declaration as by the musical act itself. The chains of affiliation produced by and through transnational sound put in sync a Black diaspora amid New World revolutionary transformations from colonial slavery to the yet undefined. The future was up for grabs, and who better than musicians to summon, through heterogenous vocality and embodied dance, new knowledges of struggle and the sensational unity felt across distant regions? Anti-colonial Latin American movements only deepened the Afrodiasporic soundtrack to the age of revolution, and Black musicians were practically omnipresent in the insurgent armies across the Americas, from the Black Union troops in the Civil War South to the Afro-Mexican *jarabe* guitarists who accompanied the revolutionary Mexican general Albino Garcia in 1810.[92] In these liberation movements, a performance culture inspired by the Haitian Revolution animated insurgents on and off the battlefield.[93]

These common wind cultures were not carbon copies of those in Haiti, and Louisiana had at least one revolutionary Black anthem that predated the Haitian Revolution: that of the maroon St. Malo in the Cyprus swamplands, whose martyrdom by Spanish troops in 1784 was memorialized in collective song.[94] But Raquel Rivera's observation regarding New York *bomba* practitioners in 2010 also rings true in the nineteenth-century Caribbean: "Haiti was the historical and mythical bridge linking the traditions of Puerto Rico, the Dominican Republic, and even the southern United States."[95] It is significant that revolutionary "French" songs and the Haitian-inflected contradanza were censured in Louisiana by the colony's Spanish administration in 1793, who explicitly feared their ability to incite an uprising of the enslaved.[96]

Both Pierre and Alice Zeno sang within this social world inflected by the common wind, where insurgent information communicated through song generated both power and community. As their intertwined stories foreshadow, *Brassroots Democracy* often employs a methodology that Marisa Fuentes describes as "filling out miniscule fragmentary mentions or the absence of evidence with spatial and historical context," a practice in which "our historical interpretation shifts to the enslaved viewpoint in important ways."[97] Context, as we have seen, is vital for this music history from below, and the occlusions that result when we leave it unstudied yield depoliticized narratives regarding early jazz. Perhaps this is nowhere more apparent than the scholarly treatment of Alice Zeno's song. Her inability to recall Senegambian songs led jazz scholars like Tom Bethell to conclude that both she and her son, George Lewis, had "not an African but an American past"; it compelled Charles Hersch, in his otherwise insightful analysis of racial boundaries and their influence on music culture in New Orleans, to observe that Zeno's mother had "rejected the African language"; and it informs Randall Sandke's argument that "all racial hues" performed "more or less the same repertoire before the advent of jazz." None of these authors comment on the "Song from Haiti," and to date it has remained unpublished: its only print representation is in the word "Creole" in William Russell's interview transcription in the Hogan Jazz Archive.[98]

Alice Zeno could not have predicted the ideological burden that future scholarship would place on her apparent forgetfulness. Zeno's Africanness—or, specifically, her problematically perceived lack of it—served as a barometer for metrics of acculturation, African American identity, theories of cultural diffusion, New Orleans historiography, and jazz itself. The lack of care given to Zeno's connection to Haiti, however, is part of a larger Western tendency that Michel-Rolph Trouillot describes as "the silencing of the Haitian Revolution," which as he explains is "only a chapter within a narrative of global domination." Only when we "bring forward the perspective of the world" in understanding the robust tradition of resistance that flows from that revolution will we hear the sounds of brassroots democracy.⁹⁹ Context helps us hear how Zeno's song was one of several that belonged to a century-long common wind, an exchange that tirelessly spread the underground news of the Haitian Revolution and its political afterlives through expressive culture in Louisiana and the Caribbean basin.

BRASSROOTS DEMOCRACY AS CREOLIZATION

Despite impressive breakthroughs in transnational and interdisciplinary work by historians of the nineteenth-century Black Atlantic, its expressive cultural matrix of traditions and institutions need further study. Historians continue to sidebar embodied knowledge and expressive culture and take for granted a definition of archives based exclusively in the written word. As Elsa Barkley Brown notes in her advocacy for a more dynamic historiography, "few historians are good jazz musicians; most of us write as if our training were in classical music. We require surrounding silence."¹⁰⁰ Yet silence for the fugitive cultural workers of the common wind meant social death. Such knowledge was important for enslaved runaways, like the tambourine-playing Pierre, to pass on—despite the risk of being identified. A theory and practice of improvisation was a vitally important piece of this embodied knowledge that was created through a traumatic yet sometimes triumphant process.

With this in mind, one might consider how the Haitian Revolution inadvertently created the conditions for a rich legacy of intercultural improvisation to take root in Louisiana. The Haitian Revolution catalyzed two waves of African diasporic migration to Louisiana. The first was within the Saint-Domingue exodus, where thousands of free and unfree people of color among Louisiana's new arrivals encountered a long-established Afro-American community, with its own distinguished history of slave revolt and marronage.¹⁰¹ Then, after Napoleon's failed campaign to reenslave Black Saint-Domingueans compelled the French emperor to sell Louisiana to the United States, slave traders unleashed another forced migration of African descendants.¹⁰² Between 1804 and 1862, 135,000 enslaved people were sold in New Orleans in auctions that one survivor of slavery, William J. Anderson, described as "hell on Earth."¹⁰³ They traveled hundreds of miles by foot, in chains made of iron, financed by international banks, to harvest fields of cotton whose bales would turn New Orleans into "the point of union" between European and American capital.¹⁰⁴ "Thus the coffle," notes Edward Baptist, "chained the early American republic together." Its metal bound the international division of labor necessary to cohere global capitalism's nineteenth-century dynamism.¹⁰⁵

Not one but two waves of intra-diasporic cultural exchange were catalyzed by the Haitian Revolution and the new geography of abolition and slavery that it precipitated. Studying Afro-Louisianan cultural mixture during these six decades contextualizes the multivoiced aesthetics and political valences of brassroots democracy. These pivotal years marked the convergence of transatlantic capitalism with the Industrial Revolution. This era boasted unprecedented profitability for enslavers and textile manufactures, which manifested as relentless overwork and torment for the enslaved migrants. Thus, the foundation of brassroots democracy was not just strategic but also an ethical imperative. In the heart of the Reconstruction era, this movement cultivated a commoning, cooperative popular culture that merged philosophical insights and expressions of liberation from descendants of Haiti, Virginia, and colonial Louisiana. This process is known as creolization, and its proximity to other terms used throughout this book deserves further clarification.

In Louisiana, "Creole" refers to a distinct community of Louisianans descended from families in the French and Spanish colonial period. "Creole" New Orleans, as Tregle points out, was not a powerful identity in Louisiana before Anglo-American annexation. Yet, after 1803, "origin in the soil became . . . the very essence of the concept *creole*, precisely because it gave the older residents the most profound warrant of the right not to be dispossessed in their own land."[106] By Reconstruction, free Afro-Creoles became known as "Creoles of color," but even before such naming they had long constituted a uniquely liminal position. In both French Saint-Domingue and Spanish Louisiana, free persons of color "were not simply people of color who happened to be free," explains Parham: "as their numbers grew, they were seen as belonging to a distinct social group with whom whites cultivated many different kinds of social and business relationships."[107]

Martinican philosopher Édouard Glissant's use of the term "Creole," meanwhile, is different from the Louisianan term. It centers on the intermixing of various cultures living in geographic proximity due to migration, enslavement, and agricultural production, as seen in the African diaspora in the Caribbean.[108] Creolization describes the mechanism by which the cultural and semiotic expressions of heterogeneous peoples were shared and made anew in cohabitated communities in conditions not of their own choosing.[109] Glissant's definition of creolization can help animate the sense of fugitive cultural reciprocity described above, thereby situating the musical and political exchanges between Southern African Americans with Creoles of color from French Louisiana and Haiti as a specific expression of a centuries-long world-historic process.[110]

This vision of creolization is particularly applicable to the constellations of improvised musical culture that came to define Afro-Louisiana. In fact, the cultural interaction between enslaved Louisianans and Haitian migrants within

Louisiana's expanding plantation machine might be considered a "secondary creolization," since both cultures had emerged from parallel creolization processes through forced migration and enslavement.[111] For both early nineteenth-century immigrants to New Orleans and resident Afrodescendants, the musical aspects of creolization, including the creation of new vocabularies of scales and rhythms, were a means by which displaced Afro-diasporans made sense of their world and created new forms of identification where words might fail.[112] Secondary creolization propelled new musical fusions into the early twentieth century, as distinct peoples improvised through difference, sharing musical instruments, performance techniques, and suppressed histories of resistance.[113] As intercultural communities improvised new languages and methodologies to create meaning in a fractured world, creolization can be thought of as improvisation on a long-term, world-historic scale, in which improvisation is both an input and an outcome. Put differently, improvisation is a process by which creolization became constituted; and improvisation emerges as a specific technology of music-making out of that same creolization.

Indeed, for Glissant, creolization is most apparent in the hybrid musical forms produced by enslaved peoples whose expressive power broke through the social death of enslavement. "These musical expressions born of silence: Negro spirituals and blues . . . jazz, biguines, and calypsos . . . salsas and reggaes . . . This was the cry of the Plantation, transfigured into the speech of the world."[114] Glissant's theorization of the plantation as a kind of unwitting factory of subaltern speech reinforces the deep link between plantations, capital accumulation, and zones of intercultural communication. *Brassroots Democracy* situates the plantation as the manifestation of an emergent capitalist world-system based on accumulation through overwork and dispossession that would come to define the nineteenth century and regimes of capital accumulation thereafter.[115] It was a model of a new kind of commodity production and even a new kind of slavery, which accelerated dramatically in Louisiana until the Civil War. The enslaved workforce of these industrialized agrarian fortresses developed a sophisticated and nuanced critique of capital, which became enunciated in aphorisms, speeches, and songs. As capital themselves, enslaved people could be mortgaged, traded, and insured. As the following chapters explore, their popular culture and political lexicon reflected an awareness of their condition as capital.[116] Despite their dehumanization and reduction into tools of production and financial instruments, enslaved people developed a technology of congregation and consensus-building completely antithetical to the institutions that held them in bondage. While performing intricate labor whose scale and intensity is difficult to fully comprehend, they created complex polyphony whose beauty moved mountains. These workshops that produced immense wealth through unparalleled death were thus home to a class of artistic innovators who held the contradictory and impossible condition of the "commodity who screams."[117] In sum, there exists a dialectic between the plantation and communal music forms produced therein, and this book centers this contradiction to suggest the music's power as antidote to the crisis that produced it.[118]

The prevailing view in much jazz scholarship holds that Creoles of color were culturally Eurocentric and differentiated themselves from African Americans to maintain social privileges. Thomas Brothers, for instance, writes in his brilliant biography of Louis Armstrong how Black Americans experienced significant social barriers and even discrimination at the hands of Afro-Creole society: "Creoles were wary of these [African American] plantation immigrants. As they watched them arrive in imposing numbers, the Creoles asserted a multidimensional sense of cultural difference. They produced a package of social barriers that Armstrong was forced to deal with if he wanted to advance musically." Brothers explains that Afro-Creoles "embraced Eurocentric musical standards and scorned everything else," including Black vernacular musical traditions, giving way to a racial regime determined by pigmentation and skin phenotype: "differences in skin color were constantly noticed and regarded as primary markers of social difference."[119]

Historical evidence does suggest that Creole of color and African American unity could be elusive. For instance, one cooperative bakery opened by Creoles of color in New Orleans, rooted in principles of utopian socialist thought, appears to have made little inroads with African Americans.[120] Overtly conservative Black Protestants found the dominant Afro-Creole culture to be too libertine. Some Haitian-descended Creole of color activists, like Pierre-Aristide Desdunes, had an interest in Vodou and had even travelled to Haiti to study it; while the *Southwestern Christian Advocate*, New Orleans's Methodist periodical, denounced "the Hodou [sic] shout and Ebo dance" as a legacy "of the dark days of slavery."[121] In one case, a raffle organized by Creoles of color to raise funds for an orphanage was condemned as gambling. Others interpreted the reluctance of Creoles of color to join their church community as elitist.[122]

Yet the emphasis on these social divisions has masked another archive: one of solidarity. Such solidarity was certainly contested and contradictory, but it was forged in a social movement animated by internationalism. Partially because of their relative absence in jazz literature, these more radical, Atlantic-oriented Creole of color community members who sought alliances with African Americans are the subjects of this book's first half. As Fred Moten reminds us, "it's not difficult to point out complexities, crossings and antagonisms—the point is what to make of them—just as it's not enough to say this or that is an instance of internationalism."[123] These Creoles of color attempted to unite with African Americans and poor whites who hoped to own land of their own, particularly in the aptly named "Unification Committee" of 1873.[124]

As alluded to previously, religious and linguistic difference plagued the cohesiveness of these movements. But religious communities were not divided by neat lines. William E. Montgomery observes that the postemancipation African American church had two distinct sources: a formally organized, denominational church—which found its congregation predominantly in the urban areas and populated by those free during slavery—and an "invisible" church, rooted in the spiritual, ethical, and ecological worldviews of the formerly enslaved.[125] In Louisiana, the rise of the Baptist church and the subsequent emergence of the Sanctified Church was part of the latter tradition, and it created a space for Black working-class spirituality that was more polyphonic and syncretic than the African American Methodist leadership who denounced "Hodou."[126] Zora Neale Hurston's ethnography of Black churches in 1930s New Orleans provides a powerful window into the sonic world of plantation migrants to New Orleans. Amid the hallowed halls of the Sanctified Churches in the vibrant Third Ward, Hurston describes "a liquefying of words" as an electrifying symphony of jubilation unfurled. Hurston writes how preacher and congregation orchestrated a shared rhapsody of soulful catharsis: "One and all based on a dance-possible rhythm." "Jagged" harmonies resonated with intensity, as a lead and respondents "sung unceasing variations around a theme with . . . signing of the piece is a new creation."[127] In Louisiana, the heterophonic elements of the Black Sanctified Church emerged through decades of institution-building on plantations. Its democratic and polyphonic ethos contributed the core aesthetic and ethical valences of brassroots democracy.[128] As Donald Marquis and Thomas Brothers observe, its angular phrasing, repeated-note riffs played against harmonic motion, and dialogical call-and-response structure all fed into the musical grammar from which Buddy Bolden's legendary Eagle Band drew from, as well as that of plantation-to-urban migrants such as trombonist Harrison Barnes and clarinetist-drummer Willer Parker.[129]

As fifteen thousand Civil War Black migrants freed themselves by escaping to Union-controlled New Orleans in 1862, many Creoles of color were probably not entirely prepared to understand exactly what they were hearing when these forms of worship and congregational music-making crossed their ears.[130] But for others, it may not have been entirely out of the ordinary. Plantation cultures among French-speaking enslaved people also included improvisation and call-and-response cadences. Songs transcribed on the "Good Hope" plantation in St.

Charles Parish before the Civil War are described as such: "[They sing] a rude corruption of French. . . . An orchestra of singers, the leader of whom—a man selected both for the quality of his voice and for his skill in improvising—sustains the solo part, while the others afford him an opportunity, as they shout in chorus, for inventing some neat verse to compliment some lovely *danseuse* [dancer], or to celebrate the deeds of some plantation hero."[131] Although sparse, the description of an improvisational lead and an improvised chorus does bear more than a passing resemblance to the Sanctified performances Hurston observed in 1930s New Orleans's Black Baptist churches. Such a correlation may not be so surprising, since, as Phyllis Lewis-Hale points out, "the Afro-Creole folk song developed under the same conditions as did the Negro spiritual on the Louisiana plantation of the late 18th and 19th centuries."[132] The social relations of the plantation, and the counter-plantation expressive culture of its workers, highlight the importance of music in sustaining an oppositional consciousness among both English-speaking Black migrants from the Old South and French Creole-speaking descendants of enslaved Saint-Domingue migrants during the longue durée of Louisiana slavery.

The generation of Creoles of color who contributed to proto-jazz were familiar with these plantation songs, and their songbook was incorporated into Reconstruction events and mass meetings.[133] But a dearth of commentary prevents us from gleaning how Reconstruction Afro-Creoles perceived or related to the songs of either French-or English-speaking plantation migrants. Some Creole of color musicians later in the century complained emphatically about the new sounds that Black artists invented on the clarinet, trumpet, and other instruments.[134] Others embraced it, and perhaps earlier than the conventional timeline. In 1885, Economy Hall, a long-established Creole of color organization with roots in the antebellum era, hired the Eagle Band to perform at a civil rights mass meeting as part of a larger initiative to build alliances with African Americans—they invited Frederick Douglass to speak later that year.[135] The activist orientation adopted by this Creole of color fraternal order demonstrate how, within Reconstruction and post-Reconstruction social movements that fought to dismantle antebellum class and caste orders, cultural and religious differences could be superseded in struggle. Just as African Americans, then, ought not be defined monolithically by the conservative positionalities of the Black Methodist ministers who had access to print media, neither should an elitist Catholicism stand in for the politics and aesthetic tastes of all Creoles of color. Prior to the Civil War, many Creoles of color were drawn to spiritualist societies and Freemasonry, which appealed to them precisely because of its association with the anti-elitist values of the 1848 French Revolution and the Second Republic.[136]

To what extent is the claim that Creoles of color were Eurocentric borne out by a close examination of this community's musical preferences? Antebellum Creole of color musicians, like their descendants through the 1880s, embraced a formal and prideful pursuit of musical excellence, engaging in a distinguished learning path alongside musicians from the prestigious French opera house and accomplished itinerant performers from Latin American and European conservatories.[137] But recent scholarship has challenged the conventional understanding of French cultural adaptations by Afro-Franco populations in the New World. Rather than read Black and mixed-race peoples as passive recipients or unwitting propogandists of French culture, this turn places a renewed emphasis on individuals' agency to selectively and creatively appropriate aspects of French cultures through African, Black Atlantic, and Latin American epistemologies and cultural practice. Writing on the radical politics of Louisiana's Creoles of color, Georgette Mitchell critiques the tendencies of scholars to assume European mimicry for their dissident ideals. "Contrary to popular belief, this uprooted, aqueous being is not a mere offspring of Romantic thought that has been transplanted in the French Caribbean along with colonial rule."[138] Similarly, Crystal Eddins has noted how historians of Haiti have "attributed the impetus for the [Haitian] revolution to a trickle down of political and philosophical ideas from the French Revolution."[139] And Hilary Beckles has identified this historiographical tendency as one that paints African diasporans as "devoid of [their own] ideas, political concepts and an alternative socio-political vision."[140] These intellectual legacies have deformed our understanding of Creole of color activism in Reconstruction Louisiana. Several historians have attributed their creation of communes to French socialist utopian thought, but as Caroline Hossein notes in her discussion of the "Black social economy," an Afro-Atlantic cooperative economic ethos was informed by Black peoples' historic entry to the capitalist market as commodities themselves: "Africans and the African diaspora were creating social economies long before the French concept of the *économie sociale* even emerged."[141] And nowhere in the nineteenth-century world were such cooperative economies more present, and more commented upon, than in Haiti, which experienced the most rapid population growth in the nineteenth-century Caribbean and where forests and agroecology replaced plantations in what Johnhenry Gonzalez refers to as a "maroon nation." Haitian farmers, notes Gonzalez, built "fiscally illegible landscape[s]" that resisted the plantation designs of Haiti's postindependence rulers. For these maroon farmers, "the collapse of sugar exports and the destruction of the plantation infrastructure represented success."[142]

By overlooking the lateral connections between the Black Caribbean and New Orleans, as well as the complex nuances of transculturation, it could be said that using the word "Eurocentric" to describe Afro-Creole engagement with French music is, itself, Eurocentric. Louisianan Creoles of color themselves often centered their political geography not in France but in the Black Caribbean. "For us," explained the Creole of color poet Joseph Rosseau in 1862, "to be Louisianan is to be Haitian."[143] Afro-Franco subjects who embraced elements of French literature and culture were not shy about making critiques of racism and European imperialism known. "When [Aimé] Césaire wrote his tremendous attack upon Western Civilization, *In Return to My Native Land*," noted C.L.R. James, "he was able to make this ferocious attack upon Western civilization because he knew it inside out.... He had spent some twenty years studying it."[144] There is perhaps no better example for the present discussion than that of a group of Haitian soldiers in combat against Napoleon's troops during the revolution. In a remarkable moment, these soldiers transformed "La Marseillaise," the French national anthem, by infusing it with Creole and African words, a powerful act symbolizing their resistance that confused the white soldiers intent on re-enslaving them. Fumi Okiji, in her discussion of this incident, suggests that

> the African and creole dialects that disfigure the French language provides a metaphor for the dialectical movement of the unfolding of freedom in this age of revolution. The manner in which these dialects break and reset the language, speaks to how the Haitian revolutionary forces offer a reconstituted understanding of liberty to the world. Europe's anthem disarticulated by Africa's sound, practically unrecognizable. French's freedom thoroughly transfigured by literal enslavement and race, by a place at the margins, by illegitimate participants (from the perspective of Europe, thoroughly ill-prepared for the occasion). A contribution to the standard that is revolution.[145]

This is how we should hear the "French" music performed by New Orleans's Afro-Franco Creoles, who also sang "La Marseillaise" in their battle with British forces in 1815: rife with critique, contradiction, and conjoined with Afrodiasporic permutations in ways both explicitly sounded and forbidden. To appropriate or master European forms did not mean acquiescing to the colonial racial order. To the contrary, "French negroes," as the United States press frequently commented, were profoundly destabilizing to the white-Black dichotomy that served as the ideological justification for womb-based enslavement, and were often accused of circulating abolitionist ideals. In South Carolina, some of those accused were executed.[146] Creolization therefore surfaced as a dynamic and impactful political critique woven into the sonic tapestry of antislavery and emancipatory movements, and New Orleans's Afro-Creole community would likewise challenge

Europe's attempt to monopolize terms like *liberté*, *égalité*, and *fraternité* in the service of colonial power.

Moreover, mastery of French concert music did not preclude other musical interests. Even the most seasoned classical musician performed over a rhythmic substrate popular in the nineteenth century that was deeply implicated with generations of African creolization in the Caribbean: the *habanera*, which the first two chapters of this book discuss in greater depth. What's more, the Creole of color intelligentsia were also in tune with the vernacular Black cultures produced by francophone plantation workers. "Chère, mo lemmé toi," a French Creole song popular in both Haiti and Louisiana, was sung at a Reconstruction mass meeting held at the Mechanics' Institute in 1876.[147] As Thomas Fiehrer has observed more broadly of Creole New Orleans, "elites and masses participated in the same aesthetic experiences. The gap between folk and elite-lore had yet to widen and the respective domains of the classical and vernacular were still to formalise."[148] Creole songs from both plantations and urban New Orleans were prominent in Black musical circles in the 1870s. Caroline Vézina has documented at least eighty Creole-language songs in circulation among New Orleans musicians during the last three decades of the nineteenth century.[149]

The first chapters of *Brassroots Democracy* concern themselves with the political imagination that shaped radical Afro-Creoles' world by exploring the tangible actions they took to realize their vision. These individuals served as potent bridges to Black Atlantic cultures in the Caribbean Basin, and their aspirations for freedom were central to their endeavors. It was not uncommon to witness African American activists and politicians sharing the stage with Creole of color musicians, fostering a sense of camaraderie during various events. For instance, in 1885, during a civil rights rally in New Orleans, an extraordinary collaboration unfolded. The chorus of Fisk University, a historically Black college and university (HBCU) located in Nashville, Tennessee, joined forces with the Excelsior Brass Band, one of New Orleans's pioneering Black brass bands.[150] Notably, the Excelsior Brass Band comprised several talented Creole of color musicians, including the renowned clarinetists Lorenzo and Louis Tio, and were such a frequent feature at Black Republican events that P. B. S. Pinchbeck, Louisiana's first African American lieutenant governor, personally treated them to drinks.[151] These events held significant importance as symbols of unity and artistic expression. They foretold the influential fusion of talents from two distinct musical traditions—a pivotal precursor to the "birth" of jazz. Such displays of solidarity set the foundation for the transformative power that jazz music would later wield.

Moreover, the term "brassroots democracy" denotes the space that connected jazz to these earlier forms of brass band music-making—a space beyond formal music, yet animating it. Louisiana's Reconstruction events exemplified one such site where music played a vital role in facilitating interethnic and intra-class coalition building. This generative blend of cultures propelled the momentum toward the consolidation of brassroots democracy. This book emphasizes the intra-Caribbean and Latin American connections forged by both Creoles of color and African Americans within the tapestry of the Black Atlantic. Reconstruction's social movement provided a context for Creoles of color to reimagine their Haitian ancestry as a revolutionary legacy with meaningful lessons for the present moment. Activist Édouard Tinchant, for instance, proudly announced in both published communications and at Reconstruction mass meetings that he was a "son of Africa . . . of Haitian descent."[152] While some Creole of color musicians, like Jelly Roll Morton, denied his Haitian ancestry, it is noteworthy that a Haitian identity was emphasized by a significant number of Creole of color musicians through a variety of performance practices.[153] Sidney Bechet expressed the clearest articulation of this circum-Caribbean identity when he interpreted the music of Haiti with his so-called "Haitian Orchestra" in 1939.[154] Abbey "Chinee" Foster recalled playing "Haitian drums" early in his career.[155] Lizzie Miles did not overtly interpret Haitian rhythmic or melodic devices but did record a homage to this identity in her song "Haitian Blues" in 1923.[156] Each of these artists found it important to recover their buried connection to Haiti in repertoire choice, song lyrics, band names, and in instrument use. That each of these Creoles of color were also important stylistic influencers who incorporated elements of African American popular culture suggests that their invocation of Haiti shared something in common with Reconstruction activists of a previous generation: Haiti was imagined as a symbol of Black unity across the diaspora.

Some Afro-Creoles certainly played up distinctiveness with African Americans in belittling ways as a last-gasp attempt to have their identity recognized by the white state and civil society. In contrast, the architects of brassroots democracy retained a connection to their unique history but understood that meaningful progress in their collective quest for freedom and equality hinged on the interconnectedness and collaboration among individuals and communities commonly dispossessed. They were internationalists. By the end of the nineteenth century, all Louisianan descendants of Africa, including formerly enslaved individuals from Saint-Domingue, English-speaking African Americans, and long-standing free people of color, faced legalized segregation as "negroes." It is no surprise that the African descendants of colonial Louisianans or Saint-Domingue migrants engaged in a fierce struggle to uphold a cultural identity that spanned over a century as Southern law forcefully erased their distinctiveness and claims to historicity.[157] But some Creole of color musicians, like Daniel and Mamie Desdunes, George Guesnon, and Avery "Kid" Howard, found a means to integrate their performance traditions into the unique "blues epistemology" developed by the African American working class.[158] The assault on Creole identity within an anti-Black legislative framework made this renewed project of secondary creolization a strategic and spiritual imperative. For many Afro-Creoles, one's identity as a jazz musician was literally a response to, and partial substitute for, the erasure of Creole identity: "The tragedy is that Creoles were forced to choose [to be white or Black Americans], since an identity based on Créolité was no longer an option," explains Bruce Boyd Raeburn. "Perhaps this is why identity as a jazz musician—a creative professional judged by merit—mattered so much on both sides of the color line."[159]

Centering this secondary creolization challenges the notion that African American music is solely a fusion of "European" harmony and "African" rhythm and foregrounds the interactions within the African diaspora as part of what J. Lorand Matory calls a "live-dialogue" between Black communities across the Atlantic world.[160] This live dialogue can be also thought of as a series of intercultural improvisations, whose echoes spanned from the Haitian Revolution through Black Reconstruction. Zeno's recollection of her grandmother's song reveals that this live dialogue between Haiti and the Black South was alive and well through Reconstruction. Here lay the countervailing impulses to "Creole snobbery," through which Afro-Creole activists attempted to sow solidarity, and music was an important part of this ecology of intention and collective action.[161] In the examples I will discuss in this book, Creole of color musicians are found performing alongside African American civil rights leaders in the Reconstruction and post-Reconstruction period with an impressive frequency, such as clarinetists Lorenzo and Louis Tio at an 1885 civil rights rally where they performed between speeches by Daniel A. Straker of South Carolina and Bishop Henry M. Turner of Georgia. Afro-Creole activist musicians also participated in direct action campaigns to desegregate public institutions, such as the Haitian-descended cornetist-violinist Daniel Desdunes who led a successful sit-in campaign in 1892. Others contributed to a counterculture that affirmed Black women's experiences, such as Mamie Desdnues, who composed an oppositional anthem for Storyville's sex workers known as "Mamie's Blues." African American musicians and religious leaders, such as Methodist minister A. E. P. Albert and the Black dockworker organizer and band manager William Penn, also struggled for cultural "fusion" between New Orleans's different African-descended factions.[162] Social movements, then, were the spaces where "secondary creolization" came to life in music.

The impetus for *Brassroots Democracy* goes beyond merely establishing the participation of these musicians in social movements. While they certainly did participate, this book explores how such experiences transformed them, and their communities, profoundly. Witnessing the potential of collective power, many recognized the possibilities that came with political organization. Others became aware of its limitations, sometimes through witnessing the betrayal by whites or others in their ranks, in other moments by experiencing the raw efficacy of violence. All learned concretely the ways music could organize multitudes—to commemorate, to resist, to congregate, to heal—and how important such affective labor was to sustain a civic ethos rooted in collective self-determination. Above all, the musicians described in these chapters developed a profound identification with resistance: as a culture and a way of life. This lived commitment was often passed down to future generations, shaping the values of their children and extended family members. The music created by these future generations became an authentic expression of their shared dedication to liberation.

BRASSROOTS DEMOCRACY'S ORGANIZATION

Jacques Attali claims that music is "an affirmation that society is possible . . . Its order simulates the social order, and its dissonances express marginalities."[163] Acknowledging the nonlinear and fragmenting history of plantation modernity's sacrifice zones, *Brassroots Democracy* is necessarily dissonant in its organization—its structure seeking to replicate the inter-epistemic processes at play in the contingent improvisation under study. It is isomorphic in the sense that its apparently disjointed structure itself maps an interdisciplinary and unbounded musical practice whose cleavage with grassroots movements is impossible to separate. This book reconstructs the history of the music and analyzes the existing jazz paradigm, which often begins in Congo Square as an imagined reconstruction of Africa. While the West African influences of American Black music are central to the present study, it situates Africanity as historically and locally constructed, especially in relation to the plantation complex within which an overwhelming majority of African peoples in the Americas were embedded.[164] The process came to have a very particular meaning in revolutionary Haiti, informing its emancipation diaspora's musical cultures and communicative matrix.

The first chapter, "The Common Wind's Second Gale: The Desdunes Family" on the Haitian Louisianan Desdunes family, opens with Daniel Desdunes, a renowned cornetist and violinist who performed with a popular band that bore his name. He leveraged his fame as a musician to draw attention to a Freedom Ride that tested Louisiana's segregationist laws—a case he won. Through a fine-grained recounting of the work of Daniel and his father, Rodolphe, the chapter explores how Haitian Louisianan political culture became actualized in musical performance and mutual aid institutions throughout Reconstruction in Louisiana and, later, in Omaha, the Desdunes' adopted home through the Great Migration.

Chapter 2, "Mamie Desdunes in the Neo-Plantation: Legacies of Black Feminism among Storyville's Blues People" explores the music of Daniel's sister Mamie Desdunes, an accomplished pianist and singer who mixed Haitian rhythmic traditions and storytelling conventions in the blues form as early as 1895. Her work denounced a patriarchal sex industry that she participated in. Her signature composition "Mamie's Blues" (also known as "219 Blues") suggests that not only was a gendered perspective foundational to blues and early jazz, but also that women musicians theorized the continuities of plantation economies with New Orleans's red-light district, Storyville.

Chapter 3, "La Frontera Sónica: Mexican Revolutions in Borderlands Jazz," situates Haitian and Louisiana cultural exchanges in a nation not typically associated with the African diaspora: Mexico. In focus is the Tios, a Creole of color family that included several clarinet prodigies. The Tios fled the repressive New Orleans white supremacist government to resettle in Veracruz, Mexico, in the late 1850s, where they built a free Black colony predicated on communal agriculture.[165] They returned to New Orleans in 1877 and contributed to New Orleans's clarinet tradition by training generations of woodwind players. While the Tios have been discussed in early jazz scholarship, less consideration has been placed on the tradition of radical solidarity between the antislavery factions of Mexico and the ways their support inspired African-descended peoples in New Orleans. The history of Mexican and African American musical influence suggests that dialogue between sonic cultures is not the outcome of political solidarity but a precursor to it, and the musical internationalism of brassroots democracy was a modality of a larger anti-colonial political project.

The first half of this work, then, shines a light on two specific trans-Caribbean lineages. The social movements and musical aesthetics of the common wind were made manifest by the Desdunes and the Tios, revealing the concrete and complex linkages between early jazz and Crescent City activism. Their collective work contributes to a multigenerational and granular history of brassroots democracy as both a grassroots and an internationalist practice, a fidelity to both local issues and regional contexts that could be heard in the music itself. While individuals and musicians remain present, the second half of this book focuses more deliberately on the institutions created by counter-plantation movements and their synergy with brassroots democracy. Chapter 4, "Sowing Freedom: Abolitionist Agroecology in Afro-Louisiana," explores the internal gardening systems of enslaved communities across the Caribbean to illustrate the impact of land reform politics and the commune movement in Louisiana. This chapter examines the lives of musicians such as Kid Ory, who grew up as an impoverished sugar worker and later sustained himself as an urban farmer in Los Angeles, to consider how brass bands were integrated into the daily life of Black and Creole of color communities in the plantation belt—that is, how these bands were embraced as an expression of the commons they struggled for.

Chapter 5, "Black Reconstruction and Brassroots Democracy: Sonic Assembly in the Post-Civil War South," explores the role and evolution of brass bands and public musicking in the Black Civil War and Reconstruction culture. While this is a theme in other sections of the book, chapter 5 makes the strongest association between the takeover of public space and the expansion of the public sphere within Black brass band cultures. The interaction of brass band performance with emancipation and jubilee generated a new form of sonic politics in the Civil War and Reconstruction South. The radically participatory nature of both assemblies and brass bands suggests that Black music's ability to infuse political spectacle with an affective consensus was central to Black Reconstruction.

Finally, chapter 6, "Black Unions and the Blues: Dockworkers' Activism and New Orleans Jazz" centers New Orleans's powerful Black dockworkers unions, which included many important jazz musicians. The African American Longshoremen's Protective Union Benevolent Association (LPUBA) was pivotal in this movement. In 1900 the LPUBA was led by William Penn, an African American activist who had previously served as the business manager of the Excelsior Brass Band.[166] The LPUBA, the largest Black union in the South, underscores how New Orleans's Black working class created new forms of culture and political organizing to continue fighting for day-to-day gains in the quality of their life, emphasizing the significance of music within their movement. If farmers fought for control over land and production, and grassroots assemblies spoke to issues of space and democratic governance, dockworkers' unions contested the organization and ownership of time and the quotidian rhythms of work. Freedpeople struggled not only to be free, but to define the nature of work and its rhythms on their own terms, and the aesthetic importance of shared, communal time became a modality by which musicians shaped their cultural labor.

Brassroots Democracy explores early jazz and Black brass band culture more broadly as the expression of a socializing musical technology that contested slavery, racism, ecocide, patriarchy, capitalism, and imperialism through these overlapping histories. This venerated connection between sonic assembly and participatory democracy; between self and other, healing and struggle; between the local and the global, improvisation and creolization—the bridge between the counter-plantation and the promised land—is what the title of this book speaks to. The afterlives of these movements informed commoning projects in defiance of US empire in the Caribbean and Latin America, and the institutions and individuals to which this book is devoted thus had enormous importance in setting the tenor and tone of this unauthorized music for generations to come.

ONE

The Common Wind's Second Gale
The Desdunes Family

> The nation-state sees the entire territory as its performance area; it organizes the space as a huge enclosure, with definite places of entrance and exit.
> *Ngũgĩ wa Thiong'o*[1]

> Kreyon pèp la pa genn gonm
> (The people's pen has no eraser)
> *Haitian Proverb*[2]

One question has long occupied jazz historians: when did the music we call "jazz" really begin? The question is impossible to answer—the music was not referred to as such during its development, though researchers who take on this task may look to the memories of trombonist George Fihle: "Younger musicians about 1892 began to 'swing.' Older men used lots of Mexican music." Fihle specifically credits "swinging" to "Dan Desdunes," recalling, "[We] played jazz, [and] would always swing the music, that was [our] novelty."[3] While what such swinging consisted of, exactly, is not explained, we are left with a sense that something changed in 1892 among brass bands, and that the new music was different from the Mexican-derived music of an earlier generation.[4]

The year 1892 marked another kind of transformation. It was the year that Daniel Desdunes—the very same Creole of color violin and cornet player to whom Fihle attributed the development of swing—crossed the color line in public transportation. On February 24, Desdunes boarded a Louisville and Nashville Railroad train with a first-class ticket to Mobile and took a seat in a car reserved for whites only.[5] It was a strategic action years in the making. The Separate Car

Act, which required "equal, but separate" train car accommodations for Black and white passengers, was passed in 1890 by the Louisiana state legislature to stymie gains made by the state's Black and Afro-Creole populations under the 1868 Louisiana Constitution.[6] In response, an activist collective named the Comité des Citoyens coordinated the sit-in. The group organized with a diverse group of allies—meetings might include a former African American governor of Louisiana (P. B. S. Pinchback), a Cuban revolutionary exile (Ramón Pagés), and Desdunes's father, Rodolphe, a Creole of color activist of Haitian descent who helped found the organization.[7] Rodolphe expressed how their civil rights case was part of a larger strategy to contest anti-Black violence in the Comité's newspaper, the *Crusader*: "No theory of white supremacy, no method of lynching, no class legislation, no undue disqualification of citizenship, no system of enforced ignorance, no privileged classes at the expense of others can be tolerated, and, much less, openly encouraged by any citizen who loves justice, law, and right."[8] As his writings suggest, Desdunes and the collective had a double mission: to wage legal battle and to organize through the case by disseminating propaganda challenging the Jim Crow laws.[9] Comité member Daniel Desdunes, precisely because his profile as an innovative musician brought the attention of New Orleans's concertgoing public, was selected as the first test case.

The incident was closely followed in local and national press to see if the segregation laws passed by Louisiana's legislature were constitutional. The *New York Times* depicted a particularly dramatic showdown. According to its correspondent, a stressed conductor yelled, "You can't ride in this car!" Desdunes refused to budge, and a private detective riding on the train took it upon himself to arrest the Freedom Rider—but only after hailing backup from local police. Even with several officers escorting him, Desdunes "used some harsh language and made resistance."[10] The tense scene was a pretense, for the arrest was carefully orchestrated, and the railroad company, wary of the costs associated with operating racially segregated train cars, cooperated with the choreography. Even the "detective" had been hired by the Comité.[11] The event was a form of street theater designed to gain exposure for the upcoming case.[12] The state of Louisiana set Desdunes's bond at $500—the equivalent of approximately $14,000 in today's currency—demonstrating the New South's commitment to bankrupting and criminalizing emergent civil rights organizations.[13] Nonetheless, Desdunes prevailed. Because the train was moving between states, the court determined that his ejection violated the Commerce Clause of the United States Constitution. The broader constitutionality of "separate but equal" institutions for white and Black, however, was left unaddressed. This issue would not be resolved until four years later in the better-known case brought by Desdunes's friend and fellow

Comité member, the shoemaker Homer Plessy, whose defeat in *Plessy v. Ferguson* set a sixty-eight-year precedent for American apartheid.[14] In the intervening years, however, a victory had been briefly secured, segregation's legal basis was weakened, and a generation was further politicized.[15]

This search for jazz's beginnings, then, leads to a rather startling observation—that both a new musical form and a new civil rights campaign congealed in 1892, embodied by the same person who was supported by a coalition of musicians and organizers. New questions emerge: How did the fusion of brass bands and anti-racist rebellion inform swing's new structure of feeling? What were the connections between brassroots democracy and Haitian activism in the Crescent City? These topics are interrelated, for no other reason than Daniel Desdunes's own identity as a Haitian-descended activist musician who agitated for anti-racist grassroots democracy. But they were interrelated at the level of music as well. For decades, rhythmic substrates of the Cuban-Haitian *tresillo* and *habanera* rhythms had permeated New Orleans Creole music, whose popularity was reinforced by the Mexican military bands that performed regularly in the 1880s and '90s.[16] Yet what Fihle meant by "swing" likely suggests a proximity to African American musical traditions that spoke to a different sense of feel. Desdunes's reinterpretation of brass band rhythm reflects, as Eric Lott has written about another epoch, how "the music attempted to resolve at the level of style what the militancy combated in the streets."[17] The rhythmic subtexts that made "swing" swing derived from this creative dialogue between urban to rural African American musical traditions with those of Haitian and Afro-Caribbean migrants, with each group contributing unique practices of freedom and agency through embodied, intergenerational knowledge.[18] Their fusion in the person of Daniel is but one part of the legacy of an overlooked Haitian-descended family who engaged deeply with both New Orleans music and politics.

This chapter explores the lives of Rodolphe and Daniel Desdunes. Their musical and organizational labor illustrates how multigenerational Haitian Louisianan folkways—the common wind—were mobilized through counter-plantation organizing and popular music to defy the state's ability to order racial space. Haiti was not ancillary to the printed statements and political imagination of his family, and at the time of writing, the Haitian Embassy in Washington, DC, proudly includes a biography of Rodolphe Desdunes on its website.[19] This chapter will first consider the ways Reconstruction-era Afro-Creole activists invoked Haiti to guide their politics and geography of freedom and emancipation. It will then explore points of consensus and tension with African American activists of the same epoch. Swing and the cinquillo complex, two different rhythmic substrates with distinct senses of feel, were expressions of the unique cultural identities of both groups, and their fusion in early jazz was one way solidarity was enacted through musical performance. The chapter concludes with Daniel Desdunes's legacy as a brass band instructor at an interracial orphanage in Omaha, Nebraska. Here, his experiences as an innovative musician and community organizer in New Orleans would inspire a productive synthesis of Black arts and networks of mutual aid. His life, as well as that of his father's, reveals how brassroots democracy was an organic expression of revolutionary cultural currents from the Haitian Revolution and its diaspora that profoundly inflected the tenor of jazz musicianship not only in New Orleans but throughout the Americas at large.[20]

ON BEING HAITIAN: NEW ORLEANS CREOLES OF COLOR THROUGH THE CIVIL WAR ERA

For us, to be a Louisianian is to be Haitian.
Rousseau, "Souvenirs"

In 1907, Rodolphe Desdunes published a fifteen-page pamphlet entitled *A Few Words to Dr. DuBois 'With Malice Toward None.'* Desdunes, in phrases alternating lavish praise and pointed criticism, attacked Du Bois's elitism. Du Bois had recently opined that Black Southerners lacked book learning and industrial skills. "The Negroes of the South," retorted the elder Desdunes, "do not deserve to stand under the indictment which . . . that declaration conveys."[21] Rodolphe Desdunes's overture to Du Bois may seem surprising, given the latter's prolific scholarship lifting up the contributions of the Black working class. Who was this Creole of color from Louisiana to call out the venerable W. E. B. Du Bois?

Desdunes "took a broad view of the struggle," writes Rebecca Scott, a struggle that encompassed "the principles of the French and Haitian Revolutions, the Louisiana Constitution of 1868, and the history of the fight for equal rights across the Caribbean."[22] Desdunes's political education started at a young age, when he studied Radical Republican ideals in a New Orleans school founded by a once-enslaved Haitian emigrant, Marie Justine Couvent.[23] Desdunes himself descended from Haitian immigrants, and the connections were ongoing: his parents and brother were part of a group of Creole of color families who briefly emigrated to Haiti in 1858. This ongoing two-way travel between the Black republic and New Orleans is one possible explanation for Alice Zeno's knowledge of a Haitian song dated to the 1850s.

Rodolphe came from a family of justice-minded activists. His brother, Pierre-Aristide, fought in the Civil War, motivated by the promise of emancipation for four million enslaved African descendants. Rodolphe did not see wartime combat

FIGURE 1.0 Photo of Rodolphe Desdunes, date unknown. Photo courtesy of Amistad Research Center, Charles Rousseve papers, Box 9, Folder 20.

but served in the racially integrated Metropolitan Police to defend Reconstruction's gains from right-wing white terroristic violence. In 1874, he was injured by a confrontation with a white supremacist militia at the Battle of Liberty Place.[24] The Desdunes family belonged to the tight-knit circle of radical Creoles of color and contributed to the war of ideas that animated Black Reconstruction. Now considered a century ahead of its time, the 1868 Louisiana Constitution that this group influenced included the strongest anti-racist provisions in the nineteenth-century world, and its novel language of "public rights" was developed by Black and mulatto revolutionaries during the Saint-Domingue uprising.[25] As Joseph Logsdon and Caryn Cossé Bell note, Desdunes and those of his generation took positions that "placed them in the political vanguard of the entire nation."[26] Louisiana's radical Creole of color activists fought for the most expansive suffrage laws in the United States, for agricultural cooperatives to replace plantations,[27] for women's rights,[28] for a robust and desegregated public school system, and for a culture of interracial solidarity. These innovations had everything to do with the meaning and messaging of the Haitian Revolution, exemplifying Westenley Alcenat's argument that "the idea of Haiti became a radically subversive alternate to American citizenship."[29] Perhaps in this period, we can say that the idea of Haiti radically altered and expanded the meaning of American citizenship.

Rodolphe Desdunes was deeply inspired by both the idea of this "radically subversive alternative" and the actual politics of Haiti. It was late in Desdunes's life—decades after the defeats of both Radical Reconstruction and the 1890s civil rights movement—when he expressed his disagreements with Du Bois. Yet he still proselytized for a vision of social change inspired by the saga of the Haitian Revolution, looking to the Black republic's history for lessons of decolonization and revolutionary leadership. Du Bois (whose father, Alfred, was Haitian) had, in Desdunes's assessment, uncritically accepted Toussaint Louverture as Haiti's great Black hero. "Louverture was willing to see the island remain under French control," Desdunes notes, before quipping in language that Du Bois was sure to understand that "Toussaint Louverture was the Booker T. Washington of Haiti."[30] While the comparison may be an overstatement, Louverture was complicit with French rule and plantation agriculture, perhaps a result of a naive belief in the Enlightenment, a point reinforced in modern scholarship.[31] Desdunes contrasts Louverture with Jean-Jacques Dessalines, Haiti's Black emperor who was born into slavery, and who Desdunes celebrates for pursuing authentic independence and initiating trans-Caribbean slave revolts. Dessalines's legacy is more complex than Desdunes acknowledges in this letter—while David Nicholls describes him as "a spokesman for the disinherited," most contemporary historians demonstrate Dessalines's commitment to the plantation system through a heavily militarized regime. Vodou songs in nineteenth- and twentieth-century Haiti both celebrated and condemned the Black general.[32] Nonetheless, Desdunes self-consciously aligned himself with what he understood to be the most anti-colonial and uncompromisingly radical legacy of the Haitian Revolution to argue that Southern freedpeople were revolutionary subjects—an opinion that Du Bois himself argued forcefully twenty-eight years later in *Black Reconstruction in America*.

In his words to Du Bois, Desdunes embodied the consciousness of Afro-Creole activists who came of age during Reconstruction and self-consciously identified their work with the memory and example of Haiti. This cadre was the second gale of the common wind, and looked to the Black Republic and its world-changing Revolution to animate their participation in the Civil War and the social revolution that followed.[33] They were not far off the mark, either: contemporary historians have noted the parallels between the Haitian Revolution and the United States Civil War, despite their very different outcomes.[34] It was not only their certain class and caste politics but their understanding of geopolitics that animated their will to fight. Desdunes continued to proselytize, decades after heart-crushing defeats of equal rights provisions and the consolidation of white supremacist rule, channeling what Christopher Hodson has called Afro-Creoles' "particular vantage point" wherein "Louisiana emerges as an energetic offshoot of the greater Caribbean patched hastily onto the fabric of the United States." This particularly Atlantic perspective understood the catastrophic end of Reconstruction "less as national tragedies and more as American manifestations of a trans-Atlantic reckoning."³⁵ These reckonings, however, swung both ways, and Rodolphe's keen sense of history lent clarity to his analysis as he considered the political openings that transatlantic revolutions and social movements offered, even when defeated. This worldview animated the participation of the Desdunes family in the Civil War, during Reconstruction, and as 1890s Freedom Riders.

By zooming out from Rodolphe Desdunes to the community of activists with which he organized, we can further grasp the Afro-Atlantic kaleidoscope that shaped the worldview of this community of radical Afro-Creoles. Édouard Tinchant, a Creole of color Union army veteran and Reconstruction activist, had a story that was Atlantic in scope and one in which Haiti figured prominently. His grandmother, Rosalie of the "Poulard" nation, was enslaved in Senegambia and forcibly transported to Haiti; in the tumultuous years of the Haitian Revolution, she gained her freedom.³⁶ Tinchant's mother, Elisabeth, was a Haitian émigré who fled Louisiana for France during the especially oppressive years leading up to the Civil War. Tinchant grew up in Paris, where he was radicalized as a student by Napoleon III's violent repression of the Paris Commune of 1848. He became an avid anti-imperialist and Radical Republican. He moved to New Orleans two years before the battle of Fort Sumter and fought in the Civil War on the side of the Union army. During Reconstruction, he participated in Louisiana's Constitutional Convention of 1867–68, where he fought for universal suffrage for both men and women and later became an outspoken school board president.³⁷

What grounded each of Édouard Tinchant's transatlantic journeys was that he self-consciously identified, in his words, as "a son of Africa . . . of Haitian descent," and he fought to "defeat, reverse and obliterate this tyrannical aristocracy that forced our father to expatriate and which, ever since our earliest years, he has taught us to hate." His connection to France did not blind him to its imperialism. In protests at the French consulate and in letters to more conservative Creoles of color, he defended the Mexican Revolution against French invasion in 1862. He also claimed to be "in early and ardent sympathy with the Cuban cause" in a letter to Cuban independence leader Máximo Gómez in 1899 while the nation was under US occupation.³⁸ Tinchant understood his anti-imperialist internationalism as an embodiment of his Haitian ancestry, and this connection was made apparent in his various letters and speeches, which altered the tenor of Louisiana's Reconstruction Constitution. As Rebecca Scott notes, "during the last months of 1867 and the first months of 1868, this French-born man of Haitian ancestry helped to hammer out the most radical state constitution the South had ever seen."³⁹

This radical faction of Creoles of color foregrounded their Haitian identity to inspire daring alternatives to the plantation order in the context of postwar Louisiana's tumultuous political changes. Before the Civil War, many had visited the island nation. In 1858, facing increased repression, at least five hundred eighty-five Afro-Louisianans moved to Haiti, including New Orleans Creole of color Romantic poet Joseph Colastin Rousseau.[40] Rousseau continued publishing in Haiti, and in December 1862 (months after New Orleans had been seized by the Union army) he published a groundbreaking article for the port-au-Prince *L'Opinion Nationale* that invoked Pan-Africanist ideas to build the case for Haitian and Afro-Louisianan solidarity. "[I write] in order to shine a light upon these Louisianians, so that everyone, and most especially our Haitian brothers, might learn more about who these people are, because for us, to be a Louisianian is to be Haitian."[41] Rousseau's declaration as a Haitian Louisianan was an early expression of Black internationalism in print media. This was no passive inheritance—Rousseau constructed it.

Rousseau's testimony was not the first public example of Creole of color solidarity with Haiti. In 1832, New Orleans Creoles of color coordinated a fundraising campaign for hurricane victims in Les Cayes and Jérémie on Haiti's southern peninsula.[42] Seven years later, Haitian president Jean-Pierre Boyer's son visited New Orleans—during a time when Southern senators routinely denounced Haiti and wielded devastating economic and political sanctions.[43] Adorning the walls of the long-standing mutual aid association composed of New Orleans Creoles of color, La Société d'Économie et d'Assistance Mutuelle, was a portrait of Haitian president Alexandre Pétion, and its library contained numerous books by Haitian writers.[44] And in schools organized by Creoles of color, Haiti was part of the curriculum. A fourteen-year-old Creole of color named Lucien Lamanière wrote to a fictional pen-pal "J. H. Sauvign" in 1861 as part of a school assignment: "I am going next year and I invite you to come[,] we will go to Paris together before coming back to New Orleans, we will go and visit that fine country called Hayti and if you are not satisfied of those two countries, we will go and visit Mexico the finest country after Paris."[45] Young Lamanière's imagined itinerary shows how some Creoles of color reproduced an Atlantic conception of freedom constructed within, and transmitted from, the revolutions in Haiti, Mexico, and France. They hoped to one day advance their legacies in Louisiana.

The Desdunes family was a nodal point between Haiti and Louisiana. Sometime in the mid-1850s, Rodolphe Desdunes's father, Pierre-Jérémie, convinced Haiti's Emperor Faustin-Élie Soulouque to allow Black Louisianan emigration to Haiti. Rodolphe describes this clandestine meeting in his history of New Orleans Creoles of color, *Our People and Our History* [Nos hommes et notre histoire]

(1911). He writes how his uncle Emile, while born in New Orleans, "was Haitian by education and custom," and thus "Emperor Soulouque, acting on [the] basis of reports he received, decided to send Emile Desdunes to New Orleans to inquire into the condition of all people of Haitian descent." He apparently did a good job: Desdunes mentions that his uncle "justified all his [Soulouque's] expectations," and he was given responsibilities as an emissary. He facilitated the voyage for hundreds of New Orleans families of color.[46] Emile Desdunes also attempted to break the United States embargo of Haiti by encouraging New Orleans merchants to establish a line of packets.[47] In 1859, he appealed to African Americans in both the North and South, publishing in the *Cincinnati Daily Press*: "In Hayti he will have no superior. Here he can never dream of arriving at equality. Let the free Negroes emigrate by all means, and infuse American energy, skill and republicanism into the Hayti Republic. By so doing they will escape from their degraded and insecure position, and enter on a new and brilliant field that surpasses Liberia in every respect."[48] Soulouque was of such interest to New Orleans Afro-Creoles that a blind Creole composer, Henri Fourier, wrote an "epic song" titled "Proclamation de Soulouque Aux Haitiens." Despite the differences with Louisiana Creole, this song's Haitian Creole lyrics, which aligned with Soulouque's non-elite origins, suggest that the dialect resonated with (and was intelligible to) New Orleans Creoles of color.[49] The tone of the piece, narrated from the point of view of the deposed emperor, appears to poke fun at Soulouque and his fall from power. The composition makes evident a New Orleans market for songs that detailed Haitian current events, a page in a common wind songbook that Alice Zeno would eventually contribute to.

Among those who responded to Soulouque's invitation and traveled to Haiti was Rodolphe's brother, Pierre-Aristide, an important activist-poet during the Civil War and Reconstruction. While in Haiti, Pierre-Aristide frequently visited the grave of one of his idols, the Haitian poet Coriolan Ardouin, who Pierre-Aristide cherished for playing "the very fibers of his heart" like a "lyre."[50] He also studied Haitian Vodou at a relative's home who had fought in the Haitian Revolution.[51] These experiences influenced his own class politics: decades later Pierre-Aristide wrote essays on Karl Marx's philosophy of capitalism.[52] Pierre-Aristide's study of Haitian Vodou and radical politics, as well as his spiritual kinship with Joseph, reveals that both he and his brother understood their alignment with the Black republic in political, cultural, and spiritual registers.

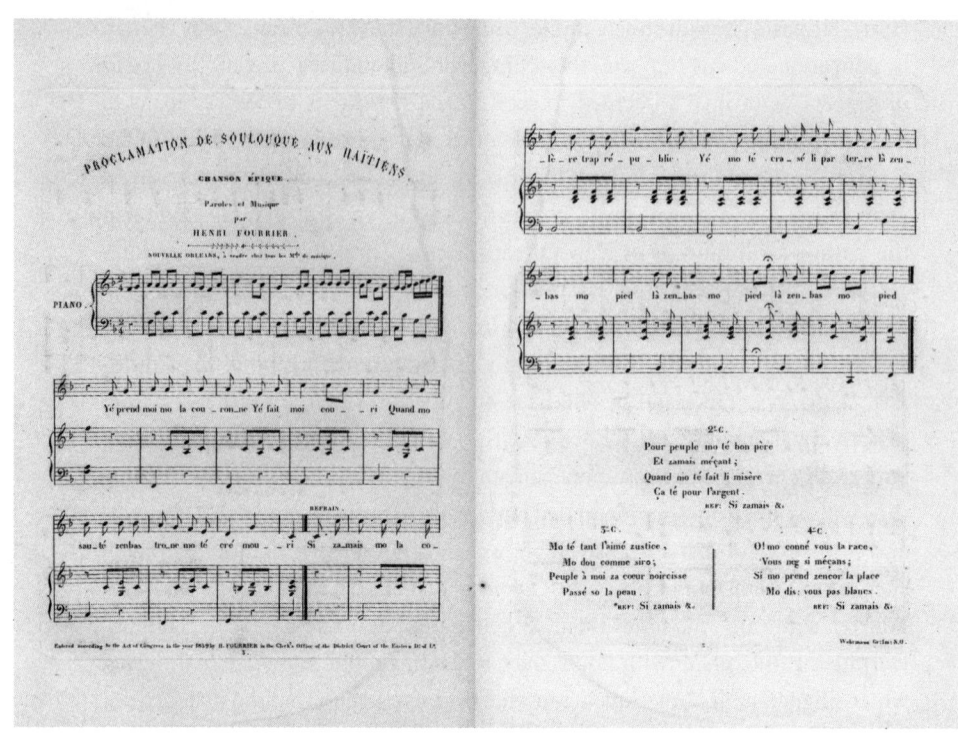

FIGURE 1.1 «Proclamation de Soulouque aux Haïtiens» by Henri Fourrier, ca. 1859. Courtesy of Louisiana State University Archives, TN 55771.

THE CIVIL WAR AS THE UNFINISHED HAITIAN REVOLUTION

[The] defeat inflicted upon the French expeditionary army in November 1803 should be reduced to no more than a skirmish in a titanic confrontation with the architects of the racialization of the human species.

Jean Casimir[53]

Quite impossible to free them here and now without a San Domingo.

Union General Benjamin Butler[54]

In his autobiography, Louisiana's centrist Republican governor Henry C. Warmoth expressed his antagonism toward the Desdunes brothers. Warmoth, who moved to Louisiana during Reconstruction from his home state of Illinois and later became the proud owner of a sugar plantation, was threatened by the counter-plantation politics of these Afro-Creole radicals. "They thought to establish an African State Government . . . [they] urged the negroes of Louisiana to assert themselves and follow Hayti."⁵⁵ Warmoth invoked Haiti to discredit his opposition from the Left, but there is a truth in his perception of this faction's politics. Their sense of the "possible" was not limited by the politics of the United States; they were aware of, and receptive to, the revolutionary movements in Haiti's that shattered its plantation complex.

The *New Orleans Tribune*, founded by the Creole of color Louis Charles Roudanez, was the first Black daily newspaper in the United States.⁵⁶ Its articles, published in English and French, called for the unthinkable to the Union military leadership who occupied New Orleans: universal male suffrage; plantations to be confiscated and its land and machinery given to freedpeople; and the creation of cooperatives that would destroy the hegemony of private property. In language that echoes the most radical Marxian tracts of its time, its editors announced: "Our basis for labor must now be put on a democratic footing. There is no more room, in the organization of our society, for an oligarchy of slaveholders, or property holders. . . . Slavery is dead, but 'free labor' lives, and 'free labor' is to be killed."⁵⁷ By November 1865, the Freedmen's Aid Association, organized by Roudanez and others, claimed it had supported fourteen farms of "independent laborers" where "about seven hundred men, women, and children lived and worked" in collective labor arrangements organized democratically by freedpeople.⁵⁸ Afro-Creole radicals also created a "People's Bakery" in New Orleans that sourced materials from these occupied plantations. Organized like a workers' co-op, hundreds of New Orleans freedpeople were co-owners and producer-consumers.⁵⁹

Inspiring these projects was an internationalist imagination that engaged directly with the legacies of Haitian maroons and French socialist thought. With articles contributed by Victor Hugo, Afro-Guadeloupean activist Melvil Bloncourt, and others across the Atlantic, they challenged their New Orleans readers "to broaden their visions to areas beyond the English-speaking world."⁶⁰ As Anna Brickhouse writes, these writers "presented [their] own Haitian affiliation not . . . as a matter of shared aristocratic, slave-holding privilege, but instead as a shared revolutionary heritage on which [the paper's] readership could draw for political inspiration in the present."⁶¹ Indeed, the *Tribune* editors pointed to the examples of the Haitian and French Revolutions and asked: do "our proposals" truly "sound like the impossible dreams of poetry and fiction?"⁶² Their radical vision inspired African Americans across the country. In October 1865, Frederick Douglass wrote to the *Tribune*: "I am proud that a press so true and wise is devoted to the interests of liberty and equality in your Southern latitude. . . . Every upward movement in the South on our behalf is instantly felt here.

You may depend upon me to do what I can in the right direction here."⁶³ The spirit of transcending the "outer limits" of a historical era, to believe in "impossible dreams," came from this direct engagement with radical legacies abroad, animating these activists, their African American allies, and their coalitional Reconstruction activism.

As these *Tribune* articles make evident, two major factions—African American plantation refugees and radical Afro-Creoles—quickly developed frameworks for organizing together in pursuit of land reform, autonomy, and commoning social relations. While a sector of Creoles of color, including Armand Lanusse, signaled support for the Confederacy at the onset of the Civil War, it is evident that a considerable contingent of Afro-Creole leadership grew increasingly radicalized during the war years and broke with the conservative members of their community.⁶⁴ They understood the need to forge a broad, grassroots political alliance with freedpeople as early as the winter of 1864. At a mass meeting in December of that year, Oscar J. Dunn, born enslaved but emancipated before the war, initiated the assembly by declaring, "We regard all black and colored men as brothers and fellow sufferers."⁶⁵ The second speaker that night, Dr. J. P. Randolph of New York, proclaimed that he no longer represented mulattos but now stood proudly as an "African."⁶⁶ After a mass meeting in mid-January, the *Tribune* celebrated how "seated side by side [were] the rich and the poor, the literate and educated man, and the country laborer, hardly released from bondage."⁶⁷ Even conservative Creoles of color understood that in one-drop-rule society, their fate would be sealed with those of freedpeople. "[Perhaps we once] held ourselves aloof from the slaves," an unnamed Creole of color told Whitelaw Reid in 1865, but now "we see that our future is indissolubly bound up with that of the negro race in this country." This reality demands solidarity, declared Rodolphe Desdunes's colleague, for "we have resolved to make common cause, and rise or fall with them. We have no rights which we can reckon safe while the same are denied to the field hands on the sugar plantations."⁶⁸ Initially, some leaders presumed that the formerly enslaved would be foot soldiers, deferential to freeborn leadership. Yet to overstate these airs of "noblesse oblige" would be to overlook the deep progressivism and idealism that underlay these efforts to transcend long-standing racial, class, legal, and caste divisions and unite, according to the *Tribune*, "all classes of society . . . whether black, yellow or white . . . in a common thought: the actual liberation from social and political bondage."⁶⁹

While radical Creoles of color opened the door to an alliance with freedpeople, they closed ranks against reactionary members of their own community who did not get with the program. In an open letter published in the *Tribune*, Édouard Tinchant chastised Armand Lanusse for betraying "our brothers of African descent" when the latter showed wavering loyalty to the Union occupation of New Orleans.[70] The ultimate scorn was shown to Creoles of color who attempted to pass as white, a practice known as "jumping the fence."[71] Rodolphe Desdunes, for instance, called it "a moral depression that seems to represent the last degree of impotence."[72]

But it was popular song that enforced the Afro-Creole consensus to rise or fall with their sisters and brothers of African descent. As Dr. Randolph and Oscar Dunn sat side by side in mass meetings throughout the 1860s, "jumping the fence" became ridiculed by a Creole of color melody in Louisiana.[73] The song's refrain, often heard at bars, picnics, and political events, directed a cutting insult to one perpetrator: "Ah, Toucoutou, we know you! . . . No soap will make you white." Desdunes praised the song's erstwhile author, a musician-barber known as "The Creole Beaumont," and saluted its ability to enforce an anti-racist consensus.[74] "The song," he wrote, "will suffice to prove his genius and to show *how* our people reacted to the foolish controversy over the color of the skin."[75] "Ah, Toucoutou" made it clear that this vocal group of Afro-Creoles rejected the "wages of whiteness."[76] They attacked both those who would pass as white and the lack of political conviction that would lead one to abandon their identity in exchange for privilege. This anthem of intra-Black solidarity impacted some progressive-minded Creole of color musicians into the twentieth century. One was the trumpeter Mike DeLay. DeLay remembered that his family frequently criticized those who "jumped the fence." He exhibited an admiration for African American musicianship, and he claimed Louis Armstrong as his most important influence. He hated the racism of rural Louisiana, and he celebrated his father for influencing his anti-racist politics. He was "a Frenchman," DeLay explained, "But I mean, so what? . . . My father missed opportunities because he married a Negro wife. He was so wonderful. He couldn't get anything . . . [what] he went through in life for us."[77] His comments embody Thomas Fiherer's observation of New Orleans: "Despite the textbook image of racially torn Reconstruction, the 1880 federal census indicates the persistence of multi-racial households, frequently led by French or Cuban-born patriarchs."[78] DeLay's collaboration with African American artists in the 1890s and early 1900s was made possible by the Reconstruction culture that activists like Tinchant, Desdunes, and Beaumont enforced within their own ranks and in the city at large. Brassroots democracy's Reconstruction genesis had much to do with the ability of popular song, in the mouths, chests, and legs of multitudes, to perform a commitment to social justice in a moment when divisions among New Orleans's African descendants had the potential to disrupt a revolutionary project.

In their study of the Atlantic world economy, Peter Linebaugh and Marcus Rediker have emphasized how power's great fear in the seventeenth and eighteenth centuries was the amalgamation of the underprivileged strata: a many-headed hydra. Wherever possible, they mobilized racial and nationalistic divisions to subvert the foundations of any such fusion.[79] Union army leadership, who hoped to maintain the plantation system and export cotton and sugar to fund the war effort, were no different in this regard from preceding Southern hegemons. They were threatened by the radical vision articulated by Afro-Creoles and especially their critique of plantation labor. In the spring of 1865, 474,000 freedpeople had worked at one moment or another as federally supervised laborers in the Union-occupied South.[80] The *Tribune*, fighting for Black land ownership, denounced the Union brass as an "oligarchy" and demanded the abolition of the army's Bureau of Freed Labor for its abusive conscription of freedpeople. For instance, Black refugees in New Orleans who were caught stealing food were often sent to work on plantations; in one case, Black soldiers who mutinied against an abusive white colonel who had whipped them were sentenced to hard labor. In dialogue with African Americans who resisted these wartime labor arrangements, the *Tribune* writers described the military plantations as "not far removed from slavery."[81]

These words rankled the Union military, which, despite exceptions, was plagued by white supremacy.[82] Already in 1863, General Banks complained that Afro-Creole officers were "a source of constant embarrassment and annoyance" and forced most of them to resign.[83] In 1865, in response to their growing militancy in the *Tribune* and the success of their communes, Union General Hubert went on the offensive and attempted to sow division between Creoles of color and African Americans. He admonished Afro-Creoles for their culture of participatory democracy and encouraged African Americans to break ranks with their cooperative projects. "There has always been a bitterness of feeling among the slaves and the free colored. . . . If instead of assembling in mass meetings and wasting your time in high sounding resolutions, you would devote yourselves to assisting in the physical and moral improvement of the freedmen, you would do some practical good."[84] General Hubert's critique is a familiar one. As Rebecca Scott has noted, Afro-Creole radicals were often attacked by the Right for their skin tone as a way of delegitimizing their activism's integrity. This "line of attack aimed at associating the radicals with personal light-skin privilege, and with indifference to the real interests of former slaves," a claim made that ignores the legacies of "many of the radicals pushing for equal public rights [who] were also concerned with reforming the tax structure to make land more easily available for rent or purchase by the freedpeople."[85] Deep into the 1870s, for instance, Rodolphe Desdunes zigzagged through Republican meetings, supporting the labor activism of African Americans in the countryside while advocating for equal access to public institutions.⁸⁶ General Hubert's attack on "mass meetings," like Governor Warmoth's attacks on the Afro-Creoles who attempted to establish an "African state government," betrayed their fear of the intra-caste, intra-racial, and intra-class organizing among thousands of activists who resisted the designs of the plantation system.

Nonetheless, the attempts of Hubert and others to sow division between Afro-Creoles and African Americans was only possible because there remained a faction of Creoles of color who were apathetic or downright hostile to African American freedom dreams.⁸⁷ The attitudes of Desdunes, Roudanez, Tinchant, and other Afro-Creoles were not representative of the whole Afro-Creole community.⁸⁸ Many Black artists active in the 1890s and early 1900s later recalled the anti-Black prejudice they experienced at the hands of Creoles of color. "The worst Jim Crow around New Orleans was what the colored did to themselves," remembered bassist Pops Foster. "The lighter you were the better they thought you were. The [Creole of color] Francs Amis Hall was like that. The place was so dicty that they wouldn't let us come off the bandstand because we were too dark."⁸⁹ The banjo player Johnny St. Cyr similarly claimed that "the mulattoes were actually more prejudiced than the white people at that time."⁹⁰ These forms of social exclusion were clearly traumatizing for African American musicians, and played out in the aesthetic arena as well. Some Creole of color musicians openly resisted learning how to improvise, rejecting what Brothers refers to as the African American "plantation vernacular."⁹¹ Bassist Paul Dominguez contrasted his community of Afro-Creole "real musicians" with the "ratty" approach of African Americans who "can't tell you what's there on the paper, but they just play the hell out of it."⁹² The attempt to remain a distinct cultural-linguistic community, now facing obliteration due to repressive anti-Black legislation, undoubtedly fueled the psychological barriers Creoles of color erected. "Even as their economic status began to wane in the nineteenth century," argues David Ake, "Creole society strove to maintain staunchly middle-class values, priding itself on appearing well mannered and well educated (in the European sense) and living within an overall Francocentrism . . . the rift between the two populations [African Americans and Creoles of color] was a real one."⁹³ "[By] avoiding extensive contact with Afro-Americans," concurs Arthé Agnes Anthony, "they were able to separate themselves—at least psychologically—from other blacks."⁹⁴

Rodolphe Desdunes, however, complicates this tidy division between African Americans and Afro-Creoles. It may have been during his years of coalitional activism that he met Clementine Walker, an African American woman with whom he would have an affair and father the influential early jazz pianist Mamie Desdunes (b. 1881). Such multifamily arrangements were not uncommon in nineteenth-century Creole of color middle-class society, but a partnership between an English-speaking African American and a francophone Afro-Creole was less documented.[95] While the nature of their extramarital relationship is unclear, they had five children together over a period of eleven years, and Mamie received a piano education growing up, suggesting that Rodolphe did provide for his second family in a manner consistent with Afro-Creole middle-class values. Due to the oppression of Jim Crow, however, by the first decade of the twentieth century, all of Desdunes's children—including Daniel, who would become a janitor—were working class.[96]

In the arena of civil rights, radical Afro-Creoles' commitment to an alliance with African Americans was not limited to the Reconstruction era, and activists in this community continued to push for unity with African Americans even when others in their community expressed hostility. The Comité des Citoyens, which coordinated Daniel Desdunes's sit-in, represented a continuation of their organizing experiences during Radical Reconstruction. Within this organization, Rodolphe and Pierre-Aristide helped found the *Crusader*, a new organ dedicated to "industrial and economic questions... and particularly we shall devote space to questions of labor. Our special aim, in fact, shall be to make a great Republican Labor organ through which the working classes can at all times be heard and have their grievances made known and their wrongs righted."[97] These activists refused to leave questions of class off the table as they challenged the classificatory systems of white racial power. Then, in 1895, during the height of the Comité's legal work and campaign of public pressure in *Plessy v. Ferguson*, Rodolphe published translated excerpts from Joseph Saint-Rémy's five-volume work, *Pétion et Haïti*, in the *Crusader*. This work detailed Haitian president Alexandre Pétion's progressive land reform policies to Black English-speaking audiences in the Jim Crow South.[98] Much like the *Tribune* of the 1860s, the ethos of the *Crusader* reinforced an Afro-Atlantic perspective to the battle over civil rights—"public rights" in the lexicon of African-descended Saint-Domingue agitators a century earlier—and varied musicians read the periodical.[99] The clarinetist Lorenzo Tio, for instance, took out ads in the *Crusader* for his performances in 1895.[100]

As white supremacists overthrew Reconstruction and instituted segregation and Black dispossession known as "Redemption," leading African Americans called for solidarity with Creoles of color and demanded unity in the face of a growing fascist backlash.[101] One was A. E. P. Albert. Born into slavery on a plantation where he had only spoken French Creole, in 1863 Albert joined an exodus of 223,000 other enslaved people in the Lower Mississippi Valley who abandoned the plantations where they had been held in bondage by escaping to

Union-occupied territory.¹⁰² When Albert arrived in New Orleans, he learned English in a Freedmen's School and joined the Methodist Faith. He then enrolled in the Atlanta-based Congregational Theological University. He returned to New Orleans several years later as an influential religious figure in the African American community, and graduated from Straight University in 1881 with a Bachelor of Divinity. He soon became the editor of the influential Methodist periodical, the *Southwestern Christian Advocate*, a position never held before by an African American.¹⁰³

Writing in 1888, Albert celebrated Black political unity in a moment when Reconstruction seemed like a distant memory and anti-Black violence ran rampant across the South. He suggested that intra-Black social divisions between antebellum enslaved and free people were insignificant: a "fusion" had occurred between those free before the war and those freed from the war. But he paused when he thought of his home state. "A notable exception exists in Louisiana where the fusion is not so thorough . . . [but] this results not so much from the perpetuation of antebellum lines of division as from difference in language and religion." While culturally distinct, he rejected the arguments of General Hubert and others who argued that Afro-Creoles and African Americans had fundamentally different interests: "But among the blacks and those of mixed bloods, who were freed as a result of the war, there is perfect unity, and only *one* voice." He noted Black unity came about despite diversity of skin color. He celebrated that "the Negro of this land is inexplicably mixed, representing all the hues from lily white to jet black." He condemned those who propagated the idea that the Black community had "two voices" as "a dangerous enemy who . . . inspired father and mother to rise against their children."¹⁰⁴

Albert considered a movement for cultural "fusion" to be essential, from both a pragmatic and an ethical perspective. This fusion had been underway some years earlier in the brass-band-imbued public sphere. At the Mardi Gras parades of 1871, the *Louisianan* noted how "every shade of complexion, natural, political and Religious, all mixed in one indiscriminate procession and paraded New Orleans from early morn till long after the shades of night had closed over us."¹⁰⁵ Albert's call for self-conscious creolization was also, however, a late-1880s call to resurrect a Reconstruction-era organizational culture that included intercultural performance in an ethos of unity. At the Mechanics' Institute in 1876, a joint event featuring president-elect Rutherford B. Hayes and former governor Henry C. Warmoth featured a "liberal supply of music," ranging from Civil War–inspired "fife and drum in the lobby," to "music by the band" in between Warmoth's speech and others, this band performed a rendition of "that old negro melody . . . *Chere mo l'aimain toi*," a French Creole love song popular on the plantations and also popular in Haiti, suggesting the band included Black and Afro-Creole musicians.[106] The *New Orleans Democrat*, a white supremacist Democratic periodical, editorialized that this song was "added to soothe the savage breasts of the politicians"—"savage" being a euphemism for "Africa" and a reference to the Black Republicans who held state office.[107] One African-descended politician present who had been born into slavery was James Lewis, a steamboat steward who had escaped to freedom and enlisted in the first Black Union regiment of the Civil War. Lewis, who worked as an educator on plantations after the war, had escaped many near-death experiences at the hands of ex-Confederate white supremacists.[108] He was present at the Mechanics' Institute during the 1866 New Orleans riot, when a white militia deputized by New Orleans Sheriff and Confederate veteran Harry Hayes massacred a parade of Black Louisianans celebrating suffrage. In testimony to US Congress, Hayes's reasoning for opening fire was because the marchers had a brass band.[109]

In these examples and others, James Lewis and a coalition of African American, Creole of color, and white Republican activists were met with material and symbolic violence when they integrated brass bands with Reconstruction mass meetings. Yet the repression and attacks against Black political mobilization only made these mobile institutions more urgent. As the poet and cultural theorist Fred Moten asks: "How would you recognize the antiphonal accompaniment to gratuitous violence—the sound that can be heard as if in response to that violence, the sound that must be heard as that to which such violence responds?"[110] A coterie of Haitian-descended activists thought through this very question. Founded in 1836 by Creoles of color, La Société d'Économie et d'Assistance Mutuelle (hereafter referred to as Société) was a mutual aid society with numerous members of Haitian descent, including Reconstruction-era political activists. Several of its members had been killed by white nationalist paramilitaries, known as the White League, when the latter attempted a coup in 1874. In response, the Société's new president, Myrtil Piron, vowed in 1875 to publicly parade as frequently as possible for celebrations, funerals, and strategic political moments—and required "one corp of musicians" to march at the head of each procession. Although the Société's meeting minutes were written in French, they chose to refer to these bands in English, as "brass bands." Noting that these English words "jumped off the page" of Société meeting notes, Fatima Shaik explains that these sonic institutions and their naming responded to the activist and revolutionary energy of the age: "It was a heated and very important question, an issue of culture and language in this time of change." The Société's members had an identity firmly rooted in the Afro-Franco-Creole Atlantic, and this admission of an English phrase into their vocabulary reflected that a new style of music had been born that simply did not have the same meaning in French. "Brass bands," forged through the Black Reconstruction struggle and its intercultural imperatives, became a term that, as Shaik writes, "expressed them [the Afro-Creoles of the Société]—their pride, steadfastness, style, virtue, and optimism."[111]

The invocation of brass bands in English also reflected a larger strategic initiative that aimed at consolidating a united front with African Americans through cultural organizing. In 1885, at the very moment that its membership invited Frederick Douglass to speak at an Emancipation Day event, the Société began to hire the Eagle Brass Band and other African American musicians to shake up its traditional offerings of waltzes and French music.[112] Etymologically, sonically, and socioculturally, the Société's embrace of brassroots democracy reflected how creolization was an improvisatory and political act. By incorporating Black musical vernaculars while deepening their relationship with leading African American activists, the Société, like other activist Creoles of color, recognized that building a united front between the "old freedmen" and the "new freedmen" was a cultural process as much as a political one.[113] The Société's progressive orientation toward African American culture is one explanation for why their meeting space, the Economy Hall, would host "hot" Black and Black-inspired bands like the Golden Rule, when other Creole of color societies would not.[114]

These intercultural legacies deepened within brass bands themselves. Joe Oliver, the son of an African American Baptist preacher from Louisiana's sugar districts with no French ancestry, moved to New Orleans, became fluent in Creole, and studied with Manuel Pérez, a Creole of color musician of Afro-French Mexican heritage. Perez embraced Oliver's Black Baptist influences and improvisational abilities and hired him in the Onward Brass Band in 1904, fast becoming "quite chummy."[115] Pérez did not charge for his music lessons—he "taught anyone" that he considered deserving for free—but he demanded excellence from his students.[116] But Pérez was as much a student as Oliver. Their mutual commitment to the music reflects that collaboration was not happenstance. Creole of color clarinetist Albert Nicholas described how brass bands were spaces that fostered unity in difference by sounding multitextured polyphony. "Brass bands were mixed bands. Creole and [African American] uptown [musicians] in a brass band—they were solid. They were one, Joe Oliver and Manuel Pérez, see?"[117]

Brass bands, then, were simultaneously forms of public activism and vehicles for intercultural solidarity. Ascribing such ideological frameworks to these late nineteenth-century musicians might be seen as overly specious, but reading the *Tribune*, the *Crusader*, and the *Southwestern Christian Advocate* reveals that calls for intra-African solidarity were very much prevalent from the 1860s through the 1890s. More than any other institution, brass bands' sociomusical practice invoked the "fusion" called for by A. E. P. Albert. This interpretive framework of solidarity, however inconsistent and contradictory it may prove when applied to the Afro-Creole community as a whole, nonetheless provides another way of understanding how Creole of color musicians came to internalize African American musical aesthetics beyond narrow economic self-interest. Unlike white early jazz musicians who, with the exception of anarchist Antonio Maggio, did not entertain performing for progressive or radical political causes, pre- and proto-jazz Afro-Creole musicians such as Lorenzo Tio and Isidore Barbarin performed at civil rights rallies alongside African American activists and musicians throughout the nineteenth and into the twentieth century.[118]

Daniel Desdunes was a young child when the Société's regular brass band parades commenced their challenge to the white supremacist state, whose procession routes were blocks away from his History Street home. Brass bands were especially important to reinforce communal solidarity across racial lines, including among white allies. In 1881, for instance, Black dockworker James Hawkins was killed by a police officer while he and others were on strike, and brass bands were provided by the mutual aid societies and labor organizations who were present, including the Afro-Catholic "St. Joseph Colored Society."[119] As brass bands marched through the streets, they honored those martyred by white supremacist violence and defied the will of those who would see freedpeople return to a state of servitude. Young Black and Afro-Creole musicians like Desdunes were educated by these mobile institutions, what Johari Jabir calls "Black communal conservatories," and were impressed at their ability to turn "segregation into congregation."[120]

Daniel later majored in music at Straight University, where he would have had access to a robust education in both Afro-Creole and Southern Black musical traditions: its music department had a prominent African American choral music program whose choirs performed at civil rights events while Desdunes was a student.[121] A. E. P. Albert, who published well-known work on "plantation melodies," attended the school as well.[122] Later in his career in Omaha, Daniel expertly directed large Black choirs that performed spirituals.[123] The university's law students had included Daniel's own father and the Afro-Creole Louis André Martinet, a cofounder of the *Crusader* who crafted the legal theory for both Daniel's Freedom Ride and *Plessy v. Ferguson*.[124] Daniel's interest in African American culture and civil rights activism was a perfect fit for Straight University, which was a hotbed of militancy and whose lecturers often included outspoken Black activists. One visiting lecturer, the prolific poet and journalist Frances Ellen Watkins Harper, called for intra-Black unity and women's suffrage in order to challenge "the relentless hostility of the enemies of our race and human progress."[125]

Rodolphe Desdunes reflected years later on this turbulent period when his son came of age. By the 1900s, their rights had been stripped by Louisiana's white supremacist legislature. "It is more noble and dignified to fight, no matter what, than to show a passive attitude of resignation," he explained. "Absolute submission augments the oppressor's power and creates doubt about the feelings of the oppressed."[126] The brass bands fielded by the Société were one means by which the feelings of the oppressed could be unequivocally sounded. Daniel became an innovative, community-oriented bandleader and participated in a direct-action sit-in against segregation within his upbringing in this interwoven nexus of sonic celebration and anti-racist community organizing. His decisions reflected his immersion in a culture of activism and musical solidarity in which Afro-Louisianan brass bands embodied resistance to racialized apartheid and the white supremacist ideology by which it was maintained. Brassroots democracy provided the joyful and resilient strains of resistance during Daniel's childhood. He continued his father's legacy of coalition building by learning how to swing.

SWING AND THE INTERSUBJECTIVE INTERNATIONAL

Since the eighteenth century, Black artists have creolized European set dance traditions such as the *quadrille* and the *contradanza*, so much so that their variations became the standard.[127] Diasporic rhythmic interchange through apparently European forms was not dissimilar to the Haitian appropriation of *liberté, égalité, et fraternité* during the revolution: the popular music of the Enlightenment became the unwitting refuge of a fugitive ideoscape—the common wind.[128] On the levees in port cities across the Atlantic, a "motley crew" of Black dockworkers reinvented set and couple dance traditions through a network of subterranean polyrhythms and participatory performance practices, suturing diasporic African musical cultures within the beating heart of New World commodity exchange.[129] This transcontinental remix propelled vernacular dance forms whose virtuosity seemed to defy physics to white observers. Lafcadio Hearn, in a Cincinnati riverfront bar in the late 1870s, noted how African American "men patted juba and shouted; the negro women danced with the most fantastic grace, their bodies describing almost incredible curves forward and backward; [their] limbs intertwined rapidly in a wrestle with each other and the music," adding: "amid such scenes does the roustabout [dock laborer] find his heaven."[130] Not only musical languages but whole instruments became deconstructed. Hearn remarked in New Orleans some years later that "Creole negroes" played the piano "exactly like a banjo"—itself a diasporic invention with ties to Haiti and Jamaica.[131] The cultural labor of tens of thousands of mobile Black workers would eventually culminate in a dramatic reordering of American popular culture whose consequences musicians, historians, and musicologists are still finding reasons to theorize in innovative and compelling ways.[132] At the turn of the twentieth century, it was in New Orleans where Afro-Atlantic approaches to musical time portended a profound shift in United States popular music, transforming the quadral time feel that threatened to constrain ragtime's polyrhythmic potential.[133] The name attributed to this breakthrough in feeling was swing.

Butch Morris, the African American cornetist and composer-conductor, once explained: "It's not swing I'm after, it's the essence of swing I'm after, the very thing that makes swing. The thing that musicians create between each other is what I am after."[134] Morris points to a force that animates swing—an ethos, a social relation—between musicians. Precisely because it refers to both this sociomusical signifier of community as well as a set of shared rhythmic conventions, a concrete definition of swing remains an elusive pursuit. In the context of its rhythmic qualities, what George Fihle characterized as swing likely described the music that accompanied the new two-step dance ("deux temps" in French-language programs of the time) that became popular in the 1890s, in which syncopated accents and rhythmic displacements arose through the amalgamation of 6/8 or 12/8 time signatures with 2/4 or 4/4 marches.[135] While sources are scarce, this timeline also coincides with the memories of Afro-Cuban New Orleanian cornetist Manuel Pérez, who referred to the 1890s as a period of "syncopated evolution" in interviews with Belgian journalist Robert Goffin fifty years later.[136] The unique fusion gives rise to a distinct sensation of "uneven" eighth notes, reflecting two parallel time signatures running concurrently.[137] Fumi Okiji describes the resulting effect as a "ghostly presence," wherein a "Yoruba Elewe rhythmic complex" is superimposed "over metronomic insistence."[138] In brass bands of the era, this was probably most noted in the "big four," a signature blend of anticipation and displacement in which the bass drum deviates from the straight march every fourth beat.[139]

Although Fihle attributes swing to Desdunes, swing appears to have already been in circulation, introduced by African American migrants through institutions of their own making. Trombonist Kid Ory was one of several musicians who attributed its source in New Orleans to Black Baptist and Pentecostal churches, claiming the choirs during service "would get to swinging."[140] This 12/8 against 4/4 rhythmic complex, audible in so much twentieth-century African American music, differed from that prevalent in Haiti and Cuba, in which interlocking patterns of repeated figures create different rhythmic "keys," such as *tresillo*, *habanera*, *clave*, and *cinquillo*. The commonality of many of these rhythmic figures (also called "cells" to express the metaphor of an organism) across the

Caribbean and parts of Latin America led Samuel Floyd to coin this intraregional musical language as the "cinquillo complex," which he thinks of as a "circum-Caribbean" Black culture that developed in a coeval (or simultaneous) fashion across the Americas.[141] Ned Sublette distinguishes swing's looping 12/8 feel from this cinquillo complex, arguing that they are relatively incompatible. Sublette further suggests that swing's 12/8 structure can be heard in contemporary Senegambian and Guinean music, as well as pentatonic, riff-based improvisations strongly evocative of the blues. His enticing conclusion is that swing rhythms came to New Orleans in the French Colonial period, when the majority of the enslaved were Bamana or Bambara from this region Sublette calls "griot Africa," while the cinquillo family was more likely brought by the enslaved who emigrated from Saint-Domingue following the Haitian Revolution, a significant plurality of whom descended from Kongo.[142]

Yet the cultural tapestry of Louisiana is not as straightforward as Sublette suggests—and neither is the noncompatibility of these distinct rhythmic feels. Recent scholarship has complicated the ethnic and cultural homogeneity of even the first generations of enslaved migrants in colonial Louisiana that Sublette draws on. During Spanish colonial rule, hundreds of enslaved workers were transported to New Orleans from Veracruz, some of whom had previously lived in Cuba, and others who were of the Gago, Foules, Meczara, Genoah, Zanfara, and Cano kingdoms North and South of the Senegal and Niger Rivers. In total, these enslaved migrants had African, Mexican, and Cuban roots and routes.[143] Kingston and Dominica accounted for two-thirds of Louisiana's slave trade from 1722 to 1790.[144] Louisiana's enslaved populations thus exhibited considerable cultural heterogeneity even before the arrival of Saint-Domingue enslaved migrants from 1804 to 1811, who included, as Jean Casimir notes, "Ibos, Kongos, Mandingas, Toucouleurs, Peuls, Hausas . . . at least twenty-four different groups that use their own criteria to identify themselves."[145]

Complicating the ethnic homogeneity of these forced migrants does not imply that African history is unimportant to the development of New World African cultures and political philosophies.[146] But, in addition to its potential erasure of other groups, the efforts to endow a singular West African "feeder" culture as an all-encompassing explanatory device might limit the agency and innovation of the forced African migrants of the Atlantic. Matory characterizes this organicist conception of cultural retention as a "certain passivity, involuntariness, absence of strategy, and political guilelessness and neutrality that seem quite foreign to the processes that have in fact shaped African and African American cultures over time."[147] "Rather than either Old World folkways or New World environments," argue Eltis, Morgan, and Richardson, "we need to encompass both and become much more thoroughly Atlantic." By focusing on overlapping transformations, they hope to complicate the view that enslaved "migrants remained conservatively attached to traditional ways," so that "we might also view them as experimenters and improvisers."[148]

Perhaps a discussion of what made Desdunes's band "swing" can be enriched by this notion—a swing not only of overlapping meters, derived from historically determined and unidirectional African "feeder" cultures, but rather as an improvisational, culturally conversational practice in which a practiced intersubjectivity was a vital component. In the language of Nathaniel Mackey, we are rethinking swing "from noun to verb."[149] Such a definition is more congruent with the twentieth- (and twenty-first-) century usage that Butch Morris pointed to. Here is a conception of swing in which cohabitating an imagined consciousness is crucial—what Ralph Ellison compared to a boxer who can "step into his opponents' sense of time."[150] This intentional inhabitation of alterity has profound implications for the (de)construction of the Western "I" subject. Okiji thinks of swing as a kind of sociomusical critique, whose refusal to abide by the oppositional logic of a principle and subordinate beat "ridicules the imposed polarization" implicit in Western dualism. "[Swing's] Syncopation should not be seen as an opposing pole to the main beat but as a shaking of that beat, a loosening of the soil around its roots, preparing the ground for its displacement. The doubleness of swing, the holding both counted-out beat and the plethora of micro (and quantum) movements away from it, convulses the structure."[151] Saxophonist Fred Ho has similarly argued that swing cannot be explained with a reductive notion of syncopation. Ho highlights how swing's interactive ethos generates "a shared communal bond of time, motion and energy. . . . Swing can be in time, in different time and in no time!"[152]

Would this idea of swing have resonated in turn-of-the-century New Orleans? Some testimonies from musicians of the era describe swing as boundless yet fiercely interdependent play, not dissimilar to the definitions Ellison, Morris, Okiji, and Ho all point to. The early jazz trombonist Jim Robinson, a plantation-to-urban migrant who was born the same year that Desdunes began to swing, related that stepping into each other's rhythm was the central element of the new music: "Now if them people don't work together, you can blow your brains out and you can't, you ain't getting nowhere. . . . That drum and that piano and that banjo and bass, that must work together."[153] Similarly, drummer Zutty Singleton, born in 1898, suggested that he could not even play without sharing a lived sense of time with those he was musicking with. "So many guys can play when the beat ain't there, but man, I can't do anything 'til everyone is right in it. Then I can play."[154] Singleton's words suggest that there was nothing inevitable or "organic" about sharing time with others—as many, apparently, did not—and that to "swing" required a shared commitment, the product of each participants' conscious decision to be "right in it."

Overcoming obsessive virtuosity in favor of a shared ontology was the major component of this swing ethos. "When musicians from other places . . . played hot, they just played fast," recalled the banjo player Emanuel Sayles. But New Orleans musicians developed a beat that swung—known colloquially as the "Negro New Orleans beat"—whereby one could "play hot and at the same time be playing in a groovy tempo where you [could] dance or clap your hands or join."[155] Sayles is probably referring to the tendency of musicians to play slightly behind the "hot" beat to maintain its intensity while creating a sensational pleasure by slightly resisting it. In all these accounts, the unidirectional energy of "fast," or a "show-off" method, is rejected in favor of this collaborative, commoning gesture: a "working together" where community members could come together through a "groovy tempo" as bodies and micro-rhythmic displacements were shared and innovated upon in an improvisatory, kinesthetic framework. Black New Orleanians thus developed an intersubjective practice that could synchronize participants' bodies to polyrhythms by synergizing dance, movement, and musical affect.[156] New Orleans was an epicenter for swing and other Black rhythmic innovations and diffusions to rural Louisiana, the Gulf Coast, and northern urban centers of Black culture. Sayles relates that bands from New Orleans were hired in Mobile, Alabama, in the 1920s because the Mobile bands "didn't have that New Orleans beat that people were going crazy about." He later explains the same was true in Orlando, Florida, where "the colored people . . . get really excited" upon hearing "[our] New Orleans swing."[157]

By refusing to give a metric reduction of what made "swing" swing, these artists prioritize the social aspects of the music, sharing their experience of the swing sublime without divulging a metric blueprint. Coming from this latter positivistic camp, European and white American ethnographers of this era struggled to explain what they were hearing. The German composer and pianist Albert Friedenthal, while visiting Louisiana in the early twentieth century, found it impossible to adequately notate what he called Afro-Creoles' "rhythmic sharpness." Explaining his choice to tie triplet figures to eighth notes, he felt obliged to apologize for the orthographic awkwardness: "Though they are complicated, they are not faulty."[158] Among white Americans, Alan Lomax was one who scratched at this breach, noting in his study of Creole of color musicians that there was "actually more syncopation throughout than can be indicated." While transcribing a downbeat in the music of Creole of color clarinetist Alphonse Picou, he explains: "This note might just as well have been written as the last sixteenth of the previous beat. Triplets might be substituted."[159] The revolution would not be transcribed—as it was not only metric. What was being played was a social relation made audible in sound.

Swing's syncretic sociality, which weaves perception, community, and quantum-rhythmic responsibility into a unified musical practice, has important implications for an alternative perception of time resonant with a larger Black Atlantic rhythmic episteme. In his study of the rhythmic patterns of early jazz, John Doheny draws attention beyond specific rhythms themselves to "how musicians operating outside the bounds of how European musical tradition *conceived* time-patterns." He argues that European rhythmic systems based in metric notation imply division, wherein a unitary value (a measure) is divided into distinct fractional units (four quarter notes, eight eighth notes, etc.). In contrast, Doheny suggests Afro-Cuban drummers approach this same rhythm from an "additive" framework. Within this conception, a constant succession of rapid pulses underlies musicians' decisions and rhythmic patterns are played in dialogue with this relation to a living, emergent time. "Where metric rhythm forms shorter (rapid) notes as divisions of a longer (slower) beat, additive rhythm forms longer notes as cumulative fusings of rapid beats," explains Doheny.[160] This difference, while seemingly subtle, may inform the insult of jazz musicians to those who do not, or cannot, swing—as playing "square"—a spatial metaphor whose insult also connotes the divisive quadrality of plantation geography.[161]

Although Doheny focuses on Afro-Caribbean musical cells, bebop trumpeter Dizzy Gillespie is one African American jazz musician of several who expressed how the perception of additive rhythms informed his own approach: "You know what I'm thinking about, to my time? [Sings] I'm filling up the bar and then if I want to hit anywhere, I got the correct hit. Instead of thinking '1, 2, 3, 4,' I'm thinking 1 and 2 and 3 and 4 and chuk-a-tuk-a-chuk-a-tuk-a . . ." Gillespie then starts singing faster subdivisions without a mathematical value attached and dancing different parts of his body—his chest, shoulders, and torso—to varying beats. "I might miss the note, but not miss the time."[162] The bassist Charles Mingus combined each of these definitions in his description of his rhythmic concept, which integrated intersubjective improvisation, collective world-making, and micro-variations to the pulse that prioritized dialogue over metric discernment. He explained that he "imagine[d] a circle surrounding each beat—[where] each guy can play his notes anywhere in that circle and it gives him a feeling he has more space. The notes fall anywhere inside the circle but the original feeling for the beat isn't changed."[163]

This spatiality—an undercommons expressed, in part, by the sensation of "additive" rhythm that permitted precise yet spontaneous rhythmic interchange—

has been theorized by Fred Moten to express a revolutionary alternative to Western ontologies of time, race, and space: "Must revolutionary subjectivity also be geometric, geographical subjectivity? If it must, how will it successfully detach itself from empire's spatial obsessions? How are the complex dis-articulations and re-articulations of space and subjectivity productive of theoretical insight and political possibility?"[164] Swing's sociality overcame binary ontologies that racial capitalism and the Enlightenment had inscribed between self and other, humanity and nature, Blackness and modernity. This was a utopian language, which resisted the "stultifying temporal logical of a broken-down present" in order to open up new experiences of being in resistance to the axiomatic colonial divisions of the human subject.[165] Its resistance to binary temporality resonates with flutist Nicole Mitchell Gantt's nonhierarchical performance practice that seeks to undo "siloed binaries . . . gender binaries, racial binaries, class binaries." "My intent," explains Gantt, "was to inspire alternative realities for how we, as people, relate to one another by redefining *difference*."[166]

Time became not a metric but a relation. It was precisely this relation that allowed musicians to communicate with each other, and themselves, multiple time signatures simultaneously, and improvisatorially move between each at will to explore difference in an additive, and not divisive, manner. Mingus's spatial imagination expressed what was already, in fact, happening on the bandstand—as musicians could *already* play "anywhere in the circle," able to make quantum adjustments in dialogue with others. His emphasis on human interdependence outweighs the quantitative Euclidean grid. In much the same way that Jim Robinson described the ideal rhythm section, Mingus continued: "The pulse is inside you. When you're playing with musicians who think this way you can do anything."[167] Mingus was not the first Black musician to identify an internalized pulse shared through an improvising community. Robert Charles Ball wrote in 1927 how he and others on a Louisianan plantation would enjoy "dancing largely to an inward music, a music that was felt, but not heard." But Ball was not writing in the present tense. He was reflecting on his enslavement and the dancing form he and his community had improvised, what later was known as Juba. "We tried to express in motion the particular feelings within our own selves."[168]

West African precedents certainly provide a metacontext for the polyrhythmic pulse that Ball, Mingus, and Gillespie allude to. Yet, as Valerie Kaussen has observed about Haitian *kombit* cooperative farms, "[their] utopian dreams were most certainly derived from the modern transcultural experience of enslavement and revolution."[169] The experiences of the enslaved and their descendants mattered—specifically, their cultural and intersubjective methods for building community and bodily connection in a world fractured by human commodification.

Swing's emergence in the activist culture of turn-of-the-century New Orleans bears more than a passing connection to this legacy. What Ball, Mingus, Gillespie, Sayles, and Robinson describe is not only an additive, generative pulse recreating itself from the annals of cultural memory. The dancers on the Louisiana plantation where Ball was enslaved expressed a social relation of solidarity forged inside and against the plantation and its afterlives. Their cultural labor, and those of their descendants, helped overflow the categories of a divisible, quantifiable time organized by capital, and reasserted the primacy of immanent, historical time—creating a world where an awareness of permanent change and qualitative transformation came about in relations of intersubjectivity, not objectification.[170] In 1890s Louisiana, these socializing temporalities became known as swing. And they developed in dialogue with another counter-plantation rhythmic tradition marked—much like swing—by additive rhythm, overlapping time signatures, and the ability to "step into another's time": the Haitian Cuban cinquillo complex.

CINQUILLO CONSCIOUSNESS AND THE INTRATEMPORAL INTERNATIONAL

When Desdunes began to swing, it was in dialogue with an African American counter-plantation tradition whose adaptive socialities became urgently relevant for Creole of color civil rights organizers. Their adaptations were another expression of the effort to build the "fusion" that A. E. P. Albert called for. But Afro-Creole musicians did not forgo the circum-Caribbean rhythmic lexicon they often referred to as "Mexican" or "Spanish" music. As trombonist George Fihle noted in his remarks that began this chapter: "Older men used lots of Mexican music." This nomenclature was partially due to the explosive performances of Mexican wind bands that toured New Orleans in the 1880s through the turn of the twentieth century. La Banda del Octavo Regimiento de Caballería, which performed at the New Orleans Cotton Centennial from 1884–1885, featured repeated *habanera* and *danza* rhythms through massive orchestral arrangements that mesmerized New Orleans audiences and set off a craze for Mexican music. Mexican they were, but their music had been thoroughly transformed over recent decades by musicians from Cuba, especially in Veracruz. Cuban observers of the concerts attested to the similarities between their national musics and rhythmic feel.[171] A New Orleans observer in Cuba similarly remarked that the Mexican bands he heard on tour there were "very strongly affected by African influence—full of contretemps."[172] The African and Afro-Cuban rhythmic substrate that were present in this style of Caribbean brass band repertoire is the subject of this section—what many call the cinquillo complex.[173]

Desdunes's only surviving composition—"Happy Feeling Rag" (1912)—is overlaid by this rhythmic complex, abundant with reinterpreted habanera and cinquillo rhythms in amorphous and emergent permutations. Rather than suggest that George Fihle was wrong in his memory of Desdunes's swing, the present discussion seeks to think through the social meanings attached to rhythmic kinship: specifically, how swing's emergence led to both musical traditions bumping up against one another, as a practice of internationalism in a moment of crisis. Fred Moten argues that such creolizations, secondary or otherwise, are consistently fraught: in the context of a "shared diasporic legacy that is always articulated in close proximity to intra-diasporic conflict," specifically characterized by "African American musicians' persistent denigration and distancing of Caribbean rhythms and sonorities" as well as "[Afro-]Caribbean disavowals of an African-American identity that is conceived as both dominant and abject," there arises the imperative to make these multiple time feelings mutually comprehensible and interactive, so that the "anti- and ante-American, musico-democratic assertion of The Black American International" can be embodied in musical and affective form.[174]

In the context of struggles against Union generals and, later, white Redemption militias, this practice of Black internationalism was a political necessity in post-Reconstruction Louisiana. As Clyde Woods explains: "Freedom to the Afro-Creole population had come to mean more than just the abolition of slavery; it meant planning for and creating a new society," a society characterized by "permanent democratic communities on lands that were free from the violent racial and economic enclosures that so far had defined their lives." Woods describes the articulation of this vision as a "Blues agenda" that "necessitated an internationalism among Afro-Louisianans, Haitians, and their allies that imagined, and planned, the end of plantation-bloc domination and of the empires that fostered it."[175] Yet this fusion, between the Haitian Revolution's emancipatory diaspora and African American freedpeople who had been displaced due to the internal slave trade in the United States, required that distinct lexicons, both linguistic and musical, be reconciled.

Written twenty years after Desdunes began to swing, "Happy Feeling Rag" showcases how Afro-Caribbean and Haitian Cuban rhythms were consistently present in the development of Desdunes's music. This cinquillo complex is characterized by overlapping ostinanti (repeated figures) that together create polyrhythm. Yet an underdiscussed aspect of its cellular approach is that the cinquillo complex implied its own multiplicity of time signatures through which skilled musicians could alternate in dialogue with others. Desdunes's use of habanera is apparent in Figure1.2, as well as the flipped cinquillo rhythm associated with the Cuban danza pianist Ignacio Cervantes (1847–1905), who also influenced ragtime composer Scott Joplin and jazz pianist Jelly Roll Morton.[176]

Within the New Orleans context, such rhythms have often been linked to what Jelly Roll Morton referred to as "Spanish" (in contemporary parlance one would say Latin American) traditions. But Black commentators of the era linked the rhythm's presence in the Crescent City to the 1791–1810 Saint-Domingue exodus.[177] These invocations of diaspora were imbued with the internationalism called for by Haitian Louisianan activists in New Orleans. The cinquillo and its sibling rhythms—the tresillo and the habanera—were the markers of a diasporic undercommons, and these rhythms often morphed into one another in the hands, lungs, and embouchures of vernacular artists. This "cinquillo consciousness" embodied an international, unauthorized, and subterranean public sphere in the nineteenth-century Caribbean, and its varied rhythms in the plantation Americas (tresillo and habanera) frequently underlay lyrical critiques of enslavers and empire.[178] Jerry Wever refers to the habanera as an "Afro-Caribbean creole rhythmic substratum," and while its notation in nineteenth-century sources does not appear particularly complex or syncopated by contemporary standards, the habanera was in fact a notated reduction of a nuanced four-against-three polyrhythmic pattern that became rearticulated within a 2/4 time signature over the course of nineteenth-century creolization in Cuba, Puerto Rico, Veracruz, and Haiti—not unlike the 12/8 looping sensation also imputed into a 2/4, and then a 4/4, march feel.[179] The habanera, then, signaled not only a rhythm but also a practice of temporality. The closely related tresillo was often referred to as an "elastic triplet" and sometimes even notated as such, implying, much like Lomax's description, a liminal rhythmic gesture whose "in-betweenness" was the point.[180]

This critical hearing of the habanera and tresillo is supported by the writings of late nineteenth-century Haitian composers in the Western art music tradition, who exhibited a profound anxiety when trying to notate the habanera's parent-sibling rhythm, the cinquillo. One Haitian composer, Theramene Menes, attacked composers who, hoping to assimilate the time feel of Haiti's rural musicians, notated a quintuplet or quintolet (5 against 2) rhythm as an alternative interpretation of the cinquillo rhythm found in nineteenth-century Haitian *meringue*. This very debate was reproduced in countless high-pitched vitriolic debates across the Caribbean as "learned" composers hoped to tame this paradigm-shattering infrastructure of feeling with duplet or triplet representations.[181] Cuban anthropologist Fernando Ortiz, frustrated that these rhythms were not played evenly, referred to them as the "improperly named cinquillo" and the "wrongly named tresillo."[182]

Yet these debates reveal that the habanera was, in fact, "swung" in the sense

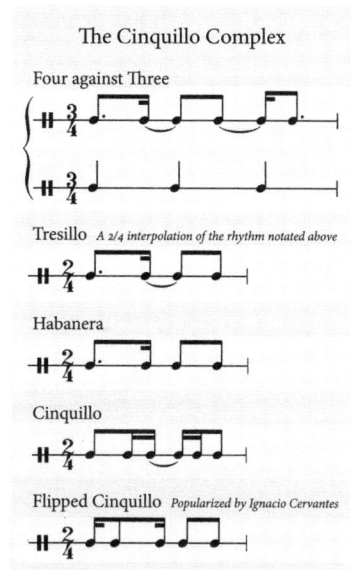

FIGURE 1.2 *Left*: "Happy Feeling Rag" by Daniel Desdunes. The variations of the flipped cinquillo popularized by Ignacio Cervantes are highlighted in black boxes, while tresillo-accented bass lines are highlighted with grey boxes. Courtesy of the History Harvest project at the University of Nebraska-Lincoln. *Right*: Notations of the tresillo, habanera, cinquillo, and flipped cinquillo rhythms, and their relationship to a "four against three" rhythmic pattern, above. Compiled by author.

that it contained complex implied polyrhythms that surpassed what Western notation's positivistic reductions was capable of rendering. These legacies live: contemporary *tumba francesa* drummers in Eastern Cuba (a tradition widely considered to be the creolized result of nineteenth-century Saint-Domingue forced migration) continue to "swing," or impose this quintolet polyrhythm, against the cinquillo, as do, according to Paul Austerlitz, ceremonial Vodou drummers in modern-day Haiti.[183] Thus, just as jazz musicians in the late nineteenth- and early twentieth-century United States found methodologies to subtly suggest overlapping time signatures through micro-rhythmic variation, so, too, did their counterparts in the Haitian diaspora in the Americas—and likely in Louisiana through the dawn of Jim Crow. Testimonies from early jazz musicians suggest that it was at this very moment that musicians began to incorporate both temporalities, of swing and cinquillo. The trumpet player Manuel Pérez noted that fellow Afro-Creole Lorenzo Tio, who performed polkas, danzas, schottisches with an habanera-inflected rhythmic substructure—what Gushee

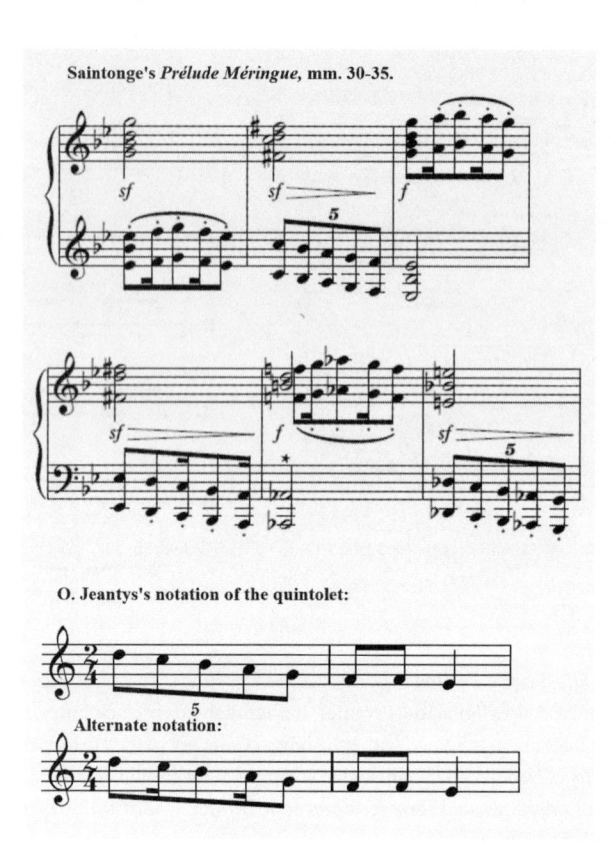

FIGURE 1.3 *Top*: Saintonge's *Prélude Méringue*, mm. 30–35. *Bottom*: O. Jeantys's depiction of how "the quintolet['s] . . . five eight notes can be replaced, according to one's tastes, with a group of three eighth-notes and two sixteenth-notes, written in the following manner." These two Haitian art music composers alternated cinquillo rhythms with evenly-divided quintuplets, implying that the "feel" of the cinquillo lay somewhere in between the two and was playfully and deceptively alternated by Haitian musicians. The excerpt of Saintonge's *Prélude Méringue* is derived from an analysis in Harned's "The Haitian Méringue," 55. The O. Jeantys example is sourced from Largey, "Ethnographic Transcription," 16.

called "Mexican" music—changed his feel during this time. "[Tio] went along with the new music."[184] Laurence Gushee uncovered evidence of what this meant: that the Tio and Doublet's Orchestra performed "two-step" pieces, so associated with the early swing feel.[185]

Caution must be exercised in arguing that the cinquillo complex and its influence in New Orleans early jazz music was structurally equivalent to their uses in Haiti or Cuba. Christopher Washburne convincingly argues that "Caribbean influence was so tied to its developmental stages that the rhythms became part of the rhythmic foundation of early jazz," and there are indeed numerous examples of tresillo, cinquillo, and habanera rhythms in early jazz recordings or ragtime piano rolls.[186] Some noted examples include the "B" section of W. C. Handy's "St. Louis Blues," the bridge melody of Scott Joplin's "The Entertainer" (which is a verbatim cinquillo rhythm), and in the drum parts of Joe Oliver's "Buddy's Habit" and Freddie Keppard's "Adam's Apple."[187] There is, however, a structural difference between these Black artists and their Caribbean counterparts. These rhythms did not function as "rhythmic cells"—a term used to describe underlying rhythmic patterns that serve as the building blocks of a musical composition, akin to how cells form the structure of an organism. These invocations of the cinquillo complex are more often used, instead, as exciting subsections, like bridges, breaks, and out-choruses. This is why, when asked if "those old Creole tunes" formed the basis of early jazz standards, the early jazz banjo player Johnny St. Cyr did not quite say yes: "I couldn't put my finger on a particular number, but they'd get a lot of those riffs and breaks from those old tunes."[188] Matt Sakakeeny notes these rhythms are not recorded among brass band rhythm sections until the mid-twentieth century. "When the[se] rhythms are present in contemporary recordings of New Orleans jazz," he explains, "they are merely present; not the substrate layer but an added later; sometimes only insinuated or 'implied.'"[189]

This distinction might seem subtle but is in fact quite important, since it suggests that Black musicians in New Orleans were actively and creatively negotiating varied cultural materials instead of copying whole traditions outright. By being present but not systematic, cinquillo, habanera, and tresillo rhythms were selectively incorporated. But such a selection process does not suggest they lacked importance, or their integration was devoid of intentionality; quite the opposite.[190] It would be a mistake to suggest these were only "rhythms in the air." Within early jazz bands, these breaks of a swing groove with cinquillo-based riffs were practices of diaspora, invoking the historical legacies—the roots and routes—of their intercultural collectivities. In the 1880s in Cuba, the introduction of cinquillo rhythms in the newly formed music style, *danzón*, caused fear and disapproval among the white upper class, who heard this music's invocation of Blackness and Haiti as a threat to their cultural hegemony.[191] Indeed, in an era where white observers were so quick to demonize or exoticize polyrhythmic complexity, the presumption of sociopolitical apathy on the part of diasporic practitioners who included these passages may be an equivalent interpretive violence.[192] These rhythms signified belonging in a transnational community through their invocation, even and especially when this early nineteenth-century referent had folded into a subordinated and substituted past.[193] While Morton referred to them as a "Spanish tinge," he riffed on a cycle of substitution by which "French" and "Spanish" would come to stand in for Haitian and Martinican, Cuban and Mexican. Morton's choice of Spain as his referent might have reflected his own contradictory racial politics, but it was also consistent with nineteenth-century nomenclature in New Orleans that referred to Latin American cultures by their European colonizer.[194]

Desdunes was conversant in both swing and cinquillo, and a core part in formalizing their unity at the very moment when he helped launch a new civil rights movement in 1892. What Olly Wilson identifies as Black music's "heterogeneous sound ideal" thus, in 1890s New Orleans, had an Afro-Atlantic genesis as well as a verifiable connection to civil rights organizing.[195] Wilson points to "variable" and "fixed rhythmic group[s]" in African American music, and perhaps this might be a meaningful way to think through the interaction between swing and the cinquillo complex. A rhythmic feel, then, cannot be reduced to a single pattern but rather is a composite generated by several instruments that play repeated interlocking parts and leave room for improvisation—in this case, improvisations that can invoke the interplay between African American and Afro-Creole cultural forms.[196]

As discussed in the introduction, diasporic rhythms played by maroon musicians had circulated in Louisana as early as 1810, through a clandestine network of underground Black institutions that included barber shops, ships, wharves, and taverns. Their interlocking polyrhythms popularized a framework for intercultural improvisation which became salient in the 1890s, pointing to the convergence of a political movement and a cultural shift in New Orleans with echoes across the Black Atlantic. The habanera and tresillo patterns in Daniel Desdunes's work gestured to a constellation of rhythms and an experience of "stretched" temporality that converged with the similar gestures found in swing. Daniel's sister Mamie Desdunes also made the habanera/tresillo rhythmic figures the foundation of the bass line in her signature composition "Mamie's Blues," whose right-hand melodies and vocal part were swung. This Afro-Louisianan creolization speaks to how musical innovation animated the intra-Atlantic horizon of the counter-plantation movement. Plantation capital's positivistic episteme was a cultural technology that reduced both Black workers' bodies and the alluvial soils of Louisiana into objects of capital accumulation, and thus arose a cultural technology to contest this objectification of soil and souls.[197]

ACTIVIST JOY: EUPHORIA AS A COMMONS

The processional forms in which swing and the cinquillo complex circulated were also similar in important ways. The marching traditions of New Orleans second-lining and Haitian *rara* were both attached to social mobilization, as subalterns could consolidate an oppositional and affirmational political voice throughout vernacular dance and polyphonic music-making that reappropriated public space. These mobile concerts were vehicles by which both individuals and whole communities learned how to step into the time of the other. New Orleans's unique step was an oft-commented subject by musicians. The trombonist Sonny Henry, reflecting on his career in brass band marches, remembered: "[When] I came here [to New Orleans] I had to learn how to walk all over again."[198] There was nothing "natural" about these collectively decided-upon gestures and movements; much like the music and the political ideas that came to represent the Black counter-plantation movements in New Orleans and Haiti, stepping, strutting, shuffling, or shimmying were carefully selected through a multitude of practitioners who signaled their approval or dissent through a movement's repetition, innovation, or disuse. This act of moving in unison not only highlights the significance of communal learning through collective action, but also underscores the importance of rhythmic synchronization to foster solidarity and project unity.

Rara is, according to Elizabeth McAlister, "the unofficial culture" of Haiti, and the "public mouthpiece of the popular class" of people, whose theatrical and spiritualized musical-processional mobilizations travel through distant villages and urban centers alike as a "reminder that the peasants are in the majority in Haiti."[199] Rara evolved into a vibrant spectacle, as a cavalcade of bamboo *vaskin* horns, drums, maracas, bells, whistles, trumpets, and saxophones reverberate with militarized and sequined costumes alike. Musicians and their devotees form small "battalions," embarking on journeys through neighborhoods and villages in aesthetic showdowns to ascertain which band can command the most admirers. From its inception, rara battalions have been powerful emblems of Black governance and rightful land possession in Haiti, often accompanying social movements. As of this writing, rara has rippled out to the communities of the Haitian diaspora, and its processional practices have been employed in contemporary protests and celebrations in Boston, Miami, and New York.[200]

Rara and second-lining both invoke euphoria within a distinct activist modality. This affect produces a transformational inclusivity that laid the foundation for an ethos of communal renewal in the plantation Caribbean. Within nineteenth-century Louisiana, these processional forms of music making, often in the affective register of joy, accompanied not only celebrations but also funerals, strikes, and slave revolts—including the uprisings led by the maroon leader Halou in 1790s Saint-Domingue and Charles Deslondes in 1811 Louisiana, whose similar musical and performative characteristics were recounted by traumatized planters in each society.[201] Eugenio Giorgianni identifies these moments as part of Congolese diasporic civic spirituality expressed through processional music, wherein "joy is seldom synonymous with happiness, rather, it is an affect . . . on the edge between bliss and self-destruction." This joyful cultural dimension resisted the annihilating processes of slavery and colonialism through music and other bodily performances; it has been a continual resource of resistance that exemplifies another register, beyond rhythmic interchange, in which the countercultures of Black Louisiana and Haiti become synchronized and mutually constitutive.[202]

Indeed, the continuities of street-parading traditions of New Orleans, Cuba, and Haiti are a frequent topic in recent literature. Scholars such as Richard Brent Turner, Zada Johnson, and Freddi Williams Evans have traced their connections. These authors have all demonstrated how Haitian, Louisianan, and Cuban musicians not only shared West and Central African–music influences, but also mobilized processional music to creolize colonial carnival celebrations, thus creating a vibrant space where Afrodiasporans could talk back to power by orchestrating practices of healing and belonging that resisted Black social death.[203]

Contemporary practitioners supplement these readings. Juan Pardo, a contemporary Mardi Gras Indian, cites as his "first musical inspiration" his Haitian Panamanian grandparents, who imparted upon him the beauty of "clave rhythms."[204] In 2013, the second-liner Fred Johnson, speaking at an awards dinner before the twentieth-anniversary parade of the Mardi Gras krewe named "Black Men of Labor," referred to their parades as a "dance across the Diaspora," theorizing the movements of their bodies in the streets as a way to connect the archipelagos of New World African culture.[205] The connections between the Afro-Atlantic and New Orleans second-lining tradition are actively remembered, enacted, and lived to the present day.[206]

Haitian rara ceremonies mirror New Orleans's second-lining through a rhyming repertoire of sociospatial affects. One contemporary New Orleans second-lining clarinetist, Dr. Michael G. White, described how band parades transform existence itself through collective social action. "The crowd grew larger and the music and the dancing increased in intensity, the entire scene was converted into a kind of spiritual dimension in which there was total freedom, a uniting of souls, and a constant reinterpretation of earthly reality."[207] Similarly, Haitian American novelist Edwidge Danticat writes eloquently of collective metamorphosis through rara parades: "At last, my body is a tiny fragment of a much larger being. I am part of a group possession, a massive stream of joy.... There is nothing that seems to matter as much as following the curve of the other bodies pressed against mine. In that brief space and time, the carnival offers all the paradoxical elements I am craving: anonymity, jubilant community, and belonging."[208] The words of White and Danticat are emblematic of the intersubjective ideal previously described in musicians' experience of swing. If the ego, as Joel Kovel has argued, is the capitalist form of the self, then this politicized pageantry of the Black Atlantic where self and other, humanity and the cosmos, anonymity and belonging, all disintegrate into one another is something akin to its antithesis—a phenomenology of the commons.[209] Jazz improvisation's liberatory and ego-destructive valences find resonance within this space. "Because jazz finds its very life in an endless improvisation upon traditional materials," writes Ralph Ellison, "the jazzman must lose his identity even as he finds it."[210] Like several other jazz musicians, John Coltrane used the metaphor of the commons to describe his own improvisational process: his ideas, he explained, were drawn from "a big reservoir that we all dip out of."[211] As Sidney Bechet explained about his own performances with Louis Armstrong, "Each person, he was the other person's music."[212] Here we see the jazz commons emerging in dialogue with a network of maroon ecologies—from Haitian rara paraders to New Orleans Mardi Gras Indians—and thus synchronizing a diaspora fragmented by colonial power through the activist euphoria of a resonant shout, a macro-antiphonal demand for freedom that invokes power beyond human domination.[213] These humanizing collectivities were responsible, then, for reproducing the sovereign universe of the counter-plantation and its commoning social relations in a mobile, active, and participatory form that could adapt to the unique emotional and political needs of each current moment and location.[214] "The process itself," explains Amiri Baraka, "is the most important quality because it can transform and create, and its only form is possibility."[215]

Like the Black Louisianans who developed the impetus for swing, Haiti's counter-plantation farmers were not only cultivators of the soil but cultivators of ideas, and the revolution they pioneered creolized the Enlightenment. Pierre-Aristide Desdunes's visit and study in Haiti demonstrates that their legacy was not confined to the dismantling of the shackles of slavery, momentous as that achievement was.[216] In the face of an embargo that strangled Haiti's diplomatic and economic bonds with its neighbors, the musicians of the common wind sparked a radiant hemispheric interculture that infused Louisiana's emerging practice of brassroots democracy with a philosophy of the commons. Both Reconstruction- and Jim Crow–era activists were led by a diverse African-descended population who synchronized several languages, visions of freedom, and rhythms of life in order to work together. The confluence of swing and the cinquillo complex run parallel to the negotiation of emancipatory traditions of the Afro-French Atlantic and African Americans in the United States South. Their fusion in the work of Daniel Desdunes helps us understand why New Orleans was an epicenter for a new rhythmic feeling that would animate Black cultural production for the subsequent century. The legacies of this historic convergence would soon spread into the Midwest.

MUSIC AND MUTUAL AID: RECONSTRUCTION LEGACIES IN OMAHA

Daniel Desdunes was significant figure in the New Orleans music scene, but he made an arguably bigger impact in his adopted home of Omaha, Nebraska. After the defeat of Louisiana's equal rights provisions with the *Plessy vs. Ferguson* case, Desdunes spent the better part of eight years on the road with the African American choral and minstrel group the Original Nashville Students. He soon became musical director of its accompanying ensemble, the Peerless Orchestra, where he directed a band that included Laura Prampin, considered the era's "the greatest colored lady cornet soloist."[217] But after touring the country, Desdunes became exhausted with New Orleans's hardened racial landscape. He joined an overlooked but significant wing of the Great Migration to the United States' Great Plains. Daniel and his wife, Madia Dodd, his eight-year-old son, Clarence, and his parents, Rodolphe and Mathilde, moved to Omaha in 1904.[218] Starting as a janitor, within three years Daniel Desdunes had built one of Omaha's leading Black bands. However, what earned him accolades from Paul Whiteman, John Philip Sousa, and Calvin Coolidge was his creation of what was probably the early twentieth century's most prolific interracial music programs.[219] Based at a Catholic orphanage known as Boys Town, Desdunes founded Father Flanagan's Boys' Band. The group toured the country, and was invited to play at events for organizations across a wide ideological and demographic spectrum, including one rather bizarre invitation from the Ku Klux Klan (an invitation that Desdunes declined).[220] Both Desdunes's music and his important role as a community educator bore imprints of his upbringing as a radical Creole of color and his early civil rights activism.

While New Orleans is a celebrated incubator of Black musical innovation, the importance of Omaha's Black community in the development of African American culture is less recognized.[221] But it was significant. As Jesse Otto notes, "Many of the musicians who played in black orchestras in Omaha went on to become big names in the history of jazz," including alto saxophonist Preston Love and drummer Buddy Miles.[222] Love himself described the city as an important "hub" for Black musicians: "If New York, Chicago, and Kansas City were the major leagues of jazz, Omaha was the triple-A. If you wanted to make the big leagues, you came and played in Omaha."²²³ David Krasner observes that Omaha attracted African Americans from across the South, who produced a Black culture that was "a complex mixture of ideas and movements—migratory, urbanized, intellectualized, fragmentary, literary, oral, folk, jazz, blues, rhythmic, Western, and Afrocentric—that created a complex, hybrid form."²²⁴ Creating "complex, hybrid" forms was a task at which the Desdunes family excelled, and Daniel laid a foundation for both local musicians and other New Orleans migrants, like Nat Towles, to move and build a musical life in this midwestern city.²²⁵ Just as part of Haiti's history happened in New Orleans, parts of New Orleans history happened in Omaha.

Desdunes's contribution in Nebraska's largest city can hardly be overstated. Omaha's Black bandleaders have long upheld a tradition of nurturing prominent musicians, many of whom had been attracted there from other parts of the country. "Dan Desdunes," according to Otto, "was largely responsible for beginning this tradition."²²⁶ Desdunes influenced not just a particular musician or institution but a whole culture, setting a model for community-based teaching just as the midwestern wing of the Great Migration achieved critical mass. He led a dizzying array of bands: the Desdunes Orchestra,²²⁷ a marching band named the First Regimental, his "famous saxophone orchestra,"²²⁸ his "colored jazz orchestra,"²²⁹ another called Dan's Jazz Hounds,²³⁰ and his "syncopated syncopators,"²³¹ to name a few. Alongside his frequent performances for the city's Black parades and pageants, Desdunes worked to desegregate Omaha's public life through his musical activity. Richard Breaux credits the "all-African American Dan Desdunes Band" for "crack[ing] the color wall" in Omaha when the band marched at the invitation of the Union Pacific Railroad at the annual Ak-Sar-Ben Parade.²³² That a Creole of color musician who had led a direct-action sit-in was, thirty years later, a prominent musical figure in an overwhelmingly white city was an irony that was lost on Woodrow Wilson, the president who resegregated the federal government.²³³ The band's performance during Wilson's 1916 visit to Omaha reportedly "thrilled" the president, while the accompanying general John J. Pershing praised them as "one of the best trained bands I have ever heard."²³⁴

In a climate where racism and white supremacy were becoming increasingly strong—the Omaha branch of the NAACP fought unsuccessfully to cancel the screening of *The Birth of a Nation* (1915) at the Rialto Theatre—Daniel Desdunes produced his own concerts that dramatized emancipation and the struggle against slavery.²³⁵ The *Indianapolis Review* glowingly reviewed a concert in Omaha that located Daniel's output within his father's activist legacy:

Perhaps one of the most helpful colored men in our midst is Mr. Daniel Desmumes [sic], the son of the distinguished writer and historian, Mr. R. L. Desdunes, of New Orleans. When Mr. Desdunes came to Omaha four years ago there was no musical organization among the colored people. He organized the Desdunes orchestra, and later, making a combination of Omaha talent in his race, he produced [the play] *Forty Years of Freedom*, which was a distinct success.... His plays, which he composed and presented, have been pronounced by the press and public as artistic successes.[236]

Desdunes also frequently played for Emancipation Day festivities; in 1909, at an event that was declared "the Fourth of July for the colored race in America," he performed for "several hundred" African Americans and a "small scattering of white people." For decades, Daniel furnished the music at these events; in 1927, one particularly large celebration, he directed a chorus of a hundred fifty voices that sang "Negro spirituals."[237] He did not abandon politics, nor did he escape the possible consequences of furnishing music in such endeavors: after he played for a Republican meeting in 1920, he lost his job in a real estate business and was forced to put up an ad to sell his silver-plated Besson French trumpet and, a few months later, his Victrola.[238]

Daniel uplifted the emancipation struggles of Black Americans within similar mutual aid and benevolent socieities to which he belonged in New Orleans. The Colored Knights of Pythias, of whose New Orleans branch Homer Plessy was a member, hired Desdunes to form a band shortly after the cornetist had moved to town;[239] by 1915, he had created and trained "an elite group of African American musicians" who became the official band of the Omaha Chamber of Commerce.[240] Desdunes's cultural leadership in Omaha may even explain how the term "jazz" was introduced to the city. Its first print appearance, in 1917, was in Omaha's Black weekly newspaper, *The Monitor*, in an advertisement for a charity ball where the "Desdunes Jazz Orchestra" was scheduled to play.[241] As Dan Vernhettes has surmised: "Dan Desdunes was mainly responsible for the fact that jazz played an important part in the history of Omaha."[242]

Press coverage from Desdunes's decades in Omaha ring with praise. Reading these writers' accounts, it seems that his influence and diversity of styles knew no bounds. One Omaha periodical claimed that "there were other Negro instrumentalists in Omaha, but there were none with more music."[243] He received national press, too: in 1914, at a performance on Thanksgiving night at Kansas City's Convention Hall, the *Kansas City Sun* celebrated "Capt. Dan Desdunes, easily the greatest Negro bandmaster in America, and a composer of recognized ability."[244] The *Chicago Defender* would comment on Desdunes's broader impact on the regional Black music scene of the 1920s: "Dan Desdune, [sic] whose band is one of best known in Omaha, Neb . . . is the father of success to many musicians now ranking [as] top notchers. He is a good trainer in this line."[245] As he toured the Plains, he maintained connections to Creole of color communities in New Orleans. On December 10, 1927, the *Defender* noted that "Dan Desdune's Entertainers" [sic] were making their annual tour, and that "all of the gang speak French fluently."[246] Desdunes, it seems, recruited New Orleans talent to live in Omaha. His connections to the Omaha Chamber of Commerce and regular performance schedule certainly would have helped up-south migrants get a footing. Jeff Smith, a virtuoso cornetist who moved to Omaha from New Orleans and had previously played with the Black comedian Billy Kersands, explicitly credited Desdunes's assistance and encouragement for his move.[247]

The most salient continuation of his father's legacy was Daniel Desdunes's organizational work, particularly through his efforts to combat inequality through Boys Town. In December 1917, Father Edward J. Flanagan, an Irish immigrant priest, established Boys Town as a racially integrated anti-poverty center for young boys who were homeless or formerly incarcerated.[248] Judges began to release delinquent orphans into his care in 1917.[249] Many of those he took under his wing were young boys of color, as Jim Crow and white supremacist backlash wreaked havoc on African Americans in Omaha as in other parts of the United States.[250] Flanagan voiced strong opinions about inequality. He denounced wealth as a "dangerous enemy" and wrote of Omaha's elite: "Without being conscious of its insidious influence, they permit it [wealth] to glorify them in the scarlet cloak of pompous worldliness, of an exaggerated and, often, domineering influence, using that power of money which a mere accident may have invested them in, to the detriment of the cause of God's chosen ones—the poor and the suffering."[251] Flanagan caught a lot of flak for making such statements, especially among the donor class. But his words earned him one early admirer: Daniel Desdunes.

Daniel Desdunes convinced Flanagan to create a "show wagon troupe" where students could perform on the road to raise money for the center.[252] Desdunes trained fifteen of Flanagan's youth for a minstrel show in January 1921. It was considered a huge success and the students "enthusiastically wanted more," and so Desdunes returned and drilled the students for several months. By April of the next year, he announced: "We now have a band of thirty-two pieces that any school in the West would be proud to possess. On May 1st this band will start to tour the States through the summer months and thus help raise funds for their permanent home which is now being built on Overlook Farm."[253] The sixteen-acre farm Desdunes refers to was located eleven miles west of Omaha. Flanagan envisioned this space as home to five hundred boys at a time. He boasted that it was "[o]ne of the finest farms in Nebraska," and claimed it would grow no less than "89 varieties of fruit trees, five varieties of grapes and . . . [would be] stocked with cattle, horses, calves, pigs, chickens, etc." He stressed the link between rurality and health. "Beautifully located on a hill, the farm," he explained, "will provide a splendid setting for the new home and will afford our boys plenty of room to play and the finest of fresh air and sunshine, so necessary to their growing bodies."[254] Flanagan promised the boys that it would be the "mecca of their dreams," and he held it as a viable alternative to incarceration: "There are no iron bars, no steel windows here, we win over a boy through a planned program of activities to develop his mind and broaden his interests."[255] Daniel used the sheet music sales of his tresillo- and cinquillo-inflected "Happy Feeling Rag" to fundraise for the center, which he also played with the youth band on Omaha's *Woodmen of the World* (WOW) radio station.[256]

Flanagan's plans, and Desdunes's fundraising, bore fruit. Using teams of mules, boys planted corn, alfalfa, and potatoes; they tended fruit orchards and vegetable gardens. When a severe drought hit the Midwest in 1933, the boys formed "bucket brigades" to water vegetables. By the late 1930s, increased crop yields and livestock production made the farm nearly self-sufficient. Music was integrated into the daily life of the farm: boys awoke to the "trumpeter's reveille" at 6:30 a.m.; radio listening was encouraged; plays, musicals, and band instruction were part of their ongoing activities. Also by the late 1930s, a form of supervised self-government was practiced by the youth, with slates of candidates and a justice system whose punishment was limited to additional chores.[257] This project did only alleviate poverty; the very practice of managing such institutions trained a generation. As Caroline Shenaz Hossein notes, "Collectively run institutions can deepen the theory and practice in the social economy for Black people."[258] Cooperatively run communities further the "social learning" function of social movements, notes George Lipsitz, through "acts of social contestation" that build an alternative ethos and economy.[259] For these youth, and for their adult supporters, communalism was made real, and it was powered by music—a connection that embodied the commoning legacy of brassroots democracy.

While Father Flanagan was motivated to create an alternative to the rapidly expanding system of mass incarceration, other ideologies informed the creation of Boys Town and Overlook Farm. Both the agricultural model and Flanagan's critique of conspicuous wealth were clearly influenced by the ideals of agrarian socialism that had spread like wildfire throughout the nation's heartland in the first decades of the twentieth century. "It comes as something of a surprise," writes Jim Bissett, "that the strongest state expression of socialism occurred, not in the urban citadels of the American working class."[260] Instead, it came from rural towns in Kansas, Nebraska, North Dakota, Oklahoma, Wisconsin, and other midwestern states.

These movements were influential because of their innovative, cooperative economics and their ability to mobilize economically diverse sectors of midwestern society—including those traditionally defined as capitalist. The German-born Oscar Ameringer, who had previously worked with New Orleans's Black and white dockworkers' unions, described the Socialist Party's "summer encampments" and fundraising with the help of "loyal" bankers. "What? Chambers of commerce, merchants, bankers, supporting such subversive activities as socialist encampments? Why not? A good number of them were members of the faith."[261] In a similar vein, Desdunes's connections to the Omaha Chamber of Commerce, the colored Knights of Pythias, and the Republican Party were not contradictory to his work with Boys Town and Overlook Farm. They were all extensions of his goals as an organizer: to achieve social justice and dignity for the oppressed through diverse coalitions mobilized by a vision for expansive, interracial democracy.

Daniel's musical practice modeled his passion for economic democracy that manifested in his work with Father Flanagan. His marching band at Boys Town, named Father Flanagan's Boys' Band, was drilled up to be one of the best youth bands in the country. Touring each summer, sometimes reaching New York and California, was a sophisticated, and arduous, operation: in 1922, four wagons, four sets of horses, two adults, and ten boys traveled twenty miles a day to show destinations.[262] The band impressed John Philip Sousa, who claimed that their rendition of his composition "Stars and Stripes Forever" had touched him more deeply than any other rendition he had ever heard.[263] Paul Whiteman, the white entrepreneurial big band behemoth known as the "King of Jazz," guest-conducted Father Flanagan's Boys' Band in 1928 and was stunned by their accomplishments: "In all my travels, and they have been far and many, I have yet to see a musical band composed of comparative youngsters go through some of the most difficult pieces like veterans."[264] The band played for Calvin Coolidge, receiving a private invitation to perform at his Spearfish Canyon, South Dakota, "summer Whitehouse."[265] Its national renown foregrounded Black youth and poor people, all while raising money for the educational components of Boys Town.

Desdunes did all of this as a volunteer.[266] His work kept Boys Town afloat, since, in those early years of the Overlook Farm, "other than private donations, the revenue generated by the show troupe was the only income the home had."[267] The band also challenged a virulent anti-jazz discourse. During a decade when

FIGURE 1.4 Photograph of the Dan Desdunes Band outside of a train car number 6920. Desdunes is on the far right. Date and location unknown. Courtesy of Douglas County Historical Society, UNAC0422.

jazz was associated in many white spaces with African American depravity, the school's newsletter celebrated Father Flanagan's Boys' Band proudly and described how Desdunes had prepared the boys to play "some real jazz music."[268]

During almost every generation of Creole of color activism and institution building, orphanages and schools were spaces of cooperative, progressive learning among racially and economically diverse student bodies. Daniel's continuation of his father's and uncle's legacy was not some sort of ethereal inheritance. Rodolphe Desdunes was alive during his son's work with Boys Town, and the elder Desdunes was very much a part of Black Omaha's cultural fabric. He contributed regularly to the city's Black newspaper, the *Omaha Monitor*; on at least one occasion, he used the platform to attack a conservative Black New Orleanian, Reverend Alfred Lawless Jr., who had publicly embraced the doctrine of segregation.[269] Desdunes also published French poetry in the *Omaha World-Herald*.[270] His friend John Albert Williams—a journalist, political activist, and an influential minister in the Nebraska Episcopal Church—praised Desdunes (who was now visually impaired) as "Omaha's Blind Negro Poet," a testament to the degree to which he was now claimed as one of Omaha's own.[271] Rodolphe, a product of the Couvent School, a "nursery school for revolution in Louisiana," would not have failed to appreciate the significance of his son continuing a sister project in their adopted home of Omaha.[272]

CONCLUSION

> In waging this battle I do not fear
> [The] Unleashing [of] white reprisals upon Black men
> Because I feel, boiling within my veins of iron,
> A creative power giving birth to worlds!
>
> Pierre-Aristide Desdunes[273]

Rodolphe Desdunes succumbed to cancer of the larynx in August 1928, just nine months before Daniel died from meningitis. Rodolphe's remains were transported back to New Orleans, where he was buried in the family tomb in St. Louis Cemetery, next to his Creole of color comrades.[274] Daniel, though, was interred in Omaha, and at his funeral his impact on Omaha was made plain. His funeral drew huge crowds where "prominent Omaha businessmen mingled with colored mourners"; both the Desdunes's band and the Father Flanagan's Boys' Band performed.[275] The Boys Town Band (renamed the Desdunes Boys Town Band) continued after Daniel Desdunes's passing, surviving well into the 1960s. Praise by one particular commentator seems to suggest a sustained impact on Omaha's Black activists. Harrison J. Pinkett, a civil rights lawyer with the NAACP and friend of W. E. B. Du Bois, lived in Omaha. Pinkett celebrated Daniel Desdunes as "the father of negro musicians of Omaha" in his 1937 *An Historical Sketch of the Omaha Negro*. Pinkett further elaborated that he was a "fine, cultured gentleman who found time to aid the Negro people in all of their worthwhile fraternal and civic efforts" and who was personally responsible for elevating almost every Omaha orchestra leader to start their career.[276] Pinkett, an activist himself, knew of Desdunes's work with the Comité des Citoyens, and understood that Desdunes's commitment to the music was part of a praxis of communal transformation.

While Daniel never produced a written statement that explained his rationale for his work, his son, Clarence, channelled both his father's and grandfather's activism when he argued for Black citizenship and political rights on the basis of musical accomplishment. Clarence had been born in New Orleans in 1896 and moved with his parents to the Midwest, graduating from high school in Omaha. He was a successful violinist who toured the South and became popular in New Orleans as well as Omaha, and was praised as "a marvelous bandleader and a fine violinist" by the trombonist Elmer Crumley.[277] In a 1920 column in Omaha's Black newspaper *The Monitor*, Clarence wrote, "The black man has the brains as well as the spiritual endowment necessary to understand and appreciate music in a high degree; he can point with pride to the musicians who emphatically deserve to be called artists, and another quarter century of artistic striving will bring them into the front ranks of artistic achievement."[278] While Daniel's father, Rodolphe, identified as a radical Creole of color of Haitian descent who allied with Louisiana's Black freedmen as a fellow member of the African diaspora, Clarence Desdunes was unequivocal in asserting his connection to United States Blackness. Clarence reveals that the "sons of Africa of Haitian descent" did not disappear. Their unique vantage point informed a distinguished activist legacy, realized through the construction of sonic commons and autonomous institutions, and their cultural labor generated important reservoirs within a broader Black freedom tradition as their struggle and musical aesthetics converged ever deeper with those of English-speaking African Americans.

The legacy of cooperative economics, the influence of Haitian internationalism, and the struggle for social change through musical performance that are central to the Desdunes family story all reflect an Atlantic legacy. Reevaluating the musical changes in 1892—in what made "swing" swing—makes visible the bursts of Haitian musical-performance culture that appear like brilliant auras in the testimonies of rhythmic creolization within Louisianan musical histories. The politicized social consciousness heard in Daniel Desdunes's musical activism was more than coincidental; it was the common wind in another register. Daniel brought these lessons to Omaha's African American cultural scene and contributed to a renaissance of Black culture of the Great Plains; he self-consciously utilized his skills and his commitment to economic democracy to create a self-sufficient orphanage, reimaging the legacy of brassroots democracy and its visions of democratic mutual aid in a new home. These projects live squarely in the tradition of Creole of color anti-capitalist experiments during Radical Reconstruction, an inheritance he shared with his sister, Mamie, who revolutionized the blues in New Orleans's Storyville district. Despite Daniel's inspiring career, Mamie had an equal, if not greater, impact on the music and its counter-plantation imaginaries.

TWO

Mamie Desdunes in the Neo-Plantation
Legacies of Black Feminism among Storyville's Blues People

> Let the World be a Black poem.
> *Amiri Baraka*[1]

The resonant, insurgent, testimonial poetry of Afro-Atlantic music has long inspired a global imaginary that discerns within a rupture of the Enlightenment's blockade on the meaning of human being. Julio Cortázar, the Argentine writer exiled in Paris, penned these words about a blues written sixty years earlier by the New Orleans pianist Mamie Desdunes.

> Mamie's Blues . . . [is a] bird who migrates or emigrates or immigrates or transmigrates, roadblock jumper, smuggler, a blues which is inevitable, is rain and bread and salt, something completely beyond national ritual, sacred traditions, language and folklore: a cloud without frontiers, a spy of air and water, an archetypal form, something from before, from below.[2]

Cortázar, who later organized fellow exiles to denounce the human rights abuses of Argentina's fascist military government known as El Proceso, represented the song as antidote to modernity's barbaric violence.[3] He paid tribute to Mamie Desdunes in his famous "anti-novel" *Rayuela* (Hopscotch) (1963), writing that her blues summoned "a betrayed origin," revealing how "perhaps there have been other paths and that the one they took was maybe not the only one or the best one."[4]

This chapter explores what Cortázar meant. That is, it suggests that "Mamie's

Blues" can be heard as both the polyphonic expression of the Black New Orleans working class and a "betrayed origin" in the history of jazz and brassroots democracy. Recent scholarship and musicians' own testimonies support this claim. Contemporary musicologists now consider the piece to be the first twelve-bar jazz blues,[5] an opinion shared by Buddy Bolden's trombonist, Willie Cornish, who asserted that the song was one a New Orleans musician "had to know."[6] Jelly Roll Morton recalled it was "among the first blues that I've ever heard,"[7] and concluded, "Mamie first really sold me on the blues."[8] Then a teenager working as a roustabout on the docks, Morton went to extreme lengths to study with the song's composer, Mamie Desdunes. "Of course, to get in on it, to try to learn it, I made myself . . . the can rusher," a person responsible for delivering heavy barrels of beer to the brothels where Mamie Desdunes played.[9] The thought of the eleven-year-old Morton carrying heavy barrels of beer through an overpoliced red-light district to the most upscale brothels in the United States would be almost comical if it did not reveal the twisted deprivation in which Black artistry was forced to toil.

It might be difficult to entangle the various performance practices and mediated images now associated with the blues from this era of early jazz. As Elijah Wald explains, jazz and blues are "one tradition that has been marketed in different ways to different audiences."[10] The blues, like swing, can be a challenging topic to discuss with precision because it simultaneously refers to an interconnected cluster of concepts both musical and sociological: it is a scale (constructed through the minor pentatonic with an additional flatted fifth); a twelve-bar harmonic form (which Desdunes seems to have been among the first to codify); a genre and style (closely linked to early jazz but also one with its own routes and roots); and a social philosophy. Mamie Desdunes's signature composition embodied and prefigured each of these elements, and, in addition to Morton, she passed her poetic knowledge on to the African American trumpeter Bunk Johnson, who Louis Armstrong praised for possessing "the best tone of all."[11] Johnson, like Morton, became a can rusher to study with Desdunes and explained in 1949 that he "knew Mamie Desdoumes [sic] real well. Played many a concert with her singing those same blues. She was pretty good looking—quite fair and with a nice head of hair. She was a hustling woman. A blues-singing poor girl. Used to play pretty passable piano around them dance halls on Perdido Street."[12] Relying on census data, historian Peter Hanley has suggested that Johnson and Desdunes were next-door neighbors, and that "there seems little doubt that Bunk and Jelly Roll knew each other well in their early youth and probably competed with each other for the job of Mamie Desdunes's 'can rusher.'"[13]

Morton and Johnson both boasted to have "invented" jazz. Perhaps their early training with Mamie Desdunes gave them the confidence to make such assertions. For all of Morton's claims to creating a variety of widely shared songs and conventions, he was quite careful to credit Mamie Desdunes for "Mamie's Blues" on every possible occasion. Just one such example is found in a letter to his record label representative: "Mamie Desdume [sic] wrote Mamie's Blues in the late [18]90s. I don't like to take credit for something that don't belong to me. I guess she's dead by now, and there would probably be no royalty to pay, but she did write it."[14]

Desdunes is a fascinating figure. Born out of wedlock to Rodolphe Desdunes and Clementine Walker in 1881, Mamie was connected to a lineage of Haitian-descended activists who maintained close connections to the Black republic throughout the nineteenth century. Like her relatives, Mamie fused arts and political critique, creating a new form of music that embodied her connection to the Haitian diaspora. But unlike her family members, she did so from the point of view of a woman working in the quasi-dystopian sexual economy then known as "the District," and today as Storyville. Recent literature has complicated the depiction of Storyville as the site of "good times," highlighting the intersection of the New South variant of capitalism, sex tourism, violent white supremacy, and the disciplining of Black women's bodies.[15] "Mamie's Blues" is a remarkable work because it provides testimony of, and critiques these conditions.

Writing about Mamie Desdunes is difficult due to the paucity of extant documentation. Besides her death certificate and census records, we lack any "hard" empirical evidence to substantiate many claims made about her. In 1908 she died—at age thirty-one—of tuberculosis, about a decade too soon to record any of her performances. She left no sheet music, and her name does not appear in ads for Storyville's bordellos. Yet it is precisely this archival gap that makes her presence in assorted interviews so suggestive. We only know Mamie Desdunes's name because of her profound influence on a coterie of early jazz musicians who attest to both her impact as a mentor and the importance of her innovative signature composition "Mamie's Blues." The song's celebration of Black women's sexuality was a refrain for a generation of Storyville's blues people. Indeed, her resonance suggests that blues women responded to the District's dystopian playground through a new expressive culture called the blues.

There is one exception to this archival silence. In 1893, the *New Orleans Picayune* reported that a "colored girl named Mamie Desdunes" lost two fingers after being run over a train.[16] This amputation fascinated Jelly Roll Morton, who frequently commented on her disability that somehow did not preclude her masterstrokes of early blues piano. Perhaps he could not help but notice that Mamie's cut musical voice was an allegory for a dismembered Black body politic.¹⁷ At the exact time when "Mamie's Blues" emerged as a rebellious anthem for marginalized Black women sex workers, Confederate statues symbolizing white solidarity prominently showcased a societal structure that had erased a Black presence in the public sphere. The blues was intrinsically opposed to this symbolic regime of white supremacy, bringing to mind Amiri Baraka's critique of Western "artifact worship" that he contrasted with Black expressive culture: "Music, dance, religion, do not have artifacts as their end products, so they were saved."¹⁸ "Mamie's Blues," whose alternative stanzas denounced sex trafficking and celebrated Black women's erotic agency, contested the psychic labor that such statues, police patrols, white mobs, and their attendant discourses performed. This struggle was all the more important in the context of New Orleans's interracial sex tourism economy where Mamie Desdunes worked, a workplace that so obviously contaminated the myth of European racial purity that Confederate statues projected.

More specifically, this chapter considers how "Mamie's Blues" challenged the colonization of pleasure by the plantation. The song and the genre of social criticism to which it belonged and prefigured take aim at the anti-Black, patriarchal sexual violence through which Storyville was constituted. This analysis takes its cue from historians of the Enlightenment who have found that many philosophies of "Freedom" were constructed through their symbolic opposite: Black enslavement. Scholars including Jennifer Morgan and Marisa Fuentes have suggested that the supposedly "natural" category of the family became coherent and normative in the nineteenth-century United States only as ties of African kinship were systematically destroyed through forced reproduction and the separation of children for resale in the internal slave trade. That is, Black families were destroyed so that white families could transmit intergenerational wealth. "Reproduction (and thus enslavability) was tethered to enslavement in a way that foreclosed the possibility that kinship might destabilize capital," explains Morgan. "To be enslaved meant to be locked into a productive relationship whereby all that your body could do was harnessed to accumulate capital for another."¹⁹ Similarly, Darlene Clark Hine identifies a postbellum "culture of dissemblance" as a psychic response developed by Black women who struggled in a "relentless war" to control and defend their sexuality and bodily autonomy threatened by rape and commodification. "In the face of the pervasive stereotypes and negative estimations of the sexuality of Black women," writes Hine, "it was imperative that they [Black women] collectively create alternative self-images and shield from scrutiny these private, empowering definitions of self."²⁰

"Mamie's Blues" continued the resistant and analytic legacies that Morgan and Hine identified: as oral literature that wrestled pleasure out of white definitions.²¹

Indeed, the sexual pleasure of whites had long been a fulcrum by which Southern capital in enslaved people expanded, and New Orleans was infamous for its slave auctions that marketed light-skinned fancy girls for this very reason.[22] White enslavers' experiences of pleasure were produced through the erotic annihilation of Black bodies. Many prominent plantation owners, including Thomas Jefferson, held sex slaves as property.[23] Storyville reproduced this locus of plantation pleasure by creating a prostitution market that catered to antebellum fantasies of mixed-race sexual slaves; this was an integral part of New Orleans's tourism economy and the rapacious capitalism of the so-called New South.[24] Its reassertion of gender hierarchies was fundamental for reconstituting white supremacy and containing the unbounded optimism of Reconstruction. Gender was an important ideological terrain where freedom and unfreedom were enacted since, as Hannah Rosen notes, "both the hopeful visions of former slaves and the terror that ultimately dashed their hopes were frequently expressed through discourse and practices of manhood and womanhood." The gendered discourse of the neo-plantation was put into practice in the District.[25]

Mamie Desdunes's musical work challenged how this discourse defined Black womanhood, and in doing so negated the plantation's hold on postemancipation Black erotic and political life. Her work challenged what Avery calls "the conspiracy of silence," a pervasive norm that had historically deterred Black women from vocalizing their personal encounters with sexual abuse, oppression, and trauma.[26] She was a visionary woman artist who anticipated Black women blues singers who could, in the words of Farah Jasmine Griffin, "raise a level of consciousness about the manner in which black women have come to know and feel about their bodies," in order to "provide a path out of this prison."[27] Here, the prison had a location: Storyville, the red-light district that animated the Southern plantocracy's recapture of Black sexualities. This chapter considers brassroots democracy as an effort to reclaim pleasure from these demonic grounds.[28] Spaces of shared sensuality, connoted in lyrical meanings, timbral elements, and manipulations of time, created a reparative sociosonic commons. Black women musicians' songs alone could not heal the trauma of ongoing sexual violence. But they did provide a path out of the prison as one part of a "a multifaceted struggle to determine who would control their productive and reproductive capacities and their sexuality."[29] Their dissident anthems struck chords with collectivities of sex workers, musicians, and activists who named the forces of disciplinary and economic power that held them in new and old forms of bondage while they endeavored to create a culture of pleasure and healing.

The second half of the chapter explores the resonance of Mamie Desdunes's Haitian identity in the work. Haitian women and their descendants in New Orleans produced a well-documented body of oral literature on sexuality, power, and the domestic. This chapter considers these women, and their ostensibly free descendants, as intellectuals whose thinking on reproduction and sexuality were fundamental for the development of United States culture at large. As Angela Davis has famously argued, the blues' vernacular meditations on sex and pleasure were an outgrowth of the "sexual dimensions of [Black] freedom," as "freely chosen sexual love became a mediator between historical disappointment and the new social reality of an evolving African American community."[30] Here I foreground the Haitian intellectual histories that helped articulate this moment. Alongside her family's connections to Haiti, Mamie Desdunes's link to this variant of the "common wind" that circulated critiques of slavery's gender relations is made audible in her use of habanera-based polyrhythm in her bass line.

The piano was crucial in the development of brassroots democracy, despite not being a brass or wind instrument itself. It was an orchestral instrument that could project multiple voices at once, capable of producing polyrhythmic, polycultural interpolations, and ensembles like those of Desdunes were important spaces of innovation. As Robin D. G. Kelley has shown in his biography of Thelonious Monk, within the jazz tradition it was developments on the piano that often prefigured changes in the music at large.[31] The left and right hands of Mamie Desdunes were a convergence space between the intellectual histories of the Haitian diaspora and Southern African Americans. By centering sex workers and musicians of color's values and understanding of themselves, "Mamie's Blues" offers another genealogy of jazz and brassroots democracy: one that is antipatriarchal, sensuous, and Atlantic in scope. It is this betrayed origin to which I now turn.

LOCATING MAMIE DESDUNES IN STORYVILLE

Storyville was contested terrain, and one in which Black women attempted to shape the terms and conditions of their employment. The blues was a song form that was produced by the working class of a sex tourism economy, and at its heart expressed an analysis of gender and power. Historian Lara Pellegrinelli has pointed to Jelly Roll Morton's recollection that "chippies" (sex workers) congregated outside brothels, "singing the blues," to argue that the blues emerged as a women's vocal tradition among those employed in the sex industry.[32] Pianist Manuel Manetta claimed that it was "Women who sang mostly blues," including "Mary Jack the Bear" and "Mamie Desdume" [sic], singling out the latter as "a madam who had a house on Villere Street."[33] Blues standard-bearers Memphis Minnie and Bessie Smith were also part-time sex workers.[34] These occupations were not ancillary to their artistic output, as their cultural work confronted and narrated the logic of this sexual marketplace. This was a class of artistic innovators who experienced the contradictory and impossible condition of the "commodity who screams,"[35] a rupture humanizing allegedly subhuman subjects.

Mamie Desdunes's only recorded composition, a blues widely shared in early twentieth-century New Orleans, compels a critical reading. The song's first stanzas suggest an interrelationship between feminized poverty and patriarchal family structures. Liberation, however, is possible, through genuine erotic pleasure:

> I stood on the corner, my feet was dripping wet
> I stood on the corner, my feet was dripping wet
> I asked every man I met
> Can't give me a dollar, give me a lousy dime
> Can't give me a dollar, give me a lousy dime
> Just to feed that hungry man of mine
> I got a husband and I got a kid man too
> I got a husband and I got a kid man too
> My husband can't do what my kid man can do
> I like the way he cook my cabbage for me
> I like the way he cook my cabbage for me
> Look like he set my natural soul free.[36]

Themes in these lyrics locate "Mamie's Blues" within what Davis identifies as a "black working-class legacy" of Black blues feminism.[37] Desdunes's narrative personifies feminized poverty exacerbated by intersecting social forces. Yet there is also agency and self-determination. Many Black women were primary breadwinners and heads of households. In multiple censuses, Mamie Desdunes was registered as the head of her household, even when she was married.[38] Desdunes's independence was reflected in her lyrics: while her song's protagonist is married, she does not shy away from sexual pleasure ("cooked my cabbage") outside of that relationship. In fact, it is only with her "kid man" that she feels her "natural soul" set free. Mamie Desdunes thus preceded by decades several conventions employed by later women blues singers, such as the use of double entendre to express sexuality and the narrating of gendered power struggles within the household and marketplace. For instance, Ma Rainey, who spent considerable time working with some of Mamie Desdunes's New Orleans collaborators, used this lyrical technique in several songs, including her self-exposition as bisexual in "Prove It on Me Blues" (1928).

Desdunes contrasts the social limitations imposed by poverty with liberation enabled by sexual exploration. This duality has a long history in blues lyrics, such as in Bessie Smith's (1926) "Young Woman's Blues," Ida Cox's (1939) "One Hour Mama," and Ethel Waters's (1925) "No Man's Mamma Now." Each of these songs openly discuss sexuality within (and in opposition to) patriarchal power structures. They also postdate "Mamie's Blues" by thirty years or more.[39]

Sung during the height of New Orleans's progressive movement, which emphasized social order and the patriarchal family, Mamie's vocal embrace of extramarital sex is quite striking. This was reflected in Desdunes's own life experience. In 1898, Mamie Desdunes moved in with warehouse worker George Duque, marrying him in 1900. They appear to have split almost immediately, because, according to a city directory, by 1901 Mamie was using her maiden name and residing alone at the same address.[40] By the end of her life, Mamie and George had apparently smoothed things over. The 1910 city directory showed George as a resident of the house, and in Mamie's death certificate, she took George's last name. While there is no evidence that Mamie or George's sexual activities caused these breakups, it is clear that the two did not form a traditional nuclear family. Mamie herself was born out of wedlock to Rodolphe Desdunes and Clementine Walker. Rodolphe's other illegitimate children, including Mamie's younger sister Edna and younger brothers John and Louis, moved in with the pianist during the 1910s. Her untraditional household and work in the musical sector of New Orleans's sex economy reflected her participation in what J. T. Roane calls a "dark agora," a "unique Black vernacular landscape that challenged the predominant vision of orderly urban life."[41] It is significant that the state itself often arrested Black working-class women for the crime of maintaining a "disorderly house," a charge that, Storyville's quasi-legal prostitution notwithstanding, most frequently targeted Black sex workers.[42] What was read as "disorderly" by the white republic was actually a complex and fluid understanding of marriage and the extended family household, social structures that necessitated differentiated visions of community that exceeded the heteropatriarchal nuclear family. Mamie Desdunes embodied this ethos in her work, her lyrics emphasizing openness to life's many opportunities for emotional and sexual connection.[43]

The fourth stanza of "Mamie's Blues" expands the song's social criticism, relocating sexuality outside the domestic sphere by highlighting the hierarchical social relations that undergirded the Gulf Coast's sexual economy. Morton sings this stanza in his 1939 recording, and it is also present in Bunk Johnson's 1944 rendition.[44] In these extended lyrics, Desdunes laments the disappearance of a loved one through a sex trafficking network that linked New Orleans to the Gulf Coast of Texas. The refrain "Number 219 took my baby away" may refer to a train that connected New Orleans with Texas oil boomtowns, while the third line expresses hope that "the 217 may bring her back someday." According to Charles Edward Smith, Morton recounted that the 219 train "took the gals out on the T&P [Texas and Pacific Railway] to the sporting houses on the Texas side of the circuit . . . [and] the 217 on the S. P. [Southern Pacific] through San Antonio and Houston brought them back to New Orleans."[45] Sporting houses were euphemisms for brothels, and Morton's explanation implies that the reference to the sex trafficking ring was widely understood.

The introduction of the 219 train, a symbol of sexual servitude and industrial modernity, changes the meaning of the previous stanzas. The region's sex industry is now the engine of feminized poverty. Desdunes not only explores the violence of this expropriative sexual economy; she also restores the silenced voices of vulnerable migrants. Few scattered historical records survive of these trafficked migrant sex workers destined for oil boomtowns.[46] Often having few social connections in the towns where they arrived, such workers were especially vulnerable to exploitation.[47]

Desdunes foregrounds the social history of a class of invisible migrants whose pain lay at the intersection of commercialized sex, displacement, and modernity. These same forces animated the lifeways of those who made Storyville their new home. Thousands of Black migrants escaped white violence and repression in the sugar parishes, constituting the first wave of the Great Migration, whose primary vector was rural to urban rather than south to north.[48] The women of Storyville embodied the proletariat of a new sexual economy and were both artistic innovators and meaning-making audiences of the blues. Desdunes developed a vernacular critique of capitalism's "progress" and Black women's captivity therein. In the process, she both archived and aestheticized iterant workers' struggles.

Like later blues songs, the train in "Mamie's Blues" showcases the dark side of "progress." While New South capitalists celebrated industrial development, others experienced a new wave of enclosure and displacement. Desdunes depicts the 219 train as a symptom of capitalist modernity and its anti-women violence.[49] Here, geographic mobility does not equate with social mobility. Quite the opposite. Instead, the train is a technology that commodifies Black bodies. It reflects how the trading of sexual slaves during plantation slavery had evolved to claim Black women's bodies with modern machinery. Desdunes's spotlighting of these subaltern workers speaks to a genre of "decolonial poetics produced by diasporic communities" that, in the words of Katherine McKittrick, "depict city death not as a biological end and biological fact but as a pathway to honoring human life."[50] Desdunes's narration of dispossession and its emotional costs denormalizes "the fungibility of the captive body."[51] It places this invisible economy on the aural stage for all to hear and says: "Enough."

"Mamie's Blues" fuses with strains of Black theological thought. The verses of Genesis 2:17–19 render a patriarchal theology in the creation myth of the cosmos, and perhaps Desdunes was subtly deconstructing these myths in dialogue with sex worker violence.[52] Blues and Christianity intersected liberally in early twentieth-century New Orleans. There are widely cited accounts that trumpet player Buddy Bolden attended Baptist services, often in the same halls in which he performed the previous night, as part of his project to translate Black liturgical aesthetics into popular instrumental music.[53] A litany of early twentieth-century blues repertoire employed biblical motifs and appropriated religious channels of expression.[54] Angela Davis considers the blues to have been condemned by some Black church leaders specifically because it "drew upon and incorporated sacred consciousness and thereby posed a serious threat to religious attitudes."[55] Whether or not "Mamie's Blues" directly referenced (or critiqued) scripture with its numerology, it certainly channeled a sacred sense of sexuality and mourned the loss of those disappeared by demonic forces.

"Mamie's Blues" shines a light on this social reality, telling a story sufficiently familiar to strike a chord with Storyville's Black counterpublic. Certainly, the veracity of either the 219 train—or Morton and Johnson's rendition of the piece—should give us pause. The song certainly confirms to what Bryan Wagner describes as "[Black] music's capacity to convey hypothetical experience—experience that could be imagined but not known and felt but not named—[that] was celebrated by collectors who took its artifice for authentic self-expression."[56] Yet I nonetheless hear a multiplicity of gestures in this song that destabilizes the male outlaw archetype who dominates the imagination of such blues song collectors, and opens up productive questions for the gendered performativity of an emergent blues culture. How do we make sense of that fact that Jelly Roll Morton and Bunk Johnson were, along with dozens of male other musicians of the era, expected to simulate a woman's orgasm when they sung the third stanza of this blues one "had to know"? Perhaps they performed the song for each other during what Pops Foster remembers as "Mondays at the lakes," the industry day off for "the pimps, hustlers, whores, and musicians" who would "go out there for picnics and to rest up."[57] Community was also improvised in Storyville's after-hours clubs that catered to those in the industry. "After four o'clock in the morning, all the girls that could get out of the houses—they were there," remembers Morton, where he claims musicians and sex workers were "one big happy family" and where the music would "go on from four o'clock in the morning at a tremendous rate of speed, with plenty of money, drinks of all types, till maybe twelve, one, two, three o'clock in the daytime."[58] In these dark agoras, musicians and sex workers were expected to take care of—and care for—one another; their friendships "indexed small-scale rebellions in the realm of intimacies [through] the reappropriation of care and other forms of labor to cultivate dynamic worlds."[59] The scene was not always as idyllic as Foster and Morton represent, but many musicians, including Louis Armstrong (whose mother was a sex worker) and Manuel Manetta, remember receiving encouragement from women singer sex workers who, as audience members, cheered them on as they got their feet wet in New Orleans's Black musical underground.[60]

"Mamie's Blues" has a dual imperative: on the one hand, it reclaimed sexuality and desire from the social relations of the plantation that structured Storyville's labor market while theorizing the political forces that conscripted Black women into this sexual economy. On the other hand, Desdunes's rendering of the erotic as a practice of genuine liberation was linked to a broader postemancipation cultural transformation. "[What] is most striking is the way the blues registered sexuality as a tangible expression of freedom," explains Angela Davis. "Sexuality thus was one of the most tangible domains in which emancipation was acted upon and through which its meanings were expressed."[61] Saidiya Hartman likewise reminds us that for Black Philadelphian migrants from the South during the Great Migration, "an everyday act of fucking" should be thought of as "the center of this revolution in a minor key." Both blues lyric and its hybrid tonality became poignant repositories of a new structure of feeling rooted in women's erotic agency in and against a white supremacist dystopia.[62]

THE POLITICAL ECONOMY OF STORYVILLE

Mamie Desdunes's work contributed to a Black counterpublic sphere while plantation capitalism regrouped in Louisiana. *Harper's Weekly* reported in 1899 that Storyville had become the New South's most prosperous tourist district, processing hundreds of thousands of dollars annually and becoming the "the chief winter resort of those who journey southward to escape the winters in the North."[63] Most, however, were less interested in the climate and more interested in the legalized prostitution that the Story Act enabled. The president of the Whitney Bank and other "men of capital" lobbied to pass the Story Act and earned enormous profits from speculating in the new red-light district. Real estate moguls like Bernardo Galvez Carbajal evicted Black low-income families to rent to the city's emboldened tourism industry. The Colored Veterans Benevolent Association, which supported Black Civil War veterans, was one of many evicted. When the city constructed its new train system in 1910, it was built in the heart of Black New Orleans at Canal and Basin Streets. The train's elevated tracks entering and leaving the city ensured that the bordellos of Storyville were abundantly visible and within walking distance for tourists. Black cultural institutions, businesses, and communities were destroyed by these invasions of capital.[64]

Meanwhile, in Louisiana's rural parishes, white supremacist politicians organized violent militias to wreak havoc on Black Reconstruction organizers.[65] From 1880 to 1900, New Orleans's population increased by 30 percent as some forty thousand fled the plantations of Louisiana and Mississippi. In the Crescent City, they became part of a Black underclass that supplied sex workers to Storyville.[66] In 1900, Black women made up 38 percent of this workforce, and were often the lowest paid, earning as little as fifteen cents per transaction.[67] Trombonist Kid Ory marveled at how the shift system of prostitutes functioned like "clockwork."[68] Likewise, one madam described the almost industrial regularity and emotional toll of the work: "It was a life regular as sunrise: regular joy, misery, hope, lack of hope, and ideas of suicide. A shrug-off of the present, a numb idea of the future, too. We all lied to each other about the future, and to ourselves as well."[69]

The sonic liberation choreographed by Mamie Desdunes and other blueswomen became more important as Storyville's system of sex work deepened the city's social contradictions and extractive logics. Storyville, as Sherrie Tucker suggests, "provide[s] instructive glimpses into diverse gender systems and women's participation in early New Orleans jazz," including how they made sense of alienated time and commodified bodies.[70] The district's frenetic dystopia enacted gender ideologies that, as in slavery, transformed the bodies of Black women into objects of commercial exchange, albeit within a changed legal landscape. In sum, as Emily Epstein Landau notes, "The racial order of the slave plantation was reinscribed in the early twentieth century though the sexual organization of Storyville," the product of a brand of capitalism whose principal commodity, "female sexuality," was "put at the service of the white male patron . . . the only kind of Black sexuality allowed."[71] Landau's analysis grapples with how "Storyville repackaged coercion as servile sex (or wage labor), reproducing for the liberal economy the sexual economy of the slave plantation."[72] This continuity between antebellum and postbellum sex work, and between slavery and capitalism writ large, was grasped and critiqued by Mamie Desdunes and other blueswomen. These were women whose bodies were the point of sale. If white men's access to Black women's bodies on the plantation was reinvented in "modern" Storyville, then so, too, was the commoning ethos of brassroots democracy and the improvised, affective resistance that humanized and honored Black women who were the commodity.

Much of musicians' and sex workers' anger was directed at the intense police presence tasked with protecting the investments of this neo-plantation, a common consequence of gentrification.[73] As musician Danny Barker recounts, "There was a charge, that a person could be arrested for, called 'D and S' (dangerous and suspicious) whereby the police had the power to arrest anyone who could not walk to the phone booth to call his or her employer." Those with informal or self-employment often had no such recourse, so "most arrests were Negroes who frequented barrooms and gambling joints during working hours."[74] Barker also recalled that "it was the custom of the police to whip, kick and brutalize the young pimps when they were arrested and locked up for vagrancy, loitering and having no visible means of support."[75] These forces of white supremacy were omnipresent. Jelly Roll Morton remembered that "police were always in sight, never less than two together."[76] Police brutality was a major concern for Black musicians in New Orleans. Bassist Pops Foster recalls that "when I'd go to work I'd be careful to stay on the side of the street where I knew the cops . . . in those days if you were drunk out on the streets the cops would put you in jail until you sobered up."[77]

Black women resisted the alliance of capital and disciplinary power, forming the core of a new generation of outspoken Black leaders who challenged Southern-style apartheid and racial capitalism. Women-led strikes and a culture of militancy were present across the South, from the Atlanta washerwomen's strike of 1881 to New Orleans women who destroyed the mule-drawn carts of strike-breaking scab longshoremen in 1907.[78] In 1881, for instance, the *New Orleans Picayune* reported that the police had arrested "negresses who showed [threw] cooking utensils upon the police." These women had interrupted their detention of an African American man, Henry Williams, whose labor organizing was considered "inciting a riot." Revealing their sheer tenacity, the reporter noted: "It took seven officers of the law to arrest . . . the negro women."[79] Critiques of the police were widely shared in popular song. "Buddy Bolden's Blues," by the paradigm-shifting African American trumpet player, references the arrest of a friend of Buddy Bolden's, Frankie Dusen, in 1904 for "loitering."[80] In 1900, these acts of police aggression reached a boiling point when the Black activist Robert Charles took a stand against the system of white supremacy. Charles worked a number of jobs, from canecutter to dockworker to construction worker, but he always made time for activism in the back-to-Africa movement, working closely with the prominent Black bishop Henry M. Turner of Georgia.[81] (Turner's own Crescent City resonance was informed by brassroots democracy. He kept an active presence in New Orleans in these decades, speaking at an 1885 civil rights event at the Cotton Centennial alongside the Excelsior Band, which included the clarinetists Lorenzo and Louis Tio.)[82] When another Afro-Georgian, the farmworker Sam Hose, was barbarically lynched in front of thousands, Charles became more militant.[83] Charles, after being manhandled by an officer, broke free and orchestrated a solitary uprising against the police forces of New Orleans. He shot down one officer and wounded another, igniting a fiery wave of racist violence perpetrated by white mobs—groups who had for the last thirty years maintained a sophisticated apparatus of anti-Black violence, momentarily destabilized by Charles's act of defiance. Charles managed to kill seven of these paramilitaries before his house was set on fire; he was killed while escaping the building, his body paraded around the city as a trophy.[84] Several musicians were embroiled within the wave of white supremacist violence that followed. Notably, the following decade the "Robert Charles Ballad" became popular—a commemorative ode to the Black revolutionary, which was circulated widely during Mamie Desdunes's career, triggering yet more police repression. "This song was squashed very easily by the [police] department," explained Jelly Roll Morton.[85]

In Storyville, Black women defied this status quo in myriad ways, most frequently by causing public disturbances, antagonizing police, and stealing from white upper-class clientele. Mamie Desdunes herself was arrested in 1896 for "disturbing the peace," often an euphemism for publicly reviling police. From hundreds of similar arrests, such as that of sex worker Adeline Smith in 1908, one gleans widespread resistance.[86] Theft by sex workers, such as stealing a client's wallet, was common. In this context, organized robbery should be understood as "skillful affirmations of communal resources" rather than violations of legal ownership.[87] Clipping was one technique developed by sex workers. "While one jives [has sex with] you," explained Danny Barker, "another creeps or crawls in and rifles your pockets."[88] Clipping was class-conscious in its targets. As pianist Clarence Williams recalled, "There was never a holdup or robbery that I could remember. You could drink and never be afraid that anybody'd taken your money."[89] Black musicians and sex workers did not report experiencing such thefts.

Black women's regular, spontaneous acts of opposition indicate that sex workers were not afraid to challenge New Orleans's disciplinary apparatus. Nonetheless, their acts of decentralized rebellion were met with state violence. In 1906, the police poisoned the sex workers of Willie Piazza's brothel, causing hospitalizations.[90] Sex workers of the Crescent City became a "cipher" through which public order and political authority was enforced and contested, and where the New South could prove it had disciplined the Reconstruction-era revolutionary imaginations of the Black working class.[91] But the latter's "unorganized, evasive, seemingly spontaneous" resistance was precisely where the dissident political consciousness of the blues took root.[92]

These actions coalesced into organized and legible activity. In 1918 sex workers and musicians held a mass meeting to protest police violence. "The police in

New Orleans were making it tough for the madames and their girls to make a dollar (that is, a peaceful one)," explains Danny Barker. "So they spread the news and called a meeting of all the big shots in the District, the pimps, madames, whores, gamblers, hustlers, bartenders and all the owners of joints." Held on a Sunday evening at Peter Lala's—"the District's number one cabaret"—the event included speeches as well as performances by Joe Oliver's band. Barker suggests that organizers of this event strategically used specific songs and styles from Joe Oliver's repertoire to arouse the sentiments of their audience:

> [Madame] Ready Money told Joe Oliver to play the blues real sad, which he did. Then, when the crowd returned to their seats, she had the drummer Ratty Jean Vigne roll his snares and she pleaded sadly with tears in her big blue eyes for attention. You could hear a pin drop as she informed the gathering of the many humiliating abuses she had constantly received from the brutal police of New Orleans which they all knew so well. She then told them of her plan to organize them. She proposed that each person present come up to the table where she stood, sign their name and pledge twenty dollars as an active member, which most of them did. She had Joe Oliver play the spiritual ["] Down by the Riverside ["] so the crowd could march up to her and rally to the cause.... She blew kisses to the crowd and yelled, "We'll show them goddamned police!" Everybody screamed, yelled and clapped their hands and they balled till the next morning to the music of Joe Oliver.[93]

Danny Barker's account, unfortunately, cannot be verified as the Economy Hall's meeting notes from this time period are missing.[94] Yet its veracity is perhaps less relevant than the social world Barker points to. As Storyville was closed in 1917, a police presence was certainly on the rise, making such a gathering both conceivable and quite logical. Much like "Mamie's Blues," Oliver's music sounded both profound pain and a liberated future. Madame Ready Money collaborated with Joe Oliver to aestheticize sex worker struggles, for which his blues vocabulary was quite capable. This event was so successful that the following week, another concert was organized, this time under the helm of a benevolent society organized by and for sex workers. An advertisement saved by Barker reveals its level of detail.

"Black Sis," "Rotten Rosie," and "Lily the Crip" were sex workers ("sporting girls") who held leadership positions in this organization. By their very presence in this advertisement, they announce their intention to act as political subjects and resist intimidation and stigmatization. They demand recognition as workers, women, and human beings. Women's blues reflected and contributed to this process, weaving antipatriarchal collectivities that challenged the legacies of the

> The First Grand Ball and Soirée to be given at the Economy Hall
> May 2, 1919, by the
> HELPING HAND BENEVOLENT AID AND PROTECTIVE
> ASSOCIATION
>
> Organized on April 7, 1919, for the aid and protection of sick, needy, helpless, disabled, aged and persecuted Sporting girls and Madames who are confined to hospitals, pest houses, houses of correction, criminal institutions, jails and penitentiaries.
>
> *Officers*
>
> Black Sis: President
> Rotten Rosie: Vice President
> Mollie Hatcher: Secretary
> Mary Meathouse: Recording Secretary
> Warmbody Stell: Financial Secretary
> Barrel of Fun: Sgt. at Arms
>
> Ready Money: Treasurer
> Ida Jackson: Ex Officio
> Lily the Crip: Delegate
> One-Arm Edna: Sick C'ttee
> Bird Leg Nora: Trustee
> Bob Rowe: Director
>
> Reverend Sunshine Money: Pastor

FIGURE 2.0 Advertisement for the Helping Hand Benevolent Aid and Protective Association Ball. Reproduced in Barker, *Buddy Bolden and the Last Days of Storyville*, 68.

plantation and its racial and spatial logic.[95] Joe Oliver's presence at both events is significant, as it suggests that musicians worked alongside sex workers in ways that were not merely exploitative or ancillary.

This was the movement that "Mamie's Blues" contributed to and was shaped by. Just as Desdunes evinced a concern for the unnamed women shuttled away to Beaumont, Texas, to work far from home in conditions they could not control, the Helping Hand Benevolent Aid and Protective Association expressed a commitment to furnish "aid and protection" for the "sick, needy, helpless, persecuted, disabled, aged and persecuted sporting girls," "confined" to hospitals and penitentiaries. The focus on disability and its implicit critique of the hospital, the prison, and the mental institution (where Buddy Bolden was then languishing) as sites of disciplinary power anticipates Foucault's observation that "as medicine, psychology, education, public assistance, 'social work' assume an ever greater share of the powers of supervision and assessment, the penal apparatus will be able, in turn, to become medicalized, psychologized, educationalized."[96] These activists' language is also a pre-echo of twenty-first-century movements that fight for the rights of sex workers and those who are functionally diverse. Their horizontal decision-making process mirrors the work of Daniel and Rodolphe Desdunes in Omaha and New Orleans, another manifestation of brassroots democracy's insurgent assembly. Much like the music played, here new identities and social relations were improvised, rehearsed, and enacted.

Joe Oliver's concerts for the benefit of sex workers serve as windows into the nature of the ideological and political battles that roiled New Orleans's sex industry and its workers' relationships with the state, police forces, and white civil society during the first decades of the twentieth century. These moments of rebellion underline a culture of resistance and solidarity among the Black and Creole of color working people of the district, whose structures of commoning, mutual aid, and disobedience directly informed the lives and concerns of the first generation to record the music now called jazz. This narrative is rarely employed when jazz historians discuss Storyville, but the archival and anecdotal evidence presented certainly supports this reading. And if we take such a culture as our point of departure, we can hear in the blues and early jazz a dissident consciousness that contained the seeds of a new world, where chains of affiliation, intimacy, and pleasure were reimagined within a broken world.

Amidst Storyville's matrix of racial and sexual capitalism, New Orleans sex workers produced a vibrant counterpublic that honored and acknowledged Black women's pain as the basis for building an intersectional movement for social justice. Mamie Desdunes was an innovative composer who helped construct this common sense by creating one of the most popular, and perhaps the very first, twelve-bar blues. The blues were primarily and initially a gendered counterculture, one that contested the social forces laying claim to Black bodies as commodities. And, as with the vernacular critique of slavery's social and sexual relations sung in Saint-Domingue, Senegal, and across the Black Atlantic, these songs were sung during the point of transaction, as piano players often performed alongside prostitutes at regular gigs in brothels. Much like the socializing counter-plantation music generated by the Afrodiasporic workforce toiling on rural plantations, the paradox of the blues is that a progressive, antipatriarchal musical form was generated within workshops of expropriated sexual labor. Desdunes lived in this world and thus was able to mount her critique as one who had experienced its alienation firsthand.

Informing Mamie Desdunes's artistry and political voice is her identity as a descendant of Haitian migrants. Desdunes's connection to the Haitian diaspora informed her invocation of a nineteenth-century Black Atlantic tradition that spoke truth to gendered power, not only through her lyrics but also in the embodied knowledge of the habanera.

THE SPANISH TINGE AND THE HAITIAN DIASPORA

In her 1923 composition "Haitian Blues," New Orleans vocalist Lizzie Miles recounts her abuse at the hands of an unfaithful husband:

> Daddy's been cheating
> he's been mistreating
> gave me a beating for some abuse
> Now I've learned my lesson
> and I'm confessin'
> I wish that I had never been born
> I'm leaving town
> 'cause I've got the Haitian Blues.⁹⁷

Miles, who was descended from Haitian émigrés, seems to imply something particularly "Haitian" about being the victim of abuse, an abuse whose locus is New Orleans.⁹⁸ The following section historicizes the performance cultures of Haitian women and their descendants in the Crescent City, considering how sexualized violence informed the development of a musical counterculture. "Mamie's Blues" is part of this tradition, and the song reinterpreted Haitian Cuban musical devices in its bass line based on habanera rhythms. These bass lines were born of a complex, contested creolization process in which not only musical devices but also competing narratives of race, gender, and human bondage were negotiated in the music. These songs belong to a transatlantic vernacular culture described by Lisa Ze Winters as a "subversive negotiation of sexual and racial economies imposed by European colonialism and American slavery." Afrodiasporic women's biting social commentary through song was recorded in Saint-Domingue, French-controlled Senegal, and New Orleans.⁹⁹ While Desdunes's lyrics commented on women's sexualities within and against the sex industry at large, she simultaneously overlaid a rhythmic cadence that semiotically evoked Creole of color identification with Haiti.¹⁰⁰

Mamie Desdunes and Lizzie Miles's works were not aberrations but extensions of a nineteenth-century Caribbean tradition that talked about, and talked back to, slavery's patriarchal social relations. Overlaying shared rhythmic conventions, these motifs congealed a diasporic hermeneutics that resisted slavery and coerced sex. This "gendered common wind" present in early jazz and blues, as well as its links to radical cultures of the Haitian Revolution, can be heard in Desdunes's piano playing. Hidden within Jelly Roll Morton's statement that "Mamie could really play those blues" is his fascination at her ability to seamlessly overlay African American and Afro-Caribbean traditions: improvisation as intercultural presencing.

Born of wedlock, to suggest that Mamie's identity was "Creole of color" would be reductive, as she may have been alienated from her father while she worked in an industry that well-educated Creoles of color publicly reviled.¹⁰¹ Jelly Roll

FIGURE 2.1 "Mamie's Blues" as played by Jelly Roll Morton in the 1938 Library of Congress Sessions. In addition to the habanera and tresillo bass line figures, the "three against four" phrase is notable. Transcribed by author.

Morton, for instance, was disowned by his grandmother when she discovered he had been performing in the District.[102] The fact that Mamie sang in English also differentiated her from other Creole of color singers.[103] Her training as a pianist, however, suggests that she was raised and educated within Creole of color familial and gendered conventions.[104] The Haitian-derived rhythms in "Mamie's Blues," such as the habanera and tresillo, are the foundation of its left hand ostinatos. Several scholars have noted that tresillo, habanera, and cinquillo rhythms are all based on a similar set of rhythms that are rooted in different interpretations of a "4 against 3" hemiola and a more general license to move in the liminal space between duple and triple time feels.[105] These rhythms are characteristic of several genres of Afro-Cuban and French Afro-Caribbean music and also have a marked presence in African American music.[106] They are prominent in Jelly Roll Morton's performances of "Mamie's Blues" and became a major part of his piano style, such as in his 1905 composition "New Orleans Blues."

These rhythmic conventions became organically linked to a brand of Black Atlantic politics and antipatriarchal storytelling with roots in the Haitian Revolution. As discussed previously, refugees from Haiti more than doubled the population of New Orleans from 1791 to 1811, and tripled the size of the city's free community of color.[107] The musicologist Christopher Washburne has observed that "the musical influence of the Saint-Domingue refugees was vast," adding that cultural practices, institutions, and creolized rhythmic traditions like the tresillo first arrived with the Haitian immigrants.[108] Johnson notes that "barbed observations about racial and sexual hierarchies and the violence that became a matter of course under such regimes" accompanied these musical forms.[109] Sexuality was a terrain of struggle, violence, and refusal in the Black Atlantic, and these histories implicated the cinquillo complex. The incisive observations within these habanera-based songs traveled with enslaved musicians to Jamaica, Puerto Rico, Cuba, and Louisiana.

Adjectives denoting European heritage—"Spanish" and "French"—have long served to erase Haitian and Cuban contributions to New Orleans musical culture, reducing creolization processes to banners of European empires. For example, Baby Dodds characterized Creole of color conventions as "French and Spanish style, blended together."[110] Jelly Roll Morton perhaps did most to popularize the term and concept of the "Spanish tinge." In an interview with Alan Lomax, he explains, "Of course you got to have these little tinges of Spanish in it . . . in order to play real good jazz."[111] Other Black commentators who published in this era, however, explained that the habanera rhythm expressed a cultural lineage that connected the music of Louisiana to the Caribbean. According to one of Morton's collaborators, Walter "Foots" Thomas: "I always felt his melodies came from New Orleans but that his rhythms came from Latin [American] countries."[112]

As jazz saxophonist Steve Coleman succinctly explains, "Rhythm is movement, and it needs to be studied as movement, not as notation."[113] These rhythms traveled across bodies and boundaries, connecting and communicating a diaspora largely trapped in plantation isolation. They stood as markers of creativity, imagination, and healing, intertwining the past with the present. Reflecting on the migrants from Saint-Domingue—those voluntary, those forced, and those white, Black, and Creole of color—Sara Johnson surmises: "All [emigrant Saint-Domingue] groups used the mnemonic properties of music, theater, and dance to link memories of home with responses to the new communities encountered during the course of migration. . . . Counterposed to this nostalgia for the 'good old days,' what many of these black performers were marking as Saint-Domingueness/Frenchness among both themselves and for outsiders was their own association with revolutionary struggle."[114]

Thus, the "French" contradanza and the tresillo and habanera rhythms were performed by both the descendants of white refugees, such as Louis Gottschalk, and the descendants of free people of color and African Americans, such as Mamie Desdunes. But their invocations could summon very different meanings, especially based on the political leanings of the listening public. Maud Cuney Hare, born in Galveston, Texas, in 1874, provides an example of how one's positionality affected how the habanera was heard. Cuney Hare was an African American activist and accomplished pianist. When she attended the New England Conservatory of music in 1890, the conservatory attempted to dislodge her from her dormitory because of white complaints of her Blackness; she refused to leave, and after a campaign in her support that included W. E. B. Du Bois, the school relinquished. (Cuney Hare later worked with Du Bois as the music columnist of *The Crisis*.) In 1921, she published a compilation entitled *Six Creole Folk-Songs*, which documented the music of Afro-Creole Louisianans.[115] The songs are replete with habanera bass lines quite similar to those present in "Mamie's Blues." Cuney Hare, who wrote the compilation during the US occupation of Haiti (which she opposed), explains that these songs—"mainly African in rhythm"—were "brought to South American countries and to the West Indies, thence to Louisiana." "Distinct from the mountain song of Kentucky, the Negro Spiritual or the tribal melody of the Indian," they constituted a Creole of color "gift to the folk-song of America."[116] Cuney Hare characterizes the "West Indies," namely Haiti, as an important way station in the Afro-Atlantic's musical genealogy. Analyzing the compilation's sardonic and sarcastic elements, Cuney Hare observes that "songs of mockery, pointed at times with cruel satire, were common among the Creole songs of Louisiana and the Antilles [Haiti]." Cuney Hare also addresses these songs' treatment of gender and sexuality, noting that the song "Caroline" "sheds light into the tragedy as well as the romance of the young Creole slaves," for "marriage, that state of blissful respectability[,] [was] denied to the multitude either by law or social conditions."[117] Cuney Hare suggests the gender politics of the piece must be understood as a response to Southern slave laws and their disregard for Black families and their romantic partnerships.[118] Her interest in Haitian culture extended beyond this analysis and was important for her own work; she collected West Indian instruments and directed the play *Dessalines, Black Emperor of Haiti* in 1930 at the Fine Arts Theater in Boston.[119]

Compiled and published in the first two decades of the twentieth century, Cuney Hare's anthology reflects how African American musicians of the period understood the habanera rhythm and the social commentary it informed: as a Haitian ("West Indies") derivation, and a feature of satirical songs that subjected gender and plantation sexual relations to analysis, critique, and ridicule. Cuney Hare may have been perceptive to this phenomenon because Saint-Domingue Black women produced a well-documented body of oral work. Saint-Domingue's widespread practice of interracial sex was disavowed in the colonial public sphere, despite the fact that "gens de couleur" comprised 22 percent of the colony's free population in 1775, and 44 percent by 1788. But enslaved and free women of color developed a means to break this taboo in song and poetry, illuminating its contours for both white and Black publics.[120] In contrast, the United States' antebellum African American musical culture, as Angela Davis notes, addressed sexuality more reluctantly until the postemancipation blues era.[121]

In this underground vernacular culture, African-descended women critiqued their exclusion from the public sphere—and legitimate marriage—by celebrating their own sexual powers. For example, the late eighteenth-century poem "Lisette" was sung from the point of view of an enslaved woman. The song's eponymous narrator chastises her lover for escaping to town to have sex with a mistress, insulting her because:

> Her butt is no more than a packet of bones.
> She has not a tooth in her mouth,
> Her tits are like the sugar cane trash we feed the pigs.
>
> Bonda li c'est paquet zos.
> Li pas teni dents dans bouche,
> Tété li c'est blan cochon.

In contrast, Lisette recites a litany of her own positive attributes: she sings like a bird (Mon chanté tant com zozo), her breasts remain upright (Teté moins bougé debout), and she is in her sexual prime: "I have a canal / And no shortage of water for it" (mon gagné canal / D'yo pas lé manqué li).[122] Deborah Jenson has called "Lisette" the "earliest [recorded] example of female-narrated dissing in the New World African diaspora."[123]

This erotic agency and penchant for ribald mockery traveled with the Saint-Domingue refugees.[124] Beside New Orleans, the Caribbean locale most impacted by the Saint-Domingue exodus, Santiago de Cuba, was also the site of Haitian performance practices whose "barbed observations" shined a spotlight on white supremacy and sexual violence. Emilio Bacardí y Moreau, a Cuban historian with planter émigré ancestors from Saint-Domingue, overheard such a piece sung during an Afro-Cuban *tumba francesa* performance.[125]

> Those white men from France, oh shout it!
> They use their [white] wives as a pillow
> For caressing black women.
>
> Blan lá yó qui sotíi en Frans, oh, jelé!
> Yó prán madam yó servi sorellé
> Pú yó caresé negués.[126]

Tumba francesa—which translates to "French dance"—is a creolized dance and music practice still performed in present-day Eastern Cuba. Its diffusion in colonial Cuba in the early nineteenth century was linked to the diverse Saint-Domingue migrants, differing depending on both economic circumstances and racial backgrounds. Free people of color and elite mulattos—known as *negros francesas*—created mutual aid and recreation clubs whose music and dance culture gravitated around the Saint-Domingue–inflected contradanza.[127] While ballroom dances fell out of fashion with elite white Cubans, Grant notes that "the francesas of color may have held onto performative activities that recalled their French Creole traditions." Simultaneously, tumba francesa was developed by enslaved migrants on the regions' coffee plantations, and, as Bacardi's transcribed song indicates, their songs might insult both the masters' fetishization of Black female "property" and the undesirability of their white wives.[128] As with jazz's "Spanish tinge," tumba francesa's name—"French dance"—is a misnomer that hides the complexity of Pan-African creolization among enslaved Saint-Domingue migrant communities in Santiago de Cuba.[129] Among both free and enslaved Saint-Domingue migrants, habanera and cinquillo rhythms deepened within a practice of diaspora, a severed connection to revolution. "The 'negros francesas' had also played a very important role in the formation of Cuban music," writes Alejo Carpentier, "by bringing a fundamental rhythmic element that was slowly incorporated into many folkloric genres of the island: *the cinquillo*."[130] This rhythmic cell would become the foundation of an Afro-Cuban style in the late nineteenth century that provoked white disgust before becoming assimilated as a national Cuban culture: danzón.[131]

Recent scholarship has complicated this tidy and linear genealogy of Saint-Domingue/Haitian materials "creating" tumba francesa and the cinquillo patterns played in 1870s danzón—a story in which, according to Hettie Malcomson, "the brutality of slavery, imperialism and war are generally downplayed," while "influences and transformations are rarely conveyed as multiple processes."[132] The implication of this pause is important. It recognizes the ways in which canonical thinking reproduces a unidirectional model that limits our understanding of the dialogue and agency of cultural actors across the diaspora.

Yet asserting that Haitian influence was an important force in the formation of these various cultures does not imply a static, bounded, and linear process devoid of slavery's memory, as Malcomson identifies with nationalist discourses of danzón. Haiti's distinct process of historical formation requires a different model for thinking culture and nationality. As Jean Casimir notes, the people who would become Haitians were made up of

> Ibos, Kongos, Mandingas, Toucouleurs, Peuls, Hausas . . . at least 24 different groups that use their own criteria to identify themselves. These people have

life projects totally unrelated to the plantation, although they cannot carry them out while the dominant system remains in force. These are the people of Saint-Domingue; social actors who see their neighbors beyond any assessment based on their intended essence or within their pigmentation.

This vision of the human person that is imputed to the captive workers as a minimum common denominator supposes a shared history. That logical requirement encapsulates perhaps the most important difference between Haitians and the original populations of America, Asia, and Africa. These latter human groups coexist centuries and centuries before meeting the West, while Haitians are born in the process of resisting genocide and ethnocide. They are invented within the West and never exist on their own. Their link with the French metropolis is constitutive and sizable factions cannot imagine themselves without this alter ego. The identity that Haitians build on a daily basis moves away from the West, without ever cutting the umbilical cord. More than at a crossroads, everything indicates for now that an identity and loneliness are manufactured in a dead end.

It is not about considering such circumstances as an advantage or a disadvantage; simply to appreciate the peculiarity and complexity of Haitian history and the innovations constituting the human group. In the process of fighting colonial empires infinitely more powerful than themselves, the motley variety of ethnic groups eventually came together.[133]

Casimir's reading of Haiti and Haitianess is complex, and unpacking the debates around its veracity would overwhelm the present discussion.[134] But his gesture to this identity's radical plasticity rooted in its confrontation with the West helps us reorient how we think through migratory Saint-Domingue or Haitian culture: not as a fixed essence or even a stable nationality at all, but as repertoires of expressive culture that invoked an invitation to contribute to a regional process of revolution. This is why the cultures of the enslaved refugees of Saint-Domingue inspired new movements in the areas they touched down upon. It is why white Cuban planters were alarmed by what they referred to as their "intellectual culture superior to that of other slaves who were not French property."[135] And finally, it is why colonial governors banned African-descended Saint-Domingue refugees altogether for fear of their corruptive influence.[136]

The cultural forms and aesthetics that Afro-descended Saint-Domingue enslaved and free migrants introduced to both Cuba and New Orleans encoded an aesthetics that could be embodied and recombined according to agential actors' own needs and desires. But they were often remixed in a way that was understood by the slave power as profoundly destabilizing for the cultural hegemony of the colonial planter class. Reagan Patrick Mitchell's study of the habanera-adjacent bamboula rhythm, another migratory rhythm unleashed by the Saint-Domingue exodus, is insightful in this regard. "The ostinato, both as sonic modality and metaphor, expands possibilities for understanding how the bamboula rhythm exists as a continuum," a continuum that changed meaning based on one's social location and political ideology. "Expanding the conception of ostinatos from a musical standpoint to encompassing reflexive engagements allows us to see the constant re-embodiment of diasporas, literally and conceptually, in rhythmic and melodic cells."[137] In the late nineteenth-century Caribbean, these rhythmic cells proliferated through a variety of new musical forms, leading to an endless combination and recombination of diasporic identity and helping to consolidate a Black Atlantic grammar whose connection to Haiti was not lost on those who outlawed or circumscribed its dissemination.[138]

In this regard, it is important to emphasize that many Afro-Cuban practitioners of tumba francesa take seriously the dance form as an archive of intra-island collaboration and even solidarity. As the refrain of one carnival song from Santiago de Cuba explains: "My Mom and Dad come from Haiti; I dream of Haiti" (Mi mamá y mi papá vienen de Haiti; sueño de Haiti).[139] Afro-Cuban dancer Gaudiosa Venet Danger, a "great-granddaughter of Africans" who who was taught the partices of tumba francesa from her mother, identifies its cinquillo rhythmic substrate with Haiti. As she explains: "I, as a little girl, already knew that this thing in the tumba francesa had come to Cuba from— from Haiti, back in the 1800s or something."[140] Venet Danger and the tumba francesa community are not alone in making this assessment. The influence of the Haitian cinquillo (also known as the Haitian contradanza) is celebrated by danzón practitioners in Mexico and Cuba.[141] In contemporary Veracruz, Haitian migrants' centrality to the development of danzón is a narrative embraced by "nearly every danzonero in the port city."[142]

Linked to this conception of tumba francesa's Haitianness was how its vernacular dance deconstructed colonial social relations through mimicry, creating a space for the enslaved to insult their erstwhile masters or narrate abuse and violation in an unauthorized public sphere. As Venet Danger summarizes, "It is said that tumba francesa arose as an imitation of the slaves at the dances that their French masters used to do in the salons, at first in the form of mockery."[143] Tumba francesa was rooted in cinquillo rhythms whose dance forms mocked the physicality and affective mannerisms of enslavers, much like the "cakewalk" in the United States South.[144]

Lyrically, tumba francesa songs incorporated and adapted Haitian Creole language and its lexicon of critical theory and spirituality.[145] When Cuban independence leader Carlos Manuel de Céspedes witnessed freedpeople dancing to "songs, in French Creole, that refer to our [Cuban] revolution," it was most likely at a tumba francesa ceremony.[146] Today, the song-dance form is still used to critique hegemonic powers, as the lyrics of a 2004 song indicate: "¡Bush, vete a la mierda! (Bush, go to hell!)."[147]

The consistency of these rhythmic figures deserves further elaboration, since they portended not only to specific cells but also implied ways of feeling that were historically constructed. Diverse rhythm sections across the Black Atlantic were not background to the melody; they did not "frame" lyrics and were certainly not a blank canvas over which one would paint the melody. As the Puerto Rican musicologist A. G. Quintero Rivera reminds us, "in the [Afro-Puerto Rican] *bomba*, our most important music from the slave plantation, the importance of the rhythm is such that the *melody accompanies the percussion*, instead of the other way around."[148] Rivera pays special attention to how rhythms originating in counter-plantation drumming traditions became transliterated into the figures played by melodic and harmonic instruments. Rivera refers to these instruments, which included clarinets, basses, and *cuatros*, as "camouflaged drums." Their creolized parts reflected a cultural negotiation by which Afro-Creole composers could embed Afrodiasporic cultural forms within the national musics of the late nineteenth-century Caribbean.[149] By mediating or masking the expression of Afro-Atlantic musical aesthetics, cinquillo-based patterns and the rhythmic temporalities of the common wind could be made more acceptable to island elites.[150]

The cinquillo's proximity to performances that critiqued colonial orders gesture to a world beyond binary divisions of gender and race. This is what Cuney Hare heard in the habanera bass line, in all its implied polytemporality. Rather than simply being a canvas for the lyrics in "Mamie's Blues," the ostinato itself became framed by a feminist subject matter while gesturing to its own marooned dislocations many generations in the making. Its genealogy connected the history of Saint-Domingue and Haitian migrants through the Caribbean while creating complex constellations of meaning in new spaces and new places.

Mamie Desdunes's use of the habanera in her blues composition holds a significance that overflows a piano reduction. She connects early blues to Afro-Caribbean cyphers of culture and resistance, challenging the idea of an insular Black South as one in a chain of artistic innovators who ensured this rhythm of the common wind would become a structural element of jazz's rhythmic lexicon.[151] While the habanera became a less explicitly referenced element of blues or early jazz, it remained a rhythm that could be activated in a variety of different contexts.[152] The habanera became further camouflaged, transfigured, and reinvented as new diasporas and new transformations of the plantation and the counter-plantation created opportunities for, and necessities of, African American musical creolization. During the critical reign of Storyville, the habanera's intercultural groove was crucial for an emergent generation of brassroots democracy practitioners who reclaimed segregated space from the specter of the plantation and martialed a collective will to contest subjugation and alienation. In Louisiana, the habanera resonated because its attendant gendered culture spoke to a specific social history: the common wind's counterrevolution and the planter class's attempt to break the will of those inspired by the Haitian Revolution.

THE GENDERED CINQUILLO IN AFRO-LOUISIANA

The example of tumba francesa is instructive for our study of the Saint-Domingue diaspora in New Orleans because enslaved migrants traveled to Louisiana and Santiago de Cuba at relatively the same time. A second wave in 1810 included thousands of Santiago de Cuba's Saint-Domingue planters, and the enslaved people held in bondage, forced to leave Cuba after Napoleon's invasion of Spain.[153] Variations of the dances that contributed to tumba francesa and their linked social commentary were reproduced in Congo Square and Afro-Louisianan culture writ large. Recent music scholarship has detailed how Congolese dance forms creolized in Haiti, such as the calenda and the *bamboula*, based on the Kikongo *mbila a makinu*, were performed not only in Congo Square but also on the levees surrounding New Orleans.[154]

New Orleans was another destination for the cinquillo rhythm and the biting sexual commentary it often accompanied. In 1874 Camille Thierry, a free man of color, published an Afro-Creole song from New Orleans, "Lament of an Aged Mulatta." Its lyrics are reminiscent of the style of the Haitian "female-narrated dissing" heard in "Lisette."[155]

> Listen! When I was in Saint-Domingue,
> Negresses were just like jewels;
> The whites there were ninnies,
> They were always after us.
> In a household,
> Never any fighting,
> The love of a white meant adoration!
> They weren't stingy,
> They were very rich,
> A good *bounda* [ass] was worth a plantation!

> Times have changed, we are sleeping on straw,
> We, whom the planters celebrated . . .
> Before long a lower-class white
> Will be calling us riff raff![156]

In Afro-Creole poems and songs, as Jenson asserts, Haitians and Haitian Louisianans theorized "the power of the 'bounda'" to have "been enough to rearrange hierarchies."[157] Yet the bounda is also a marker of descent. Its former power—when it was worth a plantation—had disappeared. The tripartite social structure of colonial Saint-Domingue had been replaced by two tiers in United States–ruled Louisiana, and one of the ways that the insurgent women of Haiti were symbolically contained was through the "Quadroon ball." Quadroon balls were, in fact, as Emily Clark makes clear, "a Haitian import" adapted by free women of color in the 1820s to take advantage of New Orleans's male-dominated marriage market.[158] Louisiana was different from Haiti, however, and these balls ultimately degraded into carnivalesque, ritualized prostitution with white men.[159] Historian Daniel Rosenberg describes these "humiliating, exploitive" events as representative of the "limits [that] surrounded the freedom of free Blacks."[160]

Quadroon balls did more than satisfy white male desire. From the perspective of Saint-Domingue refugee women of color, these relationships could be a path to economic security and (in some cases) freedom, if not autonomy. While it is coercive and on a spectrum with sexual slavery, it is not simply victimhood. These balls nonetheless performed a social order, one that contained the disruption of gendered and racial hierarchies occasioned by the early phase of the Haitian Revolution. White exiles from Saint-Domingue complained about the ascent of women of color. "You cannot imagine these orgies, called patriotic fêtes," complained a white Dominguan exile in Philadelphia, lamenting that at such events, "the women of color in their former home, proud of having become the idols of the day, were given the leading place."[161] Following the 1792 reorganization of the colonial government, Jacobin French commissioners dispatched to Saint-Domingue took free women of color as mistresses. Saint-Domingue's new civil commissioner, Léger-Félicité Sonthonax, married a woman of African descent.[162] In the gendered performances of the New Orleans Quadroon ball, one can see how politicized Haitian immigrants became "fully mastered by the white men," so that, according to Emily Clark, "the danger of Haiti was [symbolically] mastered."[163] Such rituals of domination made the counternarratives of the creolized habanera and its attendant dance forms all the more urgent.

In many respects, Storyville took its cues from these Quadroon balls. Lulu White's "Mahogany Hall" was an homage to the deforested tree species associated with Haiti, a symbolic enactment of Caribbean ecocide in a New South sex factory.[164] Brothels' frequent ads for "amber fluid" (mixed-race) women illustrated the link between antebellum fetish and antiwomen violence throughout the century.[165] But instead of containing the Haitian Revolution, Storyville symbolically "mastered" a different social revolution: Reconstruction and its freedom dreams. Storyville thus took a page from an old playbook: it would restore the racial and gendered hierarchies that had animated plantation slavery through expropriating Afro-Louisianan sexuality as a commodity. As W. E. B. Du Bois wrote of the decades after emancipation: "The slave went free; stood a brief moment in the sun; then moved back again into slavery," and the ideological artifice that consummated this new slavery was expressed in ads marketing mixed-race sex workers—"amber fluid."[166] Storyville's practice of sexual commodification was not developed by Southern leaders in a vacuum. Across the South, rape and other forms of sexual violence targeting Black women leaders were employed by a white nationalist movement called "Redemption," which terrorized Black communities to dismantle Reconstruction governments and their brassroots base.[167]

A Black vernacular culture emerged to counter the narratives of the Quadroon balls that resonated through the century. One song, whose first printed attribution was in 1811 by a "Habitant d'Hayti" was performed for decades in Louisiana, including in a New Orleans second-line in 1885.[168] Alternatively called "Pauvre piti Mamselle Zizi" and "Caroline," this piece depicts feminized poverty and partner abuse in what Ruth Salvaggio calls an "echo within the chambers of a long song about woman who bear the labor and burdens of a historic pain."[169] The song, as notated by journalist George W. Cable's piano reduction in 1886, includes a habanera bass line. This song broke down the walls of white domesticity and its unspoken violence against Black women, and, according to some accounts, was performed in second-lines in the late 1880s.[170]

In the 1830s, the Creole of color poetry collection *Les Cenelles* critiqued the institution of *plaçage* (common-law marriages between white men and women of color) and took aim at the racialized sexual economy it reproduced. Plaçage was the pivot, the point, of Quadroon balls, and the poems that critiqued it touched a deep psychic nerve, becoming so popular that they were set to songs and recited from memory by free Black audiences.[171] Jerah Johnson considers these poems to be "the single most important piece of antebellum black literature ever written."[172] Armand Lanusse's poem "The Young Lady at the Ball" lambasted the lavish displays of white men's wealth that concealed rape and sexual slavery: "the glitter which surrounds you and charms your eyes / Is only a deceptive prism which conceals death."[173] Floyd Cheung argues that these poems "anticipate another African-American genre of social complaint: the blues."[174] Like New

FIGURE 2.2 A habanera variation, notated in measures 5-9 of Cable's piano reduction of "Caroline," is highlighted in grey. Also of note is the use of triplets over four sixteenth notes on b beat four in measure 1 of Cable's piano reduction, pointing to the "three over four" hemiola, also highlighted in grey. This transcription was initially published in George W. Cable's essay "Dance in Place Congo," and the arrangement done by John Van Broekhoven of a song sung by "Negro Creoles" in St. Charles Parish. According to Cable, the song translates to: "One, two three, that's the way, my dear. Papa says no, mama says yes; 'Tis him I want and he that will have me. There will be no money to buy a cabin." See also Krehbiel, *Afro-American Folksongs*, 139.

Orleans blues, these pieces of social criticism were a form of address that often critiqued the intersection of political economy and gendered power relations implicit in sex work, and their corresponding musical pieces were often set to habanera and tresillo rhythmic lines.

Congo Square was also a space of political education where critiques of gender hierarchies and plantation social relations circulated through cinquillo-based rhythmic substrates. Here, performances of the Franco-Creole song "Dialogue D'Amour" narrated the destruction of sugarcane crops as a metaphor for the "lost love" of planters' lost profits. The song, in keeping with the tradition of biting satire, was a "song of derision" and frequently accompanied by the Congolese-diasporic dance creolized in Haiti, the calenda.[175] The title appearing in Cuney Hare's sheet music reduction of this song, "Dialogue D'Amour," includes the subtitle "song of mockery." In this "dialogue," a woman implores a man:

If your love can be so great, my dear
Sir, If your love can be so great, my dear
Sir, If your love can be so great,
Then give me your silver.
[Man]: All of my cane is burned, Marianne,
Is burned, Marianne,
All of my cane is burned,
And ruined am I.
[Woman]: If plantations are lost, my dear Sir,
If your cane is destroyed, my dear Sir,
If your cane is burned,
Then love is lost in flames!

The song certainly repeats, or prefigures, lyrics heard in "Mamie's Blues," such as Desdunes's invocation to "spare a dime." The tone of "Dialogue D'Amour" is defiant, sarcastically speaking truth to power. It was, after all, a "song of mockery." The "lost love" could be a tongue-in-cheek critique of the master's power, which has evaporated with the destruction of his sugarcane. Sugarcane, a phallocentric symbol of authoritarian power and enslaved overwork, was an object of scorn among the Afro-Louisianans and was burned en masse in the German Coast Uprising of 1811.[176] It also could very well be a "Quadroon" asking for her payment from her pledged lover. In this sense, it follows the tradition of "the ability to drag sexual issues into the public sphere," which Mimi Sheller has associated with musical practice in Haiti and Jamaica to manifest "erotic agency."[177] And once again, this song utilized, like "Mamie's Blues," a habanera bass line.

FIGURE 2.3 *Top*: "Tumba Francesa Drumbeats (Toques de Tumba Francesa)" whose foundational rhythm, the catá (also the name of a wooden, cylindrical idiophone), oscillates between a tresillo and cinquillo pattern. See Galis Riverí, *La percusión en los ritmos afrocubanos y haitiano-cubanos*, 113. *Bottom*: Cuney Hare's reproduction of "Dialogue d'Amor." Here, again, we see the habanera in the bass and triplet-based melodic figures over two- and four-beat divided bass lines in the context of a barbed and sardonic reimagining of plantation hierarchies. This piano reduction assigned to the pianist's left hand what had initially been a percussive figure performed in Congo Square not dissimilar to the "toques de Tumba Francesa."

The distinct double valence of the blues—its invocation of sexual liberation within an oppressive sexual economy—echoes this genre of Haitian diasporic aural critique. These rhythms sonically marked spaces of prostitution and sex work. By the time of Storyville's emergence, sex workers were the working class of a highly profitable regime of sexual capitalism, whereby sex tourism became the centerpiece of the New South's consumer-centric economy.[178] The cinquillo- and tresillo-derived rhythms of the Haitian diaspora were so prevalent in prior conjunctures (conjunctures that rhymed with the present) that these ostinatos continued to serve as cultural responses to the psychic, political, and affective contradictions embedded in commodified sex.

Mamie Desdunes, the daughter of a proud Haitian-descended activist, composed "Mamie's Blues" within this tradition. Her composition can be heard as a late nineteenth-century manifestation of a Haitian and circum-Caribbean women's critique, whereby sexual violence, the Black body, and the erotic were enunciated within popular musical culture and conveyed to a Black counterpublic. Performed both for a concertgoing public and during the moments of transactional sex, it was an anthem that refused consent. "It is more noble and dignified to fight, no matter what, than to show a passive attitude of resignation. . . . Absolute submission augments the oppressor's power and creates doubt about the feelings of the oppressed."[179] These words penned by Mamie's father, Rodolphe, reflect how the early blues pianist crafted the popular response of the Black working-class to the same conditions that prompted her father's legislative path that challenged the constitutional basis of segregation in *Plessy v. Ferguson*. But her intervention sprung not from the theory of public rights but from the vernacular theory of patriarchal racial capitalism embodied in Afro-Caribbean dance-music forms like tumba francesa and bomba.[180] But the fascinating thing about Mamie Desdunes's work is that—if Morton's rendition is to be accepted as more or less faithful to the source material—she sang the blues. "She could really sing those blues." Indeed, each pitch that Morton chooses to sing in dialogue with this habanera bass line is based on the blues and gospel scales that permeated in the 1890s, corresponding with the migration of plantation fieldhands to the Crescent City. Perhaps Mamie was channeling the cultural inheritances she identified with her African American mother, Clementine Walker.

By merging the expressive culture of Southern African Americans with elements derived from the cinquillo complex, Desdunes was able to put Black working-class women's erotic agency in historical perspective, weaving their dissident vocality into that of the diaspora. The space between her hands and her voice briefly became a decolonized contact zone.[181] She invoked the practices of symbolic negation in which Black women in Haiti and Cuba had also played a

FIGURE 2.4 In this version of "Mamie's Blues" Morton's vocal line emphasizes blues and gospel scale-derived vocal melodies, as would Louis Armstrong's vocal rendition of the same song a few months later in May 1940. Here, Morton interchanges a habanera bass lines with his blues / gospel verses. Transcribed by the author from Morton, "Mamie's Blues," J.S. 695, Commodore Records, 1939. Notwithstanding the thoughtful intervention of Asher Chodos in "The Blues Scale" (2018) and the potentially colonial implications of notating a delimited blues scale, I find myself persuaded by the compelling evidence presented by jazz organist Radam Schwartz in his 2018 master's thesis, "Organ Jazz," which highlights the enduring and fundamental significance of these particular blues and gospel pentatonic-based scales in the development of jazz vocabulary. For insights on these scales' connection to African American liturgical traditions, see Williams-Jones, "Afro-American Gospel Music," 380.

circumscribed, yet tangible, role of signaling dissent, illuminating the dialectics of the counter-plantation encounter. This oral technology of resistance had circulated through the Black Atlantic for the better part of a century, a product of revolution and enslavement, and it continued to play an important role in the age of Storyville. The habanera channeled this tradition in the hands of an expert artist and truth-teller.

CONCLUSION

> Money ... transforms fidelity into infidelity, love into hate, hate into love, virtue into vice, vice into virtue, servant into master, master into servant, idiocy into intelligence, and intelligence into idiocy ... [It] serves to exchange every quality for every other, even contradictory, quality and object; it is the fraternization of impossibilities. It makes contradictions embrace.
>
> *Karl Marx*[182]

Reflecting on a concert by the Chicago-based blues musician Memphis Minnie, Langston Hughes declared himself moved by the force of her voice and guitar, whose power was capable of overcoming the rhythms of commerce of the bar where she was performing. "Memphis Minnie's music is harder than the coins that roll across the counter," he wrote. Hughes wondered whether she was aware of her intervention: "Does that mean she understands? Or is it just science that makes the guitar strings so hard and loud?"[183] Hughes's comments on the power of this music to overcome the system of exchange and extraction that engendered women's commodification bring us to the question of a blues consciousness. Through what personal or communal histories and experiences did "Mamie's Blues" resonate so deeply with Jelly Roll Morton, Bunk Johnson, Willie Cornish, and so many others? The musicians who worked in "the district" suggested that they did understand. They were aware of the intersection of wealth, sex, and race; they understood that the Black body was coerced by market relations, commenting on it frequently in recorded interviews.

"Mamie's Blues" offered heartfelt descriptions of these otherworldly spectacles of race and power that spoke to the social reality of proletarianization as the dreams of Reconstruction were dashed. Like alchemy, its poetry turned stories of oppression, suffering, and violence into a space of analysis, thought, and potentially action. And such lessons informed the genealogy of brassroots democracy and its critical understanding of gender and power throughout the century. Storyville was "shut down" by government ordinance in 1917, but the contested nature of the erotic and the sex industry did not suddenly cease to be an important topic for blues women singers. Yet the currents of early jazz and their interaction with this sex economy became less pronounced than their classic blues counterparts. Admittedly, the lines were not so firmly drawn, and the recording industry was only beginning to set boundaries between genres that would mark clean divisions between the two. Yet, in a strange twist, jazz's slow acceptance as an art form among mainstream American society also reproduced bourgeoise and patriarchal ideologies that separated the (male) artist from social and political concerns in producing "his" art. When exceptional women instrumentalists "made" it, they were often marketed in ways damaging to their careers, and their contributions became posthumously distorted or marginalized.

Mamie Desdunes not only challenges a male-centric reading of early jazz but also deals directly with the question of Black women's bodies, their desire as well as their containment, as foundational to the music. The embrace of her song by Jelly Roll Morton, Bunk Johnson, and countless others suggests that this variant of social commentary was widely disseminated. It points to how the new music was a space in which Black women (and men) "could discuss, plan, and organize this new world," writes Clyde Woods about the blues epistemology. That is, they are "the cries of a new society being born."[184] This sovereign universe contextualizes brassroots democracy's foundation, a common wind realized in artistic resistance, in which the weapons of the weak became the soundtrack of the future.

Mamie Desdunes offers us a lesson in jazz that does not center stars, careers, or egos, but rather social movements and intangible lessons from the narrow cracks offered by glimpses in census archives, death certificates, and a polyrhythmic bass line. Her song demonstrates women's agency and cultural influence within a social context that many modern-day commentators have written off as factories of patriarchal pleasure. It suggests that Black womanist and feminist stirrings were important forces that catalyzed the creation of new art forms, foundational to the blues and jazz itself. By navigating the painful and contradictory negotiation with the erotic through centuries of slavery and capitalist commodification, artists like Desdunes manifested new directions that contributed to brassroots democracy's liberatory lineages.

"Mamie's Blues," like the work of the Desdunes family as a whole, demonstrates how interaction between Afro-Caribbean and African American culture was endemic to the music precisely because this creolization was never apolitical. Within the forms of music that traversed the pathways of forced migration and human enslavement, oral traditions that critiqued the spiritual bankruptcy and sensual impotency of the white plantocracy created new languages to describe oppression and provided doors to one's self-actualization. They motivated new generations of artists to resist in the face of overwhelming violence against body and soul, to overthrow bondage both erotic and economic. This is why I agree with Julio Cortázar that "Mamie's Blues" is "a cloud without frontiers, a spy of air and water, an archetypal form, something from before, from below." We would do well to continue to study its intercultural aesthetics and hear what it can tell us about gender, women's agency, and the history of Black Atlantic resistance over the past several centuries.

THREE

La Frontera Sónica

Mexican Revolutions in Borderlands Jazz

Lorenzo and Louis Tio must have been at a loss for words. Like the rest of the Excelsior Brass Band, these two clarinetists were to perform inside a goliath thirty-three-acre outdoor structure between Charles Street and the Mississippi River in February 1885. Eight years earlier, the brothers moved to New Orleans as teenagers from Tampico, Mexico, where they had lived with hundreds of other Afro-Louisianan refugees who had fled the antebellum United States.[1] But after several decades living in a nation that had abolished slavery since 1829, these Creoles of color returned. Many Black Louisianans had written to family members in Mexico to share the news of a great social revolution, Reconstruction, which had the potential to destroy racial and caste prejudice in the South and the plantation model that sustained it.

Yet by 1885 the social opening occasioned by Reconstruction was all but closed. The fair at which the Excelsior Brass Band would play at was not intended to celebrate communitarian futures, but rather, slavery's afterlives. New Orleans had won the bid to be the host city for the National Cotton Planters Association's hundredth-anniversary celebration of the United States' first shipment of cotton. This commodity so associated with slave labor became the centerpiece of a carnivalesque event whose sheer scale defied any comparison of the time. Over one million global attendees visited a giant miniature city whose main building was the largest wooden structure in the world.[2] At worlds' fairs of the decade, international investors enjoyed ornate lounges while they listened to revisionist historians of slavery defend Southern virtues. White families visited whole "villages" of imagined Asians, Africans, Afro-Americans, Mexicans, and Cubans, displayed on the entertainment avenues of the fair alongside "monkey houses."³ Their depictions were so offensive that anti-lynching activist Ida B. Wells organized a boycott of these events.⁴ The New Orleans variant was built on top of a plantation itself, as this was a veritable celebration of the plantocracy and their victory over the Black working class of Louisiana. World's Fairs like the New Orleans Cotton Exposition reflected and accelerated structural changes in global capitalism. Karl Marx believed that they exemplified how capitalism could abolish national boundaries, and Walter Benjamin saw them as modern temples where the devout undertook a "pilgrimage of the commodity fetish."⁵ Capitalism's renewed vigor was powered by the dispossession of farmers and the destruction of noncapitalist forms of exchange. The world had entered a dangerous and vicious era of imperialism, led by financial capital allied with European and local armies that renewed extractive economies in Africa, Asia, and Latin America.⁶ In Mexico, a new government led by Porfirio Díaz had consolidated its power by 1884. In the Porfiriato, the Mexican state now prioritized foreign direct investment and the capture of communal lands in Mexico's many semiautonomous "Indian Republics." José T. Otero, the vice governor of Sonora, had in 1879 warned of "an anomaly whose existence is shameful for Sonora . . . a separate nation within the state."⁷ Otero was referring to the Yaqui nation in the lands between the Rio Yaqui and the Pacific Ocean, where Yaqui Indigenous people had practiced virtual autonomy within New Spain since 1571. For decades, the Yaquis had capably resisted land grabs from Sonora's elite, and Otero wanted the Mexican army to intervene on the latter's behalf.

The Yaquis' fate was sealed in New Orleans. The Porfirian elite to which Otero belonged participated enthusiastically in the New Orleans Cotton Exhibition.⁸ Of all nations, Mexico was the second-largest financial contributor to the fair and shipped huge quantities of minerals to entice investors by its elaborate exhibit.⁹ Mexico's ambassador to England, Sebastian B. de Mier, claimed that "the exhibition of New Orleans changed foreign opinion in our favor" and investors were "surprised" by Mexico's "natural riches . . . [and our] efforts to exploit them."¹⁰ One white attendee bragged to the *Times Democrat* that he had bought the rights to transfer his "entire cotton farm" onto fertile Yaqui-owned lands in Sonora.¹¹

Having already sold mining and land concessions in their territory to American and British investors, Díaz swiftly authorized military force against the Yaqui nation. Thus began a genocidal war with few comparisons in recent human history. In 1885, the Mexican government estimated the Yaqui population stood at 20,000; by 1907, that number was reduced to 2,723.¹² Between these years, thousands of captured Yaquis were forcibly transferred to the Yucatan Peninsula, where they

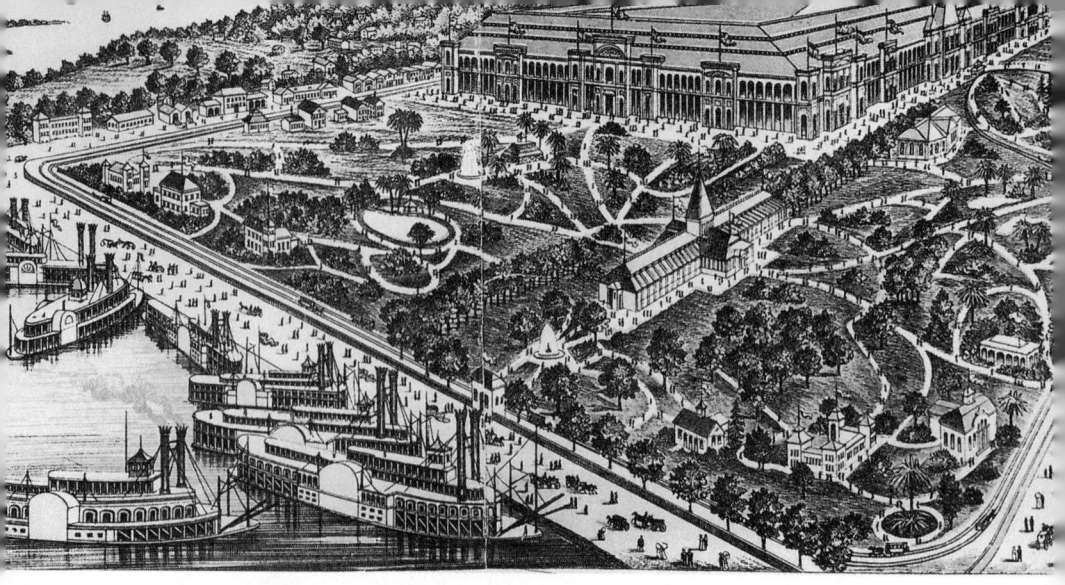

FIGURE 3.0 "World's Industrial and Cotton Centennial Exposition, New Orleans," date unknown, courtesy of the *Times-Picayune*.

were enslaved labor to harvest henequen. Henequen is an agave-like plant key in twentieth-century rope production, and the plantations where it was harvested were monopolized by the Chicago-based International Harvester Company. Two-thirds of the transferred Yaqui population died from overwork and deprivation.[13]

The Sonoran governor Ramón Corral claimed that although the "sacrifice" of the Yaquis was tragic, it brought about "the basis for the beginning of a period of civilization." Corral became one of the richest men in the state and was the first investor of the Bank of Sonora.[14] At the conclusion of the Porfiriato, over 127 million acres of communal, uncultivated, or unoccupied lands, which accounted for more than half of Mexico's cultivable farmland, were handed over to private parties.[15] The rapid levels of industrialization in the late nineteenth-century United States and Mexico generated record levels of profit for investors. This profit was powered by racialized violence that systematically targeted and eliminated noncapitalist forms of living, including in the US South.[16]

Indeed, forty-five miles from the New Orleans Cotton Centennial, violence against Black sugar workers was on the rise. Denied communal lands, activists now struck back against slavery-like conditions on plantations. They organized with the Knights of Labor and marched with brass bands to connect distant plantations.[17] In 1887 in the cane fields surrounding Thibodaux, Governor McEnery sent in military-grade equipment to suppress striking laborers. After witnessing a gatling gun mow down unarmed cane cutters for the crime of refusing to work, the heiress to slavery Mary Pugh wrote in her diary that the violence "excelled

[sic] anything I ever saw even during the [Civil] war."[18] A report from the *New Orleans Weekly Pelican* depicted the indiscriminate violence: "Lame men and blind women shot; children and hoary-headed grandsires ruthlessly swept down. The negroes offered no resistance; they could not, as the killing was unexpected."[19] After years of Reconstruction activism that built communes, cooperatives, and Black political power, the "Redemption" movement bloodily announced that Black organizing would be met with counterinsurgency tactics. Planters, perceptive of the role that music played in fomenting opposition, banned Black brass bands from Thibodaux for several years; many musicians, including a young John Robichaux, moved to New Orleans.[20]

Commenting upon such violence, the Mexican historian Paco Ignacio Taibo II explains that for the Porfirian elite, "the present is progress and there was an excess of Yaquis and their communal vision of the world."[21] The same can be said for Louisiana plantation bosses and the financiers from New York who sought to put an end to Black workers' struggle for the commons.[22] But ideas could not be destroyed so easily. Indeed, when the Tios arrived at the Cotton Exposition in February 1885, they came not to pay homage to cotton but to perform for a civil rights rally attended by three thousand and defended by a Black militia. Multiple activists traveled from across the Deep South, such as bishop Henry M. Turner of Georgia and the lawyer and professor Daniel A. Straker. Originally from Barbados, Straker moved to Kentucky to teach in a Reconstruction-era Freedmen's School. In 1876, he was elected to South Carolina's State House of Representatives. In less than a year, he was forced from office at gunpoint by a white supremacist coup.[23] On the grounds of the Cotton Centennial, he called for a world where "the antagonism of race, the hatred of creed and parties, the prejudices of caste, and the denial of equal rights may disappear from among us forever."[24]

Straker was not the only attendee who crossed international borders. Some hours earlier before his speech, the eighty musicians of la Banda del Octavo Regimiento de Caballería (hereafter referred to the Eighth Cavalry Band) played on the exhibition's grounds. The Eighth Cavalry Band's performances at the New Orleans Cotton Festival were legendary, influencing musical trends in the city for decades. Díaz appreciated the strategic power of music in projecting Mexican nationalism and sanitizing his human rights abuses. Yet the musicians had an agenda of their own. The band stayed six months in the Crescent City, and several of its members relocated to the French Quarter permanently. When Mexican Florencio Ramos decided to stay in New Orleans, he effectively deserted a military post that had provided health insurance and social security, choosing instead to become New Orleans's first full-time saxophonist.[25] Many brass band musicians had come from territories confiscated by Díaz's mass land expropriation, where they had received musical training enabled through resistant communal autonomy. Juventino Rosas, for instance, was an Otomi Indigenous violinist and trombonist who performed at Chicago's World Colombian Exposition in 1893. He had grown up in without access to land but with access to musical instruments. As a child, Rosas and his father busked in Santa Cruz, Guanajuato, to survive; he later composed one of the most popular songs in late nineteenth-century New Orleans, "Sobre las Olas," which was performed frequently by the Eighth Cavalry Band.[26]

Mexico's variant of brassroots democracy had a pronounced influence on the Black musicians of the Crescent City. Mexican musicians have been credited with introducing the clarinet and the saxophone to New Orleans music communities as well as reinforcing habanera-inflected rhythms within a Cuban danzón-influenced style. Several Mexican or Mexican-descended musicians became the teachers of a formative generation of Black and Afro-Creole artists, including Joe Gabriel, Bunk Johnson, and several others.[27] Mexican newcomers to New Orleans complemented long-standing patterns of migration from Cuba and other parts of Latin America, and Bruce Boyd Raeburn suggests that 24 percent of first-generation jazz performers born before 1900 were of Spanish American heritage, including the Tios.[28] As Gaye Theresa Johnson eloquently puts it, "the presence of Mexican musicians in early jazz both complicates *and* underscores African American histories and sensibilities fundamental in its creation."[29] The genealogy presented here connects anti-colonial and antislavery movements in two Gulf sites and animates a critical history of musical instruments (such as the clarinet), harmonic techniques (such as ragtime's "three over four"), and rhythms (including the habanera and tresillo).[30]

The life story of the Tios provides a cartography of cultural activism that cuts across empires and diasporas. Their cross-border genealogy connected the Excelsior to the Eighth Cavalry Band in a moment of celebration and danger. These musical geographies severely complicate nationalist, US-centric narratives, and foreground bottom-up histories at the US-Mexican border: *la frontera*. The cross-border imagination that such solidarity generated is yet another liberatory lineage from which the practitioners of brassroots democracy were able to select and remix as they struggled to build a new world.

This chapter considers the rebel soundscapes produced at the borders of Spanish America and Afro-Louisiana and their impact on brassroots democracy. Their sociosonic engagements constitute what I call the *frontera sónica*, an aural repertoire of Black, Indigenous, and Mexican convergence spaces that manifested maroon ecologies and new commons. Their strikingly polycultural musical forms appear anachronistic within the context of plantation slavery and its Jim Crow sequels, pointing to new worlds of possibility and alternative social relations grounded in subaltern solidarity. The frontera sónica is traced in the following pages through both the Tio family and the multiethnic, improvised community into which they were born, the Eureka colony. This commune belonged to distinguished archipelago of multinational communities, such as the Black Indigenous mestizo rebel territory known as *la Comanchería* in 1830s Texas, or the African American land colony known as "Little Liberia" in 1920s Ensenada. All of these expanded what Laura Hooton calls "relations of reciprocity,"[31] a reciprocity prefigured by musicians whose expressive culture embodied their repressed legacy.

Much of the literature on these so-called Black colonies in Mexico emphasizes their short-lived nature and the sometimes disastrous consequences for those involved.[32] The frontera sónica offers a way to think through these alternative experiments through transmission of oral and aural repertoire, whose success and historical relevance is not measured through the creation of stable states nor long-term settlements. These bold experiments belonged to the genre of possibilities that Raúl Coronado calls "worlds not to come"; they projected, in the words of Ernesto Bassi, "visions of potential futures."[33] More than failures, each of these spaces were culturally generative communities that sounded communitarian futures in a dangerous present.

Indeed, the activists and musicians involved in these efforts did not necessarily interpret the ephemerality of their efforts as a negative.[34] The counter-plantation festival at the heart of the Cotton Centennial is but one episode in which Black freedpeople and Mexican musicians improvised new musical cultures, weaving spontaneous, insurgent auralities in the heart of danger, only to fade back into the social fabric of the city. In this, their transient nature was an advantage, responding to the situatedness of plantation states and disciplinary regimes with an illegible mobility.

The borderlands are a useful site to study this deterritorialized creolization process because the fluidity of the nineteenth-century US-Mexican border was both a limit and an aperture: as Sean Kelley notes in his study of the five thousand enslaved fugitives who escaped bondage through Mexico, "the continual redrawing of the boundaries between the United States, Texas, and Mexico in the nineteenth century prompted slaves to view the border as a symbol of liberation."[35] It is precisely these shifting, unstable boundaries that made the space-making activity of communal music-making so vital. Here, the borderlands are what

Gloria Anzaldúa describes as "the emotional residue of an unnatural boundary," as well as, in the words of Alex Chávez, a "relational process of sonic enactment and reception."[36] That is, a site of violence, but also possibility, history, and spirit.[37]

And yet the story of la frontera sónica does not end, nor start, there. New Orleans's unique status as both an imperial port city and a meeting ground of Latin American exiled revolutionaries created the conditions for an archipelagic, terraqueous counterpart of the frontera sónica. Within this second set of coordinates, this chapter considers the transborder spaces within the Gulf urban entrepôts of Havana, Veracruz, and New Orleans, employing what Jessica Swanston Baker calls "a multicentric conception of Caribbean cultural production through archipelagic listening."[38]

As the vignette that opened this chapter suggests, this study of the frontera sónica explores the social history of the clarinet as a particular vessel that uniquely embodied these connections. The clarinet was rarely, if ever, performed by African American musicians before the advent of the Mexican military bands or the arrival of the Tios, and its unique multiphonics complemented the rich textures of cornets and trombones, endowing it with the ability to fulfill a unique role that expanded and deepened the world-creating affect of brassroots democracy. "The clarinet, especially," writes Thomas Brothers, "often seems like a one-man effort to reproduce the heterophonic richness of a congregation," drawing a connection between the sociomusical practices of the Black Baptist church with Black clarinet practice. Yet Brothers is quick to clarify that in his hearing of clarinet, and Black music in general, there is little room for the creolizing solidarities produced in the frontera sónica. "Jazz," he explains, "is no musical gumbo but the product of direct and vigorous transformation of the plantation vernacular.... The arguments for a substantial contribution from the Creoles in the creation of jazz are based partly on mistaken notions about the role of Latin dance rhythms."[39] Brothers uplifts the centrality of African American aesthetics but does so in a way that precludes the possibility of either solidarity or meaningful intercultural exchange with other racial subalterns in the Gulf and Caribbean.

A wave of scholarship that has considered the Latin American influence on this music often critiques this line of thinking. "Latin American music styles shared a common history with jazz and each has played seminal roles in the other's development, intersecting, cross-influencing, at times seeming inseparable," argues Christopher Washburne. "Regardless, in much of the jazz literature, their relationship has been diminished or downright ignored."[40] Robin Moore's work on the "sustained and ongoing interactions" between Latin American and early jazz musicians has, in his words, "never generated much interest among mainstream jazz scholars and represents the efforts of individuals with a particular interest in Latin America who publish in niche journals rather than those central to jazz studies." Thus obscured is early jazz's connection to "broader Afro-descendant struggles to forge diasporic ties, challenge racial stereotypes, and underscore commonalities among diverse international communities."[41] Certainly, the music is often presented in such a way that, as Robin D. G. Kelley notes in his discussion of Ken Burns's documentary *Jazz*, "jazz is not only the exclusive property of the United States, but it has been a premiere manifestation of this nation's democratic ethos."[42] Yet, in the case of Thomas Brothers's work, his motivation is not necessarily to hew a nationalistic line but to foreground how Black plantation workers, dispossessed by racial capitalism and the destruction of their robust social movement, created community and resilience through musical agency. Sensitive to the danger of explaining away all Black aesthetic inspiration as a by-product of another culture, Brothers implies that this argument, in its most extreme variants, contains its own ideological bias.[43]

These two bodies of scholarship, both inspired by the music and the musicians who produced it, are thus not in dialogue. One avenue unexplored by both, and which could articulate new points of convergence between plantation migrants and itinerant Latin American musicians, is attending to the syncretic interface of political and ideological alliance with expressive culture. This is the framework that brassroots democracy provides. As the counter-plantation festival that opened this chapter demonstrates, a call-and-response between the cultural and sociopolitical worlds of early jazz's "plantation vernacular" and "Mexican music" (or "Spanish tinge") permeated throughout New Orleans brass band traditions.

This chapter explores the material and aural landscapes manifested by the Black, Indigenous, and Mexican communities within the dynamic sphere of the frontera sónica. Despite the linguistic diversity that marked these communities, they developed a communitarian grammar that resounded social relations hitherto unrealized, becoming the basis for potent musical inventions. The changing languages of resistance drafted between these peripheralized subalterns are an important tributary of brassroots democracy's creolized polyphony. Their collective cultural labor pointed to possibilities unimagined by the architects of planation slavery and its afterlives.

This history of the frontera sónica then pivots to the Tios' own multinational history within this borderlands matrix—as cigar rollers, Mexican communalists, and clarinetists. Their story invites us to reinterpret New Orleans, not just as slavery's Southern entrepôt but also as an unintended sanctuary. One node in a network for refugees, it sheltered many Latin American exiles whose radical dreams for the future directly impacted Afro-Louisianans. Included in this cohort was the exiled Indigenous statesman and future Mexican president Benito

Juárez, who successfully planned the overthrow of Antonio López de Santa Anna. He conceived his revolutionary strategy while working as a Crescent City cigar roller, amid a community of Black and Afro-Creole coworkers.[44]

The chapter concludes by considering the contributions of the Tios in light of the dichotomous framework presented here. It delves into the flourishing danza and danzón traditions that were prevalent in the 1870s Mexican communities of their upbringing and in 1880s and '90s New Orleans. This exploration reveals that early jazz clarinet music was both the expression of an African American plantation vernacular *and* the manifestation of an intra-Gulf, working-class movement. This bottom-up cosmopolitanism embraced the danzón's idiomatic clarinet phraseology and the anti-colonial legacies with which they were tied.

MEXICAN INDEPENDENCE AS AN ABOLITIONARY FORCE

In the face of the advancing British forces outside New Orleans, an ancestor of Lorenzo Tio—their great-uncle, the Guadeloupean Louisianan clarinetist Louis Hauzer—volunteered in the free colored militia of the United States Army, placing himself in a precarious situation.[45] Hauzer, along with other soldiers of color, braced themselves for potential harm or even fatality. Positioned in strategically questionable locations and under the command of General Andrew Jackson—a man notorious for his disdain for Indigenous and African communities—he and his unit stood resolute against the advances of British troops.[46] Yet their resistance was marked with a unique defiance: their battle hymn was not the United States national anthem, but instead the resonant strains of "En Avan' Grenadié," a battle song originally vocalized by Haitian troops in their struggle against Napoleon's forces. Its refrain exhorted, "Go forward, grenadiers, he who is dead requires no ration."[47]

This song is revealing, as much for its anti-monarchical imagination as for the Black Atlantic culture it celebrated within the battalion. It also raises a question: Who did Hauzer, born in Jamaica but a lifelong Louisianan, learn it from? The likely answer lies in the recent arrival in New Orleans of several hundred seafaring revolutionaries whose nationalities were an assortment of Haitian, French, and Mexican. Many of them were veterans of the Haitian War of Independence who had chosen the Crescent City to launch anti-Spanish operations in coordination with the nascent Mexican Republic. El Grito de Delores, Mexico's declaration of independence, had been issued by Miguel Hidalgo y Costilla in 1810, and Black soldiers of fortune resonated with its call for racial equality and self-government.[48] The Haitian-born Sévère Courtois joined the likes of Joseph Savary and Mexican General José Bernardo Gutiérrez to push into Spanish-controlled

Texas under the Mexican flag. The presence of these soldiers in New Orleans likely opened networks for the Tios, either commercially or diplomatically.[49] Not long after, in 1822, Louis Marcos Tio, Lorenzo and Louis's grandfather, stayed in Haiti for a summer with seven other Afro-Louisianans, as the Tios developed a commercial network that spanned from Tabasco, Mexico, to Pensacola, Florida—almost the entire radius of the Gulf.[50] These developments provoked anger among white Louisianan customs officers, who in 1817 complained of a "system [of] audacity" organized "by a motley mixture of freebooters and smugglers . . . under the Mexican flag."[51]

When these soldiers helped achieve the independence of Mexico, they contributed to a regional creolizing event that inspired new freedom dreams expressed in popular song. This was true despite the fact that many of these soldiers of fortune, including, another ancestor of Lorenzo, Joseph Tio, raided Spanish slave ships and resold its human cargo—a legacy that complicates unequivocally republican assessments about this community of privateers.[52]

Nonetheless, as Theodore Vincent notes in his study of the dramatic entrance of Black and Indigenous Mexicans to the public sphere of the postcolonial nation, "for both Mexico and Haiti, independence was also a social revolution."[53] Mexico's freedom from Spain was a resounding moment in global abolition, and its constitution's antislavery provisions profoundly destabilized slavery in the borderlands of Texas and Mexico.

Indeed, as soon as Solomon Northup was forcibly transferred to Bayou Boeuf, a cotton plantation in Louisiana, the subject of conversation among other enslaved peoples was Mexico. "During the [US-] Mexican war I well remember the extravagant hopes that were excited," he explains in his memoir *Twelve Years a Slave* (1853). He and other Africans on the plantation hoped that, sooner rather than later, they "would hail with unmeasured delight the approach of an invading army." It was not to be. "The news of [US] victory filled the great house with rejoicing, but produced only sorrow and disappointment in the [slave] cabin." According to Northup, enslaved people paid close attention to the political events that led to the US-Mexican War, and they saw Mexico as a military power capable of delivering them from slavery. It had not been long since "a concerted movement" of mass exodus to Mexico had been organized by an enslaved man named Lew. "Lew flitted from one plantation to another, in the dead of night, preaching a crusade to Mexico, and, like Peter the Hermit, creating a furor of excitement wherever he appeared," reported Northup. "At length a large number of runaways were assembled; stolen mules, and corn gathered from the fields, and bacon filched from smoke-houses, had been conveyed into the woods." The plan was betrayed, according to Northup, by an opportunistic enslaved man who outed the would-be fugitives. Nonetheless, it was a "subject of general and unfailing interest in every slave-hut on the bayou, and will doubtless go down to succeeding generations as their chief tradition."[54]

Lew was an enslaved man with "Mexico in his head," a disease that enslavers diagnosed in Africans who sought to cross the border to liberate themselves from bondage.[55] Had Lew and his group escaped, they may have become part of some four to five thousand people who "stole themselves" from their master through the Underground Railroad to Mexico.[56] Mexican campesinos and mariners were participants in this process in both grassroots and institutional registers. In 1834, for instance, the Mexican citizen Domingo Hernández was arrested in New Orleans for carrying a "black slave" in his steamship to freedom in Matamoros.[57] Runaway slave ads printed in Texas described groups of runaway slaves "piloted to Mexico by Mexican peons," and in 1851, Manuel Flores, a head official in Guerrero, killed a Texas enslaver who crossed into Mexican territory to reenslave "Manuel," a resident African American.[58]

Enslaved United States Africans responded to Mexico's powerful antislavery legislation and popular base that set it apart from other New World anti-colonial revolutions—the overwhelmingly Indigenous, mestizo, and Black makeup of the Mexican liberation armies. *Mestizaje*, the discourse of racial mixture and color-blind citizenship that undergirds modern Mexican nationalism, has obscured the profound African presence in colonial Mexico and the importance of Black troops to its independence.[59] By 1810, Mexican *afrodescendientes* officially constituted 10.2 percent of the Mexican population, a number that some scholars have suggested is underrepresentative.[60]

While Lew did not escape from the plantation where he and Northup were enslaved, many others did. Felix Haywood, once enslaved in San Antonio, recalled how "hundreds of slaves did go to Mexico and got on all right. We would hear about them and that they were going to be Mexicans. They brought up their children to speak only Mexican." Felix summarized: "In Mexico you could be free."[61] Black exodus was often a collective endeavor. In 1835, the second-largest slave revolt in North American history was initiated by dozens of African Americans on the lower Brazos River. They burned plantations, collected tools, and joined the Mexican army or disappeared into the woods. Anti-Anglo insurgents in Texas also included "French negroes," including one named Raphael, who fought with Native Americans and Tejano Mexicans against Texan slaveholders. When captured by Texas Rangers, he "claimed to have always been free."[62] Whether this individual was from Haiti, or a Creole of color insurgent from New Orleans or another Gulf city, is unknown, but his presence raises some interesting questions about the transatlantic character of Mexican solidarity with African Americans.[63]

Black-Mexican alliances in the Texas border region produced both maroon ecologies and their attendant musical and expressive cultures. Benjamin Lundy, one of the most prolific white American abolitionists of the mid-nineteenth century, traveled first to the Mexican border town of Matamoros by way of New Orleans to make contact with radical Afro-Creoles committed to resettling African American refugees in Mexico.[64] In the new dawn of independent Mexico, Matamoros (which translates to "kill the moors") shed the genocidal legacy inscribed in its name as it became a center for anti-colonial and antislavery agitation at the border of the United States Southwest.[65] It emerged as the vibrant "center of diplomatic activity" between Shawnee, Cherokee, Kickapoo, African Americans, and Afro-Creoles who united with the Mexican army and attempted to build new homelands while fighting back against slavery's westward sprawl.[66]

Lundy paints a striking image of a multinational society. He describes in detail a "singular" type of polycrop agriculture, with "many fine cabbage plants and young radishes" alongside onions and "corn, waist high." Lundy even received medical treatment for his dysentery from the plants grown in local orchards and gardens—especially camphor and laudanum, "remedies [that] I believe are without parallel." Among these maroon ecologies, a dynamic performance culture took shape, which Lundy compared to the collective music-making practices he had witnessed in Haiti some years earlier. "In the evening I went to see a *fandango*," he wrote on December 14, 1834, where "several hundred persons, mostly of the lower classes, but many of them well dressed, had met in a spacious yard, and were dancing by moonlight. It was very much like the Haytian [sic] fandangos."[67] *Fandangos*, vibrant celebrations of dance and music with roots in the late baroque-era traditions of Spain and Portugal, morphed into unique expressions of post-independence Mexican culture, intertwining with New World and Afrodiasporic musical nuances. They are infrequently, if ever, compared to the communal musical gatherings found in nineteenth-century Haiti.[68] Yet Lundy heard in the Mexican borderlands how Haitian and Afro-Louisianan soundscapes were part of a larger, regional counter-plantation spirit marked by their interrelationship with the abolitionist spirit of the common wind. Hosted by the Afro-Creole Louisianan expat Nicholas Drouet, he attended "a respectable meeting of coloured people . . . formerly of New Orleans" who promised financial assistance for Lundy's plan to create "an asylum for hundreds of thousands of our oppressed colored." Lundy met the General of Mexican forces who also "expressed his warm approbation of my plan of colored colonization, and encouraged Drouet to introduce his colored brethren into this country."[69]

Drouet was not the first Louisianan Afro-Creole to resettle in Matamoros. As early as the 1820s, Louisianan Creoles of color migrated to the city and left a distinctive fingerprint. The 1853 census counted four hundred fifty Black or mulatto residents out of a population of eleven thousand.⁷⁰ One of them, the architect Mateo Passemont, built the Matamoros cathedral Nuestra Señora del Refugio in a manner similar to his previous work, the St. Louis Cathedral in New Orleans.⁷¹ Some of these Afro-Louisianan families renounced their identification with the United States: the extended Rivier family and Henry Powell of New Orleans settled in Matamoros in the 1830s and declared themselves to be "Hayitanos" instead of "Americanos" when they applied for their *cartas de seguridad* needed to obtain Mexican citizenship; many had mixed families with Mexican spouses.⁷²

The anti-slavery cultures that blossomed in the US-Mexico borderlands were not mere happenstance. The values espoused by radical anti-colonial insurgents, especially noted among figures of African descent like José María Morelos and Vicente Guerrero, ensured that the War of Mexican Independence became a crucible for anti-caste social justice.⁷³ Veracruz, on Mexico's Gulf Coast and a longtime destination for New Orleans merchants, was especially important to these abolitionist politics. As early as 1673, Black and mulatto subjects outnumbered mestizos in Veracruz, and the expansion of the plantation sugar economy by the end of the seventeenth century only increased the African-descended population further.⁷⁴ The enslaved joined the independence army in large numbers and ensured the insurgency did not capitulate during the several years of bloody stalemate that characterized its middle period.⁷⁵ Following Mexico's attainment of independence, Afro-Mexicans held prominent roles within the ranks of revolutionary forces and played a vital part in the political landscape during Mexico's initial federal phase (1824–1830).⁷⁶ These dynamics alarmed US Southern leaders. In 1825, the South Carolina senator Robert Y. Hayne complained that Mexican generals "proclaimed the principles of 'liberty and equality,' and have marched to victory under the banner of 'universal emancipation.' You find men of color at the head of their armies, in their Legislative Halls, and in their Executive Departments. They are looking to Hayti, even now, with feelings of the strongest confraternity."⁷⁷ These were the very same optics later that inspired men like Lew, and his community on the Bayou Boeuf plantation, to pray that Mexico would defeat the United States Army in Texas.

The Black freedpeople of Veracruz were important to these infrapolitics of emancipation, and Afro-Veracruz's history was deeply linked to patterns of sugar production and similar vectors of plantation and counter-plantation resistance, as we have seen in Saint-Domingue and Louisiana. Much like in New Orleans, marronage was a prominent means of escape from this oppressive society. Gaspar Yanga and a community of maroons inaugurated the Americas' first free Black village when they were granted an independent settlement, San Lorenzo de los

Negros, in 1609, after years of disrupting shipments and skillfully evading capture.[78] Also similar to New Orleans, Haiti, and Santiago de Cuba, enslaved and free Black Veracruzano musicians shared news, gossip, and cultures of erotic agency through music and dance. In 1763 and 1779, the dances "El Chuchumbé" and "Zacamandú" emerged as daring expressions of cultural dissent, each brimming with erotic ecstasy and featuring lyrics that openly ridiculed the sexual indiscretions of local priests. Both were banned by the Spanish Inqusition.[79] It is speculated that the influences of "El Chuchumbé" may have traveled to Veracruz from Cuba by way of Afro-Cuban enslaved migrants.[80]

Afro-Vercruzana music's ability to remake and desegregate public space was remarked upon by the independence activist Antonio López Matoso. In 1816, Matoso witnessed a communal music-making session—a fandango—in the Plazuela of Santo Domingo. Here he heard an *arpa jarocha* (a Veracruzana harp), a flute, and a *bandurria* (a plucked chordophone from Spain similar to the mandolin) accompanying a "great pageant of ladies and gentlemen, all of them black and tie-dressed and one of them dancing a *zapateado* [patterned footwork] without moving from one place." He asked "un curro con mucho salero" (a laborer with a lot of style) what he was seeing, and responded: "This is called tango."[81]

Today, these performance practices are called *son jarocho*. According to Antonio García de León Griego, this Veracruzano style serves as a regional manifestation of a neo-African influence merged with elements from Spain's late baroque period. Within its rhythmic language, musicians cleverly overlay duplet and triplet rhythms, a fusion that showcases the melding of New Spain's music into a unique "Afro-Andalusian" Caribbean sound.[82] Son jarocho musicians (also knowns as *jaraneros*) are revered as heralds of the insurgent soundscapes that reverberate through the Black Atlantic.[83] Their mastery in channeling popular resistance through poetic improvisation not only forged bonds of unity but also drew the ire of the ruling classes throughout Mexican history. A maestro like Arcadio Hidalgo wielded his musical craft as both a weapon and a beacon during the struggles orchestrated by Flores Magon's anarchist Partido Liberal Mexicano. Hidalgo was immortalized by Mexican author Juan Pascoe who described him as "the Mexican grandfather: Black, Indigenous, jaranero, zapateador, singer, poet (and revolutionary at that), an eternal adversary of Porfirio Díaz."[84] Not only maestros but collective groups of workers could immortalize their struggle through the son jarocho tradition. In the 1920s, Veracruz longshoremen collectively wrote the "la Conga del Viejo" as they initiated a strike at the Port of Veracruz. Laborers convened at the shipyards in mid-December, gathering pots, pans, improvised slogans, and brass instruments, invoking ad hoc assembly through Veracruzano brassroots democracy.[85] Indeed, these Afro-Mexican processional forms continue to resist state power and capital. In 2018, jaraneros from Veracruz and Baja California performed with Arturo O'Farrill's Afro-Latin Jazz Orchestra on both sides of the US-Mexican border wall in Tijuana in protest of the anti-immigrant and anti-Black policies of US president Donald Trump. In the Playas de Tijuana, they collaborated with renowned African American jazz musicians, including violinist Regina Carter and cellist Akua Dixon.[86] The event is still remembered by local musicians and activists as a powerful symbolic disruption of US hegemony. This binational concert echoed the African American and Mexican solidarities that had inspired nineteenth-century African Americans on the planation of Bayou Boeuf to escape not North but South.

The currents of abolitionist thought known as the common wind were strong not only in expressive culture produced by Afro-Mestizos but also through their concrete actions.[87] In 1858, a slave ship that had accidentally docked near Tamiahua was rushed by local officials who liberated the human cargo on board.[88] Apparently aware of these grassroots abolitionist politics, Veracruz emerged as an important destination for African American runaways. In August 1855, John T. Pickett, the US consul at Veracruz, complained in 1855 that "there [are] here a number of refugiated negro slaves from the States of Louisiana, Texas" who were now considered "worthy and peaceful Mexican citizens." He was furious that Veracruz was "fully abolitionized."[89] Veracruz also had a history of Haitian migration. Toña la Negra, one of the masters of the Mexican *bolero* tradition, was born in Veracruz. Her family narratives proudly trace back to her grandfather, Severo Peregrino, a Haitian immigrant who arrived in the mid-nineteenth century.[90]

In Veracruz, African American refugees would have met African-descended refugees from another slave society undergoing throes of rebellion and repression: Cuba. In the 1840s, the Mexican government welcomed five hundred Afro-Cuban exiles who had been banished by Spain for their suspected role in fomenting slave revolt.[91] Their arrivals were public and inspiring events. One day in the 1840s, Albert Gilliam witnessed in Tampico, just north of Veracruz, "the arrival of some twenty to thirty free exiled negroes from Havana" who "elicited much attention."[92] Some Black Cubans, like Francisco de Sentmanat y Zayas (1802–1844), visited New Orleans frequently to recruit Afro-Creole soldiers while building a political career in Mexico. Sentmanat was the governor of the state of Tabasco for several years in the 1840s until he was killed by forces loyal to Santa Anna, and his remains were sent to New Orleans for burial.[93] Late in the nineteenth century, a Mexican ambassador remarked that the emigration of Cubans "continues at an extraordinary pace, especially to Mexico," and gradually Veracruz emerged as a major hub for the Cuban independence movement.[94]

While the cultural impact of refugee African Americans in Veracruz remains

FIGURE 3.1 Edouard Pingret, "Músico de Veracruz," ca. mid-nineteenth century, oil on paper, courtesy of the Colección Banco Nacional de México. The musician depicted here appears to be simultaneously playing a *ravel* (a particularly resonant violin), a *jarana* and, with his feet, a type of *tololoche*, a bass-like instrument developed by Mayan and other Indigenous musicians throughout the colonial period. On the *tololoche*, see Schechter, *Music in Latin American Culture*, 43.

undocumented, Cuban immigrants were widely acknowledged for the tresillo and habanera rhythms and sonorities they contributed to Veracruzano society, brought by both traveling musicians and in an interoceanic market for sheet music.[95] As the Afro-Cuban poet Nicolás Guillén (1902–1989) joked, the port of Veracruz "is the only possession that Cuba has duly conquered and colonized."[96] During the latter part of the nineteenth century, Cuban independence groups flourished in Veracruz, and Mexican and Cuban popular music became sites of political education linked to Black Atlantic resistance.[97]

Veracruz's *corrido* culture embodied these political solidarities. Corridos are a tradition of Mexican ballad, usually performed by a single guitarist-singer, much like rural blues. In fact, their connection to the African American blues has been much commented upon. Both are characterized for their mobility, their ability to relate and contextualize current events, and as expressions of the popular imagination.[98] One of the instrumental numbers most frequently learned by rural Southwest-US Black guitarists was "Spanish Fandango," a standard beginner piece in formal instruction manuals that were sold with guitars. The song was so popular that many blues players continued to refer to its trademark "open G" tuning as "Spanish."[99] W. C. Handy credited his famous composition "Memphis Blues" to his time "on a plantation in Mississippi" when "I was awakened by a Negro singing a typical 'Blues' accompanying himself with a guitar tuned in the Spanish key and played in true Hawaiian style with a knife."[100] This influence was so pervasive that Baby Dodds describes New Orleans blues as played "with a Spanish accent."[101] Perhaps most importantly, both blues and corridos are symbolically organized as metonymies for struggles of working-class people in opposition to the plantation complex.[102] Especially during the Porfiriato, corridos projected the "social justice" perspective of campesinos that, according to Catherine Héau, "fundamentally meant communal ownership of land and free access to essential resources such as water, wood, grasslands, and parcels for cultivation."[103] Similarly, Clyde Adrian Woods argues that the blues emerged from "a growing New Orleans Black working class attempting to impose its social vision upon a region organized around its brutal exploitation."[104] One corrido, written by Ignacio Trejo in the late nineteenth century, lamented that the city of Cuautla was "surrounded by sugar mills . . . that is your greatest misfortune," and called for the rural campesino proletariat to organize against these ecocidal systems within the ecoharmonic flow of the Earth: "Wake if you are asleep . . . the waters of *Teara* flow generously around you."[105]

While corridos predominantly echo through time as a rich oral tradition, one notable instance saw ink meeting paper: in the hands of Antoni Vanegas Arroyo in 1897 Veracruz. His song paid homage to the Afro-Cuban revolutionary general Antonio Maceo—a visionary who dreamt of a Cuba aligned with the abolitionist spirit of its sister nations, "Santo Domingo and Haiti," as a beacon of new republicanism.[106] Maceo, who spent several years in exile in Haiti, resonated profoundly with the Afro-Cuban and Afro-Mestizo communities of Veracruz. His reach also extended to the Crescent City. In New Orleans, where he and his family settled between 1884 and 1885, he developed a strong base of support that echoed with Veracruz in rhythms of camaraderie and solidarity.[107] Maceo gave speeches and raised funds for the revolution at events organized by the Cuban cigarmakers' union, whose president, Ramón Pagés, was a collaborator of Rodolphe Desdunes in the Comité des Citoyens.[108] Desdunes and the Comité were inspired by the exiled Afro-Cuban insurgent, and the *Crusader* covered the Black general with admiration in the 1890s.[109] Maceo's appearance in popular song in Veracruz, and Black activist newspapers in New Orleans, reflected how an intra-Caribbean circuit of abolitionist and anti-colonial insurgency was both interdisciplinary and international, transforming the democratic corrido culture into a vehicle for intra-Gulf political education.

From fandangos in the maroon borderlands to fandangos at (and against) the wall, in the corridos that contested sugar plantations and celebrated Afro-Cuban revolutionaries, and in the abolitionist solidarities that animated refuge for the enslaved in threat of lynching and war: these are but a fraction of the history of African American and Mexican political and cultural exchange. This might also include the banjo's appearance among the Mixteca chordophone tradition in the late nineteenth century; Black boxer Jack Johnson's musical clubs in Tijuana; and Charles Mingus's childhood in Nogales, Arizona, whose Women's Club organized joint programs of "Mexican music" and "American Negro folk songs."[110] At first glance, these events may appear as historical quirks, isolated moments whispering of humanity's unpredictable cultural dance. Yet, when woven together, the outline of another image emerges, like a spectral microfilm projected behind the traditional history of jazz, a new map, an imagined and actualized archipelago of connection, in which geographically and historically separated communities living on the periphery of social exclusion in their respective societies forged new cultural languages through engagement with affective alterity.

The *frontera sónica* resounded to the accumulated geographies of liberation that resonated through African and Mexican reciprocity. The freedom dreams in Mexico's African-derived popular music help us hear why the Tio family and other Afro-Creoles would find Mexico, and specifically Veracruz, an attractive destination. The port of Veracruz had enjoyed, at least since the eighteenth century, a reputation as "one of the most cosmopolitan urban areas in the world," and a large number of the products traded between Asia, Africa, Europe, and America passed through and were distributed along its coasts.[111] More cynically, one might point to how Afro-Creoles' acclimation to New Orleans meant they possessed a hard-earned social capital as survivors of yellow fever, which, due to Veracruz's nonstop trade with the Crescent City, often broke out in both cities simultaneously.[112] But the musicality of both Veracruz and nearby Tampico would prove to be important for the Tio family to call the latter a home—and, in turn, the Tios' prior transnational connections to Mexico would prove to be equally important to ensure their success in a new land.

THE FOUNDING OF EUREKA: THE TIOS IN VERACRUZ

> New Orleans . . . is one of those Gulf cities that all seem like sisters, but is larger, more developed; in this category we can find Tampico, Veracruz and Campeche, and it has something of all of them, and Veracruz above all . . . with a drop of African soul at its heart.
>
> Justo Sierra Méndez[113]

It was quite a sight. The New Orleans port bustled with hundreds of Afro-Louisianans, waiting for passage with all their earthly possessions in tow. "Scarcely a week passes but a large number of free persons of color leave this port for Mexico or Hayti," reported the *New Orleans Daily Delta* in 1860.[114] Most had spent the previous months liquidating their assets and organizing their documents—baptismal records, marriage certificates, and their freedom papers that proved they were not enslaved—in order to start fresh.[115] This was the moment when the parents and extended family of clarinetists Lorenzo and Louis Tio relocated to Veracruz. This group included the Afro-Creole musician Louis Hauzer and his nephews, Louise Hauzer (1830–1903) and Thomas Tio (1828–1878).[116] As Rodolphe Desdunes sardonically explained about this historic exodus, "There are times in the life of a suffering people when it is good to have a change of climate."[117] Desdunes was referencing the *Dred Scott* decision of 1857, which set a devastating juridical precedent that the *Chicago Tribune* condemned as "forever excluding the African from the common equality conceded to all others, and even closing the door of national justice to him as an outlaw."[118] As Anglo-American racism became increasingly abhorrent, the Hauzers and Tios had been preparing for a change of climate, and *Dred Scott vs. Sanford* was the last straw. For years, they had set the groundwork for the Eureka colony, a multiracial cooperative society like those that had flourished in Matamoros in the 1830s and '40s.

The Tios worked directly with representatives of the Mexican state and local Veracruzano society to ensure their safe passage and the legal standing of their commune. Surviving notarial documents, issued between Mexican president Ignacio Comonfort and the Jamaican-born New Orleans Afro-Creole Nelson Fouché, provide a unique window into how the colony was to be organized. "Los condueños de Cofradía" (the co-owners of the brotherhood) offered "2,500 acres of land to a hundred families," as well as livestock, medical care, and a promise to the Afro-Louisianans to "help you obtain other relief with the most favorable conditions." Perhaps most importantly, at the very moment when the United States rendered them effectively stateless, the emigrants were to be granted Mexican citizenship.[119] A final document that ratified these commitments bears the signature of Thomas Tio and Auguste Dorestan Metoyer. On the Mexican side was the signature of president Benito Juárez.[120] Metoyer had arrived in Mexico years earlier, building community and rallying local support; he became the godfather of Teofilo Santaman of Tampico at the latter's baptism in 1856.[121] These relationships also reflected the long-term trading and political partnerships that Creoles of color had developed with Gulf Mexicanos, networks the Tios also rode. Perhaps most central for our discussion, Auguste Metoyer was the grandfather of acclaimed cornetist Arnold Metoyer, who taught several important early jazz musicians.[122] Two grandfathers, of two of New Orleans's most important musical educators in the early twentieth century, would be the founders of a Afro-Creole cooperative society in Veracruz.[123]

Of all New Orleans jazz musicians, the three clarinetists of the Tio family—Louis, Lorenzo Sr., and Lorenzo Jr.—most powerfully embody the convergence of the frontera sónica and the development of brassroots democracy. It is hard to overstate the influence of the Tio family among New Orleans musicians of color. They mentored an upcoming generation of jazz musicians including George and Achille Baquet, Alphonse Picou, Tony Girdina, Harold Dejan, Eddie Cherrie, Elliot Taylor, Louis Cottrell Jr., "Big Eye" Louis "Nelson" Delisle, Sidney Bechet, Omar Simeon, Jimmie Noone, and Willie J. Humphrey.[124] As Jelly Roll Morton succinctly explained, "These were the men who taught all the other guys how to play clarinet."[125] In multiple interviews, this generation of New Orleans clarinetists recalled the Tios' exacting discipline, their specialized embouchure that supported warm and robust tonal production, a solfège technique that required students to develop an "inner ear" and hear melodic phrases as part of sight reading, and a methodology to produce linear phrases that emphasized strings of connected eighth notes.[126] But even more than this, they remembered their lessons with the Tios as an almost supernatural experience that washed away the mundane, describing the brothers as mentors who impressed upon them a lifelong commitment to musical self-development that could withstand the social and cultural restrictions placed upon peoples of color. As musicologist Charles Kinzer emphasizes: "The Tios are perhaps the first significant pedagogues in the history of jazz, and their chief contribution lies in the establishment and maintenance of a norm for the training of jazz woodwind players in and beyond New Orleans."[127] As with the Desdunes siblings, the Tios' family history similarly carried New Orleans into the wider world. Did Lorenzo and Louis Tio, born in Mexico, carry the histories of Veracruz and Tampico with them as well?

Discussions continue to unfold concerning the scope of Mexican influence on the Tios' musical evolution and clarinet style. José Castañeda, a Mexican musicologist, has explored the potential interactions between the Tios and the polychromatic musical cultures of Tampico and Veracruz during their youth. Conversely, Charles E. Kinzer posits that without concrete evidence of the Tios attending a music school in Mexico, it is difficult to affirm that their childhood in Mexico significantly influenced their musical careers.[128]

But the Tios were not only musicians. In Veracruz, their parents were, first and foremost, communal farmers. Later in Tampico, they became cigar rollers within a Gulf economy, an occupation that overlapped with anarchist, anti-colonial, and Black Atlantic ideologies. In order to think through the multiple modalities of this cultural influence—not just expressive culture but a whole world of interaction that includes cooperative work and alienated labor—I endeavor here to paint a nuanced picture of the Tios' upbringing in Mexico, shedding light on their social history, particularly their work as cigar rollers. The sociomusical parallel between the brass band traditions of rural and urban Mexico with that of Louisiana is another point of connection—what brassroots democracy sounded like in Veracruz. Finally, this section explores danzón—a musical style developed in Cuba in dialogue with the country's African and Haitian cultures—and its intrinsic link to the nascent stages of jazz, a subject meticulously examined by scholars Alejandro Madrid and Robin Moore in their recent work.[129] I seek to augment this discussion by suggesting that proto-danzón elements, percolating through Veracruz via Cuban influences, played a pivotal role in steering the stylistic evolution of the clarinet in New Orleans, influencing the Tios in a documentable manner.

Thus, this cultural history of the Tios and their interaction with Mexico emphasizes the threads of grassroots cultural exchanges that blossomed from deep-seated political solidarity of oppressed subalterns at the US-Mexico border, a symphony of interconnected influence: the frontera sónica. I contend that the Tios broadened the scope of this creolized soundscape within Louisiana, in a time where white supremacist forces directly attacked the Afro-Creole and African American social movements that animated an anti-racist democracy that was rapidly fading away. Their performance alongside the civil rights activists, such as Daniel Straker in 1885, represented the ways that brassroots democracy was expanded through this engagement with communitarian and counter-plantation vectors of Mexican and Afro-Cuban cultural forms. Indeed, this was an interaction that the Tios helped facilitate.

Solidarity as Survival

At the most elementary and most important level, Lorenzo and Louis Tio carried the history of Mexico into New Orleans. This was a result not only of their place of birth but also of the pivotal role played by Mexican land grants and the unwavering support of individual Mexican families in their lives. They owe their existence, in many ways, to these connections. Los condueños de la Cofradía, who donated the land for Eureka, established a creative mechanism to blur the line between private and communally held property. Surpluses generated from land sales were distributed into a separate fund, acting as an equalizing agent: "the product of these sales [is intended] to foment the colony and to assist the poorest families," explained its founding documents.[130] This surplus-redistribution mechanism signaled that poverty alleviation and commoning were essential to the functioning of the colony. Mexican liberals, engaged with lawfare (and eventually warfare) with the clergy and large landowners, were inspired by their model. A report produced later by the Mexican government stipulated that "the illustrious owners of the land of the Brotherhood offered still other auxiliary lands to the colonists. . . . If only this example was imitated by other landowners in the Republic, who possess huge quantities of land which they cannot cultivate, [and which] they leave barren . . . !"[131] Mexico's liberal government thus understood these Louisianan Afro-Creoles as allies in their struggle against the church and landed interests during the period of the *reforma*, consummated by Benito Juárez.[132]

The Tios would have been aware of the political dynamics surrounding their move to Mexico. The invitation of Creoles of color from New Orleans was part of a larger positioning of Veracruz as a bulwark in the struggle against conservative forces, and both Mexican liberal leadership and the press publicly announced the imagination attached to their solidarity. As *El Progreso*, a Veracruz newspaper, wrote in 1857: "We believe that the establishment of Black colonies honors our country, whose individuals come to enjoy the rights of man, that our fundamental code grants to all races, without distinction."[133] In 1861, Matías Romero, Mexico's ambassador in Washington, was asked whether he would accept Black migration to Mexico following the Civil War. He explained: "We desire immigration . . . particularly if they come cast out and persecuted from a country that considers them as an inferior race."[134] (He also encouraged the US government to recognize Haiti.) The Eureka colony's connection to the Black Atlantic was not lost on the Mexican government. In 1860—a year after the Eureka commune was consummated—the Veracruz maroon Gaspar

FIGURE 3.2 This 1857 map of Eureka reveals not only the scope and scale of the colony but also the colonists' invocation of Afro-French, Haitian, and Mexican culture and politics. A "plaza of cowboys (*vaqueros*)" adjacent to a street (above lots 43 and 44) is named after Alexandre ("Alejandro") Dumas, the famed Black French writer whose father had been born in Saint-Domingue. Another street (above lots 61 and 62) is dedicated to Victor Séjour, a New Orleans-born man of Saint-Dominugean descent whose short story "Le Mulâtre" is set during the Haitian Revolution. Lucien Lampert, for whom another street is named (below lots 61 and 62), was a renowned Afro-Creole pianist-composer born in New Orleans and then living in Paris. All three of these streets, then, are named after influential Afro-Franco artists. For more on Séjour see chapter 1. Plano de la colonia de Eureka, Veracruz, Luis N. Fouché, R. M. Núñez, Fortunato Mora. Courtesy of the Mapoteca Manuel Orozco y Berra.

Yanga, who founded the first independent Black settlement in the New World, was recognized as a national hero by the Juárez government, and a statue in his honor was inaugurated soon after.[135] Juárez himself was living in Veracruz at this time, locked in a Civil War with Mexican conservatives who opposed Juárez's "Law of Nationalization of the Ecclesiastical Wealth" that prohibited the Catholic Church from owning properties in Mexico. That he took time to honor a maroon hero in the midst of a debilitating Civil War reflected his understanding of the importance of Afrodiasporic militancy in Mexico's current historic moment. This celebration of Blackness certainly appears anachronistic in light of the ideology of mestizaje that would contribute to Afro-Mexican erasure in the mid-twentieth century, suggesting the influence of this New Orleans Black and Afro-Creole underground on Juárez.[136]

Juárez had likely met the Tios before. Much like the Tios who fled anti-Black repression through the solidarity shown by Veracruzanos, Benito Juárez had escaped danger by living in New Orleans, where he was assisted by the city's Afro-Creoles. In 1853, the Crescent City's French Quarter was set afire when Juárez arrived, along with the core cadre of Mexican liberal revolutionaries who opposed Santa Anna's conservative military dictatorship.[137] The high number of Spanish-language newspapers—the second highest in the United States during the 1850s—facilitated a Latin American counterpublic sphere to which Juárez and his comrades could contribute.[138]

Later, Mexico's first Indigenous president, Juárez's presence in the Cresent City reveals how New Orleans was a Gulf meeting point for diverse Latin American exiles. He collaborated not only with exiled Mexicans but also with Pedro Santacilia y Palacios, a Cuban independence activist who smuggled arms to Mexican revolutionaries in Ayutla and Acapulco.[139] Santacilia later operated a meeting and support center for Cuban *independentistas* in Veracruz.[140] The meeting of these two reflected, as Rafael Rojas notes, how "New Orleans functioned, in the mid-nineteenth century, as a strategic place for intellectual and political communication between Mexico and the Caribbean."[141]

New Orleans's Creole of color community facilitated this Latin American underground. The son of Zapotec farmers, Juárez was a visibly Indigenous Mexican man in antebellum New Orleans and faced considerable risk of violence. He rented a house from a free Black woman—an "[Afro-]French woman who had been a chorus girl, Madame Doubard." Juárez caught yellow fever, and based on the accounts of other Black women innkeepers during this time, this woman may have helped him survive.[142] While Juárez is reported to have recovered by "pure chance," in-demand women of color healers known as "fever doctors" were considered essential to withstand the disease in nineteenth-century New Orleans. (Even this knowledge reflected Veracruz and New Orleans connections: Jalap, a laxative derived from a tuber found in Veracruz, was one of a variety of herbs used by these Black women doctors.)[143] Some of these women ran inns. It is plausible that this future Mexican president, later celebrated for leading a "second struggle for independence, a second defeat for the European powers, and a second reversal of the Conquest" in his defense of the country's sovereignty from French imperial forces, might have perished had it not been for Black women healers in New Orleans.[144]

Juárez was employed by the city's Creole of color community through his work in New Orleans's cigar industry. News of liberation movements, theories of value and worker organization, and the struggle against slavery were discussed and debated on the floors of cigar-making workshops in Havana, New Orleans, and Veracruz.¹⁴⁵ This culture was aural, performative, and musical. What made cigar rolling distinct from other workplaces was *el lector* (the reader) who narrated current events and radical tracts from inter-Atlantic newspapers while others worked. New musical forms and political consciousness developed hand in hand. The Cuban ballad form *la trova*, as Ned Sublette notes, emerged in Santiago de Cuba because "cigar rollers were entertained by having readers read to them, but the workers also sang while they sat twisting up tobacco all day. A group of cigar rollers could work out songs on the job, a cappella, then go out at night with a guitar, serenading."¹⁴⁶ Dialogues erupted through speech, music, and emancipatory ideas, informing new intercultural aesthetics in the process.

Brassroots democracy's vernacular political culture was partially developed through the musical and political ideas circulated on cigar factory floors. Harlem Renaissance writer James Weldon Johnson wrote in his fictionalized autobiography that in these workshops he learned "not only to make cigars, but also to smoke, to swear, and to speak Spanish. I discovered that I had a talent for languages as well as music." With a significant Afro-Cuban population and a commitment to anti-colonial republicanism, Johnson noted that "cigar-making is one trade in which the colour line is not drawn." In Louisiana, the Creole of color cigar roller Eugenia Lacarra shared this sentiment.¹⁴⁷

When New Orleans Creoles of color self-exiled to Mexico in the 1850s and '60s, it was due in part to the relationships formed on these cigar room floors. It is no coincidence that former New Orleans cigar roller Benito Juárez, was the president of Mexico as the Eureka colony was taking root. Ignacio Comonfort directly appealed to Louisiana's free people of color, insisting that they would have "the same rights and equality enjoyed by the other inhabitants [of Mexico] without at any time having to feel ashamed of their origin" as he signed the documents chartering the free Black colony.¹⁴⁸ Creoles of color thus became citizens of the Mexican republic just as they were officially denied US citizenship.

Radical Creoles of color certainly spoke and wrote in a manner familiar to Latin American radicals. The Haitian-descended, Creole of color cigar factory owner Édouard Tinchant came of age in Paris, and his politics were shaped by the emancipatory ideals of the 1848 French Revolution. He railed against the French invasion of Mexico in newspapers and protests; he would have been an ideal coworker or boss for Juárez.¹⁴⁹ According to Celeste Gómez Vincent, a descendant of Louisiana Creoles of color who moved to Veracruz in the nineteenth century, Juárez worked in Tinchant's factory, where he met other Haitian-descended Creoles.¹⁵⁰ This traffic went two ways: Tinchant's brother, don José (Joseph) Tinchant, later received Mexican citizenship in 1875 and operated a cigar factory in Veracruz.¹⁵¹ The Mexican revolutionaries found refuge in New

FIGURE 3.3 As this artistic diorama imagines, Benito Juárez (center) and fellow exile José Maria Mata of Veracruz (left) likely worked alongside Black and Creole of Color cigar rollers while in New Orleans. "Benito Juárez y José María Mata en Nueva Orleans, Liberales en el exilio." Courtesy of the Galería de Historia, Museo del Caracol, Mexico.

Orleans thanks to this sympathetic population that shielded them from retributive political violence, helped them find employment, offered care when they were ill, and provided a sense of community. And Creoles of color may not have received citizenship, land grants, subsistence, and tools from the Mexican state had their struggle not been understood as a shared one.

The cigar shop was thus an integral part of the Gulf frontera sónica, and its brand of aural politics and musical improvisation informed brassroots democracy. Many New Orleans jazz musicians worked as cigar rollers themselves, including valve trombonist Anthony Pages, Manuel Pérez, George Fihle, Natty Dominque, and multiple members of the Tio family, to name only a few. As Dominque recalled in an interview, musicians "would maybe work in New Orleans two nights a week or probably three nights a week. Well, that wasn't enough to support their family. Well, that was compulsory, then: working making cigars in the daytime."[152] Its itinerant nature and robust aural workplace culture made it attractive to musicians. A quarter of New Orleans brass and jazz band musicians between 1880 and 1915 reported that their day job was "cigarmaker."[153]

Perhaps most crucially, this was an Atlantic occupation with skills that political refugees could transfer abroad. Edmond Dédé, a New Orleans Creole of color violinist-composer born in 1827, worked as a cigar roller for Joseph Tinchant in the early 1850s. After studying composition in Mexico City, he worked again as a cigar roller in New Orleans before moving to Antwerp, Belgium, where he was hired as a bookkeeper and roller in Tinchant's new cigar factory there. Dédé eventually relocated to Bordeaux, France, where he was employed as the assistant conductor at the Grand Théâtre, later moving to the Théâtre l'Alcazar, and news of his exploits earned him a devoted Crescent City fan base. When Dédé decided to perform again in New Orleans in 1893, his concerts were organized by members of the Comité des Citoyens (see chapter 1), including Daniel Desdunes and his father, the cigar-seller Rodolphe Desdunes. Rodolphe's daughter Agnes performed in a vocal quintet at one of these concerts. Perhaps the Citizen's Committee longstanding ally, the cigar roller and revolutionary Cuban exile Ramón Pagés, greeted Dédé during his stay as well.[154] The Tios took advantage of parallel Atlantic circuits linked to cigar rolling, and it seems the occupation sustained them in their adopted home: in the 1871 Tampico census rolls appears a "Luis Marcos Tio" [sic] who is listed as "*tabaquero, Americano, casado, no tiene propriedad, sabe escribir*" (married, American, cigar roller, does not own property, knows how to write).[155]

In the Gulf, cigar rolling was simultaneously a political, cultural, and sonic world that was synonymous with Latin American radical movements.[156] Sara Hudson suggests that "the most critical locations that birthed change in Mexican political landscapes across the nineteenth century were not legislatures with their political rhetoric nor courtrooms with their judicial reckonings, but rather New Orleans's cigar factories with their day-to-day conversations."[157] Its hyperbole aside, Hudson does showcase the bottom-up nature of this aural workplace, and it is likely that exiled Mexican revolutionaries developed the Plan of Ayutla while rolling. Indeed, it was on these floors where Creoles of color built the political relationships to move en masse to Veracruz and Tampico, where the Tios could sustain themselves throughout their nearly two decades in Mexico.

Louis Marcos Tio's occupation as a tobacco roller became essential to his survival following the devastating arson of Eureka in 1862—a catastrophe that may have been inflicted by wandering marauders or as a consequence of the migrants' apparent Francophilia as the Second Franco-Mexican War raged. Yet this perception did not appear to resonate broadly among the Mexican populace, as numerous local families generously extended support to the Tio-Hauzer family during this distressing time, helping salvage the remnants of their shattered utopian dream.[158] In her memoir, Lorenzo Sr.'s aunt Antoinette Tio depicts their family moving throughout the city of Tampico, relying on the goodwill and kindness of Mexican homeowners who provided them refuge: don Igancio Iscareña, don Juan Acosta, and many others. Louis Tio had been born in Eureka; it was in these more nomadic, urban years that Lorenzo Sr. was born. They would remain in Tampico until they were fifteen and ten years old, respectively, learning clarinet and interacting with Spanish-speaking mestizo families on a regular basis.[159]

While these Afro-Creole clarinetists studied a French musical repertoire, there is no evidence that the Tios lived insular lives in Mexico. The family, it should be remembered, was musical. It seems that they would have been hard-pressed to tune out the noise of one of the most vibrant musical cultures on the planet.[160] Even if one focuses only on the rarefied classical solo repertoire they later rendered on the clarinet while on tour in the Black minstrel circuit, one finds similarities to the music performed in their immediate proximity. One clarinet solo that Lorenzo Tio performed in 1898, titled "Sonámbula," was based on an opera performed in nearby Taclua, Mexico, while the Tios were growing up in Tampico, as evidenced by Mexican newspapers advertisements of the era.[161]

The Tios likely absorbed Veracruz and Tampico culture and the musical gulf winds that flowed into these port cities with strong Afro-Mexican and Afro-Cuban cultural connections.[162] In the port city of Tampico, a hub for Cuban and French Caribbean immigrants, the Tio family would have heard Afro-Mexican and Afro-Cuban influences that resonated throughout the Gulf.[163] Their integration of this rich blend of cultural influences was particularly evident in their 1898 performance in Oskaloosa, Iowa. Here, Lorenzo Tio showcased his skill and versatility as a clarinetist in the danzón-inspired composition "Trocha (Cuban Dance)." The song is structured by habanera and flipped cinquillo rhythms, a testament to the Tios' deep-rooted connection with the diverse Gulf currents in their development.[164]

From Cuerpos Filarmónicos and Danzón: Creolizing Clarinet

Living in Tampico, the Tios were youth when the explosion of brass band culture emerged through the institution of *cuerpos filarmónicos*, brass bands managed by campesino mestizo and Indigenous communities. These bands expressed forms of localized citizenship and challenged both state and clerical authority. They ensured that Mexico's "Indian Republics" and the social relations of communal ownership and participatory democracy would not be eliminated by Díaz's so-called *tecnicos* (technicians) of progress.[165] Community-organized brass bands or *bandas de vineto* (wind bands) were another point of convergence between Veracruz and Black Louisiana. Just as changes in markets, technologies, and politics can be considered regional and global rather than strictly national, the social solidarity found in Louisiana's Black brass band culture also had significant overlap with its neighbor to the South. Powerful markers of local identity, cuerpos filarmónicos allowed, as Paul Friedrich argues, "musical specialization" to compensate "for restricted access to the means of subsistence" because the ruling class increasingly appropriated communal land, known as *terrenos ejidales*, from Indigenous communities.[166] Highly demanding—with sometimes twelve-hour practices—the bands were financially supported and populated by the local community and particularly strong in Indigenous *pueblos* (towns).[167] For example, when a Nahuatl Indigenous *ayuntameinto* (town hall or council) in the community of Huitzilan assembled in 1867 to create a cuerpo filarmónico, they required a financial contribution according to each family's means, and a refusal to donate resulted in imprisonment.[168] Similarly, in 1872 in Zapotitlan, a municipality with an Indigenous Totonac majority, the musician Mariano Rojas was imprisoned by mayor Lorenzo Diego for losing his clarinet and neglecting to replace it or come to practice.[169]

Scholars such as Tore C. Olsson and Gregory Downs have argued persuasively that the Porfiriato and the New South were linked by patterns of land centralization in which self-sufficiency and self-governance practiced by rural communities was neutralized.[170] In the words of Olsson, the "reordering of the countryside" in both "the US cotton South and the diverse plantation zones of Mexico . . . largely benefited landlords while eroding the last semblances of independence and self-sufficiency among the rural majority."[171] Yet legacies of self-sufficiency and communal autonomy were reproduced through collective brass performance. Demands such as those made on Rojas were so stern because these ensembles were a significant site of self-government and cultural independence. This symbolic transfer occurred, in part, because bands were funded by the sale of titles to village commons that the *Ley Lerdo* and, later, the Porfiriato's capitalist-minded government mandated.[172] Cuerpos filarmónicos compensated for the loss of the commons and maintained an alternative commons in sound as music came to construct "locally specific forms of citizenship."[173]

Clarinet was crucial to ensembles across the country in which members of *las clases populares* (the popular or working class), amid traumatic social dislocations, created communal bands to defend forms of collective self-governance. Zapotec and Mixtec Indigenous village authorities in Oaxaca hired music teachers and purchased hundreds of instruments, including Bb and Eb clarinets, thereby "preventing the State from appropriating their goods and capital," writes Sergio Navarrete Pellicer, while "gaining ground over the priests themselves in decisions about the administration of community funds in the hands of the Church and in the organization of their own ritual practices."[174]

Louisiana and Veracruz were thus linked by a brass band tradition that built on older forms of autonomy and social organization. But, whereas in the mid-nineteenth-century US South, clarinet repertoire was monopolized by Western art music, in Veracruz and Oaxaca the clarinet was associated with a popular-class cultural insurgency in which communal bands resisted state centralization efforts by reinventing democratic self-governance. And thus, Mexican musicians in New Orleans performing the clarinet represented a new sound and spirit of this instrument, reflecting a bottom-up identity-making matrix: brassroots democracy.[175] In refutation of the narrative that jazz was a product of African rhythm and European harmonic and instrumental know-how, the clarinet's social history in Mexico proved a more compelling metaphor than European genius to suggest its resonance in the Crescent City. And, indeed, Mexico, specifically Veracruz and Tampico, patterned a compelling parallel history from which Afro-Louisianans might hear a similar long song.

Danzón ensembles became prevalent in late nineteenth-century Mexico, connected to the rhythms of social change and revolution. Ignacio Cervantes, who popularized a proto-danzón form known as danza in his cinquillo-based piano compositions, was an outspoken supporter of Cuban independence, living in exile in Mexico and the United States for various years.[176] He influenced Mexican composers such as Antonio Vanegas Arroyo, whose "Cuba Libre" was a habanera/danza piece.[177] Cervantes's rhythmic devices were found in the work of ragtime and jazz composers like Scott Joplin, Jelly Roll Morton, and Daniel Desdunes.[178] With their large horn and rhythm sections, multisectional compositional forms, improvisational sections, and roots in Afro-Gulf culture, New Orleans jazz and the Cuban danzón may have had more similarities than differences.[179] As Mexican musicologists Jesús Flores y Escalante and Patricia García López have documented, jazz ensembles in 1920s Veracruz and Yucatan, such as Orquesta Veracruzana, had previously been danzón ensembles and frequently alternated between the styles in concert.[180] Code-switching was facilitated by the structural similarities produced within a circulatory system of cultural exchange.[181]

At the level of political imaginaries attached to music, danzón embodied a fervent desire for self-determination and liberation from European hegemony, similar to the autonomous ethos expressed by late nineteenth-century cuerpos filarmónicos and New Orleans brass bands prevalent in the rural districts. "Its rise to prominence represents a cultural revolution of sorts that paralleled the armed rebellion against Spain," writes Robin Moore, "[and] remained controversial for several years as a result of its strong association with Afrocubans and Haitians."[182] The structural resemblances between danzón and early jazz, evident in the 1906 danzón recording of "La Patti Negra," which features jazz-like improvisations on various instruments including the clarinet and trumpet over tresillo rhythms, have led Moore to propose that the "emergence of the early New Orleans jazz sound is part of a larger, overlooked regional phenomenon." According to Moore, this connection has been neglected in mainstream jazz scholarship "because such work contradicts nationalist discourses within the United States that have become so closely intertwined with jazz."[183]

The exact level of correspondence between these two forms is complex to assess, since African Americans developed unique rhythmic and aesthetic traditions that cannot be reduced to Afro-Cuban and Mexican cultural flows. A prime example of this complexity is the significant role played by the modified minor and major pentatonic scales, commonly referred to as the blues and gospel scales respectively. The gospel scale significantly influenced the musical lexicon of Louis Armstrong and other early jazz improvisers, forming a large portion of their improvisatory language.[184] New Orleans certainly shared hybridized Afro-American forms with the Veracruzano and Cuban musical styles, but, while orchestrally similar, danzón's *timbal* drum pulsed cinquillo rhythms constantly under these arrangements, thereby employing a cellular structure that was distinct from early jazz's own more intermittent use of cinquillo and habanera rhythmic patterns.[185] Alejandro Madrid and Robin Moore nonetheless point to the presence of Latin American cornet players in the cohort of early jazz musicians as "one of the most direct ways that improvisatory danzón performance practice may have spread to New Orleans."[186] Jack Stewart noted another trend, highlighting how the distinctive "mariachi sound" popularized by Mexican brass players in New Orleans was characterized by two features: the widespread use of triadic two-part writing for trumpets and a tendency to play these instruments with brilliance and intensity.[187] Cornets, however, had been played by substantial numbers of African American musicians at least since the Civil War, and a multigenerational school of Black brass within an improvisatory framework was reaching a critical mass by the late 1880s.[188]

The clarinet, on the other hand, was not common in Black musical circles until the performances of the Eighth Cavalry Band. The sheet music collection of popular Creole of color brass bandleader John Robichaux, housed at the Hogan Jazz Archives, had only three manuscripts that featured clarinet in the years of 1819–84; among songs published after the performances of the Eighth Cavalry Band's arrival, 2,797 manuscripts feature clarinet.[189] As W. C. Handy recalled, "before the time of [Robert] Leach and Tio, European and Mexicans played the clarinets in Negro bands where these instruments were used at all."[190] Simply put, before 1885, the clarinet was not an instrument of the common people or popular power in Louisiana; in Mexico, it was.[191] The clarinet was so identified as Mexican that clarinetist August Laurent, who studied with Lorenzo Tio Jr., thought that the Tios were Mexican simply because they played this instrument. And in some sense he was not mistaken, since Louis Tio had been born in Veracruz and raised in Tampico.[192] Drummer Abbey "Chinee" Foster described Lorenzo Tio Jr. as "Indian," a reference to the Indigenous musicians who performed in the Mexican bands in the United States, such as the famous Otomí composer Juventino Rosas whose composition "Sobre las Olas" became widely played in New Orleans and across the world for several decades.[193] In addition to the Tios, numerous clarinetists and saxophonists were from Mexico or of Mexican descent, including Florencio Ramos, a "Vascaro" whose last name remains unidentified, and Alcide "Yellow" Nuñez;[194] these musicians, according to Moore and Madrid, "undoubtedly had some exposure to and appreciation for the danzón."[195]

By homing in on clarinet culture as a bounded expression of the regional interaction in the frontera sónica, we can clearly observe stylistic similarities between Cuban Mexican danza and danzón with the music the Tios may have played. Because we lack transcriptions or musical examples of the elder Tios—although we know that danza "Trocha (Cuban Dance)" was in their repertoire—the evidence to support their New Orleans contribution is limited to the recorded output of Lorenzo Jr. during his performances with the Armand J. Piron Orchestra.[196]

These recordings help us appreciate how danzón clarinet conventions influenced Lorenzo Tio Jr. and jazz clarinet at large. In the late nineteenth century, danza and danzón compositions for the clarinet frequently utilized two distinctive patterns. The first showcased step-by-step note sequences, or scalar-based lines, which were occasionally interrupted by larger intervals, inducing a register shift and fluidly leading into the subsequent phrase. The second, identified as the "sawtooth" pattern, was characterized by arpeggiated sequences where chord tones were presented in a vertical fashion. This "sawtooth" nickname actually derives from jazz clarinet lines (and not that of danzón) but the phenomenon it refers to is present in both: the tendency to disrupt a linear arpeggiated progression, reversing direction with sudden register shifts often on offbeats, producing an effect akin to auditory acrobatics.[197] Here is one example of each tendency. The following excerpt is a segment from what is acknowledged as one of the first danzónes, penned by Afro-Cuban composer Miguel Failde in 1879.[198]

In "Las Altura de Simpson," the clarinet plays a medium up-tempo scalar line whose stepwise motion is interrupted by major and minor thirds, creating forward motion and "breaking" the scale on offbeats. It reverses from an ascending to a descending direction in the third measure, only to find unison with the cornet on the climactic descending cinquillo phrase at the conclusion, invoking this Afro-Haitian-Cuban rhythm to conclude the phrase. This inno-

FIGURE 3.4 Falide, "Las Alturas de Simpson," Section B, mm. 17–21. Also published in Mata, "Felipe Valdes," 12.

vative approach to composition not only broke new ground, but also opened up avenues for creative expression, where the linear melodies were replaced by intercultural musical storylines.

Now consider the following melodic fragments played by Lorenzo Tio Jr. on "Bouncing Around." Performed some five decades later, it nonetheless showcases similar clarinet writing, especially in its structural role in relation to the cornet. Stepwise scalar lines, punctuated by a concluding minor third that alters its direction thrice within the phrase, mark the opening gesture. Following another scalar line characterized by unexpected, offbeat shifts, the latter part of the phrase makes its entry on the offbeats, harmonizing with the cornet and surrounding chord tones, hinting at the forthcoming invocation on the sawtooth pattern. As the piece progresses into the second half of the A section, the disrupted scalar phrases escalate in their intervallic drama, navigating not merely by thirds but also by fifths. Diverging from the danzón, when transitioning to the B section, the piece embraces a transformative "swing" segment, where a rhythmic 6/8 pulse takes over the erstwhile straight eighth notes, ushering in a period of chromatic experimentation as opposed to the earlier diatonic phrases. Notably, in measures 31 and 32, the composition incorporates gospel phrases that resonate well within the respective tonal centers of C and F, marking a distinct departure from the structural and rhythmic patterns observed in the danzón examples. This gesture fosters an intercultural composition that invokes a musical vocabulary associated with African American musicians—a point to which we will return later.

Returning to the danza and danzón tradition, Ignacio Cervantes's "Invitación," a piece he likely wrote in the late 1860s or 1870s, utilized the "sawtooth" pattern discussed earlier. Descending and arpeggiated passages are frequently interrupted, giving rise to what can be described as arpeggiated ruptures. These ruptures, marked by abrupt intervals and unexpected shifts in tonality, often

FIGURE 3.5 "Bouncing Around" performed by Lorenzo Tio Jr. with the A. J. Piron's New Orleans Orchestra, mm. 1–10. Much like the arrangement of "Las Alturas de Simpson," the cornet plays background figures, intermittingly joining the clarinet in rhythmic unison. Transcribed in Kinzer, "The Tio Family."

reverse directions on offbeats. Furthermore, the rhythmic motif employed that interrupts the repetition of the sawtooth pattern—a flipped cinquillo rhythm—creates a forward-moving undercurrent that is also evocative of the Haitian and Afro-Cuban musical lexicons that underlaid danzón. In addition, the first four measures of this segment feature a habanera rhythm in the bass line. These same components—flipped cinquillo rhythms, habanera-inflected bass lines, and sawtooth arpeggios—are prominent in African American composer William Tyres's 1896 "Trocha: A Cuban Dance" which Lorenzo Tio Sr. performed in Oskaloosa, Iowa.

The heartbeat of "Invitación" emphasizes the rhythmic dissidence between Cervantes's flipped cinquillo and the accumulated waves of sawtooth arpeggios, and this style influenced the repertoire that Lorenzo Tio Sr. was featured on. His son, Lorenzo Tio Jr. applied these concepts to improvisation. He similarly employs sawtooth patterns and a flipped cinquillo throughout "Bouncing Around" in his solo breaks.

FIGURE 3.6 *Top:* An excerpt of "Invitación" by Ignacio Cervantes. This excerpt makes evident the use of broken arpeggios, or "sawtooth" phrases (highlighted in black), and the flipped cinquillo (highlighted in grey) that would become associated with the Cuban composer. *Bottom:* "Trocha: A Cuban Dance," composed by the African American composer and freedman William Tyers, utilized this same combination of elements, and are highlighted with the same scheme. The piece was published by the New York-based F.A. Mills.

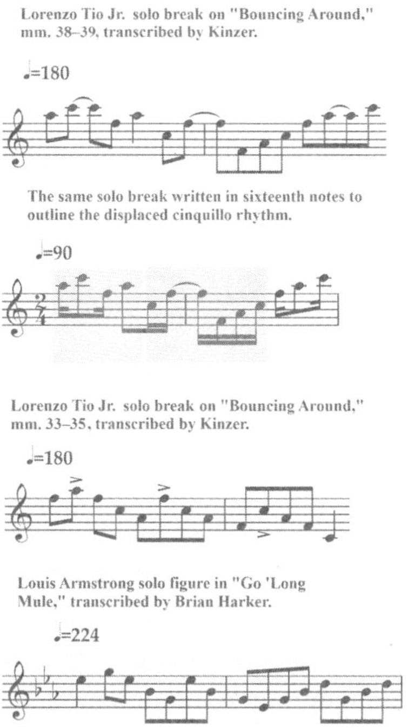

FIGURE 3.7 Lorenzo Tio solo breaks in "Bouncing Around" that utilize the sawtooth pattern, as well as one example of a sawtooth pattern by Louis Armstrong. As Brian Harker makes evident, such sawtooth arpeggios were first popularized in New Orleans clarinet vocabulary. These shapes became foundational to Armstrong's playing and the development of trumpet and cornet improvisatory languages in early jazz. See Harker, "Louis Armstrong and the Clarinet." Also of note is how Lorenzo Tio Jr. combines the flipped cinquillo pattern with the sawtooth shape in one of his solo breaks.

Lorenzo Tio Jr.'s solos reflect how, in both danza/danzón and early jazz, clarinets became stewards of the rhythmic and improvisatory frameworks produced by an Afro-Caribbean counter-plantation culture. Indeed, in addition to their shared sawtooth arpeggios and rhythmic patterns, danza and danzón influences on instrumental practices in New Orleans are apparent in the improvisational role that the clarinet takes on in second-lining, which mirrors the function of secondary melodic instruments in danza/danzón variations in Puerto Rico and Cuba. In Puerto Rican *seis* music, for instance, improvisation happens solely within the "second voice," an accompaniment that resembles the obbligato (secondary melodic line) in classical music.[199] A similar phenomenon can be observed with Cuba's proto-danzón styles. In his history of the Cuban danza, Alejo Carpentier has described how Santiago de Cuba's "free blacks" redistributed polyrhythmic and improvisatory functions from the percussion section into the second melodic-harmonic voice. Carpentier specifically mentions clarinetists as players of this "camouflaged drum."[200] The rhythms in danza and proto-danzón, as demonstrated here, are powerfully marked by cinquillo, habanera, and a variety of permutations.

In this context, the clarinet became a unique vessel for transmitting a specific improvisatory practice that emerged in a Gulf borderlands—not only between Cuba, Puerto Rico, and Mexico, but also between melody, harmony, and rhythm section roles. This is because the improvised obbligato is exactly the role the clarinet plays in New Orleans second-lining. As David Bradbury explains in his description of Louis Armstrong and Joe Oliver's performances in Lincoln Gardens: "The trombone chose notes in the bass or the tenor register, often using glissandos in what was called the tailgate style, from the wagons which often carried New Orleans bands; and the clarinet was *free* to create an obbligato out of a bubbling line of quavers [eighth notes]."[201]

Similarly, the liner notes of the *Smithsonian Collection of Classic Jazz* explain how "New Orleans jazz is played in a kind of counterpoint or polyphony in which a trumpet . . . states a melody . . . Simultaneously, a clarinet improvises a counter-melody or a kind of obbligato."[202] There is nothing inevitable or natural about an obbligato being improvised, and given the intense flows of refugees and musical-political culture between New Orleans and Havana through Veracruz, the fact that the secondary melodic voice in Puerto Rican seis and Cuban danza does so as well is striking. So, too, is the way that Afro-Caribbean, and specifically Haitian-derived, rhythms were "camouflaged" into these very secondary melodic parts—a tradition that would be reproduced in New Orleans.[203] Perhaps, then, as the habanera freed ragtime from the European quadral bass, the clarinet's improvising of the obbligato, with sawtooth arpeggios and disrupted scalar motion, marked the supplanting of the practices of the French Opera in favor of brassroots collective improvisation inspired by the frontera sónica.

The Tios left Tampico for New Orleans in 1877, meaning they lived in the Gulf Coast as early danzón percolated, as it eclipsed the stylistically similar (as far as the clarinet was concerned) danza. If the Tios were somehow not exposed to danza or danzón's clarinet vernacular in Veracruz or Tampico, they would soon have another opportunity to as they heard the performances of the Eighth Cavalry Band. As discussed earlier, this eighty-person Mexican brass band played at major citywide events, like Mardi Gras in 1885, and overlapped with the Excelsior Brass Band performances at the Cotton Centennial, a band to which the Tios belonged.[204] A testament to their sweeping popularity, the New Orleans music publisher Junius Hart published sixty-three piano transcriptions of the band's Mexican repertoire, in which habanera rhythms are extremely prevalent. The Eighth Cavalry Band, then, transmitted and reproduced these soundscapes that came to be called the Spanish Tinge. Despite no clear evidence of improvisation, the band's repertoire was diverse, encompassing mazurkas, scottishes, French operatic numbers, the compositions of Frédéric Chopin, and occasional Mardi Gras songs.[205] They were particularly renowned for their danzas, often used to

FIGURE 3.8 La Banda del Octavo Regimiento de Caballería poses for a photo in Chicago at the World's Fair Exposition in 1898. Courtesy of the private collection of Daniel Vernhettes.

conclude concerts. The band's director, Encarnación Payen, explained in 1891, when the band returned to the Crescent City, that "only Mexican music" was played during their encores.[206] In 1886, the *Butte Semi-Weekly Miner* reported on "the return of celebrated Mexican band that was here last year . . . Its execution of Mexican danzas and of the soft National Airas of that country was pronounced unsurpassed, and the band was generally regarded by critics as the best ever heard in this country."[207] Clarinet solos held a significant place in their repertoire, and pieces like "Sonnambula" often featured the clarinet. This piece was later performed by Lorenzo Tio, Sr. in Iowa.[208]

The danzas captured the fascination of the New Orleans populace and local music publishers alike, indicating a burgeoning market for this genre in the city, with an extensive array of danzas advertised and circulated. Among these was "El Nopal (Cactus Dance)," published in 1889, which incorporated habanera rhythms and its variations in the bass, coupled with a flipped cinquillo in the melody—elements associated with the work of Ignacio Cervantes. Another piece, "Danse Mexicane"—published by the Paris imprint C. Nicosias and circulated in New Orleans—featured broken arpeggios over habanera rhythms, though the exact date of its publication remains uncertain.

Perhaps most revealing in this regard are the words of one Cuban observer in New Orleans who, upon hearing the Eighth Cavalry Band, couldn't help but note the rhythmic similarities between their Mexican music and the music of his own country. "The *danza* is at the base of these melodies," writes the reporter, "but it appears under a thousand different forms."[209] A reporter with the

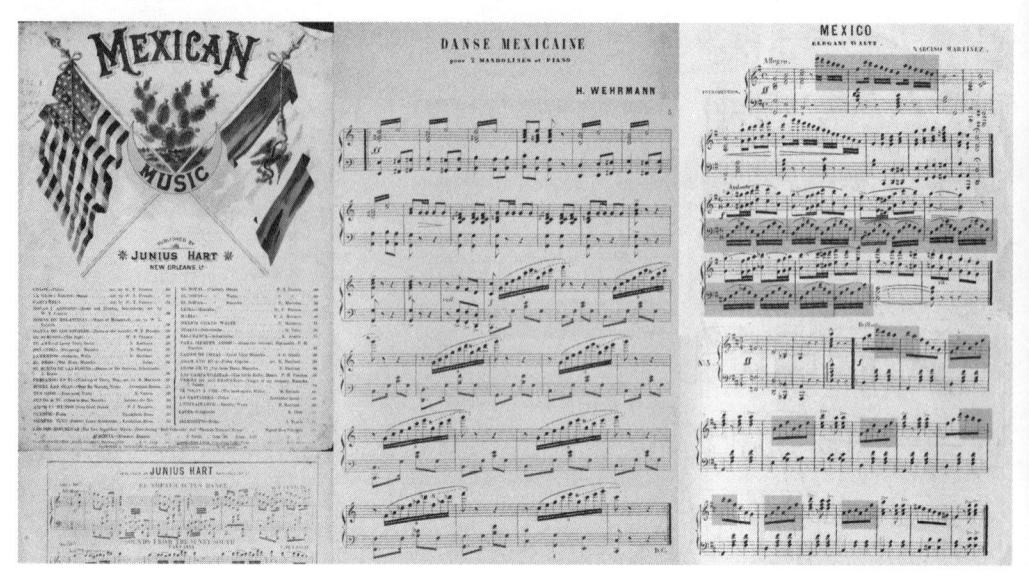

FIGURE 3.9 A compilation of various pieces sold by New Orleans music publisher Junius Hart in the late 1880s and 1890s. *Top Left*: A catalogue of their considerable offerings of "Mexican Music," reflecting this repertoire's popularity. *Bottom Left*: "El Nopal/Cactus Dance" (1892) which, true to its invocation of danza, is replete with habanera rhythms counterposed with flipped cinquillo patterns. *Middle*: "Danse Mexicana" (date unknown) in which habanera rhythms form the cellular structure of the piece. *Right*: "Mexico: Elegant Waltz," (1884) composed by Narisco Martinez and played by the Eighth Cavalry in New Orleans, features numerous ascending and descending sawtooth shapes, highlighted in black. Courtesy of the William Ransom Hogan Jazz Archive, Howard-Tilton Memorial Library, Tulane University, Box 02, Folder 24; Box 52, Folder 20; Box 35, Folder 15. For a discussion of how a New Orleans danza and danzón craze was precipitated by the "Mexican Band's" performances (and the sheet music they inspired), see Madrid and Moore, *Danzón*, 130; Raeburn, "Beyond the Spanish Tinge," 13.

Louisiana Democrat described this as "wild variations on the left [side] of the band."[210] Its Pan-American invocation was remarked upon by another reporter, who exclaimed that the band was "a great national school of music for the New World."[211] Along with its actual repertoire, it was an innovative sense of groove that made Mexican musicians so influential in New Orleans, creolizing existing repertoire with new structures of feeling that reinvented the old. "The Band even played Chopin's Funeral March in double quick-step!" exclaimed one shocked listener.[212] At other moments, the band would break out into group singing, which reportedly thrilled audiences, later emerging into a practice among New Orleans jazz bands.[213]

But thrill became disgust for many whites when the Eighth Cavalry Band began to work with Black musicians in the city. The *New Orleans Item* on June 22, 1891, published a letter from a reader that protested the presence of a "Negro drummer" in the band and insisted that the band instead "give employment to the local musicians . . . in the interest of the community."[214] This commentator appealed to Mexicans' whiteness in an attempt to paint Black Americans as a foreign and unwanted element from which they had to set themselves apart. As Toni Morrison notes, "In race talk the move into mainstream America always means buying into the notion of American blacks as the real aliens."[215] Yet, despite the oppressive racial hierarchies present in the Crescent City, Mexican musicians taught and worked with Black musicians into the twentieth century. They continued to play alongside civil rights events, such as on March 14, 1885, when they played before a "a colored representative from Brownsville, Mr. McElwee," who advocated for "the colored race and [to] increase their facilities for education."[216] Perhaps it was some of their own experiences with US racism and imperialism, made crudely real when the band was forced to perform alongside a sanitized reenactment of the bloody United States invasion of Veracruz;[217] or when the St. Louis musicians' union attempted to prevent Mexican immigrants from joining in 1890;[218] or perhaps in 1885 when an ex-Confederate soldier shot the cornet player Rodolfo Rodríguez four times for the crime of making love with his white daughter. (Rodríguez miraculously survived and returned to Mexico City; the band was forced to raise funds through a concert to pay for his treatment; and Louisiana stalled the criminal case until the assailant died of causes unrelated, provoking a diplomatic crisis.)[219] Or perhaps it was even a response to this aforementioned commentator, who later in his letter took the opportunity to attack the Mexican band for its "semi-barbaric harmony," an oft-used refrain against Black music of the era.[220]

Whatever their reasons, several Mexican musicians worked with Black musicians and contributed to the cultural fabric of their adopted home, taking on African American and mixed-race students. The multi-instrumentalist Joe Gabriel, a prominent Black bandleader from Thibodaux, learned trumpet from a "Mexican" who he recalled would "play his high C . . . first thing in the morning."[221] Tubist Martin Abraham, who may have had Mexican parentage, remembered: "I learned [guitar] from a Mexican professor who lived here for a while and died in New Orleans. I learned to play Spanish guitar and we had an orchestra of Mexicans who used to work in town." Before he switched to Tuba, Abraham played guitar in the area around Royal Dumaine, Ursulines, and Decatur streets around 1907 for "Mexicans, Puerto Ricans, and Spanish" who had "lived there for years…all you would see is Mexicans." These singers serenaded their mothers or sweethearts or friends outside their homes late at night with Cuban songs like "La

Paloma." "There was wine, food, everything you could mention," remembered Abraham. "These were serenades, you know."²²² Bunk Johnson studied with Wallace Cutchey, a Mexican music teacher who Johnson believes played with the Eighth Cavalry Band. Lorenzo Sr.'s son Louis R. Tio claimed that his family had a close collective friendship with Mexican band member Louis Chaligny who remained in New Orleans, although Chaligny's name does not appear on any of the rosters of the band to date.²²³ Saxophonist Florencio Ramos, a saxophonist with the Eighth Cavalry Band, did indeed stay, and played flute in the French Opera orchestra (with whom Lorenzo Tio Sr. had previously performed) and taught woodwinds on Canal Street.²²⁴

By transmitting instrumental techniques and new sociomusical frameworks, Mexican musicians had a decided impact on brassroots democracy. This was a chain of subterranean diplomacy, providing decolonial inspiration for creolized interpolations of space, feel, and identities beyond colonial whiteness and racial apartheid. The clarinet became a vehicle to express this communication across diasporas, adding a borderlands voice to a brass band culture that sat in between multiple roles: melodic, rhythmic, and harmonic support in its obbligato space.

Having just moved from Tampico seven years earlier, it would have been exceedingly strange for the Tios to not have interacted directly with these Mexican musicians. At the very least, the Tios were well positioned to lead bands influenced by the popular new style, since, as clarinetists, their instrument was suddenly much in demand due to the Mexican band's powerful influence. With the overwhelming likelihood of having been exposed , while in Tampico, to the habanera and danza rhythms that the Eighth Cavalry Band played the Tios also benefited from familiarity with styles that were to become popular with Black and Afro-Creole musicians. These were the "older men [who] used lots of Mexican music" that George Fihle described (see chapter 1).²²⁵

But there was a strong African American vernacular tradition associated with the clarinet as well, one with which the Tios had a complex relationship. These were also the years in which, in the onslaught of white supremacist violence in the sugar parishes, tens of thousands of African Americans fled to New Orleans— "huddling for protection," in the words of W. E. B. Du Bois, and infusing Black Baptist soundscapes into instrumental music traditions. (New Orleans's city directory showed twenty Black Baptist churches in 1885, a number that more than doubled to fifty by 1900.)²²⁶ The clarinet's improvisatory role in early jazz was consolidated through the simultaneous popularity of the Mexican band (and the cultural and educational labor of Mexican musicians) with the transliteration of African American church-derived heterophony into the clarinet's weaving obbligatos.²²⁷

This phenomenon represented another facet of the vibrant cultural mosaic in the Gulf borderlands, where Black, Mexican, and Afro-Cuban influences informed one another. Black artists were at the forefront of this creolizing process, creating innovative musical languages that reflected a new cultural movement. Matt Sakakeeny describes this as New Orleans's musical "circulatory system," a network of cultural exchanges that both predated and defied Louisiana's rigid Jim Crow system of racial segregation, fostering a climate of internationalism that facilitated creolized cultural identities.[228] As the Eureka colony makes clear, this creolization was not a passive inheritance but actively constructed through and alongside transnational political solidarity.

THE TIOS AND AFRICAN AMERICAN CULTURE

Ironically, Lorenzo and Louis Tio did not contribute as performers to the improvisatory heterophonic revolution that came to be associated with jazz clarinet, although they did teach generations of clarinetists who would. They had a complex and contradictory relationship with Black expressive culture after moving to New Orleans in 1877. On the one hand, by the 1880s Lorenzo Sr. and Louis Tio could be found performing with the Onward Brass Band and Excelsior Brass Band, two of the most in-demand Black bands in New Orleans, while rolling cigars on an as-needed basis. On the other hand, these Creole of color musicians were "classically" trained—a contemporary of Louis Tio's remembered that he was one of the "five Negroes in the whole French Opera"[229]—although cornetist Isidore Barbarin recalled that unlike their European counterparts, "they played anything."[230] Their performances encompassed parades, steamboat excursions, picnics, dances for benevolent societies, and dances at Economy Hall.[231] Nonetheless, numerous interviews suggest that Lorenzo Sr. and Louis Tio were stubbornly resistant to embrace the Black plantation vernacular on clarinet and actively resisted the attempt to transform the clarinet into an instrument that could play the blues.[232]

The Tios' racial politics were complex, and, if the testimonies of various musicians are correct, they were threatened by the development of a new style rooted in the Black plantation vernacular; they sometimes registered this critique with language that could be construed as anti-Black. When Sidney Bechet showed off extended techniques and scooped his notes, Lorenzo Tio reportedly reprimanded him: "No, no, no, we don't bark like a dog."[233] Yet I find myself fundamentally diverging from the perspectives articulated by Thomas Brothers, who asserts that the rigorous approach the Tios adopted in teaching their students long tones is indicative of a Eurocentric, colonizing auditory aesthetic, whose practitioners sought to amass cultural capital through a refined sound. Brothers writes: "When the Tios and the Creoles heard rough uptown [African American] musicians, they heard . . . an inability to control passion and aggression, which also manifested through promiscuity and problems with the law. . . . Given that situation, it seems unlikely that they [the Tios] could have done much to create jazz."[234] I argue, however, that this viewpoint neglects a tradition in jazz music pedagogy, as well as the Tios' own aesthetic development. First, a closer examination of the recordings showcasing Lorenzo Jr.'s solos reveals his scooping techniques and use of the blues scale, particularly evident in his recordings of "Red Man Blues," "West Indies Blues," and "Louisiana Swing" with Armand Piron's New Orleans Orchestra, to which I will return later.

Second, it is worth noting that long tone practice is not isolated to Afro-Creoles but is echoed in the teachings and techniques of renowned African American saxophonists of a later generation, such as John Coltrane and Grover Washington Jr.—both of whom emphasized the practice of long tones with suppressed vibrato as a foundational aspect of tonal development, despite themselves soloing with vibrato, growl, screeches, and a variety of extended techniques.[235] As Grover Washington Jr. explained in a master class at the University of Pittsburgh, "Adjust your embouchure so that you don't hear any wavering. You shouldn't hear any wavering, regardless [of] what note you're playing. You should always strive for a solid note. A note has to start softly and gradually, develop into a clear tone and eventually trails off. . . . Sound is part of a musical vocabulary that you have to learn to properly use."[236] Long tones were and continue to be a means of achieving a deeper, multifaceted tonal practice grounded in the cultivation of a robust embouchure and heightened inner aural acuity.

This poses the question of whether a dedicated scholarly inquiry should approach the Tios' pedagogical and sociocultural legacy in a manner that transcends the limited scope of Eurocentric interpretation posited by Brothers.[237] I believe, clearly, that it should, for reasons both "local" to the Tios and more methodological: namely, that the mutual influence between Mexican and Latin American cultures with those of African America challenges the Eurocentric blinders that informs the coloniality of our knowledge. The Tios' lives and musical work martial concrete counternarratives to the dominant discourse of jazz as African rhythm blended with European instruments and harmony. "Too often," explains Gregory Downs, "transnationally inclined U.S. historians look to Europe for the circulation of ideas, and to Latin America for the movement of people and raw commodities," a racialized geography of knowledge unfortunately reproduced in many art forms' canonical histories.[238] Independently of the historical framing we attach to them, the Tios made significant contributions to a wider circuit of Black culture that included the national Black minstrel circuit, the Excelsior Brass Band, civil rights rallies, and their significant work as pedagogues.

Here it is important to emphasize that Lorenzo and Louis Tio developed meaningful relationships with Black artists. African American dockworker-bassist Pops Foster, who was outspoken about prejudice exhibited by Creoles of color to African American musicians, remembers that "Papa [Louis] Tio was a nice old guy." Apparently, as Foster relates, Tio often fell asleep when he drank alcohol. One night, while asleep at the bandstand, Pops Foster replaced his clarinet with a broomstick. Joe Oliver turned to Tio and asked, "'Tea, you gonna play this next number with us?' Tio said, 'I've been playing all night, man. Don't you like my playing?' Joe said, 'What are you playing with?' He said, 'My clarinet,' and took a look at it. Then he turned to me [Foster] and said, 'You did this.'"[239]

The playful exchange does not negate the resistance that the elder Tios demonstrated to adopting Black musical styles. But it contributes to another narrative of the Tios: that they were professional musicians who were interested in befriending those they played with, and made enduring friendships in both New Orleans's Black community and at the national level. By the turn of the century, they began performing in African American national music circuits by joining the Black minstrel troupe Richards and Pringle's company in 1897, parting ways thereafter to join different ensembles.[240] In this and other ensembles on the Black minstrel circuit, their impact was felt across the country, and they frequently earned accolades from the Black press.[241] Some of these associations are recorded through open letters written by Lorenzo Sr. and published in the *Indianapolis Freeman*, a common form of communication for performers on the minstrel circuit who lacked stable addresses for most of the year. Lorenzo Sr.'s familiarity with this organ is in itself a clue that he was attuned to African American culture and politics. In November 1898, Lorenzo Tio Sr., now the clarinetist with Oliver Scott's Refined Negro Minstrels, sent his regards to Daniel Desdunes.[242] A year later, Tio sent a letter to the African American comedian Billy Kersands who was in the Richard and Pringle's tour. Scholars of minstrelsy, including Eric Lott and Mel Watkins, explain how Kersands was a complex figure emblematic of Black minstrelsy's contradictions at the turn of the century. He critiqued and challenged white American racial attitudes within the limited zone of the minstrel show, and had a following among working-class African Americans.[243] In 1899, Lorenzo Sr. published an open letter to Kersands to celebrate his new ensemble and greet the comedian. He wrote: "Lorenzo Tio . . . wishes to state to all friends in the profession that he would be pleased to hear from them . . . Hello Billy Kersands. I will meet you soon in Donaldsonville, La., regards to you, and kindest respect to your wife, and wishing success."²⁴⁴ Kersands is the only artist Lorenzo Sr. mentions by name in this correspondence other than his brother, Louis, who was also on the road at the time. By committing to a future get-together back together in Louisiana, Lorenzo Sr. is making his allegiance with the most popular Black comedian of his day well known to readers of the *Freeman*. Indeed, he seems to be bragging about this friendship.

The unique social space of the "road" partially explains how the Tios may have come to know Black artists better. Multiple musicians' interviews tesify how Black and Creole of color antagonisms in late nineteenth-century New Orleans were reinforced by the intense economic competition for limited jobs, an intentional by-product of Jim Crow.²⁴⁵ On the minstrel circuit in a "mixed" Creole of color and Black performance troupe, this disincentive for solidarity was absent. When the famed Black trumpeter W. C. Handy shared a bill with Lorenzo Tio Sr. in Portland, Oregon, with Manhara's Minstrels, he did not refer to him as a Creole; he described him as "the first of the top-notch clarinetists of our race."²⁴⁶

The relationship between Lorenzo Sr. and Kersands suggests that the Black minstrel circuit was an important space for African American and Creole of color collaborative performance. They represent a scene whereby the collective labor of African-descended musicians from distinct parts of the country united to reinvent the popular cultural form based on misrepresenting their own cultural legacies.²⁴⁷ Daniel Desdunes was another performer who occasionally performed in the same minstrel outfits as the Tios, and the Tios used their seniority in the ensembles to help support their students and find them employment. George Baquet, who performed with Gideon's Minstrels and Nashville Students company in Memphis, Tennessee, in 1901, credited Louis Tio for recommending him.²⁴⁸ These groups often played at independent African American vaudeville houses, what Lynn Abbott and Jack Stewart describe as a "subcultural network of little theaters" with an "uninhibited, self-determined environment." It was here that "some of the first commercial reverberations of blues and jazz were felt."²⁴⁹ The Tios, Daniel Desdunes, and other New Orleans Creoles of color made important contributions to this nascent, Black cultural underground during the rise of Jim Crow.

It was not until Lorenzo Jr. came of age, however, that a Tio clarinetist embraced Black expressive culture by incorporating blues-based improvisation. Lorenzo Tio Jr. had a deep connection to the development of jazz clarinet, coming of age during and participating in the heart of New Orleans's jazz revolution.²⁵⁰ Tio Jr. played with, and for, Black musicians, and was as talented a sideman as he was a composer. As Peter Bocage remembers, "He was all musician. . . . He could play jazz, too, and he could play anything you put up there in front of him. . . . He was gifted; he could fake, and he knowed the chords and everything. You see, that's what it takes."[251] Lorenzo Jr. played with both New Orleans–born Creoles of color and with plantation-to-urban Black migrants, such as in the Tuxedo Band led by former canecutter William Bébé Ridgley.[252] As Bruce Boyd Raeburn notes, this band "created relationships that subverted the dehumanizing effects of racism," and Lorenzo Tio Jr. both shaped and was shaped by this socializing process.[253]

Like his father and uncle, Lorenzo Jr. was also an important teacher of the next generation. His students included Sidney Bechet, whose professional career began in earnest in the early 1910s, when he succeeded Lorenzo Tio Jr. in Bunk Johnson's Eagle Band, which was composed of Buddy Bolden alumni.[254] Although Lorenzo Sr. likely did not improvise, Lorenzo Jr. did. This intergenerational transition both complicates and extends the argument for danzón's influence on the improvised obbligato in early jazz, and points to African American creolizing influences in late nineteenth-century New Orleans among Creole of color musicians. Indeed, Tio's mastery of African American blues sonorities is evident in his solos on "Red Man Blues," a transcription of which is reproduced later in this chapter (see figure 3.10). This solo is almost entirely constructed on the major and minor pentatonic scales (also known as gospel and blues scales).[255] His open sound and wide vibrato in these performances reflect both Black New Orleanian conventions in clarinet aesthetics. But they also reflected how African American practices were resonant with the Black Atlantic–inspired music heard in the Spanish-speaking Gulf of the same era, such as those heard in the 1930 recordings of Puerto Rican *plena* group Canario y su Grupo or the 1931 recording of Cuban group Alfredo Brito and His Siboney Orchestra.[256]

Lorenzo Jr. retained important circum-Caribbean cultural connections. He performed in Chicago in 1917 with the Mexican Louisianan cornetist Manuel Pérez.[257] Also of Cuban ancestry, Pérez was born into a Creole of color family of Spanish, French, and African descent. Like Lorenzo Jr., one of his great-grandfathers was an officer of the free Black regiment that fought in the Battle of New Orleans, one of several early jazz musicians who claimed descent from this ensemble.[258] Lorenzo Jr. later joined Armand J. Piron's Society Orchestra, which by the 1920s had become the preeminent dance band in New Orleans.[259]

With the renamed Armand Piron's New Orleans Orchestra, Tio played some high-profile dates in New York City; they performed in the Roseland Ballroom for the summer months of 1924, preceding the Fletcher Henderson jazz orchestra, which included a young Louis Armstrong on cornet.[260] The group returned to New Orleans, but Lorenzo Jr. had a transformational experience in New York, and moved to Harlem in 1930 with his family at the peak of the Harlem Renaissance. He worked with a theater orchestra, where he doubled on clarinet and alto saxophone, and he may have performed with Jelly Roll Morton when the pianist was in town.[261]

An analysis of Lorenzo Tio Jr.'s performances with Armand Piron's New Orleans Orchestra comprise the few recordings we have of the clarinetist. Especially revealing about his style was his use of the blues and gospel scales, which Tio likely further developed in Harlem. His phrases employ a variety of tonal techniques and inflections, especially pitch bends up to (and down from) a note, rapid vibrato on upper register long tones, and a bright, energetic approach. There are some truly magic moments on this recording in particular, as Peter Bocage's trumpet and Tio's clarinet at times finish one another's musical phrases; at others, Tio weaves around Bocage in the heterophonic tailgate style described earlier. Tio constructs almost every single phrase in "Red Man Blues" using either the blues or gospel scales. His evolving experimentation of this language reveals how he, like Desdunes, adopted African American musical vocabulary, and did so within the circuits of circum-Caribbean lexicons that had been favored by Creole of color musicians in previous generations. His ability to fuse these languages together in his clarinet improvisation was another expression of how solidarity between Afro-Creoles and African Americans became more fully consolidated through these intercultural improvisations of early jazz.

Indeed, Lorenzo Tio Jr. had an impact on African American musicians in Harlem beyond the tight-knit circle of New Orleans up-south migrants. Louis R. Tio, Lorenzo Jr.'s brother, claims that Lorenzo wrote the melodies for the jazz standards "Mood Indigo," "Sophisticated Lady," and "Moonglow" recorded by Duke Ellington.[262] These claims are corroborated by the Creole of color clarinetist Barney Bigard, who studied extensively with Lorenzo Jr. before playing with King Oliver and later in Duke Ellington's orchestra from 1927 to 1942.[263] That Tio's former student was a member of Duke Ellington's orchestra for fifteen years highlights how his family's pedagogical practice was important to the development of jazz beyond New Orleans. Through Bigard, Tio's composition "Dreamy Blues" passed to Duke Ellington, as the former shared it with the latter during a rehearsal. As jazz historian Al Rose surmises: "All of us in New Orleans knew that tune ["Mood Indigo"] and we knew it was the Tios'."[264] According to Kinzer, early Ellington releases of the recording listed the song as "Dreamy Blues," which was the name of a song also played by Lorenzo Tio Jr. and the Piron Orchestra. Further supporting the claim is that eventually Bigard himself would be credited as a co-composer, but twenty-five years after the song's 1930 release.[265]

This contribution to the jazz repertoire places Lorenzo Tio Jr. at the intersection of New Orleans style and big band swing. Much like Desdunes's move to

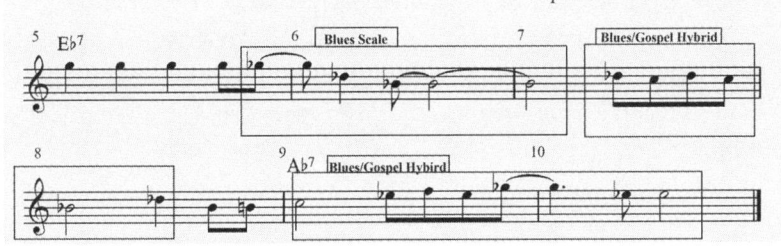

FIGURES 3.10 a and b *Top*: Black and white photo of A. J. Piron's Society Orchestra, New Orleans, 1920. Lorenzo Tio Jr. is in the front row, third from the left, with a tenor saxophone and a clarinet by his feet. The other musicians are A. J. Piron, violin and leader; Steve Lewis, piano; Louis Cottrell Sr., drums; Louis Warnecke; alto saxophone; Peter Bocage, trumpet; Charlie Bocage, banjo; Bob Ysaguirre, tuba; and John Lindsey, trombone. Courtesy of the Louisiana State Museum 1978.118(8).05935. *Bottom*: Lorenzo Tio Jr.'s 1925 Solo on "Red Man Blues" with the A. J. Piron's New Orleans Orchestra, measures 5-9. Tio's use of blues and gospel scales and lower neighbor tones to the third of the subdominant reflects an engagement with a distinctly African American, blues-based language prevalent in early jazz. Based on recordings of prominent swing bands of the era, his move to Harlem soon after this time period would have deepened his commitment and mastery of this language. This solo was transcribed by the author in dialogue with Charles Kinzer. From Piron's New Orleans Orchestra, "Red Man Blues," Victor (19646-B), 1925.

Omaha, Tio's move to Harlem reflected how the ripples of brassroots democracy reverberated and interfaced with other emancipatory strains of African American culture. It reinforces the multifaceted impact on the development of jazz clarinet and his contributions as a composer, player, and pedagogue who contributed an important timbre and technique. Ellington's famous "mike-tone" (whereby the overtones of the lower register of the clarinet interacted with an upper-register, muted trombone) would have sounded different, or been nonexistent, had a clarinetist recorded with less robust tonal production as Bigard—who forged his embouchure within the exacting long-tone regime of the Tio school.[266]

Lorenzo Tio Jr. got out on the scene and had the potential to make a larger impact. In 1932, he began running the house orchestra at the Nest, a popular nightclub and dance hall on 133rd Street in Harlem. Sidney Bechet joined his old teacher in the ensemble after returning from Paris the same year. Bechet recalled that swing-era trumpetist Roy Eldridge, who later played in Charles Mingus's Newport anti-festival, made a guest appearance with the band.[267] The band provided financial stability for Tio, but on Christmas Eve 1933 Lorenzo Jr. died of heart disease at Harlem Hospital. The *Louisiana Weekly* wrote in his obituary that "Lorenzo Tio Jr . . . contributed to the gaiety of 'America's Most Interesting City' and its reputation as a musical center for more than half a century."[268] It was not mistaken.

CONCLUSION

Isidore Bordenave, a New Orleans Creole of color of Haitian and Cuban descent, had moved to Zamora Gutierrez, Veracruz, in 1858, later marrying Agustina Azuara. After several decades in Mexico, he paid a visit to New Orleans in 1909. Although he had a "very pleasant" time with family, he emphasized in a letter to his sister-in-law later that "New Orleans is a dead city for me. Here [in Mexico] I enjoy life—in a desert, it's true, but life without any of the foolishness that makes the American Republic a dark ship." Reflecting on how his behavior and personality had changed while in the Jim Crow South, he continued, "I was unable, due to prejudice, to act as I would here, [and it] bled my heart and left a dark veil on the good time enjoyed."[269]

Like Bordenave, many Afro-Louisianans experienced the "dark ship" of the United States in the first decade of the twentieth century. But while most jazz musicians in the late 1910s who left New Orleans sought greener pastures in the North, Lorenzo Tio Sr. decided to move farther South. He followed generations of freedom seekers who employed the mobility and the informal citizenship of the borderlands to build a new life outside the United States.[270]

In contrast to the hopelessness of Jim Crow racial oppression in the US, Mexico was on the precipice of a revolutionary change. This was at the very beginning of Porfirio Díaz's overthrow; Díaz announced "free" elections in 1907 in response to major labor unrest that began in Veracruz. In 1906, the textile industry went on strike, spreading into a wildcat general strike that engulfed several states, involving tens of thousands of workers that identified with varied strains of anti-capitalism.[271] The governor of Veracruz, Teodoro A. Dehesa, expressed his solidarity with the strikers and condemned the Díaz government. These acts of dissent threw fuel on the fire that was the Mexican Revolution, which began in earnest 1910.[272] It was during these years that Lorenzo Sr. was in direct communication with the Mexican consulate. According to his son Louis R., "He writ them and told them that he wants to come back to Mexico. Well, the consul sent him a letter back . . . get all these papers set up, come on back to Mexico, all transportation would be paid."[273] One wonders whether the elder Tio was excited about the prospect of playing clarinet in Veracruz. It seems like he was confident he would be able to build a musical career there, and so, too, did the Mexican state, which identified the Tampico-born clarinetist as a renowned musician with Mexican roots, worthy of a travel subsidy. Once again, the legacy of the frontera sónica opened spaces of refuge for racial subalterns that dramatically changed the aesthetic codes of Gulf expressive culture.

Sadly, Lorenzo Tio Sr. passed away from pneumonia before said travel could take place. As Louis R. Tio reflected, "Had he lived we never would have been here [In New Orleans] . . . we [Lorenzo Jr. and I] would've been back in Mexico." But the remaining family decided to stay in the Crescent City. Had they moved, would they have participated in the popular movements of the Mexican Revolution, like other Gulf cigar rollers? Maybe they would have crossed paths with Jack Johnson, the first Black world heavyweight boxing champion who held the title from 1908 to 1915, whose open defiance of white supremacy provoked white rioting.[274] Johnson self-exiled to Tijuana, where he opened up two jazz clubs and started a land company, and traveled the country at large. He openly pledged allegiance to the Mexican Revolution; in a speech before a "cheering crowd" in Nuevo Laredo, he declared: "If the gringos invaded Mexico, American blacks would stand alongside their Mexican brothers."[275] Many Black and Afro-Creole jazz musicians answered Jack Johnson's invitation to move to what he described as "Latin America, the garden of the world," which, he reasoned, "offers us all the golden privileges of a land that has never known racial prejudice." Mexico, he wrote, "was willing not only to give us the privileges of Mexican citizenship, but will champion our cause."[276]

African American musicians influenced a younger generation of Mexican musicians, setting the stage for a still-strong Baja California jazz scene. Mexican jazz musicians including saxophonist Cheché Sánchez and trumpetist Jesus Avilés El Panchón grew up listening to these musicians. Later Sánchez moved to Mexico City.[277] According to Mexican jazz historian Abel Montelongo, the Tijuana sound became the foundation of jazz across the republic.[278] Tijuana's Afro-Mexican jazz scene was one moment in a chain of the multinational improvised societies that grew in the cracks of the border, and their musical afterlives reproduced the memories and echoes of worlds-not-to-be. The alternative emancipations of the frontera sónica were a resource, always in the liminal space between the residual and emergent, between enslavement and freedom—a sonic geography that could reproduce polycultural democratic spaces in the shadow of the plantation complex.

Despite, and partially because of, the frontera sónica's resonance, Mexico was not and is not a society free of the stain of anti-Blackness. Only in 2015 did the Mexican census begin to permit Mexicans to select Afro-Mexican as an identity, and Black Mexicans routinely experience discrimination in Mexican society, just as they did in the nineteenth and twentieth centuries.[279] Discourses of mestizaje, or racial mixture, are often mobilized to assert that anti-Black racism is not a serious issue, further stifling awareness and debate. José Vasconcelos, Mexico's first secretary for education in the postrevolutionary period, banned jazz from Mexican public schools partly for its affiliation with Blackness while he wrote *La raza cósmica* (1925), which laid the foundation of mestizaje as a national ideology of race mixing.[280] One nationalist Mexican trade union complained how their children, through listening to jazz, had become "passionate about the novelty of the saxophone's howls" and lost touch with Mexican music, although it was Mexican musicians who had initially introduced the saxophone to New Orleans forty years earlier.[281]

Yet the experiences of the individuals whose collective labor built the frontera sónica tell a story extending beyond their individual lives as well the nation-states within which they were born. Gerald Horne observes that the perception of the border and Mexico as avenues to freedom persisted among African American cultural workers even amid the Mexican state's efforts in the 1920s to curb their migration.[282] The popular, bottom-up movements in nineteenth-century Mexico extended the republican and democratic character of New World revolutions at the very moment when Haiti's isolation and the United States' expansion of slavery threatened the very meaning of hemispheric independence from European empire. Abolitionist movements rarely retained an enduring presence in Mexico's halls of power. But the multidirectional and consistent convergences between U.S. Black and Mexican peoples in the border region suggest that the way they construed and lived had a dynamic effect on the very system of caste organization under which their communities were classified. The frontera sónica transmitted material culture, orchestration and composition techniques, and theoretical legacies by which the democratic ethos of brassroots democracy could expand in new directions. Its hybrid aesthetic forms infused transnational, improvised communities with style and cultural resources that could destabilize the anti-Black and anti-Indigenous narratives of ascendant plantocracies that attempted to mold the world in their image. The music that solidarity enabled, the solidarity that must be heard as responding to that music: this legacy would forever be embedded in the jazz clarinet.

FOUR

Sowing Freedom
Abolitionist Agroecology in Afro-Louisiana

Though descended from a Senegalese woman brought against her will to Louisiana, New Orleans clarinetist George Lewis was not, like his mother, Alice Zeno, able to speak fragments of the Wolof language.[1] Yet Lewis did practice a multigenerational legacy that dated back to the Middle Passage: he and his family had a garden. Lewis spent "idyllic" years raising chickens and hogs, keeping a vegetable garden with his wife. He sometimes played clarinet outside with their plant and animal life.[2] This garden was located in Mandeville, a small Louisiana town located in the sugar parish of St. Tammany, and constitutes one expression of a transcontinental Black practice that took on a special significance in the Atlantic world: the proliferation of ecologically restorative and nutritionally rich small-scale agricultural production in the cracks of the plantation system. The archipelagos of Black Atlantic gardens created much-needed sustenance for the enslaved and their kin, but they did more: they pointed toward another possible way of life and economic development to the plantation model. This path, despite massive effort, resistance, and some flashes of success, was ultimately denied to Black American freedpeople after the conclusion of the Civil War.[3]

Lewis's brief recollection of his family's garden is an expression of a centuries-long inheritance, built and tended by generations of enslaved dissidents whose refusal of plantation agriculture led them to leave their own imprints in both soil and soul, an inheritance seen again in George Washington Carver's work as an agronomist; Mrs. Hamer's Freedom Farm; the New Community Inc. in southwest Georgia; Cooperative Jackson in modern-day Mississippi; and other efforts to preserve, maintain, and advance Black-led agriculture as an act of social justice.[4] When their efforts to cultivate land of their own were restricted by either government edict or paramilitary violence, Black plantation workers could find meaningful autonomy in communal music-making. A Chicago periodical, for instance, noted in 1920 that "Jazz is Blamed for Lack of Farm Labor . . . Easy Jobs at High Prices Cause Acute Shortage of Help on the Farms in Grain Belt."[5] While there was nothing easy about the complex maneuvers that highly trained African American improvisers had to navigate in racially segregated urban nightlife, the article nonetheless correctly identifies how music making provided a means off the plantation.

Black music-making and land practices are both negations of the plantation society, sites where freedom was—and is—*enacted*. The metaphor of brassroots democracy begins with a recognition of the value of the "grass"—the foundational, indigenous plants that keep the soil in its place; protect the land from disaster; provide home to the most microscopic of organisms; and serve as the base for a food cycle, allowing every other thing to live. Without this reminder of the ecological implications of grassroots, the metaphors of both grassroots and brassroots are lost. Gardening sites, along with public brass and Black music more generally, sounded alternative futures through aesthetic choices generated by participatory and decentralized structures that were generations in the making.

An astonishing number of New Orleans jazz musicians were born in the sugar parishes, where their lives intersected by both industrial monocrop agriculture and the communal farming alternatives. Joe Banks, Joe Gabriel, Willie James, Louis James, Neddy James, Albert Jiles Jr. and Sr., Isaiah "Big Ike" Robinson, Jim Richardson, Big Ike K, Mutt Carey, Louis Nelson, Chris Kelly, Sam Morgan, William Bébé Ridgley, Sonny Henry, Punch Miller, Harrison Barnes, Jimmy "Kid" Clayton, Pops Foster, and John Casimir were just a few of the plantation migrants who brought traditions of work songs and the historical memory of plantation resistance into the early genomes of jazz.[6] The history of early jazz in New Orleans compels students of brassroots democracy to take seriously the interconnectedness of the city with the sugar country. The agroecological habitus of this community of transplanted plantation players was a practice of autonomy, and their green thumbs an index of a fugitive freedom fought for in the provision grounds at the margins of the sugar fields.[7]

This industrial-capitalist transformation of the countryside in the post–Civil War South stood in stark contrast to the social order imagined by freedpeople. Frederick Douglass was one of many who suggested that the deprivation of Black land ownership robbed the Civil War of its emancipatory potential. In an 1893 speech, he noted that "Russia's liberated serf was given three acres of land

and agricultural implements with which to begin his career of liberty and independence"; in contrast, the United States Civil War "ended slavery... But to us no foot of land nor implement was given. We were turned loose to starvation, destitution and death." Douglass invoked a philosophy of the land, not as a source of capitalist extraction but as foundational for an ecological, communitarian society: "Life is derived from the Earth."[8]

Douglass captured the common sense of millions of African Americans who envisioned a new social order based not on cash cropping but on collective nutrition and socioecological interdependence. And they fought to enact it. Eric Foner notes that when enslavers fled plantations in territories conquered by Union troops, Black workers "sack[ed] the big houses and destroy[ed] cotton gins; they then commenced planting corn and potatoes for their own subsistence."[9] "They destroy every thing [sic] on the plantation," complained the planter John Minor, and noted that "the most of them think, or pretend to think, that the plantation & every thing [sic] belongs to them."[10] When freedpeople destroyed sugarcane and cotton, they also destroyed plantation hierarchies, reclaiming the land and restoring its metabolic process. Freedpeople in the American South were joined in their destructive rebirth of agricultural society by comrades across oceans and centuries: revolutionaries in Cuba, Jamaica, and Haiti all burned cane for ceremonial and practical reasons, an act rich with symbolism that returned phosphorus and nitrogen that had been robbed from the soil in order to power Europe's emerging capitalist social relations.[11]

In the transition to freedom, provisional gardens managed by enslaved Africans and their descendants were expanded to form the basis of a new social system to replace plantation agriculture.[12] In Louisiana and across the South, surpluses generated from these lands were redirected toward the development of new institutions: schools, churches, and collective provisions for all. Many freedpeople pooled resources to rent or buy land.[13] Others simply claimed the plantation as their own, and transformed its ghastly sugar and cotton monocultures into vibrant ecologies. The subjectification of Black Louisianians into a rural wage-labor proletariat by a Southern aristocracy allied with Northern capital was a violent and complicated process, and several strikes and music-adorned demonstrations between the end of the Civil War and the turn of the twentieth century slowed the creeping hegemony of cane planters over Black laborers.[14]

Music played a paradoxical role in this transition to wage labor within the reconstituted plantation. Freedpeoples' reluctance to work on plantations was a major obstacle for planter profit, a condition that violence alone could not address. In 1874, the *New Orleans Picayune* reported that "large sections of the State are overrun by lawless bands of negroes, who visit plantations, stop all work, threaten the lives of the peaceful and contended laborers, and fill the county with terror."¹⁵ Instead of raising wages, several planters hired musicians to perform for and offer musical training to rural laborers. The influential trombonist Kid Ory, who grew up on the Woodland plantation, remembered that Henry Peyton's renowned band from New Orleans performed on plantations during the harvest season. Festivities of drink and music, funded by planters, became the scene where new contracts were signed. In other cases, they enticed migrant workers to settle down. Ory himself traveled to a plantation across the state because he "thought he might get a chance to hear Claiborne Williams's band."¹⁶ He was tricked, for the band never arrived, and Ory was stuck in a predatory contract.

Other planters took further steps in using music to undermine demands for Black land ownership, such as the planter and former governor Henry Clay Warmoth, who hired brass band musicians from New Orleans to teach canecutters and their families how to play and march. According to one musician, "The plantation owners wanted to keep the people interested and wanted them to learn something other than farming."¹⁷ These programs did not spring from planter altruism but were a means to stabilize an exploitative labor regime, yet Black working-class communities were not "duped" by these sonic institutions. Their very existence embodied a contested social contract and reflected the contradictory desires of planters and the plantation workforce. As with cuerpos filarmónicos developed by Mexican Indigenous communities in the same era, Black Louisianans found in these bands a means to continue a dream denied. With their historic struggle for the commons interrupted by violence and political machination, the plantation brass bands became all the more important to fashion self-identity, facilitate collective action, and institutionalize cultural resistance. One "professor" hired by Warmoth, James Humphrey, African American musician born on the Cornland plantation. Shaped by Civil War and Reconstruction militancy, Humphrey understood musical education as means of self-determination and cultural autonomy. In addition to his planter-paid salary, Humphrey was partially compensated in figs and seeds shared by Black farmers, revealing how bartering and noncapitalist exchange structured relations between Afro-Louisiana musicians in the late nineteenth century. These solidarity economies were enabled by, and rooted in, Black land practices with centuries of history.

This chapter traces how brass bands came to embody the ecosocial vector of Black politics, channeling new social relations embedded in the movement for brassroots democracy. When musicians trained by these mobile musical schools eventually migrated to New Orleans, they brought with them unique techniques and relationships to groove, time, and collective music-making. George Lewis was asked whether any other trumpet players sounded like Chris Kelly (born and raised on Warmoth's Magnolia plantation). He responded, "Not exactly, no. I know a lot of fellows tried to play like him . . . till he died he had that tempo."[18] This ineffable sense of time was what Lewis identified as unique to Kelley and the Magnolia plantation. Musicians who grew up on the plantation remembered that their march step was different from that in New Orleans.[19] Bassist Sylvester Handy suggested that these influences—this "feeling"—was the dominant catalyst for the transition from pre-jazz to jazz forms: "Jazz comes from the country, not from New Orleans . . . blues and jazz feeling came from the country."[20] The bassist Steve Brown, one of the few white jazz musicians of the era to openly admit to mining Black music for inspiration, emphasized that "we took ideas from out in through the country" and that "hot music . . . drifted in from the plantations."[21] Perhaps none more than trombonist Jim Robinson, born and educated in brass on the Deer Range plantation, articulated how these musical aesthetics were born of collectivity, communication, and interdependence rather than individualistic virtuosity:

> Now if them people don't work together, you can blow your brains out and you can't, you ain't getting nowhere. Now, if that banjo and that drum are going just as fast as a cyclone, [and] you can't execute your horn like you want to . . . It's too fast, understand? But as long as that drum and that piano and that banjo and bass, that must work together. Well, that's the whole thing. Any man got a band should get that together: that drum and bass and banjo and piano. Because that's the main thing; that's your background, and if that's clicking, your band got to go right.[22]

In Jim Robinson's words, the sublime in this music is not a result of "blow[ing] your brains out"—that would only get you "nowhere." The destination, "the whole thing," is rather in the shared sense of time and space, one that rejects dystopian regimes in neo-plantation spaces like turn-of-the-century Storyville or prisons in favor of communitarian efforts of building, breathing, growing, and creating. Time, breath, and the body become expressions of a commons created through collective cultural labor, in which to participate effectively is to surrender oneself to a chain of being born in musical activity.[23]

The collectivist orientation in both gardening and plantation music-making were new expressions of a Black Atlantic struggle to redefine time, subjectivity, and labor. Permaculture-based Black agricultural production demonstrated both African and Indigenous American influence—but the context in which these gardening techniques were deployed nonetheless manifested something new, responding to the dehumanizing, ecocidal, and "rational" conditions of the plantation mode of production. When independently grown foodstuffs formed the basis of an impressive array of internal markets, as they did in Jamaica or in New Orleans's Congo Square, they were still products of a process where capital's alienated relation to the land was disavowed and transcended. The musical practices of jazz's rural-to-urban migrants were both an extension and a substitute for practices of collectivity developed in these gardening complexes. As the Barbadian poet Kamau Brathwaite wrote "Circles" dedicated to jazz trombonist Melba Liston: "music will never come out of your green horn in squares / because it does not grow on cotton wool plantations."[24] For it was not only foodstuffs grown in these garden beds, but new social relations, new practices of freedom, and new peoples.

We should consider, then, the idyllic musical spaces of brass bands as part of a pantheon of alternative institutions forged by plantation dissidents in which new political imaginations could take root. They can be thought of as what Jean Casimir, in his masterful study of Haitian history, calls the "self-managed republican plantation or the counter-plantation."[25] A French observer offers a rich account of how the plantations in Artibonite, Haiti, became converted to garden plots during the Haitian Revolution. "We followed the cultivators to the cotton fields," he wrote about his experience in 1799. "There we saw that they had each taken a piece of land as their own garden plot and were spending all their time on it, in spite of the strict prohibitions on doing this issued by the general in chief Toussaint Louverture."[26] These farmers built communal economies rooted in small regional markets that formed an alternative to Louverture's vision of export agriculture.[27] Casimir considered these spaces a "new universe [that] structured itself as a space of resocialization, repersonalization, and recivilization."[28]

These counter-plantation practices were common to Haiti, Jamaica, and Louisiana. In each of these slave societies, enslaved and later freedpeople cultivated alternative concepts of spatial order in their personal gardens and collective provision grounds, resisting what B. W. Higman calls the "total imperial design on man and the land" which attempted to apply "the rules of monocultures at every level."[29] Sites of Black production were so drastically different from the plantation agriculture that surrounded them that visual studies scholar Jill Casid suggests they were "counter-colonial landscapes . . . resistance in the plantation machine."[30] Congo Square, initially conceived as a market for non-export nutritional crops, was so filled with Black and Indigenous garden produce that architect Benjamin Latrobe opined in 1820 that the city would starve without its foodstuffs.[31] Across the Black Atlantic, enslaved and liberated Africans measured autonomy by their access to and control over land, where they fashioned a different geometry of existence and new relations of production and exchange. It is telling that the most stable postindependence governments in nineteenth-century Haiti paid their soldiers not in bullion but in land.[32]

Counter-plantation spaces incubated alternative political ideologies and new practices of music, alongside forms of worship, kinship, and community, and though it would be naïve to say that provisions grounds yielded uncomplicated emancipation, gardens were crucial for survival during slavery as much as during freedom.[33] Provision sites in the Black Atlantic, like among other oppressed peoples around the globe, were sites of cultural creation and resistance to oppression, with crop choice and nonmarket production, ecological stewardship, and preservation of African foodways (and the cosmologies they animated) each manifesting vectors toward self-determination.[34] Judith Ann Carney and Richard Nicholas Rosomoff show how the yards and garden plots attached to the enslaved's dwellings were the home of complex land practices where "the African components of the Columbian Exchange," crops such as okra, sesame, guinea squash, millet, sorghum, rice, and black-eyed peas, became introduced to New World diets.[35] Informing this "agrarian creolization" was that many of the enslaved Africans who survived the Middle Passage were skilled farmers.[36] Mande-speaking rice cultivators in the region between the Senegal and Gambia rivers were especially sought out by Louisianan and South Carolina enslavers for their ability to create sophisticated hydraulic systems, and rice's existence in the Americas was the result of an unwilling technology transfer.[37] Afro-Atlantic lexicons were often transmitted with the foodstuffs themselves; for example, Louisiana gumbo, a roux-based soup, derives its name from the Bantu word for okra, *nkombo*.[38] These words retained a power that could be evoked by cultural workers across generations. *Nkombo/Echoes from the Gumbo* was the name of a revolutionary magazine edited by Kalamu ya Salaam in the late 1960s and '70s. Its writers were linked to the grassroots organization Black Southern Theatre, which appropriated sites of slaveholder violence—plantations, sugarhouses, and cotton fields—in order to create free-jazz-inspired Black radical theater during the Black Arts movement. *Nkombo* organized its poetry as a cookbook.[39]

In addition to foodstuffs, medicine was a major component of home gardens across the Afro-Atlantic, and new herbs and remedies were spread through the migrations of Afrodiasporic and Indigenous bodies of knowledge. Jalap, a laxative derived from a tuber found in Veracruz, was one of a variety of herbs used by women of color healers known as "fever doctors" in nineteenth-century New Orleans; in Santiago de Cuba, a medicinal drink called *tifey*, produced by soaking the aerial parts of artemisia absinthium with rum, became widespread among Afro-Cubans after Haitian migration to the region during the United States occupation of Haiti (1915–34).[40] Louis Armstrong was one of several Black musicians who recalled being treated for tuberculosis by herbal remedies his mother prepared, suggesting that these counter-plantation knowledges literally kept musicians, and the music, alive.[41] Okra and aloe, transported to the Caribbean from West African enslaved migrants, were used as a contraceptive among enslaved women across the South to prevent forced and unwanted pregnancies, infuriating enslavers. Cotton root, cedar berries, and camphor were also administered.[42] Native American herbal knowledge also passed hands to African Americans and especially to African American women, who utilized such knowledge in the art of healing both in maroon communities and on plantations. Boston King, who had been enslaved on a South Carolina plantation before he secured his freedom by joining the British Army during the American Revolution, remembered his mother was able to cure the sick by "having some knowledge of the virtue of herbs, which she learned from the Indians."[43] Harriet Collins, interviewed in Houston, Texas, about her experience of enslavement, similarly described how her mom had taught her "a lot of doctorin' what she learned from old folks from Africa, and some the Indians learned her."[44] Embedded within these circuits of exchange from below were not only the goods themselves but the constellation of ideas attached to them, and their very transmission reflected a commoning practice that shared knowledge between subalterns within the oppressive arena of plantation production.[45] The Jamaican historian and philosopher Sylvia Wynter surmises that the "culture [of the garden plot] recreated traditional values—use values. This folk culture became a source of cultural guerilla resistance to the plantation system."[46]

An ecocritical perspective on the labor history of early jazz reveals how the conditions of plantation work, especially sugar work, made counter-plantation ideals not only desirable but necessary. How these institutions and grassroots organizing spaces influenced jazz and early jazz musicians tells us much about brassroots democracy—the seeding, then rooting, then flourishing of a new sound and new dream that was never meant to take hold in the ground in which it was transplanted.[47]

THE DEATH WORLD OF SUGAR
AND THE LIFE WORLD OF GARDENS

The ruins of the Plantation have affected American cultures all around.
Édouard Glissant, Poetics of Relation

A sardonic and startling paradox lies at the core of the plantation complex: the more fertile the land and the richer the soil, the less actual food was grown, and the higher the rate of malnourishment for the enslaved workforce. Higher white profits eventuated more Black deaths, with the perceived usefulness of soil as its vector. Food historian Sam Bowers Hilliard puts it mildly: "The southern plantation had no inherent characteristics that necessarily inhibited food production," but "abundant evidence [shows] that food shortages did occur and that agriculturists in some areas made no real effort to provide foodstuffs enough for their own use."[48] Second slavery, the modernization of plantation agriculture that occurred in the United States from roughly 1800 to the Civil War, linked ravenous financial speculation in the United States to the rapacious consumption of Black bodies in the Southwest frontier.[49] Just as Black bodies were tortured and wasted to produce capital, so too, was the soil from which cash crops were grown. By the early 1900s, five million acres of once-nutrient-rich land were unusable due to soil erosion from plantation monocrop agriculture.[50] Second slavery's incessant need for territorial expansion—a dynamic that fed the sectional hostilities that resulted in the Civil War—was induced, in part, by this metabolic rift. As Timothy Johnson notes, forgoing crop rotation or composting meant that Southerners' ability to continue cotton and sugar cultivation "hinged on the native fertility of the land"—that is, they had to expand to new soil or cease production.[51] Indigenous genocide and imperial wars, like the United States' invasion of Mexico, were ghastly in their cynical violence, but from the perspective of a plantation manager they were not irrational. They were the logical by-products of an economic-ecological productive apparatus that ever necessitated new lands, and new enslaved hands to work them.[52]

Lacking a moral compass with regard to their property, a few perceptive planters nonetheless realized the profound illogic of monocultural crop production. In 1842, South Carolina's state agricultural surveyor Edmund Ruffin denounced the "barbarous usage" of soil by growing cotton on the same land year after year.[53] This ecological rift was acutely felt in Louisiana, where a planter's journal in 1850 urged crop "diversification" and argued, "This sugar mania should give place to a little interest in other things on a plantation besides sugar cane."[54] But "competitive pressures" prevented even self-interest from prevailing, and such was especially true in New Orleans. According to a visitor in 1853, one "may search the world over to find the science of such money-making reduced to such perfection, and become of such all-engrossing influence, as in New Orleans."[55]

Louisiana's plantation Black Belt was a brutal setting for the confrontation between the plantocracy, the demands of commodity production, the laws of nature, and the well-being of Black bodies. In 1910, the United States census noted that alluvial soil made up one-third of Louisiana's land, one of the highest proportions in the world, much of it located in what was called the sugar bowl of the Delta.⁵⁶ Soil richness was a harbinger of Black overwork. Because "river bottoms" were often actually lower than rivers, levees ten to thirty feet tall were erected to prevent flooding. These geoengineering requirements prohibited all but the wealthiest planters from entering the field.⁵⁷

The scale at which these monocultural commodity factories developed can scarcely be understated. Filling the void left by the Haitian Revolution, Louisiana quickly overtook Saint-Domingue's previous sugar output and challenged the rest of the Caribbean for supremacy. As the agricultural journal *De Bow's Review* commented in 1853, "there are but few estates either in Mexico, Cuba, or any of the West India Islands which equal . . . the average plantations in Louisiana."⁵⁸ The Saint-Domingue migrant chemist Antoine Morin invented granulated sugar in 1795, within a year of Eli Whitney's invention of the cotton gin, and both industrial revolutions of United States slavery transformed rural Louisiana.⁵⁹ From 1824 to 1861, cane sugar emerged as southern Louisiana's principal cash crop, and the enslaved population in the sugar region rose more than sixfold, from 20,000 to 125,000.⁶⁰ William Russell, a British observer in the sugar estates south of Baton Rouge, called the view "one of the most striking of its kind in the world. If an English agriculturist could see six thousand acres of the finest land in one field, unbroken by hedge or boundary, and covered with the most magnificent crops of . . . sprouting sugarcane . . . he would surely doubt his senses."⁶¹ What provoked wonder for Russell was traumatic and disturbing for the African American traveler Nancy Prince. Approaching the Crescent City from the Mississippi River in 1853, she chose not to disembark when she was overcome by the sight of "poor slaves, who were laboring and toiling, on either side [of the Mississippi River], as far as could be seen with a glass."⁶² Despite many days of travel, she decided to stay in her ship instead of entering this "historic hell."⁶³

Louisiana's poor climate for growing sugar—it could not grow year-round, as it had in Saint-Domingue—did little to stall its ferocious expansion.⁶⁴ "Thoroughly disgusted with everything connected with sugar," wrote a Rapides Parish planter in an 1852 letter after losing a crop due to an early frost. "This is one of the incidents of this climate by which a man is foiled in making any fair calculation on planting . . . in my opinion [it] is the last spot that any man should hold land or risk sugar proper."⁶⁵ Yet other planters found a way to run the "race against time" by compressing the fourteen to eighteen months necessary for full maturation of sugarcane into just nine months. Their technique would be to induce overwork, and the method of enforcement was torture.⁶⁶ Thomas Hamilton remembered that "the fatigue is so great that nothing but the severest application of the lash can stimulate the human frame to endure it."⁶⁷ Frederick Douglass referred to Louisiana's sugar factories as a "life of living death." These conditions were not only capital-intensive but life-intensive. Unlike on most cotton plantations, sugar regions saw not an increase but a natural decrease of the population of enslaved workers.[68] Planters of sugar in Louisiana thus shared with their Saint-Domingue sugar-producing predecessors a genocidal status quo characterized by excessive Black mortality even by the standards of the United States South.[69] Observing its natural population decrease of 13 percent a year, sugar historian Michael Tadman explains bluntly: "The demographic experience of Louisiana's sugar slaves was unique by US standards."[70]

Sugar production, however, was deadly everywhere the crop was produced. Population loss among the enslaved workers on Surinam's sugar plantations between 1752 and 1850 was 50–100 percent higher than on coffee plantations in the same region.[71] "Few groups in human history have been more interested in profit seeking," wrote Trevor Burnard about sugar planters, "and less concerned about the morality with which they treated the human capital."[72] In the planter's gaze, these values were transmuted into the crop itself. One Barbados planter marveled at sugarcane's destructivity, with a fascination that bordered on the erotic. "It was a strong and lusty Plant, and so vigorous, as where it grew, to forbid all Weeds to grow very near it; so thirstily it sucked the Earth for nourishment, to maintain its own health and gallantry."[73] The plant was the perfect metaphor for the extractivist, matricidal European project in which the decimation of Black and Indigenous bodies was twined with the rupture of metabolic exchange with the land. Sugarcane's "gallantry" was a potent phallic symbol for the imposition of a patriarchal world order on the graves of the Ciboneys', Arawaks', and Caribs' matri-centric civilization.[74]

Planters were much more willing to risk their workers' lives than their crops. Work routines simply would not accommodate the nutritional needs of enslaved people to reconstitute their bodies.[75] The carnage was so obvious that even one planter complained: "We very often find planters comparing notes and making suggestions as to the most profitable modes of tilling the soil . . . but how seldom do we find men comparing notes as to their mode of feeding, clothing, nursing, working, and taking care of those human beings intrusted [sic] to our charge?"[76] What was an economic and logistical challenge for planters was thus experienced as genocide through overwork and starvation by generation after generation of enslaved laborers.[77] Beyond the cane itself, the creation of ditches and the logging of cypress in swamps despite the threat of death by snakes or mosquitos made for, in the words of Robert Paquette, "a world in which each day's tasks claimed life by the inch."[78] During the grinding season, beginning in mid-October or early November and lasting the following six to ten weeks, these agricultural factories operated twenty-four hours a day as enslaved workers incessantly executed the impossible. Solomon Northup recalled working "without intermission" to keep pace with the sugar mills.[79] One commentator claimed that being assigned the grinding season was "as equivalent to a death warrant." Pregnancies during these periods often resulted in miscarriages; in the instances when childbirth did occur, it could prove fatal for the mother.[80] The formerly enslaved man Edward De Bieuw of Lafourche Parish recalled that "My ma died 'bout three hours after I was born" and explained: "He [my dad] said ma was hoein'. She told the driver she was sick; he told her to just hoe right-on. Soon, I was born, and my ma die[d] a few minutes after they brung her to the house." Many children were born stunted.[81] After emancipation, similar conditions on sugar plantations meant life was fragile. Musician Kid Ory recalled of his mom's passing: "To this day, I have never learned what caused her illness or her death. I don't think it could have been from some old age ills because she wasn't that old."[82] She lived, and worked, as a canecutter on a sugar plantation.

Ory's words remind us of what is at stake when jazz musicians relate their childhood memories on plantations. Their ancestors, survivors of second slavery, were enslaved workers entrapped in one of the nineteenth century's most brutal amalgamations of climate, capital, and horrific violence. Bechet remembered that the music of his allegorical grandfather, the maroon Omar, was an escape vector with which he and his community could "forget all about the fields" by "work[ing] the music to the beginning and then start it all over again . . . a new beginning that could begin *them* [plantation workers] over again."[83] But music also spoke to a way of remembering, remembering a mode of ecosocial production more ancient than the empire of cane stalk that surrounded them. The Black Atlantic farmers and gardeners knew what nineteenth-century European observers would take several additional decades to fully grasp. It was in 1867 when Karl Marx observed how capitalistic production "disturbs the metabolic interaction between man and the earth, i.e., it prevents the return to the soil of its constituent elements consumed by man in the form of food and clothing," leading him to conclude that "all progress in capitalist agriculture is a progress in the art, not only of robbing the worker, but of robbing the soil."[84] But while nineteenth-century philosophers and scientists perceived the contours of this crisis, it was the gardeners of the Black Atlantic who put into practice a viable alternative.[85] Their ecosocial practice reverberated within the communitarian, dialogical sonic ethos of brassroots democracy. Time, instead of a barometer of human sacrifice needed to produce sugarcane, became in the hands of counter-plantation musicians a relation of pleasure and solidarity.

LOUISIANNA SUGAR PRODUCTION 1859, BY PARISHES *Crop in Hogsheads*
● OVER 15,000   ● 10,000–15,000   ● 5,000–10,000   ● UNDER 5,000

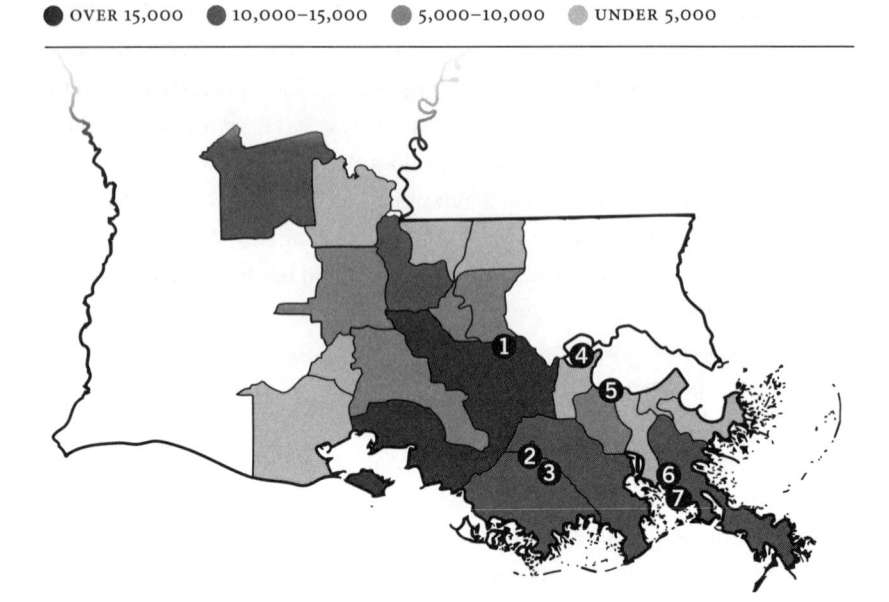

EARLY JAZZ MUSICIANS BORN ON SUGAR PLANTATIONS
OR IN SUGAR DISTRICTS

❶ Pops Foster
McCall Plantation

❷ John Robichaux
Joe Gabriel
Albert Jiles Sr.
Albert Jiles Jr.
Neddy James
Isaiah "Big Ike" Robinson
Near or in Thibodaux

❸ Sonny Henry
Harrison Barnes
Sam Morgan
Isaiah Morgan
Magnolia Plantation

❹ Kid Ory
Woodlawn Plantation

❺ Thomas "Mutt" Carey
Jack Carey
Near Hahnville

❻ Jim Robinson
Chris Kelly
Deer Range Plantation

❼ William Bebé Ridgley
Plantation in Jefferson

FIGURE 4.0 The birthplace of several early jazz musicians, juxtaposed with Louisiana sugar production at the outset of the Civil War by parishes. For these sugar production statistics, see Sitterson, *Sugar Country*, 48.

MAPPING GARDEN VALUES ONTO MUSIC: WORK SONG AS A STRUGGLE OVER TIME

> That little gal was borned rich and free.
> She's the sap from out a sugar tree;
> But you are as sweet to me;
> My little colored chile.
> *Katie Sutton*[86]

The consumption of soil health and human bodies powered the plantation. Yet within these large labor camps, the enslaved created prolific gardening spaces where new futures were imagined, born, and regrown—where, perhaps most visibly, Black farmers were able to create alternatives to the plantation's geometry of production through repurposing African and Indigenous knowledge systems. Walking through the "negro village" on Westmoreland estate, Jamaica, in 1816, Matthew Lewis commented that the divisions between home, garden, and individuals' possessions was blurred by a botanical abundance: "The whole village is intersected by lands, bordered with all kinds of sweet-smelling and flowering plants."[87] Philip Henry Gosse marveled at the litany of trees in the enslaved's gardens—papaw, coconut, shaddock, lime, star apple, mango, breadfruit—and an undergrowth that included "the lively tender green of the Plantains and bananas planted in regular avenues, the light tracery of Yams, the Chochos, the Melons and Gourds, the numerous sorts of Peas, and other climbers, among which several species of Passion-flower throw their elegant foliage . . . these are the originary, might I saw universal, features of a Jamaican Negro-garden."[88]

Part of their beauty lay in their disruption of the planation's quadral geometry. The plantation was marked by straight, neatly ordered lines demarcating monocultural grids; in contrast, noted the attorney James Simpson in 1832, it was "impossible" to "make any survey of the land by the negroes, and they generally cultivate it in a straggling way."[89] These "straggling" landscapes were both fiscally and spatially illegible to Euro-American planters, and they did not conform to its gardening ideal. In 1844, the influential landscape architect Andrew Jackson Downing asserted that "the mind can only attend . . . to one object, or one composite sensation, at the same time," and therefore concluded that "there is something unpleasing in the introduction of fruit trees among elegant ornamental trees."[90] Yet mixtures of fruit trees and ornamental trees, not to mention dozens of other plant species, were exactly what was present in the "negro gardens" that Matthew Lewis encountered. This intercropped sublime was an important manifestation of the "social, linguistic, epistemological, and psychological labor" enslaved and maroon gardeners performed to execute their vision of social and ecosocial harmony.[91]

Such practices are broadly resonant with other nineteenth-century Afro-Atlantic communitarian activities. The Senegambian practice that Robert Thompson refers to as "randomizing the flow of paths" is presented as a means to slow the movement of evil.[92] This belief that evil travels in straight lines catalyzed an African American response in the form of superstitions, especially manifest, according to Jacqueline L. Tobin and Raymond G. Dobard, in "quilts, their decoration, their construction techniques, and their final placement on actual graves [that] all reflect the concern of keeping unwanted evil and/or spirits away."[93] In contrast, straight lines were the preferred shape of plantations, the landscape design in which cane made its world-altering weight felt. "The best [way to plant]," explained British planter Richard Ligon, "is by digging a small trench of six inches broad, and as much deep, in a straight line, the whole length of the land you mean to plant . . . and so continue them the whole length of the trench, to the land's end."[94] Thompson argues that the irregularities of Afro-Atlantic geometries indicate "resistance to the closures of the Western technocratic way," and it is difficult to imagine a more dramatic enclosure than plantations.[95] The straight lines of plantation boundaries and endless fields of upright cane, stood as geoengineered monuments to Afrodiasporic commodification. The uncanny uniformity that marked their environs was not lost on their enslaved workforce.

Black gardens were built on principles of ecological design, and their nonlinear geometries expressed an epistemological grammar with powerful resonance in the musical aesthetics of the Black Atlantic. The "impossible" incongruity of intercropping was correlative to the endemic hemiolas within Afro-Caribbean music, which thrives on the experience of multiple time signatures weaving in and out of perception.[96]

Yet rhythmic intercropping is only the entry point to what is, in fact, a multifaceted and extensive dialectic between Black land practice and music making. Here it bears emphasizing that, across the plantation Caribbean, music and sound were used to coordinate the production of communal foodstuffs and resistance to monoculture. For instance, in Jamaica, the conch shell signaled to enslaved people when their shift growing sugar was done and the time to work their self-managed provision grounds, or what they called the "shellblow grounds," had begun.[97] Conch shells were accompanied by song and social commentary and could be heard not only at the provision grounds but also where the crops grown there were traded or sold. "At the out-ports, the conche-shell [*sic*] and negro song are heard for miles up the stream," explained one British military officer.[98] When

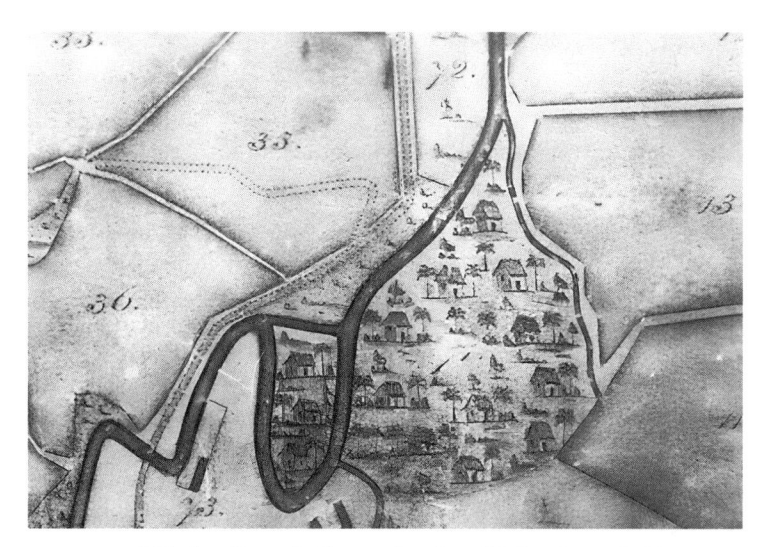

FIGURE 4.1 A Black or "negro" village in the plan of Esther Estate, St. Mary, 1818, by Stevenson and Smith. Its lack of demarcations, and its proliferation of coconut trees, stand in stark contrast to the straight lines of the plantation monocultures surrounding it. Courtesy of the National Library of Jamaica, also in Higman, *Jamaica Surveyed*, xii.

sugar plantations were burnt *en masse* in the winter of 1831–32 near Montego Bay, planters were terrified at the sudden effectiveness of these conch shells—not to announce their scheduled shifts but to coordinate collective arson of biblical proportions. "The conch shell was heard to blow in every quarter, accompanied by huzzahs and shouts from the infatuated slaves," reported a traumatized witness, while another observed how "whole fields, each perhaps contained twenty, thirty, forty acres or upwards were thus ignited," and "the sky became a sheet of flame, as if the whole country had become a vast furnace."[99] The aurality of the conch shell announcement, tied to the provision grounds, could just as swiftly encode the intent to burn to ash the sugar fields. This resonant body martialed collective resistance in the largest slave revolt in Jamaican history.

The conch shell is but one piece of sonic culture that commented upon and challenged the hegemony of sugar and monoculture writ large. As in Jamaica and Haiti, Louisianan Black culture identified sugar as a source of Black exploitation and overwork, as documented in the following song:

Old debble, Lousy Anna [Louisiana]
Dar scarecrow for poor n—r
Where de sugar-cane grow to pine-tree
And de pine-tree turn to sugar.[100]

Sugarcane was responsible for the destruction of the great pine forests as well as turning Black workers into "scarecrows"—practical automatons who resembled the living dead due to the brutal working conditions involved in harvesting the crop. The antebellum Afro-Creole song "Dialogue D'Amour" similarly identified sugar as a subject for scorn and envisioned its destruction in flames through the imagined perspective of a plantation owner: "Toutes mes cann' sont brulées, Et je suit ruiné" (All my cane is burned, and I am ruined).[101] Mocking the enslaver as his designs on the land are foiled by a rebellious workforce, this song reminded enslaved communities that there was nothing natural or inevitable about King Sugar. The dissent sung by the enslaved developed an analytic framework to understand sugar: destructive to all life forms that had the misfortune of coming into contact with its monocultures, while ultimately an ephemeral source of power of panicked planters that could be reversed with the lighting of a single spark.

In addition to signaling their rejection of planation monocultures, work songs interacted with plantation temporalities and social space in nuanced ways. Songs overheard by a planter in Saint-Domingue during plantation labor would be "improvised on the spot" and "mixed in jokes, and all the line broke out laughing without stopping work," often at the expense of abusive masters.[102] A work song echoing through eighteenth-century Barbados not only denounced a "bad master" but also melded English and French syllables, evidencing Édouard Glissant's reading of plantations as realms of both social obliteration and creolization. In these places, the workforce, silenced in the body politic of the slave society, could nonetheless birth new social and cultural epistemes through the expressive power of musical rhapsody.[103] These vocalized analyses, oscillating between quotidian and macrostructural themes, synergized with rhythm coordination to influence labor dynamics, often resulting in a deliberate deceleration of work processes. One planter banned "drawling tunes" on his plantation because "their motions are almost certain to keep time with the music."[104] One African American Texan performing prison labor explained that singing "kept a man from being singled out for whipping because he worked too slowly," and that songs were selected because "you can either slow it up or make it fast . . . When you're working and the Convicts get tired and they say 'Come on, you all, let's rock a while,' and they get together [by slowing down the beat] . . . that's the way they fool the boss."[105] Labor solidarity was mediated through sound and could provide protection from abusive overseers who punished slowdowns or individual expressions of weariness. These gestures of a musically mediated social relation were also attacks on the plantation machine writ large, reducing plantation productivity by altering the collective pace of work by rhythm in song.

Some songs explicitly announced their intention to decelerate the pace of work. One song heard in Pee Dee County, South Carolina, told this story:

Sheep and the goats
Going to the pasture:
Sheep say to goats,
"Can't you walk a little faster?"
Goat say to sheep,
"I have a sore toe"—
"Excuse me goat, I did not know."[106]

The allusion to "sheep" is a compelling metaphor for those who remained unaware of the collective action to slow down the rhythm of labor and deprive plantation owners of product. Work songs could speed up work, too, when it served the needs of the singers. Enslaved women cotton spinners on George Johnson's plantation in Virginia used song to accelerate so they make their quota and avoid threading by night: "Keep yo' eye on de sun, See how she run, Don't let her catch you with your work undone." As the son of one of these spinners, Bob Ellis, explained, this song "made the women all speed up so they could finish before [the] dark catch 'em, 'cause it mighty hard handlin' that cotton thread by fire-light."[107]

Whether by speeding up or slowing down, Black work songs made it clear that while planters held a monopoly on violence, their rule over time was contested. Devonya Natasha Havis writes that the work song should be considered "a vernacular critique of expenditure for a 'monstrous Other' [that] altered time and the different time altered Work . . . the 'work song' transforms time and launches a critique of work as labor."[108] Shona Jackson, similarly, has argued that the struggle between forms of labor involves a metaphysical distinction between "Pre-Columbian time" and "time as progress." Progress meant death and decimation for the enslaved workers who generated "advances" for planters.[109] Notably, enslaved people referred to the time cycles of crops that nourished their bodies, rather than those that consumed them, to establish an ecoharmonic time flow. "Good peach time" and "in watermelon time" were how formerly enslaved Wallace Turner and Moses Fletcher described the dates of significant events.[110] Indeed, songs and rituals that honored watermelon harvests marked important autonomous festivities within Black plantation life. "Frequently, in the height of the watermelon season," notes Arthur Anison Winfield Jr., "permission would be granted the slaves to have a grand feast to which the slaves for miles around were invited. Much singing and dancing went on at these feasts."[111] While planters organized elaborate events to celebrate the sugar and cotton harvest, the alternate harvest festivals of enslaved peoples highlighted their own foodways in distinction to the commodity-ways of the abusive planter class, a cultural terrain by which the counter-plantation challenged the symbolic hegemony of the planation.[112] These cultures directly animated the practice of brassroots democracy, as New Orleans jazz bands were often hired to play at "watermelon parties."[113] Watermelons were subject to vicious and racist caricature in the postbellum era precisely because they symbolized Black independence and an alternative temporality to the cultures of cotton, sugar, and rice. As William Black notes, the watermelon was "a symbol of black freedom, as African Americans used the fruit to both celebrate and enact their emancipation."[114]

Watermelon, domesticated in continental Africa four to five thousand years ago, is an excellent example of a counter-plantation cultivar, and a brief description of its planting techniques in the United States South is one means by which we can appreciate the nuanced interaction between land practice and Black culture.[115] Unlike rice, watermelon cultivation was not an export crop for enslavers, and less is known about how African Americans planted the crop in the antebellum period. But as a crop widely grown by smallholder farmers in West and Northwest Africa during the transatlantic slave trade, it is noteworthy that intercropping is an important part of its cultivation among contemporary smallholder African farmers. Indigenous farmers in Mali's Tombouctou region sow watermelon with beans in order to fertilize the watermelon with beans' microbial nitrogen.[116] In other regions, watermelon is also intercropped with maize or millet by planting watermelon and cereal seeds in the same hole, which allows its vines to protect the cereal seeds from weeds.[117] Watermelons are drought-tolerant crops that could not be transported long distances before modern refrigeration and so were inherently uncommodifiable in the nineteenth century. The crop's abundance in the garden plots of Black plantation workers, and the festivals that honored the nourishment it provided, is but one example of the interrelationship between Afro-Atlantic agroecology with symbolic culture and musical temporalities. In the Haitian festival of Manje Yam, yams are harvested from the soil while a percussion ensemble performs; later, the soil is adorned in banana leaves, which return nitrogen to the soil and represent the passage of the lwas' sacred boat to the city of Ifẹ.[118] Across the diaspora, from Ghana to Curaçao the millet harvest festival is a time of celebration. In Curaçao in particular, a society of communal labor, the *seú*, orchestrates the millet's harvest to the beat of drums, cow horns, and the *agan*—a plow repurposed as a musical instrument. After the harvest, a second festivity known as *seú sera* takes place, whose dance, the *wapa*, imitates the motions associated with planting and harvesting.[119] Enslaved African and African-descended farmers challenged slavery's metabolic rift with inspired agrobotanical technologies and techniques of congregating, reinforcing the ecoharmonic temporalities activated in their collective music-making practices.

Music embodied and reproduced this contest between contradictory imperatives, between the quest for planter profit versus the production of autonomous life, and the feeling of time and the meaning of sound itself were two modes in which coordinated musical activity intervened. Work song resounded an alternative conception of time that could not be reduced to a singular ontology, and was mobilized in the ongoing, concrete struggle over work rhythms and the priorities of production.[120] In a parallel manner, the spatiality of the plantation was contested through the mediums of sound and dance. Elizabeth Ross Hite, enslaved in Louisiana's sugar parishes, remembered she and others repossessed the sugar mill after the master went to sleep. "The slaves had balls in the sugar house. They would start late and was way out in the field where the master could not hear them. Not a bit of noise could be heard." As to not alert the planters, these revelers danced by low candlelight, and by the next day they had to hide any post-dance weariness or a "whipping would follow." In these spaces, the values of the counter-plantation become articulated to resocialize the antisocial world of the planation. The site of mutilation and overwork became a fleeting space of renewal where "the slave had some fine times" doing "the buck dance and the shimme" and "shake[ing] their skirts."[121] These mid-nineteenth-century performances of the shimmy—a dance whose horizontal torso movements became synonymous with the jazz age and scandalized conservative commentators in the 1920s—are thought by some commentators to have been influenced by the fusion of cultures resulting from Afro-Louisianan and Haitian creolization in the sugar plantations.[122] Haitian-influenced dance was commented upon in other regions as well. On Georgia's rice coast, white observers documented a nineteenth-century dance called "the sioca," which they described as "a voluptuous dance imported from San Domingo [Haiti]."[123] Much like the polycropping techniques employed by Black farmers today, Elizabeth's dancing of the shimmy shows how the countercultural forms developed by the enslaved in plantation spaces would prefigure African American culture for the next century.[124] "For three centuries of constraint had borne down so hard that, when this speech took root, it sprouted in the very midst of the field of modernity; that is, it grew for everyone," explains Glissant on plantation aesthetic innovation. "This is the only sort of universality there is: when, from a specific enclosure, the deepest voice cries out."[125] Glissant's metaphors of "sprouting" and "taking root" point to an understanding of creolization as a land practice.

Elizabeth Hite's kinesthetic alchemy went beyond remapping the plantation. Her movements pointed to how the recuperation of bodies through dance was a strategic necessity to both live and resist. As Fred Moten asks: "What's the revolutionary force of the sensuality that emerges from the sonic event . . . ? To ask this is to think what's at stake in the music: the universalization or socialization of the surplus, the generative force of a venerable phonic propulsion, the ontological and historical priority of resistance to power and objection to subjection, the old-new thing, the freedom drive that animates black performances."[126] In light of Hite's possible creolizing of Haitian dance movements, we might consider a Haitian expression, "Vous signé *nom* moi, mais bous pas signé *pieds* moi" (You signed my *name*, but you haven't signed my *feet*), to explore the connection between a maroon conception of freedom and dance as an embodied resistance where sensuality and self-determination are conjoined in a politics of bodily and ecological renewal. Haitians' rejection of a "signed" name critiqued legible formations of property ownership in enslaved people (or, in some eras of postindependence Haiti, in rural permits to travel).[127] "Feet" thus might mean escape or it might mean the "historic materiality" of soil and the body, what Mimi Sheller formulates as "erotic agency."[128] But more literally, it refers to dancing, like the dancing in a parade or rara, movement in defiance of slavery and racialized policing.

As in Louisiana, then, Caribbean sacred and secular dance forms often use the lower body—the "winding of the hips, the shaking of the bottom, or the stomping of the feet" that activates a different physicality than ballet, which emphasizes "high" movements.[129] These dialectics between the body, the Earth, and the social movement are reflected in the song of at least one Haitian-descended early jazz musician.[130] Pianist Jelly Roll Morton's "Black Bottom Stomp" is based on the dance called the "Black Bottom," the name given to both a neighborhood in Detroit and the rich alluvial lands found in the heart of the Black Belt, where large numbers of enslaved peoples and their free descendants lived and worked the land. Morton transliterated the dance rhythm to form the foundation of his piece. The song summons an ecosocial space associated with self-sufficiency during emancipation, and the dance that commemorated it was a bridge between soil and soul. Douglas Henry Daniels argues that

> Morton kept alive the dance traditions associated with Haitian and West African dance traditions . . . [by] drumming with their feet, [they were] turning the dance floors (or the earth, when in rural areas) into a giant drum that resounded with the sound of shoes or bare feet. Moreover, this was a way of communicating with the ancestors who are generally associated with the soil

and the ground, of letting them know that they were still perpetuating the traditions so close to the heart of African religion and spirituality.[131]

Other African American jazz musicians composed "stomps," such as Mary Lou Williams's "Messa Stomp," Hot Lips Page's "Good for Stompin,'" and the standard "Stompin' at the Savoy," named after the Harlem club.[132]

"Stompin'" and striking the ground were part of a repertoire of eco-musical activity associated with the decidedly nonanthropocentric spirituality of Haitian migrants. In Santiago de Cuba, another destination for Saint-Domingue enslaved and free people of color during the revolutionary period, the farmer Dalia Timitoc Borrero remembered a Haitian spiritual leader named Santiago Fiz on a coffee farm she grew up on in the 1930s. Fiz sang songs from "the war of the Haitians against the French" and "while he sang . . . beat the ground with a stick like they did in Haiti[,] calling to his ancestors."[133] The Haitian art music composer Werner Jaegerhuber points to a similar motion when he claimed as his inspiration "the Negro with hands injured by work and disdain [who] strikes the earth intent on thus entering in contact with the gods, and from there drawing solace."[134] Here, the Earth was a conduit for healing, whose contact, perhaps, might begin to repair the damage done by compulsory labor on monocrop plantations. These repeated stomps, across islands and generations, reproduced the embodied knowledge and its attendant genres, in which divisions of two and three were part of a greater one.

"Unsigned" or "unbounded" feet were thus an aesthetic practice that foregrounded a connection to the Earth commons as the basis for community and mutual recognition. This embodied knowledge in dance movement was linked to new forms of social organization and emancipatory ideologies in the nineteenth-century Americas.[135] Across the Caribbean and Gulf worlds, enslaved people and maroons developed new vernacular dance languages at the same time that a revitalized counter-plantation common sense cohered. Accounts from varied sources show that distant communities increasingly registered their indignation with the positivistic and rational worldview that justified the extraction of value from their body and the earth. For example, despite being combatants in hiding, the fugitive maroons of El Potrero in Veracruz wrote to the Spanish Crown in 1805. While demanding their freedom, they apologized sardonically for the informality of the parchment used. "We don't use stamped paper for we are runaways," they wrote, "but may it be known that this paper values as if it was stamped, and may our master pay later for the seal, for we have granted him multitude of *pesos* [sic] through our labor."[136] Much like Haitian farmers' rejection of a "signed name," here formerly enslaved people declared that their uncompensated labor, which had fueled the operations of the Spanish Empire in New Spain since its colonization, granted their letter a legitimacy that superseded the symbolism attached to royal communications.

Black planation workers in the United States South in the post–Civil War couched their claims to the land in a similar theory of value. The Georgia minster Bayley Wyatt gave the following sermon to his parishioners in 1867: "Our wives, our children, our husbands has been sold over and over again to purchase the lands we now locate upon; for that reason, we have a divine right to the land." Pointing out how the "large cities in the North ... grow up on the cotton and the sugars and the rice that we made," Wyatt argues that both the plantation South and the urbanized North had been powered by extracted labor and financial value produced by Black bodies; and this ill-got wealth could only be repatriated through the restitution of land.[137] Samuel Childress, a Tennessee freedman, called for land distribution on the same principle. "Our race has tilled this land for ages; whatever wealth has been accumulated South has been acquired mainly by our labor.—The profits of it, have gone to increase the pride and wickedness of our old masters."[138] Radical Creoles of color in Louisiana, in ongoing dialogue with Haitian artists and political movements throughout the nineteenth century, felt similarly.[139] They wrote in the *New Orleans Tribune* in 1864 that "no true republican government" could exist "unless the land and wealth in general, are distributed among the great mass of the inhabitants. . . . No more room [exists] in our society for an oligarchy of slaveholders or property holders."[140]

Nonbinary rhythms in movement, embodied knowledge that connected the healing powers of the Earth to the human body, and the rejection of private property created by slave labor—these interdisciplinary ephemera united a counter-plantation diaspora. The African-descended peoples of the plantation Americas imagined and experimented with new social relations and cooperative cultural mechanisms even as flight, revolution, and war made them populations on the move. Increasingly active during the age of the Haitian Revolution, "mobile commoning" drew upon deep forms of experience living outside binary structures of property and ownership.[141] The Martinique-born economist Malcom Ferdinand explains that these commoning practices created "*the first modern anticolonial and antislavery utopias* by demonstrating this striking fact: it is through care and love for Mother-Earth that it is possible to rediscover one's body, explore one's humanity, and emancipate oneself from the Plantationocene and its slaveries."[142] In the case of the maroons in Louisiana's Cyprus swamplands, among the inhabitants of the Great Dismal Swamp of Virginia, and as evidenced by Veracruz's free Black communities fluent in Nahuatl, these mobilities allowed for alliances with Indigenous communities, adding new dimensions to the relational connection to the land and the other.¹⁴³ The sophisticated resource-sharing mechanisms produced within these clandestine Afro-Indigenous agroecologies remind us that commoning is a practice focused on the production of autonomous life against the ecocidal, genocidal, and matricidal machinery of plantation capitalism.¹⁴⁴ The crucial role played by women of the African diaspora in sustaining maroon ecologies of the Afro-Atlantic—whether through orchestrating autonomous markets, curing the sick as herbal medicine practitioners, or coordinating the planting and cultivation of nonexport crops—is central to these new social relations that prefigured a world beyond plantation capitalism and its regimes of capital accumulation through patriarchal ecocide.¹⁴⁵

Early twentieth-century New Orleans jazz musicians were intimately connected to the maroon genesis of mobile commoning, from Sidney Bechet's surrealist writings on the maroon communities of his allegorical grandfather, to the lives of Lorenzo and Louis Tio, who were born in a commune in Veracruz founded by refugee Afro-Creoles who fled Louisiana in 1859.¹⁴⁶ The symbolism of Afro-Indigenous maroon alliance is vividly reproduced in the dancing traditions of the diaspora. In Haiti's coastal commune of Léogâne, rara season is called an "Indian festival" whose processions are, according to McAlister, "fleeting yearly remembrance of the 250,000 Taínos who died in the first few years after Columbus' fateful 1492 arrival in Haiti."¹⁴⁷ Even Haiti's naming in 1804 was an anti-colonial gesture that honored the original Taíno inhabitants of the land, and the solidarity they showed to escaped Africans, by adopting the Taíno name for the island.¹⁴⁸ Mardi Gras Indians likewise honor the rich history of Afro-Indigenous maroon communities, which were so disruptive in the eighteenth century that the French colonial government commissioned a special task force to repress a much-feared "Red and Black" alliance.¹⁴⁹ New Orleans's Black brass bands reproduced the praxis of these mobile commons, as much for their support of the Black cooperative institutions with which they were connected (labor unions, orphanages, schools, and fraternal societies) as in their production of new relational forms of hearing and sounding that embedded soulful, intersubjective phenomenology as a corollary to radically participatory democracy.¹⁵⁰ From provision grounds to sugarhouses, plantation geographies were repurposed by enslaved plantation laborers to sow new phenomenologies that could cohere a body and soul under constant assault.

Colonial governments, perceptive of the expressive power of these forms and their potential threat to plantation production, moved to silence them with a series of restrictive laws.¹⁵¹ Plantation states used sound control as a strategy to limit insurgency—for instance, in 1837 Louisiana, the city council only permitted "free negroes and slaves to host dances at the Circus Square from midday till dusk [solely] under police supervision," a duration later curtailed to merely two and a half hours in 1845 and further confined from May to August.[152] These provisions evolved in tandem with expanded sugar production, reflecting planter anxieties that music and dance could incite a sequel to the Haitian Revolution in Louisiana.[153]

Yet not all plantation owners prohibited Black music. Many required it, with the threat of the lash for those who did not comply. Frederick Douglass even remembered that enslaved people were compelled to sing while they worked: "A silent slave is not liked by masters or overseers."[154] One South Carolina planter who had been having trouble with productivity and discipline supplied the enslaved with fiddles and drums and "promoted dancing."[155] Something structural was at play: enslavers depended on Black music to sustain the social order of the plantation as much as enslaved workers reinvented it to cultivate a resistant culture. Planters, in essence, found themselves in an awkward dependency on Black creativity for their cash crops to be harvested. Perceptive of its ability to interact with the work processes, planters attempted to channel the music's power toward their own ends.

For enslavers, Black music evoked an affective resonance as well. Just as enslavers were consumers of the diverse crops grown in the "negro gardens" (and without which they would have suffered malnutrition or starved), they were dependent on the music of their enslaved workers for entertainment and emotional connection.[156] "So strangely they vary their time, as 'tis a pleasure to the most curious ears" remembered one Barbados enslaver.[157] In Philadelphia, a white planter exile who had fled the Haitian Revolution fantasized years later that he might return to his plantation in Abricots and listen to the enslaved's "tambourines and bamboulas."[158] That this memory, in particular, resonated so many years later suggests the ambiguities and paradoxes of slave society. One anonymous planter in the US South wrote: "I allow dancing, ay, I buy a fiddle and encourage it, by giving the boys the occasional supper."[159] One Colonel Buckingham enjoyed the "tolerable musicians" among the enslaved on his plantation, who "having formed a band, played occasionally in the summer evening in the lawn before the hall, for the amusement of the family."[160] Plantations required music simply to function: it was impossible to coordinate the backbreaking, endless, highly synchronized work without it. But planters were emotionally dependent on Black music for the same reason they were dependent on Black gardens: enslaved workers were the only people on the plantation committed to social reproduction and responsible communal stewardship. Their music reflected these social bonds that the planter would not—or could not—produce.

DESTROYING SERFDOM IN THE LAND:
AFRO-LOUISIANAN COMMONING

> "Agroecology is political; it requires us to challenge and transform structures of power in society. We need to put the control of seeds, biodiversity, land and territories, waters, knowledge, culture and the commons in the hands of the peoples who feed the world."
>
> La Via Campesina, "Seed Laws That Criminalise Farmers"

In 1865 at Fort Smith, Arkansas, a Union General was approached unexpectedly by a freedman. The latter skipped the pleasantries and got right to the point: "I want some land," he asserted. "You do nothing for me but give me my freedom." The general was taken aback: was emancipation not something to be grateful for? Is freedom not enough? "It is enough for the present," responded the man. "But I cannot help myself unless I get some land; then I can take care of myself and my family; otherwise I cannot do it."[161] This interaction was emblematic of a conflict that would roil the South for decades to come: many thousands of freedpeople measured their freedom not only or primarily in the framework of the liberal democratic tradition—of the right to vote—but by access to land. Wary of being converted into a wage-earning agrarian proletariat, they asserted that without direct control over the natural assets and production tools embodied by land, liberation could be empty and meaningless.[162] Nor did they consider this liberation an individual journey—it was conceptualized as communal in scope, and mutual aid societies self-organized by freedpeople embodied this cooperative ideal.[163]

Nowhere were such cooperatives more apparent, and more illegible to plantation capitalism, than in the agroecologies Black freedpeople sowed in the soil.[164] One Union general in Harper's Ferry, who derided free African Americans as "lazy" for not picking cotton, was struck by their "corn-fields [that] rejoiced in gigantic stalks."[165] A song by the Wisconsin Commandery in Georgia captured this ecological transformation: "How the sweet potatoes even started from the ground, While we were marching through Georgia!"[166] The transformation of the ecological geography of the South was undeniable, even and especially when freedpeople had no legal title to the land they transformed.

In Louisiana, these projects were realized vigorously. Much to the chagrin of both conquered Confederates and Union military leadership, by 1864 Louisiana produced only 5,400 tons of sugar—a 98 percent decline from its 1861 yield—as Black Louisianans effectively executed a general strike of the sucrose industry while expanding their independent production into commune-scaled endeavors.[167] As with Afro-Caribbean maroon ecologies from Jamaica to Haiti, communal music-making powerfully intertwined with new forms of cooperative economics. Decades later, for instance, music instructor James Humphrey was paid by his rural African American students in sweet potatoes. These maroon ecologies and the diets they enabled were enactments of emancipation. "Munching the yam," wrote Ralph Ellison in his 1952 novel *Invisible Man*, "[I became] suddenly overcome by an intense feeling of freedom," endowing Ellison's narrator with a self-knowledge that helped him resist the "crummy lie they [white Americans] kept us dominated by."[168] Ellison's words reinforce that emancipation was not only political and economic: it was a cultural and phenomenological experience—it had a taste, a taste that could only be produced from these intercropped ecologies that constituted freedom.

By collectively producing intercropped foodstuffs in the work camps where they had been enslaved, Black Louisianans initiated a revolution both social and ecological. The records of military officials of the Freedmen's Bureau, set up to supervise the transition to wage labor, detail the scope of these efforts. In January 1865, a community of freedmen requested of the Freedmen's Bureau "the opportunity of working the Place among ourselves," and their request was granted. But freedmen did not want to grow what they called "slave crops," such as cotton and sugar. According to one military observer, this was a political decision: these crops, in the eyes of the enslaved, "had enriched the masters, but had not fed them."[169] An African American work song of the era captured this sentiment: "N——s pick the cotton, n——s pick it out, white man pockets money, n—— goes without."[170] Southern cotton picking saw increases in productivity throughout the nineteenth century without any technological innovations, except the instruments and techniques with which to torture Black enslaved laborers. Their increased efficiency was so dramatic that the price of cotton declined by 85 percent between 1790 and 1860, despite its demand quintupling in the same time period. "Thus torture," writes Edward Baptist, "compelled and then exposed left-handed [creative] capacities, subordinated them to the power of the enslaver, [and] turned them against [enslaved] people themselves. And thus untold amounts of mental labor, unknown breakthroughs of human creativity, were the keys to an astonishing increase in cotton production that required no machinery—save the whipping-machine, of course. With it, enslavers looted the riches of black folk's minds, stole days and months and years and lifetimes, turned sweat, blood, and flesh into gold."[171]

This stealing of Black minds and souls in service of commodity production powered the Industrial Revolution, and portends to another extraction equally profound as the material degradation of bodies. As Gil Scott-Heron poised in song a century later: "And what about Mississippi, The boundary of old? Tell me,

Who'll pay reparations on my soul?"[172] The accounts of the formerly enslaved in both song and written testimony, announcing their rejection of cotton and sugar in favor of ecological intercropping, pointed to one practice of renewal: they would recuperate soul and soil on their own terms, through ecologies of their own making. Their crop choices were not only a matter of survival but a means to de-weaponize Black ingenuity and creativity that had been instrumentalized by enslavers.

Predictably, Louisianan freedpeoples' quest to reclaim their bodies, their social relations, and the crops they grew was met with planter antagonism. One planter in Bayou Black complained that "much trouble has resulted" from Black agricultural self-sufficiency, as he could not discipline hands to work his plantation.[173] Some conservative Freedmen's Bureau agents were committed to "breaking up . . . colonies of squatters." More radical officers marveled at their success. The example of these counter-plantation endeavors impressed upon one agent that only the "small farms" of freedmen could "destroy the serfdom of capital."[174]

Although African American land tenure practice varied during the Civil War and its aftermath, cooperative social arrangements appear to have been very present in Louisiana. One Freedmen's Bureau agent noted, "A crop had been planted by the people on the place, in which all were to share."[175] In New Orleans, inspired by the efforts of freedmen, the Creole of color editors of the *Tribune* declared: "Slavery is dead, but 'free labor' lives, and 'free labor" is to be killed."[176] The cooperative ethos was advocated by African American activists across the United States, including Martin R. Delany, then a Freedmen's Bureau agent. Considered a leading proponent of Black emigration to Liberia, in this decade he advocated instead for a Black land commons in the South: "Get up a community and get all the lands you can—if you cannot get any singly."[177] Meanwhile, in Austin, Texas, the *Free Man's Press* explained in 1868 that "[a] good way" to become independent "is to club together and buy a piece of land and divide it up into lots."[178]

Without systematic records of Louisiana's Black communes, it is difficult to know how many were created. But based on letters sent between Freedmen's Bureau officials, in just three parishes—Plaquemines, St. Charles, and Lafourche—there were at least nineteen in operation in 1865, and the largest had seven hundred fifty acres in cultivation, with over half dedicated to food production.[179] One Union official touring Lafourche reported "corn planted on all of these plantations which is claimed by the negroes . . . they stored it in warehouses attached to their cabins."[180] If these communes had been allowed to take fruit, the history of the South, and the United States, would have been dramatically different. But Northern liberals were obsessed with maintaining the sanctity of private property and capitalist social relations and resisted any redistribution of planter land. A *New York Times* editorialist wrote in 1867: "It is a question, not of humanity, not of loyalty, but of the fundamental relation of industry to capital: and sooner or later, if begun at the South, it will find its way into the cities of the North. . . . An attempt to justify the confiscation of Southern land under the pretense of doing justice to the freedmen, strikes at the root of all property rights in both sections. It concerns Massachusetts quite as much as Mississippi."[181] Northern elites, confronting a powerful proto-socialist movement in their own states, were fearful that land reform in the South would spark a social revolution in the North. They were also heavily invested in sugar plantations.[182]

Emboldened by these discourses in the North and milquetoast congressional commitment to Black land ownership, planters like the Louisiana governor Warmoth attacked Afro-Creole and Black activists struggling for land reform as "follow[ing] Hayti," and fought in Louisiana's state legislature to prevent meaningful land reform.[183] With the power of the state on the planters' side, cooperatives gave way to private property as freedmen were forced to either work again as hands on sugar plantations or migrate elsewhere.[184] These dynamics led to ongoing inequalities that informed the development of racial capitalism for the next century. Between 1880 and 1910, the rate of property ownership for Black people in the Southern states lagged significantly behind that of whites. By 1910, less than a quarter of Southern African Americans owned the land they toiled on.[185]

Their resistance did not end there, however. Even after the 1877 Compromise energized ex-Confederate paramilitaries as Union troops withdrew from the South, organized rural labor endured significantly longer in Louisiana's sugar districts than in cotton country—by some estimates, by more than a decade.[186] The unique conditions of sugar plantations partly explain the success of collective organizing strategies among Louisiana freedpeople relative to Black activists elsewhere. Unlike sharecropping arrangements in the cotton-picking districts, on sugar plantations, hundreds of freedpeople lived in direct proximity, creating opportunities for collective culture and resistance to flourish. Interviews with jazz musicians who grew up on these sugar plantations reveal that mutual aid societies were well established, and mass meetings were a frequent occurrence, often twinned with brass band marches and communal music-making.[187]

MUSICAL TRANSFIGURATION: BRASS BANDS AS ESCAPE AGRICULTURE

> The poem is not a mill for
> grinding sugar cane
> *Aimé Césaire*[188]

Trombonist Sonny Henry hated working in the cane fields. He grew up on the Magnolia plantation of two or three hundred. His school was on the plantation, as was the Baptist church he attended. Henry's family and others did not care for the name Magnolia and instead knew it as the "Governor Warmoth plantation." In this labor camp, the former governor may as well have had the power of a head of state. Warmoth, a Reconstruction politician who claimed to fight for Black equality but resisted calls for land redistribution, seemed indifferent to the reality that young men like Henry did not continue their school past the seventh grade. For that matter, he did not seem to mind assigning backbreaking work for eighty cents a day, work Henry described as "sun-up until sun-down."[189] Trombonist Harrison Barnes remembered the precision needed by the "first-class" workers, like himself, to prepare the endless rows for sugar planting by keeping rows level and straight, with little room for error. "You have the measuring stick and you put it down and you have sticks, you know, that make those rows straight." If one failed to execute this quadral schematic, one would be assigned to work a machine "all day," collecting and processing cane.[190] The work was so intense that during grinding season one of the few outlets of Black culture, dances, came to a halt.[191] Later in his life, now harvesting rice, Barnes remembered being forced to work through the rain and pools of water the soil had accumulated. It all reached a breaking point: "I told my mother, I say, 'I ain't going back there. I ain't going out there no more.'" He took a chance: with half of his savings, he bought a ticket to New Orleans to join other plantation migrants in the Crescent City's emerging Black brass band culture.[192]

How Barnes and Henry made it off the plantation is one of the ways that the denied autonomy in the fields could become realized in musical performance. Indeed, where Magnolia plantation lacked in health care, education, and meaningful economic mobility, it excelled in one area: brass band education. Twice a week, Warmoth hired an accomplished musician, James Humphrey, to teach a predominantly youth band of sixteen members how to play and march. The scenes described by his pupils are strikingly picturesque against the grim backdrop of these work camps. Attired in a swallowtail coat, Humphrey was met by adoring students at the local train station, who were eager to accompany him

FIGURE 4.2 The Woodland Band, ca 1905, Kid Ory's first band, in LaPlace, Louisiana. *Left to Right*: Edward Robinson, Kid Ory, Chif Matthews, Raymond Brown, Stonewall Matthews, Harry Forster. Courtesy of The William Russell Jazz Collection at The Historic New Orleans Collection, acquisition made possible by the Clarisse Claiborne Grima Fund, MSS 520.1527

to practice or, sometimes, to his quarters—he might have to spend the night if practice went late. Humphrey taught bands all across the sugar plantation belt, and by the time Henry started learning how to play at fifteen years old (the same age when his schooling ended), Humphrey had developed a system. "The first thing he would do, that battery—that's the first thing he would get straight first—that's the bass and the trombone and the drum," Henry described. Next, Humphrey would teach trumpets, then clarinets and the rest of the band. Often he would write out specific exercises and songs, on the fly, for his ensembles based on their musical needs or just what the moment called for. "I gone tell you," explained Henry, "the way he taught the boys, I think it was the right way."[193]

History would agree with Henry's assessment. Among New Orleans's sizable population of transplanted plantation players, finding an instrumentalist who was not taught by Humphrey is difficult. They were not only great players with a distinct sensibility in their time feel and tone, but they were also, crucially, able to read notated music, and thus able to join the elite Black parade bands of New Orleans. At times, Humphrey might be contracted to teach bands on five different plantations at the same time, each with sixteen or more musicians. At a time when literacy remained out of reach for most Black Americans, musicians such as Chris Kelly, William Bébé Ridgley, and Kid Ory developed a command of notated music systems and movement techniques through their studies with "the Professor." Humphrey not only taught musicians; he also accompanied them on marches through the plantation districts: "We used to go from place to place," explained Henry, such as "Woodland [plantation], and used to go to St. Sophie, and go to Deer Range, and other places." Some of these plantations were only accessible by boat, and bands would ride a ferry to make these trips—repurposing the mercantile geography by creating festive, cross-border events on the other side of the river.[194]

Why did Warmoth and other planters hire teachers like Professor Humphrey? The answer lies in an important weapon wielded by sugarhands: their strategic refusal to work. As early as February 1866, the West Baton Rouge *Sugar Planter* called attention to the plantations idle from lack of hands: "A substitute for negro labor must soon be procured."[195] In 1871, the Scottish journalist Robert Somers observed how in Louisiana's sugar country, "the great law of demand and supply in the matter of labour operates here under curious circumstances, the supply neither knowing what it is worth nor what it wants."[196] Somers refused to acknowledge what was plainly apparent to many Freedmen's Bureau officers during Reconstruction: this "supply" did not want to provide alienated labor at all, and especially not growing the slave crops. In 1877, for instance, Black labor leader Rayford Blunt urged rural workers to resist the "white aristocratic miscreants" with labor strikes and work stoppages, which provoked the white supremacist *People's Vindicator* to call for paramilitaries to "inaugurate a new system of agriculture by planting [lynching] Blunt."[197] Planters became especially angered when workers refused to sign annual contracts. According to one enraged observer in April 1869, Black laborers congregated "in and around the cities and towns, where they scarcely ever pretend to engage in regular labor; they talk politics and lead profligate and corrupt lives and subsist in the most wretched manner."[198] Black people's very presence as social and political beings, unengaged in capitalist labor, was seen as disorderly and even apocalyptic for the reconstructed planter class.

Plantation managers, short on labor, resolved not to improve schools, wages, or democratic rights for freedpeoples. As the Thibodaux Massacre of 1887— described in chapter 3—demonstrates, they often called upon paramilitary or state violence to enforce labor discipline when well-timed harvest-season strikes threatened the sugar economy. But many had a carrot that accompanied the stick. These planters hired brass band instructors from New Orleans to entice recalcitrant workers back to the fields—a reluctant acknowledgment, like the one made by their antebellum predecessors, that Afrodiasporic music was needed to ensure social reproduction within their antisocial plantation machine.

Arguing that the formation of the Black subject and its continual subjugation should be considered the nucleus of modernity, Fumi Okiji has written that "black subjectivity was encoded from the start with irresolvable contradictions," contradictions latent in its own artistry. "Black expression is never innocuous," she notes, "but rather both complicit in its own subjugation and a critical weapon against it."[199] Such an analysis resonates with the experiences of Black sugar workers and the musical institutions built to repress their demands for land reform and an ecological society. They helped maintain entire families—Sonny Henry had fourteen siblings on the plantation; Harrison Barnes had eight—locked into intergenerational relationships of semi-serfdom in which escape from servitude could require unimaginable risk. Yet these compensatory bands also reproduced the communitarian social relations that resisted the quadral, divisionary, extractive logics that reduced their bodies and the land around them into productive inputs and projected profit. Their proximity to other independent African American institutions, from garden beds to the Black churches and schools on plantations, help historicize the profound synergy between ethics and aesthetics that underlays brassroots democracy.

Many future New Orleans jazz musicians were born in the sugar districts, joining a musical culture embedded in solidarity and revolt. Music accompanied strikes, celebrations, and the ongoing production of foodstuffs. Workers lived close together, as during the antebellum period, and maintained gardens and orchards from which they could subsist. Pops Foster, born on the sugar plantation of an ex-Confederate, remembered: "There were three or four hundred shacks where the field hands lived about a mile from the house. . . . They had bitter-orange trees, big black fig trees, and pecan trees. Us kids could ask to go through the gate and get the fruit if we wanted, but we'd climb the fence and steal it. If we got caught, we got a good lickin.'"[200] These "three to four hundred" shacks paint the image of a company town, and not scattered, isolated farmhouses. In addition to providing a meaningful diet and opportunities for communal renewal, the gardens adjacent to cabins provided herbs and plants essential for medicinal healers, often women. Pumpkin seed tea was used to cure bladder infections; tonics to "refresh the blood" were made from okra; flaxseed treated pneumonia.[201] For some, the techniques young musicians learned while tending orchards and communal farms saved their lives as adults. Kid Ory grew vegetables and raised chickens during the Great Depression while a janitor in Los Angeles, also feeding the New Orleans clarinetist Joe Darensbourg who briefly lived with him between jobs.[202]

The physical, social, economic, and spiritual responses of Black worker-residents to plantation societies complicate reductive or pastoral renderings of rurality. Sugar plantations were small cities marked by heavy industry. Mark Twain, during his tour of the United States South, described the plantation where Henry and Barnes grew up as "a wilderness of tubs and tanks and vats and filters, pumps, pipes and machinery."[203] As historian Robert Shugg has detailed, plantations during the transition from Reconstruction to Redemption came under the management of a "new, capitalistic sugar aristocracy, organized in corporations and financed by banks," with more than half either born in the North or funded by Northern investment.[204] Early jazz trombonist Kid Ory remembered with disdain how massive sugar refineries breathed black smog that darkened the sky and whose thunderous processing was audible miles away.[205] As early as the antebellum era, sugar plantations were so large and industrialized that they resembled towns. "We had a sugar house right on the plantation," recalled the freedwoman Catherine Cornelius. "You know it was a big plantation cause I remember well they was standing on the levee when General Butler was on his way to the siege of Vicksburg. He said, 'girls what town is dis?' I said, 'Dis aint no town, dis a plantation.'"[206]

These giant labor camps became central to the Industrial Revolution a generation prior. Now, a new wave of capitalist agriculture was underway, and workers were pushed to their limit as planters extracted every ounce of value they could. Music coordinated their activity and could help keep body and soul alive for another day. William Bébé Ridgley, one jazz musician who grew up cutting cane, remembered that their "[work] songs could've mixed" into the repertoire of early jazz, which "wouldn't be the same thing, but [would have] some of the words, some of the stuff like that."[207] One of the songs often sung in the cane fields was "When the Saints Go Marching In," marking the massive rise of the Black Baptist church and its powerful influence in the Louisiana plantation districts. Emancipation provided the opportunity for African Americans to create independent churches, and Baptism's ecstaticism, and its symbolic use of water, powerfully connected to the quest for self-determination.[208] One way these songs entered the early jazz repertoire was from the experiences of young cane cutters who needed this music to get through the day, and sometimes even to survive: Kid Ory remembered it was "hot as hell" working in the fields in the summer, and youngsters like himself and Louis James continually filled up water in buckets at the river and brought them to canecutters.[209] Punch Miller remembered that when he and others cut cane, "almost everyone would be singing . . . 'I want to leave this place and find a better home.'"[210] Sonic enactments of marronage, through a collective body of songs developed in the cane fields and field culture,

FIGURE 4.3 "A Sugar-House on the Bayou Teche Louisiana," *Harper's Weekly*, April 1900.

prefigured how music would serve as a means of imaging and enacting a new world—both in theory and practice.

Some of the future musicians of the sugar parishes were not initially exposed to brass band music, but they found ways to create expressive culture despite the semifeudal relations of plantation life. In lieu of extreme poverty, many had to not only grow their own foodstuffs but also fashion their own musical instruments. Louis James describes his first instrument as "his heel," which he would "rub on the floor to produce a bass sound" with a comb and tissue paper.[211] Around the same time, and across the state, Sam and Isaiah Morgan created their own instruments out of repurposed metal tubes. "The boys sang and blew through the pipes with the drummer keeping time on the lard can and it was all really remarkable[,] the harmony they could get out of that junk," remembered Florence Dymond, the owner of the Belair plantation, who apparently found these Black workers' ingenuity, despite their starvation wages, remarkable.[212] Self-sufficient instrumental creation techniques were part of a centuries-long inheritance; as Salim Washington has poetically observed: "Africans in the West invented the hambone and the shuffle stomp of the ring shout when drumming was outlawed in the American South; transformed the pan, or steel drum, a product of the West's waste and pollution in Trinidad, into an instrument that can evoke beauty."[213]

Heterophonic, improvised, communally realized and reinvented: Black instrumental ecologies were also informed by the ethos of the Black Baptist church. Sonny Henry recalled that the brass band he played in in his late teens included "hymns and 6/8s," while Harrison remembered vividly the music in the Magnolia plantation's Macedonia Baptist church. There he heard "no piano, just sing[ing] anthems, jubilees. They'd word it out, then they'd sing that strain. Then they'd word it out again and sing some more. Jubilee songs—fast. Sometimes when they, sometimes they would start clapping their hands on the jubilee, yeah. Sometimes the sisters would shout, you know? Just a like a person would dance there. At socials they would be shouting. I don't know what they call it; it wasn't dancing, but it was so near dancing, I don't know what it is."[214] Barnes, like many other musicians from the plantation districts, brought these sounds into his trombone and the musical strains of early jazz. He even joined the New Orleans Free Mission Baptist Church later in life, accompanying the church choir on his trombone.[215] Like communal gardens and provision grounds, Black Baptist churches were important spaces where the heterophonic richness and multivocality could be explored on relatively autonomous terms and a collective ecology of voices developed and encouraged. As Thomas Brothers explains, "During these post-Reconstruction decades, spiritual energy was bursting out in all directions, articulated through some of the most potent forms of expressive culture ever created," and most Black Louisianan churchgoers—an estimated 62 percent—were Baptists by 1890.[216]

Reconstruction Black churches, like the occupied plantations where Black farmers sowed new commons, were born in a moment of jubilee. Indeed, these churches' invocation of maroon ecologies is palpable in the injunction of freedmen working in Charleston who, as they created their own church, proclaimed that they were finally able to worship under "their own vine and fig tree" where "none shall make us afraid."[217] As institutional repositories of the struggle against the Southern plantocracy, Black churches were later instrumental to Southern labor organizing, particularly in the 1930s and 1940s during the age of industrial unionism.[218] James Lawton, a Methodist minister and important strategist of the 1960s civil rights movement, explained the counter-plantation valences of the Black church in 2020: "We will not be silent while our economy is shaped, not by 'freedom,' but by plantation capitalism which continues to cause domination and control rather than liberty and equality for all."[219] Melanie L. Harris considers the spirituals of the Black church as intimately connected to the ecological history of African Americans and especially to the gardens Black Americans grew. "It was normal for my own mother, Noami, to teach me that the best way to grow plants, beans, and flowers was to sing to them. . . . Perhaps the greatest songs I've ever heard sung in the garden were African American spirituals. . . . Listening is a core part of singing. I learned this early, and the more I listened the louder the music of the earth grew."[220] This power of communal political mobilization and its cultivation of deep listening emerged through Reconstruction freedpeople's vision of an ecological republic, for, as Justin Behrend observes, churches "offered freedpeople an opportunity to practice their faith as they saw it, but freedpeople also used churches as spaces to share information, to convene with friends and family, and share risks through mutual security," thus helping to "establish democratic practices and ground local freedpeople's religious affiliation in networks that extended beyond" the plantations on which they were housed.[221]

These connections manifest in Zora Neale Hurston's ethnography of 1930s Sanctified churches in New Orleans. Barnes's descriptions of the music of Magnolia's Baptist church and its democratic ethos, it seems, were not exclusive to rural Louisiana. Like Barnes, Hurston drew specific attention to the call-and-response quality between the preacher and the congregation, both apparently improvising off each other: "Chants and hums are not used indiscriminately . . . if the preacher should say: 'Jesus will lead us,' the congregation would bear him up with: 'I'm got my hah-hand in my Jesus's hands.'" If in prayer or sermon, the mention is made of nailing Christ to the cross: "Didn't Cavalry tremble when they nailed Him down." Hurston emphasizes the malleable nature of sermons and prayers that create a liminal space between language and music, as humming and chants emerge from "a sort of liquefying of words." This malleability is applied to the sermon itself, wherein innovation and creativity are encouraged by the audience and community: "The individual may hang as many new ornaments upon the traditional form as he likes, but the audience would be disagreeably surprised if the form were abandoned. Any new and original elaboration is welcome, however, and this brings out the fact that all religious expression among Negroes is regarded as art." As Barnes also identified, Hurston wrote that these songs "are one and all based on a dance-possible rhythm."[222] Bassist Pops Foster wrote of the Holiness Church in New Orleans that the connection to motion was more explicit: "They'd clap their hands and bang a tambourine and sing."[223] In the case of Foster, Barnes, and other plantation workers, these songs emerged in the rhythmic interchange between the church, the plantation fields, and the gardens their families maintained. As Melanie L. Harris remembered, it was in such gardens where she developed "an agricultural epistemology that was spiritual in orientation" while singing spirituals to the regenerative polycultures cultivated and perfected by Africans in the Americas despite generations of genocidal trauma. "I noticed that we all seem to be singing the same song."[224]

In the 1870s–90s, religious and secular melodies, and communal-congregational modes of music making, proliferated through both work songs and the improvised, invented instrument traditions at the very moment that a politicized rural brass band culture was taking shape. In Thibodaux, a town in the heart of the sugar bowl and located forty-seven miles from New Orleans, a local Democratic newspaper complained that "the air was rent by the jarring sounds of a colored brass band" at a Republican mass meeting.[225] Halls on plantations or plantation towns became sites for brass band performances and linked urban and rural outposts of Black life. "Excursion from New Orleans to Thibodaux by colored lodge," announced one newspaper, describing how a "procession paraded through the principle [sic] streets of the town—preceded by a fine band of music in full uniform from New Orleans," and "also by the colored band of Thibodaux— at night a grand ball was held at Waverly Hall."[226] Rural-urban musical exchanges aestheticized and facilitated the consolidation of brassroots democracy and its attendant forms of political consciousness produced in the enacted freedom of plantation takeover through brass band procession.

One concrete way brassroots democracy was realized was the commitment of bands to fundraise for Black schools on plantations. In 1882, a local newspaper reported on "entertainments by teachers and patrons of Corp. Colored School." There, the Lafourche Band "furnished the music on said occasion free of charge.

Profit—$52.00."²²⁷ Similarly, in 1885, for the "Teachers Institute program," "an audience of more than 500 people assembled in the hall" to hear "music by the colored band that volunteered its services." Music in support of education opened other opportunities for teaching and learning. After the band concluded, "Mr. Shieb spoke upon the subject of education after the band had played several excellent pieces," and "Prof. Puckette addressed the audience on the subject of spelling."²²⁸ James Humphrey himself performed for charities, social aid and pleasure clubs (SAPCs), and orphanages on plantations.²²⁹ Since plantation owners eschewed their responsibilities to provide education, brass bands became vehicles for pooling communal resources and deepening long-standing structures of solidarity and mutual aid.

Plantation brass bands were more broadly linked to mutual aid associations that existed among plantation workers. Sonny Henry recalled in an interview how rural SAPCs funded the bands while also serving as guarantors of musical excellence. To become a part of a band, one joined "a fraternity lodge . . . that's the onliest way they'd be in it." Beyond its musical components, Henry explained membership's other benefits: "[when] you're sick they give you a little benefit" and "they gave meetings sometimes twice a month" that addressed topics ranging from Louisiana politics to upcoming events. Historians have highlighted how New Orleans's social aid and pleasure clubs provided health insurance and funerals and were spaces for political decision-making in urban contexts, but their rural counterparts were working powerfully toward similar ends.²³⁰ But the Louisiana plantation countryside was home to parallel cooperative institutions, such as Masonic lodges and other Black mutual aid societies, reinforcing networks that connected rural workers to their urban counterparts.²³¹ When white supremacists massacred striking Black sugar workers in Thibodaux in 1887, brass bands were banned by Thibodaux's mayor shortly after, compelling Thibodaux's influential bandleader John Robichaux to move to New Orleans.²³²

CONCLUSION

Although he never directly commented on the several bands he financed on his plantation, Republican governor-turned-planter Warmoth took the business of culture seriously. Warmoth's ledger records that he paid brass band instructor James Humphrey $5.55 for his visits—more than the weekly wages of a sugar laborer—alongside purchasing band uniforms and instruments for his workforce and their children.²³³ Humphrey, an accomplished solo cornetist and Drum Major for the Grand Army of the Republic, a Union army veteran fraternal organization, had traveled to Los Angeles, Indianapolis, and elsewhere in performances that commemorated the Union cause as a war to end slavery. He also played in the Bloom Philharmonic Orchestra, conducted by Louis Tio and populated by the city's best Creole of color musicians.[234] His students remember he could speak French. His grandfather was Alexandre Humphrey of the sugar town of Hahnville, and he was one of the entering classes at Straight University, an African American college created after the Civil War in 1869, which the Haitian-descended activist-musician Daniel Desdunes also attended.[235] Just as Desdunes had created accessible music programs in Omaha, Humphrey created music programs throughout the plantation districts, such as at Bulb Orphanage in Plaquemines Parish. Like Édouard Tinchant, he bucked traditional gender roles and encouraged both of his daughters to play the bass. One, Lillian, played with the Bloom Philharmonic, and his other daughter, Jamesetta, helped him teach at Bulb Orphanage.[236]

In 1897, Humphrey began working at Magnolia, spending weeks on the road as he traveled to Deer Range, Pointe à la Hache, St. Sophie, Ironton, Bellaire, Oakville, and Jesuit Bend. His student Willie Parker remembered how "old Humphrey had all that work."[237] During these years, Humphrey trained a generation of innovative New Orleans jazz musicians, including Chris Kelly, Sam Morgan, Sonny Henry, Harrison Barnes, Jimmy "Kid" Clayton, and John Casimir, who each brought traditions of work songs and the historical memory of plantation resistance into their music. Gene Miller notes that Humphrey's plantation students "became some of the best jazz musicians in New Orleans; many of them eventually led their own bands and made recordings."[238] The Professor played a role in that process, securing some of his own students their first gigs in New Orleans. Humphrey's grandson remembers that "Jim Humphrey used to bring his country boy bands down [to New Orleans] to play big Mardi Gras parades," which were so cold that "sometimes the valves would freeze on the horns," revealing the commitment and mutual trust developed between teacher and students.[239]

Most often, would-be musicians did not have the cash to pay for extracurricular private lessons and instead exchanged crops grown in their gardens for lessons with Humphrey. His grandson recalled how his grandfather "used to bring us pecans, sweet potatoes, sugar cane and all from the country. He also made a garden, and from the figs in it, he made enough to pay the taxes."[240]

This barter economy reveals that Black workers in the sugar parishes were still cultivating gardens and provision grounds, perhaps on the same land their families worked since slavery, and these items circulated in economic circuits of Black people's own making.[241] In fact, Humphrey's own garden, inspired by his students, shows that he was a student himself who learned crop preparation techniques with the plantation workers whose sound he helped develop. His grandson remembered that "[Humphrey] had a garden for food and I think teaching music was a labor of love."²⁴² These forms of Black rural agency point to an underlying synergy between these two spaces of expression and self-development, an interplaythat concretely "bore fruit." The interaction of these semi-autonomous economies, of music and gardening, laid one foundation for the rural-urban alliance that animated brassroots democracy.

Brass bands such as those taught and led by James Humphrey were transformed by Black sugar workers. Their music reproduced a commons that could activate both geographic and social mobility, creating opportunities for planation workers to contribute to an emerging creolized culture that would come to be called jazz. These structures of affiliation and solidarity would allow up-south musicians in Chicago to resist dehumanizing farm labor to the point where white periodicals would complain of social upheaval. Musicians not only performed in New Orleans but were supported by a dynamic plantation dance hall scene, which was frequented by musicians in the sugar districts as well as those from New Orleans, including a young Louis Armstrong. These plantation brass bands were vehicles for a collectivism that had previously been observed in the commoning projects of the United States South. Musicians living on, moving between, and migrating from sugar parishes recreated forms of cooperative labor through musical performance, ensuring that their counter-plantation ethos would be foundational to the practices of improvisation and shared decision-making that underscore brassroots democracy.²⁴³

FIVE

Black Reconstruction and Brassroots Democracy

Sonic Assembly in the Post-Civil War South

> Blow your trumpet, Gabriel!
> Blow louder, louder,
> And I hope that trumpet might blow me home to the new Jerusalem.
> *"Blow Your Trumpet, Gabriel"*[1]

Jubilee, the long-prophesied day of freedom, was a decidedly *aural* event, maybe the most concentrated outpouring of sonic joy in US history. Scenes of emancipation were announced by sound, manifesting a world turned upside down. In 1862, Union troops arrived in Thibodaux, Louisiana to the "strains of fifes and the beating of drums," while newly emancipated masses sang in multipart harmony "Oh the Lord's name be praised!"[2] In Charleston on April 4, 1865, Colonel Woodford "was received with prolonged shouts and deafening cheers" and a four-thousand-person parade, whose chant of "We know no masters but ourselves" was heard past the city's borders to the plantation environs.[3] George Arnold, hospital steward in the 4th US Colored Infantry, remembered Wilmington's freedom parades "With banners floating! With their splendid brass bands and drum corps, discoursing the National airs and marches."[4] Only weeks before, the curfew for enslaved and free people of color had been 9:00 p.m. Deafening brass band performances symbolically washed away the old order as those held in human bondage processed the psychological weight of slavery. One emancipated man, nearly ninety-three years old, was too weak to leave his house, but the music of the Union troops "had revived him, and he felt so happy that he came out; and there he stood, with his long white locks and his wrinkled cheeks, saying, 'Welcome, welcome!'"[5]

"Emancipation," notes Anthony Kaye, "was not a single instant at all but a process."[6] Nonlinear, archipelagic, cathartic, and chaotic, it is striking that many freedpeople in vastly different locales and stages of the war were united by one thread: they remembered their initial moment of freedom as a musical event. Hannah Crasson, who had been enslaved on a plantation near Raleigh, North Carolina, recalled: "The first band of music I ever heard play, the Yankees was playing it. They were playing a song, 'I am tired of seeing the homespun dresses the Southern women wear.'"[7] Catherine Williams, also a freedwoman of Raleigh, remembered how enslaved peoples learned of their freedom through sound: "We were not afraid of them, none of us children, neither white nor colored; they played such pretty music . . . we run after the band to hear them play."[8] "The Yankees rocked the place" is how Hattie Rogers retold her emancipation moment in New Bern, the city that was to become home to enslaved refugees from across the South.[9] Timothy Thomas Fortune, W. E. B. Du Bois's mentor and author of the first Black Marxist interpretation of Reconstruction, was eight years old when freedom came to the village of Marianna, Florida, where he was enslaved.[10] He writes: "The soldiers had dress parade twice a day and all the urchins of the village were on hand to watch it. They thought it was the grandest thing ever. They were transported by the drumbeating and the bugle blowing. The bugle call for afternoon drill and parade was heard for miles around and was the first and sweetest music the freed people had ever heard. Have they ever heard any sweeter since? I doubt it."[11]

The emancipatory sound of brass was forever etched into the ears of Fortune, Crasson, and millions of others. Soldiers' diaries, enslaved peoples' testimonies, and newspapers are replete with these sound images, like the "drumbeating and bugle blowing" or the "tocsin [bell] of freedom," summoning sonic memories associated with self-actualization for readers and writers.[12] This "sweetest music" ever heard was sounded for "miles around," and its ability to project a new social order across geographies of racial terror made it simultaneously so treasured by Black commentators and so hated by white planters. It was precisely the materiality of Black sounds that made this association so palpable. Sound is more than symbolic: it vibrates bodies whose voices, in turn, swell. Loudness from below is a collective expression of power and potential, and this potential is experienced in the body, as the harnessing of air and the self-emancipation of muscular and anatomic devices converge with others acting in concert to prefigure collective action. The future, in other words, was felt.[13]

This Civil War cultural revolution initiated by Black freedpeople was invoked decades later by New Orleans clarinetists Sidney Bechet and George Lewis, who started their musical education on the fife in Civil War–descended Field Bands. Lewis played fife in "kid parades . . . Field Bands. [They'd] have a drum, a couple of fifes, three of four boys I knew could fife, at that time."[14] Unlike in the North, fife and drum bands were exclusively a Black phenomenon in the South because of their links to Black liberation.[15] Similarly, the clarinetist George Lewis remembered the "advertising" he and other musicians were contracted to perform during the Great Depression. Musicians would be sent "to different clubs" in "columns." Upon arriving, the musicians would sing "Gettysburg March," at which point the club members "would come in with their regalia or their banners, you know, representing the club. And then they would go to the bar." Not only a New Orleans ritual—Lewis remembers that "they used that tune, also, in the country"—these episodes point to lines of descent between Louisiana jazz and the radical sonic, visual, and performative traditions generated by brassroots democracy in the Black Southern revolution called Reconstruction.[16]

Previous chapters of this book have highlighted Afro-Louisianans as participants in the "live dialogue" of the Afro-Atlantic, with a focus on trans-Caribbean aesthetic feedback loops and the transmission of an interculture simultaneously sonic and sociopolitical.[17] But there is a danger in overlooking the cultural and political exchanges that occurred more properly within the United States Black South. Just as much as the circum-Caribbean or the US-Mexican borderlands, the US South is characterized by movement, intercultural encounters, and the exchange of emancipatory ideas and music, especially during the social revolution of Black Reconstruction. The true victor of the Civil War, as understood by W. E. B. Du Bois, was not the Union army of the North; nor was its driving conflict a "war between states." Rather, its decisive moment was the general strike of a revolutionary Black proletariat—the enslaved—who destroyed the plantation economy and the enslaver plutocracy's monopoly on violence through mass refusal to work, desertion, and revolutionary warfare.[18] Steven Hahn has similarly referred to the Civil War as "the greatest slave rebellion in modern history," which transformed a slave society that was "by far the largest, most economically advanced, and most resilient in the Americas."[19]

Music was central to the political movements that animated Black Reconstruction, and its implications for brassroots democracy is the subject of this chapter. Even before slavery had been abolished, enslaved people in Atlanta took advantage of wartime chaos to hold "Negro balls" in local hotels. Billed as a fundraiser for the Confederate army, one such event nonetheless concerned whites who saw the entrance of Black women and men into public life as a sign that Black subordination was actively challenged.[20] Music and dance precipitated the opening volley of a cultural struggle that Tera Hunter calls a "war of nerves" between enslaved workers and a crumbling master class, the latter of which perceived their cultural hegemony rapidly disintegrating. Hundreds of displays of daily defiance, large and small, prefigured the conflicts that would characterize an unstable social order during Reconstruction.[21] Music in mass meetings, parades, and collective improvisations around campfires reproduced this defiant and jubilant infrastructure of feeling that propelled emancipation. As one freedwoman remarked in 1864, "Some will look upon these times as if nothing but politics, mass meetings, drums and fifes and gilt muskets were all the go."[22] This chapter tends to the core of our definition of brassroots democracy: the practice of performative assembly that laid the foundation for the simultaneous and syncretic expansion of public and musical spheres. As Johbir Janwir explains, "Just as conjurers healed the slave body with a mixture of efficacious materials, newly free Africans in America attempted to heal the body politic and cure society's ills through a tradition of organized protest with musical accompaniment that expressed alternate social visions of democracy."[23]

Although neither improvised solos nor collective improvisations were documented in the brass bands of the Civil War or Reconstruction period, improvised music was recorded in the Black Civil War regiments in a variety of forms. Improvisational modes of group composition helped coalesce a Reconstruction civic spirituality that could claim victory even in bleak moments by channeling the power of now, conjoining the agency of artist-activists and the listening power of the audience in a political context of epic proportions. Heble, Fischlin, and Lipsitz observe that "the actions of the listener or receiver of the improvised performance are every bit as significant . . . as the performance, for to discern the performance the listener must in a sense cocreate it."[24] Listening so deeply so as to recreate the sociosonic experience of musical improvisers became a kind of intersubjective training, which enabled organizers to make sense of the diverse political, social, and spiritual epistemologies of a newly constituted multitude.

A story relayed by Union general Henry G. Thomas about the Black troops in his division explores how both emotional and political consensus was achieved through improvised song. Through the repeated performances (and revisions) of these improvised works, Black musician-soldiers continuously recreated the democratic culture by which such songs were collectively composed:

> Any striking event or piece of news was usually eagerly discussed by the white troops. . . . Not so with the blacks; important news…was usually followed by [a] long silence. They sat about in groups, "studying," as they called it. They waited, like the Quakers, for the spirit to move; when the spirit moved, one of

their singers would uplift a mighty voice, like a bard of old, in a wild sort of chant. If he did not strike a sympathetic chord in his hearers, if they did not find in his utterance the exponent of their idea, he would sing it again and again, altering sometimes the words, more often the music. If his changes met general acceptance, one voice after another would chime in; a rough harmony of three parts would add itself; other groups would join his, and the song would become the song of the command.[25]

These improvisatory vocal traditions fused affective and sociopolitical dimensions of Black music-making, prefiguring a cultural technology that would be essential to Black Reconstruction. While apparently sonic decisions, these processes also modeled participatory democracy, as they were literally born of it. Rather than conceptualize democracy in the framework of liberal theory, wherein legitimacy lies in "winning" an election and "defeating" the opposition through majoritarian rule, this ethos was persuasion, not defeat; conversation, not conversion; and dialogue, not domination.[26] Such a conception resonates eloquently with a democracy in and of sound: if the collective spirit does not move, the song cannot move forward. These practices of consensus-building through trial and error, call-and-response, had immense implications for the participatory character of Reconstruction politics and portended music's importance in the decades between the Civil War and Jim Crow. Improvised music enacted what political discourse envisioned, and by rehearsing new social relations, it produced respond-ability and accountability. Much more than authored by a single great composer, these pieces were born out of the performance situation itself, demonstrating how improvisation was a testimonial in which "the particulars of encounters are inscribed."[27] The encounters of brassroots democracy—mass meetings and public celebrations in which an apartheid state was outadministered by a grassroots, Black-led multiracial movement—inscribed within improvised cultural forms the capacity to embody and reproduce this revolution's communitarian ethos.

As this chapter explores, collective improvisation existed alongside, and often in tension with, the expectations of white military generals who led bands that performed marching or military music. Likewise, freedpeople generated a diametrically different vision of democracy, one frequently at odds with established power brokers in the Republican Party. Understanding the vision of democracy that emerged during Black Reconstruction is essential to understanding the New Orleans collective improvisation traditions that came to fruition in the era's music-making practices. The white conservative journalist James S. Pike, in his attack on the supposed ineptitude of Black legislatures, is instructive in this regard. Pike misread Black communal mechanisms for creating polyvocal narratives through trial and error, call-and-response. Commenting on Black legislators' tendency to quote the previous speeches of their colleagues during their own discourses, he claimed that "the negro is imitative in the extreme. He can copy like a parrot or a monkey, and he is always ready for a trial of his skill." In response to the affective modalities of the Black Reconstruction chamber, he complained: "He notoriously loves a joke or an anecdote, and will burst into a broad guffaw on the smallest provocation." Such emotional intelligence was also apparent in the musicality of these spaces, and Pike remarked angrily of Black legislators "dancing as it were to the music of his own voice, forever." Yet in the same passage, he unwittingly revealed an organized political body with a deep commitment to plurality, with mechanisms in place to ensure that no single voice would be allowed to dominate:

> The old stagers admit that the colored brethren have a wonderful aptness at legislative proceedings. They are "quick as lightning" at detecting points of order, and they certainly make incessant and extraordinary use of their knowledge. No one is allowed to talk five minutes without interruption, and one interruption is the signal for another and another, until the original speaker is smothered under an avalanche of them. Forty questions of privilege will be raised in a day. At times, nothing goes on but alternating questions of order and of privilege ... Some of the blackest members exhibit a pertinacity of intrusion in raising these points of order and questions of privilege that few white men can equal.[28]

Pike's contradictory insults of these Black legislators, who are simultaneously incapable of original thinking and "quick as lightning," reveal he is incapable of understanding this process of decision-making whose method supersedes the content produced. As the jazz pianist Ojeda Penn explains, "in jazz it is the improvisational process [and] not the actual music composed which is the artifact."[29] Black legislators, especially attuned to questions of "privilege," ensured racial and class biases rooted in antebellum hierarchies would not determine who would be the leading voice in the South Carolina House. Indeed, Pike's description of these assemblies resembles the social philosophy embedded in "Gumbo ya ya," a Louisiana Creole phrase that translates to "everyone talk at once."[30] As Elsa Barkley Brown explains, "To some listening to such a conversation, *gumbo ya ya* may sound like chaos. We may better be able to understand it as something other than confusion if we overlay it with jazz, for *gumbo ya ya* is the essence of a musical tradition where 'the various voices in a piece of music may go their own ways but still be held together by their relationship to each other.'"[31] This radical relationality embedded in the processes of proposal, refinement, and group incorporation is one present in the Black avant-garde's collective musical improvisation traditions, which continue to flourish at the time of this writing.[32]

CELEBRATION AND ASSEMBLY: THE CIVIL WAR BLACK REVOLUTION

> Celebration is the essence of black thought, the animation of black operations, which are, in the first instance, our undercommon, underground, submarine sociality.
>
> Fred Moten[33]

The celebration culture of the United States Black South exploded in Louisiana with a particular intensity. Inoculating a pro-Union musical culture was a core strategy of the Federal troops to pacify Confederate sympathizers in occupied New Orleans. Nicknamed the "Dancing Master," in 1862 General Banks "gave a monster concert with artillery accompaniment" followed by a series of "balls to dance the fair creoles to loyalty."[34] Apparently not only white Creoles but also Black and Creole of color New Orleanians attended. One New Orleans public school teacher recalled in 1865, at the inauguration of a public school, that "many blacks and mulattos, as well as Federal soldiers, were invited to join in a dance."[35] As became the norm in other parts of the Union-occupied South, music lessons were administered by wartime teachers.[36] The conservative *Louisiana Democrat* complained that at newly desegregated schools, children sang and performed "such delightful symphonies as 'hang Jeff Davis on a sour apple tree[,]' 'John Brown's body lies a moldering in the grave,' and other approved Black Republican melodies."[37] This new musical culture was so widespread in New Orleans public schools that, in 1865, eight thousand white students staged a walk-out in protest of what they derided as pro-Union "musical patriotism."[38]

Among African Americans, it was specifically brass bands that fused this wartime aural culture with the freedom valences of the moment. James Calhart James, recently freed from slavery, recalled a song that he and others in bondage had sung. It prefiguratively symbolized brass instruments through an internalized soundscape heard in one's inner ear: "Oh where shall we go when the great day comes, And the blowing of the trumpets and the banging of the drums. When General Sherman comes, No more rice and cotton fields, We will hear no more crying. Old master will be sighing."[39] The song James and others collectively composed reveals how brass instruments, fife, and drums—largely inaccessible to the enslaved—took on specific meanings in Black musical culture during the Civil War and Reconstruction, contributing to an aural counterpublic where freedpeople debated ideas and politics. This genre of sounds—blowing of trumpets, banging of drums, the singing of freedpeople, the sighing of overthrown masters—fused with the physical act of marching. The blare of cornets and the pounding of marching drums inspired dreams of freedom because of their association with the war against the slave power. In these moments of sonic gathering, Black and Afro-Creole New Orleanians reclaimed streets as sites of mutual aid, attired in vibrant threads that emboldened their polyphonic performances.[40]

This dynamic project of social reorganization is the context in which Black Brass bands became institutionalized.[41] Heble, Fischlin, and Lipsitz write that Black brass bands' "communication, organization, coordination, culture, and interpretation as mediated through improvisation practices . . . cannot be disassociated from the communitarian sources that make [this] music possible."[42] What were these "communitarian sources"? Newspapers, interviews with freedpeople, and congressional reports historicize this claim. We can hear a dynamic struggle for public space and the public sphere, where proposals such as universal suffrage irrespective of race and gender, robust land redistribution, and the creation of an activist state to manage public investment were just three of the revolutionary proposals carved out through collective meetings organized by freedpeople.[43] The decision-making process was in many ways more important than the specific proposals. Justin Behrend notes that "the major task of democratization was not necessarily the extension of suffrage rights but the creation of a democratic ethos"—another expression of the brassroots democracy's radical expansion of the political in collective sound, demonstrating in practice a model more antiphonal than representational models of democracy where subjects' participation is reduced to "the consent of the governed."[44] These practices were active, not passive; participative, not prohibitive; vocal, not silent. Power differentials between factions of the Black communities were negotiated within a form of improvisatory governance based on extensive and sometimes painful dialogue.[45] As James S. Pike complained of South Carolina's State House: "They were of every hue, from the light octoroon to the deep black . . . Every negro type and physiognomy was here to be seen, from the genteel serving-man to the rough-hewn customer from the rice or cotton field . . . [they wore] dirty garments of the field; the stub-jackets and slouch hats of soiling labor." He concludes, with disgust: "These were the legislators of South Carolina."[46]

What most alarmed Pike was not their dress, but that these legislators possessed a hard-earned confidence that the white supremacist journalist lacked. Black workers in stub-jackets had secured a decisive victory over their enslavers, a fate that was unthinkable fifteen years earlier. The importance of Civil War military experience for these Black activists was transformative. Their primary motivation, to overthrow slavery and reunite families separated by the trade in flesh, was clear enough: as one Black soldier related, he fought so that "the Rebels would be whipped so bad that Gabriel's trumpet would not resurrect them."[47] But army service did not only represent the opportunity to take up arms against the "slave power." Joining the Union army was one means by which the formerly enslaved could flee the severely circumscribed worlds of the plantation, where power resided in near-absolute forms within individuals such as overseers and masters, and opportunities for nonclandestine collective organizing among a broader community were severely repressed.[48] The Civil War occasioned an aperture to expand the translocal at a scale scarcely imaginable years earlier.[49]

As in other diasporic contexts throughout the plantation Americas, music was instrumental in building new collectivities because the Black Civil War armies were remarkably diverse. Civil War Black regiments included those free before the war and those who had liberated themselves from bondage; practitioners of Protestantism, Catholicism, and Islam; former plantation hands, ironworkers, and musicians; each soldier equipped with different literacies.[50] Even among English speakers, regional variations in the Black vernacular sometimes led to confusion. Frederick Douglass remembered, upon hearing the enslaved workers on the Lloyd plantation to which he had been forcibly transferred, "[I] could scarcely understand them when I first went among them. . . . [They spoke] a mixture of Guinea and everything else you please."[51] While it is not clear if he served in the Union army, Norice Wilkerson, a freedperson in Hilton Head, South Carolina, claimed to have been a soldier in the Haitian Revolution, and fought in Toussaint Louverture's army before being captured, reenslaved, and shipped to the United States. He spoke French and Spanish fluently and sang songs from the Haitian Revolution upon request.[52]

The mobility made possible by the Civil War produced spaces of learning and creolization, and refugees from across the South who converged in Louisiana or elsewhere were a diverse group. Some of them had been family members separated by the internal slave trade; many were total strangers. The "journey of ideological change," as Anthony Kaye refers to enslaved people's wartime transformation, began when enslaved people "redrew the entire map of their social terrain."[53] All of these peoples, with their own relations and identities, had to conceive of a way to make themselves mutually intelligible—to be heard.

If assembly describes the means by which these emerging multitudes developed new political processes, then improvisation refers to the methodology by which new musical and expressive codes were enacted—codes that facilitated organized communication, fostered mutual trust, and reflected new subjectivities interpolated through shared sound.[54] The twinned process of assembly and improvisation mirrored the communal character of postwar Black churches, as freedpeople overwhelmingly chose to create independent spaces of worship free from white control.⁵⁵ Across the South, churches took many forms, from structures built by the community members on occupied plantations to abandoned railroad cars in the city.⁵⁶ The multilayered vocal traditions that imbued their congregational form of music making were many generations in the making, and these aesthetics took on a new power as visions of jubilee were confirmed by prophecy's deliverance. Yet it was in Civil War military units where such spirituals and local styles may have been first shared in spaces of relative autonomy. Across the South was this new music resounded and refined, dreamt up and enacted by groups of both erstwhile strangers and kinfolk from faraway plantations.

These vocal traditions were shared alongside the musical education African Americans received in military brass bands.⁵⁷ Black soldiers credit these bands for personal growth, collective enjoyment, and the opportunity to articulate their vision of a new social order. When visiting his brother in Memphis, Tennessee, Major Daniel Densmore of the 68th United States Colored Infantry had the chance to see the band of another Black regiment, the 7th United States Colored Heavy Artillery, perform in Court Square. He commended the group and appreciated the cultural politics it played in the heart of the slave power. "All negroes played in Court Square, a place of resort for the aristocracy, and some of the fine ladies looked quite vexed at what they considered the insult. But the band played well and showed the difference between the negroes as soldiers and as slaves a year ago."⁵⁸ Band performances remapped the social and sonic geography of Southern cities, performing Black autonomy and effecting planter anguish in nearly equal measure. Emily LeConte remembered how on July 4, 1865, a "brass band played continuously. I could not stand it. It was too humiliating and made me realize our condition too keenly." When the band finally stopped, "the negroes were left to make their own music. Hundreds of voices singing strange negro songs and hundred of feet [sic] dancing weird negro dances made a terrible noise."⁵⁹ Pike described these moments as "the spectacle of a society suddenly turned bottom side up."⁶⁰ The aurality of the counter-plantation and its powerful structure of feeling rendered the South's ancien régime physically sick and psychologically disoriented, as Black soldier musicians constructed new identities through the overtone-rich textures of interlocked cornets, alto horns, and baritones, overlaid on top of snare drums, bass drums, and cymbals.⁶¹

Black soldiers were so committed to their music that when some regiments lacked the resources to procure their own instruments, each would pool their army pay to buy musical instruments of their own.⁶² The "magicians," as Desmore called them, organized dance bands that performed at night, a source of "great merriment" for Black troops often stationed on dreaded and dangerous fatigue duty.[63] When music was not had, it was a cause of great concern and comment by Black soldiers: Captain Emilio of the 54th Regiment complained on the River Road campaign that they were sustained "with only the tinkle, tinkle of pans and cups striking their bayonets for music" with no drums, fife, or brass. Even so, Emilio's complaint reveals that the 54th made music in a variety of manners, and, when musical instruments could not be had, even repurposed cooking gear and weapons could be reimagined as a percussion ensemble.[64] Bands also served vital psychological purposes in the context of the terrifying violence soldiers might see in battle, articulating beauty within chaos and embodying freedom from bondage. Although he did not serve in the Civil War, Anthony Stewart, who freed himself from slavery by joining the British Army during the War of 1812, remembered how "the martial music . . . had driven from my mind entirely the bloodshed and carnage of the battle field [sic]; besides, I was sick and tired of being a slave, and felt ready to do almost any thing [sic] to get where I could act and feel like a free man."[65]

Spirituals were also commonplace in the self-organized spaces of Black soldiers, creating comfort and camaraderie, finding recognition of their past pain as a "fellow sufferers." But music was also a space of improvised political commentary built from two different types of aurality: one *effective* (through political and topical discussion) and the other *affective*. There was a good deal of improvisation in these creolized spaces where erstwhile strangers created a new culture. Captain Scroggs mentions in his dairy that the members of a popular Black regimental band, the "Ebony Tooters," would "discourse enchanting music, *especially when not attempting to play any particular tune*."[66] As many contemporary improvising musicians relate, it is the endings that are the most difficult and potentially most rewarding element to coordinate within a collective improvisation, and for this reason they can be the most sublime and even the most humorous moments of an extended performance.[67] Colonel Higginson related that songs improvised by Black soldiers in their nighttime quarters might last an indeterminate time, and then, "Suddenly there comes a sort of *snap*, and the spell breaks, amid general singing and laughter. And this not rarely and occasionally, but night after night."[68] This cadre of nighttime experimentalists were planting the seeds for a postwar musical culture, and judging from the "snap" endings and humorous reactions, its mode of production was collective improvisation—a jam.

Improvisation was a potent tool for group solidarity because it could provide "real-time" political analysis. Drummer boys, according to Colonel Higginson, would "often sing a song" as companies marched: "They constantly improvised simple verses, with the same odd mingling,—the little facts of to-day's march being interwoven with the depths of theological gloom, the same jubilant chorus annexed to all"; elsewhere he related that "drummer boys would make up songs as they went along, mixing lines of their own hymns with descriptions of what they were doing, and all shouting out the chorus very loud."[69] Higginson reveals that religious hymns were interspersed with relevant analysis of daily life, an integration of the secular and sacred through improvised songs.[70] These military bands were appropriated by Black musicians for their own needs, shaped by an African American philosophical and spiritual tradition that read the war through the Old Testament. Beyond instilling military discipline, these improvised songs spoke to band music as a living document that could help synchronize Black soldiers' understandings of ongoing developments within the war and the politics of the military.

Higginson detested these drummers: he describes them as constantly "laughing and utterly unmanageable," and asserts that they were "not my favorites by any means, for they were a roguish set of scamps, and gave me more trouble than all the grown men in the regiment."[71] Yet Higginson was dependent on them for his career as an essayist: he frequently wrote about the music of his regiment, which he vigorously transcribed, in *Atlantic Monthly*. His extractivist ethnologies compared Black music to plant species.[72] As Jabir has pointed out, Higginson's patronizing, eroticizing, and scientific-racist attitudes betray a profound contradiction in the white abolitionist politic, and his accounts of Black music-making must be read and heard against the grain to account for the Black epistemologies that Higginson distorts or erases.[73]

His accounts nonetheless relate that Black music challenged racism within the military itself, something that irritated the colonel immensely. Black soldiers experienced significant prejudice within military ranks, and many white commanders were resistant to Black recruitment until they realized it was necessary to win the war.[74] Having just escaped slavery, freedpeople found themselves, as Ira Berlin and colleagues show, "enmeshed in another white-dominated hierarchy which, like the one they had escaped, assumed their inferiority."[75] Music was one way that Black soldiers constructed an oppositional culture within military ranks. One issue they organized around was pay inequity which left them earning seven dollars a week to white soldiers' thirteen dollars. They would not accept "a laborer's pay," but that of a soldier, a demand that changed even the campfire music.[76] Higginson complains about one song that would abruptly become silent as he walked by: "Ten dollars a month / Three of that for clothing! / Going to Washington / To fight for Lincoln's daughter." He was not moved by their musical activism and wrote of this song with racialized paternalism: "Their nonsense is as inscrutable as children's."[77]

Agitation for equal pay was made scrutable by a perilous organizing campaign that Black soldiers undertook while uniformed. At least one Black soldier, William Walker, was court-martialed and executed for his protest.[78] Black soldiers read the account of this execution in the Black daily, the *New Orleans Tribune*, which took a critical position on military racism and presented Walker as a martyr.[79] Yet it would not have been surprising if Walker's martyrdom was kept alive through campfire song, as songs for equal pay spread across the Black Southern regiments. Finally, Congress passed an equal pay law in July 1864, guaranteeing all white and Black privates sixteen dollars a week, a significant increase from Black soldiers' earlier pay of seven dollars. Within Black companies, the victory was met with an immense and choreographed celebration. The first payday under the new law, in October 1864, took on a festive air. "Two days have changed the face of things," wrote an officer with the 54th Massachusetts Regiment after the news broke. "The fiddle and other music long neglected enlivens the tents day and night. Songs burst out everywhere; dancing is incessant, boisterous shouts are heard, mimicry, burlesque, and carnival; pompous salutations are heard on all sides."[80] Sergeant John Shorter of the 54th Massachusetts Regiment, stationed in Folly Island, South Carolina, describes the planning process for a local celebration, for "it was thought by the wise ones that an event of so much importance to us and ours deserved it." Shorter was appointed to a committee to prepare a program of festivities, including a band-led parade. He reported, proudly, that the festivities began with band music: "The assembly was sounded." Indeed, the celebration linked equal pay to the larger struggle for Black liberation, as listeners heard "in the most beautiful language our triumph, its legal bearing, the slave power, the past sufferings of our race, and 'the bright future which awaits it as the reward of its wisdom, patriotism, and valor.'" Of the military band, he wrote, "There could be nothing finer than their performance." The music continued well after the parade, at a celebratory supper afterward, where "gentlemen sang that night who were never known to sing before."[81] The consolidation of the singing voice and the political voice was, for these unnamed soldiers, a mutually constitutive process.

The military struggle was thus overwhelmingly musical for Black soldiers who performed and improvised a new cultural language. Campfire songs shepherded sonic spaces to develop an affective and effective consensus, mocking their white superiors in coded language that responded to the intricacies of national and military politics. Celebratory songs at parades thereafter announced a new feeling, that something unprecedented had taken place: a successful campaign for Black rights in the wartime arena. Indeed, in Shorter's account, what emerges as the fruit of this political struggle is not only equal pay but the augmenting and consolidating of a Black political *voice*. Yet this voice is not only semiotic; it is aural, affective, and, above all, musical. Thus emerged new leadership, new vocabularies, new sounds, and new musical subjects: "Gentlemen sang that night who were never known to sing before." The improvisatory moment became inscribed in the improvisation itself and the genre it produced. These Black soldiers were not alone in choosing song as the ultimate metaphor of jubilee. As the African American poet Frances Ellen Watkins Harper orated at a fundraiser for the war effort in 1864: "Tell me if the whole world of literature . . . can equal the *music* of these words: 'I grant you full, broad, and unconditional freedom.'"[82] The cultural intervention of Black liberation in the US South was heard by Harper and others as a musical injunction on a grand historical scale, and the improvisatory music discoursed by Black soldiers and later Reconstruction activists expanded the beauty of this insurgent, inclusive aurality that the written word could only approximate.

Military brass band performances, therefore, were rehearsals for revolution—one called Reconstruction. The myriad practices of grassroots activism—such as community-centered education, collective decision-making, and organized self-defense—were linked to the ongoing production of brass band music rooted in these Civil War experiences and their various articulations of affective labor. Brassroots democracy created spaces for quiet voices to sing; invoked joy and instilled motivation in trying times; rallied assemblies for self-defense or political celebrations; and aestheticized the cooperative social relations that Black communities would struggle to institutionalize as a guiding ethos for local governance. For these reasons, its musical forms were bound to the grassroots movements that gave these ensembles life and meaning. Both wings, a cultural front and an institutionally oriented politics, aimed to generate more democratic possibilities in legislatures and in the streets—sometimes on the plantation itself. They helped create and consolidate a Black body politic and challenged the attempt of the "white republic" to institute post-slavery apartheid.[83] Even after Reconstruction was overthrown, brass bands continued to summon these visions to defend these expanded public and musical spheres, endowing everyday life with an affective consensus born of social change.

THE RADICAL BANDS OF YIELDED STREETS: BRASSROOTS DEMOCRACY DURING RECONSTRUCTION

>They know when I make that roll, they got a certain distance.
>
>*Art Blakey*[84]

In an 1887 article in the *Alexandria Gazette* titled "Disgraceful Proceedings," the white conservative newspaper denounced "a large crowd of disorderly negro men, women and children, headed by a negro band, [who] paraded some of the streets." The paraders and their band were celebrating the electoral defeat of a white supremacist Democrat, Judge Stuart. Particularly "disgraceful" for the writer was how "the mob passed his [Stuart's] house, they yelled, jeered and discharged cannon crackers, and then proceeded to a lot, near the local depot, where, with shouts and dances, they burned Judge Stuart in effigy." The procession then congregated by the store owned by the victor, Mr. Corbet, who celebrated the "victory they had won in the hot-bed" of the Democratic Party. Well after the fall of Reconstruction and with white supremacy all but institutionalized, this spectacle nonetheless reminded the writers of the sounds and spectacles of Black Reconstruction governments: "The action of the negroes last night showed what they would do if their party should ever get into power again."[85]

In account after account of white supremacist newspapers from the late 1880s, nothing so disturbed their peace of mind as the music of a Black brass band. It almost always brought back memories of the most "disgraceful" moments of Reconstruction. In 1889, a journalist in Anderson, South Carolina, bemoaned how a Black band led "the largest and most enthusiastic Republican or negro meeting" in recent memory. With "a crowd of negroes ... estimated at about 500," the band marched to the courthouse in Anderson, South Carolina. Black men and women came from far away to the call of African American Republican organizer Henry Kennedy. "It was equal to a circus to the lookers-on," wrote the correspondent, "and brought back forcibly to the minds of our citizens the scenes and incidents that often occurred when the thieving carpet-baggers would come around on their campaign tours."[86]

The outrage of the white press provides a window into just how central Black band music had become in the Black grassroots movements of the postwar South. Brass bands were heard inaugurating mass meetings, during election campaigns, and in the social events of everyday life, both within Radical Republican spaces and conservative white circles. For instance, in 1872 the *Wilmington Star* editorialized that the city's white elite should fund the training and recruitment of white musicians, and rapidly. "We will then be no longer dependent upon a Radical band for our musical enjoyment."[87] It is certainly interesting that the *radical* nature of the band was of particular concern. In these bands' performative style, white ears heard the forces of Radical Reconstruction. White supremacists were right to be concerned: Black bands helped drive voters to polls, inaugurate mass meetings, adorn parades, and legitimize—or delegitimize—elections. This interconnected nexus of music, activism, and democratic expansion in the Reconstruction years is another way to define brassroots democracy—as a set of communitarian practices, both musical and social, which ensured that new political knowledge and participatory decision-making were enacted by Black activists and white allies.

Prior formations of sound and social movement in jubilee celebrations and Black military bands brought extra layers of history and signification to bear on these forms of musical assembly. Their musical associations, like those of the Civil War, were as threatening to a recalcitrant white press as they were empowering to Black activists. Symbolic and material, hopeful and cautious, looking to the future while honoring the past: Black musicians performed these phenomenologically dense gestures while grinding, day-to-day, as laborers, organizers, and intellectuals. As Mark Johnson notes, these Reconstruction musicians "did more than bang on drums and toot on horns. They generated enthusiasm, made political statements, and enforced their community's political norms and boundaries."[88] They reminded listeners both Black and white of their victory in the Civil War, the Thirteenth and Fourteenth Amendments, and candidates who earned their present-day support.

War and its aftermath changed Black musicians, for obvious reasons that nonetheless shocked white supremacist sensibilities. For example, James H. Alston was an Alabama shoemaker and an enslaved Civil War musician forced to use his musical talents in the army of Confederate General Cullen A. Battle.[89] At some point in the Civil War, Alston managed to secure his freedom and played drums for the Union army. When Alston came back from the war, Battle angrily remarked that the once-enslaved drummer was a changed man.[90] Alston served as the president of the Tuskegee Republican Club in 1867 and was then elected to the Alabama Legislature for Macon County between 1868 and 1870. A hostile sheriff, William Dougherty, claimed that Alston had "a stronger influence over the minds of the colored men in Macon county" than any other individual.[91] Alston was not only an elected official but, importantly, an organizer. In 1867, he was tapped by national leadership to organize a local Union League. Conceived as vehicles for mobilizing Black voters, Union Leagues quickly outgrew this narrow mandate and developed into what Julie Saville describes as "part political machine, part labor union, part popular tribunal, part moral or intellectual improvement body, part renters' association, part retail cooperative."[92] Union Leagues, complained one Alabama overseer, taught freedpeople to imagine and to demand that "they were to have the lands and the growing crop upon it."[93] Likewise, the Alabama Labor Union, of which Alston was an early member, explicitly organized around demands made by Black farmworkers and was part of the first attempt at a modern agricultural union among Black Alabamans, including George Washington Cox of Tuscaloosa and James K. Green of Hale.[94] These activists not only discussed labor contracts and strategies for agitation but also the acquisition of land—including, through their Committee on Labor and Wages, collectively, via an installment plan.[95]

Violent backlash was an ever-present threat to Black organizing. In 1868, for example, the Ku Klux Klan attempted to intimidate Alston to order other freedmen to abandon rented land and return to work on white-owned plantations. He refused, and two years later, he and his family were attacked at night, with gunshots fired into their house. He survived, summoned backup, and after a protracted standoff between armed Black freedmen against the Ku Klux Klan and the Democratic-controlled police forces, some of his followers were arrested and he was ordered to leave the county. Alston later testified at the congressional Ku Klux Klan hearings that it was Cullen Battle, the Confederate General who had forced Alston to use his musical talents in a war to defend his own enslavement, who led the movement to expel him.[96] Ironically, the very groups that Alston would later lead also employed music to forward the cause of Black liberation.

The music played by Reconstruction activists had profound martial and cultural functions reminiscent of the Union military experience for both Black activists and white supremacists, who interpreted the dispersal of musical instruments by the Union League to freedpeople as an act of aggression.[97] North Carolina railroad baron and Confederate army veteran Josiah Turner detested Union Leagues for their opposition to the railroad. He claimed they assembled at night "at the call of drum and fife." These sounds, again, summoned negative associations: "We knew then that this was all leading to trouble and blood."[98]

Music, especially drumming, appears to have had a similar role in Macon, Mississippi, in 1875. During a tense mass Republican meeting two days before the election, where fifteen hundred mostly unnamed freedpeople were harassed by hundreds of armed White Leaguers. One Republican organizer remembered, "On account of the state of feeling we decide to take the negroes off the streets . . . We told the colored men to get their drum and fife and call them down there. The white men got hold of the drum and cut it all to pieces. In fact, they had given notice before that the beating of the drum would be a signal of war."[99] While drumming languages had provided Black Carolinians with a military communication infrastructure as far back as the 1739 Stono Rebellion, the long roll emerged out of a particular Civil War sonic vocabulary.[100] Colonel George Sutherland remembered "the sudden awakening in the night by the alarm of the 'long roll' . . . which seems to say, 'Arise, oh men! To your death.' No one knows what is coming; how near the danger is, or how great it is." Black drummers and veterans retained the sonic language of the Civil War to fight for autonomy in the Reconstruction era.[101] For example, in Meriwether, South Carolina, in 1874, the all-white Sweetwater Sabre Club fired into Black militia leader Edward "Ned" Tennant's home. Tennant survived and called on his drummer to sound the "long roll," summoning two hundred members of his militia from surrounding plantations to confront the sixty white paramilitaries.[102] This was not Tennant's first near-death experience at the hands of white reactionary violence. He had previously managed to escape a similar militia ambush in Edgefield. He stealthily navigated for twenty-five miles to federal officials, deftly traversing in a country "swarming with whites looking for him" and surviving on the creeks and outskirts of Sumter Forest by blending into its soundscapes and ecosystems.[103]

As during the antebellum period and the Civil War, music was a call to arms. In South Carolina, Ned Tennant relied on the skillful technique of his militia drummer to survive an attack. In Alabama, James Alston's experience as a military drummer was not ancillary to his talent as an organizer: Once a drummer for he who claimed to be his master, he now drummed for his people. "The habits and rituals of race," writes Barbara Jeanne Fields on the transition from slavery to freedom, "became new in essence, even when they persisted in form."[104] The changing aesthetics of Black drum performance in the postwar South were the expressions of a revolution that was simultaneously cultural, economic, and political. Drum rolls redeveloped a centuries-old technology of counter-plantation communication to survive and organize in an unstable, violent era with a balance of power that was continuously in question. The words of the jazz drummer Art Blakey that began this section suggest that these drumming techniques retained the ability to communicate spatial and temporal imaginaries within Black musical publics. These patterned mnemonics have much to do with the organizing during the Reconstruction to Redemption periods and the struggle to retain the right to self-defense and communal autonomy.

Drum-featured musical performances were commonly used to index social progress and Black advancement during Reconstruction. In 1874, in Claiborne County, Mississippi, the boundaries of Southern society were tested when Ellen Smith married Haskin Smith. Ellen's parents owned the Port Gibson Hotel; before the Civil War, they had also claimed ownership of Haskin Smith himself. Now free and a Republican politician, the marriage caused the predictable stir, and

Ellen's father, William, threatened to kill Haskin. When the newlyweds returned to Port Gibson after a short honeymoon, a "cadre of armed bodyguards"—Black volunteer militias—"paraded" Haskin Smith through the town, a move that historian Justin Behrend suggests "may have upset white Democrats even more than the marriage."[105] Such parades were common throughout the South, often linked to social and political struggle. In 1866, the federal officer James W. Johnson witnessed a march, "with red colors flying," of Black workers protesting to demand better contract terms.[106] The pro-Confederate historian John Abney Chapman remembered how Black militiamen and bands marched through the streets of Edgefield, South Carolina, in 1870; he claimed they were followed by "every Negro man *and woman* [who] thirsted to be enrolled," and this mobilization of thousands was a marker of the "disintegration of the old order of things that was taking place all around."[107] He was right: across the reconstructing South, spectacle and its attendant music were powerful technologies of communication, unifying Black freedpeople while projecting a new political order.

Within these mobile spaces grew a new commons, organized around the takeover of public space. Radical marches "symbolized the revolutionary transformation in social relations wrought by emancipation," writes Eric Foner.[108] Herein lies the core of brassroots democracy's power: its appropriation of public space and its ability to reproduce the energy of jubilee to direct the ongoing social revolution in the South. Mobility and presence were made possible and spiritualized by musical rituals, and it is impossible to imagine this democratic revolution without music. "For former slaves," argues Thanayi Michelle Jackson, "the ability to move about the city at will was one of the first enactments of freedom, and the organized marching of black people was an early indication of their collective mobilization."[109] This Black political ritual was so consistent that many whites considered countermobilization a lost cause, leading one white Missourian to observe, "The whites have, to a great extent—greater than ever before—yielded the streets to the negroes."[110] Of course, these marches happened not only within cities but across miles of rural counties and Louisiana parishes. As late as the 1890s, jazz musicians such as Sonny Henry and Ben Kelly recall brass band parades that started at the church on the Magnolia plantation and proceeded to march south to the Woodland, St. Sophie, and other plantations in the sugar belts, defying planters who wished to keep rural laborers isolated and unorganized.[111]

In her study of the "Emancipation Circuit," Thulani Davis highlights how freedpeoples' construction of these networks was a major development in and of itself, deeply linked to the political content of Reconstruction but also durable beyond its demise. "The circuit is an achievement that emerged as a product of displacement during the Civil War and emancipation," Davis explains, "created by people defined by overt fugitive status, and characterized by the understandings people had of being fugitive, of displacement, and of fugitive status provoking policing and resistance. After emancipation, these understandings persisted and informed how Reconstruction was built on the local level." In the crucible of Black communities' struggle against police power and paramilitary violence that criminalized political organizing and cultural expressions of emancipation, African American autonomous institutions—like churches, families, schools, mutual aid societies, and labor unions—ensured social reproduction through linking diverse constituencies in a choreography of interdependence. "The process by which freedpeople engaged citizenship and built a palimpsest of layers of organizing structures," Davis explains, "allowed the continued pursuit of community interests after Reconstruction, often movements that happened across the region." One expression of this interlinked circuit was the advent of blues singers, who Davis considers avatars of Black postbellum cultural identity. Their travels through this post–Civil War spatial configuration charted by Reconstruction activists rode and renewed the same geography frequented by union organizers, preachers, and teachers.[112]

Indeed, the sociomusical work of James Alston and Sonny Henry in the plantation countryside suggests that brassroots democracy was a powerful vector in the consummation of this circuit (see also chapter 4). Musicians created mobilities at both local and interregional levels, producing new political spaces that could be activated again from without. In many ways, their work envisioned the Emancipation Circuit before it was institutionalized in more legible formations. Black activists and musicians deployed sound to revitalize the civic life of both the countryside and the cities, collapsing rural and urban divisions and creating an aural counter-public through musical performance. It was precisely the spread of this new polis that was so problematic for the planter class. These networks of communication remapped old geographies of enslavement based in feudal agriculture, imbuing urban architecture and rural landscape with the sonic logos of community, even challenging the common sense of apartheid. In 1872, the *North Louisiana Journal* noted how bands at Republican meetings activated audiences "composed of both white and black citizens."[113] Whether through protest parades, workers associations, or mass meetings where a shared political outlook was developed, this music played an important function in this new type of public space, one both aural and ideological.

The ties of this music to grassroots democracy were very visible in their connection to the voting process. Postbellum voting was very difficult, especially in rural parishes where "regulators" would unleash violence on Black voters. Black organizers coordinated trips to the polls, ensuring that would-be voters received relevant ballots while defending themselves against violence. They also prevented bribery and oversaw ballot counting—a self-organized system that Steven Hahn describes as "in essence, a military operation."[114] In Greene Country, Georgia, despite mounting political violence by the Ku Klux Klan, the once-enslaved community activist Abram Colby helped organize column after column, in military formation, to march to the polls with voters and Black community members for the 1872 election. Like the emancipation parades, voters carried flags, banners, and cornstalks. They projected unity in spirit and their step through song, resulting in a remarkable turnout of more than twelve hundred of Greene County's fifteen hundred eligible Black voters. The county was carried for Ulysses S. Grant.[115] Brassroots mobilities contributed to what Thulani Davis calls a "circuit born of abolition," and their capacity to rehearse new social relations was further honed and developed in the context of forging affective consensus—a consensus that not only emerges from, but is constitutive of, this shared mode of aural production.[116]

Musical ritual was often put to use in the service of enforcing African American community voting norms: in Lincoln County, North Carolina, one "conservative" Black man associated with the Democratic Party was surrounded by Black Republicans who surrounded his home with the sound of "tin pans and horns," as well as displays of guns and pistols. They sang a song that denounced his recent Democrat vote. Its chorus rang: "He had voted himself into Slavery."[117] These were part of a constellation of tactics to enforce group solidarity. Black women were recorded ripping the clothes of Black men in public who succumbed to pressure from white bosses or militias to vote for white supremacists.[118] These scenes reveal that voting was treated as a communal activity in which women, while denied the vote, still had substantial power. As Elsa Barkley Brown has explained, one's vote was a "collective" possession in which the community as a whole had the final say—what we might think of as a commons.[119]

Public music-making likewise could be heard during rallies in which the *right* to vote was being fought for. On the Fourth of July following the Emancipation Proclamation, Black and white New Orleanians then living under Union military occupation made their voices heard though a massive parade and rally at the grandstand at the base of Canal Street. As night fell, a torchlight parade, complete with marching bands and an array of red, white, and blue banners, led to a feast of "twelve bacon hogsheads" while the Black preacher Reverend James Keelan extolled the company of a multiracial and multilingual audience: "Fellow citizens, this is the first time for eighty seven years that the son of Africa is permitted to join in a public celebration of the Fourth of July—yet he had the right, according to the Declaration of Independence." His remarks continued: "Our country has given us our rights—we have now but to defend them." Keelan's speech was, according to the event's organizers, "the first time on any public occasion in the South, among white men, a colored man spoke to a public audience like a man."[120] This "miscegenated" gathering in 1863 outraged former Confederates, and a week later in New Orleans, white rioters rampaged through the South's largest city, lynching random Black men whom they blamed for the war.

Despite the threat of violence, participants traveled from far distances to participate. One freedman in Montgomery justified both his attendance at parades and the political determination of freedpeople more broadly when he intoned at a mass meeting in 1867: "We'd walk fifteen miles in wartime to find out about the battle. We can walk fifteen miles and more to find out how to vote."[121] These were spaces of political education as much as celebration. Here, in the heart of the former slave power, the music demanded a world that the old powers would resist with a ferocity rarely rivaled in history.

REMIXING THE STATE: BLACK FIRE COMPANIES AND BRASS BANDS DURING REDEMPTION

> The spectacle . . . is a world view transformed into an objective force.
> *Guy Debord*[122]

One fateful day, the life of clarinetist Willie Parker of the Eagle Band was changed. Parker was raised by his godmother in St. Sophie plantation in Plaquemines Parish, in the sugar country seventy-three miles southeast of New Orleans. He received a music education from brassroots formations from a young age, playing drums "every night of the week" in the Terminal Band that existed on the plantation, with James Humphrey providing instruction.[123] When he finally met his mother, it was a life-changing experience. "And my mother didn't see me till I was nineteen years old. And how she come to see me!"[124] The occasion was the annual fireman's parade. Recalling his encounter, Parker jumps from his dramatic reunion with his mother to a vivid description of the day's festivities, which were punctuated by the Black Vigilance Fire Company and the Excelsior Brass Band:

> Oh, that used to be a big day once. The fourth of March, fireman's parade, boy, firemens they didn't have no, no car, automobile like they got now. They used to pull the wagon, you know, the fire department. Long red rope, long, eight, nine blocks long and cars hook on to them every company had its position and that rope enters on to all of them, and pulled them all along. Band of music and everything. I know the band here, you've read of it, called Excelsior Brass Band, old man George Baquet was the leader of that band and the fireman

didn't have to hire—didn't have to sign no contract with them or nothing, just tell 'em, "we want you for tomorrow night." All right, they gonna be there . . . the firemen made them a present of a suit, full dress suit, red, white, and blue. Blue pants and a big red cape, blue coat with red stripes in it. Oh, they had caps, you know, they had pretty uniforms. Yeah, the firemens made 'em a present, of that. They used to do all the fireman's work.[125]

As in the Civil War and Reconstruction—from 1867 through 1877—these brass band parades were spaces of communal reintegration and healing. But Parker was attending this parade in 1904, when the Republican Party and the Black electorate had been all but banished. Yet, decades later, Reconstruction and the revolutionary legacy of the Civil War were reproduced in these parades, which still articulated modalities of Black power and organization; they still mediated the concerns and wishes of the Black community through spectacle and negotiated sound; they still provided a space for congregation. According to Parker, bands understood these events as such and participated in these communal endeavors by not requiring payment, accepting in-kind services instead. The clothing they were gifted from the fire company seems to have been an important element—an essential part of a counterspectacle, performing statecraft from below.

Militarized costumes—"planned after the style of the Prussian military," with "helmet hats," cords, plumes, brass buttons, epaulets, and stripes, in some cases—signaled to paraders' would-be paramilitary harassers that they would continue to memorialize the victories of the Civil War and Reconstruction.[126] Here, memory took on intense political dimensions, and its sound was an important aspect of "memory activism."[127] Their association of music, militancy, and commandeering of public space threatened Democratic paramilitaries and white supremacist activists with reminders of Black liberation and white humiliation. The performances of the Excelsior Brass Band and the Black Vigilance Fire company demonstrate what Shana Redmond has observed in another context: how "Black musics have remixed the modalities of the state in order to foster alternative exercises of freedom and justice," creating kinds of anthems that "helped to sustain world-altering collective visions . . . that make the listening audience and political public merge."[128] These civic lessons speak to a participatory public sphere that is more inclusive, and where power is more decentralized, than that envisioned in the US Constitution or hegemonic democratic frameworks. Such world-altering "visions" were triggered aurally, from one generation to the next. After the fall of Reconstruction, volunteer fire companies carried on this vision during and despite an age of anti-Black violence.[129]

Black fire companies provided a symbolic import as counterinstitutional and counter-plantation formations whose members were disciplined and uniformed. There was a dire need for such entities within the Black community: with the 1877 ascendency of Democratic rule in Louisiana, the White League quickly assumed the role of the state militia and the new governor Francis T. Nicholls forced Black militias to disarm.[130] The New Orleans City Legislature was particularly eager to annul the permits for the Colored Veterans Benevolent Association—located in Storyville, an epicenter of early jazz culture, in 1899 for being a "nuisance."[131] As the tide turned on Reconstruction and organized paramilitaries attacked Black labor and civil rights activists, music and public performance were still utilized to create community to withstand racial violence. Fire companies were some of the most important autonomous Black institutions in the Reconstruction and post-Reconstruction epochs. And, as the story of Willie Parker demonstrates, the formative generations of pre-jazz musicians interacted directly with these organizations, as did most Black Louisianans.

Fire companies, like all public institutions, became battlegrounds over space and power in the Reconstruction South, a terrain of conflict in the struggle between brassroots democracy and white supremacist silencing. Black fire companies were created in response to the abuses of power by white fire departments. In 1867, a Black man in New Orleans was gravely injured by a white fireman who impaled him with a ladder, possibly an act of anti-Reconstruction violence. After this incident, a contemporary observer noted that "there was a concerted attack by colored men on the firemen."[132] In the same year, a white fire company in the city was accused of interfering with a "colored procession" by "sending a [false] fire alarm during its progress."[133]

Perhaps because of their costumed apparel and their association with the state, Black fire companies were instrumental in the post-Reconstruction fight against white supremacy, even as Black militias and Union Clubs were disbanded.[134] Music was never far removed from these displays of communal resilience. In 1883, John A. Pope, the president of a Black fire company in Mobile, Alabama, celebrated the birth of his son Odeil by founding the Excelsior Brass Band (not to be confused with New Orleans's Excelsior Brass Band).[135] The band was conceived as an appendage of the Creole Fire Company, and several Black and Creole of color firefighters, such as Alex Terez, joined the musical outfit. The band became the most prominent of the city's Mardi Gras brass bands. Still active today, Mobile's Excelsior Band leads most of the city's parades and its ranks are populated by, according to Joey Brackner, "the finest of veteran musicians."[136]

Post-Reconstruction Black fire companies used their numbers, their uniforms and military discipline, or their music to challenge the paramilitary violence of the White League. In 1887, five hundred members of the Black Vigilance Fire Company visited the town of Thibodaux, where White Leaguers were engaged in a campaign of violence aimed at intimidating organizers of a budding labor movement, just as they had done in the neighboring parishes of Ascension, St. James, and St. John the Baptist.[137] There, the Black Vigilance Fire Company "serenaded" the white supremacist mayor in satiric song. Unfortunately, "the gentleman was either absent or did not want to receive negro *serenaders*," reported the *Weekly Pelican*. It must have been quite a spectacle to see five hundred uniformed Black men taunting a white man who refused to leave his home during a campaign of white violence in the countryside. Afterward, the firemen "repaired to Eureka Hall, where dancing was indulged to a late hour."[138] The dancing, and probably the serenading, would have been accompanied by a band—possibly the Excelsior Brass Band, which employed the Tio brothers.[139]

The music of Black fire companies amid the white supremacist counterrevolution named "Redemption" illustrates how, as in prior epochs, Black music commanded public space and generated an affective consensus among grassroots activists in a struggle to counteract the antidemocratic violence that threatened their movements for autonomy. Yet by the early twentieth century, the militant activism of Reconstruction radicals—of plantation seizures and sit-ins, of agricultural cooperatives and interracial constitutional conventions—had faded into the background. Yet, as Robin D. G. Kelley reminds us, "The collapse of an organization does not necessarily signify the destruction of a movement or the eradication of traditions of radicalism."[140] Brass bands attached to fire companies continued a tradition of radical procession, opening a space for public memory to disrupt a white supremacist culture based on forgetting by infusing counter-plantation culture into daily life. Reconstruction-era Black militias who had guaranteed a measure of self-defense for Black grassroots activists were channeled through the regalia and sound of Black fire companies, who provided localized and symbolically charged outlets where momentum and energy from previous epochs could be sustained during a time when other militant action was circumscribed.[141] Their performances extended the hopes of Reconstruction by redeploying the theatrical and musical language of brassroots democracy from decades prior. That many future jazz musicians would receive training or inspiration from these bands is no coincidence, for jazz was the expression of brassroots democracy as the New South imposed plantation relations over Black Louisianans.

CONCLUSION

> And from that mighty music the beginning
> Of jazz arose, tempestuous, capricious,
> Declaring to the whites in accents loud
> That not entirely was the planet theirs.
> O Music, it was you who permitted us
> To lift our face and peer into the eyes
> Of future liberty, that would one day be ours.
>
> *Patrice Lumumba*[142]

The sonic-spatial technology that brassroots democracy fostered in the post–Civil War period provided important tools for Black musicians organizing in the cane fields, in Storyville, and in the streets of New Orleans through the jazz age and beyond. Its ability to respiritualize segregated public space through communal music meant that the geographic *range* of Black brass musicians was important. Even and especially in the long night of white supremacy and segregation, Black brass music's presence across a city or countryside could be healing for young men and women grappling with the reinvented slave power. A young Louis Armstrong recalled the Onward Brass Band passing through a baseball game he played in as a child, and pointed to the range of this band. When Armstrong heard the high notes of Joe Oliver's trumpet, it shattered the isolation he and other poor Black youth were confined to, and the band transformed the day, and the lives, of community members in the parade's aural radius. Armstrong explains:

> McDonald Cemetery was just about a mile away from where the Black Diamonds [Armstrong's baseball team] was playing the Algiers team. Whenever a funeral from New Orleans had a body to be buried in the McDonald Cemetery, they would have to cross the Canal Street ferryboat and march down the same road right near our ball game. Of course, when they passed us playing a slow funeral march, we only paused with the game and tipped our hats as to pay respect. When the last of the funeral passed we would continue the game. The game was in full force when the Onward Band was returning from the cemetery, after they had put the body in the ground, they were swingin' ["] It's a Long Way to Tipperary.["] They were swinging so good until Joe Oliver reached in the high register beating out those high notes in very fine fashion. And broke our ball [game]. Yea! The players commenced to dropping bats and balls . . . and we all followed them. All the way back to the New Orleans side and to their destination.[143]

For Armstrong, the city's racial geography was transcended through this sonic congregation. It was not only Joe Oliver's heavens-splitting upper register but the distance that the band could be heard. It "broke" not only physical distance but social distance too; they crossed the river and marched through neighborhoods where they could not have traveled alone. Oliver was part of a movement that challenged apartheid's sound barrier. Danny Barker claims that Buddy Bolden's sound could be heard ten miles away. "New Orleans has a different kind of acoustics from other cities," he explained.[144] Jelly Roll Morton likewise commented on the sheer size of Bolden's sound by using a theological metaphor strikingly similar to those of Black musicians in the Civil War: he referred to Bolden as "the blowingest man since Gabriel."[145] Like the Reconstruction brass bands from which they descended, New Orleans brass bands in the second-line tradition challenged the white republic's monopolization of sound and its ordering of public space. They boldly traversed segregated racial orders, utilizing bassroots democracy's jubilant sociability and sheer volume to augment the impact of musical ideas and communal gathering. This alchemy between desegregation, social imagination, and earth-shaking sound summoned thousands of devotional listeners to Gabriel's new flock, a radical act of assembly.[146]

Such assembling was a novel form of communal antiphony that negotiated the contradictions between representation, popular sovereignty, and collective decision-making. Prefigured in the communal musical creation process heard in Civil War campfires, it was reproduced in jazz, for jazz, as the Jamaican American Harlem Renaissance writer A. J. Rogers wrote, exhibited a "mocking disregard for formality" as "a leveler."[147] The music itself came to embed these norms—this social relation transliterated in sound, not alienated but communicated through affect, energy, and intention. The World Saxophone Quartet, saxophonist Oliver Lake explained, does not have a single "leader"; rather, they "know that the music is the leader of the band."[148] The cultural technology of brassroots democracy was refined over three historical periods: the Civil War, Reconstruction, and Jim Crow. This chapter delved into the first two. It is to this latter period that we now turn.

SIX

Black Unions and the Blues

Dockworkers' Activism and New Orleans Jazz

> Whenever I went to the Apollo [and] I would hear Louis Armstrong . . . the music and the response was such that I know all the power is hidden in them there, it's waiting to come out, and the day when it comes out and it takes a political form it is going to shake this nation as nothing before has shaken it.
>
> C. L. R. James[1]

Willie Parker, a clarinetist who once "hauled tobacco . . . [in] great big hogsheads, couldn't put but four of 'em on a wagon," played an integral role in the 1907 historic interracial dockworkers' strike. This historic movement brought New Orleans commerce to a standstill, shutting down its major port and bringing New Orleans's shipping barons to their knees. By 1958, now a jazz clarinetist, Willie Parker still openly supported the strikers. Recalling his activist days in an interview, he narrated the killing of a "scab" laborer by strikers, and proclaimed: "[They] ought to kill all them old scabs, people striking and they don't wanna help them out."[2] Parker felt differently about this man's death when he found out "[it was] a friend of mine—my father's god child."[3] Nonetheless, the ease with which Parker utters this line is striking. Almost fifty years after the strike, the importance of class consciousness was still common sense for this clarinetist, highlighting the enduring impact of the movement on the musicians of the era.

Willie Parker's commitment to labor solidarity was not an anomaly. The depth of the Black community's involvement in the 1907 strike was profound. Wives and mothers of the mostly-male strikers furnished food supplies to their families through any means necessary, especially those who worked in white men's kitchens. They smuggled food at home at night under their aprons, which "contributed greatly toward holding out," remembered union activist Oscar Armeringer.[4] The *Picayune* complained that African American women direct-action activists attacked a scab who transported cotton to the docks by mule-drawn wagon. "By sheer strength [they] lifted the float from the muddy street and held it suspended, while others of the band, skillfully using wrenches, removed the wheels. The float was left a wreck in the middle of the street."[5]

Nor was Parker the only musician to have experienced the power of organized labor close at hand. The ranks of professional musicians daylighting as dockworkers exploded with Black rural-to-urban migration by the turn of the twentieth century. Musicians as diverse as Jelly Roll Morton, Louis Armstrong, George Lewis, Pops Foster, and Willie Parker all spent a significant part of their early lives loading and unloading cotton, tobacco, bananas, coal, and other commodities whose distribution led to New Orleans's reemergence as the financial center of the South.[6] Songs like "Roustabout Rag" and "Roustabout Shuffle" attested to the impact that these spaces had on the musicians as songs increasingly became indexes of Black dockworkers' occupational life.[7] Dock work was both the site of improvised musical community and brutal experiences of exploitation. Their expressive culture was so commented upon in the nineteenth century such that, as Gushee explains, "roustabouts . . . made the New Orleans levee one of the wonders of nineteenth-century America."[8] The work itself required accompaniment and improvisation, and as longshoreman-activist Stan Weir recalled, longshore workers' vernacular culture make fellow workers "an audience" as "self-respect and socialization" was fashioned through cooperative labor.[9] Musical socialization on the job, however, was not an adequate compensatory salve. Jelly Roll Morton remembered that as the worst-treated dockworkers of all, roustabouts "would carry on their backs all kinds of things . . . looked like a man couldn't carry so much. Singing and moving to rhythm of songs as much as they could . . . They were just like in slavery."[10]

But dock work did not dehumanize and destroy these musicians. As Black workers began to organize to control the labor process on the docks, powerful Black unions emerged that eventually became the strongest in the entire country. As a result of intense negotiations, the assertion of Black labor power, and tactical alliances with white unions, Black musicians found near-constant employment on the docks and representation within the trade union movement.[11] Their music increasingly disseminated Black aesthetics and forms of communal music-making to other groups of workers. This unique experience of proletarianization facilitated intercultural languages, and even interracial spaces, in a city marred by Jim Crow and white supremacy. As New Orleans dockworker historian Daniel

Rosenberg attests, "Unionism bore on a range of activities . . . At levee union dances, parades, funerals and parties, Black dockworker-musicians experimented with the new improvised forms of the period before crowds of levee laborers."[12] Black dockworkers' unions established halls that hosted and protected the new music from government shutdown, while musicians created new senses of time and rhythm within these spaces that resonated with dockworkers' attempts to shape the temporalities of the labor process. Buddy Bolden's new behind-the-beat music was often described as capable of releasing communal joy, and this practice of collective slowdown was not dissimilar to the practice of slowing the pace of production of the job. These practices of temporality were not developed in a vacuum: Bolden often performed at dockworkers' union halls and in their Labor Day celebrations.

The organizational synergy between dockworkers and African American musical practices reveals how resistance to a reinvigorated capitalism infused the cultures of early jazz with practices of brassroots democracy. Whether at parades, funerals, Baptist churches, or at protests, the influence of the new blues-based music was all-encompassing within the daily operations of dockworkers' unions and vital in the development of participants' class consciousness. Union organizers and their working-class base socialized through and to the music, especially in the social halls bought and maintained by union dues.

New Orleans waterfront unions' exemplary success during the initial years of Jim Crow and New South capitalism had a lot to do with their relationship to this revolutionary music. Black music facilitated spaces of interracial solidarity by creating new languages that became a vehicle for communication between multiethnic workers, deepening the impact of the labor movement beyond ensuring wages and jobs to creating a genuine working-class culture founded in solidarity and mutual respect. Musician-dockworkers redefined everyday life, starting with the experience of time, organizing a dissident and dissonant critique of capitalist temporalities by developing participatory structures of feeling. Despite these idyllic moments, paternalistic attitudes exhibited by white union leadership toward Black workers disrupted solidarity and the cultural efforts to build a unified movement. Yet, by 1907, Black union leaders ultimately prevailed by negotiating power-sharing with their white counterparts, reflecting how this Black resistance tradition was capable of strategically moving between race-based mobilization and class-based alliances when the opportunity structure allowed.[13] In both their musical expressions and their activism, Black dockworkers articulated a distinct rhythm of freedom and autonomy that can be heard in their music. These worker-musicians did more than critique capital: they embodied an alternative. They enacted what Robin D. G. Kelley in another context has called the "task [that] might have been the most important of all": the creation of "alternatives to Jim Crow capitalism" during the bleakest times of Southern violence against Black peoples. The activating and reimagining of a communal phenomenology through a shared sense of time was one of the powerful legacies that both dockworkers and dockworking musicians left for future generations of jazz practitioners.[14]

These legacies speak to a musical form so powerfully able to make and unmake time, space, and sociality, that it compelled C. L. R. James to predict that it had the power to shake the nation. The resistant temporalities that Black music constructed in dialogue with Black organized labor were one of the liberatory lineages from which brassroots democracy grew.

BLACK TEMPORALITIES IN THE RHYTHMS OF DOCKWORKER STRUGGLE

"Their unionism was far more than a matter of hours and wages. It was a religion, and their only hope of rising from the depths of a slavery more cruel in many respects than chattel slavery," attested the German American socialist author, artist, and organizer Oscar Ameringer in 1902 after attending a meeting with "the Negro union in their own labor temple."[15] Ameringer had spent decades lending his skills to the American labor movement; he emigrated from Bavaria to Cincinnati, Ohio, at the age of sixteen and joined the American Federation of Labor (AFL) as a cabinet maker, flutist, and cornetist.[16] In Columbus, Ohio, he became editor of *Labor World*, a socialist periodical, where he first began a prolific career in left-leaning journalism that earned him the unofficial honorific "the Mark Twain of American Socialism."[17] When he came to New Orleans with the AFL in 1902 to organize brewers and dockworkers, Ameringer held these Black workers in high esteem: "With a wisdom born of suffering," he claimed that "as strikers, there could be no better"; while they might "lose the shine of their skins, grow thinner as the weeks go on," in the end they demonstrated more solidarity than their white counterparts. "There were a few breaks on the part of the white men," noted Ameringer, "[but] none on the Negro side."[18]

Black dockworkers made up the rank and file of the historic interracial strikes of the late nineteenth and early twentieth century, whose disruption of international trade and Jim Crow sent shockwaves through the white supremacist commercial and political establishment. State Senator Charles C. Cordill, a segregationist strongman with "almost dictatorial power," was assigned to negotiate with the strikers.[19] Cordill began his career by massacring a coalition of white and Black farmers joined together in the "Country People's Ticket" in Tensas Parish in 1878.[20] When Senator Cordill discovered New Orleans dockworker unions' "50–50" arrangement, whereby Black and white workers were each equally represented in both jobs and union leadership, he was furious. As Ameringer paraphrased him: "The ideah! The ve'y ideah! White men conspirin' with n--s against the honoah and propser'ty of the gre'at po't of N'yo'l'ns; against the honoah and propsepr'ty of the gre'at State of Louisianah itself!"[21]

Cordill was ineffective in suppressing Black organizing in the nine-week strike in 1907 that shut down New Orleans's docks and drew national and international attention. His mid-negotiation outburst was quickly answered by the Black dockworker A. J. Ellis:

> Please sit down, Senator. We're not here to save the honor and prosper'ty of the great State of Louisiana. We is here to settle the strike. That's what they sent you down here for. Your job is to see to it that we work the longest possible hours at the least possible pay. Our job is to make your crowd pay us the highest possible wages for the lowest possible amount of work. Now, let's get down to business. What's more, we've won the strike already, else you gentlemen wouldn't be here to talk compromise, honor, and prosperity.[22]

While a logical enough explanation of labor demands—as few working hours for as much compensation as possible—Ellis articulates a battle not only over the quantity of work or wages but over the control of time itself. His insistence that workers determine the rhythm and pace of work speaks to a philosophical point of departure among the Black labor movement in post–Civil War Louisiana, one that would have profound implications for the aesthetic priorities of jazz musicians in New Orleans at the turn of the century.

The struggle over time was a theme that connected urban and rural labor struggles throughout a multigenerational battle in Louisiana and the Caribbean at large. Stephanie Camp referred to the practice of enslaved women regulating the pace at which they worked, and their frequent attendance at clandestine parties, as "stealing time and space for themselves."[23] In 1867, freedmen in the Concordia Parish were ordered to go to work when a plantation owner blasted a horn. Instead, the freedmen deserted the plantation, marched to the office of the local Freedmen's Bureau agent, and protested with a revealing complaint: "Haven't we been working ten hours a day all summer for a share of the crop, and now you begin to keep our time!"[24] Columbian, calendrical time was simply not how Black communities measured their lives or their responsibilities. Births, the commencement of field labor, marriages, separations through sale, the onset of hearing loss, major uprisings, significant deaths—the central life events for individuals, families, or communities—were positioned in time by the enslaved by associating them with another well-known event. Henry Clay Bruce, enslaved in Virginia and northern Mississippi, remembered how his parents marked births in relationship to a meteor shower in 1833—"the years the stars fell."[25] As Anthony Kaye notes, the "folk chronology" of enslaved people was "a complex technique of mapping time by the proximity of events" defined by place and "the horizons of collective memory."[26]

This understanding of time as a shared resource—whose rhythms would be self-determined by Black communities—was anathema to late nineteenth-century industrial capitalism and the logistical expectations of global commodity markets. Black dockworkers led the defense of this right as they fought to set limits on the number of bales that could be loaded into ships, fixing their day's alienated labor to the task instead of the clock. The West India and Pacific Line complained in 1886 that the seventy-five-bale daily load limit enforced by the screwmen's union "operates very unfairly . . . against the regular lines that make their living out of this port . . . [whose] time is very valuable."[27] Another steamship manager complained that the labor rules "gave ship owners very little opportunity to figure on a definite time for the departure of their vessels."[28] In their refusal of clockwork, W. E. B. Du Bois theorized that Black workers "brought to modern manual labor a renewed validation of life," what he described as "a gift . . . usually known as 'laziness.'" He predicted that its "contribution to current economics will be recognized as of tremendous and increasing importance."[29] Black workers resisted the idea of time as something to be subdivided, administered, or controlled from without. That such a treasured phenomenology would belong in the hands of an adversarial managerial class was an unacceptable infringement.

Collective music-making was one means by which these workers asserted their power to manage, experience, and organize time. The formalized agreements on the docks were only one facet of a pattern of daily resistance to the rhythms of work imposed by capitalist shipping firms and their local bosses. They were also mediated by the songs sung by Black dockworkers themselves—"singing and moving to rhythm of songs as much as they could," in the words of Morton.[30] Philosopher Devonya Natasha Havis's theorizing of Black aural traditions applies powerfully to the docks: "The 'work song' transforms time and launches a critique of work as labor."[31]

Temporalities became increasingly politicized, and slowness in musical practice was associated with Black rebellion. When dance hall owners asked the Juvenile Protective Association, a white middle-class "reform" organization, "What can we do to make our dance halls more respectable?" they answered: "Speed up your music."[32] Jazz musicians often recalled how Black audiences demanded the new, slow music. Bassist Pops Foster, himself a longshoreman, remembered: "They'd dance with no coats on and their suspenders down. They'd jump around and have a bunch of fun. They wanted you to play slow blues and dirty songs so they could dance rough and dirty."[33] Foster was not the only musician to associate slowness as a fundamental part of a new structure of feeling. Emanuel Sayles remembered that even when music was played fast, it still had a pulse that emerged from this new feeling of time: "When musicians from other places . . . played hot, they just played fast . . . That's what people called playing hot." But New Orleans musicians could "play hot and at the same time be playing in a groovy tempo where you [could] dance or clap your hands or join."[34] Playing behind the beat was a cultural marker associated with Black rebellion, threatening white supremacy both at the workplace and in the cultural sphere. Black musicians and their working-class audiences could summon, through the blues's stretched temporality, alternative epistemologies to a capitalist order struggling for dominance. These breakthroughs in time, according to Charles Hersch, invited "listeners to cast off their established identities and try on new modes of being."[35]

At the center of this temporal revolution was trumpeter Buddy Bolden, who had a personal relationship to Black union leadership. Growing up, his next-door neighbor, E. S. Swann, was a dockworker who became president of the Longshoremen's Protective Union Benevolent Association (LPUBA). Bolden's brother-in-law, Alex Reed of the Union Sons Relief Association, was also a union man.[36] Bolden's repertoire reflected the Black working class's critique of time and the working conditions of New Orleans's dock economy. "Don't Go Way Nobody," written by Percy Cahill in 1906 but attributed to Bolden's band, explicitly connected the exploitation of dockworkers to capitalist time management:

> I've worked on the levee front
> Right in the broiling sun;
> I've worked on every steamboat too
> That ever dare to run
> Worked at the docks
> From morn till night,
> And burnt out lots of men;
> When the whistle blew to knock off
> The boss would yell out then:
>
> (*Chorus*)
> Don't go way nobody
> Don't nobody leave,

Cause I need somebody
To help me I believe,
Stay right here, and be nice,
I don't want to tell you twice
Don't go way nobody
Don't nobody leave.

The piece symbolically depicts the conditions of levee work. Despite the long hours and high levels of burnout described by the singer, an ungrateful boss would still use the whistle, mobilizing sound to discipline longshoremen and squeeze some more value out of the workforce. The next verse depicts a robbery during railroad travel, connecting this extraction of value to everyday theft:

I used to be a railroad man,
Had wrecks most every night;
The reason that I quit the job,
Was getting too much fight.
I saw a man, hold up a train,
Passengers were in dread;
He held a big gun in his hand,
And this is all he said:

(*Chorus*)
Don't go way nobody
Don't nobody leave,
Cause I need somebody
To help me I believe,
Stay right here, and be nice,
I don't want to tell you twice
Don't go way nobody
Don't nobody leave.[37]

Tellingly, the words of the boss, "Don't go way nobody," reappear in the mouth of a thief, comparing the levee foreman to the railroad robber as those who participate in the expropriation of the Black working class. The sheet music cover art depicts the boss only with his white hand, reaching from offstage to grab a disoriented Black man. The song is interesting, not only for its anti-capitalist messaging but because it inverts the celebration of the outlaw as a glorified antihero and symbol of Black defiance that was common in African American culture at the time.[38] In this example, the robber is interchangeable with an

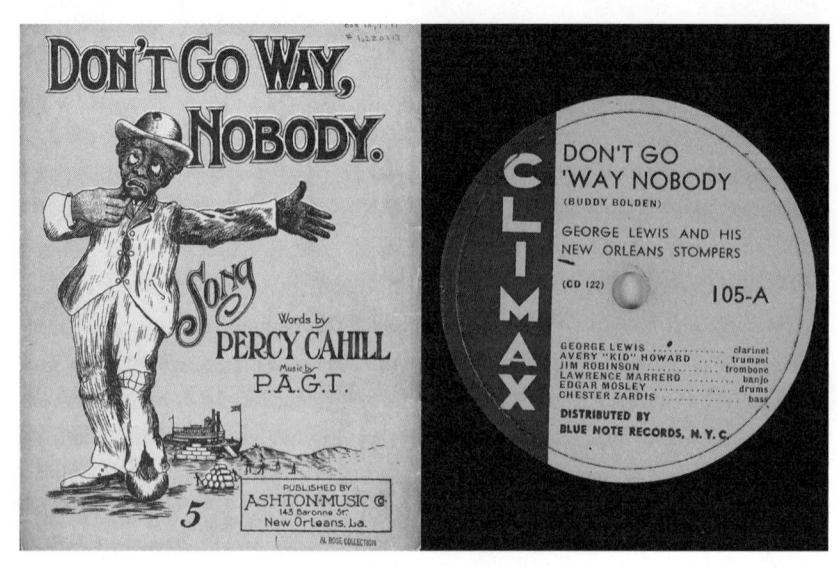

FIGURE 6.0 *Left*: "Don't Go 'Way Nobody" 1906 sheet music. Courtesy of the William Ransom Hogan Jazz Archive, Addendum. *Right*: The label on a George Lewis 78 RPM record incorrectly attributes the composition of "Don't Go 'Way Nobody" to Buddy Bolden. This "error," however, highlights the strong association of the song with Bolden, who effectively made it his own. George Lewis and his New Orleans Stompers, *Don't go 'Way Nobody*, Blue Note Records, 105-A, in possession of author.

overseer at the docks, and the nature of value and the power of elites to define what constitutes crime is called into question. Resistance cannot be accomplished through theft but by directly challenging the organization of the labor process and its management of time.

Bolden's frequent performances of "Don't Go Way Nobody" at Longshoremen's Hall mirrored union political education. Its two antagonists both command the listener: "stay." The boss commands with a whistle, the thief with a gun: the disciplinary power of the foreman's sonic directive was backed by violence. Bolden and his audiences resisted what Foucault described as "the rhythm imposed by signals, whistles . . . orders imposed on everyone [as] temporal norms" that "teach speed as a virtue."[39] This piece was such an important part of Bolden's repertoire and so resonant with his audiences that he often began his concerts with it.[40] Multiple musicians remembered the violence of such weaponized sounds in the countryside. Trombonist Harrison Barnes described an enormous bell at the Magnolia plantation, so large it could be heard across the river. Every morning, it rang at four thirty to wake up the worker-residents; fifteen minutes later, it rang as an order to get to work. Another bell rang at seven, signaling a thirty-minute breakfast. As Barnes related: "Be on the job when the bell rings."[41] Various work songs of the era directly called out the disciplinary nature of these bells and whistles, imagining workers in control of its time management. One in circulation in the late 1800s included the following refrain: "I could pull the bell, I could blow the whistle, I could pull the bell, An' let the engine run."[42] This song aestheticized a political consciousness that had marked the transition from slavery to freedom. As early as 1864, a Black woman defiantly explained to the plantation-owning Mandeville family: "Answering bells is played out."[43] Across several decades, Black Louisianan workers understood the link between sound and disciplinary power, especially where it corresponded to the rhythmic demands of an emergent capitalism. It is no coincidence that "Don't Go Way Nobody" was popular on the plantation where Barnes grew up..

The lyrics of working-class blues songs played by Buddy Bolden and others contested the sonic languages tied to alienated labor, calling into question capitalists' attempts to monopolize the organization of time. Just as A. J. Ellis explained the motivation of the union and the workers they represented—to be masters of their own time—Bolden and the musicians who played with him created new rhythms and temporalities rooted in the worldview of Black audiences. As Charles Hersch notes, "Routinizing industrial labor monopolized time in a particularly dehumanizing way. Improvising musicians controlled time and how it felt—for what is music but sound unfolded in time?"[44]

DOCK WORK IN HISTORICAL CONTEXT

> Memory in our works is not a calendar memory; our experience of time does not keep company with the rhythms of month and year alone; it is aggravated by the void, the final sentence of the Plantation.
>
> *Edouard Glissant,* Poetics of Relation, *72.*

From 1887 through 1923, New Orleans was home to the most powerful and numerically large Black Union, not only in the South, but in the entire country: Longshoremen's Protective Union Benevolent Association (LPUBA).[45] Dockworkers' ability to shut down the docks brought the city's commerical elite to its knees so frequently that the city government of New Orleans, which was responsible for the United States' second-largest port, had to create several commissions to study the "problem of the docks." Their findings are revealing. "One of the greatest drawbacks to New Orleans is the working of the white and negro races on terms of equality," expressed the results of one such investigation in 1908.[46] Senator C. C. Cordill, speaking on the 1907 strike, remarked: "Do I understand you to say that twelve white men and twelve negroes dominate the commerce of this port?" an astonished Cordill asked. "Well, we are practically under negro government."[47]

The success of the dockworkers' unions in frightening white elites does not suggest that the road to trade unionism was an uncomplicated or easy process. Black labor organizing took place in the most difficult of political environments. For many commentators, Southern antagonism to labor unions has had historic, even world-historic, implications. In 1931, economist George Sinclair suggested that the South's hostility to organized labor reflected a continuity with plantation power structures. "The South," he wrote in the 1930s, "is still an authoritarian society. The cotton industry has reproduced for its owner the position of power held by the masters of plantations."[48] C. Vann Woodward, twenty years later, built on this thesis when he wrote that by the 1880s, the South "came to be regarded . . . as a bulwark of, instead of a menace to, the new capitalist economic order."[49] Even when union membership grew in the United States as a whole, it declined in the South, with implications for the labor movement and power relations of the whole country. "Union weakness there [in the United State South] undermined unionization and social reform throughout the United States," notes Friedman. "Of the 160,000 union members in 1880, fewer than 6 percent lived in the South."[50]

New Orleans Black dockworkers' unions thus were quite exemplary organizers, mobilizing workers and achieving victories that were so unexpected, they left New Orleans's white supremacist commercial elites speechless. In the face of tremendous violence, Black dockworkers were able to invoke a powerful postemancipation revolutionary tradition in the plantation districts, where many of them had migrated from, challenging white supremacy across Southern society.[51] Black dockworkers, according to an observer, "wiped out the Jim Crow law in the chief centers of their lives—[the] working place and union hall."[52] These organizations not only fought for better wages or control over the labor process; they performed cultural and ideological labor, too. Black waterfront union organizers were deeply committed to cultivating a militant working-class consciousness that identified capital as their antagonist. Longshoreman Thomas P. Woodland, president of the Black Central Labor Council, which represented all Black organized labor in New Orleans, argued in 1916 that:

> The capitalist class owns the factories, land, ships, railroads, in fact all the means by which wealth is produced and distributed . . . in order to emancipate ourselves from the influence of the [capitalist] class that is hostilely arrayed against the wage-working class, the wage-working class must organize and oppose the

power of capital with the power of organized labor and must champion their own interests on the docks, in the cotton presses, the team drivers, in fact, every class of labor that is connected with the shipping interest of the port of New Orleans... The class-conscious power of capital with all its camp-followers, is confronted with the class-conscious power of labor... There is no power on earth strong enough to thwart the will of such a majority conscious of itself. The earth and all its wealth belong to all.[53]

New Orleans's Black dockworker resistance was, for Woodland, a crucial node in a regional movement against the power of international capital. Recognizing the strategic importance of the logistics sector in New Orleans's crusade to rebrand itself as a hub of international commerce, Woodland expressed how dockworkers understood their struggle in global terms, as a lightning rod of global working-class consciousness.

Woodland was not alone in openly embracing currents of socialist politics. The life of A. J. Ellis demonstrates the depth of radicalism in the Black labor movement. Before his career as a dockworker, he had traveled much of the world as a jockey, an occupation in which many Black athletes had found national and worldwide success until the sport was resegregated in the twentieth century.[54] In Europe, this chapter of his life came to an end when he suffered an accident. He became a seaman for the Hamburg-American Line and eventually joined the German Seamen, which Ameringer explains was "the reddest of the German unions." Apparently, this experience affected Ellis deeply, as he acquired "a fair smattering of German, and more than a fair understanding of the *Communist Manifesto* ... [he] swallowed whole the theory of the class struggle and uncompromisingly."[55] He brought this brand of radical politics to New Orleans and served as a longtime dock labor leader.

By 1903, Ellis was fully committed to New Orleans's dockworkers unionizing. He would often tell the press in their frequent coverage of him, "I am a union man and will be until death."[56] In newspapers of the time, his presence in meetings is described in almost mythic terms, where he was said to "orate ... for half an hour with volubility and a vehemence that showed his deep earnestness" powered by his "very strong voice and cast iron lungs."[57] Ellis was a critical negotiator with the white screwmen's union in the early 1900s, when he and other Black screwmen—whose ability to screw barrels of cotton into the decks of ship required a highly trained hand and were considered the most skilled labor on the docks—came to a half-and-half agreement. "We, the colored Screwmen, have not departed from any of our agreements except that we were tired of being used as an instrument to starve our brother workmen, the white men, and who have the same right to live that we have,"⁵⁸ reads a statement signed by Ellis. Some white screwmen apparently agreed with Ellis's approach, as their representative noted in the *Picayune* that they could make no progress "as long as black was pitted against the white in the race for levee work."⁵⁹

In many ways, Ellis was a precursor to African American and Afro-Caribbean maritime radicals who joined the communist movement in the early twentieth century. The Alabama-born communist James W. Ford (c. 1893) and Suriname-born mariner and charter member of the American Communist Party Otto Huiswoud (c. 1893) met in Hamburg, Germany, in 1930 to from the Negersekretariat (Negro Secretariat), whose goal was to create a radical trade union for "Negro workers throughout the world" and challenge colonial hegemony in the Caribbean and Africa.⁶⁰ As Gerald Horne reminds us, "travels made for a certain cosmopolitanism, a broadened outlook and an acute awareness of exploitation. Together, these traits were a ready recipe for radicalism."⁶¹

A. J. Ellis and Thomas P. Woodland were instrumental in organizing internationally, as well, activating the same trans-Caribbean and Atlantic networks that activists such as the Desdunes family participated in. While not officially associated with dockworkers' unions, Ramón Pagés shared circles with them. A Cuban revolutionary and leader of the so-called Spanish cigar-making community in New Orleans, Pagés sailed to Cuba to fight for its freedom from Spain in 1898. While in the US, he agitated for universal "public rights" regardless of color or class at an equal rights meeting in New Orleans convened by Rodolphe Desdunes.⁶²

During the late nineteenth and early twentieth centuries, these international labor movements mirrored the growing influence of Southern capital in the Gulf region. This period coincided with a surge in trade between New Orleans and Latin American markets, driven by US finance capital and military expansion into neighboring countries. The Louisiana Tehuantepec Company, for instance, acquired land in Mexico's Tehuantepec Isthmus as early as 1857, displacing Zapotec Indigenous communities to facilitate the transportation of Louisiana's slave-produced commodities to the Pacific Ocean. Notably, one of the company's key investors was Louisiana senator John Slidell, later to become the Confederacy's ambassador to France.⁶³ In 1880, United Fruit Company made New Orleans its base of operations for the colonization of banana plantations in Central America and the Caribbean, and the city became a major importer of commodities grown on tropical plantations.⁶⁴ Hundreds of new migrants, including the Jamaican Panamanian jazz pianist Luis Russell, migrated from these disrupted economies to New Orleans. Russell's father was one of over fifty thousand migrants from the West Indies who worked on the Panama Canal, one the United States' most prized imperial possessions.⁶⁵

In response to the expanding influence of international capital, dockworkers in New Orleans began organizing on an international scale. In 1903, the city hosted a convention of Southern dockworkers, drawing delegates from across the American South and even Veracruz, Mexico, which still maintained a Creole of color community.[66] According to the *Picayune*, it was "one of the most significant moves in the labor world in recent times" and workers considered it akin to a new international.[67] Like generations before them, Black labor leaders tapped into the long-standing rhythms of Black internationalism to forge new bonds of solidarity across borders and seas in the era of the New South.

Within this backdrop, New Orleans jazz musicians came of age amid a cultural tapestry shaped by an improvised cosmopolitanism. Danny Barker, a resident of the French Quarter, recalled the sounds of dockworkers singing the blues on their way to work. He would occasionally hear the screams of segregated pleasure boat patrons when their whites-only river packets were intentionally showered with "cinders and fire."[68] For Barker, this soundscape held a central place in his childhood development, a vivid world where he freely roamed, welcomed by many who knew his grandparents. It was in this milieu that Barker received a treasured gift, a Japanese doll, reflecting the emergence of an international working-class culture in the New Orleans port.[69]

While a doll may not be a musical instrument or a song, it symbolized a larger ecosystem of exchange and reciprocity among strangers, revealing a profound, not-to-be-taken-for-granted solidarity. This doll gifted by a Japanese sailor became part of the symphony of the polyglot port, where soundscapes, cultural languages, and affective spaces contributed to Barker's deep sense of rhythm and life. These exchanges, albeit small, bridged the gaps created by global capitalism's profound dislocations, fostering creolization and developing a new common sense. New symbols and new musics reached ears of people of faraway lands brought suddenly and violently close by global capitalism, reproducing bonds, even fleetingly, that modernity had fractured.

The cultural exchanges extended to music, with Black New Orleanians incorporating elements introduced by overseas workers. For example, percussionist Abbey "Chinee" Foster's use of "Chinese" cymbals and tom-toms was influenced by Chinese immigrants who had created a vibrant Chinatown.[70] Clarinetist Willie Parker's choice of the name "Eureka Brass Band" was inspired by acquaintances from the West Indies with a band of the same name.[71] Drummer Albert Jiles Jr. recalled he played his first gigs in Chris Kelly's band at a party at Co-operators Hall that included "a lot of Jamaicans." "At that time," he remembered, "great numbers of them came to New Orleans, mostly without passports, jumping off ships, etc." The Jamaican presence at Co-operators Hall was well known to both musicians and authorities, whose raids on the hall inspired the song "I'm Going Home to Jamaica," also known as "West Indian Blues."[72] These connections to the music and musicians of Jamaican origin in New Orleans were crucial to the transmission of Garveyism. The New Orleans jazz singer Esther Bigeou recorded a version of "West Indian Blues" in 1923 that explicitly celebrated Marcus Garvey's Black power consciousness.[73]

Coterminous with US penetration into Latin America, a Pacific arena of US capital expansion deeply implicated Louisianan sugar technicians such as W. C. Stubbs, the former state chemist for Louisiana who visited Hawaii's behemoth "plantation centers" to "study the agricultural possibilities of these islands."[74] Hawaiian performers touring through the Pacific incorporated veiled critiques of US expansionism into their productions, using their art as a countercolonial political praxis.[75] It was during these decades that the bottlenecking technique of sliding a metal object across guitar strings, ubiquitous in early blues, was likely was introduced by Kānaka Maoli Hawaiian musicians.[76] The shared open tuning of Hawaiian slack guitar, blues guitar, and Mexican guitar traditions facilitated this cross-pollination.[77] Hawaiian guitarists began performing in New Orleans as early as 1885 at the Cotton Centennial, and by 1914, newspaper advertisements for Hawaiian guitar music were increasingly commonplace.[78] Segregation laws paradoxically created opportunities for Black and Native Hawaiian collaboration, as Kānaka Maoli musicians often lodged with African American families while touring the segregated South.[79] The African American "sacred steel" tradition, associated with the Church of the Living God, also benefited from this cross-cultural exchange, with practitioners studying under Kānaka Maoli guitar instructors in the 1930s.[80] In 1929, New Orleanian Walter "Fats" Pichon recorded the song "Wiggle Yo' Toes" with the Kānaka Maoli guitarist Bennie Nawahi.[81]

Through these musical collaborations, the internationalism of Union organizers was made real and organic. A new wave of cultural exchange was underway against the backdrop of a new age of enclosure and white supremacist attack. Racialized capitalism was challenged by the musical collaborations of displaced subalterns in these underdocumented yet influential collaborations. "Their very noise promised a music beyond the racial orders of colonialism and settler colonialism," argues Denning, "a music beyond the commodity forms and labor processes of capitalism: this remains an unfilled promise and unfinished revolution."[82] These converging temporalities and rhythms of struggle from abroad only strengthened the vision expressed by Woodland: that the dockworkers' struggle not only sought to liberate Black workers in New Orleans but dislocated workers the world over.

Among the port-city working class, dockworkers shared obvious affinities with maritime workers such as pearl divers and whalers. On a typical boat deck, one might see African Americans, West Indians, Polynesians, and Native Hawaiians working together as early as the 1700s.[83] Sea shanties produced by multiracial whaling ships throughout the nineteenth century likely played a role in the development of New Orleans's distinctive port-city soundscape. Scholars have meticulously documented how an array of languages—including French, German, Norwegian, Italian, Welsh, Swedish, Spanish, Pidgin English, Dutch, Russian, Greek, Japanese, Egyptian, South Asian, Chinese, and West African—converged in song, contributing to a rich and complex aural culture among whalers.[84]

Their structure and links to labor certainly shared commonalities with the work songs of the roustabouts that Morton remembered helping withstand the working conditions of the docks, so reminiscent of a plantation. In 1888, Laura Alexander Smith wrote that in the lyrical poetry of shanties "a strict regard for sense is not of so much importance as the rhymical flow of united words and melody—especially in songs of the sea, where the union of syllables with sounds must be well suited to the 'work' which they are meant to enliven and facilitate." As with Puerto Rican bomba and the Haitian diaspora cinquillo, these songs inverted the traditional hierarchy of melody and accompaniment. Instead, the lyrics framed rhythmic patterns that engendered compelling narratives of their own, deeply entwined with collective labor experiences.[85]

For New Orleans dockworkers like Morton, these songs flowed like an unspoken current, a deeply ingrained rhythm so woven into their daily lives that its significance may have become almost invisible. Yet it was on these docks where musicians like him and Willie Parker expanded their ears and their sense of the world. Barker's cherished Japanese doll, then, carried meaning, and his memory of it was no mere happenstance. "Over the long term," argues James Revell Carr, "the cosmopolitan tastes of sailors spilled over into mainland musical practices, turning port cities like New Orleans, Liverpool, and Honolulu into crucibles for the creation of innovative new approaches to music."[86]

The international division of labor that interconnected dockworkers, sailors, and plantation workers found its most vivid expression in the songs and musical techniques brought by rural and global migrants. These encounters nurtured cultural cohesion in the port city, transforming dissonance and incompatibility into intercultural polyphony. They imparted a global perspective on both culture and the struggle for workers' rights, thereby perpetuating a counter-plantation tradition that spanned centuries. These erstwhile strangers developed bonds rooted in militant action and created a "community based on class, on ship and ashore."[87] Marcus Rediker names this the "motley crew," and suggests that "its collective power animated the entire port city economy." Indeed, the motley crew "unified itself" through its "common cooperative work," creating commoning spaces in the most complex and dangerous of social conditions.[88]

The exchange of expressive culture propelled these new formations to coalesce, and each of their vernacular musical traditions informed brassroots democracy's liberatory lineages. By the 1920s, African American-inspired-musical practice was adopted by both Kānaka Maoli musicians and Oaxaca Indigenous Mixtec musicians, the latter of whom adopted the Afrodiasporic banjo and incorporated it into long-existing musical forms.[89] One Lebanese Mexican banjoist who lived in the Tehuantepec city of Ixtepec, Tito Enríquez, was a socialist organizer and jazz club owner. Remarkably, in proximity to the Louisiana Tehuantepec Company's activities, a neighborhood bearing Enríquez's name still stands to this day, bearing testament to the enduring legacy of this common, cooperative work that built a bottom-up transnational music culture.[90]

As Woodman and actvists organized a dockworkers' international, early jazz musicians contributed to a parallel international. This international could not coordinate a mass strike, like the LPUBA was in 1907. But their brass bands were able to contribute dynamic new repertoire to that strike. Indeed, Black brass bands accompanied LPUBA marches from its inception, an 1872 strike that inspired wildcat strikes in other industries and generated mass community support.[91] The symbiotic relationship between the union and the musicians was unmistakable; the union relied on the musicians, while the musicians, in turn, relied on the union. The affirmative counterculture they co-created was built on an inclusive framework that embraced the cultural knowledges of fellow sufferers caught in plantation capitalism's increasingly global matrix. Not only did dockworkers' union activism create a context within which displaced laborers from abroad could synchronize with Afro-Louisianans in acts of cultural reciprocity; dockworkers helped institutionalize one of Black New Orleans's archetypal institutions: the jazz funeral.

FUNERALS AND THE DOCKS: PUBLIC MOURNING, BRASS BANDS, AND ORGANIZED LABOR

Anthropologist Helen Regis participated in the 1996 second-line funeral of Nathaniel Grey, a former Grand Marshall in the Young Men Olympian Association. In the company of brass bands, Regis experienced how the "layering of simultaneous performances" created an "inclusiveness and aesthetic intensity" that clashed with bewildered white onlookers as the procession "moved through the invisible boundaries of everyday apartheid." Regis added, "[I]t is not uncommon to experience the active engagement of the police in this antagonistic dance." White violence has long been used to silence Black funerals.⁹² In 1890, an article in the *Picayune* described "a small-sized riot" between "a crowd of Negroes and whites, during which rocks, bricks and clubs were freely used, and several persons were slightly injured." They suggested that the source of the problem was "a colored procession" headed by the Onward Brass Band, which was paying homage to Mrs. Johnson, a mother of one of the musicians. The paper complains that the "usual crowd of Negroes who follow up parades of this kind were on hand in force and took charge of the sidewalk as is their custom"; the paraders were confronted by "[a] force of young white men" who "pelted them with rocks."⁹³ The *Daily States* called for "benevolent societies to abolish the custom of brass bands at funerals" and denounced "the hideous brass band and long lines of vari dressed [*sic*] and tired men traveling through mud and slush at funerals."⁹⁴ Musicians themselves often recalled racialized violence at Black funerals. Trombonist Sonny Henry, for instance, remembers how attackers might have bricks, rocks, knives, and brass knuckles. "[They'd hit you] anywhere they could hit you, they'd hit you on the bottom of your feet, if you run."⁹⁵

Attacks on Black mourning intend to disrupt the communal sociability heard in brass bands' multilayered voicings, which ushered both the living and the dead through a collective rite of passage. As Robin D. G. Kelley has written, "mourning is not a lonesome isolated act but a public expression, a collective acknowledgment of the dead that refuses to suppress our rage and anger."⁹⁶ Mourning is an unacceptable utterance of Black historical consciousness, one that white New Orleans attacked systematically. Brass bands' lament and celebration were threatening for white New Orleans society and its vision of social order. As white supremacists dismantled Reconstruction and Black political power, they also sought to limit these sonorous tributes to the deceased through both paramilitary and legal channels.

Black dockworker unions did much to normalize and defend these defiant utterances. In the history of New Orleans's Black mourning, the 1881 funeral "negro teamster" James Hawkins takes on special importance. Hawkins was killed by a police officer at nine o'clock in the morning on the tenth day of a waterfront strike. The St. Joseph Colored Society provisioned pall bearers and a brass band. Black and white labor organizations attended in large numbers, each with their respective bands. Their combined number reached two thousand to three people. At this funeral for a Black laborer, numerous participants were white laborers and their family members. They assembled at "colored church on Levee," from which the mourners and their bands began their processional in the streets. In this moment, white and Black workers, Catholics and Protestants all both mourned together within the soundscapes of Black brass bands, sharing a sonically adorned collective catharsis and in the context of a highly visible and emotionally charged dock strike.⁹⁷

The murder of Hawkins drew enormous commentary from all sectors of the press. The *Daily Picayune* dramatically declared him a martyr in the "war between labor and capital."⁹⁸ The *St. Landry Democrat* was alarmed by the implications of the strike and this framing of Hawkins's death. "The people of the Crescent City realized the fact that a great public calamity was upon them—that a gigantic labor strike had been inaugurated in the metropolis of the south." The paper argued that "Hawkins had created a disturbance of the peace and an attempt was made to arrest him when he resisted the officers who thereupon shot him," suggesting his killing was justified. Its writers implored the strikers to give up their unrealisitic demands: "It is folly to suppose that capital can be whipped into submission. It is worse than folly to attempt to do so."⁹⁹

The *Weekly Louisianian*, a Black newspaper, took the opposite point of view— that Hawkins's extrajudicial killing was completely unjustified, and that his sacrifice should be motivation to further challenge inequities created by capital. "The authorities and our merchants are blind to these barbarous outrages . . . officers with their hands dyed in the blood of colored men with no condemnation whatsoever. Must we strike back, or shall we be protected by the law?" Yet the paper noted with approval the interracial character of the funeral. "It was a source of satisfaction to see the sympathy expressed by the white laborers association. Their popular indignation were [sic] expressed by the large numbers who turned out to pay their last tribute of respect to the unfortunate man."¹⁰⁰

Perhaps these scenes help contextualize how brass bands were so threatening to the white republic and its vision of the New South. As participants stepped together, they weaved a "social synchrony," generative of social belonging that had the potential to disrupt white supremacy.¹⁰¹ White laborers sided with the position of the Black newspaper over the reasoning of the *St. Landry Democrat* when they honored the martyrdom of a fellow waterfront worker whose life was taken to silence the strikers. The recent creation of Cotton Men's Executive Council, which included representatives from thirteen Black and white waterfront unions, institutionalized a framework for expressing this Black-white solidarity, although it did not go as far as to create an integrated union.¹⁰² But this temporary disruption of Southern racial order was forged in the streets— through strikes, through funerals, and especially through the textured weaving of joy and lament heard in cornets, trombones, and drums.¹⁰³ Black brass bands made these appropriations of public space an invitation to form new collectivities that could resist policing by capital or the state. As trumpeter Gregg Baker relates: "The music on the street dictates the mood and the atmosphere of *what goes on* in the street."[104]

Although print archives do not reveal their thinking on brass bands, it is evident that Black union leadership treasured these mobile musical institutions. Many had decades-long relationships with brass bands and their attendant benevolent societies. William H. Penn, president of the LPUBA, embodied a bridge between New Orleans's Black musical communities and the labor movement.[105] He was the business manager of the Excelsior Brass Band in the early 1880s, which included some of New Orleans's most distinguished Black and Creole of color musicians, including Louis and Lorenzo Tio Sr., serving with "great success."[106] He emerged as a union leader following the white on Black violence in 1894 that destroyed the interracial alliance that had existed since the 1880s. He was partially successful in rebuilding these ties.[107] At his death, the otherwise conservative *Times Picayune* called him "a power for good in the colored labor world" and noted in his dying moments that Penn had "many good friends, both white and colored, coming instantly to his assistance and relief."[108]

Penn's death tells us much about his life, his funeral an archive of the social networks between diverse sectors of Black New Orleans. His stroke commenced in the middle of fraught negotiations with shipping firms during a freight handlers' strike. But being a union organizer and representing the Black working class in a confrontation with global capital was only one part of his schedule. The *Picayune* reported that more than seventeen hundred benevolent association members from more than a dozen organizations attended Penn's funeral, plus a "long concourse of friends," interspersed with at least two brass bands. The varied mourners and institutions present reflected Penn's profound participation in New Orleans's varied benevolent associations. The *Weekly Pelican* estimated that Penn belonged to at least twenty-five. His participation in one in particular, *Jeunes Amis*, of which Daniel Desdunes was a member and where Excelsior clarinetist Lorenzo Tio frequently played, hints at the links between Creole of color and African American musical affinities and political activism.[109] Indeed, having managed Lorenzo Tio not long before in the Excelsior Brass Band, he may have treasured the Mexican-born clarinetist's distinct sound when he played. Penn was also the treasurer of the Odd Fellows from 1875 through the 1880s.[110] In the Odd Fellows, he would have worked closely with Sumpter J. Watt, the president and, later, permanent secretary, of the Black freight handlers' union.[111] In 1876, Penn's name was on the roster of a Republican mass meeting, around the same time that Rodolphe Desdunes was chairman.[112]

Penn fused his labor organized with a commitment to civil rights activism and was also a member of the Equal Justice Association, credited for almost single-handedly defeating the Louisiana Republican Party's "Lily-White" faction, which nearly sent an all-white delegation to the national Republican Convention in Chicago in 1893. The organization, later named the the Equal Rights League, would include the Black screwmen union leader A. J. Ellis, as well as Penn's eventual replacement in the LPUBA, president E. S. Swann, a man born into slavery who who served with Rodolphe Desdunes in the Metropolitan Police. Penn's connections show how deeply ingrained Black dockworking activism was within a larger ecosystem of movements and communal structures of Black New Orleans. As Thulani Davis notes in her work on the abolitionist network of Black institutions she calls the "Emancipation Circuit," "the foundational structures for [African American] community building and activism of all sorts emerged from a matrix of early benevolent societies and trade associations with overlapping membership and local roots."[113] Penn's work as the manager of the Excelsior (a major entity within this network were bands) facilitated access to musicians and was strategically essential to project and maintain Black unions' legitimacy in the community at large.

Black dockworkers strengthened the political power and cultural autonomy of Afro-Louisianans through these lateral alliances, because the LPUBA was a uniquely powerful Black organization whose bargaining power sometimes enabled it to protest Jim Crow in the city's public sphere. In 1902, the *Picayune* reported: "Negro Entertainments Seriously Affected by the Operation of the Jim Crow Car Law," offering a rare criticism from the white press toward the economic consequences of apartheid. "The Jim Crow Law is playing hob [sic] with colored entertainments and public functions of the race," the newspaper noted, "where crowds would expect transportation in a short space of time, and as a natural result is knocking the Railways Company out of considerable revenue."[114] What was the occasion for the lost revenue? The *Picayune* continues:

> It is a time-honored custom of the colored people of New Orleans to hold a big memorial service and pay honor to their dead on the last Sunday in the month of November. This day is observed by the Longshoremen's Protective Union and Benevolent Association, which Association has over 1,000 members. [sic]
>
> This year, last Sunday, the service was abandoned. William H. Penn, President of the Longshoremen's Association, explained yesterday that it was true that the customary observance had been given up this year owing to the Jim Crow Law.
>
> "There was nothing else to do," said he. "We could not get transportation service in the cars. Under the law, when four colored people get in a car [it] is full. At that rate, not any oftener than cars run, it would have taken a day and

night to have gotten our folks up to Carrollton, and another day and night to have gotten them back. It is an iron-clad rule of the Association that every member is fined $1 who does not attend the memorial services and who is not there on time. Holding the observance would have resulted in most all our members being fined."

It is said colored balls and entertainments are being discontinued because of the inability of the members of the organization to go in bodies or to get to their places in a reasonable length of time. They say there will be no colored parks or picnics next summer under the Jim Crow Law.[115]

By foregrounding the economic damage resulting from the LPUBA's withdrawal from the transportation economy, the *Picayune* foregrounded the disruption of Black cultural life by acknowledging the marked restriction on group mobility within the Black community. Not only the funeral itself but "colored balls and entertainments" were discontinued by the LPUBA, suggesting that they had an outsize role in organizing musical activities and social events in Black New Orleans life.

The LPUBA's level of organization and collective commitment to mourning—which fined those who did not attend—demonstrates how seriously the union's rank and file took this ritual of collective memory. In these highly choreographed yet improvised practices, community members, mourners, and bands moved en masse to honor the dead to struggle for the living. The Carrollton pilgrimage, even when interrupted as in 1902, illustrates the synchronicity between the struggles on the docks and every other aspect of Black life. Every moment, from dancing to strategizing to rituals of the most quotidian to the most festive, was part of a living, dynamic, antiphonal movement that hinged on the political power and dignity of the Black working class.

Over the course of the late nineteenth and early twentieth centuries, the resilience and determination of Black dockworkers' unions in New Orleans took on a profound and symbolic significance within the vibrant tradition of the city's brass bands. Their unwavering spirit of resistance found its most poignant expression during solemn funerals held to honor labor leaders and those who had sacrificed their lives in the struggle for workers' power. A potent amalgamation of labor activism and musical artistry, these funerals served as a testament to their enduring defiance in the face of pervasive inequality. New Orleans brass bands, infused with the ethos of the labor movement, were a conduit for this unique fusion of protest and remembrance. The music they played at these gatherings resonated not only with the cadence of rebellion but also with the rhythms of solace and solidarity. Beyond the musical realm, Black dockworkers channeled their activism into political engagement and participation in various cultural institutions. In doing so, they forged spaces where their voices could be heard and their identity affirmed, even in a world ever dominated by white supremacy. In essence, the legacy of Black dockworkers in New Orleans encapsulated a powerful interplay of labor, music, politics, and culture, carving out a place for themselves in a society rife with racial capitalism, and leaving an indelible mark on the collective memory of a music to come.

LONGSHOREMEN'S HALL: MOVEMENT-BASED ART MAKING

Pops Foster was one of the most important bass players New Orleans ever produced. His career as a sideman spanned the bands of King Oliver to bebop avatar Charlie Parker. His family moved to New Orleans with tens of thousands of other rural-to-urban migrants at the turn of the twentieth century, and he began working on the docks. His reflections on his hybrid life capture the duality of the night for New Orleans's Black dockworker-musicians who labored on levies and at lawn parties during the first decade of the twentieth century. "It was pretty rough playing and working a full[-time] job too," he explained. Sleep deprivation and force of will were required to get through the weekend, and "Monday was your roughest day."

> You might play a dance from eight that night till four o'clock the next morning. You'd go home then, hang up your tuxedo, put on your overalls and leave about 5:00 a.m. and catch the streetcar to the stables. There you'd pick up your mule team at 6:00 a.m. and start out for the docks to pick up a load at 7:00 a.m. . . . You could [then] sleep because your mules would follow the wagon in front.

Even on Mondays, Foster might have a gig at Longshoremen's Hall, so after getting home after his shift, he would "get a little shuteye, and start playing at eight o'clock."[116]

While protests manifested the demands of Black organized labor, and funerals embodied a spiritualized political culture, such spaces and practices were not to decide the major operational and governance aspects of Black waterfront unions. This is what union halls purported to do. Over time, these spaces evolved to serve multiple functions extending way beyond this mandate. In the context of our elaboration of brassroots democracy, union halls provided a space for an interconnected network of activities including church services, blues-based performance culture, and political mass meetings, which would all entertain decades of longevity. Space and place were policed in New Orleans and elsewhere, and few public spaces were open to New Orleans's Black community. Unions built on the covert practices of fraternal orders like the Prince Hall Masons created spaces for an interdisciplinary Black working-class culture to percolate under a single roof, enabling exchanges between religious, musical, and political communities. As Rosenberg notes, "Performers like Buddy Bolden made their reputations at labor-hosted and union-sponsored social functions in halls."[117] These were spaces where, for one dollar, one could dance to music "made by your neighbors"—and fellow workers.[118] Both were true for Buddy Bolden, whose father was a drayage worker who moved cotton bales, and whose next-door neighbor was LPUBA president E. S. Swann.

Attendees at such dances were aware that they were present in the heart of not only organized labor but a special kind of Black cooperative society. Many dancegoers may have come earlier in the week to drop off dues, which supported a wide range of activities. Unions organized funerals and protests, as well as medical and life insurance for members and their families. They organized civil rights commissions that agitated within Republican political circles, held fish fries, took out obituaries in the *Picayune* for deceased members, and provided a range of other social services. In this respect, Black waterfront workers organized spaces strikingly similar to benevolent societies more generally. These can be best conceptualized as institutions of the counter-plantation, formations that operated against the slaveocracy's reinvented form as the "white republic."[119] They provided a space for participatory democratic life and collectively run social services among Black communities when the state refused to do so. Benevolent societies writ large, for instance, were the greatest providers of health care for Black New Orleanians, one of the strong motivations for four-fifths of New Orleans's Black residents to join to such groups.[120] Healthcare was an important issue for Black people and a site of racial discrimination, both in terms of access and in the quality of treatment, and musicians were no exception. The Creole of color bassist McNeal Breaux recalled that in the late 1920s his father was killed in a hospital. "He went into the hospital with a perforated lung, and they took out the wrong lung and he died." Asked if he sued, he responded, "Are you kidding? A black man in Louisiana suing a white doctor?"[121] Breaux's comments suggest that Black musicians, as with other members of their community, were painfully aware of the brutal disparities in access to health care and their exclusion from juridical channels. It was precisely this social exclusion that made membership in benevolent societies essential for Black New Orleanians. The LPUBA was thus both a union and the foundation of an entire ecology of social services and cultural activities. In these spaces, the vision of political economy Black workers fought for on the docks was created within their own ranks, echoing centuries-long commoning experiments in Louisiana and the Caribbean.[122]

Indeed, what distinguished union-owned halls, and Longshoremen's Hall especially, from other benevolent societies was their sheer operational power. Their mass membership, their dues-collecting mechanisms, and their centrality in the lives of their members made them logical patrons of several extracurricular activities. By the 1890s, they became prolific programmers of famed dances that lasted until the next morning, featuring the new music called by many at the time as "blues for dancing," and which today observers would describe as early jazz.[123] ("Buddy Bolden is the first man who played blues for dancing," is how Papa John Joseph, a bass player who migrated to New Orleans from St. James Parish, explained this cultural revolution.)[124] These performances were often sponsored by the Black union community. The operational expenses of the hall, such as garbage collection and electricity fees, were managed by the entire union and its dues. In return, revenue from balls helped pay taxes and insurance.[125] Longshoremen's Hall was located in the heart of the Uptown neighborhood that became the home of Black refugees fleeing white supremacist violence in the sugar and cotton parishes. As Clyde Woods notes, "They brought their Blues with them," forming the basis for a new musical language that was developed over decades of cooperative agrarian struggle.[126] It is no coincidence that the institutional heart of the movement to challenge brutal exploitation of the Black working class would embrace this music.

As with struggles on occupied plantations, food continued to be an expression of solidarity as well as a source of sustenance, acting as a vehicle that called community into being. "No matter what dance hall or affair you were playing in New Orleanians," recalled Pops Foster, "you stopped for an hour at midnight and had dinner. Whoever was having the dance fed the musicians. Usually you'd have a big plate of gumbo, rice, and French bread."[127] The exchange of food and conviviality had a different resonance in the union halls than in brothels in Storyville—especially when one was, like Foster, a dockworker. Nutritional sustenance, musical conviviality, medical care, and class struggle: each of these initiatives reflected the evolving contours of the counter-plantation.[128]

All forms of Black cultural life—including Black churches, Black picnics, Black funerals, and even the act of being Black in public—were attacked by white New Orleanians during the 1890s and early 1900s.[129] The power of organized labor provided a bulwark between practitioners of Black culture and the repressive power of the state. Both government ordinances and "grassroots" mobilizations of white "citizens committees" expressed their repulsion at all forms of Black life. The YMCA was but one organization that called upon "every good man and woman" in New Orleans to find sites of Black disorder, file affidavits, and go to court to displace such residents and performances from their neighborhoods.[130] Under the banner of public sanitation, self-styled progressive reformers linked prostitution and Black depravity, and used segregation laws to create "order." As Emily Epstein Landau surmises, "All sorts of entertainments fell under the rubric of 'disorder' . . . It seems that any celebratory behavior involving people of color, especially if it involved a group, was perceived as disorderly."[131]

A plethora of affidavits to city council detail just how perverse and pervasive this campaign was. Paul Capdeville wrote to the city in the last years of the nineteenth century, "We the white residents beg of your honor not to issue any more permits to negros [sic] in the eight hundred block of Adams St. for parties or Fish Frys [sic] as they are a nuisance to the neighborhood and keep them until all hours of the morning."[132] Fish fries were common sites for music and festivities, and often included multiracial crowds. These spaces were threatening to the operation of white supremacy and public "cleanliness" for their interruption of segregation and for their showcasing of Black musical culture.

For similar reasons, Black benevolent societies were attacked. One letter complained of noise at Providence Hall, which was run by the Ladies Providence Benevolent Association, of which Buddy Bolden's mother was a member. Donald Marquis wrote that the "old, old timers in the neighborhood still remember Buddy playing at Providence Hall."[133] It was a hall that clarinetist George Lewis recalled standing outside of as a young boy, late at night, where he listened to and absorbed the new music.[134] Unlike the young Lewis, the reformers detested its late-night revelry and attempted to shut it down. "Property holders and residents of the immediate vicinity," reads the petition filed on June 5, 1899, "hereby protest against the colored hall . . . known as the Ladies Providence Benevolent Association Hall, insofar as the giving of Balls, Parties, Dances and the like in said hall at such unreasonable hours."[135] Music seems to have been especially singled out by self-styled reformers. A resident and property owner wrote to the city council in 1902 to complain about "concerts" in his neighborhood. "My tenants complain that the performances are continued into a late hour of the night that the negroes become drunk and boisterous . . . in fact, while the performance lasts pandemonium reigns supreme."[136] Also in 1902, the *Times Picayune* condemned "the hoodlums and blacks" for "forcing blood" at a concert where "Kid Ory, a heavy footed labourer" was charged with murder.[137]

In 1905, Dr. T. A. Duggan brought a petition to the mayor "signed by more than one hundred citizens" calling on the mayor to stop the "isuuance [sic] of permits to any colored social club to hold festivals in Dixie Park." In addition to the "disgraceful language" that the men and women of the "colored 'social clubs'" were said to utter, the complaint's anger was directed at "a very discordant brass band playing indeterminable 'ragtime' selections" which played "all day and all night." The mayor resolved to only issue permits that would allow music until midnight.[138] Once again, the regulation of time and the surveillance of pleasure emerge as a central axis around which the struggle for public space was organized. A sampling of complaints to city council demonstrates the increasing anti-Black component of daily life, a process that reflected how "folkways were replaced with stateways" in the words of the historian J. Morgan Kousser.[139] Longshoremen's Hall, however, was rarely attacked or censored. Union halls mobilized folkways, giving them a special "expressional" character, to successfully push back against the juridical and political power of the state. Black waterfront unions' strategic bargaining power in city politics gave them the operating room to protect and house the culture.

The story of Mother Anderson is instructive in this regard. Anderson, who claimed Indigenous ancestry, was a renowned medium of the African American Spiritualist Church and was based in Chicago. She was initially hesitant to start a second church in New Orleans because, according to one of her followers, she was afraid she would be a victim of police harassment.[140] She was right to be concerned, as attacks on Black spirituality and religion at the legislative level happened early and fast with the fall of Reconstruction governments. The City Ordinance 13347 against fortune telling and magnetic healing was passed and revised several times between 1879 and 1920. It prohibited, in the words of the act, "fortunetelling, predicting future events, and all the phases of mediumship, clairvoyance, etc."[141] The "etc." signaled that the state retained the power to arbitrarily denote Black spiritual practices as illegal. The ordinance was used to attack several upstart Black Baptist churches, of which there were about fifty by 1900, which were also cited under ordinances for noise complaints.[142] Mother Anderson did open a church in 1917, and she chose to do so at Longshoremen's Hall. Apparently, the LPUBA felt they had the political strength to resist the ordinance that prohibited her form of divination—and they did, as she was not shut down in the space. She may have crossed paths here with Louis Armstrong, and Kid Ory, who also performed here.[143]

Indeed, Black churches and blues dances shared space, and many scholars have noted the profound and multifaceted influence of the Baptist influence on early jazz. Drummer Bill Matthews remembered that Bolden played with "a moan in his cornet that went all though you, just like you were in church or something . . . make a spiritual feeling go through you. He had a cup, a specially made cup, that made that cornet moan like a Baptist preacher."[144] Jason Berry has argued that Baptist performance cultures and spiritual rituals circulated among not only blues musicians but also within the wider entertainment and cultural infrastructure of New Orleans. "Rural churches released a memory stream in the ring shouts, dancing, and ecstatic worship among many of the 40,000 black folk who fled Louisiana plantation poverty between 1880 and 1910 for dreams in the shambling metropolis."[145] Thomas Brothers estimates that at least 60 percent of these Black Louisianans were Baptist and imagines that these infusions between the music and the religion, the communally based practices of Baptist churches and their particular "musical-kinetic-social interaction," happened "bit by bit, here and there"—an improvised creolization.[146] Both Berry and Brothers describe a fluid, flowing, and decentralized process by which Black Baptist and Pentecostal aesthetics became felt in early jazz.

The commoning culture of the union was inflected with this musical-kinetic-social interaction, and union halls often held church services on Sunday mornings. James Edward Porter, a longtime secretary of the LPUBA and a member of the Felicity Street Baptist Church, performed as a vocal soloist at Emancipation Day celebrations in 1894. He had also been a delegate to Baptist state and national conventions, revealing how union leadership shared leadership positions in the church. Perhaps Porter contributed to early jazz, since, as drummer Paul Barbarin explained: "The pastors in the Baptist churches . . . were singing rhythm. More so than a jazz band." Kid Ory remembers that "Bolden got most of his tunes from the 'Holy Roller Church,' the Baptist church on Jackson Avenue and Franklin," and described the interactive ethos between congregation and musician: "Oh, yeah, they had drums and piano while they sang, clapping their hands. Even the Baptists, some of the Baptist Churches had it. They'd have guests; invite a trumpet player, trombone player to come play with them. Yeah, they'd get to swinging, you know? What we're doing now we're about sixty years behind what happened, you know? I was like a guest artist on the show."[147]

Porter and Bolden were two of several musicians who frequented Longshoremen's Hall's syncretic mix of dances, church services, and labor organizing. The hall was within walking distance of Kid Ory's 2135 Jackson Avenue home (where he lived from 1910 to 1915). Other blues and jazz musicians lived nearby over the years, including Jelly Roll Morton, Johnny Dodds, Mutt Carey, King Oliver, and Mamie Desdunes. According to research done by Kid Ory biographer John McCusker, many of Ory's Black neighbors were "laborers and freight handlers," especially dockworkers. The neighborhood also included many German and Italian working-class immigrants, many of whom worked on the docks.[148]

Longshoremen's Hall was not the only labor-run space where the "blues for dancing" took hold. Bolden was also frequently featured at Union Sons Hall, which was located on the corner of Perdido and South Rampart Streets. The building was owned, and its dances were organized, by the Union Sons Relief Association. It had roots in Reconstruction and dated back to 1866, providing aid to freedpeople migrating to New Orleans. Officers of the organization were laborers in a variety of occupations, and their work was intimately tied to the union movement.[149] Bolden played here so frequently that it became known as "funky butt hall," a tribute to the reinvented sense of time and bodily connection that resisted the mechanization and alienated time of the New South.[150]

Music was one of several offerings at Union Sons Hall. Saturday night dances, lasting until five in the morning, would be turned over to fulfill a different medium of spiritual need a few hours later. "On Sunday mornings," writes Marquis, "the hall served as the First Lincoln Baptist Church."[151] This was no standard gig for Bolden, for he could call the Union Sons Hall his family: his sister, Cora, was married to Alex Reed, who was the organization's third deputy Marshall in 1904.[152] Thus, within twenty-four hours, one might attend a meeting discussing rights and strategies for the Black laborer, an all-night blues dance, and then a Baptist service, with close family, friends, and coworkers present at all three. Two of Bolden's main regular performance spaces were thus union-run halls, and these concerts directly benefited, and were defended by, organized labor. It is not an exaggeration to suggest that jazz would not have developed the way it did without the protective power and sociality of the Black labor movement.

The ability of unions to shield practitioners from police shutdown also allowed dissident messaging through music to become widespread. In addition to his depiction of working-class life and abusive bosses in "Don't Go Way Nobody," Bolden critiqued police harassment. Jazz historian Donald Marquis has shown through cross-checking the New Orleans Police Department arrest records that the lyrics of "Buddy Bolden's Blues" reference the arrest of his friend Frankie Dusen for "loitering" in 1904.[153] Police brutality was a major concern for Black residents and Black musicians in New Orleans, as Pops Foster and others attested in numerous interviews.[154] The "Robert Charles Ballad," which commemorated the Black revolutionary who attacked the white police officers who were harassing him and led to an explosion of indiscriminate white mob violence against New Orleans's Black citizens, was likely a union hall standard.[155] Musicians remember how popular songs that denounced state violence were directly repressed by law enforcement. Sidney Bechet claimed that performing Bolden's music in the Eagle Band was a potentially criminal act: "When we started playing Buddy's theme song, 'I Thought I Heard Buddy Bolden Say,' the police put you in jail if they heard you singing that song. I was just starting out on clarinet, six or seven years old, Bolden had a tailgate contest with the Imperial Band. Bolden started his theme song, people started singing, policemen began whipping heads."[156]

These were some of the insurgent forms of commentary that early jazz produced in dialogue with the labor movement. Some years later, in 1929, Blind Willie Johnson was arrested for inciting to riot because he sang "If I Had My Way in This Wicked World I Would Tear This Building Down" in front of the Customs House building.[157] Song lyrics themselves were prohibited from being uttered in public spaces if they disturbed the "peace," forcing Black musicians to find new ways to encode and transmit the meanings of such songs. One solution was to render them purely instrumental and remove the lyrics altogether. As Bechet recalled, "The Eagle Band was good for the blues, they played every Saturday night. They played Bolden's theme song, but they did not sing any words to it." But surely the words were not forgotten, and likely the performance of the song would summon, like a mnemonic device, the silenced lyrics and recall the spirit of dignified refusal in this substitutive process. Such songs influenced white radicals as well, including the composer of the popular "I Got the Blues," the Italian anarchist Antonio Maggio, who was arrested in a dragnet for the assassination of President William McKinley. The piece was "respectfully dedicated to all those have the blues," and its ethos was rooted in a working-class consciousness that Maggio, who had studied socialism, professed: "I believe that the people are the masters. Anarchy is the doctrine of equality and love."[158]

It was precisely musicians' ability to organize popular dissent and communal pride that made them effective partners for unions. The dissident consciousness they transmitted facilitated the type of base-building that union organizers needed to develop if they were to be successful in resisting the hegemony of capital and white supremacy on the docks. Such linkages between organized labor and the blues were theorized by Clyde Woods: "Later labeled Jazz, the right of individual and community self-defense, the ethic of social justice, the critique of plantation relations, the desire to create sustainable communities, and the sound of rebellion against fascism were deeply embedded in the Blues movement led by 'King Bolden.'"[159] Bolden's embodiment of such values was not incidental, but rather was the fruit of organized space-making that unions enacted. LPUBA president William Penn's prior experience as the manager of the Excelsior Brass Band thus emerges as an even more relevant detail in this arc of movement-based art making.

LABOR DAY AND THE RECLAIMING OF THE BODY

When American Federation of Labor (AFL) Samuel Gompers President visited New Orleans to celebrate the city's first labor day parade in 1902, he was taken aback. "What I have witnessed has surprised me a little," he exclaimed in response to its raw spectacle. "I have attended many Labor-day [sic] celebrations in the northern states, and this one in New Orleans stands alongside any of them for numbers in parade ... and for the fruits of organized labor."¹⁶⁰

Perhaps Gompers, who had earlier met with the "the colored [labor] organization," was surprised—or unnerved—by the stunning musical processional through which Black paraders symbolically claimed this holiday, and the mantle of labor, as their own. "Labor Day was celebrated in usual big style by the negro labor organizations," wrote the *Picayune* in 1907, reporting that the seven thousand marchers "were variously attired in new blue overalls or such apparel as they use while working." Afterward, a picnic of thirty-five hundred assembled at the City Park Race Track for "a great concourse of happy, laughing merry-makers" and "speech-making, dancing, [and] music," as speakers called for an end to child labor and for the "elimination of competition among the toiling classes." Labor Day celebrations like this combined politics, celebration, and music, full of pageantry comparable to Reconstruction.¹⁶¹

Labor Day celebrations were spaces where traditions of brassroots democracy were deepened among musicians and wider publics. They reflected another prerogative of Black working-class activism: the reclaiming of the body, away from the demands of capitalist industry and in the service of communal self-expression and solidarity. Musicians who performed in the union halls were well represented in the parades, including Buddy Bolden, who was frequently contracted for Labor Day parades by the dockworker unions. In fact, the 1906 Labor Day parade was where Buddy Bolden played his last professional gig.¹⁶² In parades, musicians Freddie Keppard, Buddy Bolden, and Louis Armstrong could play for, and inspire, new generations of musicians, as their music came to embody a Black labor alliance that cut across caste and cultural divisions. Violinist Paul Dominguez credited Buddy Bolden for "cause[ing] these younger Creoles, men like Bechet and Keppard, to have a different style altogether from the old heads."¹⁶³ The growing hegemony of Black musical aesthetics reflected the organizational power of the labor movement itself, since, as Clyde Woods wrote about the new blues-based style, "the music emerged from, and was placed at the service of, a growing New Orleans Black working class attempting to impose its social vision upon a region organized around its brutal exploitation."¹⁶⁴

The cultural work of these parades reflected another arena in which time was a site of contestation in the struggle between capital and the counter-plantation. Charles Hersch has argued that the kinetic properties of Black brass band parades spoke to their hopes to reverse the traditional hierarchies of power and value, expressed through unique fusions of physicality and displacements of time. For Hersch, the downbeat, especially "in the case of a march," compels the listener to "militarily . . . put one foot in front of another." New Orleans brass band parades, imbued with the values of the sanctified church, reversed this. "Where the downbeat represents obedience and uniformity, the upbeat, and even downbeats two and four, is a surprise, a deviation, an interruption." He suggests that these musicians "discovered and created a new experience of time for themselves and listeners, and these experiences challenged social constraints."[165] This new impulse, a shared community in time, was a powerful cultural response to proletarianization that embedded industrial work cycles into the body.

Not only were new ways of listening and moving innovated in these spaces, but so, too, were the very technical foundations of performance: the material conditions, as it were, of dozens of musicians, such as their embouchures, their finger dexterity, and their diaphragm strength. These collective schools contested a central logic of capitalism and its hold on the body. Michel Foucault argues that a "body manipulated by authority" is a constitutive part of modernity's claim on the subject. He considers the body as "directly involved in a political field; power relations have an immediate hold upon it; they invest it, mark it, train it, torture it, force it to carry our tasks, to perform ceremonies, to emit signs."[166] Black Labor Day parades retrained, or "redisciplined," bodies in the interest of developing skills, performing ceremonies, and emitting signs that were collectively created and refined within the Black community. In a sense, the parade subverted the capitalist regimentation of the body and attempted detournement to other ends. These repurposed muscles were not retrained to pack cotton bales aboard cargo ships or celebrate white masters. This was a kind of power and knowledge from below, a collective reclaiming of the body and its physical capacities, a pointillistic quiltwork of techniques, from invented mutes to diaphragm positions that encouraged multiphonics, to new subtle divisions of the beat, to new marching steps—all of which were passed among hands, mouths, feet, and ears quickly (even if it took longer to internalize them).

Not all musicians were so keen to allow their hard-won technique to become property of this commons. Cornetist Freddie Keppard was a frequent participant in parades and events organized by the LPUBA. Pops Foster remembered that "the last job I played with Freddie was a Labor Day parade, put on by the Longshoremen's Union."[167] Louis Armstrong recalled that Keppard had covered his fingers with a handkerchief during one parade as he played cornet to protect his ideas from "theft," a gesture that Louis Armstrong derided as "silly."[168] Nonetheless, the fact that Keppard felt compelled to do this at all suggests that the borrowing of techniques and ideas was a widespread practice. The Labor Day parade was one potent playground for these creative, brilliant reimaginations of what discipline might feel like. Collectively constructed, selected, and reproduced by musicians and paraders, the aesthetic practices of the activist procession embodied the initiative of the Black working class and suggested how a humane political economy might be realized from their perspective.

Sometimes, the intense muscularity associated with these new styles became conflated with masculinity. Danny Barker held that a true practitioner of the new music had "to be a working-class man, out in the open all the time, healthy and strong."[169] Similarly, Johnny St. Cyr once said that only a "working man" had "the power to play hot": "You see, the average working man is very musical."[170] In St. Cyr's analysis, jazz was explicitly working class—and depended on this association for its technique, authenticity, and masculinity. The emphasis on masculinity by some New Orleans jazz musicians obscures the women musicians who second-lined during New Orleans's early jazz days. "While it is true that women were less likely than men to play brass instruments in New Orleans marching bands," notes Sherrie Tucker, "nonetheless some did"[171]—just as they also participated in unions as workers, auxiliary members, and supporters of unionized laborers and strikers. Women musicians and paraders in Labor Day celebrations add another component to the ways in which such parades were "rehearsals for revolution" where musicians, organizers, and marchers experienced what the society they hoped to build could feel like and sound like.

CONCLUSION

The cultural commons of brassroots democracy was deeply tied to the rhythms and initiatives of the dockworkers' movement. It was sounded and enacted on docks, in union halls, at jazz funerals, and during Labor Day parades. Paul Garon's *Blues and the Poetic Spirit* (1996) argues that "the revolutionary nature of the blues" lies in its "fidelity to fantasy and desire": "the blues generates an irreducible and, so to speak, habit-forming demand for freedom." Garon explains:

> The black working-class blues singer rejects and even ridicules the repressive norms of the white bourgeoisie, negating bourgeois ideology by the mere act of non-acceptance. Although this form of rejection/negation does not necessarily comprise an effort to change society's structure, it was, historically, the principle vehicle of the poetic revolt for blacks throughout roughly the first third of this century. Other forms of revolt, although existent, did not relate to the black working class on the same level that the blues did... It is certainly worth asking why it was that no ostensibly revolutionary organization that period "adopted" the blues or jazz in any way, or even considered them sympathetically.[172]

Though Garon does not recognize it, this music was mobilized by the revolutionary dockworkers in New Orleans at the turn of the century for precisely the reasons he identifies. Its habit-forming demand for freedom was itself historically contingent, informed by the struggle for the control of the labor process and public space on the docks and New Orleans writ large. Its aesthetics, the lyrics of its songs, its rituals and performance practices all bear the imprint of the dockworkers' impact on Black public life and its insistence on another sense of time that prioritizes human dignity and community over raw productivity.

The contributions of labor organizers to Black New Orleans far exceeded the workplace. Dockworker unions were a bulwark against the fascist creep of white supremacy in the everyday life of the city, protecting Black culture from state and civilian repression. Black labor unions garnered respect and recognition, even from the white conservative press, illustrating a broad-based legitimacy that was notable. They had a power that mayors and industry owners were forced to recognize. They brought racist senators to the negotiating table even when it threatened their "honor" as white men. This is not to suggest that unions were somehow more legitimate or credible than other Black spaces. It does suggest, however, that Black dockworkers' unions were aware of their unique power, and mobilized this power to organize vibrant spaces that nurtured new forms of Black working-class culture.

In addition, militancy on the docks fueled a globally rooted analysis of power and oppression and taught working people how applying pressure on the weak points in the capitalist supply chain could result in significant material and sociopolitical gains for their community and impoverished peoples more broadly. This initiative required effort and conscious decision-making on the part of activists. While Black popular resistance to Jim Crow and Redemption was powerful, its unity with working-class and anti-capitalist politics was not inevitable. Union organizers worked overtime to link these forms of expression, to connect local hierarchies of race and class to global historical forces and Black community structures to the newest confrontation with capital.

These formations profoundly affected musicians and contributed to the zeitgeist. Their lessons informed the values of community members and compelled them to fight for a deeper cause linked to a whole world in struggle. It is why Willie Parker would say, so matter-of-factly, that scabs should be killed for defying labor solidarity on the docks; it is what Oscar Ameringer heard in the singing of Black union meetings: that "their unionism was far more than a matter of hours and wages. It was a religion."[173] Black unions were vehicles by which affective solidarities were hashed out through experimentation, vulnerability, and dialogue. Much like a club or a recording studio, they created spaces where the music could flourish and take on new meanings, as well as new temporalities, physicalities, and resonances, within the context of a cooperative culture that insisted on the possibility—the necessity—of other worlds. Brassroots democracy is the name of dynamic cipher of affect and effect, by which participatory decision-making fused with euphoric and cathartic collective music-making that challenged the racialized ontologies of capital. It is a struggle that continues to the present day.

CONCLUSION

Telegrams from the Spiritual Plane

> The oral literature of the Plantations is consequently akin to other subsistence—survival—techniques set in place by enslaved people and their immediate descendants. Everywhere that the obligation to get around the rule of silence existed a literature was created that has no "natural" continuity, if one may put it that way, but, rather, bursts forth in snatches and fragments ... That is because, in addition to this obligation to get around something, the Creole language has another, internal obligation: to renew itself in every instance on the basis of a series of forgettings.
>
> *Édouard Glissant,* Poetics of Relation, *68–69.*

Brass bands remain a vital part of the movement for Black liberation and new forms of life beyond racial capitalism. On August 6, 2020, an assortment of hip-hop artists and brass band musicians in Pittsburgh, including this author, came together for a poignant event described as a "living funeral." This gathering was a community-wide display of solidarity with Danielle Brown, who was at that time in the midst of a two-hundred-day-long hunger strike. Brown's decision to abstain from food and orchestrate her own funeral was a compelling act intended to bring attention to her late son, Marquis. In 2018, Marquis had been a student at Duquesne University, where, according to accounts from police officers who had entered his dorm room, Marquis had thrown a chair against his window and subsequently leaped through the shattered glass. He fell sixteen flights to his death. The Duquesne University Police Department, who did not require their officers to wear body cameras, refused to release the results of their internal investigation to Danielle.[1]

Musicians at the event supported the speakers, who connected Marquis's death to a legacy of racialized policing, urban apartheid, and extrajudicial murder.

During the processional that followed, marchers took the funeral to Duquesne University's doorstep. Both acts were part of a multivalent politics, since, as Sakakeeny writes, "The jazz funeral is deeply symbolic but the representational layer is only one source of its power. Collective emotions of joy and lament constitute another embroidered layer within an overriding atmosphere of mutual aid. Sound seeds this atmosphere, and the relative openness or ambivalence of the sound ... means that it can also be heard as a political act of refusal, rebellion, or something else altogether."[2] The embodiment of mutual aid and community sound are realized through the nonprofit music school The Roots of Music, which was founded in the aftermath of Hurricane Katrina by Derrick Tabb in response to the destruction of Black life and music education in its wake.[3] Its grassroots approach centers a community-based practice that combines brass band education with social programs that combat the "roots of hunger" while creating performance opportunities for about a hundred and fifty students.

The fusion of brass band activism and the struggle against racial capitalism has a special resonance at the scene of the crime itself. The Minneapolis-based brass band and activist group Brass Solidarity was formed in 2021 in direct response to the murder of George Floyd. They describe themselves as "a convergence of musicians, activists, and community members using our sound as a voice for justice and an advocate for Black Lives." According to Brass Solidarity organizer and clarinetist Anthony Afful, the group is inspired by the Black Panthers' popular education programs and is deepening its political education program: "You are only as strong as your least educated member." While being largely BIPOC musicians, the group is inclusive of all who wish to join them and often teach new members songs—and their social meanings—during performances, whether at May Day, Juneteenth, or at their weekly brass band vigils at George Floyd square. Afful describes these gatherings as serving "a larger funeral function" by offering "sonic peace."[4]

Their sonic stories alchemize; sound becomes heartbeat becomes pain becomes release, becomes resistance. Each motion converges in the rhythm of breath—the inhale, the exhale—each precious, each endowed with the divine right to breathe freely. As we contemplate their lives at these funerals too frequent, for the living and for the dead, we contemplate Black life cut short in the cruel chasm between systemic oppression and bystanders' apathy. We, the living, carry the weight of their breathless moments. We are reminded, perhaps, of what Ashon T. Crawley describes as "the hermeneutics given by black breath, black pneuma," the "intellectual practice and performance of the breathing in and the breathing out, the reciprocity of exhalation and inhalation, the giving and sharing in the commons of air."[5] These commemorative events, then, challenge the temporal and spatial trajectory emblematic of the transition from the plantation to the penitentiary, from the sugarhouse to Storyville—a ricocheting nexus of extractivist political economies and regimes of surveillance that Katherine McKittrick has discerned as "plantation futures." In opposition to these racial-spatial echoes of the plantation, and in alignment with the renewal embedded in the garden plot of the maroon republic, McKittrick underscores the act of burial as one that establishes a "spatial continuity between the living and dead" articulating "a location of black death that holds in it a narrative soundscape that also promises an honest struggle for life."[6]

These brassroots movements contend with jazz's co-optation by the neoliberal marketplace.[7] They respond to Nathaniel Mackey's call to "confront the neotraditionalism that has taken hold of late with a counter-tradition of marronage, divergence, flight, fugitive tilt."[8] Brassroots democracy remains a viable counter-plantation practice whose polyphonic subjectivities creolize new movements of resistance. Its staying power as a technology of assembly reflects a long historical durée in which Afro-Louisianan musical workers commented upon and critiqued what Marcus Rediker has identified as the four foundational violences to Atlantic capitalism: the expropriation of the commons both in Europe and in the Americas; African slavery and the Middle Passage; rationalized exploitation through the institution of wage labor; and disciplinary repression organized through prisons and the criminal justice system.[9]

Black Atlantic musicians responded to each of these violences with novel and inspiring strategies, transforming both the Atlantic world and themselves in the process. They fought back against the expropriation of the commons by building new ones, whether in the Eureka commune in Veracruz, on repurposed plantations in Louisiana's sugar districts, or in communal aid organizations with strong music education components such as the Bulbs Orphanage in Plaquemines Parish or the Boys Town Orphanage in Omaha. Their music challenged the scope and scale of slavery, helping expand the gardening complex and honoring communal labor relations. In some cases, music accompanied and prophesied the wholescale burning of cane and slavery's social relations entirely. Such music was, in essence, the aesthetic corollary to marronage: a sonic and social performative practice that imagined counter-plantation realities even while immersed in the plantation.[10] This impulse survived through centuries of change in the social relations of plantation capitalism. Black musicians built counterstructures to wage labor and the hegemony of capital through the cooperative solidarity economy of sex workers and musicians in early twentieth-century Storyville, as well as their symbiotic relationship with New Orleans's powerful Black dockworkers union during the same time period. And although this topic is outside the scope of this volume, we have seen examples of how Black music commented upon and challenged the dehumanization of the prison-industrial complex in the work of Buddy Bolden and others, a theme taken up more forcibly by hip-hop activists later in the twentieth century.[11]

It is thus understandable why brassroots democracy continues to resonate. Black music, as Paul Gilroy writes, "demands that they [musicians] ceaselessly reconstruct their own histories" reflecting a "concern with history which demands that the experience of slavery is also recovered and rendered vivid and immediate . . . [as] a powerful metaphor for the injustice and exploitation of contemporary wage work in general."[12] Such historical remixing invokes not only the legacy of slavery but also the Afro-Atlantic social relations designed to resist it: the sovereign universe of the counter-plantation, assembly and its practice of affective consensus, pleasure as a vehicle of community beyond commodification. These practices were continually reproduced, radically responsive to the current historical context due to their improvisational and dialogical mode of cultural production. The musical resistance of expropriated African workers and their descendants evolved in direct relationship to the evolving system of dispossession that continues to cast its shadow on our global relations. One could say that brassroots democracy has moved from *local defensive* actions to a *regional and national resistance* to a *global "movement of social movements"* focused on defending and extending life-centered subsistence social relations.[13] Black music formed a socializing alternative even as it was expropriated and exploited as a commodity itself—a dynamic not lost on the musicians themselves who formed collectives, innovated new structures of musical communication that resisted the commodity form, and used music to increasingly speak out against injustice and colonization as social movements waxed and waned.[14] In sites of US military occupation during the ironically named Jazz Age, African American cultural forms, often brought with US marines, inspired resistance movements to US cultural hegemony and capitalist social relations, such as in Haiti's anti-occupation "Vodou Jazz" movement.[15] As saxophonist Salim Washington has said, "the music is the antidote to the existential crisis," the existential, and now ecocidal, crisis of slavery and capitalism.[16]

As Salim Washington's words indicate, jazz musicians themselves have frequently interjected into debates on the nature of the music and its connection to histories of rebellion. Many have situated jazz protest in the Black Power and the Black Arts movements of the 1960s and 1970s. Yet clarinetist Sidney Bechet, active in early twentieth-century New Orleans, mediated on the connections between racial violence and Black self-determination through music significantly earlier. In his autobiography *Treat It Gentle* (1960), one moving passage on his grandfather suggests as such: "There was one time he had a dream about his right arm, about losing it at the elbow. After that, he'd only practice shooting with his left hand. But maybe that don't belong here. What I'm saying is that he was a musician. No one had to explain notes or rhythm or feeling to him. All the things that was happening to him outside, they had to get there to be measured—there inside him where the music was."[17]

Bechet explained the corporeal mutilation and armed resistance from his allegorical grandfather—"a slave named Omar"—in order to contour the collective resistance of enslaved African descendants in the Atlantic world to their quixotic and sometimes utopian musical expression. Even in this brief passage, the historical consciousness is striking in scope. Bechet's description of Omar's amputated arm connects him to the maroon revolutionary Bras-Coupé, whose activity in the 1830s is recorded in both Louisiana police records and collective folklore. Bras-Coupé's arm was amputated following a struggle with the police, and he lived for years in the swamps, raiding plantations and inspiring wider resistance.[18] When Bechet suggests that Omar was a major figure in Congo Square, he is attempting to thread the dialectic between white supremacist violence and musical marronage as foundational to the development of jazz.

The story of Bras-Coupé is also a piece of intra-Caribbean folklore with Haitian origins, and this connection informs how we should read Bechet's larger work and the generation of brassroots democracy practitioners with which he was enmeshed. The Louisianan legend of Bras-Coupé often includes potions that granted him bulletproof skin, and historian John Bardes observes that this same motif was preceded by "several slave oral traditions regarding revolutionary Haitian and Caribbean maroons," specifically François Mackandal. Bardes suggests that these stories must have circulated in Louisiana by Saint-Domingue enslaved people and their descendants. Not only did this story encode historic memory, but it actually had a practical application for social reproduction in that it communicated "particular religious strategies employed by historic maroons engaged in revolutionary guerrilla warfare."[19] The myth of Bras-Coupé was a distinct mode of Afro-Atlantic remembering, whereby Louisianan enslaved people incorporated Bras-Coupé and a broader Black Caribbean tradition into their own origin stories. This creative substitution reflects how Haitian performance cultures and belief systems fused with the political consciousness and cultures of Afro-Louisiana at large.[20]

Bechet's account of Omar is relevant for this study—not only because of its surrogacy of Haitian archetypes, but because it mobilizes this Haitian Louisianan oral literature to develop Bechet's own theory of Black music, in which jazz expresses the intersection of an internal musical being and group political consciousness. In this way, Bechet's reading of jazz as Afro-Atlantic inheritance and reflects how the theory of the music and the music itself are one. As his grandfather Omar struggles through the Bayou LeFourg during his daring escape, lost and confused, he hears

> a whole lot of slaves there, some free, some runaway—they was all chanting and moaning and beating on drums around this woman who had a big cast-iron pot she was boiling this potion in. They was all waiting to see what was going to happen, if this point, it would give them a sign. . . . The whole thing there kept building and building up, and those people, they were telling themselves about things that were inside them. They were telling it out to the fire and the dark and the mist, and the only way they knew to tell it was by singing about a place where they all used to be happy once—how they stand listening in that place hearing sounds. . . . That's why there was this music in them; music was all they had to forget with. Or they could use it for a way of remembering that was as good as forgetting, a way that was another kind of forgetting. This music was their need, their want. But it had to have a pride too . . . they *needed* my grandfather to love this girl just like he needed her himself so they could bring themselves together and hope.
>
> Then this potion exploded and it was a sign to them, and they set to clapping and shouting.[21]

Bechet's words might explain why the runaway musician-barber Pierre continued to play music from Haiti in New Orleans, even if it risked identifying him to his erstwhile captors: this was a music that had to continue to be produced or risk an ahistoricity worse than death. Musicians "singing about a place where they all used to be happy," to create music they could "forget with" was paradoxically a form of collective memory. Bechet shows how psychological catharsis and subjective reconstitution take place through intersubjective community building, a dialectic between individual and group that forms a core part of Black music's special power—its potion. This music and its communal healing process become a bulletproof armor for a collective subject, one that could make sense of physical torture, dismemberment, the loss of loved ones, starvation. "We don't play this or that piece," explained the saxophonist Albert Ayler. "We play sadness; we play hunger."[22]

Much of this book has focused on assembly, congregation, and new visions of society that brassroots democracy was able to summon through the collective labor of musicians. Yet Bechet's account reminds us that the music was not just "notes or rhythms." While their exteriorization was aural, these sonic ceremonies were a manifestation of an intellectual and spiritual experience unfolding "inside," a form of internal hearing. By measuring what "was happening to him" inside "where the music was," Bechet presents musical creation as a narrative device across generations to consolidate a historical consciousness among the African diaspora.[23] As he wrote elsewhere, "The part of him that was where he was now, in the South, a slave—that part was the melody, the part of him that was different from his ancestors." This was a song built in the hard material conditions of plantation production; "it was coming right up from the fields, setting itself into their feet and working right up, right up into their stomachs, their spirit." It was a melody that one "had to live, every day, working, waiting for rest and joy, trying to understand that the distance he had to reach was not his own people, but white people. Day after day, like there was no end to it."[24] Bechet's meditation reflects on how the emergence of counter-plantation consciousness through the mediation of internal pain through cathartic performance—how it was not just "notes and rhythms" included in these notes and rhythms.

Interiority is also a major theme in these quotations, but it is an interior world that is both dependent on community while also autonomous and self-activated. In Bechet's account of his grandfather, collective singing allowed his interior space to convert his social knowledge into sound. While his voice is autonomous, it is held captive by the violence of the system congealed as trauma; its transformation into aesthetic wisdom is simultaneously a psychological release. Such songs were present during traumatizing experiences in the throes of captivity, such as those experienced by sex workers in New Orleans at the turn of the century. In such spaces, music and dance provide the necessary means for group cohesion in ways both psychic and physical. In sharing a mutual vulnerability, they become one. These themes find echoes in the accounts of an anonymous African American, imprisoned in Texas in 1964, who described how work songs "would relieve the tensions." "It was made up for words as it went along," he reported. "Sometimes they would touch so close that everyone would take a liking to them and repeat them," creating one kind of shared experience. Other times, "a guy [would] be burdened and doesn't want to pass his burden on to nobody . . . So he'd sing a song, and he'd make it real sad." This incarcerated individual also suggests that such songs functioned as a hidden transcript: "You tell the truth for how you feel [in the songs], cause you can't express it, see, to the boss . . . they used to sing songs about the bosses, captains, sergeants, lieutenants, whatever they think of them."[25] In his telling, the intersection of interior pain and political critique were in shared songs, arising often within the violent environs of forced labor, whether waged or nonwaged systems.

At the center of this dialectic between an interior voice and a collective process, musicians could "measure" what had happened to them and their community and anticipate future struggles. For instance, Omar dreams of his forthcoming amputation and prepares for it by practicing shooting with his other arm. Bechet makes clear that this divination was linked to his ontology as a musician. In Bechet's account, then, Omar was a distinct interpreter of worldly oppression and historical forces, able to predict forthcoming gains and losses in the long struggle to overthrow slavery and its sequels, as well as help construct a collective phenomenology and theory of history. Paul Gilroy might say that musicians such as Omar belonged to a "priestly caste of organic intellectuals whose experiences enable us to focus upon the crises of modernity and modern values with special clarity," as "temporary custodians of a distinct and embattled cultural sensibility which has also operated as a political and philosophical resource."[26] Bechet seems to invoke this meaning as well when he writes: "He [Omar] had no house, he had no telegram, no newspaper." Still, Omar can take on his priestly role. "But he had a drum, and he had a rhythm that could speak into the drum, and he could send it out through all the air to the rest of his people."[27] He may have had no telegram, but Bechet's grandfather was still sending what saxophonist Lester Young once described as "telegrams" from the spiritual plane.[28]

Communication of information was central in this chain of music and intersubjectivity, but it was a kind of communication that linked events on the outside—"what was happening to him [Omar]"—to an inside repository of experience. The collective singing of the ritual speaks to healing, a "remembering that [was] almost as good as forgetting." In this, Bechet suggests a relationship between pain, alterity, and community to inform the virtuosic coordination of music, memory, and therapy. For, as Elaine Scarry observes in her study of torture: "Whatever pain achieves, it achieves in part through its unsharability, and it ensures this unsharability through its resistance to language."[29] Bechet places torture—via amputation, rape, and daily exploitation in the fields—at the center of his analysis of the Black musical body for, as Gilroy notes, "imaginative proximity to terror is their [Black musics'] inaugural experience" precisely because "though such terrors were unspeakable, they were not inexpressible"; music contained the unique ability to communicate "a direct image of the slaves' will."[30] This interiority lay at the intersection of the pain Omar felt and the pain his community feels. It served as a creative resource that future generations looked to for insight and solace.

This triangular relationship between collective memory, racial terror, and imaginative communitarian possibility is a kind of middle passage in reverse, an attempt to create an aesthetic corollary to the ineffable holocaust of North American slavery. It is also at the core of brassroots democracy's cathartic, utopian, and radical expansion of the public sphere. It propels its insistence to dismantle structures of racial oppression whose roots are in the commodification of human beings—"the rosy dawn of the era of capitalist production."³¹ In a world where apolitical forgetting is continuously produced by hegemonic media, we may do well to visit Ana Hofman's notion of "memory activism" and the ways in which music and sound are "able to make a rupture or open a possibility for new forms of political belonging and identifications."³² Collective singing has a particularly significant role in expanding the conventional definition of politics, as demonstrated in Hofman's study of women's choirs in former Yugoslavia:

> Unlike other forms of memory activism, singing is presumed to be "soft activism" or even "apolitical" and therefore less threatening to those in power. But it is precisely as an apparently mundane and joyful activity that choral performing enables a powerful mobilization. The strong embodied and sensory experience of collective singing is able to build ad hoc collectivities on a spatial and temporal scale that have profound political potentials or may even challenge the traditional notions of politics and the political.³³

Put differently, jazz's evasiveness to being thought of in terms of "the political" is rooted in categories and epistemologies that forfeit an appreciation of affective power. If the political is reduced to directed speech expressing a concrete demand, then surely this notion of music as collective power fails. But if we appreciate how brassroots democracy encapsulates an entire mode of production rooted in congregation, collectivity, multivocality, and avant-garde internationalism haunted by the ability to express the inexpressible (as witness to the human and ecological commodification borne by Black Atlantic history), then it would seem difficult to separate jazz from the historical forces that surrounded the people who produced it, and which produced them.

Brassroots democracy speaks to human beings' capacity to express their subjectivity and connection to land and others despite dehumanizing and desocializing work regimes. Footloose seasonal workers in the sugar harvest and forced migrants from Haiti both found ways to keep body and soul together through musical self-activity. During the age of Black labor unionizing on the New Orleans docks, mobile sailors who came and went with the tides made impressions on Louisianan Black activists and musicians; in other contexts, Black musicians were sailors themselves. Soldiers, mobile military workers, were sometimes part of deployed forces of imperialism and other times fought wars of liberation against slavery, such as when Black New Orleans brass band musicians served in Cuba in the Spanish American War and spent months at a time jamming with Afro-Cubans in the Oriente province.³⁴ In both contexts, Black military workers were carriers of subversive culture born out of the simple and profound imperative of people trying to keep body and soul together, paradoxically united by what they hoped to challenge: a regional plantation system.

Brassroots democracy is an expression of the radical democratic potential of the "motley crew" as a historic agent of creativity and change.[35] Sailors, dockworkers, smugglers, and sex workers all come together via seaport and ship, what Mary Louise Pratt might call extreme "cultural contact zones," just as brass band traditions were contact zones between Mexican and African American musical cultures, between Afro-Cuban and Haitian performance cultures and Afro-Louisianan procession.[36] Musical history from below is profoundly and inevitably cosmopolitan in ways that defy the construction of a canon. The long nineteenth century in the Caribbean basin reveals that music is a fugitive form of communication and being, especially among those in resistance to the plantation complex. Musicians revel in this radical collectivity that comes and goes, sometimes disappearing on the wind. It is creative, uncontrollable, and indestructible. This music can be heard as a component of a protean, sometimes mysterious, proletarian public sphere with its own means of communication—which overlapped with other mobile professions like those of cigar rollers, barbers, sex workers, and seasonal workers. Indeed, as we have seen, music was a powerful entity in the lives of each of these groups of mobile workers and the spaces in which they carried out collective tasks.

Perhaps most importantly, the music of brassroots democracy is an archive of the affective power of struggles past. As a form of subversive knowledge that circulates beyond the boundaries of the nation-state, it was, and is, a constant reminder that there are other worlds than this—and that the one that rules today has been contested. As Daniel Desdunes's uncle Pierre-Aristide Desdunes wrote in his poem "Thoughts of a Slave Soldier": "I feel, boiling within my veins of iron, A creative power giving birth to worlds!"[37] This music speaks of a never-going-away pain, one that plagues and propels creators to imagine new ways of being together, which can, with collective labor, transform into a redemptive power for a human species struggling to enter a new epoch. As we watch familiar forms of oppression take shape once again on our shared horizon, the music will respond.

Lips to mouthpiece, chest to cosmos, eyes drawn at the emerging police response: musicians collectively engage in the sacred act of drawing breath, against history, against the impossibility of justice, bearing witness to the lives lost in the relentless, unyielding grip of racial capitalism. We confront this stark truth: the world is ours to shape, but not at the expense of another's breath.

The music was created precisely for this reason.

NOTES

INTRODUCTION *A Long Song from Haiti*

1. Marx, *The Eighteenth Brumaire of Louis Bonaparte*, 15.

2. I capitalize "Black" and decapitalize "white," following the reasoning outlined in Harris, "Whiteness as Property," 1707–91.

3. Jackson, *Creole Indigeneity*, 44.

4. Blanchard, "Opinion: Black Protest Is Music."

5. Salaam, "The Spirit Family of the New Orleans Streets."

6. Hunter, *To 'Joy My Freedom*, 3.

7. Bechet, *Treat It Gentle*, 6. On Bechet's genealogy, see Chilton, *Sidney Bechet*, 1–3, 291–92. Bryan Wagner suggests that Bechet's depiction of his grandfather in the likeliness of the maroon Bras-Coupé poses "profound questions about jazz tradition," and that "we need to take these questions seriously. What does it mean to find, as the absence at the origin of jazz history, a slave maimed by the police?" Wagner, *The Life and Legend of Bras-Coupé*, 27. The authenticity of Bechet's autobiography has been disputed. Krin Gabbard claims that "the entire story is told in a colloquial but authoritative fashion that probably came from his editors more than from Bechet." Recent archival discoveries have highlighted Bechet's own talent as a writer in his unpublished short stories, complicating the claim that the clarinetist was not a literary artist. Jessica Teague argues that such "assumptions [are] tinged with the kind of deeply rooted racist rhetoric once used to delegitimize the stories dictated by enslaved African Americans." Gabbard, *Better Git It in Your Soul*, 138; Teague, "A Story in Sound," 49–50.

8. Ho, *Wicked Theory, Naked Practice*, 93–94.

9. For more on the political organization of freedpeople in Louisiana before the passage of the Military Reconstruction acts, see Behrend, *Reconstructing Democracy*, 83; in other areas of the South, see O'Donovan, *Becoming Free in the Cotton South*, 213–14, 225–31. On credit unions and communal lands, see chapters 1 and 4. On pre-suffrage cultures of self-governance, see White, "'It Was a Proud Day,'" 13–50; Kantrowitz, "'Intended for the Better Government of Man,'" 1009–10.

10. Ahmad, "How to Tell When the Rebels Have Won," 16–18.

11. *New Orleans Tribune*, May 30, 1867.

12. McPherson, *The Negro's Civil War*.

13. Du Bois, *Black Reconstruction*.

14. Lipsitz, *Dangerous Crossroads*, 134.

15. Hosbey and Roane use the term "Black ecologies" to describe these land practices and the epistemologies they produced. I have opted for "maroon ecologies" to emphasize the counter-plantation praxis invoked in collective music making that was tied to both Black land practice and community organizing. Hosbey and Roane, "A Totally Different Form of Living," 71.

16. Glissant, *Poetics of Relation*, 71–72 ; 1st Municipality Guard Records, August 27, 1837.

17. On evidence of Haitian brass band traditions during and after the Revolution, see Popkin, *Facing Racial Revolution*, 77, 289, 303, 309. On Afro-Louisianan militias, see chapter 3. On the postwar arena, see chapters 1 and 5. Most of the evidence of improvisation in these contexts is in drumming and vocal traditions, suggesting transfer to brass band contexts unfolded over the nineteenth century.

18. Bechet, *Treat It Gentle*, 47–48 ; Ellison, "African-American Music and Muskets in Civil War New Orleans," 303–4.

19. On Black celebrations in Louisiana, see Pierson, *Mutiny at Fort Jackson*, 14–15; see also chapter 5.

20. *Louisiana Democrat*, October 2, 1867; Vincent, "Black Louisianians during the Civil War and Reconstruction," 94.

21. Gilmore discusses the selection of liberatory lineages in her understanding of "infrastructures of feeling" in Gilmore, *Abolition Geography*.

22. Heble, Fischlin, and Lipsitz, *The Fierce Urgency of Now*.

23. Cone, *The Spirituals and the Blues*, 4–5.

24. Dawdy, "La Catrina"; Gruesz, "Delta Desterrados"; Scott, *Degrees of Freedom*; Fiehrer, "From Quadrille to Stomp."

25. Horne, *Jazz and Justice*; Sakakeeny, "Textures of Black Sound and Affect"; Sakakeeny, "New Orleans Music as a Circulatory System"; Jones, "Louis Armstrong's 'Karnofsky Document'"; Tucker, "Jazz History Remix"; Tucker, "A Feminist Perspective on New Orleans Jazzwomen"; Hersch, *Subversive Sounds*.

26. Scott, "The Atlantic World"; Woods, *Development Drowned and Reborn*.

27. Fanon, *The Wretched of the Earth*, 242–43.

28. Okiji, *Jazz as Critique*, 9.

29. Morcom, "Following the People," 474.

30. Willie Parker, interview, November 7, 1958, HJA; Stuart, "Kid Ory"; Koenig, "The Plantation Belt and Musicians Part 1"; Kinzer, "The Tio Family"; Emanuel Sayles, interview, January 17, 1959, HJA; PBS, "Freedom."

31. Iyer, "Exploding the Narrative in Jazz Improvisation," 395.

32. Camp, "Breaking the Thermometer."

33. Follett, "Heat, Sex, and Sugar," 510–39; Scott, *Degrees of Freedom*; Mintz, *Sweetness and Power*; Burnard and Garrigus, *The Plantation Machine*.

34. Thank you to Marleen Julien for providing this translation.

> Tout ayisyen depi plus de onz zan
> Tape soufèr de la plus grande misère
> Manje te cher pate ganyen larjan
> Lafin te tué déjà bokou de mère
> Anba sabbat
> Anfin benissons le seigneur
> Yo fè partir Faustin par ordre de Renard

Bondieu dans ciel
Pou finir l'injustisce
De ces hommes de crimes et de malices
Qui en voulait que general vainqueur
Geffrard rive pour finir nos malheurs
Aba la croix d'honneur
Aba le gouverneur
Aba la couronne
Sans faire mourir personne.
On "infrastructure of feeling" see Gilmore, *Abolition Geography*, 365.

35. Alice Zeno, interview, November 14, 1958, HJA.
36. Smith, *Liberty, Fraternity, Exile*.
37. Lachance, "The 1809 Immigration"; Hunt, *Haiti's Influence on Antebellum America*, 38; Saint-Méry, *Journey in the United States*, 265; Babb, "French Refugees," 375–77.
38. Moreau de Saint-Méry, *Description Topographique*, 92–93; Dial, "Consumer Choices in Martinique and Saint-Domingue"; Burnard and Garrigus, *The Plantation Machine*, 24; Sonneck, *Early Concert Life in America*, 64.
39. Dawdy, *Building the Devil's Empire*, 3.
40. Rodriguez, *Spanish New Orleans*, 31–32.
41. Kendall, *History of New Orleans*, vol. 1, 85; Sonneck, *Early Concert Life in America*, 64.
42. Dubois, "The Haitian Revolution and the Sale of Louisiana," 18–41.
43. Lachance, "The 1809 Immigration." Anglo-Americans also moved to New Orleans during this time period.
44. Hunt, *Haiti's Influence on Antebellum America*, 62–63; Johnson, *Soul by Soul*, 220.
45. Imhotep, Zhang, and Snorton, "'Hell You Talmbout'"; Paquette, "'A Horde of Brigands?'"; Rodriguez, "Rebellion on the River Road"; Dickens, *Household Words*, reprinted in *The Provincial Freedman*, April 15, 1854.
46. Edward Baptist provides the clearest evidence to date that Deslondes may have been a forced migrant from Saint-Domingue. Baptist, *The Half Has Never Been Told*, 56–58. See also *New York Evening Post*, February 20, 1811; Dormon, "The Persistent Specter."
47. Laurent, "A History of St. John the Baptist Parish."
48. Dessens, "St Domingue Refugees in New Orleans"; Dubois, *The Banjo*.
49. "Nelder, Alexander"; Brady, "Black Artists in Antebellum New Orleans." His Saint-Domingue ancestry has not been verified.
50. Bell, *Revolution*, 94.
51. Séjour, "Le Mulâtre"; Daut, "'Sons of White Fathers'"; Piacentino, "Seeds of Rebellion in Plantation Fiction"; Handley, "A New World of Oblivion"; Cagidemetrio, "'The Rest of the Story,'" 24.
52. Trotter, *Music and Some Highly Musical People*; Charles Edwards O'Neill, "Fine Arts and Literature," 78; Johnson, *The Fear of French Negroes*, 132–36.
53. Casimir, "Haiti's Need for a Great South," 17.
54. Munro, "Can't Stand up for Falling Down," 2–3.
55. In addition to the literature already cited in this introduction, see Gaspar and Geggus, *A Turbulent Time*; Sepinwall, *Haitian History*; and Dubois et al., *The Haiti Reader*; Casimir, *The Haitians*.

56. Recent literature includes Stoler, *Along the Archival Grain*; Arondekar, *For the Record*; Connolly and Fuentes, "Introduction," 105–16; Hartman, "Venus in Two Acts," 1–14; Smallwood, "The Politics of the Archive," 117–32; Kazanjian, "Freedom's Surprise," 133–45.

57. Dubois, "Afro-Atlantic Music as Archive."

58. Jabir, *Conjuring Freedom*, 18.

59. Hartman, "Venus in Two Acts," 4.

60. Scott, *The Common Wind*, 16, 96, 87.

61. Elisabeth, "Les Relations," 177–206.

62. Rugemer, *The Problem of Emancipation*; Johnson, *The Fear of French Negroes*.

63. Jong, *Tambú*, 28, 43–44; Benjamin, *Jews of the Dutch Caribbean*, 75–76; Callahan, *Songs of Slavery and Emancipation*, 67.

64. "Venezuela Song, 1801," Academia de la Historia, Caracas, Sección Civiles, Signature A13–5159-2, report of 24 Feb. 1801, in *The Haitian Revolution*, ed. David Geggus, 188; "American Song," in *Archivo General Indias, Estado*, 59, n. 6/ 6, discussed in Naranjo Orovio and Buscaglia, "Race as a Weapon," 6.

65. Pressing, "Black Atlantic Rhythm," 298.

66. Bethel, *The Roots of African-American Identity*, 145; Coffin, *Reminiscences of Levi Coffin*; cited in "Harrison, Thomas and Harrison, Isabella Benton," in Snodgrass, *The Underground Railroad*; Austin, *African Muslims in Antebellum America*; Newman, *Black Founders*, 33–34.

67. Frederick Douglass, "The Revolution of 1848," *The North Star*, August 4, 1848; Douglass, "Remarks at Dedication Ceremonies at the Haitian Pavilion."

68. Genovese, *From Rebellion to Revolution*, 97.

69. Georgia's rice coast, white observers complained of a dance called the "the sioca," "a voluptuous dance imported from San Domingo." Flanders, *Plantation Slavery in Georgia*, 171.

70. Charlie Guillard placed the ad for this runaway in the *Courier de la Louisiane* on July 23, 1810. This story is recounted in Johnson, *Slavery's Metropolis*.

71. Rodríguez, "Reflexiones sobre los defectos," 5–27.

72. Mills, *Cutting Along the Color Line*, 52–57; *Detroit Advertiser and Tribune*, February 23, 1875; Douglass, "Make Your Sons Mechanics and Farmers"; Harris, *In the Shadow of Slavery*, 240–42.

73. Soriano, *Tides of Revolution*.

74. Sawyer Lee, *Memoir of Pierre Toussaint*; Bristol, *Knights of the Razor*.

75. Marquis, *In Search of Buddy Bolden*, 41.

76. The jazz pianist Willie "The Lion" Smith, for instance, indicates that his uncle was a barbershop singer, and his mother was "Spanish, Negro, Mohawk," suggesting connections to both Spanish America, North American Indigenous ancestry, and barbershop culture. Smith, *Music on My Mind*. For Black barbershop culture and four-part harmony, see Averill, *Four Parts, No Waiting*; Hobson, *Creating Jazz Counterpoint*; Abbott, "'Play That Barber Shop Chord,'" 289–325.

77. Parham, *American Routes*, 65.

78. Le Glaunec, "Slave Migrations," 219–22.

79. Diouf, *Slavery's Exiles*.

80. Pargas, *Freedom Seekers*, 80.

81. Fiehrer, "African Presence in Colonial Louisiana," 26; Kmen, "Singing and Dancing," 1, 76, 84; Le Glaunec, "Slave Migrations," 219–22.

82. Berquin-Duvallon, *Travels*, 28–31; Liljegren, "Jacobinism in Spanish Louisiana," 47–97; Liljegren, "Lieutenant-Colonel Don Carlos Howard," 57.

83. Tansey, "Out-of-State Free Blacks," 270.

84. *New Orleans Daily Crescent*, March 1, 1850; *New York Weekly Tribune*, April 10, 1854; *New York Weekly Tribune*, December 9, 1858; *New Orleans Daily Crescent*, February 16, 1860; *New Orleans Bee*, January 10, 1855; *New Orleans Daily Orleanian*, November 22, 1857.

85. *New Orleans Daily Delta*, March 27, 1851; Tansey, "Out-of-State Free Blacks," 372; *New Orleans Bee*, July 11, 1850; Schafer, "New Orleans Slavery," 52.

86. George W. Cable, "Creole Slave Songs," 807–28; Smith, *The Music of the Waters*, 330.

87. George W. Cable, *Century Magazine*, April 1886; Smith, *The Music of the Waters*, 330; Gayarré, *History of Louisiana*, 239–41; Blackbird, "Entwined Threads of Red and Black"; Spear, *Race, Sex, and Social Order in Early New Orleans*, 30–33, 235–36.

88. The Creole lyrics are: "O zeneral Flordio! C ést vrai ye pas ca-pab'pren moin! Ya ein counan si la mer. Cést vrai ye pas ca-pab'pren moin!" Hall, "The Formation of Afro-Creole Culture."

89. Fiehrer, "From Quadrille to Stomp," 21–38.

90. *New Orleans Commercial Bulletin*, April 29, 1841; *New Orleans Picayune*, July 23, 1841; Kerr-Ritchie, *Rites of August First*, 115.

91. Rediker, "Escaping Slavery by Sea"; Scott, "Afro-American Sailors"; Dawson, "Enslaved Ship Pilots."

92. Alamán, *Historia De Méjico*, 193–94; Vincent, "The Blacks Who Freed Mexico," 257. For Black musicians in the Union army, see chapter 5.

93. In 1883, Colonel P. H. Carson marched on the twenty-first anniversary of emancipation in attire meant to manifest Toussaint Louverture. See *Washington Bee*, April 21, 1883; Blight, *Race and Reunion*, 306–7.

94. Cable, *Creoles and Cajuns*; Din, "'Cimarrones' and the San Malo Band in Spanish Louisiana," 256.

95. Rivera, "New York Bomba," 189.

96. Berquin-Duvallon, *Travels*, 28–31; Carondelet's December 1, 1796, letter to Prince of Peace, No. 85 *Reservada*, A. H. N. Estado, 3900, cited in Liljegren, "Jacobinism in Spanish Louisiana, 1792–1797," 47–97; Liljegren, "Lieutenant-Colonel Don Carlos Howard and the International Rivalry for the Mississippi Valley: 1796–1798," 57.

97. Fuentes, *Dispossessed Lives*, 4.

98. Bethell, *George Lewis*, 9; Hersch, *Subversive Sounds*, 20; Sandke, *Where the Dark and the Light Folks Meet*, 80.

99. Trouillot, *Silencing the Past*.

100. Brown, "Polyrhythms and Improvisation," 85.

101. Hall, *Africans in Colonial Louisiana*.

102. Dubois, "The Haitian Revolution and the Sale of Louisiana."

103. Anderson, *Life and Narrative*, 22; Schermerhorn, "'As I Have Seen and Known It,'" 29.

104. Flint, *Recollections*, 218.

105. Baptist, *The Half Has Never Been Told*, 36, 85.

106. Tregle Jr., "Creoles and Americans," 138.

107. Parham, *American Routes*, 96.

108. Glissant, *Poetics of Relation*; Rath, "Drums and Power," 99.

109. Glissant, *Poetics of Relation*; see also Hall, "Creolité and the Process of Creolization," 12–25.

110. Harris, "Creoleness," 23–35.
111. Dessens, "The Saint-Domingue Refugees," 53–69; Hall, "Creolization, Diaspora, and Hybridity in the Context of Globalization," 185–98.
112. Rath, *How Early America Sounded*.
113. Stanyek, "Transmissions of an Interculture," 87–130.
114. Glissant, *Poetics of Relation*, 73–74.
115. Mintz, *Sweetness and Power*; Baptist, *The Half Has Never Been Told*.
116. Kish and Leroy, "Bonded Life," 630–51; Baucom, *Specters of the Atlantic*. See the discussion in chapter 4 for more on enslaved and freedpeople's critiques of this.
117. Moten, *In the Break*, 12.
118. Saxophonist Salim Washington describes Black music as "antidote" to racial capitalism in "Black Red and Green Revolutionary Eco-Music Tour," https://vimeo.com/91707067.
119. Brothers, *Louis Armstrong's New Orleans*, 25–26.
120. Vandal, "Black Utopia."
121. *Southwestern Christian Advocate*, New Orleans, September 14, 1882.
122. Logsdon and Bell, "The Americanization of Black New Orleans," 236.
123. Moten, "The New International of Rhythmic Feeling(s)," 49.
124. Shugg, *Origins of Class Struggle in Louisiana*, 243; *New Orleans Picayune*, June 17, 1873; Williams, "The Louisiana Unification Movement of 1873."
125. Montgomery, *Under Their Own Vine and Fig Tree*, 36–37.
126. Brothers, *Louis Armstrong's New Orleans*.
127. Hurston, "Spirituals and Neo-Spirituals," 355–64.
128. Behrend, *Reconstructing Democracy*, 50–59.
129. Brothers, *Louis Armstrong's New Orleans*; Marquis, *In Search of Buddy Bolden*; Harrison Barnes, interview, January 29, 1959, HJA; Willie Parker, interview, November 7, 1958, HJA.
130. Logsdon and Bell, "The Americanization of Black New Orleans."
131. Allen, Ware, and Garrison, *Slave Songs of the United States*, 113.
132. Lewis-Hale, "From Old Creole Days," 481.
133. *New Orleans Democrat*, June 18, 1876.
134. Hersch, *Subversive Sounds*, 107.
135. Shaik, *Economy Hall*, 364.
136. Ochs, *A Black Patriot and a White Priest*; 64; Bell, *Revolution*, 186–87, 263.
137. Fiehrer, "From Quadrille to Stomp."
138. Mitchell, "Autour d'une Rosette," iii.
139. Eddins, "Runaways, Repertoires, and Repression," 4.
140. Beckles, "Caribbean Anti-Slavery," 16.
141. Hossein, "Daring to Conceptualize the Black Social Economy," 1–14.
142. Gonzalez, *Maroon Nation*, 3–4.
143. Rousseau, "Souvenirs De La Louisiane."
144. Robinson, *Black Marxism*, 183.
145. Okiji, "Haiti's Infrasonic Boom."
146. Sweet, "'Brothers Gonna Work It Out.'"
147. *New Orleans Democrat*, June 18, 1876.
148. Fiehrer, "From Quadrille to Stomp," 28.
149. Vézina, "Jazz à La Creole," 6.
150. *Times Picayune*, February 24, 1885.

151. Gushee, "Black Professional Musicians in New Orleans," 57. For the band's drink(s) with Pinchbeck, see *Weekly Louisianian*, March 25, 1882.

152. Scott and Hébrard, *Freedom Papers*, 167.

153. Gushee, "A Preliminary Chronology of the Early Career of Ferd 'Jelly Roll' Morton."

154. Porter and Ullman, "Sidney Bechet and His Long Song."

155. Abbey "Chinee" Foster, interview, March 9, 1961, HJA.

156. Lizzie Miles, "*Haitian Blues/Your Time Now*, Shellac, 10," 78 RPM (The New Emerson, 1923); Yanow, "Lizzie Miles," 402.

157. Parham, *American Routes*, 66.

158. Martyn, *New Orleans Jazz*, 83, 98; Woods, *Development Arrested*.

159. Raeburn, "'That Ain't No Creole, It's a . . . !,'" 168–69.

160. Matory, "The 'New World' Surrounds an Ocean," 159; Johnson, *The Fear of French Negroes*, 144.

161. On "Creole snobbery," see Cleaver, "The Voices of Danny Barker," 20.

162. *Southwestern Christian Advocate*, August 2, 1888; see also chapter 6.

163. Attali, *Noise*, 23.

164. Kaussen, *Migrant Revolutions*, 9.

165. Louis R. Tio, interview, October 26, 1960, New Orleans, The Hogan Jazz Archive; Kinzer, "The Tio Family," 148; "Arnold Metoyer," in Vernhettes and Lindstörm, *Jazz Puzzles*, 81; Hardie, *Exploring Early Jazz*, 82; Gehman, "L. A. Creole-Mexican Connection."

166. *New Orleans Louisianan*, July 9, 1881, 2.

ONE The Common Wind's Second Gale

1. Thiong'o, *Penpoints, Gunpoints, and Dreams*, 53–55.

2. Arthur and Dash, "Proverbial Wisdom," 278–88.

3. Gushee, "The Nineteenth-Century Origins of Jazz," 151–74.

4. Stewart, "The Mexican Band Legend," 1–10.

5. *New Orleans Picayune*, February 28, 1892.

6. Act 111 of the Louisiana Legislature was technically called the Withdraw Car Act, but it was referred to colloquially as the Separate Car Act. Klarman, *From Jim Crow to Civil Rights*, 10–39.

7. Scott, "The Atlantic World," 731.

8. Logsdon and Bell, "The Americanization of Black New Orleans," 258.

9. Desdunes, *Our People and Our History*; Battle, "New Orleans' Creoles of Color."

10. "Now for a Test Case: Colored Man Arrested for Refusing to Leave a Railway Car," *New York Times*, February 26, 1892.

11. Letter from Louis. A Martinet to Albion Tourgée, October 5th, 1891, in Davis, "More than Segregation, Racial Identity," 1–41.

12. Brook, *The Accident of Color*.

13. "Now for a Test Case." On the New South, see Kousser, *The Shaping of Southern Politics*.

14. Davis, "More than Segregation, Racial Identity."

15. Gushee, "The Nineteenth-Century Origins of Jazz"; Vernhettes and Hanley, "The Desdunes Family," 25–45.

16. Vernhettes, *Visiting Mexican Bands*, 80; Stewart, "The Mexican Band Legend"; Johnson, "'Sobre Las Olas.'"

17. Lott, "Double V, Double-Time," 597–605.

18. Johnson, "Cinquillo Consciousness," 35–58; Washburne, *Latin Jazz*; Vézina, "Jazz à La Creole"; Fiehrer, "From Quadrille to Stomp," 21–38.

19. Embassy of Haiti, "Rodolphe Lucien Desdunes."

20. Scott, *The Common Wind*.

21. Desdunes, *A Few Words to Dr. DuBois 'With Malice Toward None.'*

22. Scott, *Degrees of Freedom*, 75.

23. Daggett, *Spiritualism in Nineteenth-Century New Orleans*.

24. Vernhettes and Hanley, "The Desdunes Family."

25. Bell, "Pierre-Aristide Desdunes (1844–1918)," 282–312; Scott, "The Atlantic World."

26. Logsdon and Bell, "The Americanization of Black New Orleans," 220.

27. Bell, *Revolution*, 278.

28. Scott and Hébrard, *Freedom Papers*.

29. Alcenat, "'Children of Africa, Shall Be Haytians.'"

30. Desdunes, *A Few Words to Dr. DuBois*. See also Charles E. O'Neill's introduction to Desdunes, *Our People and Our History*.

31. West and Martin, "Haiti, I'm Sorry," 72–104; Geggus, "Haiti's Declaration of Independence," 25–41.

32. Nicholls, *From Dessalines to Duvalier*, 38–39; Dubois, "Dessalines Toro d'Haïti," 541–48; Lundahl, "Defense and Distribution," 77–103; Gaffield, "Haiti and Jamaica in the Remaking of the Early Nineteenth-Century Atlantic World," 583–614; Gaffield, "'So Many Schemes in Agitation.'"

33. Duplantier, "Creole Louisiana's Haitian Exile(s)," 68–84.

34. Zimmerman, "Africa and the American Civil War"; Hahn, *The Political Worlds of Slavery and Freedom*, 98.

35. Hodson, "Freedom Papers," 677–80.

36. That is, speakers of Pulaar, a group referred to as "Peul" in French and "Fulbe" in English. Scott and Hébrard, "Rosalie of the Poulard Nation," 116–43.

37. Scott and Hébrard, *Freedom Papers*.

38. Édouard Tinchant, Communiqué, *La Tribune de la Nouvelle—Orléans*, July 21, 1864; Tinchant, 1899 letter to Máximo Gómez; in Scott and Hébrard, *Freedom Papers*, 167,

39. Scott, "Public Rights and Private Commerce," 237–56.

40. *Pine and Palm*, October 12, 1861, October 19, 1861, October 26, 1861; cited in Dixon, *African America and Haiti*.

41. Rousseau, "Souvenirs," *Port-au-Prince L'Opinion Nationale*, December 27, 1862. Translation by Duplantier.

42. Brickhouse, "'L'Ouragan de Flammes.'"

43. Freund, *Gustav Dressel's Houston Journal*; Hunt, *Haiti's Influence on Antebellum America*.

44. Shaik, *Economy Hall*.

45. Mitchell, "'A Good and Delicious Country,'" 123–44.

46. Desdunes, *Our People and Our History*, 68.

47. *Cleveland Morning Leader*, September 16, 1858; Vernhettes et al., "The Desdunes Family," 52–94.

48. The *Daily Press* (Cincinnati, Ohio), April 19, 1859; Vernhettes et al., "The Desdunes Family."

49. Hyppolite, "Proclamation de Soulouque Aux Haitiens"; Barnes and Breunlin, *Le Kèr Creole*, 9.

50. Pierre-Aristide Desdunes Ledgers, vol. I, 207–10; quoted in Bell, "'Rappelez-Vous Concitoyens,'" 1–19.

51. Daniels, "Vodun and Jazz"; Bell, "Pierre-Aristide Desdunes (1844–1918)"; Bell, "Pierre-Aristide Desdunes," 287.

52. Pierre-Aristide Desdunes's two ledgers, given by Mr. Tureaud to Howard University, contain an essay about the French Revolution and Karl Marx's philosophy in the form of a letter to Charles Testier, his French correspondent, in the Pierre-Aristide Desdunes Ledgers, A. P. Tureaud family papers. Thank you to Dan Vernhettes for sharing this with me. Johnson, *Slavery's Metropolis*, 122.

53. Casimir, "The Sovereign People of Haiti during the Eighteenth and Nineteenth Centuries," 184.

54. Ripley, *Slaves and Freedmen*, 33.

55. Warmoth, *War, Politics, and Reconstruction*, 51, 52.

56. Roudané, *The New Orleans Tribune*; Bell, "The Common Wind's Creole Visionary," 10–25.

57. *New Orleans Tribune*, March 1, 1865; February 18, 1865.

58. *New Orleans Tribune*, November 14, 1865; Shaik, *Economy Hall*, 265; Micklin, "Louis Charles Roudanez."

59. Vandal, "Black Utopia."

60. *New Orleans Tribune*, September 4, 1866; Bell, *Revolution*, 269–270; Fabre, "The New Orleans Press," 40; Manchuelle, "Le rôle."

61. Brickhouse, "'L'Ouragan de Flammes,'" 1106.

62. *New Orleans Tribune*, September 4, 1866; Houzeau, *My Passage at the* New Orleans Tribune, 91; Logsdon and Bell, "Americanization of Black New Orleans," 238; Senter, "Creole Poets on the Verge of a Nation," 279.

63. *New Orleans Tribune*, October 10, 1865.

64. Foner, *Reconstruction*, 62–65; Blassingame, *Black New Orleans 1860–1880*; Belz, "Origins of Negro Suffrage During the Civil War," 115–30; Thompson, *Exiles at Home*, 215, 226–33.

65. *New Orleans Tribune*, December 3, 1864.

66. *New Orleans Tribune*, December 3, 1864.

67. *New Orleans Tribune*, January 15, 1865.

68. Reid, *After the War*, 244.

69. Reid, *After the War*, 233.

70. Scott and Hébrard, *Freedom Papers*, 132. The letter was actually published in *L'Union*, which was renamed the *New Orleans Tribune* some years later. To avoid confusion, I use the latter name. See Roudané, *The New Orleans Tribune*.

71. Anthony, "'Lost Boundaries,'" 291–312; Blassingame, *Black New Orleans*, 201–2.

72. Desdunes, *Our People and Our History*, 65.

73. Although the song was written before the Civil War, it gained popularity in this era. See Thompson, "'Ah Toucoutou, Ye Conin Vous,'" 232–66.

74. Joseph Beaumont (1820–1872) was also the first president of Les Francs Amis, an association of Creole of color men started in 1860. Tinker, *Les Décrits Des Langue Française En Louisiane*, 31–32; Thompson, "'Ah Toucoutou, Ye Conin Vous,'" 259.

75. Desdunes, *Our People and Our History*, 69.

76. Roediger, *The Wages of Whiteness*.

77. Mike DeLay, interview, September 14, 1970, HJA.

78. Fiehrer, "African Presence in Colonial Louisiana," 42.

79. Linebaugh and Rediker, *The Many Headed Hydra*, 174–210.

80. Blight, *A Slave No More*, 159.

81. *New Orleans Tribune*, January 15, 29, February 18, 23, March 1, 31, 1865; Houzeau, *My Passage*, 37; *Daily Picayune*, September 26, 1863, February 21, 1864; Wiley, *Southern Negroes*, 316–17; Harrington, *Fighting Politician*, 111; Eiss, "A Share in the Land."

82. Berlin et al., "Fighting on Two Fronts."

83. Harrington, *Fighting Politician*, 111.

84. Quoted in Du Bois, *Black Reconstruction*, 458–59.

85. Scott and Hébrard, *Freedom Papers*, 130.

86. *New Orleans Republican*, October 5, 1872; *New Orleans Republican*, December 7, 1875; *New Orleans Republican*, August 27, 1876; *New Orleans Republican*, March 21, 1876; Scott, *Degrees of Freedom*, 75.

87. Andrew Wegmann calls them "a middle group." Wegmann, *An American Color*, 90.

88. Nystrom, "Racial Identity and Reconstruction."

89. Foster, *The Autobiography of Pops Foster*, 105.

90. Lomax, *Mister Jelly Roll*, 99.

91. Brothers, *Louis Armstrong's New Orleans*, 303; Hersch, *Subversive Sounds*, 107–8.

92. Lomax, *Mister Jelly Roll*, 102–6.

93. Ake, *Jazz Cultures*, 16.

94. Anthony, "The Negro Creole Community in New Orleans," 57.

95. The banjo player Johnny St. Cyr was born Catholic and married a Methodist African American Methodist who inspired him to convert. Johnny St. Cyr, interview, August 27, 1958, HJA.

96. Barson, "'I've Got the Haitian Blues'"; Tucker, "A Feminist Perspective," 50; Vernhettes et al., "The Desdunes Family"; Otto, "Dan Desdunes"; Anthony, "The Negro Creole Community in New Orleans," 100–103.

97. Bell, "'Rappelez-Vous Concitoyens,'" 15.

98. Bell, "'Rappelez-Vous Concitoyens'"; Haggerty, "Land Tenure and Land Policy."

99. Scott, "The Atlantic World," 276–79.

100. "Tio & Doublet's Orchestra or String Band," *Crusader*, February 23, 1895; Gushee, "The Nineteenth-Century Origins of Jazz," 17–18.

101. Clyde Woods describes Louisiana in this period as "the epicenter of Southern fascism." See Woods, *Development Drowned and Reborn*, 59; see also Rydell, *All the World's a Fair*, 77–89.

102. Blight, *A Slave No More*, 159; Berlin et al., *Slaves No More*, 179–89.

103. Penn, *The Afro-American Press and Its Editors*, 223–27.

104. *Southwestern Christian Advocate*, August 2, 1888.

105. *New Orleans Louisianian*, February 23, 1871; Somers, "Black and White in New Orleans," 33.

106. *New Orleans Democrat*, June 18, 1876; Lescot, *Chansons Créoles*.

107. *New Orleans Democrat*, June 18, 1876, 1.

108. Christian, "Oscar J. Dunn," 139.

109. United States, Congress, House, Select Committee on the New Orleans Riots, Thomas Dawes Eliot, Samuel Shellabarger, Benjamin Markley Boyer, *Report of the Select Committee on the New Orleans Riots*, U.S. Government Printing Office, 1867, 13; Brock, "Notes on New Orleans Brass Bands."

110. Moten, "Blackness and Nothingness," 755.

111. Shaik, *Economy Hall*, 336–38.

112. Shaik, 276, 364. This most likely was not Buddy Bolden's Eagle Band, as Bolden was eight years old at the time.

113. *Southwestern Christian Advocate*, August 2, 1888.

114. Johnny St. Cyr, interview, August 27, 1958, HJA.

115. Raeburn, "'That Ain't No Creole, It's a . . . !,'" 39; Oliver, interview, April 22, 1959, HJA.

116. Brothers, *Louis Armstrong's New Orleans*, 153. "Manuel Pérez was a very patient man giving lessons," explained Natty Dominque, "but if you didn't know all of your lesson, [if you] missed one measure, he'd send you back home and give you that same lesson over. . . . He'd tell you . . . 'You're supposed to know your lesson when you get here.'" Dominque, interview, May 31, 1958, HJA.

117. Chilton, *Sidney Bechet*, 18.

118. Lief, *Anarchist Blues*; C. Kinzer: "The Excelsior Brass Band of New Orleans, 1879–89"; Gushee, *Black Professional Musicians in New Orleans*, c1880; see chapters 3 and 6 for accounts involving civil rights rallies and events in support of organized labor.

119. *Daily Picayune*, September 12, 1881.

120. Jabir, *Conjuring Freedom*, viii; Lipsitz, *How Racism Takes Place*, 51.

121. *Times Picayune*, February 24, 1885.

122. Penn, *The Afro-American Press and Its Editors*, 227.

123. *Omaha World-Herald*, September 13, 1927.

124. Karcher, "Albion W. Tourgée and Louis A. Martinet," 13–15; Hart, "Toward an Ideal of Moral and Democratic Education," 228–29; Cockrill, "Straight University's Ties to *Plessy v. Ferguson*."

125. *The Weekly Louisianan*, April 1871; Cockrill, "Activists at Straight University"; McGill, "Frances Ellen Watkins Harper and the Circuits of Abolitionist Poetry"; Hart, "Toward an Ideal of Moral and Democratic Education."

126. Logsdon and Bell, "The Americanization of Black New Orleans," 261.

127. Szwed and Marks, "The Afro-American Transformation"; Okiji, "Haiti's Infrasonic Boom."

128. Dubois, *A Colony of Citizens*, 2; Appadurai, *Modernity at Large*; Scott, *The Common Wind*.

129. Hearn referred to Black levee musicians and dancers as a motley crew in Hearn, "Levee Life," 162. For its definition as a port city proletariat, see Rediker, "A Motley Crew for Our Times?"

130. Hearn, "Levee Life," 164.

131. Bisland, *The Life and Letters of Lafcadio Hearn*, 232; Gushee, "The Nineteenth-Century Origins of Jazz," 9; Dubois, *The Banjo*.

132. Ojiki, *Jazz as Critique*; Ho, *Wicked Theory, Naked Practice*; Brennan, *Secular Devotion*;

133. Gushee, "The Nineteenth-Century Origins of Jazz"; Doheny, "The Spanish Tinge Hypothesis."

134. Bradley, *The Williamsburg Avant-Garde*, 165.

135. Gushee, "The Nineteenth-Century Origins of Jazz." Among Gushee's archival findings in this article is that the "Texas Tommy," which (in a 1910 film shot in San Francisco) was the earliest recorded swing dancing on film, was considered a New Orleanian invention in a 1911 *Variety* article by the journalist Oscar Samuels titled "New Orleans Makes a Claim."

136. Goffin, *La Nouvelle-Orléans, Capitale Du Jazz*, 69–70; cited in Gushee, "The Nineteenth-Century Origins of Jazz," 17.

137. Wilson, "The Heterogeneous Sound Ideal in African American Music."

138. Okiji, *Jazz as Critique*, 46.

139. Sakakeeny, "New Orleans Music and the Problem of the Black Vernacular," 29; Vidacovich, Riley, and Thress, *New Orleans Jazz*.

140. Peretti, *The Creation of Jazz*, 25. Johnny St. Cyr explained how "the churches always had music—singing—and the congregation would really swing." St. Cyr, "Jazz as I Remember It," 6–10.

141. Floyd, "Black Music in the Circum-Caribbean."

142. Sublette, *Cuba and Its Music*, 166–68; Hall, *Africans in Colonial Louisiana*, 41–55, 97–118. Hall initially referred to the Bamana as Bambara. For more literature that theorizes the Senegambian and Bamana influences on the blues, see Durán, "POYI!"; Coolen, "The Fodet."

143. Dawdy, "La Catrina"; 39; Ingersoll, "The Slave Trade"; Woodward, "Spanish Commercial Policy"; Vinson III, *Before Mestizaje*, 76–78.

144. Le Glaunec, "Slave Migrations."

145. Casimir, "Haití y Sus Élites," 814–15. This translation and all others are done by the author unless indicated otherwise.

146. Sweet, "'Brothers Gonna Work It Out.'"

147. Matory, "From 'Survival' to 'Dialogue,'" 37.

148. Eltis, Morgan, and Richardson, "Agency and Diaspora in Atlantic History." See also Price, "The Miracle of Creolization."

149. Mackey, "Other," 251.

150. Ellison, *Invisible Man*, 8; Anderson, "Ralph Ellison on Lyricism and Swing," 287.

151. Ojiki, *Jazz as Critique*, 46–47.

152. Ho, *Wicked Theory, Naked Practice*, 99.

153. Jim Robinson, interview, December 10, 1958, HJA.

154. Peretti, *The Creation of Jazz*, 110.

155. Chamberlain, "Searching for 'The Gulf Coast Circuit,'" 10.

156. Sakakeeny, "Textures of Black Sound and Affect."

157. Sayles, interview, January 17, 1959, HJA.

158. Friedenthal, *Musik*, 100; Cuney Hare, *The Musical Observer*, 17; Collier, *Jazz*, 195.

159. Lomax, *Mister Jelly Roll*, 280.

160. Doheny, "The Spanish Tinge Hypothesis," 13.

161. Stebbins, "Role Distance," 411; Higman, *Jamaica Surveyed*.

162. Horne, *To Bop or Not to Be: A Jazz Life*.

163. Mingus, *Beneath the Underdog*, 251–52.

164. Moten, "The New International of Rhythmic Feeling(s)," 43; Harney and Moten, *The Undercommons*, 38.

165. Muñoz, *Cruising Utopia*, 10.

166. Gantt, *The Mandorla Letters*, 10.

167. Mingus, *Beneath the Underdog*, 251–52.

168. Anderson, *From Slavery to Affluence*, 30; Bradley, "Black Geographies."

169. Kaussen, *Migrant Revolutions*, 9.

170. McKittrick, "On Plantations, Prisons, and Black Sense of Place"; Bobulescu, "The Original Time Approach of Georgescu-Roegen," 87–89; Altvater, "Ecological and Economic Modalities of Time and Space."

171. *Le Trait d'Union*, May 24, 1891; Vernhettes, *Visiting Mexican Bands*, 80.

172. Bisland, *The Life and Letters of Lafcadio Hearn*, 380.

173. Floyd, "Black Music in the Circum-Caribbean"; Johnson, "Cinquillo Consciousness."

174. Moten, "The New International of Rhythmic Feeling(s)."

175. Woods, *Development Drowned and Reborn*, 18.

176. Lomanno, "Topics on Afro-Cuban Jazz in the United States," 47; Piras, "Jelly-Roll Morton."

177. Cuney Hare, *Six Creole Folk-Songs*.

178. Johnson, "Cinquillo Consciousness."

179. Wever, "Dancing the Habanera Beat," 204–33; Manuel, "The Anticipated Bass in Cuban Popular Music"; Carpentier, *La música en Cuba*; Rodicio, "Habanera."

180. Muñoz, "Music in Puerto Rico," 116; Mikowsky, "The Nineteenth-Century Cuban 'Danza,'" 88.

181. Largey, "Ethnographic Transcription and Music Ideology in Haiti," 1–31.

182. Ortiz, *La Africanía de La Música Folklórica de Cuba*, 277.

183. Alén, "Rhythm as Duration of Sounds in Tumba Francesa"; Austerlitz, *Jazz Consciousness*, 200n53.

184. Goffin, *La Nouvelle-Orléans*, 69–70.

185. Gushee, "The Nineteenth-Century Origins of Jazz," 17.

186. Washburne, "The Clave of Jazz," 75."

187. Lamanno, "Topics on Afro-Cuban Jazz in the United States," 48; Doheny, "The Spanish Tinge Hypothesis," 8–15.

188. St. Cyr, "Interview," April 2, 1949, ALDA.

189. Sakakeeny, "New Orleans Music and the Problem of the Black Vernacular," 18. On "cellular" rhythmic structure, see Manuel, Bilby, and Largey, *Caribbean Currents*, 9.

190. Doheny has a slightly different view in "The Spanish Tinge Hypothesis," 15.

191. Moore, *Nationalizing Blackness*, 23–25; Carpentier, *La música en Cuba*, 237; Peter Manuel challenges the Haitian genesis of these rhythms in Cuban danza and danzón, but Cuban writers and musicians of the nineteenth and twentieth centuries did hear them as Haitian. See Manuel, "From Contradanza to Danzón," 52–112. On the practice of diaspora, see Edwards, *The Practice of Diaspora*, 7–13.

192. As late as 1965, Fernando Oritz, an anthropologist who valorized Afro-Cuban culture, nonetheless felt that cinquillo consciousness "rhythmically embod[ied] diabolic lasciviousness to the point of orgasmic paroxysm." Moore, "Representations of Afrocuban Expressive Culture," 43.

193. On substitution as an Atlantic World practice, see Roach, *Cities of the Dead*, 1–6.

194. Rebecca Scott notes that "Spanish" was a pseudonym for Cuban in nineteenth-century New Orleans. Scott, *Degrees of Freedom*, 78. One of Morton's collaborators, Walter "Foots" Thomas, provided a different word than Spanish for Morton's "Spanish Tinge": "I always felt his melodies came from New Orleans but that his rhythms came from the Latin countries." Balliett, *Jelly Roll, Jabbo, and Fats*, 25–26. On Morton's denial of his Haitian heritage, see Gushee, "Would You Believe Ferman Mouton?," 56–59.

195. Wilson, "The Heterogeneous Sound Ideal in African American Music," 327–340.

196. Wilson, "The Significance of the Relationship between Afro-American Music and West African Music," 3–22.Similarly, John Chernoff and Hafiz Shabbaz Farel Johnson describe how

the "beat" of an Afro-Atlantic style "emerges from the overall organization and dynamics of several rhythms combined and working together." Johnson and Chernoff, "Basic Conga Drum Rhythms," 55–73.

197. Gilroy, *The Black Atlantic*, 222.
198. Henry, interview, October 21, 1959, HJA.
199. McAlister, *Rara!*, 178.
200. Frere-Jones, "Roundtable."
201. Fouchard, *The Haitian Maroons*, 346; Paquette, "'A Horde of Brigands?,'" 72–96. These included drums, conch shells, and flags. For a discussion on the Congolese roots of such combinations of drumming and resistance, see Thornton, "African Dimensions of the Stono Rebellion."
202. Giorgianni, "Joyful Resonances," 12, 20.
203. Johnson and Evans, "Freedom Dances across the Diaspora," 39–42; Turner, *Jazz Religion*, 21.
204. Ligon-Williams, "From Maroons to Mardi Gras."
205. Johnson and Evans, "Freedom Dances across the Diaspora," 42.
206. Breunlin, *Fire in the Hole*; Breunlin and Lewis, *The House of Dance & Feathers*, 67–68.
207. White, "A Musician's Life in the Second Line," 120–21.
208. Danticat, *After the Dance*, 147.
209. Kovel, *History and Spirit*, 218; see also Strongman, "Transcorporeality in Vodou," 4–29.
210. Ellison, *Shadow and Act*, 234.
211. Kofsky, *Black Nationalism and the Revolution in Music*, 235.
212. Bechet, *Treat It Gentle*, 176.
213. Salim Washington in Barson, "Answering the Call."
214. Casimir, "Haiti's Need for a Great South."
215. Baraka, *Home*, 175.
216. Blackburn, "Haiti, Slavery, and the Age of the Democratic Revolution," 643–74; Dubois, *A Colony of Citizens*; Geggus, "The Louisiana Purchase and the Haitian Revolution," 117–29; Conrad, "Enlightenment in Global History," 999–1027; Buck-Morss, "Hegel and Haiti," 821–65; Benot, *La Révolution Française*; Nesbitt, *Universal Emancipation*; Knight, "The Haitian Revolution and the Notion of Human Rights," 391–416; Joseph-Gabriel, "Creolizing Freedom," 111–23; Scott, "The Theory of Haiti," 35–51; Gordon, *Creolizing Political Theory*, 176–87.
217. *The Freeman* (Indianapolis), May 10, 1902; *The Freeman*, January 20, 1900; Schwartz, "The African American Contribution to the Cornet of the Nineteenth Century," 61–88. On the Original Nashville Students and the complicated legacy of the African American minstrel circuit, see Graham, *Spirituals and the Birth of a Black Entertainment Industry*, 252.
218. Breaux, "The New Negro Renaissance in Omaha and Lincoln," 121–39.
219. Otto, "Contemporaries."
220. *Helena Independent*, July 26, 1925.
221. Love, *A Thousand Honey Creeks Later*, xx–xxi.
222. Otto, "Dan Desdunes," 107.
223. Preston Love quoted in Otto, "Dan Desdunes," 107.
224. Krasner, *A Beautiful Pageant*, 10.
225. Russell, *Jazz Style in Kansas City and the Southwest*, 69–70.
226. Otto, "Dan Desdunes."
227. *Kansas City Sun*, November 28, 1914.
228. The *Monitor*, October 27, 1917.

229. *Omaha World-Herald*, May 18, 1919.
230. *Omaha World-Herald*, October 30, 1921.
231. *Omaha World-Herald*, March 3 and 17, 1921.
232. Breaux, "The New Negro Renaissance in Omaha and Lincoln," 121.
233. Yellin, *Racism in the Nation's Service*.
234. "Dan Desdunes Band," The *Monitor*, August 4, 1921.
235. Breaux, "The New Negro Renaissance in Omaha and Lincoln," 130. The movie's original title was *The Clansman*.
236. *Indianapolis Freeman*, July 16, 1910. Thank you to Daniel Vernhettes for making me aware of this article.
237. *Omaha World-Herald*, September 1909; *Omaha World-Herald*, September 13, 1927; Sasse, "A History of Music in North Omaha."
238. *Omaha World-Herald*, March 20, 1920. Although there is no direct evidence that the two were related, the timing is striking.
239. Medley, *We as Freemen*.
240. Reilly and Reilly, *Historic Omaha*, 51.
241. "Grand Charity Ball! For Benefit of The Old Folks Home," The *Monitor*, November 3, 1917.
242. Vernhettes and Hanley, "The Desdunes Family," 52–94.
243. *Omaha World-Herald*, April 30, 1929.
244. *Kansas City Sun*, November 28, 1914.
245. *Chicago Defender*, March 6, 1926.
246. *Chicago Defender*, December 10, 1927.
247. *Omaha World-Herald*, November 24, 1918.
248. Boys Town, "Father Edward J. Flanagan."
249. McGlade, "A Boys Town Hall of History," 82.
250. WPA Nebraska Writer's Project, *The Negroes of Nebraska*, 21.
251. *Father Flanagan's Boys' Home Journal* (March 1920): 2.
252. Reilly and Warneke, *Father Flanagan of Boys Town*.
253. "Mr. Dan Desdunes Instructor of Our Band," *Father Flanagan's Boys' Home Journal* 5, no. 1 (April 1922): 5.
254. Reilly and Warneke, *Father Flanagan of Boys Town*, 60.
255. McGlade, "A Boys Town Hall of History," 84.
256. Desdunes, "'Happy Feeling Rag' Sheet Music."
257. Ibid.
258. Hossein, "Daring to Conceptualize the Black Social Economy," 3.
259. Lipsitz, *A Life in the Struggle*, 228.
260. Bissett, *Agrarian Socialism in America*, 3.
261. Bissett, 263.
262. McGlade, "A Boys Town Hall of History," 77.
263. "Boys' Home Has One of the Best Juvenile Bands in U.S.," *Father Flanagan's Boys' Home Journal*, May 1927.
264. "Paul Whiteman Directs Father Flanagan's Band," *Father Flanagan's Boys' Home Journal*, January 1929.
265. "Father Flanagan's Boys' Band Visits President Coolidge," *Boys' Home Journal*, September 1927, 8–9.

266. Otto, "Dan Desdunes," 19.
267. Reilly and Warneke, *Father Flanagan of Boys Town*, 69.
268. Kingsley, "Whence Comes Jass?," *New York Sun*, August 5, 1917, 3; "The Appeal of the Primitive Jazz," *Literary Digest*, August 25, 1917, 28–29; Walser, *Keeping Time*; "Our Band," *Father Flanagan's Boys' Home Journal*, April 1922, quoted in Otto, "Dan Desdunes," 114.
269. Vernhettes et al., "The Desdunes Family."
270. *Omaha World-Herald*, October 6, 1917.
271. "Omaha's Blind Negro Poet," *Omaha World-Herald*, September 12, 1917.
272. Daggett, *Spiritualism in Nineteenth-Century New Orleans*.
273. P. A. Desdunes, "Les pensées d'ún esclave soldat," in Kress, "Pierre-Aristide Desdunes," 51.
274. Medley, *We as Freemen*, 217.
275. "Homeless Boys Mourn Dan Desdunes' Death"; "Dan Des-dunes Dies"; "Dan Desdunes' Funeral Attended by Hundreds," *Omaha World-Herald*, April 30, 1929; cited in Otto, "Dan Desdunes," 107–16.
276. University of Nebraska Omaha, Criss Library. Special Collections. Repository April 28, 1937: http://unomaha.contentdm.oclc.org/cdm/ref/collection/p15301co111/id/321.
277. "Elmer Crumbley—his story as told to Franklin Driggs," *Coda* 1 (February 1959): 9.
278. Clarence Desdunes in the *Monitor*, 1920, quoted in Otto, "Dan Desdunes," 116.

TWO *Mamie Desdunes in the Neo-Plantation*

1. Baraka, "Black Art," 143.
2. Cortázar, *Hopscotch*, 67–70.
3. Gómez, "'Algo como un sí, o un siempre y un ahora,'" 251.
4. Cortázar, *Hopscotch*, 70; Roberts, "Subverted Claims," 730–45; Illingworth, "The Subtle Radicalism of Julio Cortázar's Berkeley Lectures."
5. Hobson, "New Orleans Jazz and the Blues," 12.
6. Frederic Ramsey Papers, MSS 559, Box 16C, Historic New Orleans Collection; Hobson, "New Orleans Jazz and the Blues."
7. Jelly Roll Morton, letter to Roy Carew, December 18, 1939; Russell, *"Oh, Mister Jelly,"* 223; Lomax, *Mister Jelly Roll*, 21; Vernhettes and Hanley, "The Desdunes Family," 39.
8. Lomax, *Mister Jelly Roll*, 20–21.
9. Jelly Roll Morton, *Mamie's Blues*, J. S. 695 (New York: Commodore Records, 1938).
10. Wald, *The Blues*, 93.
11. Armstrong, *Satchmo*, 53.
12. Lomax, *Mister Jelly Roll*, 21.
13. Hanley, "Bunk Johnson."
14. Jelly Roll Morton, letter to Roy Carew, December 18, 1939; Russell, *"Oh, Mister Jelly,"* 223.
15. Landau, *Spectacular Wickedness*; Adams, *Wounds of Returning*.
16. *New Orleans Picayune*, July 21, 1893. Thank you to Tom Roberts for this find.
17. Here I am invoking both Nathaniel Mackey's (and later Fred Moten's) writing on the sexual "cut" and the [im]possibility of language in the context of human commodification and its attendant traumas, as well as opening a space to think through Black disability as an important aspect of Mamie's ghostly legacy. See Mackey, *Bedouin Hornbook*, 30–38; Moten, *In the Break*, 6–10; Schalk, "Contextualizing Black Disability."
18. Baraka, *Blues People*, 16.

19. Morgan, *Reckoning with Slavery*, 5.
20. Hine, "Rape and the Inner Lives of Black Women in the Middle West."
21. Morgan, "Privacy, Slavery, and the Fictions of Domestic Space," with respondent Maria Fuentes, paper delivered at the University of Pittsburgh, February 22, 2023.
22. Landau, *Spectacular Wickedness*; Hine, "Rape and the Inner Lives of Black Women in the Middle West"; Baptist, "'Cuffy,' 'Fancy Maids,' and 'One-Eyed Men.'"
23. Clark, *The Strange History of the American Quadroon*.
24. Ayers, *The Promise of the New South*, 139–40, 158.
25. Rosen, *Terror in the Heart of Freedom*, 5–6.
26. Avery, "A Question of Survival."
27. Griffin, "Textual Healing," 534.
28. McKittrick, *Demonic Grounds*.
29. Hines, "Rape and the Inner Lives of Black Women in the Middle West," 915.
30. Davis, *Blues Legacies and Black Feminism*, 10.
31. Kelley, *Thelonious Monk*, 141.
32. Pellegrinelli, "Separated at 'Birth,'" 31–47.
33. Manuel Manetta, "Interview Digest, March 28, 1957," edited by Robert Campbell William Russell, Nesuhi Ertegun, and Richard B. Allen (New Orleans: Hogan Jazz Archive): 13.
34. Garon and Garon, *Woman with Guitar*.
35. Moten, *In the Break*, 12.
36. Jelly Roll Morton, *Mamie's Blues*, J. S. 695 (New York: Commodore Records, 1938).
37. Davis, *Blues Legacies and Black Feminism*, 25.
38. Vernhettes and Hanley, "The Desdunes Family."
39. Carby, "It Jus Be's Dat Way Sometime," 474.
40. Soard's New Orleans City Directory of 1901.
41. Roane, *Dark Agoras*, 3.
42. In the 1920s, a sex worker, Queenie Venerable, was arrested for operating a "disorderly house." Docket Books, Louisiana Division, New Orleans Public Library; Landau, *Spectacular Wickedness*, 46.
43. Edwards, "Mary Celina Mamie Desdunes Dugue"; Vernhettes and Hanley, "The Desdunes Family."
44. Jelly Roll Morton, "Mamie's Blues" (New York City, December 1939; General 4001-A); Bunk Johnson and The Yerba Buena Jazz Band, 2:19 *Blues* (Ace in the Hole, 1944).
45. Wald, "Mamie's Blues (219 Blues)."
46. Humphrey, "Prostitution."
47. Balderach, "A Different Kind of Reservation," 8.
48. Hahn, *A Nation Under Our Feet*.
49. Carby observes the critique of the railroad amongst women's blues singers in "It Jus Be's Dat Way Sometime," 476.
50. McKittrick, "Plantation Futures," 14.
50. Hartman, *Scenes of Subjection*, 23.
52. Barson, "'I've Got the Haitian Blues.'"
53. Berry, *City of a Million Dreams*, 166; Marquis, *In Search of Buddy Bolden*.
54. Levine, *Black Culture and Black Consciousness*.
55. Davis, *Blues Legacies and Black Feminism*, 8
56. Wagner, *Disturbing the Peace*, 57.

57. Foster, *The Autobiography of Pops Foster*, 16.

58. Landau, *Spectacular Wickedness*.

59. Roane, *Dark Agoras*, 3.

60. Manuel Manetta, Oral History Collection, Hogan Jazz Archive, Tulane University; Brothers, *Louis Armstrong's New Orleans*, 111.

61. Brothers, 23–24.

62. Hartman, *Wayward Lives, Beautiful Experiments*, 117–18.

63. Ralph, "New Orleans, Our Southern Capitol."

64. Sparks, "Lost Bodies/Found Objects," 29; Long, *The Great Southern Babylon*, 119–20, 160; Landau, *Spectacular Wickedness*, 145, 229–35.

65. Gould, "The Strike of 1887," 45–55; Scott, *Degrees of Freedom*.

66. United States Census Bureau; Brothers, *Louis Armstrong's New Orleans*, 4, 186.

67. Foster, "Tarnished Angels," 387–97.

68. Kid Ory, Oral History Collection, Hogan Jazz Archive; Landau, *Spectacular Wickedness*, 369.

69. Kimball, *Nell Kimball*, 86.

70. Tucker, "Jazz History Remix," 256–69.

71. Landau, *Spectacular Wickedness*, 229.

72. Landau, *Spectacular Wickedness*, 149.

73. Ramírez, "City as Borderland," 147–66.

74. Shapiro and Hentoff, *Hear Me Talkin' to Ya*, 5–6.

75. Barker, *Buddy Bolden and the Last Days of Storyville*, 61.

76. Shapiro and Hentoff, *Hear Me Talkin' to Ya*, 10.

77. Foster, *The Autobiography of Pops Foster*, 40.

78. Jones, *Labor of Love, Labor of Sorrow*; Rosenberg, *New Orleans Dockworkers*.

79. *Daily Picayune*, September 12, 1881.

80. Marquis, *In Search of Buddy Bolden*, 110.

81. Wagner, *Disturbing the Peace*, 46; Hair, *Carnival of Fury*, 3–93; Somers, "Black and White in New Orleans."

82. *Times Picayune*, February 24, 1885; Turner, *Respect Black*; Matthews, "Negro Republicans in the Reconstruction of Georgia," 147; Foner, "Henry M. Turner," 215–16; see also chapter 3.

83. Hose, accused of murdering the white farmer Alfred Cranford and raping his wife, was castrated, burned alive, and dismembered. His lynching became the subject of considerable commentary in the Black and white press and church. Grem, "Sam Jones," 35–44; Brundage, *Lynching in the New South*, 28–36, 82–84. Sam Hose's name was actually a pseudonym; his real name was Samuel Wilkes. See Wells-Barnett, *Lynch Law in Georgia*, 13.

84. Wagner, *Disturbing the Peace*, 47; Wells-Barnett, *Mob Rule*, 5–23.

85. Wagner's fascinating discussion of this song is essential to think through the politics of ethnographic research and the transference of the outlaw character onto Black voice. Unfortunately, this topic would overwhelm the present discussion. Lomax, *Mister Jelly Roll*, 57; Prince, "Remembering Robert Charles," 297–300; Wagner, *Disturbing the Peace*, 51–52.

86. Arrest Books, City Archives, Louisiana Division, New Orleans Public Library; Landau, *Spectacular Wickedness*, 46.

87. Holmes, *The Age of Wonder*, 16–17; Linebaugh, *Stop, Thief!*, 33; *City v. Freddie Crockett, et al.* (1908), Criminal District Court, Docket No. 18,051 [18,061], City Archives, Louisiana Division, New Orleans Public Library; Landau, *Spectacular Wickedness*, 291.

88. Danny Barker in Hentoff and Shapiro, *Hear Me Talkin' to Ya*, 10.

89. Clarence Williams in Hentoff and Shapiro, *Hear Me Talkin' to Ya*, 12–13.

90. *New Orleans Item*, December 22 and 24, 1906, quoted in Landau, *Spectacular Wickedness*, 281–82.

91. Smith, "Southern Sirens," iii.

92. Kelley, "'We Are Not What We Seem,'" 76.

93. Barker, *Buddy Bolden and the Last Days of Storyville*, 67–68.

94. Conversation with Fatima Shaik, June 26, 2022.

95. McKittrick, "Plantation Futures," 2.

96. Foucault, *Discipline and Punish*, 306.

97. Lizzie Miles, *Haitian Blues/Your Time Now*, Shellac, 10", 78 RPM (The New Emerson, 1923). Thanks to Michael Heller for his help with transcription.

98. Zutty Singleton said that Lizzie Miles was Jelly Roll Morton's favorite vocalist. "Zutty and Marge Singleton, Oral History," February 2, 1969, Reel I, Track I, Summary, 7. Hogan Jazz Archives. Tulane University, quoted in Tucker, "A Feminist Perspective on New Orleans Jazzwomen," 324.

99. Winters, *The Mulatta Concubine*, 61; Clark and Jones, "Transatlantic Currents of Orientalism," 189–209; Wells-Oghoghomeh, *The Souls of Womenfolk*, 228–32.

100. Mitchell, "Gottschalk's Engagement with the Ungovernable."

101. Cheung, "Les Cenelles and Quadroon Balls," 6.

102. Carter and Lindsay Jr., "The Devil's Music."

103. Vézina, "Jazz à La Creole," 38–45.

104. Tucker, "A Feminist Perspective on New Orleans Jazzwomen," 41.

105. Floyd, "Black Music in the Circum-Caribbean," 1–38; Washburne, "The Clave of Jazz."

106. Narváez, "The Influences of Hispanic Music Cultures on African-American Blues Musicians," 175–96.

107. Dessens, "St Domingue Refugees in New Orleans"; Fiehrer, "From Quadrille to Stomp"; Lachance, "The 1809 Immigration."

108. Washburne, *Latin Jazz*, 54.

109. Johnson, *The Fear of French Negroes*, 142.

110. Russell, *New Orleans Style*, 23.

111. Morton interview with Lomax, 1938; in Garrett, *Struggling to Define a Nation*, 54.

112. Balliett, *Jelly Roll, Jabbo, and Fats*, 25–26.

113. Steve Coleman, Facebook Post, January 27, 2023.

114. Johnson, *The Fear of French Negroes*, 138–40.

115. Hales, *A Southern Family in White and Black*, 100–101.

116. Cuney Hare, *Six Creole Folk-Songs*, 3; Dalleo, *American Imperialism's Undead*, 2.

117. Cuney Hare, *Six Creole Folk-Songs*, 7, 18.

118. Morgan, *Reckoning with Slavery*.

119. Cuney Hare, "Letter from Maud Cuney Hare to W. E. B. Du Bois, May 28, 1930," W. E. B. Du Bois Papers (MS 312, Special Collections and University Archives, University of Massachusetts Amherst Libraries); Riley, *Performing Race and Erasure*, 176.

120. King, *Blue Coat or Powdered Wig*, 45; Burnard and Garrigus, *The Plantation Machine*, 68.

121. Davis, *Blues Legacies and Black Feminism*, 3–24.

122. "Chanson créole," in Moreau de Saint-Méry, *Notes Historiques*, F3 ed., vol. 140 (Archives d'Outre-mer), 49.

123. Jenson, *Beyond the Slave Narrative*, 297.
124. On Jamaica, see Abrahams and Szwed, *After Africa*, 238.
125. Bacardí y Moreau, *Via Crucis*, 56; Fernandez, *Otro Golpe De Dados*,; 85; Johnson, *The Fear of French Negroes*, 141–42.
126. Fernandez, *Otro Golpe De Dados*, 85.
127. Viddal, "'Sueño de Haiti,'" 50–64.
128. Grant, "Public Performance," 188; Johnson, *The Fear of French Negroes*, 136; Bacardí y Moreau, *Crónicas de Santiago de Cuba*, 508.
129. Olavo Alén Rodríguez, "La Oralidad y La Huella Franco."
130. Carpentier, *La música en Cuba*, 130.
131. Moore, *Nationalizing Blackness*, 23–30.
132. Malcomson, "The 'Routes' and 'Roots' of 'Danzón,'" 270; see also Viddal, "Vodú Chic"; Manuel, "From Contradanza to Danzón," 52–112.
133. Casimir, "Haití y Sus Élites," 814–15.
134. For a different view that does not engage directly with Casimir, see Sweet, "'Brothers Gonna Work It Out.'"
135. Bacardí y Moreau, *Crónicas de Santiago de Cuba*, 508.
136. Arango y Parreño, in a 1791 letter to the Spanish king, argued that "the ideas of Toussaint the Black" were threatening to Cuba and that Haiti's destruction of its plantation complex was "catastrophic." Naranjo Orovio and Buscaglia, "Race as a Weapon," 4; Scott and Hébrard, "Rosalie of the Poulard Nation," 125–26.
137. Mitchell, "Gottschalk's Engagement with the Ungovernable," 81–82.
138. See the introduction.
139. Viddal, "'Sueño de Haiti,'" 50.
140. Cruz Ríos, "Testimonios de Una Misma Expresión Cultural Cubana," translated by author.
141. Madrid and Moore, *Danzón*, 117–49.
142. Frierson, "Jarocho Publics," 135–36.
143. Gaudiosa Venet Danger in Cruz Ríos, "Testimonios de Una Misma Expresión Cultural Cubana," 73–77.
144. Baldwin, "The Cakewalk," 205–18; Washburne, *Latin Jazz*, 58.
145. Gordo, "Los Cantos de La Tumba Francesa," 33–72.
146. Céspedes, *El diario Perdido*, 268–70; Ibarra Cuesta, *Encrucijadas de la guerra prolongada*, 32.
147. Coca-Izaguirre, "Análisis de Los Cantos," 91–100.
148. Quintero Rivera, "Ponce, the Danza, and the National Question," 54. For a different interpretation, see Aparicio, "Ethnifying Rhythms, Feminizing Cultures," 95–112.
149. Moore, *Nationalizing Blackness*; Lane, "Anticolonial Blackface," 223; Washburne, *Latin Jazz*, 54–55.
150. Quintero-Rivera, "The Camouflaged Drum," 27–37.
151. Washburne, "The Clave of Jazz."
152. Yanow, *Afro-Cuban Jazz*, 1.
153. Esdaile, *The Spanish Army in the Peninsular War*.
154. Dewulf, "From the Calendas to the Calenda"; Kubik, *Jazz Transatlantic*; Pettinger, "'Eh! Eh! Bomba, Hen! Hen!'"; Dunham, *Dances of Haiti*; Washburne, *Latin Jazz*, 55; Joyaux, "Forest's Voyage Aux Étas-Unis de l'Amérique En 1831," 465; Kinser, *Carnival, American Style*; Thompson, *Tango*, 115.

155. Thierry, *Les Vagabondes*; Jenson, *Beyond the Slave Narrative*, 298–99.

156. Miré! Quand mon té Saint-Domingue,
Négresses même té bijoux;
Blancs layo té semblé seringue,
Yo té collé derrière à nous.
Dans yon ménage
Jamain tapage,
L'amour yon blanc, c'était l'adoration!
Yo pa té chiches,
Yo té bien riches,
Yon bon bounda té vaut yon bitation! . . .
Temps-là changé, nous sur la paille,
Nous que z'habitants té fèté . . .
Avant longtemps yon blanc pété
Va hélé nous canaille!!!

Thierry, *Les Vagabondes*; Jenson, *Beyond the Slave Narrative*, 298–99.

157. Jenson, *Beyond the Slave Narrative*, 299.

158. Clark, *The Strange History of the American Quadroon*, 172.

159. Clark, *American Quadroon*, 83.

160. Rosenberg, *New Orleans Dockworkers*, 4.

161. Dalmas, *Histoire de la Révolution de Saint-Domingue*, 184, translated and quoted in Popkin, *You Are All Free*, 182.

162. Popkin, *You Are All Free*, 174, 177, 182–83, 186.

163. Clark, *American Quadroon*, 83.

164. Landau, *Spectacular Wickedness*, 200.

165. Blue Book, Williams Research Center, The Historic New Orleans Connection; Landau, *Spectacular Wickedness*, 212.

166. Du Bois, *Black Reconstruction*, 30.

167. Rosen, *Terror in the Heart of Freedom*, 68–71.

168. Habitant d'Hayti, *Idylles et Chansons, Ou Essais de Poësie Créole* (Philadelphia: De l'Imprimerie de J. Edwards, 1811); Epstein, *Sinful Tunes and Spirituals*, 94–95; *Historical Sketch Book and Guide to New Orlean*s; Mondor, "Listen to the Second Line," 82–90.

169. Salvaggio, *Hearing Sappho in New Orleans*, 13.

170. Mondor, "Listen to the Second Line," 82–90; Salvaggio, *Hearing Sappho in New Orleans*, 15.

171. Coleman, *Creole Voices*, xix.

172. Johnson, "Les Cenelles," 407.

173. "L'éclat qui t'environne et qui charme ta vue / N'est qu'un prisme trompeur qui récèle la mort." Lanusse, *Les Cenelles*, 108–9.

174. Cheung, "Les Cenelles and Quadroon Balls," 6.

175. Histories of the Calenda in Congo Square and its link to Haiti include Dewulf, "From the Calendas to the Calenda"; Kubik, *Jazz Transatlantic*; Pettinger, "'Eh! Eh! Bomba, Hen! Hen!'"; Dunham, *Dances of Haiti*; Washburne, *Latin Jazz*, 55; Joyaux, "Forest's Voyage Aux Étas-Unis de l'Amérique En 1831"; Kinser, *Carnival, American Style*; Thompson, *Tango*, 115.

176. Genovese, *Roll, Jordan, Roll*, 592; Martínez-Fernández, *Revolutionary Cuba*, 11; Howard, *Black Labor, White Sugar*, 42; Fick, *The Making of Haiti*.

177. Sheller, *Citizenship from Below*, 265.
178. Landau, *Spectacular Wickedness*, 168–71.
179. Logsdon and Bell, "The Americanization of Black New Orleans," 261.
180. Farred, *What's My Name?*
181. Meehan, *People Get Ready*, 3–13.
182. Marx, "The Power of Money."
183. Langston Hughes, "HERE TO YONDER: Music at Year's End," *Chicago Defender*, January 1943, 14.
184. Woods, *Development Arrested*, 39.

THREE La Frontera Sónica: Mexican Revolutions in Borderlands Jazz

1. *Times Picayune*, February 24, 1885. Mary Gehman has documented fifteen hundred names of Creoles of color with a connection to Mexico in the 1850s; see Gehman, "The Mexico-Louisiana Creole Connection," 68–76; and http://marygehman.net. On the Tios, see Gushee, "Black Professional Musicians in New Orleans, C1880," 53–63; Kinzer, "The Tio Family and Its Role in the Creole-of-Color Musical Traditions of New Orleans," 24; Kinzer, "The Tio Family," 150; Castañeda, *La Música Que Llegó Del Mar*; Rose Wynn Tio, interview, various dates, HJA.
2. NOLA.com, "The 1884 Cotton Expo."
3. Rydell, *All the Worlds a Fair*, 93–94.
4. Wells-Barnett and Douglass, *The Reason Why the Colored American Is Not in the World's Columbian Exposition*.
5. Benjamin, "Paris, Capital of the 19th Century," 146–58, in Tenorio-Trillo, *Mexico at the World's Fairs*, 16; Bird, "Aucune Usine au Monde," 299–310. Palti, Review of *Mexico at the World's Fairs*, 778–80.
6. Harman, *A People's History of the World*, 407–21.
7. Schulze, *Are We Not Foreigners Here?*, 26; Hu-Dehart, "Yaqui Resistance to Mexican Expansion," 146–58.
8. Tenorio-Trillo, *Mexico at the World's Fairs*.
9. Jiménez, "Brokering Modernity," 22; Yeager, "Porfirian Commercial Propaganda," 235.
10. Mier, *México en la Exposición*, 6–7.
11. "Mexico Exhibit," *Times-Democrat*, February 16, 1885; Rydell, *All the World's a Fair*.
12. Schulze, *Are We Not Foreigners Here?*, 31.
13. Heatherton, *Arise!*, 3.
14. Taibo II, *Yaquis*, 149.
15. Beezley, *Mexicans in Revolution, 1910–1946*, 4.
16. Olsson, *Agrarian Crossings*, 32–33.
17. Gould, "The Strike of 1887," 45–55, Scott, *Degrees of Freedom*, 77–85.
18. DeSantis, *The Thibodaux Massacre*, 142.
19. "Murder Most Foul," *Weekly Pelican*, November 25, 1887; Gould, "The Strike of 1887."
20. Brothers, *Louis Armstrong's New Orleans*, 87; Vernhettes and Lindström, *Jazz Puzzles*, 13.
21. Taibo II, *Yaquis*, 86.
22. Uzee, "Republican Politics in Louisiana," 111.
23. Phillips, "The Response of a West Indian Activist," 128–39; Foner, "Daniel A. Straker," 205–6.

24. *Times Picayune*, February 24, 1885.

25. Tuiz Torres, "Las Bandas Militares de Música En México y Su Historia," 21–44; Stewart, "The Mexican Band Legend," 3.

26. Brenner, *Juventino Rosas*, 45–49; Johnson, "'Sobre Las Olas'"; *Daily Picayune*, July 13, 1890.

27. Roberts, *The Latin Tinge*; Derbez, *El jazz en México*, 235–36; Madrid and Moore, *Danzón*, 117–50; Louis James, interview, May 25, 1959, HJA.

28. Raeburn, "Beyond the 'Spanish Tinge,'" 21–46.

29. Johnson, "'Sobre Las Olas,'" 229, emphasis mine.

30. Stewart, "The Mexican Band Legend: Part III," 1–10.

31. Hooton, "Little Liberia," 64–81; McBroome, "Harvests of Gold," 149–81; Kun, "Tijuana and the Borders of Race," 313–26; Flomen, "The Long War for Texas," 36–61.

32. Shankman, "The Image of Mexico," 43–56.

33. Coronado, *A World Not to Come*; Bassi, *An Aqueous Territory*, 4.

34. Mongey, *Rogue Revolutionaries*, 4.

35. Kelley, "'Mexico in His Head,'" 709–23.

36. Anzaldúa, *Borderlands*, 3; Chávez, *Sounds of Crossing*, 7.

37. Kovel, *History and Spirit*, 218.

38. Baker, "Archipelagic Listening," 383–402.

39. Brothers, *Louis Armstrong's New Orleans*, 45, 187.

40. Washburne, *Latin Jazz*, 113.

41. Moore, "The Danzón," 323–24, 334.

42. Kelley, "In a Mist," 10.

43. Some of this is evident in Piras, "'Ecos de México.'"

44. Rojas, *Las repúblicas de aire*, 300–316.

45. On colored militias in colonial Spain, see Vinson, *Bearing Arms for His Majesty*; Hanger, "Free Blacks in Spanish New Orleans," 44–64.

46. On Jackson's mistreatment of the free colored milita, see Petition to Andrew Jackson from Joseph Savary et al., March 16, 1815, in *Papers of Andrew Jackson*, 3: 315–16; and Bell, *The Afro-Creole Protest Tradition in Louisiana*, 59–60.

47. Kinzer, "The Band Music"; Cuney Hare, *Negro Musicians and Their Music*, 256–66.

48. Tutino, *From Insurrection to Revolution in Mexico*, 134–37.

49. Grafenstein Gareis, "Auge y Decadencia"; Puente González, "Las insurrecciones de esclavos en Haití."

50. Kinzer, "The Tio Family," 23.

51. This officer was referring to the republic of Galveston. Johnson, *The Fear of French Negroes*, 91.

52. A study of these "rogue revolutionaries" and their contradictions would overwhelm the focus of this section. Nonetheless, it is important to highlight that Joseph Tio likely engaged in the slave trade in a small-scale capacity. Others in his family did not, and maintained friendships and relationships in Haiti. This chapter suggests that Mexico's antislavery politics was one factor that contributed to the Tios' political evolution and helped them consolidate a relationship of solidarity with the African diaspora. For Joseph's resale of five enslaved people, see Kinzer, "The Tio Family," 20 On rogue revolutionaries, see Mongey, *Rogue Revolutionaries*, 17; Bassi, *An Aqueous Territory*, 68–69; Johnson, *The Fear of French Negroes*, 95, 99; Helg, "Simón

Bolívar and the Spectre of Pardocracia," 447–71. Afro-Creole ownership of human beings is complicated by their attempts to free enslaved people through purchasing them. On this, see Kotlikoff and Rupert, "The Manumission of Slaves in New Orleans, 1827–1846," 173–81; and Cole, "Capitalism and Freedom." On antebellum Louisiana's curtailing of manumission, see Kotlikoff and Rupert, "The Manumission of Slaves in New Orleans, 1827–1846," 173–74; Du Bois, *Black Reconstruction*, 402; Schafer, *Becoming Free, Remaining Free* 9.

53. Vincent, "The Contributions of Mexico's First Black Indian President," 150.
54. Northup, *Twelve Years a Slave*, 246–49.
55. Kelley, "Mexico in His Head."
56. Ford, *Rip Ford's Texas*, 196.
57. Baumgartner, *South to Freedom*, 81–95
58. *Indianola Bulletin*, May 31, 1855; *Anti-Slavery Bugle*, May 31, 1851; Pargas, *Freedom Seekers*, 206; Nichols, "Freedom Interrupted," 251–74.
59. Vinson III, *Before Mestizaje*; Vincent, "The Blacks Who Freed Mexico."
60. Beltrán, *La población negra de México*, 234; Vincent, "The Contributions of Mexico's First Black Indian President," 150.
61. Tyler and Murphy, *The Slave Narratives of Texas*, 67; Lim, *Porous Borders*, 57.
62. Flomen, "The Long War for Texas," 36–61.
63. This solidarity went two ways: Frederick Douglass denounced the United States invasion of Mexico while proselytizing in Ireland. Heatherton, *Arise!*, 72.
64. Committed to finding refuge for his free Black neighbors in Ohio, Lundy traveled more than five thousand miles on foot in North America and made two trips by ship to Haiti. He held over two hundred public meetings and was a target for political violence. He was nearly beaten to death by an enslaver in Baltimore. Greeley, *The American Conflict*; "Benjamin Lundy," *The Liberator*, April 1, 1864.
65. Mexican president Valentín Gómez Farías secretly ordered his Louisiana and Texas ambassadors to recruit African Americans to build a multinational buffer state in this area. This state was to include Indigenous, Black, and mestizo Texans (Tejanos). Aguilar, "Uprooted," 189; Cornell, "Citizens of Nowhere," 351–74; Flomen, "The Long War for Texas."
66. Flomen, "The Long War for Texas," 45.
67. Lundy, *The Life, Travels, and Opinions of Benjamin Lundy*, 143–47.
68. Gutiérrez, "Chicano Music," 150; Griego, *El mar de los deseos*, 154.
69. Lundy, *The Life, Travels, and Opinions of Benjamin Lundy*, 141–46.
70. Herrera Casasús, *Raíces Africanas*, 69–71; Pargas, *Freedom Seekers*, 227.
71. Burian, *The Architecture and Cities*, 33; Mary Gehman, personal correspondence, March 17, 2023.
72. Mareite, *Conditional Freedom*, 173, 186.
73. Afro-Mexican general Vicente Guerrero was elected the second president of the republic in 1829, supported by a base of self-governing Indigenous, mestizo, and Black communities around the country. Guerrero called for "the wooden shack of the humble laborer" to be the focus of national development instead of the palace of the rich. "If equality before the law destroys the efforts of power and of gold," he declared, "we [shall] have a republic, and she will be conserved by the universal suffrage of a people solid, free and happy." Vincent, "The Contributions of Mexico's First Black Indian President," 152.
74. López Matoso, *Viaje de Perico Ligero al país de los moros*, 31–32.
75. Vincent, "The Blacks Who Freed Mexico," 257–76.
76. Carroll, *Blacks in Colonial Veracruz*, 15.

77. Bellegarde-Smith, *In the Shadow of Powers*, 9.
78. Tardieu, *Resistencia de Los Negros*, 13.
79. Alcántara López, "Negros y Afromestizos Del Puerto de Veracruz," 175–91.
80. Carpentier, "Music in Cuba," 191.
81. López Matoso, *Viaje de Perico Ligero al país de los moros*, 31–32.
82. Griego, *El mar de los deseos*, 18; León, *Del canto y el tiempo*. Floyd also treats son jarocho as part of the Black circum-Caribbean nexus of musical forms in "Black Music in the Circum-Caribbean," 19.
83. Rolando Antonio, "El Son Jarocho Como Expresión Musical Afro-Mestiza."
84. Alcántara López, "La Mona de Juan Pascoe," 10.
85. Díaz-Sánchez and Hernández, "The Son Jarocho as Afro-Mexican Resistance Music," 197–98.
86. Sehgal, *Fandango at the Wall*, 15.
87. Malfavon, "Kin of the Leeward Port," 91–105."
88. Herrera Casasús, *Raíces Africanas*, 147–53; Hall, *An Ethnographic Study*, 28; Mareite, *Conditional Freedom*, 156.
89. Mareite, *Conditional Freedom*, 156.
90. Figueroa-Hernández, *Toña La Negra*, 11; Arce, *Mexico's Nobodies*, 255n50; Rafael Figueroa-Hernández, personal correspondence, January 10, 2023; Sublette, *Cuba and Its Music*, 252; León, *Del canto y el tiempo*, 274. Immigration records from the nineteenth century indicate Haitians did indeed move to Veracruz, albeit at a much lower rate than Cubans. Juárez Hernández, "Persistencias Culturales Afrocaribeñas En Veracruz," 154.
91. Reid-Vazquez, *The Year of the Lash*, 69.
92. Gilliam, *Travels Over the Table Lands and Cordilleras of Mexico*, 355.
93. Rugeley, *The River People in Flood Time*, 109–48.
94. García Díaz, "El Caribe en el Golfo," 47; Muller, *Cuban Émigrés*, 45.
95. Mendoza, *La Canción Mexicana*, 80, 82, 86, 97, 101, 120, 418, 437; Huet, "Lo 'Afro' en las Industrias de la Música y el Cine," 165; Smith, "Caribbean Influences on New Orleans Jazz," 31–58; Garrido, *Historia de La Música Popular En México*, 12; Linares, *La Música Popular*, 38; LaBrew, "The Brindis de Salas Family," 15–57. Cuban immigrants were attributed for popularizing the habanera rhythm, also called the "Creole dance," which became incorporated in several popular Mexican romantic songs. "La Paloma," widespread in Mexico, was initially a Cuban organ grinders' song. Nonexiled professional Afro-Cuban musicians also traversed the region, further facilitating this creolization. For instance, the Paris-trained Afro-Cuban violinist Claudio Brindis de Salas of Havana toured the Caribbean and Mexico in 1877 and 1878.
96. Díaz, "El Caribe en el Golfo," 47.
97. Bobadilla González, *La Revolución cubana en la diplomacia*, 82, 152–55.
98. Gamio, *Mexican Immigration to the United States*, 159; Narváez, "The Influences of Hispanic Music Cultures," 182; Lucero-White, *Literary Folklore*, 117.
99. Wald, *Escaping the Delta*, 47.
100. Handy, "How I Came to Write the 'Memphis Blues'"; Hobson, *Creating Jazz Counterpoint*, 84.
101. Russell, *New Orleans Style*, 23.
102. Corridos with counter-plantation and anti-capitalist messaging in the the late nineteenth and early twentieth centuries include include "El Ferrocarril" and "Corrido a la Patria." Héau, "The Musical Expression of Social Justice," 331; Garcilazo, *Traqueros*, 151–52.
103. Héau, "The Musical Expression of Social Justice," 334.

104. Woods, *Development Drowned and Reborn*, 77.

105. "Que te encuentras rodeada de ingenios, Pero esa es tu mayor ruina . . . Despierta si estás dormida . . . las aguas del Teara se transitmen abundantes." Héau, "The Musical Expression of Social Justice," 331.

106. Maceo Grajales, *Ideología Política*, 102; Zacaïr, "Haiti on His Mind," 47; Díaz Frene, "Generales mulatos y habaneras trasatlánticas," 89–129.

107. Zacaïr, "Haiti on His Mind," 58–61, 70; Casey, *Empire's Guestworkers*, 40; Scott, *Degrees of Freedom*, 77. Decades later, New Orleans resident Inez Andrews claimed to be Maceo's daughter. "Says General Maceo's Daughter Now Lives in New Orleans," *Afro-American*, January 28, 1933, 8.

108. Scott, "The Atlantic World," 726–33.

109. *Crusader*, June 22 1895; Scott, *Degrees of Freedom*, 3.

110. Salas, *In the Shadow of the Eagles*, 159; Horne, *Black and Brown*, 48; Rustin-Paschal, *The Kind of Man I Am*, ix; *California Eagle*, July 1, 1922; McBroome, "Harvests of Gold," 168; Heatherton, *Arise!*, 67; Hart, *Revolutionary Mexico*, xviii, 146; St. John, *Line in the Sand*, 152; López, "El Banjo En La Tradición Musical De La Mixteca."

111. Ryan, *Civic Wars*, 11.

112. Olivarius, "Immunity, Capital, and Power," 425–55.

113. Méndez, *En tierra yankee*, 28–32; in Dawdy, "La Catrina," 35.

114. *New Orleans Daily Delta*, January 16, 1860; Everett, "Free People of Color in New Orleans, 1830–1865," 129.

115. Kinzer, "The Tio Family."

116. Their full names are Louise Marguerite Anthenais Hauzer and Thomas Louis Marcos Tio. Due to the number of individuals discussed in this section, I chose to use their shorter names in the interest of clarity.

117. Desdunes, *Our People and Our History*, 114.

118. Urofsky, "Dred Scott Decision"; *Chicago Daily Tribune*, April 10, 1857; Oswald, "The Reaction to the Dred Scott Decision."

119. *Documents Relatif à la Colonie d'Eureka*, LRC, 1–7.

120. Metoyer's ancestor, a freedwoman Marie Thérèse Coincoin, had previously founded a Creole of color Louisiana community known as Cane River, with her husband, Auguste Metoyer, who had purchased her as a means of freeing her. While Cane River developed West African–inspired architecture, many free people of color who lived here managed plantations and enslaved other African-descended peoples. Gehman, "Metoyer in Mexico in the Mid-1800s"; Morgan, MacDonald, and Handley, "Economics and Authenticity," 44–61; MacDonald and Morgan, "African Earthen Structures in Colonial Louisiana," 161–77; Mills, *The Forgotten People*.

121. Gehman, "Metoyer in Mexico in the Mid-1800s," 1.

122. Vernhettes and Lindstörm, *Jazz Puzzles*, 162–64.

123. Act of Reorganization, Eureka Colony, August 25, 1859, Orleans Parish Notarial Archives; Kinzer, "The Tio Family," 105.

124. Stewart, "The Mexican Band Legend," 1–14; Quirarte, *Ritmos de la Eternidad*; Natty Dominque, interview, May 31, 1958, HJA.

125. Smith, "Caribbean Influences on New Orleans Jazz," 36.

126. Lomax, *Mister Jelly Roll*, 90.

127. Bigard, *With Louis and the Duke*; Interview, Leonard Bechet, April 4, 1949, Alan Lomax Digital Archives (ALDA); Kinzer, "The Tios of New Orleans and Their Pedagogical Influence," 279–302.

128. Castañeda, "La Música Que Llegó Del Mar"; Kinzer, "The Tio Family."
129. Madrid and Moore, *Danzón*, 118–121.
130. Thank you to Charles E. Kinzer for sharing this document.
131. Siliceo, *Memoria de la Secretaría de Estado*, 57.
132. Knowlton, *Los Bienes del Clero*, 1–5.
133. *El Progreso en El Siglo XIX*, August 2, 1857.
134. Schoonover, *Mexican Lobby*, 5, 7.
135. Tardieu, *Resistencia de Los Negros*, 13.
136. Vinson III, *Before Mestizaje*, 37.
137. Zúñiga, *Valentín Gómez Farías*, 191. Santacilia had been exiled for "having spread proclamations" of independence. He founded a shipping company that exported cattle to Havana and Veracruz. He often used these same shipments to smuggle arms to the Cuban independence fighters. Juárez became friends with Santacilia and they began to send the arms to Juárez's insurgent troops. Santacilia later married Juárez's daughter, Margarita Maza, and became Juárez's secretary. When Juárez boarded a ship to return to Mexico to fight with the forces of General Álvarez in 1855, Pedro Santacilia asked, "Where will we meet again?" Juárez replied, "In a free Mexico or in the afterlife."
138. Gruesz, "Delta Desterrados," 52–79.
139. Herrera Peña, "Juárez y el destierro (1853–1855)," 51–68.
140. Juárez Hernández, "Persistencias Culturales Afrocaribeñas En Veracruz," 153; Santacilia, *Apuntes Biográficos de Pedro Santacilia*, 56.
141. Rojas, "Los Amigos Cubanos de Juárez," 42–57.
142. Ridley, *Maximilian and Juárez*, 26; Smart, *Viva Juárez!*, 110–18; Foix, *Juárez*, 91–94; Roeder, *Juarez and his Mexico*, 111–12; Blancké, *Juárez of Mexico*; 56–57. The quotation comes from Iturribarría, *Oaxaca en la historia*, 168.
143. Ward, "Where Circum-Caribbean Afro-Catholic Creoles Met American Southern Protestant Conjurers," 124–38; Long, *Spiritual Merchants*, 236; Olivarius, "Immunity, Capital, and Power in Antebellum New Orleans," 425–55; Robinson, *The Diary of a Samaritan*, 239–40; Jordon, *White over Black*, 528. On "pure chance," see Roeder, *Juarez and his Mexico*, 110.
144. Hamnett, *Juárez*, xii.
145. Mormino and Pozzetta, "Spanish Anarchism in Tampa, Florida, 1886–1931," 91–128; Daniel, "Rolling for the Revolution"; Knotter, "Transnational Cigar-Makers," 409–42.
146. Sublette, *Cuba and Its Music*, 297.
147. Johnson, *The Autobiography of an Ex-Coloured Man*, 72–73; Anthony, "'Lost Boundaries," 291–312.
148. Siliceo, *Memoria de La Secretaría de Estado*, 57; Mitchell, *Raising Freedom's Child*, 43.
149. Scott and Hébrard, *Freedom Papers*, 121–25.
150. Mary Gehman interview with Celeste Gomez Vincent, July 1999.
151. Scott and Hébrard, *Freedom Papers*, 150.
152. Dominque, interview, May 31, 1959, HJA.
153. Marquis, *In Search of Buddy Bolden*, 89–91.
154. McKee, *The Exile's Song*, 73, 93, 194; Scott, *Degrees of Freedom*, 92, 151.
155. "Patron General de los Habitantes de la Municipalidad de Tampico, 1871" (Tampico, Mexico, 1871); Mary Geham, personal communication, February 25, 2023; Hudson, "Crossing Stories," 241.
156. Tinajero, *El Lector*; Knotter, "Transnational Cigar-Makers," 409–42.

157. Hudson, "Crossing Stories," 241–42.
158. Tio, "The Kinzer Family," 113.
159. Antoinette Tio, "Memoir of Antoinette Tio," 1878. Thank you to Charles Kinzer for this source.
160. Castañeda, *La Música Que Llegó Del Mar*.
161. "Programa," *El Siglo XIX*, August 8, 1857; *Indianapolis Freeman*, October 24, 1898; Kinzer, "The Tio Family," 180.
162. Castañeda, *La Música Que Llegó Del Mar*.
163. Adleson Gruber, "Historia Social de Los Obreros Industriales de Tampico," 13–15.
164. *Indianapolis Freeman*, October 8, 1898; quoted in Kinzer, "The Tio Family," 181.
165. Friedrich, *Agrarian Revolt in a Mexican Village*, 191; Tenorio-Trillo, *Mexico at the World's Fairs*, 24.
166. Friedrich, *Agrarian Revolt in a Mexican Village*, 191.
167. Starr, *In Indian Mexico*, 237; Friedrich, *Agrarian Revolt in a Mexican Village*, 191.
168. Thomson, "Bulwarks of Patriotic Liberalism," 58.
169. Ibid.
170. Downs, "The Mexicanization of American Politics," 407.
171. Olsson, *Agrarian Crossings*, 32–33.
172. Thomson, "Bulwarks of Patriotic Liberalism," 58.
173. Acevedo-Rodrigo, "Playing the Tune of Citizenship," 256–257.
174. Pellicer, "Las Capillas de Música de Viento En Oaxaca Durante El Siglo XIX," 9–27
175. Handy, *Father of the Blues*, 64.
176. Tavares Romero and Barreiro Lastra, "La influencia de la danza," 1840–45.
177. Díaz Frene, "Generales mulatos y habaneras trasatlánticas," 114.
178. Lomanno, "Topics on Afro-Cuban Jazz in the United States," 48; Piras, "Jelly-Roll Morton"; Desdunes, "'Happy Feeling Rag' Sheet Music."
179. Acosta, *Raíces del jazz latino*; García Díaz, "La Migración Cubana a Veracruz, 1870–1910," 297–399.
180. López, "El Banjo En La Tradición Musical De La Mixteca," 105–10; Flores y Escalante, *Salón México*, 74–99.
181. Floyd, "Black Music in the Circum-Caribbean"; Sakakeeny, "New Orleans Music as a Circulatory System," 291–325.
182. Moore, *Nationalizing Blackness*, 23.
183. Moore, "The Danzón," 324.
184. Williams-Jones, "Afro-American Gospel Music"; Sublette, *Cuba and Its Music*, 166–68.
185. Mata, "Felipe Valdes"; Mikowsky, "The Nineteenth-Century Cuban 'Danza' and Its Composers"; see also chapter 1.
186. Madrid and Moore, *Danzón*, 124.
187. Stewart, "The Mexican Band Legend: Part III," 4.
188. See chapter 5.
189. Lemmon, "New Orleans Popular Sheet Music Imprints," 41–61.
190. Navarrete Pellicer, "Las Capillas de Música," 9–27.
191. Acevedo-Rodrigo, "Playing the Tune of Citizenship," 256–57; Navarrete Pellicer, "Las Capillas de Música," 9–27.
192. August Laurent, interview, March 21, 1967, HJA.
193. Abbey "Chinee" Foster interview, March 9, 1961, HJA; Johnson, "'Sobre Las Olas.'"
194. Stewart, "The Mexican Band Legend," 1–14.

195. Madrid and Moore, *Danzón*, 124.

196. *Indianapolis Freeman*, October 8, 1898.

197. Harker, "Louis Armstrong and the Clarinet," 145.

198. Malcomson provides a comprehensive overview of theories of danzón's emergence and why ascribing individual originators is "hugely problematic." See Malcomson, "The 'Routes' and 'Roots' of 'Danzón,'" 269.

199. Quintero Rivera, "Ponce, the Danza, and the National Question."

200. Carpentier, "Music in Cuba," 185; Quintero-Rivera, "The Camouflaged Drum," 27–37. While Carpentier suggests that clarinets played cinquillo rhythms associated with Haitian and Afro-Cuban drummers, it is Quintero-Rivera, not Carpentier, who uses the term "camouflaged drum" to refer to the process of reproducing African-Atlantic rhythms in melodic and harmonic instruments, as opposed to percussion instruments.

201. Bradbury, *Armstrong*, 21.

202. Lichtenstein and Dankner, *Musical Gumbo*, 31.

203. Quintero-Rivera, "The Camouflaged Drum," 27–37.

204. Lemmon, "New Orleans Popular Sheet Music," 43–44; see the introduction to this chapter.

205. *Daily Picayune*, Feburary 16, 1885; *Albany Times*, July 25, 1885, 45; Lemmon, "New Orleans Popular Sheet Music."

206. *Times-Democrat*, May 23, 1891; Lemmon, "New Orleans Popular Sheet Music, 43–44.

207. *Butte Semi-Weekly Miner*, February 17, 1886; Vernhettes, *Visiting Mexican Bands*, 67.

208. *New Orleans Picayune*, December 10, 1884, May 17, 1897; Vernhettes, *Visiting Mexican Bands*, 51, 112; *Indianapolis Freeman*, October 8, 1898.

209. *Le Trait d'Union*, May 24, 1891; Vernhettes, *Visiting Mexican Bands*, 80.

210. *Louisiana Democrat*, February 21, 1885.

211. *Daily Picayune*, January 19, 1885.

212. Vernhettes, *Visiting Mexican Bands*, 104.

213. *Cleveland Leader*, July 11, 1885.

214. *New Orleans Item*, June 22, 1891; Vernhettes, *Visiting Mexican Bands*, 82.

215. Morrison, "On the Backs of Blacks."

216. *The Commercial Appeal* (Memphis, TN), April 9, 1885, in Vernhettes, *Visiting Mexican Bands*, 83.

217. *Minneapolis Review*, in Vernhettes, *Visiting Mexican Bands*, 83.

218. Vernhettes, *Visiting Mexican Bands*, 79.

219. *Daily Picayune*, May 17, 1885, 7; "Badly Shot," *Sunday States*, May 17, 1885; Jiménez, "Brokering Modernity," 228–39.

220. *New Orleans Item*, June 22, 1891; Vernhettes, *Visiting Mexican Bands*, 82.

221. There was another Mexican musician in Thibodaux who played violin. They both played classical music. Louis James, interview, May 25, 1959, HJA.

222. Kay, "Chink Martin," 18–19, 39; Martin Abraham, interview, October 19, 1966, HJA. Note that this interview is listed in the HJA archives under his alias "Chink Martin."

223. Stewart, "The Mexican Band Legend," 2; Vernhettes, *Visiting Mexican Bands*, 66.

224. Vernhettes, *Visiting Mexican Bands*, 66.

225. The John Robichaux Library: 1819–1917, Hogan Jazz Archive, Tulane University; Neprud-Ardovino, "The Jazz Clarinet," 54–105.

226. Marquis, *In Search of Buddy Bolden*, 31.

227. Brothers, *Louis Armstrong's New Orleans*, 45.

228. Sakakeeny, "New Orleans Music as a Circulatory System."
229. Zutty Singleton, interview, February 8, 1969, HJA.
230. Isidore Barbarin, interview, January 7, 1959, HJA.
231. Vernhettes and Lindstörm, *Jazz Puzzles*, 156.
232. Hersch, *Subversive Sounds*, 104.
233. Brothers, *Louis Armstrong's New Orleans*, 223; see also Albert Glenny, interview, March 27, 1957, HJA; Hersch, *Subversive Sounds*, 107–8.
234. Brothers, *Louis Armstrong's New Orleans*, 182–86.
235. Ratliff, *Coltrane*, 72.
236. Washington Jr., "University of Pittsburgh Annual Seminar on Jazz 1990," 142.
237. For more on the Tios' pedagogical practice, see Kinzer, "The Tios of New Orleans and Their Pedagogical Influence."
238. Downs, "The Mexicanization of American Politics," 407.
239. Foster, *The Autobiography of Pops Foster*, 39.
240. Manuel, *Creolizing Contradance in the Caribbean*; Largey, *Vodou Nation*; Stanyek, "Transmissions of an Interculture," 87–130.
241. Vernhettes and Lindstörm, *Jazz Puzzles*, 156.
242. *Indianapolis Freeman*, November 19, 1898.
243. Lott, *Love and Theft*, 21. For more on Kersands, see Watkins, *On the Real Side*, 113–15; Gubar, *Racechanges*, 114; Noah Cook, interview, August 30, 1960, HJA.
244. *Indianapolis Freeman*, April 1, 1899.
245. As Paul Dominguez said, "See, us Downtown people . . . we didn't think so much of this Uptown jazz until we couldn't make a living otherwise." Quoted in Lomax, *Mister Jelly Roll*, 102–6.
246. Handy, *Father of the Blues*, 78.
247. Smith, *The Creolization of American Culture*.
248. Gushee, *Pioneers of Jazz*, 38–39.
249. Abbott and Stewart, "The Iroquois Theater," 2.
250. Lomax, *Mister Jelly Roll*, 99.
251. Peter Bocage, interview, January 29, 1959, HJA. See also Kinzer, "The Tio Family," 296.
252. William Bébé Ridgley, interview, April 7, 1961, HJA.
253. Raeburn, "Foreword," 1–2.
254. Kinzer, "The Tios of New Orleans and Their Pedagogical Influence," 286. Bechet explains in his autobiography that he sought lessons with Lorenzo Jr. after his initial Creole of color clarinet teacher, George Baquet, did not help him grow as an improviser. "What he [Baquet] played, it wasn't really jazz . . . he stuck real close to the line in a way. He played things more classic-like, straight out how it was written. And he played it very serious." In contrast, as Bechet explains: "I hung around his [Tio's] house a lot. We used to talk together, and we'd play [music] to all hours." Bechet, *Treat It Gentle*, 79–80; Gushee, *Pioneers of Jazz*, 251.
255. Barson, "La Frontera Sónica," 1–23.
256. Canario y su Grupo, "Te olvidaré mejor," *Discography of American Historical Recordings*, Victor matrix BVE-55112.
257. Kinzer, "The Tios of New Orleans and Their Pedagogical Influence on the Early Jazz Clarinet Style," 288.
258. Smith, "Caribbean Influences on New Orleans Jazz," 36.
259. Kinzer, "The Tio Family," 266.

260. Tirro, *Jazz*; Kinzer, "The Tio Family," 290.

261. Wright, *Mr. Jelly Lord*, 74–82. Cornetist Lee Collins remembers that Jelly Roll Morton "wanted to talk to me about making some records with him and wanted Lorenzo Tio, Jr., and me on them." Lee Collins never made the session. Collins and Collins, *Oh, Didn't He Ramble*, 65–66. See also Kinzer, "The Tio Family," 293.

262. Kinzer, "The Tio Family," 293–94. He credits this oral history to an interview with Lorenzo Jr.'s daughter, Rose Wynn Tio. Interview by Martyn, May 11, 1990; Louis R. Tio, interview; Wellam Buad [Duke Ellington's longtime bassist], interview, May 30, 1957, HJA.

263. Bigard, *With Louis and the Duke*, 54.

264. Rose, *I Remember Jazz*, 109; Kinzer, "The Tio Family," 293–94. A blog, without much in the way of sources but possibly echoing New Orleans oral history, claims that Lorenzo Tio Jr. initially called the song "Mexican Blues."

265. Carl, "Duke Ellington Records 'Mood Indigo' 89 Years Ago Today."

266. For a discussion of Ellington's "mike-tone," see Jenkins, "A Question of Containment," 433; see also Johnson, "A Date with the Duke," 390.

267. Bechet, *Treat It Gentle*, 158–59; Washington, "'All the Things You Could Be by Now,'" 36.

268. *Louisiana Weekly*, January 13, 1934; quoted in Kinzer, "The Tio Family," 295.

269. Gehman, "The Mexico-Louisiana Creole Connection."

270. Kinzer, "The Tio Family," 148

271. Ameringer, *The Socialist Impulse*, 57; Chacón, *Radicals in the Barrio*, 186.

272. Koth, "'Not a Mutiny But a Revolution,'" 40.

273. Louis R. Tio, interview, October 26, 1960, New Orleans, HJA.

274. Heatherton, *Arise!*, 85; Gwin, "'The Selling of American Girls,'" 30–54.

275. Roberts, *Papa Jack*, 212.

276. The United States spied on some Afro-Louisianan musicians who moved to Tijuana at Johnson's incitation, but their names are unknown. See *California Eagle*, July 1, 1922; McBroome, "Harvests of Gold," 168; Heatherton, *Arise!*, 67; and Hart, *Revolutionary Mexico*, xviii, 146.

277. Lizárraga, "Baja California," 17–22.

278. "The Public Forum . . . El Foro Publico."

279. Cornell, "Citizens of Nowhere."

280. Cohen, *Finding Afro-Mexico*; Derbez, *El jazz en México*.

281. Santiago Guerrero, "La participación de los empresarios mexicanos," 240–41.

282. Horne, *Black and Brown*, 183–92.

FOUR   Sowing Freedom

1. Bethell, *George Lewis*, 10–12.
2. Sancton, *Song for My Fathers*, 87.
3. Yard, "'They Don't Regard My Rights at All,'" 201–29.
4. Hersey, *My Work Is That of Conservation*; Akuno, "Build and Fight."
5. "Jazz Is Blamed for Lack of Farm Labor," *Lincoln Star Journal*, Chicago, March 31, 1920.
6. Koenig, "The Plantation Belt and Musicians Part 1," 24–49; Raeburn, "New Orleans Jazz Styles of the 1920s," xv–xxxiv; Charters, *Jazz*.
7. Raeburn, "New Orleans Jazz Styles of the 1920s," xx–xxi.
8. Douglass, "Introduction," in Wells-Barnett and Douglass, *The Reason Why the Colored American Is Not in the World's Columbian Exposition*.

9. Foner, *Reconstruction*, 51–118.

10. Entries for February 24, February 26, and January 3, 1863, William J. Minor Plantation Diary (1861–1868), Minor Papers, Mss. 519, 294, Louisiana and Lower Mississippi Valley Collections, Louisiana State University, Special Collections, hereafter referred to as LLMVC; Lago, *Civil War and Agrarian Unrest*, 315.

11. Martínez-Fernández, *Revolutionary Cuba*; Fick, *The Making of Haiti*.

12. On collective resources management in the emancipation period, see several articles in Hahn et al., *Freedom*, vol. 1, 3, which are cited and discussed later. See also Hahn, *A Nation Under Our Feet*, 277–301.

13. Hunter, *To 'Joy My Freedom*; Delany, *The Condition*.

14. Woods, *Development Drowned and Reborn*; Rodrigue, *Reconstruction in the Cane Fields*, 162.

15. Halpern, "Solving the 'Labour Problem,'" 20.

16. McCusker, *Creole Trombone*, 31.

17. Koenig, *Music in the Parishes Surrounding New Orleans: Plaquemines*, 4.

18. George Lewis, interview, November 1, 1968, HJA.

19. Sonny Henry, interview, October 21, 1959, HJA.

20. Sylvester Handy, interview, December 13, 1961, HJA.

21. Steve Brown, interview, HJA; Collier, *Jazz*, 198.

22. Jim Robinson, interview, December 10, 1958, HJA.

23. Crawley, *Blackpentecostal Breath*, 36.

24. Brathwaite, "Jazz Music," 1–7.

25. Casimir, *The Haitians*, 157.

26. Popkin, *Facing Racial Revolution*, 275.

27. Georges, *Atlas Critique d'Haïti*, 83.

28. Casimir, *The Haitians*, 302.

29. Higman, *Jamaica Surveyed*, 291.

30. Casid, *Sowing Empire*, 196.

31. Latrobe, *Impressions Respecting New Orleans*, 47.

32. Gonzalez, "Defiant Haiti," 125.

33. For a critique of an emancipatory reading of provision grounds, see Vermeulen, "Thomas Thistlewood's Libidinal Linnaean Project," 18–38; Follett, *The Sugar Masters*.

34. Scott, *The Art of Not Being Governed*, 195, 174.

35. Carney and Rosomoff, *In the Shadow of Slavery*, 125.

36. Richards, "Culture and Community Values."

37. Carny, *Black Rice*, 162; Hall, *Africans in Colonial Louisiana*, 10; Berry, *City of a Million Dreams*, 29.

38. George, *Civil War Recipes*, 12.

39. Ward, "Southern Black Aesthetics," 143–50; Fleming, "Transforming Geographies of Black Time," 587–617.

40. Ward, "Where Circum-Caribbean Afro-Catholic Creoles Met American Southern Protestant Conjurers," 124–38; Long, *Spiritual Merchants*, 236; Olivarius, "Immunity, Capital, and Power in Antebellum New Orleans," 425–55; Robinson, *The Diary of a Samaritan*, 239–40; Jordon, *White over Black*, 528; Volpato, Godínez, and Beyra, "Migration and Ethnobotanical Practices," 43–53.

41. Brothers, *Louis Armstrong's New Orleans*, 76.

42. Morgan, *Laboring Women*, 114; Follett, "Gloomy Melancholy," 54; Perrin, "Resisting

Reproduction," 255–74; Bush, *Slave Women in Caribbean Society*, 138; White, *Ar'n't I a Woman*, 85; Morgan, "An Essay on the Causes of the Production," 117–23.

43. "Memories of the Life of Boston King, a Black Preacher," *Methodist Magazine*, XXI (1798), 105; Morgan, *Slave Counterpoint*, 619.

44. Mellon, *Bullwhip Days*, 94; Fett, *Working Cures*, 64.

45. Sheller, "Mobile Commoning," 32.

46. Wynter, "Novel and History, Plot and Plantation," 95–102.

47. Prieto, "The Uses of Landscape," 237.

48. Hilliard, *Hog Meat and Hoecake*, 21–23.

49. Baptist, *The Half Has Never Been Told*, 49; Zeuske, "The Second Slavery in the Americas," 429–39; Tomich, *Through the Prism of Slavery*, 61–71.

50. Montgomery, *Dirt*, 141.

51. Johnson, "Reconstructing the Soil," 191.

52. Genovese, *The Political Economy of Slavery*, 85–88.

53. Edmund Ruffin, Private Diary, 107, 177; Faust, "The Rhetoric and Ritual of Agriculture in Antebellum South Carolina," 541–68.

54. Franklin Planters' Banner, June 20, 1850.

55. Hall, *The Manhattaner in New Orleans*, 91–95.

56. U.S. Census, 1910. The sugar bowl extended thirty miles from the Mississippi River, seventy miles beyond the coast to the southeast.

57. Shugg, *Origins of Class Struggle in Louisiana*, 5.

58. *De Bow's Review* 15 (Dec. 1853), 647–48.

59. Hunt, *Haiti's Influence on Antebellum America*, 62.

60. Sitterson, *Sugar Country*, 28–30, 60.

61. Russell, *My Diary North and South*, vol. 1, 388.

62. Prince, "A Narrative of the Life and Travels of Mrs. Nancy Prince," 72.

63. Johnson, *Slavery's Metropolis*, 118.

64. Shugg, *Origins of Class Struggle in Louisiana*, 14; Vance, *Human Geography of the South*, 219–20.

65. K. M. Clark to Lewis Thompson, December 1853, in Sitterson, *Sugar Country*, 18.

66. McDonald, "Independent Economic Production," 276; Follett, "Heat, Sex, and Sugar."

67. Kendall, "New Orleans' Peculiar Institution," 874; Follett, "Gloomy Melancholy," 55.

68. Hamilton, *Men and Manners in America*, vol. 2, 299–30; McDonald, "Independent Economic Production," 275–99; Follett, "Heat, Sex, and Sugar"; Newman, *A New World of Labor*.

69. Garraway, *The Libertine Colony*, 240.

70. Tadman, "The Demographic Cost of Sugar," 1537. Tadam's data used Louisiana census data between 1840 and 1860.

71. Stipriaan, *Surinaams Contrast*, 316–18.

72. Burnard, "Toiling in the Fields," 3.

73. Ligon, *A True and Exact History of the Island of Barbados*, 157.

74. Ferdinand, *Decolonial Ecology*, 38–45.

75. Marshall, "Provision Ground and Plantation Labor in Four Windward Islands," 209.

76. A Mississippi Planter, "Management of Negroes upon Southern Estates," *DeBow's Review* 10, no. 6 (June 1851): 622.

77. Higman, *Slave Populations of the British Caribbean*, 374.

78. Paquette, "'A Horde of Brigands?'" 81.

79. Northup, *Twelve Years a Slave*, 161, 248–49.
80. Follett, "Heat, Sex, and Sugar," 510–39.
81. Solinger, "Racializing the Nation," 265.
82. McCusker, *Creole Trombone*, 42.
83. Bechet, *Treat It Gentle*, 39, 5.
84. Marx, *Capital*, Volume 1, 637–41; see also Foster and Clark, *The Robbery of Nature*, 31.
85. Liebig, *Letters on Modern Agriculture*; Marx, *The Poverty of Philosophy*; Foster, *Marx's Ecology*; Clark, Auberbach, and Xuan Zhang, "The Du Bois Nexus," 113–28.
86. Tick and de Graaf, "Three Slave Lullabies."
87. Lewis, *Journal of a West India Proprietor*, 85; Higman, *Jamaica Surveyed*, 262.
88. Stewart, *Gosse's Jamaica 1844-45*.
89. Stewart, 36.
90. Downing, *A Treatise on the Theory and Practice of Landscape Gardening*, 80–81.
91. Meehan, *People Get Ready*, 29.
92. Thompson, *Flash of the Spirit*, 222; Georgia Writers' Project, *Drums and Shadows*.
93. Tobin and Dobard, *Hidden in Plain View*, 49.
94. Ligon, *A True and Exact History of the Island of Barbados*, 157.
95. Thompson, *Flash of the Spirit*, 221–22; Lears, *Something for Nothing*, 15.
96. Floyd, "Black Music in the Circum-Caribbean"; Fryer, *Rhythms of Resistance*, 4.
97. Struge and Harvey, *The West Indies in 1837*, 224–25; Higman, *Jamaica Surveyed*, 263.
98. Senior, *Jamaica*, 121.
99. Waddell, *Twenty-Nine Years*, 55; Mathieson, *British Slavery and Its Abolition*, 212; Senior, *Jamaica*, 179; Zoellner, *Island on Fire*, 112.
100. McDonald, "Independent Economic Production," 278.
101. Cuney Hare, *Six Creole Folk-Songs*, 24.
102. Comte de Vaublanc, *Souvenirs Par Le Comte*, vol. 1, 177; Geggus, *The Haitian Revolution*, 17.
103. Rickford and Handler, "Textual Evidence," 221–55; Handler and Frisbie, "Aspects of Slave Life in Barbados," 5–46; Glissant, *Poetics of Relation*, 73–74.
104. "Management of Negroes," *DeBow's Review* 10 (March 1851): 328; Southern, *The Music of Black Americans*, 161.
105. Jackson, *Wake Up Dead Man*, 17–19.
106. Bass, "Negro Songs from the Pedee Country," 418–36.
107. Bob Ellis in Perdue, Barden, and Phillips, eds., *Weevils in the Wheat*, 88–89.
108. Havis, "Nimble or Not at All," 145–48.
109. Jackson, *Creole Indigeneity*, 4.
110. Kaye, *Joining Places*, 45.
111. Winfield, "Slave Holidays and Festivities in the United States," 42.
112. Vance, "The Profile of Southern Culture," 30; Faust, "The Rhetoric and Ritual of Agriculture in Antebellum South Carolina," 543.
113. Koenig, *Under the Influence*, 148.
114. Black, "How Watermelons Became Black," 64–86.
115. The exact location of its domestication is subject to considerable debate, although recent literature identifies West Africa as a likely source. See Sousa and Raizada, "Contributions of African Crops."
116. Jensen et al., "Watermelons in the Sand of Sahara." 117. Nantoumé et al., "Traditional Uses and Cultivation of Indigenous Watermelons," 461–71.

118, Penniman, *Farming While Black*, 152.

119. Allen, "The Harvest Ceremony," 13–29; Penniman, *Farming While Black*, 154.

120. Thomas, *Political Life in the Wake of the Plantation*, 5.

121. Elizabeth Ross Hite, date unknown, WPA Ex-Slave Narrative Collection, LSU. For other examples of nighttime dancing on plantations, see Jefferson Franklin Henry in Rawick, *The American Slave*, 188; Camp, *Closer to Freedom*, 69; and Charlie Crump, in Rawick, *American Slave*, 213; also quoted in Camp, *Closer to Freedom*, 69.

122. Taylor, "'Release Your Wiggle,'" 6–65; Cresswell, *On the Move*, 128.

123. Flanders, *Plantation Slavery in Georgia*, 171.

124. Cresswell, *On the Move*, 128–36; Bryant, "Shaking Things Up"; Penniman, *Farming While Black*, 152.

125. Glissant, *Poetics of Relation*, 73–74.

126. Moten, *In the Break*, 12.

127. Ardouin, *Études Sur l'Histoire d'Haïti*, volume 10, 23, n1; Sheller, *Citizenship from Below*, 166–72.

128. Sheller, *Citizenship from Below*, 55.

129. Cresswell, "'You Cannot Shake That Shimmie Here,'" 55–77; Gottschild, *Digging the Africanist Presence in American Performance*; Sheller, *Citizenship from Below*.

130. Gushee, "Would You Believe Ferman Mouton?," 56–59.

131. Daniels, "Vodun and Jazz," 117.

132. Dahl, *Morning Glory*, 437; Hot Lips Page, 1940–1944 (Classics 809, n.d.).

133. Borrero, *Montecafé*, 37–38; Casey, *Empire's Guestworkers*, 188.

134. Maximilien, "Notes on Folklore"; Largey, "Ethnographic Transcription and Music Ideology in Haiti," 15.

135. Daniel, *Caribbean and Atlantic Diaspora Dance*, 80–94.

136. AGN/Indiferente Virreinal/Caja 2506/exp.002/fs. 33–42; Malfavon, "Kin of the Leeward Port," 122–40.

137. "85: Report of a Speech by a Virginia Freedman; and Freedmen's Bureau Superintendent of the 5th District of Virginia to the Headquarters of the Virginia Freedmen's Bureau Assistant Commissioner," in *Freedom*, eds. Hayden et al. See also Guelzo, *Fateful Lightning*; Butchart, *Northern Schools*.

138. *New York Anglo-African*, December 16, 1856; Magdol, *A Right to the Land*, 257.

139. Brickhouse, "'L'Ouragan de Flammes,'" 1106.

140. Hahn, *A Nation Under Our Feet*; Mandell, *The Lost Tradition*.

141. Sheller, "Mobile Commoning," 29–52.

142. Ferdinand, *Decolonial Ecology*, 152. The literature on the Plantationocene is extensive. For an overview, see Carney, "Subsistence in the Plantationocene"; and Haraway, "Anthropocene, Capitalocene, Plantationocene, Chthulucene."

143. King, *The Black Shoals*; Sayers, *A Desolate Place for a Defiant People*; García León, "Economía y vida cotidiana," 29–45.

144. Barbagallo, Beuret, and Harvie, *Commoning with George Caffentzis and Silvia Federici*; Fortier, *Unsettling the Commons*; Harney and Moten, *The Undercommons*, 38–39.

145. Moten, "The New International of Rhythmic Feeling(s)," 31–56; Mintz, "The Jamaican Internal Marketing Pattern," 95–103; Fett, *Working Cures*, 9.

146. Bechet, *Treat It Gentle*; on the latter, see chapter 3 of this book.

147. McAlister, *Rara!*, 4.

148. Geggus, "The Naming of Haiti," 43–68.

149. Breunlin and Lewis, *The House of Dance & Feathers*, 66–67; Lief and McCusker, *Jockomo*; Blackbird, "Entwined Threads of Red and Black."

150. Olsen, "The Gift of the New Orleans Second Line," 176–89.

151. Hall, *Acts*, 113; Goveia, *Slave Society*, 156; Palmer, "Africa in the Making of the Caribbean," 48; "1740, Slave Code of South Carolina, Articles 34–37," Duhaime.org, accessed October 29, 2020, http://www.duhaime.org/LawMuseum/LawArticle-1501/1740-Slave-Code-of-South-Carolina-Articles-34-37.aspx; Jenks, *Our Cuban Colony*; Singleton, *Slavery Behind the Wall*; Handler and Frisbie, "Aspects of Slave Life in Barbados," 9.

152. New Orleans City Council Ordinances, 1856, book 11, no. 3121 O.S., Art. 1, sec. 7, 9, 11; no. 3131 O.S.; Johnson, "New Orleans's Congo Square," 151.

153. *Southern Agriculturalist*, IV (1831), 162–64; Sitterson, *Sugar Country*, 136; Franklin, *Planter's Banner*, January 13, 1853; Sitterson, *Sugar Country*, 152; Hunt, *Haiti's Influence on Antebellum America*.

154. Douglass, *My Bondage and My Freedom*, 97.

155. N. Herbemont, "On the Moral Discipline and Treatment of Slaves," *Southern Agriculturalist* IX (January 1836); Johnson, *A Social History of the Sea Islands*, 143.

156. Tobin, *Colonizing Nature*, 87.

157. Ligon, *A True and Exact History of the Island of Barbados*, 50–51.

158. Johnson, *Slavery's Metropolis*, 28.

159. "Management of Negroes," *DeBow's Review* 11, no. 4–5 (November 1851): 372.

160. Criswell, *"Uncle Tom's Cabin" Contrasted with Buckingham Hall*, 113. In planation memoirs, there are numerous examples of white masters admiring Black music.

161. Magdol, *A Right to the Land*, 141.

162. This continued to be a commonly held understanding through the Black Power movement of the 1960s. See Rickford, "'We Can't Grow Food on All This Concrete.'" For contemporary Black radical land practice grounded in ecosocialist principles, see Akuno, "Build and Fight."

163. Hunter, *To 'Joy My Freedom*.

164. On the cooperative initiatives in the post–Civil War South, see Magdol, *A Right to the Land*; Zimmerman, "Africa and the American Civil War"; Vandal, "Black Utopia"; Ripley, *Slaves and Freedmen*; Nembhard, *Collective Courage*; Dulken, "A Black Kingdom"; Behrend, *Reconstructing Democracy*.

165. Gordon, *Brook Farm to Cedar Mountain*, 48.

166. Work, "Marching Through Georgia," 354.

167. Pace, "'It Was Bedlam Let Loose,'" 389–409; Eiss, "A Share in the Land," 46–89.

168. Ellison, *Invisible Man*, 264–66, 499.

169. Pearson, *Letters from Port Royal*, 181; Foner, *Reconstruction*, 51–118.

170. Botkin, "Self-Portraiture," 895.

171. Baptist, *The Half Has Never Been Told*, 142.

172. Scott-Heron, "Who'll Pay Reparations on My Soul?"

173. Berlin et al., *Freedom*, vol. 2, 556.

174. Hahn et al., *Freedom*, 578, 632.

175. Hahn et al., *Freedom*, 627.

176. *New Orleans Tribune*, February 18, 1865.

177. Hahn et al., *Freedom*, 632.

178. *The Free Man's Press*, Austin, Texas, August 1, 1868.
179. Ripley, *Slaves and Freedmen*, 78.
180. Eiss, "A Share in the Land," 57.
181. *New York Times*, July 9, 1867; Foner, *Politics and Ideology*, 144.
182. Foner, *Politics and Ideology*, 144–47; Uzee, "Republican Politics in Louisiana," 11; Shugg, "Survival of the Plantation System in Louisiana."
183. Warmoth, *War, Politics, and Reconstruction*, 51–52; Shugg, "Survival of the Plantation System in Louisiana"; Williams, "The Louisiana Unification Movement of 1873." Warmoth would not become a planter until 1873, after his governorship.
184. Mandle, *Not Slave, Not Free*; Gould, "The Strike of 1887."
185. Hollis, "Neither Slave nor Free," 13.
186. Scott, *Degrees of Freedom*.
187. Gould, "The Strike of 1887."
188. Césaire, "Le Verbe Marronner," 368–71.
189. Sonny Henry, interview, January 8, 1959, HJA.
190. Harrison Barnes, interview, January 29, 1959, HJA.
191. Koenig, *Music in the Parishes Surrounding New Orleans: Plaquemines*.
192. Harrison Barnes, interview, January 29, 1959, HJA
193. Sonny Henry, interview, January 8, 1959, HJA.
194. Koenig, *Music in the Parishes Surrounding New Orleans: Plaquemines*.
195. West Baton Rouge, *Sugar Planter*, February 10, 1866.
196. Somers, *The Southern States Since the War, 1870–1*, 222.
197. Natchitoches *People's Vindicator*, April 21, 1877; Hair, *Bourbonism and Agrarian Protest*, 19.
198. Bouchereau and Bouchereau, *Statement of the Sugar and Rice Crops*, vii; Sitterson, *Sugar Country*, 237.
199. Okiji, *Jazz as Critique*, 3.
200. Foster, *The Autobiography of Pops Foster*, 64.
201. Gaudet, *Tales from the Levee*, 85; see also Ward, "Where Circum-Caribbean Afro-Catholic Creoles Met American Southern Protestant Conjurers," 128–38.
202. Stuart, "Kid Ory," 5–8; Darensbourg, *Telling It Like It Is*, 70; Bigard, *With Louis and the Duke*, 83.
203. Clemens, *Life on the Mississippi*, 281.
204. Shugg, "Survival of the Plantation System in Louisiana," 311–25.
205. McCusker, *Creole Trombone*, 9.
206. Tanner, *Chained to the Land*, location 1341.
207. Sonny Henry, interview, January 8, 1959, HJA; William Bébé Ridgley, interview, June 2, 1959, HJA.
208. Brothers, *Louis Armstrong's New Orleans*, 32–54.
209. Kid Ory, *Autobiography*; see also McCusker, *Creole Trombone*, 2–23.
210. Miller, "Interview Digest, August 20, 1959," 3; Hobson, "New Orleans Jazz and the Blues."
211. Louis James, interview, May 25, 1959, HJA.
212. Dymond, "Memoirs," undated manuscript, Dymond Collection, Collection 453, folder 28, Louisiana Research Collection, Tulane University, quoted in Raeburn, "New Orleans Jazz Styles of the 1920s," xxii.
213. Washington, "The Avenging Angel of Creation/Destruction," 235.

214. Barnes, interview, January 29, 1959, HJA; Sonny Henry, interview, November 7, 1958, HJA.
215. Barnes, interview, January 29, 1959, HJA.
216. Brothers, *Louis Armstrong's New Orleans*, 32–54.
217. Montgomery, *Under Their Own Vine and Fig Tree*.
218. Kelley, *Race Rebels*, 40.
219. Raymond, "James Lawson Remarks at John Lewis Funeral," 41.
220. Harris, *Ecowomanism*, location 168.
221. Behrend, *Reconstructing Democracy*, 45–46.
222. Hurston, "Spirituals and Neo-Spirituals," 355–64.
223. Foster, *The Autobiography of Pops Foster*.
224. Harris, *Ecowomanism*, location 200.
225. *Thibodaux Sentinel*, September 16, 1876; Koenig, *Music in the Parishes Surrounding New Orleans: Ascension*, 187–88.
226. June 14, 1879; quoted in Koenig, *Music in the Parishes Surrounding New Orleans: Ascension*, 74.
227. *Thibodaux Sentinel*, December 31, 1881.
228. *Thibodaux Sentinel*, June 13, 1885.
229. Koenig, *Music in the Parishes Surrounding New Orleans: Plaquemines*, 13; and Koenig, "The Plantation Belt and Musicians Part 1," 28.
230. Parr, "Sundays in the Streets," 8–30; Jacobs, "Benevolent Societies," 21–33.
231. Sonny Henry, interview, January 8, 1959, October 21, 1959, HJA.
232. DeSantis, *The Thibodaux Massacre*; Rodrigue, *Reconstruction in the Cane Fields*, 162; Gould, "The Strike of 1887."
233. Julian, "Magnolia's Music," 8.
234. Peter R. Haby, "Interview," *Footnote II* (July 1980): 8; Koenig, "The Plantation Belt and Musicians Part 1," 31.
235. Koenig, "The Plantation Belt and Musicians Part 1," 31; Savitt, "Straight University Medical Department," 175–201; Blassingame, *Black New Orleans 1860-1880*, 126.
236. Miller, "The Carpetbagger and the Professor," 10.
237. Willie Parker, interview, November 7, 1958, HJA.
238. Miller, "The Carpetbagger and the Professor," 9.
239. Willie Humphrey Sr. and Willie Humphrey Jr., interview, March 15, 1959, HJA.
240. Willie Humphrey Sr. and Willie Humphrey Jr., interview, March 15, 1959, HJA.
241. Jeffrey Gould describes ongoing garden production during the transition to wage labor. See Gould, "The Strike of 1887," 45–55.
242. Koenig, "Professor James B. Humphrey—Part II," 16.
243. Koenig, "Mandeville," 2–11; Koenig, "Buddy Petit on the North Side of Lake Pontchartrain," 34–51; Chamberlain, "Searching for 'The Gulf Coast Circuit,'" 1–18; Raeburn, "New Orleans Jazz Styles of the 1920s."

FIVE *Black Reconstruction and Brassroots Democracy*

1. Allen, Ware, and Garrison, *Slave Songs of the United States*, 3.
2. Diary of Homer B. Sprague, 13th Connecticut, April 14, 1863, vol. 2, 79–80, Papers of Homer B. Sprague, Manuscripts Division, Library of Congress, Washington DC; Frazier, *Fire in the Cane Field*, 195; DeSantis, *The Thibodaux Massacre*, 39.

3. "Department of the South: Affairs in Charleston; The Jubilee among the Freedmen: How the Slaves Celebrated Their Emancipation; Military Changes," *New York Times*, April 4, 1865.

4. Arnold, "Through the Carolinas," March 29, 1865, in *Christian Recorder*, April 15, 1865.

5. John W. Pratt, "Letter from North Carolina," February 28, 1865, in *Christian Recorder*, March 18, 1865; Jackson, "'Devoted to the Interests of His Race,'" 23.

6. Kaye, *Joining Places*, 206.

7. Crasson in *WPA Slave Narratives 1936–1938: North Carolina*, vol. XI, pt. 1, 93.

8. Williams in *WPA Slave Narratives 1936–1938: North Carolina*, vol. XI, pt. 2, 381.

9. Rogers in *WPA Slave Narratives 1936–1938: North Carolina*, vol. XI, pt. 2, 230; Glymph, *Out of the House of Bondage*, 212.

10. Fortune, *Black and White*.

11. T. Thomas Turner, *Norfolk Journal and Guide*, July 30, 1927; Sterling, *The Trouble They Seen*.

12. Foner, "'The Tocsin of Freedom,'" 131; Wideman, "Charles Chesnutt and the WPA Narratives," 72.

13. Turino, *Music as Social Life*, 28–37; Manabe, "Chants of the Resistance"; Sakakeeny, "Textures of Black Sound and Affect."

14. George Lewis, interview, November 1, 1968, HJA.

15. Evan, "Black Fife and Drum Music in Mississippi," 163.

16. George Lewis, interview, November 1, 1968, HJA.

17. Matory, "The 'New World' Surrounds an Ocean."

18. Du Bois, *Black Reconstruction*.

19. Hahn, *The Political Worlds of Slavery and Freedom*, 97.

20. Russell, *Atlanta, 1847–1890*, 110–11.

21. Hunter, *To 'Joy My Freedom*, 14.

22. *Christian Recorder*, January 30, 1864; Clark, "Celebrating Freedom," 108.

23. Janwir, *Conjuring Freedom*, 3.

24. Heble, Fischlin, and Lipsitz, *The Fierce Urgency of Now*, 61.

25. Thomas, "The Colored Troops at Petersburg," 777–79.

26. On contemporary participatory direct democracy, see Fitzwater, *Autonomy Is in Our Hearts*, 74–75.

27. Heble, Fischlin, and Lipsitz, *The Fierce Urgency of Now*, 63.

28. Pike, *The Prostrate State*, 11.

29. These words are from Brown, "Polyrhythms and Improvization," 90; Ojeda Penn, "The Message in the Music" (74th Annual Meeting of the Association for the Study of Afro-American Life and History, Dayton, Ohio, 1989).

30. Teish, *Jamalaya*, 139–40.

31. Brown, "Polyrhythms and Improvization," 85; quote from Penn, "Jazz."

32. Bradley, *Universal Tonality*.

33. Moten, "Blackness and Nothingness," 742.

34. Hoffman, *Camp, Court and Siege*, 111; Harrington, *Fighting Politician*, 94; Drayton, *Naval Letters*, 41.

35. Harris, *The Story of Public Education in Louisiana*, 54.

36. *National Anti-Slavery Standard*, June 25, 1864; Bahney, "Generals and Negroes," 195.

37. *Louisiana Democrat*, February 21, 1866; Bond, *No Easy Walk to Freedom*, 92.

38. *Boston Advertiser*, September 28, 1865.

39. Cornelius, *Music of the Civil War Era*.
40. Regis, "Second Lines," 74.
41. Sakakeeny, "The Representational Power of the New Orleans Brass Band," 123–37; Sakakeeny, *Roll with It*; Olsen, "The Gift of the New Orleans Second Line."
42. Heble, Fischlin, and Lipsitz, *The Fierce Urgency of Now*, 91, 86, 88.
43. Behrend, *Reconstructing Democracy*, 3–4.
44. Ibid.
45. Sanchez, "Teaching the Reconstruction Revolution."
46. Pike, *The Prostrate State*, 10.
47. Testimony of Isaac Hughes, quoted in Behrend, *Reconstructing Democracy*, 19.
48. Blassingame, *The Slave Community*; Gutman, *The Black Family in Slavery and Freedom*.
49. Penningroth, *The Claims of Kinfolk*; Schermerhorn, *Money over Mastery*; Camp, *Closer to Freedom*; Bardes, "Redefining Vagrancy," 69–112.
50. Hallowell, *The Negro as a Soldier*, 3–8; Curtis, *Muslim Americans in the Military*, 46–49; Dabovic, "Out of Place"; Hollandsworth, *Louisiana Native Guards*, 69.
51. Douglass, *My Bondage and My Freedom*, 169.
52. Bartlett, *Wendell and Ann Phillips*, 131–34; Powers, "'The Worst of All Barbarism,'" 145; Sweet, "'Brothers Gonna Work It Out,'" 220. As Clavin notes, "the veracity of these stories mattered little to the readers of these accounts"; rather, he points to how an "oral tradition of the revolution [that] survived among enslaved Americans is evident." Clavin, "American Toussaints," 101–3.
53. Kaye, *Joining Places*, 207.
54. Hardt and Negri, *Assembly*, 294.
55. Thornbery, "The Development of Black Atlanta," 143–45.
56. Hunter, *To 'Joy My Freedom*, 68.
57. Bahney, "Generals and Negroes," 195.
58. D. Densmore to friends at home, September 6, 1864, Benjamin Densmore Family Papers; Wilson, *Campfires of Freedom*, 147–48.
59. LeConte Diary, July 5, 1865, Electronic Edition, University of North Carolina Southern Historical Collections, https://docsouth.unc.edu/fpn/leconteemma/leconte.html.
60. Pike, *The Prostrate State*, 12; Bennett, *Black Power U.S.A.*, 298; Sanchez, "Teaching the Reconstruction Revolution."
61. Garofalo and Elrod, *A Pictorial History*, 56.
62. D. Densmore to friends at home, December 25, 1864, Benjamin Densmore Family Papers; Wilson, *Campfires of Freedom*, 171.
63. Ibid.
64. Trudeau, *Like Men of War*, 321.
65. Steward, *Twenty-Two Years a Slave*, 37.
66. Scroggs, Diary, January 2, 1865; Wilson, *Campfires of Freedom*, 154; emphasis mine.
67. John Zorn, in Bailey, *Improvisation*, 77.
68. Higginson, *Army Life in a Black Regiment*, 18.
69. Higginson, *Army Life in a Black Regiment*, 182; Higginson, "Drummer Boys in a Black Regiment," 465.
70. Such songs were also heard on the Black maritime songs of the Sea Islands. Epstein, *Sinful Tunes and Spirituals*, 180–81.
71. Higginson, *Army Life in a Black Regiment*, 135, 179.

72. Picker, "The Union of Music and Text in Whitman's Drum-Taps and Higginson's Army Life in a Black Regiment," 237; Cox, "'Half Bacchanalian, Half Devout'"; Jabir, *Conjuring Freedom*.

73. Jabir, *Conjuring Freedom*, 39.

74. Du Bois, *Black Reconstruction*, 33–45.

75. Berlin et al., *Freedom's Soldiers*, 2.

76. Friedrich, "We Will Not Do Duty Any Longer for Seven Dollars per Month," 64–73; Westwood, "The Cause and Consequence," 222–36; Belz, "Law, Politics, and Race," 197–213; Redkey, *A Grand Army of Black Men*, 114–35.

77. Higginson, *Army Life in a Black Regiment*, 221.

78. Sutherland, "The Negro and the Great War," 179.

79. *New Orleans Tribune*, April 9, 1864; Wilson, *Campfires of Freedom*, 75–76.

80. Emilio, *History of the Fifty-Fourth Regiment*; Litwack, *Been in the Storm So Long*, 85.

81. Redkey, *A Grand Army of Black Men*, chapter 7.

82. *Christian Recorder*, December 31, 1864; Forbes, *African American Women*, 200; emphasis mine.

83. Hartman, *Scenes of Subjection*.

84. Sidran, *Talking Jazz*, 105.

85. "Local News," *Alexandria Gazette and Virginia Advertiser*, November 10, 1887, 3.

86. "Republican Rally," *The Intelligencer* (Anderson Court House, SC), November 14, 1889; Johnson, *Rough Tactics*, 18.

87. *Wilmington Star*, March 16, 1872, March 17, 1874, June 7, 1876, January 19, 1877; Reaves, *Strength through Struggle*, 62; Evans, *Ballots and Fence Rails*, 159.

88. Johnson, "'The Best Notes Made the Most Votes,'" 208.

89. Fitzgerald, *The Union League Movement in the Deep South*, 168–69; Foner, *Reconstruction*, 600; Foner, *Freedom's Lawmakers*, 7; Wiggins, *The Scalawag in Alabama Politics, 1865–1881*, 148.

90. Work, "Some Negro Members," 67; Bailey, *Neither Carpetbaggers nor Scalawags*, 108.

91. Foner, *Freedom's Lawmakers*, 7.

92. Saville, *The Work of Reconstruction*, 186.

93. W. O'Berry to Paul Cameron, August 11, 1867, Cameron Family Papers, Southern Historical Collection, University of North Carolina, Chapel Hill; Fitzgerald, *Reconstruction in Alabama*, 128.

94. Foner, *Freedom's Lawmakers*, 7.

95. Montgomery, *Alabama State Journal*, November 15, 16, 1873; Montgomery, *Advertiser*, November 11, 16, 1873; Fitzgerald, *The Union League Movement in the Deep South*, 168; Foner, *History of the Labor Movement in the United States*, 402–8.

96. Bailey, *Neither Carpetbaggers nor Scalawags*, 108.

97. Edgefield (SC) *Advertiser*, August 5, 1868; Parsons, *Ku-Klux*, 231.

98. *Raleigh Sentinel*, March 16, 1870; Nelson, *Iron Confederacies*, 106.

99. US Senate, *Mississippi in 1875. Report of the Select Committee to Inquire into the Mississippi Election of 1875*, 44th Cong., 1st Sess. (Washington: Government Print Office, 1876), 1178.

100. Smith, "Remembering Mary, Shaping Revolt," 513–34.

101. Sutherland, "The Negro and the Great War," 182.

102. Evan, "Black Fife and Drum Music in Mississippi"; Zuczek, *State of Rebellion*, 148; Smith, "Dying to Vote," 42.

103. Burton, "Race and Reconstruction," 41.

104. Fields, *Slavery and Freedom on the Middle Ground*, 206.
105. Behrend, *Reconstructing Democracy*, 210.
106. James W. Johnson to A. M. Crawford, December 17, 1866, South Carolina Governor's Papers; Foner, *Reconstruction*, 122.
107. Chapman, *History of Edgefield County*, 238.
108. Foner, *Reconstruction*, 122.
109. Jackson, "'Devoted to the Interests of His Race,'" 23.
110. Williamson, *After Slavery*, 1–15.
111. Sonny Henry, interview, January 8, 1959, HJA; Ben Kelly, interview, August 11, 1960, HJA.
112. Davis, *The Emancipation Circuit*, 6, 286–90.
113. *North Louisiana Journal*, October 12, 1872; Behrend, *Reconstructing Democracy*, 164.
114. Hahn, *A Nation Under Our Feet*, 224.
115. Bryant, *How Curious a Land*, 138.
116. Davis, *The Emancipation Circuit*, 4; Barson, "Sounding Affective Consensus."
117. Bryant, *How Curious a Land*, 138.
118. Bennett, *Black Power U.S.A.*, 359.
119. Brown, "Negotiating and Transforming the Public Sphere," 107–46.
120. *Minutes of the Loyal National League of Louisiana*; Brook, *The Accident of Color*, 43.
121. *Loyal Georgian*, April 10, 1867; Sterling, *The Trouble They Seen*, 100.
122. Debord, *The Society of the Spectacle*, 12–13.
123. Koenig, *Music in the Parishes Surrounding New Orleans: Plaquemines*, 60–62.
124. Willie Parker, interview, November 7, 1958, HJA.
125. Clarinetist George Baquet was never the leader of the Excelsior Brass Band, according to existing documentation, but George Noret and Theogene Baquet were. Willie Parker, interview, November 7, 1958, HJA.
126. *Weekly Pelican*, March 8, 1879; Kinzer, "The Tio Family," 139–40.
127. Hofman, "The Romance with Affect," 303–18.
128. Redmond, *Anthem*, 4, 2.
129. Kinzer, "The Excelsior Brass Band of New Orleans," 14–24.
130. Scott, *Degrees of Freedom*, 70.
131. Landau, *Spectacular Wickedness*, 299.
132. O'Connor, *History of the Fire Department of New Orleans*, 184.
133. O'Connor, *History of the Fire Department of New Orleans*, 185.
134. Scott, *Degrees of Freedom*, 83.
135. Angela D. Davis, "Excelsior Band," *New Times Weekly*, February 11, 1988.
136. Brackner, "The Excelsior Marching Band, Mobile."
137. Rodrigue, *Reconstruction in the Cane Fields*, 174–95.
138. *Weekly Pelican*, July 23, 1887; Scott, *Degrees of Freedom*, 83.
139. Gushee, "Black Professional Musicians in New Orleans"; Kinzer, "The Tio Family"; Kinzer, "The Excelsior Brass Band of New Orleans."
140. Kelley, *Hammer and Hoe*, 228.
141. Hirschman, *Getting Ahead Collectively*, 42–43.
142. Lumumba, "May Our People Triumph," 48–49; Kalb, *Congo Cables*.
143. "Louis Armstrong," *Jazz Review*, July 1960.
144. Shapiro and Hentoff, *Hear Me Talkin' to Ya*, 38.
145. Bergreen, *Louis Armstrong*, 45.

146. Stewart, "Freedom Music," 88–107.
147. Rogers, "Jazz at Home," 223.
148. AAJ Staff, "A Fireside Chat."

SIX Black Unions and the Blues

1. C. L. R. James, unpublished autobiography; Meehan, "'To Shake This Nation as Nothing before Has Shaken It,'" 77–99.
2. Willie Parker, interview, November 1, 1958, HJA.
3. Willie Parker, interview, November 1, 1958, HJA.
4. Ameringer, *If You Don't Weaken*, 199.
5. *Picayune*, October 16, 1907; Rosenberg, *New Orleans Dockworkers*, 152.
6. Williams, *Jazz Masters of New Orleans*, 44; PBS, "Freedom"; Foster, *The Autobiography of Pops Foster*; Martyn and Gagliano, *The Fabulous George Lewis Band*.
7. Gushee, "How the Creole Band Came to Be," 89.
8. Gushee, "The Nineteenth-Century Origins of Jazz," 171.
9. Weir, *Singlejack Solidarity*, 73.
10. Rosenberg, *New Orleans Dockworkers*, 48.
11. Rosenberg, *New Orleans Dockworkers*; Arnesen, *Waterfront Workers of New Orleans*.
12. Rosenberg, "Race, Labor and Unionism," 311.
13. Earl Lewis describes a similar negotiation in *In Their Own Interests* (1993).
14. Camp, "Black Radicalism, Marxism, and Collective Memory," 230.
15. Ameringer, *If You Don't Weaken*, 199.
16. Johnpoll, "Ameringer, Oscar (1870–1943)," 5–6; Poole, Hayssen, and De Leon, *The American Labor Who's Who*, 4.
17. Blanc, "Red Oklahoma."
18. Ameringer, *If You Don't Weaken*, 197–98.
19. Williamson and Goodman, *Eastern Louisiana*, 569–71.
20. Hair, *Bourbonism and Agrarian Protest*, 72–73.
21. Ameringer, *If You Don't Weaken*, 218; emphasis in the original.
22. Ameringer, *If You Don't Weaken*, 218.
23. Camp, *Closer to Freedom*, 91.
24. *Tri-Monthly Report*, Christian Rush, October 10, 21, 1867, La. Asst. Comr., Letters Received, roll 19, Records of the Bureau of Refugees, Freedmen, and Abandoned Lands, Record Group 105, National Archives, Washington, DC; Behrend, *Reconstructing Democracy*, 69.
25. Bruce, *The New Man*, 11; Bancroft, *Slave Trading in the Old South*, 292; Kaye, *Joining Places*, 45.
26. Kaye, *Joining Places*, 45–47.
27. *Times Democrat*, December 4, 1886.
28. *Daily Picayune*, November 11, 1894.
29. Du Bois, *The Gift of Black Folk*, 14, 26–27.
30. Rosenberg, *New Orleans Dockworkers*, 48.
31. Havis, "Nimble or Not at All," 145–48.
32. Kenney, *Jazz on the River*, 35.
33. Hersch, *Subversive Sounds*, 37.
34. Chamberlain, "Searching for 'The Gulf Coast Circuit,'" 10.

35. Hersch, *Subversive Sounds*, 46–47.

36. Twelfth Census of the United States, Schedule No. 1—Population, New Orleans, National Archives, Washington, DC; Marquis, *In Search of Buddy Bolden*, 24; Arnesen, *Waterfront Workers of New Orleans*, 310n39.

37. Cahill, "Don't Go 'Way Nobody," 1906, HJA Addendum. Accessed online on July 16, 2019, via the Tulane University Digital Library at https://digitallibrary.tulane.edu/islandora/object/tulane%3A19044.

38. Levine, *Black Culture and Black Consciousness*, 407–8; Prince, "Remembering Robert Charles," 297–328.

39. Foucault, *Discipline and Punish*, 381.

40. Nissen, *Buddy Bolden's Storyville Blues*, 1–10. Although Nissen's work is historical fiction, his sharing of "Don't Go Way Nobody" as Bolden's opener is circulated among numerous jazz scholars, including Daniel Hardie.

41. Barnes, interview, January 29, 1959, HJA.

42. Botkin, "Self-Portraiture," 894.

43. Robinson, "'Worser Dan Jeff Davis,'" 37; Hunter, *To 'Joy My Freedom*, 4.

44. Hersch, *Subversive Sounds*, 47.

45. Arnesen, *Waterfront Workers of New Orleans*, 189.

46. Report of the Port Investigation Commission to the Louisiana General Assembly, May 28, 1908; Rosenberg, *New Orleans Dockworkers*, 142.

47. *New Orleans Daily Picayune*, March 28, 1908.

48. Mitchell, *Textile Unionism and the South*, vi.

49. Woodward, *Origins of the New South, 1877-1913*, 3–4.

50. Friedman, "The Political Economy of Early Southern Unionism," 386.

51. Camp, "Black Radicalism, Marxism, and Collective Memory," 218.

52. Ameringer, *If You Don't Weaken*, 214.

53. Woodland, "An Open Letter on Affiliation," 5; Arnesen, *Waterfront Workers of New Orleans*, 323–24.

54. *Louisville Courier-Journal*, May 15, 1890; Leeds and Rockoff, "Beating the Odds," 8; Hotaling, *The Great Black Jockeys*, 322, 6; for a discussion of Afro-Caribbean jockeys during slavery, see Lambert, "Master–Horse–Slave," 618–41.

55. Ameringer, *If You Don't Weaken*, 217.

56. *Times Picayune*, September 29, 1903.

57. *Times Picayune*, February 21, 1904; quoted in Rosenberg, *New Orleans Dockworkers*, 30.

58. *Times Picayune*, May 4, 1903.

59. *Times Picayune*, October 30, 1902.

60. Weiss, *Framing a Radical African Atlantic*, 6; Edwards, *The Practice of Diaspora*, 243–44.

61. Horne, *Red Seas*, 1–25.

62. Scott, *Degrees of Freedom*, 151.

63. Winberry, "The Mexican Landbridge Project," 12–18; Moore, "Correspondence of Pierre Soule," 59–72.

64. Kendall, *History of New Orleans*.

65. Martin, *Banana Cowboys*, 20; Chambers, *From the Banana Zones to the Big Easy*, 33; Read and Bucehli, "Banana Boats and Baby Food," 215; Putnam, "Jazzing Sheiks at the 25 Cent Bram," 339–59; Richard Sudhalter, liner notes to *The Luis Russell Story 1929-1934*, compact disc; Jos, *Guadeloupéens et Martiniquais Au Canal de Panamá*.

66. Mary Gehman, "L. A. Creole-Mexican Connection," Dville Press, accessed November 7, 2019, http://dvillepress.com/LCMC.php.
67. *Daily Picayune*, May 19, 20, 23, 24, 1903; Rosenberg, *New Orleans Dockworkers*, 75.
68. Barker, *A Life in Jazz*, 2–3.
69. Foster, *The Autobiography of Pops Foster*, 113.
70. Barson, "From Plantation Percussion to the Sound of Solidarity," 47–61.
71. Knowles, *Fallen Heroes*.
72. Albert Jiles, interview, July 15, 1960, HJA.
73. Martin, *Race First*, 15; Chambers, *From the Banana Zones to the Big Easy*, 90; Tucker, "A Feminist Perspective on New Orleans Jazzwomen," 56.
74. Wilcox, *Sugar Water*, 63–67; Maclennan, "Hawai'i Turns to Sugar," 97–125.
75. Imada, *Aloha America*.
76. Troutman, "Steelin' the Slide," 26–52.
77. Fellezs, *Listen but Don't Ask Question*, 32.
78. Imada, "Aloha America," 152–56; *Times Picayune*, October 6, 1912; September 19, 1915; February 19, 1917; Troutman, "Steelin' the Slide," 35.
79. Troutman, "Steelin' the Slide," 37.
80. Stone, *Sacred Steel*, 64–71, 129–30.
81. Larkin, *The Guinness Who's Who of Blues*, 292–93; Troutman, "Steelin' the Slide," 34.
82. Denning, *Noise Uprising*, 233.
83. Webb-Gannon, Webb, and Solis, "The 'Black Pacific' and Decolonisation in Melanesia," 177–206; Carr, *Hawaiian Music in Motion*, 54; Solis, "The Black Pacific," 297–312.
84. Smith, *The Music of the Waters*.
85. Quintero-Rivera, "The Camouflaged Drum."
86. Carr, *Hawaiian Music in Motion*, 68.
87. Rediker, "Afterword," 260.
88. Rediker, "Afterword," 260.
89. See the recordings from this period of Hawaiian guitarists Sol Ho'opi'i, Bob Paole, and Sam Ku, in Kanahele, *Hawaiian Music and Musicians*, 107; Troutman, "Steelin' the Slide," 49; and López, "El Banjo En La Tradición Musical De La Mixteca," 133–50.
90. Martínez Oxama, "Oaxaca," 177–88.
91. Barson, "Sounding Affective Consensus."
92. Regis, "Second Lines, Minstrelsy, and the Contested Landscapes of New Orleans Afro-Creole Festivals," 483–89.
93. *New Orleans Picayune*, 1890; Berry, *City of a Million Dreams*, 181.
94. *New Orleans Daily States*; Berry, *City of a Million Dreams*, 181.
95. Sonny Henry, interview, October 21, 1959, HJA.
96. Kelley, "Forging Futures," 200.
97. Arnesen, *Waterfront Workers of New Orleans*, 35.
98. *Daily Picayune*, September 12, 1881.
99. *St. Landry Democrat*, September 17, 1881.
100. *The Weekly Louisianian*, September 17, 1881.
101. Turino, *Music as Social Life*, 41–44.
102. Arnesen, *Waterfront Workers of New Orleans*, 34–35.
103. Sakakeeny, "Textures of Black Sound and Affect."
104. Sakakeeny, *Roll with It*, 122.

105. Arnesen, *Waterfront Workers of New Orleans*, 86.
106. *New Orleans Louisianian*, July 9, 1881, 2.
107. Arnesen, *Waterfront Workers of New Orleans*, 86.
108. *Times Picayune*, December 24, 1902.
109. Gushee, "The Nineteenth-Century Origins of Jazz," 167.
110. *Weekly Pelican*, May 14, 1887; *Southwestern Christian Advocate*, January 1, 1903.
111. *Weekly Pelican*, May 14, 1887; Arnesen, *Waterfront Workers of New Orleans*, 285.
112. *New Orleans Republican*, April 18, 1876 1876; Vernhettes et. al, "The Desdunes Family."
113. Davis, *The Emancipation Circuit*, 7; Arnesen, *Waterfront Workers of New Orleans*, 86, 185–86.
114. *Times Picayune*, December 3, 1902.
115. *Times Picayune*, December 3, 1902; Arnesen, *Waterfront Workers of New Orleans*, 187.
116. Foster, *The Autobiography of Pops Foster*, 40.
117. Rosenberg, *New Orleans Dockworkers*, 63.
118. Marquis, *In Search of Buddy Bolden*.
119. Hartman, *Scenes of Subjection*.
120. Jacobs, "Benevolent Societies," 21–22.
121. Martyn and Gagliano, *The Fabulous George Lewis Band*, 62.
122. Gessler, *Cooperatives in New Orleans*, 4.
123. Hobson, "New Orleans Jazz and the Blues."
124. Berry, *City of a Million Dreams*, 167.
125. Rosenberg, *New Orleans Dockworkers*, 58; see also *Picayune*, September 8, 1908.
126. Woods, *Development Drowned and Reborn*, 77.
127. Foster, *The Autobiography of Pops Foster*, 66.
128. Casimir, "On the Origins of the Counterplantation System."
129. Ayers, *The Promise of the New South*.
130. *New Orleans Item*, December 30, 1902; Landau, *Spectacular Wickedness*, 229.
131. Landau, *Spectacular Wickedness*, 134, 229.
132. Papers of Paul Capdeville, City Archives, Louisiana Division, New Orleans Public Library.
133. Marquis, *In Search of Buddy Bolden*, 69.
134. George Lewis and Alice Zeno, interview, November 14, 1958, HJA.
135. Letter, June 5, 1899, City Council Papers, City Archives, Louisiana Division, New Orleans Public Library.
136. City Council Papers, City Archives, Louisiana Division, New Orleans Public Library; Landau, *Spectacular Wickedness*, 142.
137. *New Orleans Times Picayune*, June 16, 1902.
138. *Daily Picayune*, August 25, 1904.
139. Kousser, *The Shaping of Southern Politics*, 262–63.
140. Guillory, *Spiritual and Social Transformation in African American Spiritual Churches*, 35.
141. City Ordinances, Book 11, Series C. S. (11714–13464), Ordinance 13347 C.S; Roberts, "The Promise of Power," 208.
142. Hersch, *Subversive Sounds*, 74.
143. Guillory, *Spiritual and Social Transformation in African American Spiritual Churches*, 35.
144. Brothers, *Louis Armstrong's New Orleans*, 43.
145. Berry, *City of a Million Dreams*, 166.
146. Brothers, *Louis Armstrong's New Orleans*, 42–46..

147. Kid Ory, interview, April 20, 1957, HJA; Russell, *New Orleans Style*, 60, 175; Giola, *The History of Jazz*, 36; on Porter see Arnesen, *Waterfront Workers of New Orleans*, 85–86. Ory's description of the Holy Roller church as a Baptist church is probably incorrect, since Holy Roller was a Pentecostal denomination. See McCusker, *Creole Trombone*, 59–60.

148. McCusker, *Creole Trombone*, 60.

149. Henry C. Dibble, notary public, March 1, 1866, incorporation papers for Union Sons Benevolent Association of Louisiana, in Notarial Archives, Civil District Courts Building, New Orleans; Marquis, *In Search of Buddy Bolden*, 67.

150. Marquis, *In Search of Buddy Bolden*, 67.

151. Ibid.

152. Edouard Henriques, notary public, February 6, 1907, minutes of a meeting of the Union Sons Benevolent Association that includes a list of officers elected on November 9, 1904, in Notarial Archives, Civil District Courts Building, New Orleans.

153. Marquis, *In Search of Buddy Bolden*, 110. The lyrics of the song are based on the lyrics of Jelly Roll Morton's 1940 recording of "Buddy Bolden's Blues."

154. Foster, *The Autobiography of Pops Foster*, 40.

155. Prince, "Remembering Robert Charles," 297–328.

156. Sidney Bechet, "Buddy Bolden Stomp," The Grand Master of the Soprano Sax and Clarinet, Columbia Record, CL 836, side 1, no 4; Marquis, *In Search of Buddy Bolden*, 111.

157. Lipsitz, "Learning from New Orleans," 459.

158. *Daily Picayune*, June 23, 1902; Lief, "Anarchist Blues," 34–42.

159. Woods, *Development Drowned and Reborn*, 77.

160. *Times Picayune*, September 2, 1902.

161. *Times Picayune*, September 3, 1907.

162. Foster, *The Autobiography of Pops Foster*, 46.

163. Lomax, *Mister Jelly Roll*, 102–6.

164. Woods, *Development Drowned and Reborn*, 77.

165. Hersch, *Subversive Sounds*, 46–47.

166. Foucault, *Discipline and Punish*, 380, 25.

167. Foster, *The Autobiography of Pops Foster*, 55.

168. Armstrong, *Satchmo*, 53.

169. Shapiro and Hentoff, *Hear Me Talkin' to Ya*, 14.

170. Lomax, *Mister Jelly Roll*, 101.

171. Tucker, "Jazz History Remix," 131.

172. Garon, *Blues and the Poetic Spirit*, 54.

173. Ameringer, *If You Don't Weaken*, 199.

CONCLUSION   *Telegrams from the Spiritual Plane*

1. Other musicians present included the Pittsburgh-based saxophonists Roger Romero and Alec Zander Redd and the emcee Jasiri X. Author's observation, August 6, 2020; Davison, "Mother of Deceased Duquesne Student."

2. Sakakeeny, "Textures of Black Sound and Affect," 2.

3. The Roots of Music, "About the Roots of Music"; see also Lipsitz, "Learning from New Orleans," 456–60.

4. Afful, interview with author, September 10, 2023.

5. Crawley, *Blackpentecostal Breath*.

6. McKittrick, "Plantation Futures," 2.

7. Chapman, *The Jazz Bubble*; Jones, "Death Sentences"; Watts and Porter, *New Orleans Suite*, 56–77.

8. Mackey, "Other," 259.

9. Rediker, "The Red Atlantic," 111–30.

10. Quintero Rivera, "Music, Social Classes."

11. Nocella and Socha, "Old School, New School, No School."

12. Gilroy, *Small Acts*, 37–38.

13. Brownhill, *Land, Food, Freedom*, 266.

14. Heller, *Loft Jazz*, 73.

15. Averill, *A Day for the Hunter, a Day for the Prey*, 56–80.

16. Salim Washington, in "Black Red and Green Revolutionary Eco-Music Tour," Barnard Vermont, February 2014, 15:06–16:14, https://vimeo.com/91707067.

17. Bechet, *Treat It Gentle*, 6.

18. *New Orleans Bee*, November 11, 1834; Marcus Christian, "Bras Coupé," Marcus Christian Papers, Archives and Manuscripts Division, Earl K. Long Library, University of New Orleans; Wagner, "Disarmed and Dangerous," 149.

19. Bardes, "The Notorious Bras Coupé," 9.

20. Roach, *Cities of the Dead*, 2.

21. Bechet, *Treat It Gentle*, 9–11.

22. Muleiro, "Mi música refleja el sufrimiento."

23. "Measurement" brings forward the violence of abstraction found in auctions of enslaved people. As one French trader noted in a New Orleans auction in 1838, "The slaves are seated on benches arranged like an amphitheater. . . . The deal is never concluded until the slave has been completely looked over, from head to foot." Joyaux, "Forest's Voyage Aux Étas-Unis de l'Amérique En 1831," 465; Hanger, *A Medley of Cultures*, 24.

24. Bechet, *Treat It Gentle*, 7, 21.

25. Jackson, *Wake Up Dead Man*, 17–19.

26. Gilroy, *The Black Atlantic*, 73.

27. Bechet, *Treat It Gentle*, 8.

28. Daniels, "Vodun and Jazz," 118.

29. Scarry, *The Body in Pain*, 4.

30. Gilroy, *The Black Atlantic*, 74.

31. Karl Marx, *Capital*, Vol. 1.

32. Hofman, "The Romance with Affect," 304.

33. Hofman, "'We Are the Partisans of Our Time,'" 161.

34. Aruan Ortiz, interview, March 28, 2022; McCusker, "The Onward Brass Band and the Spanish-American War," 24–35.

35. Marcus Rediker, paper at "Bass Lines from Below" (Boston: Organization of American Historians, April 2022).

36. Pratt, *Imperial Eyes*, 6–7. For "decolonized cultural contact zones," Meehan, *People Get Ready*, 18.

37. P. A. Desdunes, "Les pensées d'ún esclave soldat," in Kress, "Pierre-Aristide Desdunes," 51.

BIBLIOGRAPHY

Archives and Collections

Academia de la Historia, Caracas, Sección Civiles
Alan Lomax Digital Archive (ALDA)
Archivo General de la Nación (AGN), México City, México
Blue Book, The Historic New Orleans Collection
Frederic Ramsey Papers, Historic New Orleans Collection
The John Robichaux Library: 1819–1917, Hogan Jazz Archive, Tulane University
Mary W. Pugh Papers, Louisiana State University
Minor Papers, Mss. 519, 294, Louisiana and Lower Mississippi Valley Collections, Louisiana State University, Special Collections
Oral History Collection, Hogan Jazz Archive (HJA), Tulane University
Orleans Parish Notarial Archives
Pierre-Aristide Desdunes Ledgers, A. P. Tureaud family papers, Williams Research Center, The Historic New Orleans Collection.
Pimeria Alta Historical Society, Nogales, Arizona
Salmon P. Chase Papers, Manuscript Division, Library of Congress, Washington, DC
University of Nebraska Omaha, Criss Library, Special Collections

Government Documents

Arrest Books, City Archives, Louisiana Division, New Orleans Public Library
City Council Records (1899), City Archives, Louisiana Division, New Orleans Public Library
City v. Freddie Crockett, et al. (1908), Criminal District Court, Docket No. 18,051 [18,061], City Archives, Louisiana Division, New Orleans Public Library
Documens Relatif à La Colonie d'Eureka, Louisiana Research Center, Tulane University, 1860
Deôt et euripsto, *O. de Armas*, 1859
Freedom: A Documentary History of Emancipation, 1861–1867, 11 vols. (Various Publishers)
House Reports, 43 Cong., 2 Sess., No. 261, Part 3, "Louisiana Affairs," 1037–38
John Spencer Bassett, ed. *Correspondence of Andrew Jackson*. Washington, DC: Carnegie Institution of Washington, 1926
Loyal National League of Louisiana. *Minutes of the Loyal National League of Louisiana. New Orleans*: H.P. Lathrop, 1863

Memoria de la secretaría de Estado y del Despacho de Fomento, Colonización, Industria y Comercio de la República Mexicana

New Orleans Police Department Arrest Records, First Precinct, March 10, 1903, Louisiana Division, New Orleans Public Library

Official Journal of the Proceedings of the Convention for Framing a Constitution for the State of Louisiana (New Orleans, 1867–1868)

S. Congress, *Testimony Taken by the Joint Select Committee on the Condition of Affairs in the Late Insurrectionary States*, Vol. 2. North Carolina. Washington: Government Printing Office, 1872

Succession of Mary A. Deubler, Docket No. 107603, Civil District Court for the Parish of Orleans, Division C, City Archives, New Orleans Public Library

Territorial Papers of the United States, Volume 20: The Territory of Arkansas, 1825–1829. 28 vols. Washington: Government Printing Office, 1940

US Senate, *Mississippi in 1875. Report of the Select Committee to Inquire into the Mississippi Election of 1875*, 44th Cong., 1st Sess. Washington, DC: Government Print Office, 1876

William C. Binkley, ed. *Official Correspondence of the Texan Revolution (OCTR)*. 2 vols. New York: D. Appleton-Century, 1936

Interviews

Abbey "Chinee" Foster
Abraham Martin
Albert Glenny
Alice Zeno
Alice Zeno and George Lewis
Anthony Afful
August Laurent
Danny Barker
Edmond Hall
Edward "Kid" Ory
Emilie Barnes
George Lewis
Hypolite Charles
Jelly Roll Morton and Alan Lomax
Jim Robinson
Johnny St. Cyr
Louis James
Louis R. Tio
Natty Dominque
Noah Cook
Omar Simeon
Paul Barbarian
Peter Bocage
Rose Wynn Tio
Sonny Henry
Steve Brown
Stella Oliver
William Bébé Ridgley
Willie Parker
Zutty and Marge Singleton
Zutty Singleton

Newspapers and Periodicals

Afro-American (Baltimore)
Albany Times
Alexandria Gazette and Virginia Advertiser
The Caucasian (Louisiana)
Century Magazine
Charleston Daily Courier
Chicago Defender
Cleveland Morning Leader
Coda
Commercial Bulletin (New Orleans)
Courier-Journal (New Orleans)
Crusader (New Orleans)
The Daily Inter-Ocean (New Orleans)
Daily Telegraph (Macon, Georgia)

The Daily Press (Cincinnati, Ohio)
DeBow's Review
Down Beat
Edgefield (South Carolina) Advertiser
El Monitor Republicano (Mexico City)
El Progresso (Veracruz)
El Siglo XIXI (Mexico City)
Father Flanagan's Boys' Home Journal
Genius of Universal Emancipation
Harper's Weekly
Harper's New Monthly Magazine
The Helena Independent
Huntsville Gazette
Indianapolis Freeman
Indianapolis Journal
The Kansas City Sun
L'Opinion Nationale (Port-au-Prince)
La Chinaca (Mexico City)
La República (Chihuahua)
London News
The Longshoreman
Louisianan (New Orleans)
Louisiana Democrat
Louisiana Gazette
Louisiana Weekly
The Loyal Georgian
The Monitor (Omaha, Nebraska)
National Anti-Slavery Standard
New Orleans Bee
New Orleans Crescent
The New Orleans Daily Democrat
New Orleans Daily Delta
The New Orleans Democrat
New Orleans Item
New Orleans Picayune
New Orleans Republican
The New Orleans Tribune / La Tribune de la Nouvelle-Orléans
The New York Evening Post
New York Times
Omaha World-Herald
People's Vindicator (Natchitoches, Louisiana)
Pine and Palm
Plain Dealer (Cleveland, Ohio)
Planters' Banner (Franklin, Louisiana)
The Provincial Freedman
Raleigh Sentinel
Richmond Dispatch
Shreveport Progress (Louisiana)
Shreveport Times (Louisiana)
The Southwestern Christian Advocate (New Orleans)
St. Louis Post
Sugar Planter (West Baton Rouge, Louisiana)
Telegraph and Texas Register
Thibodaux Sentinel
Times-Democrat (New Orleans)
Weekly Pelican (New Orleans)
Wilmington Star

Secondary Sources

AAJ Staff. "A Fireside Chat with the World Saxophone Quartet." All About Jazz, September 29, 2020. https://allaboutjazz.com/a-fireside-chat-with-the-world-saxophone-quartet-world-saxophonequartet-by-aaj-staff.php?page=1.

Abbott, Lynn. "'Play That Barber Shop Chord': A Case for the African-American Origin of Barbershop Harmony." *American Music* 10, no. 3 (1992): 289–325.

Abbott, Lynn, and Jack Stewart. "The Iroquois Theater." *The Jazz Archivist* IX, no. 2 (December 1994): 2–20.

Abdy, E. S. *Journal of a Residence and Tour in the United States of North America: From April, 1833, to October, 1834.* 3 vols. London: John Murray, Albemarle Street, 1835.

Abrahams, Roger D., and John F. Szwed, eds. *After Africa: Extracts from British Travel Accounts and Journals of the Seventeenth, Eighteenth, and Nineteenth Centuries Concerning the Slaves, Their Manners, and Customs in the British West Indies*. New Haven, CT: Yale University Press, 1983.

Acosta, Leonardo. *Raíces del jazz latino: un siglo de jazz en Cuba*. La Habana: Editorial La Iguana Ciega, 2001.

Acevedo-Rodrigo, Ariadna. "Playing the Tune of Citizenship: Indian Brass Bands in the Sierra Norte de Puebla, Mexico, 1876–1911." *Bulletin of Latin American Research* 27, no. 2 (2008): 255–72.

Adams, Jessica. *Wounds of Returning: Race, Memory, and Property on the Postslavery Plantation*. Chapel Hill: University of North Carolina Press, 2012.

Adleson Gruber, Steven Lief. "Historia Social de Los Obreros Industriales de Tampico, 1906-1919." PhD diss., El Colegio de México, 1982.

Agawu, Kofi. *Representing African Music: Postcolonial Notes, Queries, Positions*. New York: Routledge, 2003.

Aguilar, Alfredo. "Uprooted: African Americans in Mexico; International Propaganda, Migration, and the Resistance against US Racial Hegemony." In *Human Rights, Race, and Resistance in Africa and the African Diaspora*, edited by Toyin Falola and Cacee Hoyer, 188–209. Abingdon: Routledge, 2016.

Ahmad, Eqbal. "How to Tell When the Rebels Have Won." In *The Selected Writings of Eqbal Ahmad*, edited by Carolle Bengelsdorf, Margaret Cerullo, and Yogesh Chandrani, 16–18. New York: Columbia University Press, 2004.

Ake, David. *Jazz Cultures*. Berkeley: University of California Press, 2002.

Akuno, Kali. "Build and Fight: The Program and Strategy of Cooperation Jackson." In *Jackson Rising Redux: Lessons on Building the Future in the Present*, edited by Kali Akuno and Matt Meyer, 23–45. Binghamton, NY: PM Press, 2023.

———. "It's Eco-Socialism or Death." Cooperation Jackson, February 16, 2020. https://cooperationjackson.org/blog/ecosocialismordeath.

Alamán, Lucas. *Historia De Méjico: Desde Los Primeros Movimientos Que Prepararon Su Independencia En El Año De 1808 Hasta La* Época *Presente*. 5 vols. Mexico, 1849.

Alcántara López, Alvaro. "La Mona de Juan Pascoe." *La Manta y La Raya* 13 (September 2022): 7–13.

———. "Negros y Afromestizos Del Puerto de Veracruz: Impresiones de Lo Popular Durante Los Siglos XVII y XVIII." In *La Habana/Veracruz, Veracruz/La Habana. Las Dos Orillas*, edited by Bernardo García Díaz and Sergio Guerra Vilaboy, 175–91. Veracruz: Instituto de Investigaciones Histórico-Sociales. Universidad Veracruzana, 2010.

Alcenat, Westenley. "'Children of Africa, Shall Be Haytians': Prince Saunders, Revolutionary Transnationalism, and the Foundations of Black Emigration." PhD diss., Columbia University, 2019.

Alén, Olavo. "Rhythm as Duration of Sounds in Tumba Francesa." *Ethnomusicology* 39, no. 1 (1995): 55–71.

Alén Rodríguez, Olavo. "La Oralidad y La Huella Franco – Haitiana En Cuba. Su Presencia En La Tumba Francesa, Obra Maestra de Patrimonio Oral e Inmaterial de La Humanidad." In *Para El Rescate de La Tradición Oral En América Latina y El Caribe*, 66–91. Vol. Anuario 13. UNESCO, 2005.

Allen, Rose Mary. "The Harvest Ceremony Seú as a Case Study of the Dynamics of Power in Post-Emancipation Curaçao (1863–1915)." *Caribbean Quarterly* 56, no. 3 (September 1, 2010): 13–29.

Allen, William Francis, Charles Pickard Ware, and Lucy McKim Garrison. *Slave Songs of the United States*. New York: Simpson, 1867.

Altvater, Elmar. "Ecological and Economic Modalities of Time and Space." *Capitalism Nature Socialism* 1, no. 3 (January 1, 1989): 59–70.

Ameringer, Charles D. *The Socialist Impulse: Latin America in the Twentieth Century*. Gainesville: University Press of Florida, 2009.

Ameringer, Oscar. *If You Don't Weaken: The Autobiography of Oscar Ameringer*. Whitefish, Montana: Kessinger Publishing, 1940.

Anderson, Paul Allen. "Ralph Ellison on Lyricism and Swing." *American Literary History* 17, no. 2 (2005): 280–306.

Anderson, Robert Ball. *From Slavery to Affluence: Memoirs of Robert Anderson, Exslave*. Hemingford: Hemingford Ledger, 1927.

Anderson, William J. *Life and Narrative of William J. Anderson*. Chicago, IL: Daily Tribune Book and Job Printing Office, 1852.

Anthony, Arthé A. "'Lost Boundaries': Racial Passing and Poverty in Segregated New Orleans." *Louisiana History: The Journal of the Louisiana Historical Association* 36, no. 3 (1995): 291–312.

———. "The Negro Creole Community in New Orleans, 1880–1920: An Oral History." PhD diss., University of California, Irvine, 1978.

Anzaldúa, Gloria. *Borderlands/La Frontera: The New Mestiza*. San Francisco: Spinsters/Aunt Lute, 1987.

Aparicio, Frances R. "Ethnifying Rhythms, Feminizing Cultures." In *Music and the Racial Imagination*, edited by Ronald M. Radano and Philip V. Bohlman, 95–112. Chicago: University of Chicago Press, 2000.

Appadurai, Arjun. *Modernity at Large: Cultural Dimensions of Globalization*. Minneapolis: University of Minnesota Press, 1996.

Arce, B. Christine. *Mexico's Nobodies: The Cultural Legacy of the Soldadera and Afro-Mexican Women*. Albany: SUNY Press, 2016.

Ardouin, Beaubrun. Études Sur *l'Histoire d'Haïti*. 11 vols. Paris: Dezobry, Madeleien et Ce, 1860.

Armstrong, Louis. *Satchmo: My Life in New Orleans*. New York: Da Capo Press, 1986.

Arnesen, Eric. *Waterfront Workers of New Orleans: Race, Class, and Politics, 1863–1923*. New York: Oxford University Press, 1991.

Arondekar, Anjali. *For the Record: On Sexuality and the Colonial Archive in India*. Durham, NC: Duke University Press, 2009.

Arthur, Charles, and Michael Dash, eds. "Proverbial Wisdom." In *Libète: A Haiti Anthology*, 287–88. Princeton, NJ: Markus Wiener Publishers, 2009.

Attali, Jacques. *Noise: The Political Economy of Music*. Translated by Brian Massumi. Manchester: Manchester University Press, 1985.

Austerlitz, Paul. *Jazz Consciousness: Music, Race, and Humanity*. Middletown, CT: Wesleyan University Press, 2005.

Austin, Allan D. *African Muslims in Antebellum America: Transatlantic Stories and Spiritual Struggles*. New York: Routledge, 1997.

Averill, Gage. *A Day for the Hunter, a Day for the Prey: Popular Music and Power in Haiti*. Chicago: University of Chicago Press, 1997.

———. *Four Parts, No Waiting: A Social History of American Barbershop Quartet*. Oxford University Press, 2003.

Avery, Byllye. "A Question of Survival/A Conspiracy of Silence: Abortion and Black Women's

Health." In *From Abortion to Reproductive Freedom: Trans-Forming a Movement*, edited by Marlene G. Fried, 75–80. Boston, MA: South End, 1990.

Ayers, Edward L. *The Promise of the New South: Life after Reconstruction*. New York: Oxford University Press, 1992.

Babb, Winston Chandler. "French Refugees from Saint Domingue to the Southern United States: 1791–1810." PhD diss., University of Virginia, 1954.

Bacardí y Moreau, Emilio. *Crónicas de Santiago de Cuba*. Madrid: Graf. Breogan, 1909.

Baeza, Roberto Rivelino García. "Lírica Popular Improvisada, Estudio de Dos Casos: El Son Huasteco y El Blues." PhD diss., El Colegio de San Luis, A.C., 2016.

Bahney, Robert. "Generals and Negroes: Education of Negroes by the Union Army, 1861–1865." PhD diss., University of Michigan, 1965.

Bailey, Derek. *Improvisation: Its Nature and Practice in Music*. New York: Da Capo Press, 1993.

Bailey, Richard. *Neither Carpetbaggers nor Scalawags: Black Officeholders During the Reconstruction of Alabama, 1867–1878*. Montgomery, AL: NewSouth Books, 1991.

Baker, Jessica Swanston. "Archipelagic Listening." In *Contemporary Archipelagic Thinking: Towards New Comparative Methodologies and Disciplinary Formations*, edited by Yolanda Martínez-San Miguel and Michelle Stephens, 383–402. Lanham, MD: Rowman & Littlefield Publishers, 2020.

Balderach, Amy S. "A Different Kind of Reservation: Waco's Red-Light District Revisited, 1880–1920." Master's thesis, Baylor University, 2005.

Baldwin, Brooke. "The Cakewalk: A Study in Stereotype and Reality." *Journal of Social History* 15, no. 2 (1981): 205–18.

Balliett, Whitney. *Jelly Roll, Jabbo, and Fats: Nineteen Portraits in Jazz*. New York: Oxford University Press, 1983.

Bancroft, Frederic. *Slave Trading in the Old South*. Colombia: University of South Carolina Press, 1931.

Baptist, Edward E. "'Cuffy,' 'Fancy Maids,' and 'One-Eyed Men': Rape, Commodification, and the Domestic Slave Trade in the United States." *The American Historical Review* 106, no. 5 (December 1, 2001): 1619–50.

———. *The Half Has Never Been Told: Slavery and the Making of American Capitalism*. New York: Hachette Books, 2016.

Baraka, Amiri. "Black Art." In *Transbluesency: The Selected Poems of Amiri Baraka/LeRoi Jones*, edited by Paul Vangelisti, 142–43. New York: Marsilio Publishers, 1995.

———. *Black Music*. New York: Quill, 1967.

———. *Blues People: Negro Music in White America*. Harper Collins, 1963. Initially published under the name of LeRoi Jones.

———. *Home: Social Essays*. New York: William Morrow, 1966.

Barbagallo, Camille, Nicholas Beuret, and David Harvie. *Commoning with George Caffentzis and Silvia Federici*. London: Pluto Books, 2019.

Bardes, John K. "The Notorious Bras Coupé: A Slave Rebellion Replayed in Memory, History, and Anxiety." *American Quarterly* 72, no. 1 (2020): 1–23.

———. "Redefining Vagrancy: Policing Freedom and Disorder in Reconstruction New Orleans, 1862–1868." *Journal of Southern History* 84, no. 1 (February 7, 2018): 69–112.

Barker, Danny. *Buddy Bolden and the Last Days of Storyville*. Edited by Alyn Shipton. New York: Continuum, 1998.

———. *A Life in Jazz*. Edited by Alyn Shipton. New York: Springer, 2016.

Barkley Brown, Elsa. "Negotiating and Transforming the Public Sphere: African American Political Life in the Transition from Slavery to Freedom." *Public Culture* 7, no. 1 (Fall 1994): 107–46.

Barnes, Bruce Sunpie, and Rachel Breunlin. *Le Kèr Creole: Creole Compositions and Stories from Louisiana*. New Orleans: University of New Orleans Press, 2019.

Barr, Ruth B., and Modeste Hargis. "The Voluntary Exile of Free Negroes of Pensacola." *Florida Historical Quarterly* 17, no. 1 (1938): 3–14.

Barson, Ben. "The Poetic Justice of Fred Ho: Tracing the Influence of the Black Arts Movement Poets." In *Black Power Afterlives: The Enduring Significance of the Black Panther Party*, edited by Diane C. Fujino and Matef Harmachis, 183–204. Chicago: Haymarket Books, 2020.

Barson, Benjamin. "Answering the Call: Antiphony Between the Music and Social Movements." New Music USA, September 26, 2019. https://newmusicusa.org/nmbx/answering-the-call-antiphony-between-the-music-and-social-movements/

———. "El Viento Sónico Común: Movimiento Musical y Secuelas de La Revolución Haitiana En El Jazz de Haití y Nueva Orleans." *Revista Interdisciplinar Da Mobilidade Humana* 31, no. 67 (April 2023): 1–25.

———. "From Plantation Percussion to The Sound of Solidarity: Afro-Asian Echoes in the Drum Set." In *The Cargo Rebellion: Those Who Chose Freedom*, edited by Jason Oliver Chang, Alexis Dudden, and Kim Inthavong, 47–61. New York: PM Press, 2022.

———. "'I've Got the Haitian Blues': Mamie Desdunes and the Gendered Inflections of the Common Wind." In *The Routledge Companion of Jazz and Gender*, edited by James Reddan, Monika Herzig, and Michael Kahr, 15–31. Abingdon: Routledge, 2022.

———. "La Frontera Sónica: Explorando La Historia de Las Conexiones Mexicanas y Afroamericanas En La Práctica Del Jazz." In *Paisaje Sonoro de Las Fronteras: Ruidos, Sonidos y Musicalidades*, edited by Miguel Olmos Aguilera, 1–23. Tijuana: COLEF, 2023.

———. "Sounding Affective Consensus: New Orleans' Black Longshoremen Union and the Strike as Musical Affect, 1872–1907." *Journal of Extreme Anthropology* 7 no. 1 (2023): 112-142.

———. "'You Can Blow Your Brains Out and You Ain't Getting Nowhere': Jazz, Collectivism, and the Struggle for Ecological Commons in Louisiana's Sugar Parishes." In *The Routledge Handbook on Ecosocialism*, edited by Leigh Brownhill, Salvatore Engel-Di Mauro, Terran Giacomini, Michael Löwy, and Terisa E. Turner, 201–13. Abingdon: Routledge, 2021.

Bartlett, Irving H. *Wendell and Ann Phillips: The Community of Reform, 1840-1880*. New York: Norton, 1979.

Bass, Robert Duncan. "Negro Songs from the Pedee Country." *Journal of American Folklore* 44, no. 174 (December 1931): 418–36.

Bassi, Ernesto. *An Aqueous Territory: Sailor Geographies and New Granada's Transimperial Greater Caribbean World*. Durham, NC: Duke University Press, 2016.

Battle, Karen. "New Orleans' Creoles of Color: Shattered Dreams and Broken Promises." *Loyola University Student Historical Journal* 23 (1991).

Baucom, Ian. *Specters of the Atlantic: Finance Capital, Slavery, and the Philosophy of History*. Durham, NC: Duke University Press, 2005.

Baumgartner, Alice L. *South to Freedom: Runaway Slaves to Mexico and the Road to the Civil War*. New York: Basic Books, 2020.

Baz, Gustavo. *Vida de Benito Juárez*. México: Casa Editorial y Agencia de Publicaciones de Enrique de Capdevielle, 1874.

Beard, Rick. "Louisiana's Stillborn Constitution." *New York Times*, September 11, 2014, sec. Opinion. https://opinionator.blogs.nytimes.com/2014/09/11/louisianas-stillborn-constitution/.

Bechet, Sidney. *Treat It Gentle.* New York: Da Capo Press, 1960.

Beckles, Hilary. "Caribbean Anti-Slavery: The Self Liberation Ethos of Enslaved Blacks." *Journal of Caribbean History* 22, no. 1/2 (1988): 1–19.

Beezley, William. *Mexicans in Revolution, 1910–1946: An Introduction.* Lincoln: University of Nebraska Press, 2009.

Behrend, Justin. *Reconstructing Democracy: Grassroots Black Politics in the Deep South after the Civil War.* Athens: University of Georgia Press, 2015.

Bell, Caryn Cossé. "The Common Wind's Creole Visionary: Dr. Louis Charles Roudanez." *South Atlantic Review* 73, no. 2 (2008): 10–25.

———. "Haitian Immigration to Louisiana in the Eighteenth and Nineteenth Centuries." In *In Motion: The African-American Migration Experience*, edited by the Schomburg Center for Research in Black Culture. New York Public Library Digital Gallery, 2005. http://inmotionaame.org/print.cfm?migration=5.

———. "Pierre-Aristide Desdunes (1844–1918), Creole Poet, Civil War Soldier, and Civil Rights Activist: The Common Wind's Legacy." *Louisiana History: The Journal of the Louisiana Historical Association* 55, no. 3 (2014): 282–312.

———. "'Rappelez-Vous Concitoyens': The Poetry of Pierre-Aristide Desdunes, Civil War Soldier, Romantic Literary Artist, and Civil Rights Activist." In *Rappelez-Vous Concitoyens: La Poésie de Pierre-Aristide Desdunes*, by Pierre-Aristide Desdunes, 1–19. Shreveport, LA: Les Éditions Tintamarre, Centenary College of Louisiana, 2011.

———. *Revolution, Romanticism, and the Afro-Creole Protest Tradition in Louisiana, 1718–1868.* Baton Rouge: Louisiana State University Press, 1997.

———. "'Une Chimère': The Freedmen's Bureau in Creole New Orleans." In *The Freedmen's Bureau and Reconstruction*, edited by Paul A. Cimbala and Randall M. Miller, 140–60. New York: Fordham University Press, 1999.

Bellegarde-Smith, Patrick. *In the Shadow of Powers: Dantes Bellegarde in Haitian Social Thought.* Nashville: Vanderbilt University Press, 2019.

Beltrán, Gonzalo Aguirre. *La población negra de México: estudio etnohistórico.* Fondo de Cultura Económica, 1972.

Belz, Herman. "Law, Politics, and Race in the Struggle for Equal Pay during the Civil War." *Civil War History* 22 (September 1976): 197–213.

———. "Origins of Negro Suffrage During the Civil War." *Southern Studies* 17 (Summer 1978): 115–30.

Benjamin, Alan F. *Jews of the Dutch Caribbean: Exploring Ethnic Identity on Curacao.* London: Routledge, 2002.

Benjamin, Walter. "Paris, Capital of the 19th Century." In *Illuminations*, edited by Peter Demetz, translated by E. Jephcott, 146-58. New York: Harcourt, Brace and World, 1986.

Bennett, Lerone. *Black Power U.S.A.: The Human Side of Reconstruction, 1867–1877.* Chicago: Johnson Publishing Company, 1967.

Benot, Yves. *La Révolution Française et La Fin des Colonies 1789–1794.* Paris: La Découverte, 2007.

Bergreen, Laurence. *Louis Armstrong: An Extravagant Life.* New York: Crown Archetype Publishing, 2012.

Berlin, Ira, Barbara J. Fields, Joseph P. Reidy, and Leslie S. Rowland, eds. *Freedom's Soldiers: The Black Military Experience in the Civil War.* Cambridge: Cambridge University Press, 1998.

Berlin, Ira, Barbara J. Fields, Leslie S. Rowland, and Joseph P. Reidy. "Fighting on Two Fronts: The Struggle for Equal Pay." *Prologue* 14 (Fall 1982): 129–39.

Berlin, Ira, Barbara J. Fields, Steven F. Miller, Joseph P. Reidy, and Leslie S. Rowland. *Slaves No More: Three Essays on Emancipation and the Civil War*. Cambridge: Cambridge University Press, 1992.

Berlin, Ira, Thavolia Glymph, Steven F. Miller, Joseph P. Reidy, and Julie Saville, eds. *Freedom: A Documentary History of Emancipation, 1861-1867: The Wartime Genesis of Free Labor: The Lower South*. Vol. 2. 1. New York: Cambridge University Press, 1990.

Berquin-Duvallon, Pierre-Louis. *Travels in Louisiana and the Floridas, in the Year, 1802: Giving a Correct Picture of Those Countries*. Vol. I. New York: Riley & Company, 1806.

Berry, Jason. *City of a Million Dreams: A History of New Orleans at Year 300*. Chapel Hill: University of North Carolina Press, 2018.

Bestor, Arthur E. "The Evolution of the Socialist Vocabulary." *Journal of the History of Ideas* 9, no. 3 (1948): 259–302.

Bethel, Elizabeth Rauh. *The Roots of African-American Identity: Memory and History in Antebellum Free Communities*. New York: Palgrave Macmillan, 1999.

Bethell, Tom. *George Lewis: A Jazzman from New Orleans*. Berkeley: University of California Press, 1977.

Bigard, Barney. *With Louis and the Duke: The Autobiography of a Jazz Clarinetist*. Edited by Barry Martyn. New York: Oxford University Press, 1987.

Bird, Lawrence. "Aucune Usine Au Monde: Dreaming Work in the Exposition Universelle, Paris 1878." In *Meet Me at the Fair: A World's Fair Reader*, edited by Laura Hollengreen, Celia Pearce, Rebecca Rouse, and Bobby Schweizer, 299–310. Pittsburgh, PA: Carnegie Mellon University ETC Press, 2014.

Bisland, Elizabeth. *The Life and Letters of Lafcadio Hearn*. London: Archibald Constable, 1906.

Bissett, Jim. *Agrarian Socialism in America: Marx, Jefferson, and Jesus in the Oklahoma Countryside, 1904-1920*. Norman: University of Oklahoma Press, 2002.

Black, William R. "How Watermelons Became Black: Emancipation and the Origins of a Racist Trope." *Journal of the Civil War Era* 8, no. 1 (2018): 64–86.

Blackbird, Leila. "Entwined Threads of Red and Black: The Hidden History of Indigenous Enslavement in Louisiana, 1699-1824." PhD diss, University of New Orleans, 2018.

Blackburn, Robin. "Haiti, Slavery, and the Age of the Democratic Revolution." *The William and Mary Quarterly* 63, no. 4 (2006): 643–74.

Blanc, Eric. "Red Oklahoma." Jacobin, April 13, 2018. https://jacobinmag.com/2018/04/teachers-strikes-oklahoma-socialism-sanders-unions.

Blancké, W. Wendell. *Juárez of Mexico*. New York: Praeger, 1971.

Blanchard, Terence. "Opinion: Black Protest Is Music. Learning the Melody Isn't Enough." NPR.org, June 18, 2020. https://npr.org/2020/06/18/879663904/opinion-terence-blanchard-black-protest-marvin-gaye-melody.

Blassingame, John W. *Black New Orleans 1860–1880*. Chicago: University of Chicago Press, 1973.

———. *The Slave Community: Plantation Life in the Antebellum South*. New York: Oxford University Press, 1979.

Blier, Suzanne Preston. "Vodun: West African Roots of Vodou." In *Sacred Arts of Haitian Voudou*, edited by Donald J. Cosentino, 61–87. Los Angeles: UCLA Fowler Museum of Cultural History, 1995.

Blight, David W. *A Slave No More: Two Men Who Escaped to Freedom, Including Their Own Narratives of Emancipation*. New York: Mariner Books, 2009.

———. *Race and Reunion: The Civil War in American Memory*. Cambridge, MA: Harvard University Press, 2001.

Bobadilla González, Leticia. *La Revolución cubana en la diplomacia, prensa y clubes de México, 1895–1898: tres visiones de una revolución finisecular*. Mexico: Secretaría de Relaciones Exteriores, 2001.

Bobulescu, Roxana. "The Original Time Approach of Georgescu-Roegen." *Œconomia. History, Methodology, Philosophy*, no. 7–1 (March 1, 2017): 87–109.

Bond, James Edward. *No Easy Walk to Freedom: Reconstruction and the Ratification of the Fourteenth Amendment*. Westport, CT: Greenwood Publishing Group, 1997.

Boornazian, Josiah. "Teaching Jazz History with 'Jelly Roll' Morton, 'Inventor of Jazz,' as a Focal Point for Jazz Authenticity Discourse." *Jazz Education in Research and Practice* 1, no. 1 (2020): 118–34.

Botkin, B. A. "Self-Portraiture and Social Criticism in Negro Folk-Song." In *The New Negro: Readings on Race, Representation, and African American Culture, 1892–1938*, edited by Henry Louis Gates Jr. and Gene Andrew Jarrett, 885–900. Princeton, NJ: Princeton University Press, 2007.

Bouchereau, Louis, and Alcée Bouchereau. *Statement of the Sugar and Rice Crops Made in Louisiana in 1868–69*. New Orleans: Pelican Book and Job Printing Office, 1869.

Boys Town. "Father Edward J. Flanagan," September 19, 2020. https://boystown.org/about/father-flanagan/Pages/default.aspx.

Brackner, Joey. "The Excelsior Marching Band, Mobile." Alabama State Council on the Arts, 2013. https://arts.alabama.gov/Traditional_Culture/heritageaward/excelsior.aspx.

Bradbury, David. *Armstrong*. London: Haus Publishing, 2003.

Bradley, Cisco. "Black Geographies, Networks, and Mobilities." Forthcoming.

———. *Universal Tonality: The Life and Music of William Parker*. Durham, NC: Duke University Press, 2021.

———. *The Williamsburg Avant-Garde: Experimental Music and Sound on the Brooklyn Waterfront*. Durham, NC: Duke University Press, 2023.

Brady, Patricia. "Black Artists in Antebellum New Orleans." *Louisiana History: The Journal of the Louisiana Historical Association* 32, no. 1 (1991): 5–28.

Brasseaux, Ryan A. *Cajun Breakdown: The Emergence of an American-Made Music*. New York: Oxford University Press, 2009.

Brathwaite, Edward Kamau. "Jazz Music." *Sargasso* 1, no. 1 (1984): 1–7.

Breaux, Richard M. "The New Negro Renaissance in Omaha and Lincoln, 1910–1940." In *The Harlem Renaissance in the American West: The New Negro's Western Experience*, edited by Cary D. Wintz and Bruce A. Glasrud, 121–39. Abingdon: Routledge, 2011.

Brennan, Timothy. *Secular Devotion: Afro-Latin Music and Imperial Jazz*. New York: Verso, 2008.

Breunlin, Rachel, and Ronald W. Lewis. *The House of Dance & Feathers: A Museum by Ronald W. Lewis*. New Orleans: University of New Orleans Press, 2009.

Breunlin, Rachel, ed. *Fire in the Hole: The Spirit Work of Fi Fi FI & The Mandingo Warriors*. New Orleans: University Press of New Orleans, 2018.

Brickhouse, Anna. "'L'Ouragan de Flammes' ('The Hurricane of Flames'): New Orleans and Transamerican Catastrophe, 1866/2005." *American Quarterly* 59, no. 4 (2007): 1097–1127.

Bristol, Douglas W., Jr. *Knights of the Razor: Black Barbers in Slavery and Freedom*. Baltimore: Johns Hopkins University Press, 2009.

Brock, Jerry. "Notes on New Orleans Brass Bands." *OffBeat Magazine*, July 1, 2001. http://www.offbeat.com/articles/notes-on-new-orleans-brass-bands/.

Brook, Daniel. *The Accident of Color: A Story of Race in Reconstruction.* New York: W. W. Norton, 2019.

Brothers, Thomas David. *Louis Armstrong's New Orleans.* New York: W. W. Norton, 2006.

Brown, Elsa Barkley. "Polyrhythms and Improvisation: Lessons for Women's History." *History Workshop*, no. 31 (1991): 85–90.

Brownhill, Leigh. *Land, Food, Freedom: Struggles for the Gendered Commons in Kenya, 1870 to 2007.* Trenton, NJ: Africa World Press, 2009.

Brownhill, Leigh, and Terisa E. Turner. "Ecofeminism at the Heart of Ecosocialism." *Capitalism Nature Socialism* 30, no. 1 (January 2, 2019): 1–10.

Bruce, Henry Clay. *The New Man: Twenty-Nine Years a Slave, Twenty-Nine Years a Free Man.* Lincoln: University of Nebraska Press, 1996.

Brundage, W. Fitzhugh. *Lynching in the New South: Georgia and Virginia, 1880–1930.* Urbana: University of Illinois Press, 1993.

Bryant, Jonathan M. *How Curious a Land: Conflict and Change in Greene County, Georgia, 1850–1885.* Chapel Hill: University of North Carolina Press Books, 2014.

Bryant, Rebecca A. "Shaking Things Up: Popularizing the Shimmy in America." *American Music* 20, no. 2 (2002): 168–87.

Buck-Morss, Susan. "Hegel and Haiti." *Critical Inquiry* 26, no. 4 (2000): 821–65.

Burian, Edward. *The Architecture and Cities of Northern Mexico from Independence to the Present.* Austin: University of Texas Press, 2015.

Burnard, Trevor. "Toiling in the Fields: Valuing Female Slaves in Jamaica, 1674–1788." In *Sexuality and Slavery: Reclaiming Intimate Histories in the Americas*, edited by Daina Ramey Berry and Leslie M. Harris, 33–48. Athens: University of Georgia Press, 2018.

Burnard, Trevor, and John Garrigus. *The Plantation Machine: Atlantic Capitalism in French Saint-Domingue and British Jamaica.* Philadelphia: University of Pennsylvania Press, 2016.

Burton, Vernon. "Race and Reconstruction: Edgefield County, South Carolina." *Journal of Social History* 12, no. 1 (October 1978): 31–56.

Bush, Barbara. *Slave Women in Caribbean Society, 1650–1838.* Bloomington: Indiana University Press, 1990.

Butchart, Ronald E. *Northern Schools, Southern Blacks, and Reconstruction: Freedmen's Education, 1862–1875.* Westport, CT: Praeger, 1980.

Butler, Judith. *Notes Toward a Performative Theory of Assembly.* Cambridge, MA: Harvard University Press, 2015.

Cable, George Washington. "Creole Slave Songs." *Century Illustrated Magazine* XXXI, no. 6 (April 1886): 807–28.

———. *Creoles and Cajuns: Stories of Old Louisiana.* Garden City, NY: Doubleday, 1959.

———. "The Dance in Place Congo." *Century Illustrated Magazine* XXXI, no. 4 (February 1886): 517–32.

Cagidemetrio, Alide. "'The Rest of the Story'; or, Multilingual American Literature." In *Multilingual America: Transnationalism, Ethnicity, and the Languages of American Literature*, edited by Werner Sollors, 17–28. New York: New York University Press, 1998.

Callahan, Mat. *Songs of Slavery and Emancipation.* Jackson: University Press of Mississippi, 2022.

Camp, Jordan T. "Black Radicalism, Marxism, and Collective Memory: An Interview with Robin D. G. Kelley." *American Quarterly* 65, no. 1 (2013): 215–30.

———. "Breaking the Thermometer: An Interview with Leyla McCalla." Conjuncture podcast, September 6, 2023. https://www.youtube.com/watch?v=zWitYcCmDDE.

Camp, Stephanie M. H. *Closer to Freedom: Enslaved Women and Everyday Resistance in the Plantation South*. Chapel Hill: University of North Carolina Press, 2005.

Campos, Rubén F. *El Folklore En Las Ciudades: Investigación Acerca De La Música Mexicana Para Bailar y Cantar*. México: Publicaciones La Secretaria De Educación Publica Talleres, 1930.

Canales, Isidro Vizcaya. *En los albores de la independencia: las Provincias Internas de Oriente durante la insurrección de don Miguel Hidalgo y Costilla, 1810–1811*. Mexico: Fondo Editorial de NL, 2005.

Carby, Hazel. "It Jus Be's Dat Way Sometime: The Sexual Politics of Women's Blues." In *The Jazz Cadence of American Culture*, edited by Robert O'Meally, 470–83. New York: Columbia University Press, 1998.

Cardoso, Lawrence A. *Mexican Emigration to the United States, 1897–1931: Socio-Economic Patterns*. Tucson: University of Arizona Press, 1980.

Carl. "Duke Ellington Records 'Mood Indigo' 89 Years Ago Today." *The Daily Music Break* (blog), October 17, 2019. https://dailymusicbreak.com/2019/10/17/duke-ellington-records-mood-indigo-89-years-ago-today/.

Carney, Judith Ann. *Black Rice: The African Origins of Rice Cultivation in the Americas*. Cambridge, MA: Harvard University Press, 2002.

———. "Subsistence in the Plantationocene: Dooryard Gardens, Agrobiodiversity, and the Subaltern Economies of Slavery." *The Journal of Peasant Studies* 48, no. 5 (July 29, 2021): 1075–99.

Carney, Judith Ann, and Richard Nicholas Rosomoff. *In the Shadow of Slavery: Africa's Botanical Legacy in the Atlantic World*. Berkeley: University of California Press, 2009.

Carpenter, Kyle B. "Musing on the United States Consulate in Matamoros." The Future of the Past, March 27, 2018. https://blog.smu.edu/gradhist/2018/03/27/consuls/.

Carpentier, Alejo. "Music in Cuba." *Transition*, no. 81/82 (2000): 172–228.

———. *La música en cuba*. Mexico: Fondo de Cultura Económica, 1946.

Carr, James Revell. *Hawaiian Music in Motion: Mariners, Missionaries, and Minstrels*. Urbana: University of Illinois Press, 2014.

Carroll, Patrick J. *Blacks in Colonial Veracruz: Race, Ethnicity, and Regional Development*. Austin: University of Texas Press, 2010.

Carter, Clarence Edward. *The Territory of Orleans, 1803–1812*. New York: Ams Pr Incorporated, 1940.

Carter, María, and Calvin Lindsay Jr. "The Devil's Music: 1920s Jazz." PBS Culture Shock. Accessed March 30, 2023. https://pbs.org/wgbh/cultureshock/beyond/jazz.html.

Casanovas, Joan. *Bread or Bullets: Urban Labor and Spanish Colonialism in Cuba, 1850–1898*. Pittsburgh: University of Pittsburgh Press, 1998.

Casey, Matthew. *Empire's Guestworkers: Haitian Migrants in Cuba during the Age of US Occupation*. Cambridge, MA: Cambridge University Press, 2017.

Casid, Jill H. *Sowing Empire: Landscape and Colonization*. Minneapolis: University of Minnesota Press, 2005.

Casimir, Jean. "Haití y Sus Élites: El Interminable Diálogo de Sordos." *Foro Internacional* 194, no. XLVIII (2008): 807–41.

———. "Haiti's Need for a Great South." *Global South, The* 5, no. 1 (2011): 14–36.

———. *The Haitians: A Decolonial History*. Chapel Hill: University of North Carolina Press, 2020.

———. "On the Origins of the Counterplantation System." In *The Haiti Reader: History, Culture, Politics*, edited by Laurent Dubois, Kaiama L. Glover, Nadève Ménard, Millery Polyné, and Chantalle F. Verna. Durham, NC: Duke University Press, 2020.

———. "The Sovereign People of Haiti during the Eighteenth and Nineteenth Centuries." In *The Haitian Declaration of Independence: Creation, Context, and Legacy*, edited by Julia Gaffield, 181–200. Charlottesville: University of Virginia Press, 2016.

Castañeda, Jose. "La Música Que Llegó Del Mar: El Viaje de La Familia Tio y Los Inicios Del Jazz." Unpublished manuscript, 2020.

Césaire, Aimé. "Le Verbe Marronner / The Verb 'Marronner.'" In *Aimé Césaire: The Collected Poetry*, translated by Clayton Eshleman and Annette Smith, 368–71. Berkeley: University of California Press, 1983.

César, Filipa. "Meteorisations." *Third Text* 32, no. 2–3 (May 4, 2018): 254–72.

Céspedes, Carlos Manuel de. *El diario perdido*. La Habana: Editorial de Ciencias Sociales, 1992.

Chacón, Justin Akers. *Radicals in the Barrio: Magonistas, Socialists, Wobblies, and Communists in the Mexican-American Working Class*. Chicago: Haymarket Books, 2018.

Chamberlain, Charles. "Searching for 'The Gulf Coast Circuit': Mobility and Cultural Diffusion in the Age of Jim Crow, 1900–1930." *The Jazz Archivist* XIV (2000): 1–18.

Chambers, Glenn A. *From the Banana Zones to the Big Easy: West Indian and Central American Immigration to New Orleans, 1910–1940*. Baton Rouge: Louisiana State University Press, 2019.

Chapman, Dale. *The Jazz Bubble: Neoclassical Jazz in Neoliberal Culture*. Berkeley, CA: University of California Press, 2018.

Chapman, John Abney. *History of Edgefield County: From the Earliest Settlements to 1897*. Newberry, SC: E. H. Aull, 1897.

Charles Edwards O'Neill, S. J. "Fine Arts and Literature: Nineteenth Century Louisiana Black Artists and Authors." In *Louisiana's Black Heritage*, edited by Robert Macdonald, John Kemp, and Edward Haas, 63–84. Louisiana State Museum, 1979.

Charters, Samuel B. *Jazz: New Orleans, 1885–1957*. Belleville, NJ: Walter C. Allen, 1958.

Chávez, Alex E. *Sounds of Crossing: Music, Migration, and the Aural Poetics of Huapango Arribeño*. Durham, NC: Duke University Press, 2017.

Chávez-Hita, Adriana Naveda. "El Nuevo Orden Constitucional y El Fin de La Abolición de La Esclavitud En Córdoba, Veracruz, 1810–1825." In *De La Libertad y La Abolición : Africanos y Afrodescendientes en Iberoamérica*, edited by Juan Manuel de la Serna, 195–217. Africanías. México: Centro de estudios mexicanos y centroamericanos, 2013.

Cheung, Floyd D. "Les Cenelles and Quadroon Balls: 'Hidden Transcripts' of Resistance and Domination in New Orleans, 1803–1845." *The Southern Literary Journal* 29, no. 2 (1997): 5–16.

Chilton, John. *Sidney Bechet: The Wizard of Jazz*. New York: Da Capo Press, 1996.

Chodos, Asher Tobin. "The Blues Scale: Historical and Epistemological Considerations." *Jazz Perspectives* 11, no. 2 (2018): 139–71.

Christian, Marcus B. "Oscar J. Dunn, Charles E. Nash, P. B. S. Pinchback, James Lewis." *Negro History Bulletin* 5, no. 6 (March 1, 1942): 137–39.

Clark, Brett, Daniel Auerbach, and Karen Xuan Zhang. "The Du Bois Nexus: Intersectionality, Political Economy, and Environmental Injustice in the Peruvian Guano Trade in the 1800s." In *Environmental Sociology: From Analysis to Action*, edited by Leslie King and Deborah McCarthy Auriffeille, 113–28. London: Rowman & Littlefield, 2019.

Clark, Colia. "Black Red and Green Revolutionary Eco-Music Tour, 2014." https://vimeo.com/91707067.

Clark, Emily. *The Strange History of the American Quadroon: Free Women of Color in the Revolutionary Atlantic World*. Chapel Hill: University of North Carolina Press, 2013.

Clark, Emily, and Hilary Jones. "Transatlantic Currents of Orientalism: New Orleans Quadroons and Saint-Louis Signares." In *New Orleans, Louisiana, and Saint-Louis, Senegal: Mirror Cities in the Atlantic World, 1659-2000s*, edited by Emily Clark, Cecile Vidal, and Ibrahima Thioub, 189–209. Baton Rouge: Louisiana State University Press, 2019.

Clark, Kathleen. "Celebrating Freedom: Emancipation Day Celebrations and African American Memory in the Early Reconstruction South." In *Where These Memories Grow: History, Memory, and Southern Identity*, edited by W. Fitzhugh Brundage, 107–32. Chapel Hill: University of North Carolina Press, 2015.

Clavin, Matthew J. "American Toussaints: Symbol, Subversion, and the Black Atlantic Tradition in the American Civil War." *Slavery & Abolition* 28, no. 1 (April 1, 2007): 87–113.

———. *Toussaint Louverture and the American Civil War: The Promise and Peril of a Second Haitian Revolution*. Philadelphia: University of Pennsylvania Press, 2012.

Cleaver, Molly Reid. "The Voices of Danny Barker: Reframing Contributions to African American History and Culture Through Storytelling." Master's thesis, Tulane University, 2018.

Clemens, Samuel L. *Life on the Mississippi*. New York: James R. Osgood, 1883.

Coca-Izaguirre, Manuel. "Análisis de Los Cantos En Tumba Francesa de Guantánamo." *Santiago* 130 (2013): 91–100.

Cockrill, Rachel. "Activists at Straight University." *Straight Up History* (blog), September 14, 2017. https://prcno.org/straight-university-plessy-ferguson/.

———. "Straight University's Ties to *Plessy v. Ferguson*." *Straight Up History* (blog), November 2, 2017. https://prcno.org/straight-university-plessy-ferguson/.

Coffin, Levi. *Reminiscences of Levi Coffin, the Reputed President of the Underground Railroad*. Cincinnati: Western Tract Society, 1876.

Cohen, Theodore W. *Finding Afro-Mexico: Race and Nation after the Revolution*. Afro-Latin America. Cambridge: Cambridge University Press, 2020.

Cole, Shawn. "Capitalism and Freedom: Manumissions and the Slave Market in Louisiana, 1725–1820." *The Journal of Economic History* 65, no. 4 (2005): 1008–27.

Coleman, Edward Maceo, ed. *Creole Voices*. Washington, DC: Associated Publishers, 1945.

Collier, James Lincoln. *Jazz: The American Theme Song*. New York: Oxford University Press, 1995.

Collins, Lee, and Mary Collins. *Oh, Didn't He Ramble: The Life Story of Lee Collins as Told to Mary Collins*, edited by Frank Gillis and John W. Miner. Urbana: University of Illinois Press, 1974.

Collins, R. *New Orleans Jazz: A Revised History*. New York: Vantage Press, 1996.

Comte de Vaublanc. *Souvenirs Par Le Comte de Vaublanc Ancien Ministre de l'intérieur*. Paris: F. Ponce Lebas, 1838.

Cone, James H. *The Spirituals and the Blues: An Interpretation*. Maryknoll: Orbis Books, 1992.

Connolly, Brian, and Marisa Fuentes. "Introduction: From Archives of Slavery to Liberated Futures?" *History of the Present* 6, no. 2 (2016): 105–16.

Connor, William P. "Reconstruction Rebels: The New Orleans Tribune in Post-War Louisiana." *Louisiana History: The Journal of the Louisiana Historical Association* 21, no. 2 (1980): 159–81.

Conrad, Sebastian. "Enlightenment in Global History: A Historiographical Critique." *The American Historical Review* 117, no. 4 (October 1, 2012): 999–1027.

Coolen, Michael Theodore. "The Fodet: A Senegambian Origin for the Blues?" *The Black Perspective in Music* 10, no. 1 (1982): 69–84.

Cornelius, Steven. *Music of the Civil War Era*. Westport, CT: Greenwood Press, 2004.

Cornell, Sarah E. "Citizens of Nowhere: Fugitive Slaves and Free African Americans in Mexico, 1833–1857." *Journal of American History* 100, no. 2 (September 1, 2013): 351–74.

Coronado, Raúl. *A World Not to Come: A History of Latino Writing and Print Culture*. Cambridge, MA: Harvard University Press, 2013.

Cortázar, Julio. *Hopscotch*. Translated by Gregory Rabassa. New York: Pantheon, 1987.

Cox, David G. "'Half Bacchanalian, Half Devout': White Intellectuals, Black Folk Culture, and the 'Negro Problem.'" *American Nineteenth Century History* 16, no. 3 (September 2015): 241–67.

Crawley, Ashon T. *Blackpentecostal Breath: The Aesthetics of Possibility*. New York: Fordham University Press, 2016.

Cresswell, Tim. "'You Cannot Shake That Shimmie Here': Producing Mobility on the Dance Floor." *Cultural Geographies* 12, no. 1 (2006): 55–77.

Cresswell, Timothy. *On the Move: Mobility in the Modern Western World*. New York: Routledge, 2006.

Criswell, Robert. *"Uncle Tom's Cabin" Contrasted with Buckingham Hall, the Planter's Home: Or, A Fair View of Both Sides of the Slavery Question*. New York: AMS Press, 1852.

Cruz, Filiberta Gómez. "La población afrodescendiente de la región de Tamiahua: la pesca y la resistencia a tributar a finales del siglo XVIII." *Ulúa. Revista de Historia, Sociedad y Cultura*, no. 19 (2012): 147–64.

Cruz Ríos, Laura. "Testimonios de Una Misma Expresión Cultural Cubana: La Tumba Francesa." In *Para El Rescate de La Tradición Oral En América Latina y El Caribe*, Anuario 13:73–77. UNESCO, 2005.

Cuney Hare, Maud. *The Musical Observer* XIX, no. 9–10 (October 1920): 17.

———. *Negro Musicians and Their Music*. New York: G. K. Hall & Co, 1996.

Curtis, Edward E. *Muslim Americans in the Military: Centuries of Service*. Bloomington: Indiana University Press, 2016.

Dabovic, Safet. "Out of Place: The Travels of Nicholas Said." *Criticism* 54, no. 1 (Winter 2012): 59–83.

Daggett, Melissa. *Spiritualism in Nineteenth-Century New Orleans: The Life and Times of Henry Louis Rey*. Jackson: University Press of Mississippi, 2016.

Dahl, Linda. *Morning Glory: A Biography of Mary Lou Williams*. Berkeley: University of California Press, 1999.

Dalleo, Raphael. *American Imperialism's Undead: The Occupation of Haiti and the Rise of Caribbean Anticolonialism*. Charlottesville: University of Virginia Press, 2016.

Daniel, Evan Matthew. "Rolling for the Revolution: A Transnational History of Cuban Cigar Makers in Havana, Florida, and New York City, 1853–1895." PhD diss., The New School, 2010.

———. *Caribbean and Atlantic Diaspora Dance: Igniting Citizenship*. Bloomington, IN: University of Illinois Press, 2011.

Daniel, Yvonne. *Dancing Wisdom: Embodied Knowledge in Haitian Vodou, Cuban Yoruba, and Bahian Candomblé*. Urbana: University of Illinois Press, 2005.

Daniels, Douglas Henry. "Vodun and Jazz: 'Jelly Roll' Morton and Lester 'Pres' Young—Substance and Shadow." *Journal of Haitian Studies* 9, no. 1 (2003): 110–23.

Danticat, Edwidge. *After the Dance: A Walk Through Carnival in Jacmel, Haiti*. New York: Knopf Doubleday Publishing Group, 2015.

Darensbourg, Joe. *Telling It Like It Is*. Edited by Peter Vacher. London: Macmillan Press, 1987.

Daut, Marlene L. "'Sons of White Fathers': Mulatto Vengeance and the Haitian Revolution in Victor Séjour's 'The Mulatto.'" *Nineteenth-Century Literature* 65, no. 1 (2010): 1–37.

Daudin, Guillaume. *Commerce et prospérité: La France au XVIIIe siècle—2e* édition. Paris: Presses de l'Université Paris-Sorbonne, 2005.

Davis, Angela Y. *Blues Legacies and Black Feminism: Gertrude "Ma" Rainey, Bessie Smith, and Billie Holiday.* New York: Pantheon Books, 1998.

Davis, Thomas. "More than Segregation, Racial Identity: The Neglected Question in Plessy V. Ferguson." *Washington and Lee Journal of Civil Rights and Social Justice* 10, no. 1 (April 1, 2004): 1–41.

Davis, Thulani. *The Emancipation Circuit: Black Activism Forging a Culture of Freedom.* Durham, NC: Duke University Press, 2022.

Davison, Madeleine. "Mother of Deceased Duquesne Student Continues Hunger Strike for Campus Police Reform." National Catholic Reporter, September 4, 2020. https://ncronline.org/news/mother-deceased-duquesne-student-continues-hunger-strike-campus-police-reform.

Dawdy, Shannon Lee. *Building the Devil's Empire: French Colonial New Orleans.* Chicago: University of Chicago Press, 2008.

———. "La Catrina: The Mexican Specter of New Orleans." In *Remaking New Orleans: Beyond Exceptionalism and Authenticity*, edited by Matt Sakakeeny and Thomas Jessen Adams, 35–54. Durham, NC: Duke University Press, 2019.

Dawson, Kevin. "Enslaved Ship Pilots in the Age of Revolutions: Challenging Notions of Race and Slavery between the Boundaries of Land and Sea." *Journal of Social History* 47, no. 1 (2013): 71–100.

Debord, Guy. *The Society of the Spectacle.* Translated by David Nichols. New York: Zone Books, 1967.

Delany, Martin Robison. *The Condition, Elevation, Emigration, and Destiny of the Colored People of the United States.* Philadelphia: Humanities Press, 1852.

DeLoughrey, Elizabeth M. "Provision Grounds and Cultural Roots: Towards Ontological Sovereignty." In *The Caribbean Woman Writer as Scholar: Creating, Imagining, Theorizing*, edited by Keshia N. Abraham, 205–24. Pompano Beach: Caribbean Studies Press, 2008.

Denbow, James. "Heart and Soul: Glimpses of Ideology and Cosmology in the Iconography of Tombstones from the Loango Coast of Central Africa." *The Journal of American Folklore* 112, no. 445 (July 1999): 407–8.

Denning, Michael. *Noise Uprising: The Audiopolitics of a World Musical Revolution.* New York: Verso Books, 2015.

Derbez, Alain. *El jazz en México: Datos para esta historia.* México: Fondo de Cultura Económica, 2014.

DeSantis, John. *The Thibodaux Massacre: Racial Violence and the 1887 Sugar Cane Labor Strike.* Mount Pleasant, SC: Arcadia Publishing, 2016.

Descourtilz, Michel-Etienne. *Voyages d'un Naturaliste, et Ses Observations Faites Sur Les Trois Règnes de La Nature, Dans Plusieurs Ports de Mer Français, En Espagne, Au Continent de l'Amérique Septentrionale, à Saint-Yago de Cuba, et à Saint-Domingue, Où l'auteur Devenu Le Prisonnier de 40,000 Noirs Révoltés, et Par Suite Mis En Liberté Par Une Colonne de l'armée Française, Donne Des Détails Circonstanciés Sur l'expédition Du Général Leclerc.* 3 vols. Paris: Dufort, 1809.

Desdunes, Dan. "'Happy Feeling Rag' Sheet Music." History Harvest, March 30, 2023. https://historyharvest.unl.edu/items/show/182.

Desdunes, Rodolphe Lucien. *A Few Words to Dr. DuBois 'With Malice Toward None.'* New Orleans, Self-published, 1907.

———. *Our People and Our History: Fifty Creole Portraits*. Baton Rouge: Louisiana State University Press, 2001.

Dessens, Nathalie. "St Domingue Refugees in New Orleans: Identity and Cultural Influences." In *Echoes of the Haitian Revolution, 1804–2004*, edited by Martin Munro and Elizabeth Walcott-Hackshaw, 87–115. Trinidad and Tobago: University of West Indies Press, 2008.

———. "The Saint-Domingue Refugees and the Preservation of Gallic Culture in Early American New Orleans." *French Colonial History* 8, no. 1 (2007): 53–69.

Dewulf, Jeroen. "From the Calendas to the Calenda: On the Afro-Iberian Substratum in Black Performance Culture in the Americas." *The Journal of American Folklore* 131, no. 519 (2018): 3–29.

Dial, Andrew J. "Consumer Choices in Martinique and Saint-Domingue: 1740–1780." Master's thesis, Miami University, 2012.

Díaz Frene, Jaddiel. "Generales mulatos y habaneras trasatlánticas. La independencia de Cuba desde una editorial mexicana, 1895–1898." *Historia mexicana* 72, no. 1 (September 2022): 89–129.

Díaz-Sánchez, Micaela, and Alexandro D. Hernández. "The Son Jarocho as Afro-Mexican Resistance Music." *Journal of Pan African Studies* 6, no. 1 (July 2013): 187–209.

Din, Gilbert C. "'Cimarrones' and the San Malo Band in Spanish Louisiana." *Louisiana History: The Journal of the Louisiana Historical Association* 21, no. 3 (1980): 237–62.

Diouf, Sylviane A. *Slavery's Exiles: The Story of the American Maroons*. New York: New York University Press, 2014.

Dixon, Chris. *African America and Haiti: Emigration and Black Nationalism in the Nineteenth Century*. Westport, CT: Greenwood Press, 2000.

Doheny, John. "The Spanish Tinge Hypothesis: Afro-Caribbean Characteristics in Early New Orleans Jazz Drumming." *The Jazz Archivist* XIX (2005): 8–15.

Doleac, Benjamin Grant. "'We Made It Through That Water': Rhythm, Dance, and Resistance in the New Orleans Second Line." PhD diss., University of California, 2018.

Dormon, James H. "The Persistent Specter: Slave Rebellion in Territorial Louisiana." *Louisiana History: The Journal of the Louisiana Historical Association* 18, no. 4 (1977): 389–404.

Douglass, Frederick. *The Life and Times of Frederick Douglass*. Hartford: Park Publishing Co., 1881.

———. "Make Your Sons Mechanics and Farmers." *Frederick Douglass' Paper*, March 18, 1853.

———. *My Bondage and My Freedom*. New York: Miller, Orton & Mulligan, 1855.

———. "Remarks at Dedication Ceremonies at the Haitian Pavilion," World's Columbian Exposition, Chicago, Frederick Douglass Papers at the Library of Congress, Manuscript Division, 1893.

Downing, Andrew Jackson. *A Treatise on the Theory and Practice of Landscape Gardening: Adapted to North America*. New York and London: Wiley and Putnam, 1841.

Downs, Gregory P. "The Mexicanization of American Politics: The United States' Transnational Path from Civil War to Stabilization." *The American Historical Review* 117, no. 2 (April 1, 2012): 387–409.

Drayton, Percival. *Naval Letters from Captain Percival Drayton, 1861–1865*. New York: Self-published, 1906.

Du Bois, W. E. B. *Black Reconstruction: An Essay Toward a History of the Part Which Black Folk Played in the Attempt to Reconstruct Democracy in America, 1860–1880*. 1st ed. New York: Harcourt, Brace and Co, 1935.

———. *The Gift of Black Folk: The Negroes in the Making of America*. Garden City, NY: Square One Publishers, 2009.

Dubois, Laurent. "Afro-Atlantic Music as Archive." In *Africa N'Ko: La Bibliothèque Coloniale En Débat*, edited by Jean-Bernard Ouedraogo, Mamadou Diawara, and Mamadou Diouf. Paris: Présence Africaine, 2022.

———. *The Banjo: America's Africa Instrument*. Cambridge, MA: Harvard University Press, 2016.

———. *A Colony of Citizens: Revolution and Slave Emancipation in the French Caribbean, 1787-1804*. Chapel Hill: University of North Carolina Press, 2004.

———. "Dessalines Toro d'Haïti." *The William and Mary Quarterly* 69, no. 3 (2012): 541–48.

———. "The Haitian Revolution and the Sale of Louisiana." *Southern Quarterly* 44, no. 3 (2007): 18–41.

Dubois, Laurent, and Richard Lee Turits. *Freedom Roots: Histories from the Caribbean*. Chapel Hill: University of North Carolina Press Books, 2019.

Dubois, Laurent, Kaiama L. Glover, Nadève Ménard, Millery Polyné, and Chantalle F. Verna, eds. *The Haiti Reader: History, Culture, Politics*. Durham, NC: Duke University Press, 2020.

Dulken, Danielle. "A Black Kingdom in Postbellum Appalachia." Scalawag, September 9, 2019. https://scalawagmagazine.org/2019/09/black-appalachia-kingdom/.

Dunham, Katharine. *Dances of Haiti*. Los Angeles: UCLA Center for Afro-American Studies, 1983.

Duplantier, Jean-Marc Allard. "Creole Louisiana's Haitian Exile(s)." *Southern Quarterly* 44, no. 3 (2007): 68–84.

Durán, Lucy. "POYI! Bamana Jeli Music, Mali and the Blues." *Journal of African Cultural Studies* 25, no. 2 (2013): 211–46.

Eddins, Crystal Nicole. "Runaways, Repertoires, and Repression: Marronnage and the Haitian Revolution, 1766–1791." *Journal of Haitian Studies* 25, no. 1 (2019): 4–38.

Edwards, Bill. "Mary Celina Mamie Desdunes Dugue." RagPiano.com, 2016. http://ragpiano.com/comps/desdunes.shtml.

Edwards, Brent Hayes. *The Practice of Diaspora: Literature, Translation, and the Rise of Black Internationalism*. Cambridge, MA: Harvard University Press, 2003.

Eiss, Paul K. "A Share in the Land: Freedpeople and the Government of Labour in Southern Louisiana, 1862–65." *Slavery & Abolition* 19, no. 1 (1998): 46–89.

Elisabeth, Léo. "Les Relations Entre Les Petites Antilles Françaises et Haïti, de La Politique Du Refoulement à La Résignation, 1804–1825." *Outre-Mers* 90, no. 340 (2003): 177–206.

Ellison, Mary. "African-American Music and Muskets in Civil War New Orleans." *Louisiana History* 35, no. 3 (1994): 285–319.

Ellison, Ralph. *Invisible Man*. New York: Vintage International, 1952.

———. *Shadow and Act*. New York: Knopf Doubleday, 1964.

Eltis, David, Philip Morgan, and David Richardson. "Agency and Diaspora in Atlantic History: Reassessing the African Contribution to Rice Cultivation in the Americas." *The American Historical Review* 112, no. 5 (December 1, 2007): 1329–58.

Embassy of Haiti. "Rodolphe Lucien Desdunes." *Embassy of the Republic of Haiti, Washington, D.C.* (blog). Accessed August 28, 2023. https://haiti.org/dt_team/rodolphe-lucien-desdunes/.

Emilio, Luis Fenollosa. *History of the Fifty-Fourth Regiment of Massachusetts Volunteer Infantry, 1863–1865*. Boston: Boston Book Company, 1894.

Epstein, Dena J. *Sinful Tunes and Spirituals: Black Folk Music to the Civil War*. Chicago: University of Illinois Press, 1977.

Esdaile, Charles J. *The Spanish Army in the Peninsular War*. Manchester: Manchester University Press, 1988.

Evan, David. "Black Fife and Drum Music in Mississippi." Folkstreams, 1972. http://folkstreams.net/film-context.php?id=86.

Evans, Freddi Williams. *Congo Square: African Roots in New Orleans*. Lafayette: University of Louisiana at Lafayette Press, 2011.

Evans, William McKee. *Ballots and Fence Rails: Reconstruction on the Lower Cape Fear*. Athens: University of Georgia Press, 2004.

Everett, Donald. "Free People of Color in New Orleans, 1830–1865." Master's thesis, Tulane University, 1952.

Fabre, Michel. "The New Orleans Press and French-Language Literature by Creoles of Color." In *Multilingual America: Transnationalism, Ethnicity, and the Languages of American Literature*, edited by Werner Sollors, 29–49. New York: NYU Press, 1998.

Fanon, Frantz. *The Wretched of the Earth*. New York: Grove Press, 1963.

Farred, Grant. *What's My Name?: Black Vernacular Intellectuals*. Minneapolis: University of Minnesota Press, 2003.

Faust, Drew Gilpin. "The Rhetoric and Ritual of Agriculture in Antebellum South Carolina." *The Journal of Southern History* 45, no. 4 (1979): 541–68.

Fellezs, Kevin. *Listen but Don't Ask Question: Hawaiian Slack Key Guitar across the TransPacific*. Durham, NC: Duke University Press, 2019.

Ferdinand, Malcom. *Decolonial Ecology: Thinking from the Caribbean World*. Translated by Anthony Paul Smith. Cambridge, MA: Polity Press, 2022.

Fernandez, Pablo Armando. *Otro Golpe De Dados*. Santo Domingo, Dominican Republic: Carieva Editorial, 2000.

Fernandez, Raul A. *From Afro-Cuban Rhythms to Latin Jazz*. Berkeley: University of California Press, 2006.

Fett, Sharla M. *Working Cures: Healing, Health, and Power on Southern Slave Plantations*. University of North Carolina Press, 2000.

Fick, Carolyn E. "African Presence in Colonial Louisiana: An Essay on the Continuity of African Culture." In *Louisiana's Black Heritage*, edited by Robert Macdonald, John Kemp, and Edward Haas, 3–31. Louisiana State Museum, 1979.

———. *The Making of Haiti: The Saint Domingue Revolution from Below*. Knoxville: University of Tennessee Press, 1990.

Fiehrer, Thomas Marc. "African Presence in Colonial Louisiana: An Essay on the Continuity of African Culture." In *Louisiana's Black Heritage*, edited by Robert Macdonald, John Kemp, and Edward Haas, 3–31. New Orleans, LA: Louisiana State Museum, 1979.

———. "From Quadrille to Stomp: The Creole Origins of Jazz." *Popular Music* 10, no. 1 (1991): 21–38.

Fields, Barbara Jeanne. *Slavery and Freedom on the Middle Ground: Maryland During the Nineteenth Century*. New Haven, CT: Yale University Press, 1984.

Figueroa-Hernández, Rafael. *Toña La Negra*. Xalapa, Veracruz: Como Suena, 2012.

Fitzgerald, Michael W. *Reconstruction in Alabama: From Civil War to Redemption in the Cotton South*. Baton Rouge: Louisiana State University Press, 2017.

———. *The Union League Movement in the Deep South: Politics and Agricultural Change During Reconstruction*. Baton Rouge: Louisiana State University Press, 2000.

Fitzwater, Dylan Eldredge. *Autonomy Is in Our Hearts: Zapatista Autonomous Government through the Lens of the Tsotsil Language*. Oakland, CA: PM Press, 2019.

Flanders, Ralph Betts. *Plantation Slavery in Georgia*. Chapel Hill: University of North Carolina Press, 1933.

Fleming, Julius B., Jr. "Transforming Geographies of Black Time: How the Free Southern Theater Used the Plantation for Civil Rights Activism." *American Literature* 91, no. 3 (September 1, 2019): 587–617.

Flint, Timothy. *Recollections of the Last Ten Years in the Valley of the Mississippi*. Boston, 1826.

Flomen, Max. "The Long War for Texas: Maroons, Renegades, Warriors, and Alternative Emancipations in the Southwest Borderlands, 1835–1845." *Journal of the Civil War Era* 11, no. 1 (Spring 2021): 36–61.

Flores y Escalante, Jesús. *Salón México: Historia Documental y Gráfica Del Danzón En México*. México: Asociación Mexicana de Estudios Fonográficos, 1993.

Foix, Pere. *Juárez*. Mexico: Ediciones Ibero Americanas, 1949.

Floyd, Samuel A. "Black Music in the Circum-Caribbean." *American Music* 17, no. 1 (1999): 1–38.

Follett, Richard. "Gloomy Melancholy: Sexual Reproduction among Louisiana Slave Women, 1840–60." In *Women and Slavery: The Modern Atlantic*, edited by Gwyn Campbell, Suzanne Miers, and Joseph Calder Miller, 54–75. Athens: Ohio University Press, 2007.

———. "Heat, Sex, and Sugar: Pregnancy and Childbearing in the Slave Quarters." *Journal of Family History* 28, no. 4 (October 1, 2003): 510–39.

———. *The Sugar Masters: Planters and Slaves in Louisiana's Cane World, 1820–1860*. Baton Rouge: Louisiana State University Press, 2007.

Foner, Eric. "Daniel A. Straker." In *Freedom's Lawmakers: A Directory of Black Officeholders during Reconstruction*, 205–6. New York: Oxford University Press, 1993.

———. "Henry M. Turner." In *Freedom's Lawmakers: A Directory of Black Officeholders during Reconstruction*, 215–16. New York: Oxford University Press, 1993.

———. *Politics and Ideology in the Age of the Civil War*. New York: Oxford University Press, 1981.

———. *Reconstruction: America's Unfinished Revolution, 1863–1877*. New York: Harper & Row, 1988.

———. "'The Tocsin of Freedom': The Black Leadership of Radical Reconstruction." In *Slavery, Resistance, Freedom*, edited by G. S. Boritt, Scott Hancock, and Ira Berlin, 118–40. Oxford: Oxford University Press, 2007.

Foner, Philip S. *History of the Labor Movement in the United States: From Colonial Times to the Founding of the American Federation of Labor*. Vol. 1. New York: International Publishers Co., 1947.

Forbes, Ella. *African American Women during the Civil War*. New York: Routledge, 2013.

Ford, John Salmon. *Rip Ford's Texas*. Edited by Stephen B. Oates. Austin: University of Texas Press, 1963.

Fortier, Craig. *Unsettling the Commons: Social Movements Against, Within, and Beyond Settler Colonialism*. Winnipeg: Arbeiter Ring Publishing, 2017.

Fortune, Timothy Thomas. *Black and White: Land, Labor, and Politics in the South*. New York: Washington Square Press, 2010.

Foster, Craig L. "Tarnished Angels: Prostitution in Storyville, New Orleans, 1900–1910." *Louisiana History: The Journal of the Louisiana Historical Association* 31, no. 4 (1990): 387–97.

Foster, John Bellamy. *Marx's Ecology*. New York: Monthly Review Press, 2000.

Foster, John Bellamy, and Brett Clark. *The Robbery of Nature: Capitalism and the Ecological Rift*. New York: Monthly Review Press, 2020.

Foster, Pops. *The Autobiography of Pops Foster: New Orleans Jazzman, as Told to Tom Stoddard*. Edited by Tom Stoddard and Ross Russell. Berkeley, CA: Backbeat Books, 2005.

Foucault, Michel. *Discipline and Punish: The Birth of the Prison.* Translated by Alan Sheridan. New York: Vintage Books, 1995.

Fouchard, Jean. *The Haitian Maroons.* New York: Blyden Press, 1981.

Franco-Ferrán, José Luciano. *Antonio Maceo: Apuntes Para Una Historia de Su Vida.* La Habana: Editorial de Ciencias Sociales, 1989.

———. *La Ruta de Antonio Maceo En El Caribe y La América Continental.* La Habana: Editorial de Ciencias Sociales, 1978.

Frazier, Donald S. *Fire in the Cane Field.* Abilene, TX: State House Press, 2010.

Friedrich, Otto. "We Will Not Do Duty Any Longer for Seven Dollars per Month." *American Heritage* 39, no. 1 (February 1988).

Frere-Jones, Sasha. "Roundtable: Haitian Music, Part 2: 'What Does Revolution Sound Like?'" *New Yorker*, July 9, 2009. https://newyorker.com/culture/sasha-frere-jones/roundtable-haitian-music-part-2-what-does-revolution-sound-like.

Freund, Max, ed. *Gustav Dressel's Houston Journal: Adventures in North America and Texas, 1837–1841.* Translated by Max Freund. Austin: University of Texas Press, 1954.

Frey, Sylvia R. *Water from the Rock: Black Resistance in a Revolutionary Age.* Princeton, NJ: Princeton University Press, 1992.

Friedenthal, Albert. *Musik, Tanz Und Dichtung Bei Den Krolen Amerikas.* Berlin-Wilmersdor: H. S. Schnippel, 1913.

Friedman, Gerald. "The Political Economy of Early Southern Unionism: Race, Politics, and Labor in the South, 1880–1953." *The Journal of Economic History* 60, no. 2 (2000): 384–413.

Friedrich, Paul. *Agrarian Revolt in a Mexican Village.* Chicago: University of Chicago Press, 1977.

Frierson, Karma. "Jarocho Publics and the Presencing of Blackness in the Port City of Veracruz, Mexico." PhD diss., The University of Chicago, 2018.

Fryer, Peter. *Rhythms of Resistance: African Musical Heritage in Brazil.* Middletown, CT: Wesleyan University Press, 2000.

Fuentes, Marisa J. *Dispossessed Lives: Enslaved Women, Violence, and the Archive.* Philadelphia: University of Pennsylvania Press, 2016.

Gabbard, Krin. *Better Git It in Your Soul: An Interpretive Biography of Charles Mingus.* Oakland: University of California Press, 2016.

Gaffield, Julia. "Haiti and Jamaica in the Remaking of the Early Nineteenth-Century Atlantic World." *The William and Mary Quarterly* 69, no. 3 (2012): 583–614.

———. "'So Many Schemes in Agitation': The Haitian State and the Atlantic World." PhD diss., Duke University, 2012.

Galis Riverí, Mililián. *La Percusión En Los Ritmos Afrocubanos y Haitiano-Cubanos.* Santiago de Cuba: Ediciones Caserón, 2017.

Gamio, Manuel. *Mexican Immigration to the United States: A Study of Human Migration and Adjustment.* Chicago: University of Chicago Press, 1930.

Gantt, Nicole Mitchell. *The Mandorla Letters: For the Hopeful.* Minneapolis: University of Minnesota Press, 2022.

García Díaz, Bernardo. "El Caribe en el Golfo: Cuba y Veracruz a Fines Del Siglo XIX y Principios Del XX." *Anuario* X (1995): 47–66.

———. "La Migración Cubana a Veracruz, 1870–1910." In *La Habana/Veracruz, Veracruz/La Habana. Las Dos Orillas*, edited by Bernardo García Díaz and Sergio Guerra Vilaboy, 297–399. Veracruz: Instituto de Investigaciones Histórico-Sociales. Universidad Veracruzana, 2010.

García León, Antonio de. "Economía y vida cotidiana en el Veracruz del siglo XVII: 1585–1707." *Boletín americanista*, no. 48 (1998): 29–45.

Garcilazo, Jeffrey Marcos. *Traqueros: Mexican Railroad Workers in the United States, 1870 to 1930*. Denton: University of North Texas Press, 2012.

Garofalo, Robert, and Mark Elrod. *A Pictorial History of Civil War Era Musical Instruments and Military Bands*. Charleston, WV: Pictorial Histories Publishing, 1982.

Garon, Paul. *Blues and the Poetic Spirit*. San Francisco: City Lights Books, 1996.

Garon, Paul, and Beth Garon. *Woman with Guitar: Memphis Minnie's Blues*. San Francisco: City Lights Books, 2014.

Garraway, Doris Lorraine. *The Libertine Colony: Creolization in the Early French Caribbean*. Durham, NC: Duke University Press, 2005.

Garrido, Juan S. *Historia de La Música Popular En México*. México: Editorial Extemporáneos, 1981.

Garrett, Charles Hiroshi. *Struggling to Define a Nation: American Music and the Twentieth Century*. Berkeley: University of California Press, 2008.

Garrigus, John D. *Before Haiti: Race and Citizenship in French Saint-Domingue*. New York: Palgrave Macmillan, 2006.

Gaspar, David Barry, and David Patrick Geggus, eds. *A Turbulent Time: The French Revolution and the Greater Caribbean*. Bloomington: Indiana University Press, 1997.

Gaudet, Marcia G. *Tales from the Levee: The Folklore of St. John the Baptist Parish*. Lafayette: Center for Louisiana Studies at the University of Southwestern Louisiana, 1984.

Gayarré, Charles. *History of Louisiana: The American Domination*. New York: William J. Widdleton, 1866.

Geggus, David. "Haiti's Declaration of Independence." In *The Haitian Declaration of Independence: Creation, Context, and Legacy*, edited by Julia Gaffield, 25–41. Charlottesville: University of Virginia Press, 2016.

Geggus, David, ed. *The Haitian Revolution: A Documentary History*. Indianapolis: Hackett Publishing Company, 2014.

———. "The Louisiana Purchase and the Haitian Revolution." In *The Haitian Revolution and the Early United States: Histories, Textualities, Geographies*, edited by Elizabeth Maddock Dillon and Michael J. Drexler, 117–29. Philadelphia: University of Pennsylvania Press, 2016.

———. "The Naming of Haiti." *New West Indian Guide / Nieuwe West-Indische Gids* 71, no. 1–2 (January 1, 1997): 43–68.

Gehman, Mary. "L. A. Creole-Mexican Connection." *Dville Press*, November 7, 2019. http://dvillepress.com/LCMC.php.

———. "Metoyer in Mexico in the Mid-1800s." *The Cane River Trading Company Newsletter* 25, no. 87 (May 2019): 1–5.

———. "The Mexico-Louisiana Creole Connection." *Louisiana Cultural Vistas* 11, no. 4 (Winter 2001): 68–76.

Genovese, Eugene D. *The Political Economy of Slavery: Studies in the Economy and Society of the Slave South*. Middletown, CT: Wesleyan University Press, 2014.

———. *From Rebellion to Revolution: Afro-American Slave Revolts in the Making of the Modern World*. Baton Rouge: Louisiana State University Press, 1981.

———. *Roll, Jordan, Roll: The World the Slaves Made*. New York: Vintage Books, 1976.

George, Lynn. *Civil War Recipes: Adding and Subtracting Simple Fractions*. New York: Rosen Publishing Group, 2010.

Georges, Anglade. *Atlas Critique d'Haïti*. Montreal: Groupe d'Études et de Recherches Critiques d'Espace & Centre de Recherches Caraïbes de l'Université de Montréal, 1982.

Georgia Writers' Project. *Drums and Shadows: Survival Studies Among the Georgia Coastal Negroes*. Athens: University of Georgia Press, 1940.

Gerhard, Peter. *A Guide to the Historical Geography of New Spain*. Cambridge: Cambridge University Press, 1972.

Gessler, Anne. *Cooperatives in New Orleans: Collective Action and Urban Development*. Jackson: University Press of Mississippi, 2020.

Gilliam, Albert M. *Travels Over the Table Lands and Cordilleras of Mexico, During the Years of 1843 and 1844*. Philadelphia: J. W. Moore, 1846.

Gilmore, Ruth Wilson. *Abolition Geography: Essays Towards Liberation*. New York: Verso Books, 2022.

Gilroy, Paul. *The Black Atlantic: Modernity and Double Consciousness*. Cambridge, MA: Harvard University Press, 1993.

———. *Small Acts: Thoughts on the Politics of Black Cultures*. London: Serpent's Tail, 1993.

Gioia, Ted. *The History of Jazz*. New York: Oxford University Press, 2021.

Giorgianni, Eugenio. "Joyful Resonances: Spirituality and Civic Engagement in the Music of the Congolese Diaspora." PhD diss., University of London, 2020.

Glissant, Édouard. *Poetics of Relation*. Ann Arbor: University of Michigan Press, 1997.

Glymph, Thavolia. *Out of the House of Bondage: The Transformation of the Plantation Household*. Cambridge, MA: Cambridge University Press, 2008.

Gobat, Michel. *Empire by Invitation: William Walker and Manifest Destiny in Central America*. Cambridge, MA: Harvard University Press, 2018.

Goffin, Robert. *La Nouvelle-Orléans, Capitale Du Jazz*. New York: Éditions de la Maison Français, 1946.

Gómez, Susana. "'Algo como un sí, o un siempre y un ahora.' Tópicos del habeas vox en la palabra política de Cortázar sobre la desaparición de personas." *Orbis Tertius* 27, no. 36 (November 1, 2022): 251.

Gonzalez, Johnhenry. "Defiant Haiti: Free-Soil Runaways, Ship Seizures and the Politics of Diplomatic Non-Recognition in the Early Nineteenth Century." *Slavery & Abolition* 36, no. 1 (2015): 124–35.

———. *Maroon Nation: A History of Revolutionary Haiti*. New Haven, CT: Yale University Press, 2019.

Gordon, George Henry. *Brook Farm to Cedar Mountain: In the War of the Great Rebellion 1861-62*. Boston, MA: J.R. Osgood, 1883.

Gordon, Jane Anna. *Creolizing Political Theory: Reading Rousseau through Fanon*. New York: Fordham University Press, 2014.

Gottschild, Brenda D. *Digging the Africanist Presence in American Performance: Dance and Other Contexts*. Westport, CT: Praeger, 1998.

Gould, Jeffrey. "The Strike of 1887: Louisiana Sugar War." *Southern Exposure* 12 (November 1984): 45–55.

Gould, Virginia Meacham. "The Free Creoles of Color of the Antebellum Gulf Ports of Mobile and Pensacola: A Struggle for the Middle Ground." In *Creoles of Color of the Gulf South*, edited by James H. Dormon, 28–50. Memphis: University of Tennessee Press, 1996.

Goveia, Elsa V. *Slave Society in the British Leeward Islands at the End of the Eighteenth Century*. New Haven, CT: Yale University Press, 1965.

Grafenstein Gareis, Johanna von. "Auge y Decadencia En Las Relaciones Intramericanas: México y El Caribe En Los Años 1763–1821." Conference Paper, LASA, Guadalajara, 1997.

Graham, Sandra Jean. *Spirituals and the Birth of a Black Entertainment Industry*. Urbana: University of Illinois Press, 2018.

Grant, Jacqueline. "Public Performance: Free People of Color Fashioning Identities in Mid-Nineteenth-Century Cuba." PhD diss., University of Miami, 2012.

Grau Rebollo, Jorge. "Antropología, Cine y Refracción. Los Textos Fílmicos Como Documentos Etnográficos." *Gazeta de Antropología* 21, no. 3 (2005).

Greeley, Horace. *The American Conflict: A History of the Great Rebellion in the United States of America, 1860-'65*. Chicago: O. D. Case, G. & C. W. Sherwood, 1866.

Grem, Darren E. "Sam Jones, Sam Hose, and the Theology of Racial Violence." *Georgia Historical Quarterly* 90, no. 1 (2006): 35–61.

Griego, Antonio García de León. *El mar de los deseos: el Caribe hispano musical : historia y contrapunto*. Quintana Roo: Siglo XXI, 2002.

Griffin, Farah Jasmine. "Textual Healing: Claiming Black Women's Bodies, the Erotic and Resistance in Contemporary Novels of Slavery." *Callaloo* 19, no. 2 (1996): 519–36.

Gruesz, Kirsten Silva. "Delta Desterrados: Antebellum New Orleans and New World Print Culture." In *Look Away!: The US South in New World Studies*, edited by Jon Smith and Deborah Cohn, 52–79. Durham, NC: Duke University Press, 2004.

Gubar, Susan. *Racechanges: White Skin, Black Face in American Culture*. New York: Oxford University Press, 2000.

Guelzo, Allen C. *Fateful Lightning: A New History of the Civil War and Reconstruction*. New York: Oxford University Press, 2012.

Guillory, Margarita Simon. *Spiritual and Social Transformation in African American Spiritual Churches: More than Conjurers*. Oxfordshire: Routledge, 2017.

Gutiérrez, José Ángel. "Chicano Music: Evolution and Politics to 1950." In *The Roots of Texas Music*, 146–74. College Station: Texas A&M University Press, 2003.

Gushee, Lawrence. "A Preliminary Chronology of the Early Career of Ferd 'Jelly Roll' Morton." *American Music* 3, no. 4 (1985): 389–412.

———. "Black Professional Musicians in New Orleans, C1880." *Inter-American Music Review* 11, no. 2 (1991): 53–63.

———. "How the Creole Band Came to Be." *Black Music Research Journal* 8, no. 1 (1988): 83–100.

———. "The Nineteenth-Century Origins of Jazz." *Black Music Research Journal* 22, no. 1 (1994): 151–74.

———. *Pioneers of Jazz: The Story of the Creole Band*. Oxford: Oxford University Press, 2005.

———. "Would You Believe Ferman Mouton? (A Second Look)," *Storyville* December-January (1981): 56–59.

Gutman, Herbert G. *The Black Family in Slavery and Freedom, 1750-1925*. New York: Knopf Doubleday Publishing Group, 1977.

Gwin, Catherine Christensen. "'The Selling of American Girls': Mexico's White Slave Trade in the California Imaginary." *California History* 99, no. 1 (February 1, 2022): 30–54.

Habitant d'Hayti. *Idylles et Chansons, Ou Essais de Poësie Créole*. Philadelphia: De l'Imprimerie de J. Edwards, 1811.

Haby, Peter R. "Interview." *Footnote* II (July 1980): 8.

Haggerty, Richard A., ed. "Land Tenure and Land Policy." In *Haiti: A Country Study*. Washington: GPO for the Library of Congress, 1989.

Hahn, Steven. *A Nation Under Our Feet: Black Political Struggles in the Rural South, from Slavery to the Great Migration*. Cambridge, MA: Harvard University Press, 2003.

———. *A Nation Without Borders: The United States and Its World in an Age of Civil Wars, 1830-1910*. New York: Penguin, 2017.

———. *The Political Worlds of Slavery and Freedom*. Cambridge, MA: Harvard University Press, 2009.

Hahn, Steven, Steven F. Miller, Susan E. O'Donovn, John C. Rodrigue, and Leslie S. Rowland, eds. *Freedom: A Documentary History of Emancipation, 1861-1867: Land & Labor, 1865*. Vol. 1. Series 3. Chapel Hill: University of North Carolina Press, 2008.

Hair, William Ivy. *Bourbonism and Agrarian Protest: Louisiana Politics, 1877-1900*. Baton Rouge: Louisiana State University Press, 1969.

———. *Carnival of Fury: Robert Charles and the New Orleans Race Riot of 1900*. Baton Rouge: Louisiana State University Press, 1976.

Hales, Douglas. *A Southern Family in White and Black: The Cuneys of Texas*. College Station: Texas A&M University Press, 2002.

Hall, A. O. *The Manhattaner in New Orleans*. New York: J. S. Redfield, 1852.

Hall, Gwendolyn Midlo. *Africans in Colonial Louisiana: The Development of Afro-Creole Culture in the Eighteenth Century*. Baton Rouge: Louisiana State University Press, 1995.

———. "The Formation of Afro-Creole Culture." In *Creole New Orleans: Race and Americanization*, edited by Arnold R. Hirsch and Joseph Logsdon, 58-87. Baton Rouge, LA: Louisiana State Museum, 1992.

Hall, Raymond A. *An Ethnographic Study of Afro-Mexicans in Mexico's Gulf Coast: Fishing, Festivals, and Foodways*. Lewiston, NY: Edwin Mellen Press, 2008.

Hall, Richard. *Acts, Passed in the Island of Barbados from 1643, to 1762*. London: Richard Hall, 1764.

Hall, Stuart. "Creolité and the Process of Creolization." In *Creolizing Europe: Legacies and Transformations*, edited by Encarnación Gutiérrez Rodríguez and Shirley Anne Tate, 12-25. Liverpool, UK: Liverpool University Press, 2015.

———. "Creolization, Diaspora, and Hybridity in the Context of Globalization." In *Créolité and Creolization: Documenta11_Platform3*, edited by Okwui Enwezor, Carlos Bausaldo, Ute Meta Bauer, Susanne Ghez, Sarat Maharaj, Mark Nash, and Octavio Zaya, 185-98. Ostfildern: Hatje Cantz, Ostfildern-Ruit, 2003.

Hall, Stuart, Chas Critcher, Tony Jefferson, John N. Clarke, and Brian Roberts. *Policing the Crisis: Mugging, the State, and Law and Order*. New York: Holmes & Meier, 1978.

Hallowell, Norwood P. *The Negro as a Soldier in the War of the Rebellion*. Boston: Little, Brown, and Company, 1897.

Halpern, Rick. "Organized Labour, Black Workers and the Twentieth-Century South: The Emerging Revision." *Social History* 19, no. 3 (1994): 359-83.

———. "Solving the 'Labour Problem': Race, Work and the State in the Sugar Industries of Louisiana and Natal, 1870-1910." *Journal of Southern African Studies* 30, no. 1 (2004): 19-40.

Hamilton, Captain Thomas. *Men and Manners in America*. 2 vols. Edinburgh and London, 1833.

Hamnett, Brian R. *Juárez*. Harlow: Longman, 1994.

Handler, Jerome S., and Charlotte J. Frisbie. "Aspects of Slave Life in Barbados: Music and Its Cultural Context." *Caribbean Studies* 11, no. 4 (1972): 5-46.

Handley, George B. "A New World of Oblivion." In *Look Away!: The U.S. South in New World Studies*, edited by Jon Smith and Deborah Cohn, 25-51. Durham, NC: Duke University Press, 2004.

Handy, W. C., ed. *The Blues: An Anthology*. New York: Albert and Chalres Boni, 1926.

Handy, W. C. *Father of the Blues: An Autobiography*. Edited by Arna Bontemps. New York: Macmillan Publishers, 1941.

———. "How I Came to Write the 'Memphis Blues.'" *New York Age* 7 (1916).

Hanger, Kimberly. "Free Blacks in Spanish New Orleans." In *Against the Odds: Free Blacks in the Slave Societies of the Americas*, edited by Jane Landers, 44–64. London: Frank Cass, 1996.

Hanger, Kimberly S. *A Medley of Cultures: Louisiana History at the Cabildo*. New Orleans: Louisiana Museum Foundation, 1996.

Hanley, Peter. "Bunk Johnson." Doctor Jazz, 2002. http://doctorjazz.co.uk/portnewor.html.

Hardie, Daniel. *Exploring Early Jazz: The Origins and Evolution of the New Orleans Style*. Bloomington, IN: iUniverse, 2002.

Hardt, Michael, and Antonio Negri. *Assembly*. New York: Oxford University Press, 2017.

Haraway, Donna. "Anthropocene, Capitalocene, Plantationocene, Chthulucene: Making Kin." *Environmental Humanities* 6, no. 1 (May 1, 2015): 159–65.

Hare, Maud Cuney. *Six Creole Folk-Songs with Original Creole and Translated English Text—Sheet Music for Voice and Piano*. New York: C. Fischer, 1921.

Harker, Brian. "Louis Armstrong and the Clarinet." *American Music* 21, no. 2 (2003): 137–58.

Harman, Chris. *A People's History of the World: From the Stone Age to the New Millennium*. New York: Verso Books, 2008.

Harned, William Leroy. "The Haitian Méringue Through Stylized Piano Compositions From 1880–1930." PhD diss., University of Northern Colorado, 2023.

Harney, Stefano, and Fred Moten. *The Undercommons: Fugitive Planning & Black Study*. New York: Minor Compositions, 2013.

Harrington, Fred Harvey. *Fighting Politician: Major General N. P. Banks*. Philadelphia: University of Pennsylvania Press, 1948.

Harris, Cheryl I. "Whiteness as Property." *Harvard Law Review* 106, no. 8 (1993): 1707–91.

Harris, Leslie M. *In the Shadow of Slavery: African Americans in New York City, 1626-1863*. Chicago: University of Chicago Press, 2004.

Harris, Melanie L. *Ecowomanism: African American Women and Earth-Honoring Faiths*. Maryknoll: Orbis Books, 2017.

Harris, T. H. *The Story of Public Education in Louisiana*. Baton Rouge: University of Louisiana, 1924.

Harris, Wilson. "Creoleness: The Crossroads of a Civilization?" In *Caribbean Creolization: Reflections on the Cultural Dynamics of Language, Literature, and Identity*, edited by Kathleen M. Balutansky and Marie-Agnès Sourieau, 23–35. Gainsville: University Press of Florida, 1998.

Hart, Dana C. "Toward an Ideal of Moral and Democratic Education: Afro-Creoles and Straight University in Reconstruction New Orleans, 1862–1896." PhD diss., Louisiana State University, 2014.

Hart, John Mason. *Revolutionary Mexico: The Coming and Process of the Mexican Revolution*. Berkeley: University of California Press, 1997.

Hartman, Saidiya. "Venus in Two Acts." *Small Axe* 12, no. 2 (2008): 1–14.

———. *Wayward Lives, Beautiful Experiments: Intimate Histories of Social Upheaval*. New York: W. W. Norton, 2019.

Hartman, Saidiya V. *Scenes of Subjection: Terror, Slavery, and Self-Making in Nineteenth-Century America*. New York: Oxford University Press, 1997.

Havis, Devonya Natasha. "Nimble or Not at All: The Ethico—Political Play of Indeterminancy." PhD diss., Boston College, 2002.

Hayden, René, Anthony E. Kaye, Kate Masur, Susan E. O'Donovan, and Stephen A. West, eds.

Freedom: A Documentary History of Emancipation, 1861-1867: Land & Labor, 1866-1867. Vol. 2, Series 3. Chapel Hill: University of North Carolina Press, 2008.

Hearn, Lafcadio. "Levee Life." In *An American Miscellany*, 147–70. New York: Dodd, Mead and Company, 1924.

Heatherton, Christina. *Arise!: Global Radicalism in the Era of the Mexican Revolution*. Berkeley: University of California Press, 2022.

Héau, Catherine. "The Musical Expression of Social Justice: Mexican Corridos at the End of the Nineteenth Century." In *Struggles for Social Rights in Latin America*, edited by Susan Eva Eckstein and Timothy P. Wickham-Crowley, 323–44. Abingdon: Routledge, 2012.

Heble, Ajay, Daniel Fischlin, and George Lipsitz. *The Fierce Urgency of Now: Improvisation, Rights, and the Ethics of Cocreation*. Durham, NC: Duke University Press, 2013.

Helg, Aline. "Simón Bolívar and the Spectre of Pardocracia: José Padilla in Post-Independence Cartagena." *Journal of Latin American Studies* 35, no. 3 (August 2003): 447–71.

Heller, Michael C. *Loft Jazz: Improvising New York in the 1970s*. Berkeley: University of California Press, 2017.

Herrera Casasús, María Luisa. *Raíces Africanas en la Población de Tamaulipas*. Ciudad Victoria: Universidad Autónoma de Tamaulipas, 1998.

Herrera Peña, José. "Juárez y el destierro (1853–1855)." In *Benito Juárez en América Latina y el Caribe*, edited by Adalberto Santana, 51–68. México: UNAM, 2006.

Hersch, Charles. "Unfinalizable: Bakhtin, Dialog, and Self-Expression in Jazz." In *The Routledge Companion to Jazz Studies*, edited by Nicholas Gebhardt, Nicole Rustin-Paschal, and Tony Whyton, 367–76. Abingdon: Routledge Handbooks Online, 2018.

Hersch, Charles B. *Subversive Sounds: Race and the Birth of Jazz in New Orleans*. Chicago: University of Chicago Press, 2008.

Hersey, Mark D. *My Work Is That of Conservation: An Environmental Biography of George Washington Carver*. Athens: University of Georgia Press, 2011.

Higginson, Thomas Wentworth. *Army Life in a Black Regiment*. Boston, MA: Fields, Osgood & Company, 1870.

———. "Drummer Boys in a Black Regiment." *The Youth's Companion* 61 (September 27, 1888): 465.

Higman, B. W. *Jamaica Surveyed: Plantation Maps and Plans of the Eighteenth and Nineteenth Centuries*. Kingston: University of West Indies Press, 2001.

———. *Slave Populations of the British Caribbean, 1807–1834*. Trinidad and Tobago: University of the West Indies Press, 1995.

Hill, Elyan Jeanine. "Spirited Choreographies: Ritual, Identity, and History-Making in Ewe Performance." PhD diss., University of California, Los Angeles, 2018.

Hilliard, Sam Bowers. *Hog Meat and Hoecake: Food Supply in the Old South, 1840–1860*. Athens: University of Georgia Press, 1972.

Hine, Darlene Clark. "Rape and the Inner Lives of Black Women in the Middle West." *Signs* 14, no. 4 (1989): 912–20.

Hirschman, Albert O. *Getting Ahead Collectively: Grassroots Experiences in Latin America*. New York: Pergamon Press, 1984.

Historic Structures. "Laurel Valley Sugar Plantation, Thibodaux Louisiana," June 30, 2020. http://historic-structures.com/la/thibodaux/laurel_valley_sugar_plantation.php.

Historical Sketch Book and Guide to New Orleans. New Orleans: New Orleans Press, 1885.

Ho, Fred. "Why Music Must Be Revolutionary—and How It Can Be." *Solidarity* (blog), August 2012. http://solidarity-us.org/atc/159/p3642/.

———. *Wicked Theory, Naked Practice: A Fred Ho Reader*. Edited by Diane Fujino. Minneapolis: University of Minnesota Press, 2009.

Hobson, Vic. *Creating Jazz Counterpoint: New Orleans, Barbershop Harmony, and the Blues*. Jackson: University Press of Mississippi, 2014.

———. "New Orleans Jazz and the Blues." *Jazz Perspectives* 5, no. 1 (2011): 3–27.

Hodson, Christopher. "Freedom Papers: An Atlantic Odyssey in the Age of Emancipation by Rebecca J. Scott and Jean M. Hébrard (Review)." *Journal of the Early Republic* 35, no. 4 (2015): 677–80.

Hofman, Ana. "The Romance with Affect: Sonic Politics in a Time of Political Exhaustion." *Culture, Theory and Critique* 61, no. 2–3 (July 2, 2020): 303–18.

———. "'We Are the Partisans of Our Time': Antifascism and Post-Yugoslav Singing Memory Activism." *Popular Music and Society* 44, no. 2 (March 15, 2021): 157–74.

Hoffman, Wickham. *Camp, Court and Siege: A Narrative of Personal Adventure and Observation During Two Wars: 1861–1865; 1870–1871*. New York: Harper & Brothers, 1877.

Hollandsworth, James G., Jr. *Louisiana Native Guards: The Black Military Experience During the Civil War*. Baton Rouge: Louisiana State University Press, 1995.

Hollis, Shirley A. "Neither Slave nor Free: The Ideology of Capitalism and the Failure of Radical Reform in the American South." *Critical Sociology* 35, no. 1 (January 1, 2009): 9–27.

Holly, James Theodore, and J. Dennis Harris. *Black Separatism and the Caribbean, 1860*. Edited by Howard H Bell. Ann Arbor: University of Michigan Press, 1860.

Holmes, Richard. *The Age of Wonder: How the Romantic Generation Discovered the Beauty and Terror of Science*. London: Harper Press, 2008.

hooks, bell. *Feminism Is for Everybody: Passionate Politics*. London: Pluto Press, 2000.

Hooton, Laura. "Little Liberia: The African American Agricultural Colony in Baja California." In *Farming across Borders: A Transnational History of the North American West*, edited by Sterling Evans, 64–81. College Station: Texas A&M University Press, 2017.

Horne, Gerald. *Black and Brown: African Americans and the Mexican Revolution, 1910–1920*. New York: New York University Press, 2005.

———. *Jazz and Justice: Racism and the Political Economy of the Music*. New York: New York University Press, 2019.

———. *Red Seas: Ferdinand Smith and Radical Black Sailors in the United States and Jamaica*. New York: New York University Press, 2009.

Horne, Jan. *To Bop or Not to Be: A Jazz Life*. Documentary, 1990.

Hosbey, Justin, and J. T. Roane. "A Totally Different Form of Living: On the Legacies of Displacement and Marronage as Black Ecologies." *Southern Cultures* 27, no. 1 (2021): 68–73.

Hossein, Caroline Shenaz. "Daring to Conceptualize the Black Social Economy." In *The Black Social Economy in the Americas: Exploring Diverse Community-Based Markets*, edited by Caroline Shenaz Hossein, 1–14. New York: Palgrave Macmillan, 2018.

Hot Lips Page, 1940–1944. Classics 809, n.d.

Hotaling, Edward. *The Great Black Jockeys: The Lives and Times of the Men Who Dominated America's First National Sport*. Rocklin, CA: Forum Prima Publishing, 1999.

Houzeau, Jean-Charles. *My Passage at the* New Orleans Tribune: *A Memoir of the Civil War Era*. Baton Rouge: Louisiana State University Press, 2001.

Howard, Philip A. *Black Labor, White Sugar: Caribbean Braceros and Their Struggle for Power in the Cuban Sugar Industry*. Baton Rouge: Louisiana State University Press, 2015.

Hu-Dehart, Evelyn. "Yaqui Resistance to Mexican Expansion." In *The Indian in Latin American*

History: Resistance, Resilience, and Acculturation, edited by John E. Kicza, 146–58. Wilmington, DE: Scholarly Resources, 1993.

Hudson, Sara. "Crossing Stories: Circulating Citizenships in an Américas Du Golfe." PhD diss., Yale University, 2011.

Huet, Nahayeilli. "La Estética de Las Religiones Afrocubanas En La Refracción de Escenarios Trasatlánticos." *Encartes* 1 (March 22, 2018): 84–100.

———. "Lo 'Afro' En Las Industrias de La Música y El Cine: El Caso Afrocubano En México." In *Circulaciones Culturales: Lo Afrocaribeño Entre Cartagena, Veracruz y La Habana*, edited by Freddy Avila Domínguez, Ricardo Pérez Montfort, and Christian Rinaudo, 165–88. Marseille, France: IRD Éditions, 2011.

Humphrey, David C. "Prostitution." In *Handbook of Texas Online*. Texas State Historical Association, June 15, 2010. http://tshaonline.org/handbook/online/articles/jbp01.

Hunt, Alfred. *Haiti's Influence on Antebellum America: Slumbering Volcano in the Caribbean*. Baton Rouge: Louisiana State University Press, 2006.

Hunter, Tera W. *To 'Joy My Freedom: Southern Black Women's Lives and Labors after the Civil War*. Cambridge, MA: Harvard University Press, 1998.

Hurston, Zora Neale. "Spirituals and Neo-Spirituals." In *The New Negro: Readings on Race, Representation, and African American Culture, 1892–1938*, edited by Henry Louis Gates Jr. and Gene Andrew Jarrett, 355–64. Princeton, NJ: Princeton University Press, 2007.

Hyppolite, Viv. "Proclamation de Soulouque Aux Haitiens." Tumblr. *Haitian History Blog* (blog), May 2013. https://haitianhistory.tumblr.com/post/118212683458/although-not-as-well-known-for-sponsoring.

Ibarra Cuesta, Jorge. *Encrucijadas de la guerra prolongada*. Santiago de Cuba: Editorial Oriente, 2008.

Illingworth, Dustin. "The Subtle Radicalism of Julio Cortázar's Berkeley Lectures." *The Atlantic*, March 28, 2017. https://theatlantic.com/entertainment/archive/2017/03/the-subtle-radicalism-of-julio-cortazars-berkeley-lectures/520812/.

Imada, Adria L. "Aloha America: Hawaiian Entertainment and Cultural Politics in the United States Empire." PhD diss., New York University, 2003.

———. *Aloha America: Hula Circuits through the U.S. Empire*. Durham, NC: Duke University Press, 2012.

Imhotep, Ra Malika, S. J. Zhang, and C. Riley Snorton. "'Hell You Talmbout?' Sighting Confusion in the Performance of Black Revolt." *Women & Performance: A Journal of Feminist Theory* 30, no. 3 (September 1, 2020): 331–43.

Ingersoll, Thomas N. "The Slave Trade and the Ethnic Diversity of Louisiana's Slave Community." *Louisiana History: The Journal of the Louisiana Historical Association* 37, no. 2 (1996): 133–61.

Iturribarría, Jorge Fernando. *Oaxaca en la historia*. Mexico: Editorial Stylo, 1955.

Israel, Jonathan Irvine. *Race, Class, and Politics in Colonial Mexico, 1610–1670*. London: Oxford University Press, 1975.

Iyer, Vijay. "Exploding the Narrative in Jazz Improvisation." In *Uptown Conversation: The New Jazz Studies*, edited by Robert G. O'Meally, Brent Hayes Edwards, and Farah Jasmine Griffin, 393–403. New York: Columbia University Press, 2004.

Jabir, Johari. *Conjuring Freedom: Music and Masculinity in the Civil War's "Gospel Army."* Columbus: Ohio State University Press, 2017.

Jackson, Bruce, ed. *Wake Up Dead Man: Afro-American Worksongs from Texas Prisons*. Cambridge, MA: Harvard University Press, 1972.

Jackson, Shona N. *Creole Indigeneity: Between Myth and Nation in the Caribbean*. Minneapolis: University of Minnesota Press, 2012.

Jackson, Thanayi Michelle. "'Devoted to the Interests of His Race': Black Officeholders and the Political Culture of Freedom in Wilmington, North Carolina, 1865–1877." PhD diss., University of Maryland, 2016.

Jacobs, Claude F. "Benevolent Societies of New Orleans Blacks during the Late Nineteenth and Early Twentieth Centuries." *Louisiana History: The Journal of the Louisiana Historical Association* 29, no. 1 (1988): 21–33.

Jenkins, Chadwick. "A Question of Containment: Duke Ellington and Early Radio." *American Music* 26, no. 4 (2008): 415–41.

Jenks, Leland H. *Our Cuban Colony—A Study in Sugar*. New York: Vanguard Press, 1928.

Jensen, Brita Dahl, Fatoumata Maïga Touré, Mohamed Ag Hamattal, Fatimata Aya Touré, and Aminata Dolo Nantoumé. "Watermelons in the Sand of Sahara: Cultivation and Use of Indigenous Landraces in the Tombouctou Region of Mali." *Ethnobotany Research and Applications* 9 (2011): 151–62.

Jenson, Deborah. *Beyond the Slave Narrative: Politics, Sex, and Manuscripts in the Haitian Revolution*. Liverpool: Liverpool University Press, 2011.

Jiménez, Valeria Priscilla. "Brokering Modernity: The World's Fair, Mexico's Eighth Cavalry Band, and the Borderlands of New Orleans Music, 1884–1910." PhD diss., Northwestern University, 2018.

John, Rachel St. *Line in the Sand: A History of the Western U.S.-Mexico Border*. Princeton, NJ: Princeton University Press, 2012.

Johnpoll, Bernard K. "Ameringer, Oscar (1870–1943)." In *Biographical Dictionary of the American Left*, edited by Harvey Klehr and Bernard K. Johnpoll, 5–6. Westport, CT: Greenwood Press, 1986.

Johnson, Aaron J. "A Date with the Duke: Ellington on Radio." *The Musical Quarterly* 96, no. 3/4 (2013): 369–405.

Johnson, Gaye Theresa. "'Sobre Las Olas': A Mexican Genesis in Borderlands Jazz and the Legacy for Ethnic Studies." *Comparative American Studies: An International Journal* 6, no. 3 (September 1, 2008): 229.

Johnson, Guion Griffis. *A Social History of the Sea Islands*. Chapel Hill: University of North Carolina Press, 1930.

Johnson, Hafiz Shabazz Farel, and John M. Chernoff. "Basic Conga Drum Rhythms in African-American Musical Styles." *Black Music Research Journal* 11, no. 1 (1991): 55–73.

Johnson, James Weldon. *The Autobiography of an Ex-Coloured Man*. New York: Knopf, 1955.

Johnson, Jerah. "Les Cenelles: What's in a Name?" *Louisiana History: The Journal of the Louisiana Historical Association* 31, no. 4 (1990): 407–10.

———. "New Orleans's Congo Square: An Urban Setting for Early Afro-American Culture Formation." *Louisiana History: The Journal of the Louisiana Historical Association* 32, no. 2 (1991): 117–57.

Johnson, Mark A. "'The Best Notes Made the Most Votes': Race, Politics, and Spectacle in the South, 1877–1932." PhD diss., University of Alabama, 2016.

———. *Rough Tactics: Black Performance in Political Spectacles, 1877–1932*. Jackson: University Press of Mississippi, 2021.

Johnson, Rashauna. "From Saint-Domingue to Dumaine Street: One Family's Journeys from the Haitian Revolution to the Great Migration." *The Journal of African American History* 102 (October 1, 2017): 427–43.

———. *Slavery's Metropolis: Unfree Labor in New Orleans during the Age of Revolutions*. Cambridge, MA: Cambridge University Press, 2016.

Johnson, Sara E. "Cinquillo Consciousness: The Formation of a Pan-Caribbean Musical Aesthetic." In *Music, Writing, and Cultural Unity in the Caribbean*, edited by Timothy J. Reiss, 35–58. Trenton, NJ: Africa World Press, 2004.

———. *The Fear of French Negroes: Transcolonial Collaboration in the Revolutionary Americas*. Berkeley: University of California Press, 2012.

Johnson, Timothy. "Reconstructing the Soil: Emancipation and the Roots of Chemical-Dependent Agriculture in America." In *The Blue, the Gray, and the Green: Toward an Environmental History of the Civil War*, edited by Brian Allen Drake, 191–208. Athens: University of Georgia Press, 2015.

Johnson, Walter. *Soul by Soul: Life Inside the Antebellum Slave Market*. Cambridge, MA: Harvard University Press, 1999.

Johnson, Zada, and Freddi Williams Evans. "Freedom Dances across the Diaspora." In *Freedom's Dance: Social Aid and Pleasure Clubs in New Orleans*, edited by Karen Celestan and Eric Waters, 31–42. Baton Rouge: Louisiana State University Press, 2018.

Jones, Dalton Anthony. "Death Sentences: From Genesis to Genre (Big Mama's Parole)." *Women & Performance: A Journal of Feminist Theory* 25, no. 1 (January 2, 2015): 59–81.

———. "Louis Armstrong's 'Karnofsky Document': The Reaffirmation of Social Death and the Afterlife of Emotional Labor." *Music and Politics* IX, no. 1 (Winter 2015).

Jones, Jacqueline. *Labor of Love, Labor of Sorrow: Black Women, Work, and the Family, from Slavery to the Present*. New York: Basic Books, 1985.

Jones, Shermaine M. "'I CAN'T BREATHE!': Affective Asphyxia in Claudia Rankine's *Citizen: An American Lyric*." *South: A Scholarly Journal* 50, no. 1 (2017): 37–46.

Jong, Nanette de. *Tambú: Curaçao's African-Caribbean Ritual and the Politics of Memory*. Bloomington: Indiana University Press, 2012.

Jordon, Winthrop D. *White over Black: American Attitudes toward the Negro, 1550–1812*. Chapel Hill: University of North Carolina Press, 1968.

Jos, Joseph. *Guadeloupéens et Martiniquais Au Canal de Panamá: Histoire d'une Émigration*. Paris: Éditions L'Harmattan, 2004.

Joseph-Gabriel, Annette K. "Creolizing Freedom: French-Creole Translations of Liberty and Equality in the Haitian Revolution." *Slavery & Abolition* 36, no. 1 (2015): 111–23.

Joyaux, George J., ed. "Forest's Voyage Aux Étas-Unis de l'Amérique En 1831." *Louisiana Historical Quarterly* XXXIX (1904): 465.

Juárez, Benito. *Apuntes Para Mis Hijos*. México: CEN, 1972.

Juárez Hernández, Yolanda. "Persistencias Culturales Afrocaribeñas En Veracruz: Siglo XIX." Tesis de Doctorado, Universidad Nacional Autónoma de México, 2005.

Julian, Jane. "Magnolia's Music." *The Mississippi Rag* 1, no. 9 (July 1974): 7–8.

Kafka, Judith. "Action, Reaction and Interaction: Slave Women in Resistance in the South of Saint Domingue, 1793–94." *Slavery and Abolition* 18, no. 2 (1997): 48–72.

Kalb, Madeleine. *Congo Cables: The Cold War in Africa—From Eisenhower to Kennedy*. New York: Macmillan, 1982.

Kanahele, George S., ed. *Hawaiian Music and Musicians: An Encyclopedic History*. Honolulu: Mutual Publishing Company, 2012.

Kantrowitz, Stephen. "'Intended for the Better Government of Man': The Political History of African American Freemasonry in the Era of Emancipation." *Journal of American History* 96, no. 4 (March 2010): 1001–26.

Kaplan, Sidney. *The Black Presence in the Era of the American Revolution, 1770–1800*. Amherst: University of Massachusetts Press, 1989.

Karcher, Carolyn L. "Albion W. Tourgée and Louis A. Martinet: The Cross-Racial Friendship behind 'Plessy v. Ferguson.'" *MELUS* 38, no. 1 (2013): 9–29.

Kaussen, Valerie. *Migrant Revolutions: Haitian Literature, Globalization, and US Imperialism*. Lanham, MD: Lexington Books, 2008.

Kay, George W. "Chink Martin: An Interview with George W. Kay." *Jazz Journal* 25, no. 4 (April 1972): 18–19; 39.

Kaye, Anthony E. *Joining Places: Slave Neighborhoods in the Old South*. Chapel Hill: University of North Carolina Press, 2007.

Kazanjian, David. "Freedom's Surprise: Two Paths Through Slavery's Archives." *History of the Present* 6, no. 2 (2016): 133–45.

Kelley, Robin D. G. "Forging Futures." In *A Moment on the Clock of the World: A Foundry Theatre Production*, edited by Melanie Joseph and David Bruin, 233–52. Chicago: Haymarket Books, 2019.

———. *Freedom Dreams: The Black Radical Imagination*. Boston: Beacon Press, 2002.

———. *Hammer and Hoe: Alabama Communists During the Great Depression*. Chapel Hill: University of North Carolina Press, 2015.

———. "In a Mist: Thoughts on Ken Burns's Jazz." *Institute for Studies in American Music* 30, no. 2 (2010): 8–10.

———. *Race Rebels: Culture, Politics, and the Black Working Class*. New York: The Free Press, 1996.

———. *Thelonious Monk: The Life and Times of an American Original*. New York: Free Press, 2010.

———. "'We Are Not What We Seem': Rethinking Black Working-Class Opposition in the Jim Crow South." *The Journal of American History* 80, no. 1 (1993): 75–112.

Kelley, Sean. "'Mexico in His Head': Slavery and the Texas-Mexico Border, 1810–1860." *Journal of Social History* 37, no. 3 (2004): 709–23.

Kendall, John. *History of New Orleans*. Chicago: Lewis Publishing Company, 1922.

Kendall, John S. "New Orleans' 'Peculiar Institution.'" *Louisiana Historical Quarterly* XXIII (July 1940): 876.

Kenney, William Howland. *Jazz on the River*. Chicago: University of Chicago Press, 2005.

Kerr-Ritchie, Jeffrey R. *Rites of August First: Emancipation Day in the Black Atlantic World*. Baton Rouge: Louisiana State University Press, 2007.

Kimball, Nell. *Nell Kimball: Her Life as an American Madam*. Edited by Stephen Longstreet. New York: MacMillan, 1970.

King, Boston. "Memoirs of the Life of Boston King, A Black Preacher." *The Methodist Magazine* XXI (June 1798): 105–265.

King, Stewart R. *Blue Coat or Powdered Wig: Free People of Color in Pre-Revolutionary Saint Domingue*. Athens: University of Georgia Press, 2001.

King, Tiffany Lethabo. *The Black Shoals: Offshore Formations of Black and Native Studies*. Durham, NC: Duke University Press, 2019.

Kinser, Samuel. *Carnival, American Style: Mardi Gras at New Orleans and Mobile*. Chicago: University of Chicago Press, 1990.

Kinzer, Charles E. "The Band Music of the First Battalion of Free Men of Color and the Siege of New Orleans, 1814–1815." *American Music* 10, no. 3 (1992): 348–69.

———. "The Excelsior Brass Band of New Orleans, 1879–1889: A Decade in the Development of a Vernacular Archetype." *Journal of Band Research* 29, no. 1 (1993): 14–24.

———. "The Tio Family: Four Generations of New Orleans Musicians, 1814-1933." The Louisiana State University and Agricultural and Mechanical College, 1993.

———. "The Tio Family and Its Role in the Creole-of-Color Musical Traditions of New Orleans." *The Second Line* 43, no. 3 (Summer 1991): 18-27.

———. "The Tios of New Orleans and Their Pedagogical Influence on the Early Jazz Clarinet Style." *Black Music Research Journal* 16, no. 2 (1996): 279-302.

Kish, Zenia, and Justin Leroy. "Bonded Life." *Cultural Studies* 29, no. 5-6 (September 3, 2015): 630-51.

Klarman, Michael J. *From Jim Crow to Civil Rights: The Supreme Court and the Struggle for Racial Equality.* New York: Oxford University Press, 2004.

Kmen, Henry Arnold. "Singing and Dancing in New Orleans (1791-1841)." PhD diss., Tulane University, 1961.

Knight, Franklin W. "The Haitian Revolution and the Notion of Human Rights." *Journal of the Historical Society* 5, no. 3 (2005): 391-416.

Knotter, A. "Transnational Cigar-Makers. Cross-Border Labour Markets, Strikes, and Solidarity at the Time of the First International (1864-1873)." *International Review of Social History* 59, no. 3 (2014): 409-42.

Knowles, Richard H. *Fallen Heroes: A History of New Orleans Brass Bands.* New Orleans: Jazzology Press, 1996.

Knowlton, Robert J. *Los Bienes del Clero y La Reforma Mexicana, 1856-1910.* Translated by Juan Jose Utrilla. Mexico: Fonda de Cultura Económica, 1985.

Koenig, Karl. "Buddy Petit on the North Side of Lake Pontchartrain." *The Second Line* XXXVIII, no. 4 (Fall 1986): 34-51.

———. "Mandeville: Dew Drop Dance Hall." *The Second Line* XXXVIII (Winter 1986): 2-11.

———. *Music in the Parishes Surrounding New Orleans: Ascension.* Running Springs, CA: Basin Street Press, 1997.

———. *Music in the Parishes Surrounding New Orleans: Plaquemines.* Running Springs, CA: Basin Street Press, 1997.

———. "The Plantation Belt and Musicians Part 1: Professor James B. Humphrey." *The Second Line* XXXIII (Fall 1981): 24-49.

———. "Professor James B. Humphrey—Part II." *The Second Line* XXXIV (Winter 1982): 24-49.

———. *Under the Influence: Four Great New Orleans Cornetists.* Running Springs, CA: Basin Street Press, 1994.

Kofsky, Frank. *Black Nationalism and the Revolution in Music.* New York: Pathfinder Press, 1970.

Korngold, Ralph. *Citizen Toussaint.* Boston: Little, Brown and Co., 1945.

Koth, Karl B. "'Not a Mutiny But a Revolution': The Rio Blanco Labour Dispute, 1906-1907." *Canadian Journal of Latin American and Caribbean Studies / Revue Canadienne Des Études Latino-Américaines et Caraïbes* 18, no. 35 (1993): 39-65.

Kotlikoff, Laurence J., and Anton Rupert. "The Manumission of Slaves in New Orleans, 1827-1846." *Economic Inquiry* 17, no. 4 (1980): 173-81.

Kousser, Jospeh J. Morgan. *The Shaping of Southern Politics: Suffrage Restriction and the Establishment of the One-Party South, 1880-1910.* New Haven, CT: Yale University Press, 1974.

Kovel, Joel. *History and Spirit: An Inquiry Into the Philosophy of Liberation.* Boston: Beacon Press, 1991.

Krasner, David. *A Beautiful Pageant: African American Theatre, Drama, and Performance in the Harlem Renaissance, 1910-1927.* New York: Palgrave Macmillan, 2004.

Krehbiel, Henry. *Afro-American Folk Songs: A Study in Racial and National Music*. New York: Schirmer, 1914.

Kress, Dana. "Pierre-Aristide Desdunes, Les Cenelles, and the Challenge of Nineteenth-Century Creole Literature." *Southern Quarterly* 44, no. 3 (2007): 42–67.

Kubik, Gerhard. *Jazz Transatlantic: Jazz Derivatives and Developments in Twentieth-Century Africa*. Jackson: University Press of Mississippi, 2017.

Kun, Josh. "Tijuana and the Borders of Race." In *A Companion to Los Angeles*, edited by William Deverell and Greg Hise, 313–26. Hoboken: Wiley-Blackwell, 2010.

La Via Campesina. "Seed Laws That Criminalise Farmers: Resistance and Fightback," 2015. https://viacampesina.org/en/wp-content/uploads/sites/2/2015/04/2015-Seed%20laws%20booklet%20EN.pdf.

LaBrew, Arthur R. "The Brindis de Salas Family." *Afro-American Music Review* 1, no. 1 (1981): 15–57.

Lachance, Paul F. "The 1809 Immigration of Saint-Domingue Refugees to New Orleans: Reception, Integration and Impact." *Louisiana History: The Journal of the Louisiana Historical Association* 29, no. 2 (1988): 109–41.

———. "The Limits of Privilege: Where Free Persons of Colour Stood in the Hierarchy of Wealth in New Orleans." In *Against the Odds: Free Blacks in the Slave Societies of the Americas*, edited by Jane G. Landers, 65–84. Abingdon: Routledge, 1996.

Lago, Enrico Dal. *Civil War and Agrarian Unrest: The Confederate South and Southern Italy*. Cambridge: Cambridge University Press, 2018.

Lambert, David. "Master–Horse–Slave: Mobility, Race and Power in the British West Indies, c.1780–1838." *Slavery & Abolition* 36, no. 4 (October 2, 2015): 618–41.

Landau, Emily Epstein. *Spectacular Wickedness: Sex, Race, and Memory in Storyville, New Orleans*. Baton Rouge: Louisiana State University Press, 2013.

Lane, Jill Meredith. "Anticolonial Blackface: The Cuban Teatro Bufo and the Arts of Racial Impersonation, 1840–1895." PhD diss., New York University, 2000.

Lanusse, Armand, ed. *Les Cenelles: A Collection of Poems by Creole Writers of the Early Nineteenth Century*. Translated by Régine Latortue and Gleason R. W. Adams. Reference Publications in Afro-American Studies. Boston: G. K. Hall, 1979.

Largey, Michael. "Ethnographic Transcription and Music Ideology in Haiti: The Music of Werner A. Jaegerhuber." *Latin American Music Review / Revista de Música Latinoamericana* 25, no. 1 (2004): 1–31.

———. "Haiti: Tracing the Steps of the Méringue and the Contredanse." In *Creolizing Contradance in the Caribbean*, edited by Peter Manuel, 209–30. Philadelphia: Temple University Press, 2011.

———. *Vodou Nation: Haitian Art Music and Cultural Nationalism*. Chicago: University of Chicago Press, 2006.

Larkin, Colin. *The Guinness Who's Who of Blues*. 2nd ed. Enfield, CT: Guinness World Records, 1995.

Lasso, Marita. "Haiti as an Image of Popular Republicanism in Caribbean Colombia: Cartagena Province, 1811–1828." In *The Impact of the Haitian Revolution in the Atlantic World*, edited by David P. Geggus. Columbia: University of South Carolina Press, 2002.

Lasso, Marixa. *Myths of Harmony: Race and Republicanism during the Age of Revolution, Colombia, 1795–1831*. Pittsburgh: University of Pittsburgh Press, 2007.

Latrobe, Benjamin Henry. *Impressions Respecting New Orleans: Diary and Sketches, 1818–1820*. New York: Columbia University Press, 1951.

Laurent, Lubin. "A History of St. John the Baptist Parish." *L'Observatuer* (1923) 1922.

Le Glaunec, Jean-Pierre. "Slave Migrations and Slave Control in Spanish and Early American New Orleans." In *Empires of the Imagination: Transatlantic Histories of the Louisiana Purchase*, edited by Peter J. Kastor, François Weil, and Fran Ois Weil, 204–38. Charlottesville: University of Virginia Press, 2009.

———. "Slave Migrations in Spanish and Early American Louisiana: New Sources and New Estimates." *Louisiana History: The Journal of the Louisiana Historical Association* 46, no. 2 (2005): 185–209.

Lears, Jackson. *Something for Nothing: Luck in America*. New York: Penguin, 2004.

Leeds, Michael, and Hugh Rockoff. "Beating the Odds: Black Jockeys in the Kentucky Derby, 1870–1911." Working Paper. National Bureau of Economic Research, January 2019.

Lemmon, Alfred. "New Orleans Popular Sheet Music Imprints: 'The Latin Tinge Prior to 1900.'" *Southern Quarterly* 27, no. 2 (Winter 1989): 41–61.

Léon, Argeliers. *Del canto y el tiempo*. Havana: Editorial Letras Cubanas, 1984.

Lescot, Andrée. *Chansons Créoles: Chansons Folkloriques d'Haïti*. FMT 133163. Deca, 1952.

Levine, Lawrence W. *Black Culture and Black Consciousness: Afro-American American Folk Thought from Slavery to Freedom*. Oxford: Oxford University Press, 1977.

Lewis, Earl. *In Their Own Interests: Race, Class and Power in Twentieth-Century Norfolk, Virginia*. Berkeley: University of California Press, 1993.

Lewis, Laura A. *Chocolate and Corn Flour: History, Race, and Place in the Making of "Black" Mexico*. Durham, NC: Duke University Press, 2012.

Lewis, Matthew Gregory. *Journal of a West India Proprietor*. London: John Murray, 1834.Lewis-Hale, Phyllis. "From Old Creole Days: Sampling the Afro-Creole Folk Song of Louisiana of the Late Nineteenth through the Mid-Twentieth Centuries." *Journal of Singing* 73, no. 5 (June 2017): 481–95.

Lichtenstein, Grace, and Laura Dankner. *Musical Gumbo: The Music of New Orleans*. New York: W. W. Norton, 1993.

Liebig, Justus von. *Letters on Modern Agriculture*. London: Walton and Maberty, 1859.

Lief, Shane. "Anarchist Blues." *The Jazz Archivist*, no. XXV (2012): 34–42.

Lief, Shane, and John McCusker. *Jockomo: The Native Roots of Mardi Gras Indians*. Jackson, MS: University Press of Mississippi, 2019.

Ligon, Richard. *A True and Exact History of the Island of Barbados*. London: Peter Parker, 1673.

Ligon-Williams, Robin. "From Maroons to Mardi Gras: The Role of African Cultural Retention in the Development of the Black Indian Culture of New Orleans." Master's thesis, Liberty University, 2018.

Liljegren, E. R. "Jacobinism in Spanish Louisiana, 1792–1797." *Louisiana Historical Quarterly* XXII, no. 1 (1939): 47–97.

———. "Lieutenant-Colonel Don Carlos Howard and the International Rivalry for the Mississippi Valley: 1796–1798." Master's thesis, University of Southern California, 1939.

Lim, Julian. *Porous Borders: Multiracial Migrations and the Law in the U.S.-Mexico Borderlands*. Chapel Hill: University of North Carolina Press Books, 2017.

Linares, Maria Teresa. *La Música Popular*. La Habana: Instituto del Libro, 1970.

Linebaugh, Peter. *Stop, Thief!: The Commons, Enclosures, and Resistance*. Oakland, CA: PM Press, 2014.

Linebaugh, Peter, and Marcus Rediker. *The Many-Headed Hydra: Sailors, Slaves, Commoners, and the Hidden History of the Revolutionary Atlantic*. Boston: Beacon Press, 2000.

Lipsitz, George. *A Life in the Struggle: Ivory Perry and the Culture of Opposition*. Philadelphia: Temple University Press, 1995.

———. *Dangerous Crossroads: Popular Music, Postmodernism, and the Poetics of Place*. New York: Verso, 1994.

———. *How Racism Takes Place*. Philadelphia: Temple University Press, 2011.

———. "Learning from New Orleans: The Social Warrant of Hostile Privatism and Competitive Consumer Citizenship." *Cultural Anthropology* 21, no. 3 (2006): 451–68.

Litwack, Leon F. *Been in the Storm So Long: The Aftermath of Slavery*. New York: Vintage Books, 1979.

Lizárraga, Neto. "Baja California." In *Atlas Del Jazz En* México, edited by Antonio Malacara Palacios, 17–22. Mexico City: Taller de Creación Literaria, 2016.

Logsdon, Joseph, and Caryn Cossé Bell. "The Americanization of Black New Orleans, 1850–1900." In *Creole New Orleans: Race and Americanization*, edited by Arnold R. Hirsch and Joseph Logsdon, 201–61. Baton Rouge: Louisiana State Museum, 1992.

Lomanno, Mark. "Topics on Afro-Cuban Jazz in the United States." Master's thesis, Rutgers University, 2007.

Lomax, Alan. *Alan Lomax: Selected Writings, 1934–1997*. Edited by Ronald Cohen. Abingdon: Routledge, 2004.

———. *Mister Jelly Roll: The Fortunes of Jelly Roll Morton, New Orleans Creole and "Inventor of Jazz."* New York: Duell, Sloan and Pearce, 1950.

Long, Alecia P. *The Great Southern Babylon: Sex, Race and Respectability in New Orleans, 1865–1920*. Baton Rouge: Louisiana State University Press, 2005.

Long, Carolyn Morrow. *Spiritual Merchants: Religion, Magic, and Commerce*. Memphis: University of Tennessee Press, 2001.

López, Patricia García. "El Banjo En La Tradición Musical De La Mixteca." BA thesis, Universidad Nacional Autónoma de México, 2004.

———. "El Banjo En La Tradición Musical De La Mixteca." In *Entre La Tradición y El Canon*, edited by Ana Rosa Domenella, Luzelena Gutiérrez de Velasco, and Edith Negrín, 133–50. Mexico: El Colegio de Mexico, 2009.

López Matoso, Antonio. *Viaje de Perico Ligero al país de los moros: A Critical Edition of Antonio López Matoso's Unpublished Diary, 1816–1820*. New Orleans: Middle American Research Institute, Tulane University, 1972.

Lott, Eric. "Double V, Double-Time: Bebop's Politics of Style." *Callaloo*, no. 36 (1988): 597–605.

———. *Love and Theft: Blackface Minstrelsy and the American Working Class*. New York: Oxford University Press, 1993.

Love, Preston. *A Thousand Honey Creeks Later: My Life in Music from Basie to Motown—and Beyond*. Middletown, CT: Wesleyan University Press, 1997.

Lubin, Maurice A. "Langston Hughes and Haiti." *The Langston Hughes Review* 6, no. 1 (1987): 4–7.

Lucero-White, Aurora. *Literary Folklore of the Hispanic Southwest in Spanish and English*. San Antonio: Naylor, 1953.

Lumumba, Patrice. "May Our People Triumph." In *The Truth about a Monstrous Crime of the Colonialists*, 48–49. Moscow: Foreign Languages Publishing House, 1961.

Lundahl, Mats. "Defense and Distribution: Agricultural Policy in Haiti during the Reign of Jean-Jacques Dessalines, 1804–1806." *Scandinavian Economic History Review* 32, no. 2 (July 1, 1984): 77–103.

Lundy, Benjamin. *The Life, Travels, and Opinions of Benjamin Lundy: Including His Journeys* to Texas and Mexico, with a Sketch of Contemporary Events, and a Notice of the Revolution in Hayti. Philadelphia: W.D. Parrish, 1847.

MacDonald, Kevin C., and David W. Morgan. "African Earthen Structures in Colonial Louisiana: Architecture from the Coincoin Plantation (1787–1816)." *Antiquity* 86, no. 331 (March 2012): 161–77.

Maceo Grajales, Antonio. *Ideología Política: Cartas y Otros Documentos*. Habana: Sociedad Cubana de Estudios Históricos e Internationales, 1950.

Mackey, Nathaniel. *Bedouin Hornbook*. Los Angeles: Sun & Moon Press, 2000.

———. "Other: From Noun to Verb." In *The Improvisation Studies Reader: Spontaneous Acts*, edited by Rebecca Caines and Ajay Heble, 243–59. London: Routledge, 2015.

Maclennan, Carol A. "Hawai'i Turns to Sugar: The Rise of Plantation Centers, 1860–1880." *The Hawaiian Journal of History* 31 (1997): 97–125.

Madrid, Alejandro L., and Robin D. Moore. *Danzón: Circum-Caribbean Dialogues in Music and Dance*. Oxford: Oxford University Press, 2013.

Magdol, Edward. *A Right to the Land: Essays on the Freedmen's Community*. Westport, CT: Greenwood Press, 1977.

Mahé II, John A., and Rosanne McCaffrey, eds. *Encyclopaedia of New Orleans Artists, 1718-1918*. New Orleans: Historic New Orleans Collection, 1987.

Malcomson, Hettie. "The 'Routes' and 'Roots' of Danzón: A Critique of the History of a Genre." *Popular Music* 30, no. 2 (2011): 263–78.

Malfavon, Alan Alexander. "Kin of the Leeward Port: Afro-Mexicans in Veracruz in the Making of State Formation, Contested Spaces, and Regional Development, 1770-1830." PhD diss., University of California-Riverside, 2021.

Manabe, Noriko. "Chants of the Resistance: Flow, Memory, and Inclusivity." *Music and Politics* 13, no. 1 (Winter 2019).

Manchuelle, François. "Le rôle des Antillais dans l'apparition du nationalisme culturel en Afrique noire francophone." *Cahiers d'Études africaines* 32, no. 127 (1992): 375–408.

Mandell, Daniel R. *The Lost Tradition of Economic Equality in America, 1600-1870*. Baltimore: Johns Hopkins University Press, 2020.

Mandle, Jay R. *Not Slave, Not Free: The African American Economic Experience Since the Civil War*. Durham, NC: Duke University Press, 1992.

Manning, Chandra. "Emancipation as State-Building from the Inside Out." In *Beyond Freedom: New Directions in American Emancipation*, edited by Jim Downs, 60–76. Athens: University of Georgia Press, 2017.

Manuel, Peter. "The Anticipated Bass in Cuban Popular Music." *Latin American Music Review / Revista de Música Latinoamericana* 6, no. 2 (1985): 249–61.

———. "From Contradanza to Danzón." In *Creolizing Contradance in the Caribbean*, edited by Peter Manuel, 52–112. Philadelphia: Temple University Press, 2009.

Manuel, Peter, Kenneth Bilby, and Michael Largey. *Caribbean Currents: Caribbean Music from Rumba to Reggae*. Philadelphia: Temple University Press, 2012.

Mareite, Thomas. *Conditional Freedom: Free Soil and Fugitive Slaves from the U.S. South to Mexico's Northeast, 1803–1861*. Leiden: Brill, 2022.

Marquis, Donald M. *In Search of Buddy Bolden: First Man of Jazz*. Baton Rouge: Louisiana State University Press, 2005.

Marshall, Woodville K. "Provision Ground and Plantation Labor in Four Windward Islands: Competition for Resources During Slavery." In *Cultivation and Culture: Labor and the*

Shaping of Slave Life in the Americas, edited by Ira Berlin and Philip D. Morgan, 203–21. Charlottesville: University of Virginia Press, 1993.

Martin, James W. *Banana Cowboys: The United Fruit Company and the Culture of Corporate Colonialism*. Albuquerque: University of New Mexico Press, 2018.

Martin, Tony. *Race First: The Ideological and Organizational Struggles of Marcus Garvey and the Universal Negro Improvement Association*. Dover, MA: The Majority Press, 1986.

Martínez Gordo, Isabel. "Los Cantos de La Tumba Francesa Desde El Punto de Vista Lingüístico." *Santiago* 59 (1989): 33–72.

Martínez Oxama, Óscar Javier. "Oaxaca." In *Altas Del Jazz En México*, edited by Antonio Malacara Palacios, 177–88. México: Taller de Creación Literaria, 2016.

Martínez-Fernández, Luis. *Revolutionary Cuba: A History*. Gainesville: University Press of Florida, 2014.

Martyn, Barry. *New Orleans Jazz: The End of the Beginning*. New Orleans: Jazzology Press, 1998.

Martyn, Barry, and Nick Gagliano. *The Fabulous George Lewis Band: The Inside Story*. New Orleans: Louisiana State University Press, 2010.

Marx, Karl. *Capital, Volume I: A Critique of Political Economy*. Mineola, NY: Dover Publications, 2011.

———. *The Eighteenth Brumaire of Louis Bonaparte*. Edited by Daniel De Leon. Chicago: C. H. Kerr, 1913.

———. *The Poverty of Philosophy*. New York: International Publishers, 1963.

———. "The Power of Money in Bourgeoise Society." In *Economic and Philosophic Manuscripts of 1844*, 164–70. Mineola, NY: Dover, 2007.

Mata, Gerardo Garcia. "Felipe Valdes and the Role of the Cornet in the Cuban Orquesta Tipica." PhD diss., University of Houston, 2020.

Mathieson, William Law. *British Slavery and Its Abolition 1823-1838*. London: Octagon Books, 1926.

Matthews, John M. "Negro Republicans in the Reconstruction of Georgia." *Georgia Reconstruction Quarterly* 60 (1976): 145–64.

Matory, J. Lorand. "From 'Survival' to 'Dialogue': Analytic Tropes in the Study of African-Diaspora Cultural History." In *Transatlantic Caribbean: Dialogues of People, Practices, Ideas*, edited by Ingrid Kummels, Claudia Rauhut, Stefan Rinke, and Birte Timm, 33–56. Bielefeld, Germany: Transcript Verlag, 2014.

———. "The 'New World' Surrounds an Ocean: Theorizing the Live Dialogue between African and African American Cultures." In *In Afro-Atlantic Dialogues: Anthropology in the Diaspora*, edited by Kevin A. Yelvington, 151–92. Santa Fe: School of American Research Press., 2006.

Mavounzy, Marcel S. *Cinquante Ans de Musique et de Culture En Guadeloupe 1928-1978* (Paris: Présence Africaine, 2002), 20. Paris: Présence Africaine, 2002.

Maximilien, Louis. "Notes on Folklore with Respect to the Music of Werner Jaegerhuber." Translated by Julius Wiesel. Unpublished manuscript, 1954.

McAlister, Elizabeth. "Listening for Geographies: Music as Sonic Compass Pointing toward African and Christian Diasporic Horizons in the Caribbean." *Black Music Research Journal; Chicago, Ill.* 32, no. 2 (Fall 2012): 25–50.

———. *Rara! Vodou, Power, and Performance in Haiti and Its Diaspora*. Berkeley: University of California Press, 2002.

McBroome, Delores Nason. "Harvests of Gold: African American Boosterism, Agriculture, and Investment in Allensworth and Little Liberia." In *Seeking El Dorado: African Americans in California*, edited by Lawrence B. de Graaf, Kevin Mulroy, and Quintard Taylor, 149–81. Seattle: University of Washington Press, 2001.

McCusker, John. *Creole Trombone: Kid Ory and the Early Years of Jazz*. Jackson: University Press of Mississippi, 2012.

———. "The Onward Brass Band and the Spanish-American War." *The Jazz Archivist* XIII (1998): 24–35.

McDonald, Roderick A. "Independent Economic Production by Slaves on Antebellum Louisiana Sugar Plantations." In *Cultivation and Culture: Labor and the Shaping of Slave Life in the Americas*, edited by Ira Berlin and Philip D. Morgan, 275–99. Charlottesville: University of Virginia Press, 1993.

McGill, Meredith L. "Frances Ellen Watkins Harper and the Circuits of Abolitionist Poetry." In *Early African American Print Culture*, edited by Jordan Alexander Stein and Lara Langer Cohen, 53–74. Philadelphia: University of Pennsylvania Press, 2012.

McGlade, Jacqueline Ann. "A Boys Town Hall of History: A Case Study in Public History and Exhibition Methods." Master's thesis, University of Nebraska at Omaha, 1986.

McKee, Sally. *The Exile's Song: Edmond Dédé and the Unfinished Revolutions of the Atlantic World*. New Haven, CT: Yale University Press, 2017.

———. *Demonic Grounds: Black Women And The Cartographies Of Struggle*. Minneapolis, MN: University of Minnesota Press, 2006.

McKittrick, Katherine. "On Plantations, Prisons, and Black Sense of Place." *Social & Cultural Geography* 12, no. 8 (2011): 947–63.

———. "Plantation Futures." *Small Axe* 17, no. 3 (December 21, 2013): 1–15.

McNeill, George E. *The Labor Movement: The Problem of Today, Comprising a History of Capital and Labor, and Its Present Status*. Boston: M. W. Hazen, 1886.

McPherson, James M. *The Negro's Civil War: How American Blacks Felt and Acted During the War for the Union*. New York: Knopf Doubleday Publishing Group, 2008.

Medley, Keith. *We as Freemen: Plessy V. Ferguson*. Gretna: Pelican Publishing, 2012.

Meehan, Kevin. *People Get Ready: African American and Caribbean Cultural Exchange*. Jackson: University Press of Mississippi, 2010.

———. "'To Shake This Nation as Nothing before Has Shaken It': C. L. R. James, Radical Fieldwork, and African American Popular Culture." In *Obsolete Geographies: Displacements and Transformations in Caribbean Cultures*, edited by Lisabeth Paravisini-Gebert and Ivette Romero, 77–99. Gainesville: University Press of Florida, 2008.

Mellon, James, ed. *Bullwhip Days: The Slaves Remember*. New York: Weidenfeld & Nicolson, 1988.

Méndez, Justo Sierra. *En Tierra Yankee (Notas a Todo Vapor)*. México: Palacio Nacional, 1895.

Mendoza, Vincente T. *La Cancíon Mexicana: Ensayo de Clasificación y Antología*. Mexico: Instituto de Investigaciones Estéticas, UNAM, 1961.

Meyers, Charles J., and Richard L. Noble. "The Colorado River: The Treaty with Mexico." *Stanford Law Review* 19, no. 2 (1966): 367–419.Micklin, Anna. "Louis Charles Roudanez (1823–1890)," June 30, 2008. https://www.blackpast.org/african-american-history/roudanez-louis-charles-1823-1890/.

Mier, Sebastian B. de. *México en la Exposición universal internacional de París — 1900*. Paris: J. Dumoulin, 1901.

Mikowsky, Solomon Gadles. "The Nineteenth-Century Cuban 'Danza' and Its Composers, with Particular Attention to Ignacio Cervantes (1847–1905)." PhD diss., Columbia University, 1973.

Miller, Gene. "The Carpetbagger and the Professor." *New Orleans Music* 4, no. 6 (June 1994): 6–10.

Mills, Gary B. *The Forgotten People: Cane River's Creoles of Color*. Baton Rouge: Louisiana State University Press, 1977.

Mills, Quincy T. *Cutting Along the Color Line: Black Barbers and Barber Shops in America*. Philadelphia: University of Pennsylvania Press, 2013.

Mingus, Charles. *Beneath the Underdog: His World as Composed by Mingus*. New York: Vintage, 1991.

Mintz, Sidney W. *Caribbean Transformations*. New Brunswick, NJ: Transaction Publishers, 2007.

———. "The Jamaican Internal Marketing Pattern: Some Notes and Hypotheses." *Social and Economic Studies* 4, no. 1 (1955): 95–103.

———. *Sweetness and Power: The Place of Sugar in Modern History*. New York: Penguin Books, 1986.

Mitchell, George Sinclair. *Textile Unionism and the South*. Chapel Hill: University of North Carolina Press, 1931.

Mitchell, Georgette M. "Autour d'une Rosette: Insularity and Cross-Cultural Exchange in Nineteenth-Century Poetry of New Orleans, Haiti, and France." PhD diss., Rutgers University, 2019.

Mitchell, Mary Niall. "'A Good and Delicious Country': Free Children of Color and How They Learned to Imagine the Atlantic World in Nineteenth-Century Louisiana." *History of Education Quarterly* 40, no. 2 (ed 2000): 123–44.

———. *Raising Freedom's Child: Black Children and Visions of the Future after Slavery*. New York: New York University Press, 2010.

Mitchell, Reagan Patrick. "Gottschalk's Engagement with the Ungovernable: Louis Moreau Gottschalk and the Bamboula Rhythm." *Educational Studies: Echoes, Reverberations, Silences, and Noise: Sonic Possibilities in Education* 54, no. 4 (2018): 415–28.

Mondor, Colleen. "Listen to the Second Line." In *Do You Know What It Means to Miss New Orleans? A Collection of Stories and Essays Set in the Big Easy*, edited by Bruce Rutledge and David Rutledge, 82–90. Seattle: Chin Music Press, 2006.

Mongey, Vanessa. *Rogue Revolutionaries: The Fight for Legitimacy in the Greater Caribbean*. Philadelphia: University of Pennsylvania Press, 2020.

Monson, Ingrid. *Freedom Sounds: Civil Rights Call out to Jazz and Africa*. Oxford: Oxford University Press, 2007.

Montgomery, David R. *Dirt: The Erosion of Civilizations*. Berkeley, CA: University of California Press, 2012.

Montgomery, William E. *Under Their Own Vine and Fig Tree: The African-American Church in the South, 1865–1900*. Baton Rouge: Louisiana State University Press, 1993.

Moore, John Preston. "Correspondence of Pierre Soule: The Louisiana Tehuantepec Company." *The Hispanic American Historical Review* 32, no. 1 (1952): 59–72.

Moore, Robin. *Nationalizing Blackness: Afrocubanismo and Artistic Revolution in Havana, 1920–1940*. Pittsburgh: University of Pittsburgh Press, 1997.

———. "Representations of Afrocuban Expressive Culture in the Writings of Fernando Ortiz." *Latin American Music Review / Revista de Música Latinoamericana* 15, no. 1 (1994): 32–54.

Moore, Robin D. "The Danzón, North American Racial Discourses, and Reflections on Early Jazz." *Journal of Latin American Cultural Studies* 25, no. 3 (July 2, 2016): 321–37.

Moore, Sophie Sapp. "Organize or Die: Farm School Pedagogy and the Political Ecology of the Agroecological Transition in Rural Haiti." *The Journal of Environmental Education* 48, no. 4 (2017): 248–59.

Morcom, Anna. "Following the People, Refracting Hindustani Music, and Critiquing Genre-Based Research." *Ethnomusicology* 66, no. 3 (January 1, 2022): 470–96.

Moreau de Saint-Méry, Louis-Élie. *Description Topographique, Physique, Civile, Politique et Historique de La Partie Française de l'isle Saint-Domingue*. Philadelphia: 1797.

Morgan, David W., Kevin C. MacDonald, and Fiona J. L. Handley. "Economics and Authenticity: A Collision of Interpretations in Cane River National Heritage Area, Louisiana." *The George Wright Forum* 23, no. 1 (2006): 44–61.

Morgan, Jennifer L. *Laboring Women: Reproduction and Gender in New World Slavery*. Philadelphia: University of Pennsylvania Press, 2004.

———. *Reckoning with Slavery: Gender, Kinship, and Capitalism in the Early Black Atlantic*. Durham, NC: Duke University Press, 2021.

Morgan, John H. "An Essay on the Causes of the Production of Abortion among Our Negro Population." *Nashville Journal of Medicine and Surgery* 19 (1860): 117–23.

Morgan, Philip D. *Slave Counterpoint: Black Culture in the Eighteenth-Century Chesapeake and Lowcountry*. Chapel Hill: University of North Carolina Press, 2012.

Mormino, Gary R., and George E. Pozzetta. "Spanish Anarchism in Tampa, Florida, 1886–1931." In *Hidden Out in the Open: Spanish Migration to the United States (1875–1930)*, edited by Phylis Cancilla Martinelli and Ana Varela-Lago, 91–128. Denver: University Press of Colorado, 2019.

Morrison, Toni. "On the Backs of Blacks." *Time Magazine*, 1993.

Moten, Fred. "Blackness and Nothingness (Mysticism in the Flesh)." *South Atlantic Quarterly* 112, no. 4 (2013): 737–80.

———. *In the Break: The Aesthetics of the Black Radical Tradition*. Minneapolis: University of Minnesota Press, 2003.

———. "The New International of Rhythmic Feeling(s)." *Thamyris/Intersecting* 18 (2007): 31–56.

"Mr. Dan Desdunes Instructor of Our Band." *Father Flanagan's Boys' Home Journal* 5, no. 1 (April 1922).

Muleiro, Hernán. "Mi música refleja el sufrimiento, dice a 'La Jornada' Archie Shepp." La Jornada, March 4, 2021. https://jornada.com.mx/notas/2021/03/04/cultura/mi-musica-refleja-el-sufrimiento-dice-a-la-jornada-archie-shepp/.

Muller, Dalia Antonia. *Cuban Émigrés and Independence in the Nineteenth-Century Gulf World*. Chapel Hill: University of North Carolina Press, 2017.

Muñoz, José Esteban. *Cruising Utopia: The Then and There of Queer Futurity*. New York: NYU Press, 2009.

Muñoz, María Luisa. "Music in Puerto Rico." Unpublished PhD diss., Columbia University, 1958.

Munro, Martin. "Can't Stand Up for Falling Down: Haiti, Its Revolutions, and Twentieth-Century Negritudes." *Research in African Literatures* 35, no. 2 (2004): 1–17.

Murray, Gerald F. "The Evolution of Haitian Peasant Land Tenure: A Case Study in Agrarian Adaptation to Population Growth." PhD diss., Columbia University, 1977.

Nantoumé, Aminata, Sidiki Traoré, Jorgen Christiansen, S.B. Andersen, and Brita Jensen. "Traditional Uses and Cultivation of Indigenous Watermelons (Citrullus Lanatus) in Mali." *International Journal of Biodiversity and Conservation* 4 (January 1, 2012): 461–71.

Naranjo Orovio, Consuelo, and José F. Buscaglia. "Race as a Weapon: Defending the Colonial

Plantation Order in the Name of Civilization, 1791–1850." *Culture & History Digital Journal* 4, no. 2 (December 2015): 1–8.

Narváez, Peter. "The Influences of Hispanic Music Cultures on African-American Blues Musicians." *Black Music Research Journal* 22, no. 1 (2002): 175–96.

Navarrete Pellicer, Sergio. "Las Capillas de Música de Viento En Oaxaca Durante El Siglo XIX." *Heterofonía*, no. 124 (June 2001): 9–27.

Nelson, Scott Reynolds. *Iron Confederacies: Southern Railways, Klan Violence, and Reconstruction*. Chapel Hill: University of North Carolina Press, 2005.

Nembhard, Jessica Gordon. *Collective Courage: A History of African American Cooperative Economic Thought and Practice*. University Park: Penn State University Press, 2014.

Neprud-Ardovino, Lori Fay. "The Jazz Clarinet: Its Evolution and Use in the Early Jazz Orchestras before 1920." D.M.A. thesis, University of Cincinnati, 1993.

Nesbitt, Nick. *Universal Emancipation: The Haitian Revolution and the Radical Enlightenment*. Charlottesville: University of Virginia Press, 2008.

Newman, Richard S. *Black Founders: The Free Black Community in the Early Republic*. Philadelphia, PA: Library Company of Philadelphia, 2008.

Newman, Simon P. *A New World of Labor: The Development of Plantation Slavery in the British Atlantic*. Philadelphia: University of Pennsylvania Press, 2013.

Nicholls, David. *From Dessalines to Duvalier: Race, Colour and National Independence in Haiti*. Revised edition. New Brunswick, NJ: Rutgers University Press, 1996.

Nichols, James David. "Freedom Interrupted: Runaway Slaves and Insecure Borders in the Mexican Northeast." In *Fugitive Slaves and Spaces of Freedom in North America*, edited by Damian Alan Pargas, 251–74. Gainesville: University Press of Florida, 2018.

———. *The Limits of Liberty: Mobility and the Making of the Eastern U.S.-Mexico Border*. Lincoln: University of Nebraska Press, 2018.

Nissen, Peter. *Buddy Bolden's Storyville Blues*. Lulu Press, Inc, 2014.

Njoroge, Njoroge M. *Chocolate Surrealism: Music, Movement, Memory, and History in the Circum-Caribbean*. Jackson: University Press of Mississippi, 2016.

Nocella, Anthony, and Kim Socha. "Old School, New School, No School: Hip Hop's Dismantling of School and Prison Industrial Complexes." *The International Journal of Critical Pedagogy* 4, no. 3 (September 24, 2013).

NOLA.com. "The 1884 Cotton Expo and New Orleans' First Case of World's Fair Fever," May 17, 2017. https://nola.com/300/the-1884-cotton-expo-and-new-orleans-first-case-of-worlds-fair-fever/article_21fc06f9-a1f5-56f8-8440-dee682805dfe.html.

Northup, Solomon. *Twelve Years a Slave: Narrative of Solomon Northup, a Citizen of New-York, Kidnapped in Washington City in 1841*. Auburn, NY: Applewood Books, 1853.

Nystrom, Justin A. "Racial Identity and Reconstruction: New Orleans's Free People of Color and the Dilemma of Emancipation." In *The Great Task Remaining Before Us: Reconstruction as America's Continuing Civil War*, edited by Paul Cimbala and Randall M. Miller, 122–39. New York: Fordham University Press, 2010.

O'Connor, Thomas. *History of the Fire Department of New Orleans: From the Earliest Days to the Present Time*. New Orleans: Self-Published, 1895.

O'Donovan, Susan E. *Becoming Free in the Cotton South*. Cambridge, MA: Harvard University Press, 2009.

Ochs, Stephen J. *A Black Patriot and a White Priest: André Cailloux and Claude Paschal Maistre in Civil War New Orleans*. Baton Rouge, LA: Louisiana State University Press, 2006.

Okiji, Fumi. "Haiti's Infrasonic Boom." Forthcoming.

———. *Jazz as Critique: Adorno and Black Expression Revisited*. Berkeley: Stanford University Press, 2018.

Olivarius, Kathryn. "Immunity, Capital, and Power in Antebellum New Orleans." *The American Historical Review* 124, no. 2 (April 1, 2019): 425–55.

Olsen, Margaret. "The Gift of the New Orleans Second Line." In *Neoliberalism and Global Theatres: Performance Permutations*, edited by Lara D. Nielsen and Patricia Ybarra Ybarra, 176–89. New York: Palgrave Macmillan, 2012.

Olsson, Tore C. *Agrarian Crossings: Reformers and the Remaking of the Us and Mexican Countryside*. Princeton, NJ: Princeton University Press, 2020.

Ortiz, Fernando. *La Africanía de La Música Folklórica de Cuba*. Ortiz, Fernando. La Habana: Universidad Central de las Villas, 1950.

Oswald, Alix. "The Reaction to the Dred Scott Decision." *Voces Novae* 4, no. 1 (April 26, 2018). https://digitalcommons.chapman.edu/vocesnovae/vol4/iss1/9.

Otto, Jesse J. "Contemporaries: Black Orchestras in Omaha before 1950." Master's thesis, University of Nebraska at Omaha, 2010.

———. "Dan Desdunes: New Orleans Civil Rights Activist and 'The Father of Negro Musicians of Omaha.'" *Nebraska History* 92 (2011): 106–17.

Pace, Robert F. "'It Was Bedlam Let Loose': The Louisiana Sugar Country and the Civil War." *Louisiana History: The Journal of the Louisiana Historical Association* 39, no. 4 (1998): 389–409.

Palmer, Colin A. "Africa in the Making of the Caribbean: The Formative Years." In *Slavery, Freedom and Gender: The Dynamics of Caribbean Society*, edited by Brian L. Moore, B. W. Higman, Carl Campbell, and Patrick Bryan, 40–56. Kingston: University of the West Indies Press, 2003.

Parham, Angel Adams. *American Routes: Racial Palimpsests and the Transformation of Race*. New York: Oxford University Press, 2017.

Paquette, Robert L. "'A Horde of Brigands?' The Great Louisiana Slave Revolt of 1811 Reconsidered." *Historical Reflections / Réflexions Historiques* 35, no. 1 (2009): 72–96.

Paravisini-Gebert, Lizabeth. "'He of the Trees': Nature, Environment, and Creole Religiosities in Caribbean Literature." In *Caribbean Literature and the Environment: Between Nature and Culture*, edited by Elizabeth M. DeLoughrey, Renée K. Gosson, and George B. Handley, 182–98. Charlottesville: University of Virginia Press, 2005.

Pargas, Damian Alan. *Freedom Seekers*. Cambridge: Cambridge University Press, 2021.

Parr, Leslie Gale. "Sundays in the Streets: The Long History of Benevolence, Self-Help, and Parades in New Orleans." *Southern Cultures* 22, no. 4 (2016): 8–30.

Parsons, Elaine Frantz. *Ku-Klux: The Birth of the Klan during Reconstruction*. Chapel Hill: University of North Carolina Press, 2016.

Pastras, Phil. *Dead Man Blues: Jelly Roll Morton Way Out West*. Berkeley: University of California Press, 2003.

PBS. "Freedom: A History of US. Biography. Louis Armstrong." PBS. Accessed September 11, 2023. https://thirteen.org/wnet/historyofus/web11/features/bio/B09.html.

Pearson, Elizabeth Ware. *Letters from Port Royal Written at the Time of the Civil War*. Boston: Book on Demand, 1906.

Pellegrinelli, Lara. "Separated at 'Birth': Singing and the History of Jazz." In *Big Ears: Listening for Gender in Jazz Studies*, edited by Nichole T. Rustin and Sherrie Tucker, 31–47. Durham, NC: Duke University Press, 2008.

Penn, Irvine Garland. *The Afro-American Press and Its Editors*. Springfield, MA: Wiley & Company, 1891.

Penn, Ojeda. "Jazz: American Classical Music as a Philosophic and Symbolic Entity." Invited Talk, Emory University, Atlanta, Georgia, 1986.

———. "The Message in the Music." Invited Talk, Dayton, Ohio, 1989.

Penniman, Leah. *Farming While Black: Soul Fire Farm's Practical Guide to Liberation on the Land*. White River Junction, VT: Chelsea Green Publishing, 2018.

Penningroth, Dylan C. *The Claims of Kinfolk: African American Property and Community in the Nineteenth-Century South*. Chapel Hill: University of North Carolina Press, 2003.

Perdue, Charles L., Thomas E. Barden, and Robert K. Phillips, eds. *Weevils in the Wheat: Interviews with Virginia Ex-Slaves*. Charlottesville: University of Virginia Press, 1992.

Peretti, Burton William. *The Creation of Jazz: Music, Race, and Culture in Urban America*. Urbana: University of Illinois Press, 1992.

Pérez, Elvia, Margaret Read MacDonald, and Paula Martin. *From the Winds of Manguito/Desde los Vientos de Manguito: Cuban Folktales in English and Spanish/Cuentos Folclóricos de Cuba, en Ingles y Español*. Westport, CT: Libraries Unlimited, 2004.

Perrin, Liese M. "Resisting Reproduction: Reconsidering Slave Contraception in the Old South." *Journal of American Studies* 35, no. 2 (August 2001): 255–74.

Pettinger, Alasdair. "'Eh! Eh! Bomba, Hen! Hen!': Making Sense of a Vodou Chant." In *Obeah and Other Powers: The Politics of Caribbean Religion and Healing*, edited by Diana Paton and Maarit Forde, 80–102. Durham, NC: Duke University Press, 2012.

Phillips, Glenn O. "The Response of a West Indian Activist: D. A. Straker 1842–1908." *Journal of Negro History* 66 (1981): 128–39.

Piacentino, Ed. "Seeds of Rebellion in Plantation Fiction: Victor Séjour's 'The Mulatto.'" *Southern Spaces*, 2007. https://southernspaces.org/2007/seeds-rebellion-plantation-fiction-victor-sejours-mulatto/.

Picker, John M. "The Union of Music and Text in Whitman's Drum-Taps and Higginson's Army Life in a Black Regiment." *Walt Whitman Quarterly Review* 12, no. 4 (1995): 231–45.

Pierce, Valentine. "Interview with Fred Johnson." In *Freedom's Dance: Social Aid and Pleasure Clubs in New Orleans*, edited by Karen Celestan and Eric Waters. Baton Rouge: Louisiana State University Press, 2018.

Pierson, Michael D. *Mutiny at Fort Jackson: The Untold Story of the Fall of New Orleans*. Chapel Hill: University of North Carolina Press, 2009.

Pike, James Shepherd. *The Prostrate State: South Carolina Under Negro Government*. New York: D. Appleton, 1874.

Piras, Marcello. "'Ecos de México': Young Scott Joplin and His Secret Role Model." *Current Research in Jazz*, no. 10 (2019). https://www.crj-online.org/v10/CRJ-Rosas-Joplin.php.

———. "Jelly-Roll Morton: ¿padre del jazz o tataranieto de la contradanza?" *Jazz-hitz*, no. 3 (November 16, 2020): 55–70.

Poole, Grace, Irma C. Hayssen, and Solon De Leon, eds. *The American Labor Who's Who*. New York: Hanford Press, 1925.

Popkin, Jeremy D. *Facing Racial Revolution: Eyewitness Accounts of the Haitian Insurrection*. Chicago: University of Chicago Press, 2008.

———. *You Are All Free: The Haitian Revolution and the Abolition of Slavery*. Cambridge: Cambridge University Press, 2011.

Porter, Lewis, and Michael Ullman. "Sidney Bechet and His Long Song." *The Black Perspective in Music* 16, no. 2 (1988): 135–50.

Powers, Bernard E. "'The Worst of All Barbarism': Racial Anxiety and the Approach of Secession in the Palmetto State." *The South Carolina Historical Magazine* 112, no. 3/4 (2011): 139–56.

Pratt, Mary Louise. *Imperial Eyes: Travel Writing and Transculturation*. London: Routledge, 1992.

Pressing, Jeff. "Black Atlantic Rhythm: Its Computational and Transcultural Foundations." *Music Perception: An Interdisciplinary Journal* 19, no. 3 (2002): 285–310.

Price, Richard. "The Miracle of Creolization: A Retrospective." *NWIG: New West Indian Guide / Nieuwe West-Indische Gids* 75, no. 1/2 (2001): 35–64.

Prieto, Eric. "The Uses of Landscape: Ecocriticism and Martinican Cultural Theory." In *Caribbean Literature and the Environment: Between Nature and Culture*, edited by Elizabeth M. DeLoughrey, Renée K. Gosson, and George B. Handley, 236–51. Charlottesville: University of Virginia Press, 2005.

Prince, K. Stephen. "Remembering Robert Charles: Violence and Memory in Jim Crow New Orleans." *Journal of Southern History* 83, no. 2 (2017): 297–328.

Prince, Nancy. "A Narrative of the Life and Travels of Mrs. Nancy Prince, Written by Herself." In *Collected Black Women's Narratives*, edited by Henry Louis Gates Jr. New York: Oxford University Press, 1998.

"The Public Forum . . . El Foro Publico." Accessed February 25, 2023. https://laprensa-sandiego.org/archieve/2007/november30-07/TJSound.htm.

Puente González, Jesús María. "Las insurrecciones de esclavos en Haití y el imperio español en la época de Carlos IV." Master's thesis, Universidad de Cantabria, 2012.

Putnam, Lara. "Jazzing Sheiks at the 25 Cent Bram: Panama and Harlem as Caribbean Crossroads, circa 1910–1940." *Journal of Latin American Cultural Studies* 25, no. 3 (July 2, 2016): 339–59.

Quintero Rivera, A. G. "Music, Social Classes, and the National Question of Puerto Rico." Working Paper No. 178, Washington, DC: Latin American Program, Woodrow Wilson Center for Scholars, 1989.

———. "Ponce, the Danza, and the National Question: Notes Toward a Sociology of Puerto Rican Music." *Cimarrón: New Perspectives on the Caribbean* 1, no. 2 (Winter 1986): 49–65.

Quintero-Rivera, Angel G. "The Camouflaged Drum—Melodization of Rhythms and Maroonaged Ethnicity in Caribbean Peasant Music." *Caribbean Quarterly* 40, no. 1 (March 1, 1994): 27–37.

Quirarte, Xavier. *Ritmos de La Eternidad*. Mexico: CNCA, 1999.

Raeburn, Bruce Boyd. "Beyond the 'Spanish Tinge': Hispanics and Latinos in Early New Orleans Jazz." In *Eurojazzland: Jazz and European Sources, Dynamics, and Contexts*, edited by Luca Cerchiari, Laurent Cugny, and Franz Kerschbaumer, 21–46. Boston: Northeastern University Press, 2012.

———. "Foreword." In *The Original Tuxedo Jazz Band: More Than a Century of a New Orleans Icon*, by Sally Newhart, 1–2. Charleston, SC: The History Press, 2013.

———. "New Orleans Jazz Styles of the 1920s: Sam Morgan's Jazz Band." In *Sam Morgan's Jazz Band: Complete Recorded Works in Transcription*, edited by John Joyce Jr., Bruce Boyd Raeburn, and Anthony M. Cummings, xv–xxxiv. Middleton, WI: A-R Editions, 2012.

———. "'That Ain't No Creole, It's a . . . !': Masquerade, Marketing, and Shapeshifting Race in Early New Orleans Jazz." In *The Routledge Companion to Jazz Studies*, edited by Nicholas Gebhardt, Nichole Rustin-Paschal, and Tony Whyton, 37–44. New York: Routledge, 2018.

Ralph, Julian. "New Orleans, Our Southern Capitol." *Harper's New Monthly Magazine*, February 1899.

Ramírez, Margaret M. "City as Borderland: Gentrification and the Policing of Black and

Latinx Geographies in Oakland." *Environment and Planning D: Society and Space* 38, no. 1 (February 1, 2020): 147–66.

Ramos Pedrueza, Antonio. *Rusia Soviet y México Revolucionario. Vicente Guerrero: Precursor Del Socialismo*. México: Talleres gráficos de la nación, 1922.

Ramsey, Kate. "Without One Ritual Note: Folklore Performance and the Haitian State, 1935–1946." *Radical History Review* 84, no. 1 (2002): 7–42.

Rankine, Claudia. *Citizen: An American Lyric*. Minneapolis: Graywolf Press, 2014.

Rath, Richard Cullen. "Drums and Power: Ways of Creolizing Music in Coastal South Carolina and Georgia, 1730–1790." In *Creolization in the Americas: Cultural Adaptations to the New World*, edited by Steven Reinhardt and David Buisseret, 99–130. Arlington: Texas A&M University Press, 2000.

———. *How Early America Sounded*. Ithaca, NY: Cornell University Press, 2003.

Ratliff, Ben. *Coltrane: The Story of a Sound*. New York: Farrar, Straus and Giroux, 2008.

Rawick, George. *From Sundown to Sunup: The Making of the Black Community*. Westport, CT: Praeger, 1973.

Rawick, George P. *The American Slave*. Westport, CT: Greenwood Publishing Group, 1972.

Raymond, Jonathan. "James Lawson Remarks at John Lewis Funeral." 11 Alive, July 30, 2020. https://www.11alive.com/article/life/people/john-lewis/james-lawson-john-lewis-funeral/85-353bbce3-d876-4903-8371-6ce0764c9a4c.

Read, Ian, and Marcelo Bucehli. "Banana Boats and Baby Food: The Banana in U.S. History." In *From Silver to Cocaine: Latin American Commodity Chains and the Building of the World Economy, 1500–2000*, edited by Steven Topik, Carlos Marichal, and Zephyr Frank, 205–27. Durham, NC: Duke University Press, 2006.

Reaves, Bill. *Strength through Struggle: The Chronological and Historical Record of the African-American Community in Wilmington, North Carolina, 1865-1950*. Wilmington, NC: New Hanover County Public Library, 1998.

Rediker, Marcus. "Afterword: Reflections on the Motley Crew as Port City Proletariat." *International Review of Social History* 64, no. S27 (2019): 255–62.

———. "A Motley Crew for Our Times? Multiracial Mobs, History from below and the Memory of Struggle." *Radical Philosophy*, no. 207 (2020): 93–100.

———. "Escaping Slavery by Sea in Antebellum America: A Labor History." *Revista Mundos Do Trabalho* 14 (June 20, 2022): 1–18.

———. "The Red Atlantic, or, 'A Terrible Blast Swept over the Heaving Sea.'" In *Sea Changes: Historicizing the Ocean*, edited by Bernhard Klein and Gesa Mackenthun, 111–30. New York: Routledge, 2003.

Redkey, Edwin S., ed. *A Grand Army of Black Men: Letters from African-American Soldiers in the Union Army 1861–1865*. Cambridge: Cambridge University Press, 1992.

Redmond, Shana L. *Anthem: Social Movements and the Sound of Solidarity in the African Diaspora*. New York: New York University Press, 2014.

Regis, Helen A. "Second Lines, Minstrelsy, and the Contested Landscapes of New Orleans Afro-Creole Festivals." *Cultural Anthropology* 14, no. 4 (1999): 472–504.

Reid, Whitelaw. *After the War: A Tour of the Southern States, May 1, 1865, to May 1, 1866*. London: Sampson Low, Son, & Marston, 1866.

Reid-Vazquez, Michele. *The Year of the Lash: Free People of Color in Cuba and the Nineteenth-Century Atlantic World*. Athens: University of Georgia Press, 2011.

Reilly, Hugh Reilly, and Robert Reilly. *Historic Omaha*. San Antonio: Historical Publishing Network, 2003.

Reilly, Hugh, and Kevin Warneke. *Father Flanagan of Boys Town.* Omaha: Boys Town Press, 2011.

Richards, Paul. "Culture and Community Values in the Selection and Maintenance of African Rice." In *Valuing Local Knowledge: Indigenous People and Intellectual Property Rights,* edited by Stephen B. Brush and Doreen Stabinsky, 209–29. Washington, DC: Island Press, 1996.

Rickford, John R., and Jerome S. Handler. "Textual Evidence on the Nature of Early Barbadian Speech, 1676–1835." *Journal of Pidgin and Creole Languages* 9, no. 2 (January 1, 1994): 221–55.

Rickford, Russell. "'We Can't Grow Food on All This Concrete': The Land Question, Agrarianism, and Black Nationalist Thought in the Late 1960s and 1970s." *Journal of American History* 103, no. 4 (March 1, 2017): 956–80.

Ridley, Jasper. *Maximilian and Juárez.* New York: Ticknor & Fields, 1992.

Riley, Shannon Rose. *Performing Race and Erasure: Cuba, Haiti, and US Culture, 1898–1940.* London: Palgrave Macmillan, 2016.

Ripley, C. Peter. *Slaves and Freedmen in Civil War Louisiana.* Baton Rouge: Louisiana State University Press, 1976.

Rivera, Raquel Z. "New York Bomba: Puerto Ricans, Dominicans, and a Bridge Called Haiti." In *Rhythms of the Afro-Atlantic World Rituals and Remembrances,* edited by Ifeoma Kiddoe Nwankwo and Mamadou Diouf, 178–99. Ann Arbor: University of Michigan Press, 2010.

Roach, Joseph R. *Cities of the Dead: Circum-Atlantic Performance.* New York: Columbia University Press, 1996.

Roane, J. T. *Dark Agoras: Insurgent Black Social Life and the Politics of Place.* New York: NYU Press, 2023.

Roberts, John Storm. *The Latin Tinge: The Impact of Latin American Music on the United States.* New York: Oxford University Press, 1979.

Roberts, Kodi Alphonse. "The Promise of Power: The Racial, Gender, and Economic Politics of Voodoo in New Orleans, 1881–1940." PhD diss., University of Chicago, 2012.

Roberts, Nicholas. "Subverted Claims: Cortázar, Artaud, and the Problematics of Jazz." *The Modern Language Review* 104, no. 3 (2009): 730–45.

Roberts, Randy. *Papa Jack: Jack Johnson and the Era of White Hopes.* New York: Simon and Schuster, 1985.

Robinson, Armstead L. "'Worser Dan Jeff Davis': The Coming of Free Labor during the Civil War." In *Essays on the Postbellum Southern Economy,* edited by Thavolia Glymph and John J. Kushma, 11–47. College Station: Texas A&M University Press, 1985.

Robinson, Cedric J. *Black Marxism: The Making of the Black Radical Tradition.* Chapel Hill: University of North Carolina Press, 2000.

Robinson, William L. *The Diary of a Samaritan: By a Member of the Howard Association of New Orleans.* New York: Harpers and Brothers, 1960.

Rodicio, Emilio Casares, ed. "Habanera." In *Diccionario de La Música Española e Hispanoamericana,* edited by Emilio Casares, José López Calo, Ismael Fernández de la Cuesta, and María Luz González Peña. Madrid: Sociead General Autores Y Editores, 1999.

Rodrigue, John C. "Introduction." In *War, Politics, and Reconstruction: Stormy Days in Louisiana,* by Henry Clay Warmoth, ix–xlvi. Columbia: University of South Carolina Press, 2006.

———. *Reconstruction in the Cane Fields: From Slavery to Free Labor in Louisiana's Sugar Parishes, 1862–1880.* Baton Rouge: Louisiana State University Press, 2001.

Rodriguez, John Eugene. *Spanish New Orleans: An Imperial City on the American Periphery, 1766–1803.* Baton Rouge: Louisiana State University Press, 2021.

Rodriguez, Junius Peter. "Rebellion on the River Road: The Ideology and Influence of Louisiana's German Coast Slave Insurrection of 1811." In *Antislavery Violence: Sectional, Racial, and Cultural Conflict in Antebellum America*, edited by John R. McKivigan and Stanley Harrold, 65–88. Knoxville: University of Tennessee Press, 1999.

Rodríguez, Simón. "Reflexiones sobre los defectos que vician la escuela de primeras letras en Caracas y medios de lograr su reforma por un nuevo establecimiento, 19 de mayo de 1794." In *Simón Rodríguez, Escritos*, edited by Pedro Grases, 5–27. Caracas: Imprenta Nacional, 1954.

Roeder, Ralph. *Juarez and His Mexico: A Biographical History*. New York: The Viking Press, 1947.

Roediger, David R. *The Wages of Whiteness: Race and the Making of the American Working Class*. London: Verso, 2007.

Rogers, J. A. "Jazz at Home." In *The New Negro*, edited by Alain Locke, 223. New York: Touchstone, 1925.

Rojas, Rafael. *Las repúblicas de aire: utopía y desencanto en la revolución de Hispanoamérica*. México: Taurus, 2009.

———. "Los Amigos Cubanos de Juárez." *Istor*, no. 33 (2008): 42–57.

Rolando Antonio, Pérez Fernández. "El Son Jarocho Como Expresión Musical Afro-Mestiza." In *Musical Cultures of Latin America: Global Effects, Past and Present: Proceedings of an International Conference, University of California, Los Angeles, May 28–30, 1999*, edited by Steven J. Loza and Jack Bishop, 39–56. Los Angeles: Dept. of Ethnomusicology and Systematic Musicology, University of California, Los Angeles, 2003.

Ronzón León, José. "El Panorama Epidémico En El Golfo de México. Los Puertos de La Habana, Veracruz y New Orleans En La Segunda Mitad Del Siglo XIX." *Papeles de Población* 4, no. 16 (1998): 167–79.

The Roots of Music. "About the Roots of Music." *The Roots of Music* (blog), 2023. https://therootsofmusic.org/our-team/.

Rose, Al. *I Remember Jazz: Six Decades among the Great Jazzmen*. Baton Rouge: Louisiana State University Press, 1987.

Rosen, Hannah. *Terror in the Heart of Freedom: Citizenship, Sexual Violence, and the Meaning of Race in the Postemancipation South*. Chapel Hill: University of North Carolina Press, 2009.

Rosenberg, Daniel. *New Orleans Dockworkers: Race, Labor, and Unionism 1892–1923*. Albany: SUNY Press, 1988.

———. "Race, Labor and Unionism: New Orleans Dockworkers, 1900–1910." Master's thesis, City University of New York, 1985.

Roudané, Mark Charles. "Mechanics' Institute Massacre—Stop 3 of 9 on the *New Orleans Tribune*: America's First Black Daily Newspaper Tour." New Orleans Historical, August 4, 2020. https://neworleanshistorical.org/items/show/1541?tour=104&index=2&fbclid=IwAR3dzRIyIxQ3gxIPGbnq6GkvnOBorLnZlMYxzx0-h8xlyznpeATQcy-Rx1A.

———. *The* New Orleans Tribune: *An Introduction to America's First Black Daily Newspaper*. New Orleans: Historic New Orleans Collection, 2014.

Rousseau, Joseph Colastin. "Souvenirs De La Louisiane: Moralité De La Poésie." In *L'Union*. New Orleans, LA, 1863. Originally published as "Souvenirs De La Louisiane: Moralité De La Poésie," in *L'Opinion Nationale*, Port-au-Prince, Haiti, 1862.

Rugeley, Terry. *The River People in Flood Time: The Civil Wars in Tabasco, Spoiler of Empires*. Stanford, CA: Stanford University Press, 2014.

Rugemer, Edward Bartlett. *The Problem of Emancipation: The Caribbean Roots of the American Civil War*. Baton Rouge: Louisiana State University Press, 2009.

Runstedtler, Theresa. *Jack Johnson, Rebel Sojourner: Boxing in the Shadow of the Global Color Line*. Berkeley: University of California Press, 2013.

Russell, Bill. *New Orleans Style*. Edited by Barry Martyn and Mike Hazeldine. New Orleans: Jazzology, 1999.

Russell, James Michael. *Atlanta, 1847–1890: City Building in the Old South and the New*. Baton Rouge: Louisiana State University Press, 1988.

Russell, Ross. *Jazz Style in Kansas City and the Southwest*. Berkeley: University of California Press, 1971.

Russell, William. *"Oh, Mister Jelly": A Jelly Roll Morton Scrapbook*. Copenhagen: JazzMedia ApS, 1999.

Russell, William Howard. *My Diary North and South*. 2 vols. London: Bradbury and Evans, 1863.

Rustin-Paschal, Nichole. *The Kind of Man I Am: Jazzmasculinity and the World of Charles Mingus Jr*. Middletown, CT: Wesleyan University Press, 2017.

Ryan, Mary P. *Civic Wars: Democracy and Public Life in the American City during the Nineteenth Century*. Berkeley: University of California Press, 1998.

Rydell, Robert W. *All the World's a Fair: Visions of Empire at American International Expositions, 1876–1916*. Chicago: University of Chicago Press, 1984.

Saint-Méry, Moreau de. *Journey in the United States*. Edited and translated by Kenneth Roberts. New York: Doubleday, 1947.

Sakakeeny, Matt. "New Orleans Music and the Problem of the Black Vernacular." Unpublished manuscript, 2023.

———. "New Orleans Music as a Circulatory System." *Black Music Research Journal* 31, no. 2 (2011): 291–325.

———. "The Representational Power of the New Orleans Brass Band." In *Brass Bands of the World : Militarism, Colonial Legacies, and Local Music Making*, edited by S. A. Reily and K. Brucher, 123–37. Oxfordshire: Taylor & Francis Group, 2013.

———. *Roll with It: Brass Bands in the Streets of New Orleans*. Durham, NC: Duke University Press, 2013.

———. "Textures of Black Sound and Affect, Life and Death in New Orleans." *American Anthropologist* (Forthcoming).

Salaam, Kalamu ya. "The Spirit Family of the New Orleans Streets." *Neo-Griot* (blog), May 2014. https://kalamu.com/neogriot/2014/05/25/essay-spirit-family-of-the-streets-4/.

Salas, Miguel Tinker. *In the Shadow of the Eagles: Sonora and the Transformation of the Border During the Porfiriato*. Berkeley: University of California Press, 1997.

Salvaggio, Ruth. *Hearing Sappho in New Orleans: The Call of Poetry from Congo Square to the Ninth Ward*. Baton Rouge: Louisiana State University Press, 2012.

Sanchez, Adam. "Teaching the Reconstruction Revolution." *Rethinking Schools* 37, no. 1 (Fall 2022): 27–37.

Sancton, Tom. *Song for My Fathers: A New Orleans Story in Black and White*. New York: Other Press, 2010.

Sanders, James E. *The Vanguard of the Atlantic World: Contesting Modernity in Nineteenth-Century Latin America*. Durham, NC: Duke University Press, 2014.

Sandke, Randall. *Where the Dark and the Light Folks Meet: Race and the Mythology, Politics, and Business of Jazz*. Lanham, MD: Scarecrow Press, 2010.

Sandos, James A. *Rebellion in the Borderlands: Anarchism and the Plan of San Diego, 1904–1923*. Norman: University of Oklahoma Press, 1992.

Santacilia, Pablo Prida. *Apuntes Biográficos de Pedro Santacilia*. Secretaría de Educación Pública, Subsecretaría de Asuntos Culturales, 1966.

Santiago and Guerrero, and Leticia Bibiana. "La Participación de Los Empresarios Mexicanos en el Desarrollo Económico de Tijuana, 1915 – 1929." PhD diss., UABC, 2009.

Sasse, Adam Fletcher. "A History of Music in North Omaha." *North Omaha History* (blog),

January 6, 2022. https://northomahahistory.com/2022/01/06/a-history-of-music-in-north-omaha/.

Saville, Julie. *The Work of Reconstruction: From Wage Labor to Free Labor in South Carolina, 1860–1870*. New York: Cambridge University Press, 1994.

Savitt, Todd L. "Straight University Medical Department: The Short Life of a Black Medical School in Reconstruction New Orleans." *Louisiana History: The Journal of the Louisiana Historical Association* 41, no. 2 (2000): 175–201.

Sawyer Lee, Hannah Farnham. *Memoir of Pierre Toussaint, Born a Slave in St. Domingo*. 2nd ed. Westport, CT: Negro University Press, 1854.

Sayers, Daniel O. *A Desolate Place for a Defiant People: The Archaeology of Maroons, Indigenous Americans, and Enslaved Laborers in the Great Dismal Swamp*. Gainesville: Florida University Press, 2016.

Scarry, Elaine. *The Body in Pain: The Making and Unmaking of the World*. Oxford: Oxford University Press, 1987.

Schafer, Judith Kelleher. *Becoming Free, Remaining Free: Manumission and Enslavement in New Orleans, 1846–1862*. Baton Rouge: Louisiana State University Press, 2003.

———. "New Orleans Slavery in 1850 as Seen in Advertisements." *The Journal of Southern History* 47, no. 1 (1981): 33–56.

Schalk, Sami. "Contextualizing Black Disability and the Culture of Dissemblance." *Signs: Journal of Women in Culture and Society* 45, no. 3 (March 2020): 535–40.

Schechter, John Mendell. *Music in Latin American Culture: Regional Traditions*. New York: Schirmer Books, 1999.

Schermerhorn, Calvin. *Money over Mastery, Family over Freedom: Slavery in the Antebellum Upper South*. Baltimore: John Hopkins University Press, 2011.

Schoonover, Thomas D. *Mexican Lobby: Matías Romero in Washington 1861–1867*. Lexington: University Press of Kentucky, 2014.

Schulze, Jeffrey M. *Are We Not Foreigners Here?: Indigenous Nationalism in the U.S.-Mexico Borderlands*. Chapel Hill: University of North Carolina Press, 2018.

Schwalm, Leslie Ann. *Emancipation's Diaspora: Race and Reconstruction in the Upper Midwest*. Chapel Hill: University of North Carolina Press, 2009.

Schwartz, Radam. "Organ Jazz." MA thesis, Rutgers University, 2012.

Schwartz, Richard. "The African American Contribution to the Cornet of the Nineteenth Century: Some Long-Lost Names." *Historic Brass Society Journal* 12 (2000): 61–88.

Scott, David. "The Theory of Haiti: The Black Jacobins and the Poetics of Universal History." *Small Axe: A Caribbean Journal of Criticism* 18, no. 3 (45) (November 1, 2014): 35–51.

Scott, James C. *The Art of Not Being Governed: An Anarchist History of Upland Southeast Asia*. New Haven, CT: Yale University Press, 2009.

Scott, Julius S. "Afro-American Sailors and the International Communication Network: The Case of Newport Bowers." In *Jack Tar in History: Essays in the History of Maritime Life and Labor*, edited by Colin Howell and Richard Twomey. Fredericton: Acadiensis, 1991.

———. *The Common Wind: Afro-American Currents in the Age of the Haitian Revolution*. New York: Verso Books, 2018.

Scott, Rebecca J. *Degrees of Freedom: Louisiana and Cuba after Slavery*. Cambridge, MA: Harvard University Press, 2005.

———. "The Atlantic World and the Road to *Plessy v. Ferguson*." *Journal of American History* 94, no. 3 (December 1, 2007): 726–33.

Scott, Rebecca J., and Jean M. Hébrard. *Freedom Papers: An Atlantic Odyssey in the Age of Emancipation*. Cambridge, MA: Harvard University Press, 2012.

———. "Rosalie of the Poulard Nation: Freedom, Law, and Dignity in the Era of the Haitian Revolution." In *Assumed Identities: The Meanings of Race in the Atlantic World*, edited by John D. Garrigus and Christopher Morris, 116–43. College Station: Texas A&M University Press, 2010.

Scott, Rebecca J. "Public Rights and Private Commerce: A Nineteenth-Century Atlantic Creole Itinerary." *Current Anthropology* 48, no. 2 (2007): 237–56.

Scott-Heron, Gil. "Bicentennial Blues." In *It's Your World*. Arista Records, 1976.

———. "Who'll Pay Reparations on My Soul?" In *Small Talk at 125th and Lenox*. Flying Dutchman Records, 1970.

Sehgal, Kabir. *Fandango at the Wall: Creating Harmony Between the United States and Mexico*. New York: Hachette Book Group, 2018.

Séjour, Victor. "Le Mulâtre." *Révue Des Colonies*, March 1837, 376–92.

Senior, Bernard Martin. *Jamaica, as It Was, as It Is, and as It May Be*. London: T. Hurst, 1835.

Senter, Caroline. "Creole Poets on the Verge of a Nation." In *Creole: The History and Legacy of Louisiana's Free People of Color*, edited by Sybil Kein, 276–94. Baton Rouge: Louisiana State University Press, 2000.

Sepinwall, Alyssa Goldstein, ed. *Haitian History: New Perspectives*. London: Taylor & Francis Group, 2012.

Shaik, Fatima. *Economy Hall: The Hidden History of a Free Black Brotherhood*. New Orleans: Historic New Orleans Collections, 2021.

Shankman, Arnold. "The Image of Mexico and the Mexican-American in the Black Press, 1890–1935." *The Journal of Ethnic Studies* 3, no. 2 (Summer 1975): 43–56.

Shapiro, Nat, and Nat Hentoff. *Hear Me Talkin' to Ya*. London: Souvenir Press, 1992.

Sheller, Mimi. *Citizenship from Below: Erotic Agency and Caribbean Freedom*. Durham, NC: Duke University Press, 2012.

———. *Democracy after Slavery: Black Publics and Peasant Radicalism in Haiti and Jamaica*. Gainesville: University Press of Florida, 2001.

———. "Mobile Commoning: Reclaiming Indigenous, Caribbean, Maroon, and Migrant Commons." *Praktyka Teoretyczna* 4, no. 46 (2022): 29–52.

Shugg, Roger Wallace. *Origins of Class Struggle in Louisiana*. Baton Rouge: Louisiana State University Press, 1939.

———. "Survival of the Plantation System in Louisiana." *The Journal of Southern History* 3, no. 3 (1937): 311–25.

Sidran, Ben. *Talking Jazz: An Oral History*. New York: De Capo Press, 1995.

Siliceo, Manuel. *Memoria de la Secretaría de Estado y Del Despacho de Fomento, Colonización, Industria y Comercio de La República Mexicana*. México: Imp. V. García Torres, 1857.

Singleton, Theresa A. *Slavery Behind the Wall: An Archaeology of a Cuban Coffee Plantation*. Gainesville: University Press of Florida, 2015.

Sitterson, Joseph Carlyle. *Sugar Country: The Cane Sugar Industry in the South, 1753–1950*. Lexington: University of Kentucky Press, 1953.

Smallwood, Stephanie E. "The Politics of the Archive and History's Accountability to the Enslaved." *History of the Present* 6, no. 2 (2016): 117–32.

Smart, Charles Allen. *Viva Juárez!* Philadelphia, PA: J. B. Lippincott Company, 1963.

Smith, Christopher J. *The Creolization of American Culture: William Sidney Mount and the Roots of Blackface Minstrelsy*. Chicago: University of Illinois Press, 2013.

Smith, Elizabeth Parish. "Southern Sirens: Disorderly Women and the Fight for Public Order in Reconstruction-Era New Orleans." PhD diss., University of North Carolina, 2013.

Smith, Laura Alexandrine. *The Music of the Waters: A Collection of the Sailors' Chanties, or Working Songs of the Sea, of All Maritime Nations; Boatmen's Fishermen's, and Rowing Songs, and Water Legends*. London: Kegan Paul, Trench, 1888.

Smith, Mark M. "Remembering Mary, Shaping Revolt: Reconsidering the Stono Rebellion." *The Journal of Southern History* 67, no. 3 (2001): 513–34.

Smith, Matthew J. *Liberty, Fraternity, Exile: Haiti and Jamaica After Emancipation*. Chapel Hill: University of North Carolina Press, 2014.

Smith, Michael P. "Behind the Lines: The Black Mardi Gras Indians and the New Orleans Second Line." *Black Music Research Journal* 14, no. 1 (1994): 43–73.

Smith, Pamela J. "Caribbean Influences on New Orleans Jazz." MA thesis, Tulane University, 1986.

Smith, Rosemunde Goode. "Dying to Vote: The Negroes' Struggle to Secure the Right to Vote in Upcountry South Carolina 1868–1898." Master's thesis, Morgan State University, 2008.

Smith, Willie. *Music on My Mind: The Memoirs of an American Pianist*. Garden City, NY: Doubleday, 1964.

Snodgrass, Mary Ellen. *The Underground Railroad: An Encyclopedia of People, Places, and Operations*. London: Routledge, 2008.

Soards' New Orleans City Directory of 1901. New Orleans: Soards' Directory Company, 1901.

Solinger, Rickie. "Racializing the Nation: From the Declaration of Independence to the Emancipation Proclamation." In *The Reproductive Rights Reader: Law, Medicine, and the Construction of Motherhood*, edited by Nancy Ehrenreich, 261–74. New York: NYU Press, 2008.

Solis, Gabriel. "The Black Pacific: Music and Racialization in Papua New Guinea and Australia." *Critical Sociology* 41, no. 2 (March 1, 2015): 297–312.

Somers, Dale A. "Black and White in New Orleans: A Study in Urban Race Relations, 1865–1900." *The Journal of Southern History* 40, no. 1 (1974): 19–42.

Somers, Robert. *The Southern States Since the War, 1870-1*. New York: Macmillan and Company, 1871.

Sonneck, Oscar. *Early Concert Life in America*. Mansfield, CT: Martino Pub, 1922.

Soriano, Cristina. *Tides of Revolution: Information, Insurgencies, and the Crisis of Colonial Rule in Venezuela*. Albuquerque: University of New Mexico Press, 2018.

Sousa, Emily C., and Manish N. Raizada. "Contributions of African Crops to American Culture and Beyond: The Slave Trade and Other Journeys of Resilient Peoples and Crops." *Frontiers in Sustainable Food Systems* 4 (2020): 1–24.

South Carolina Legislature. "1740 | Slave Code of South Carolina, Articles 34-37." Duhaime.org, October 29, 2020. http://www.duhaime.org/LawMuseum/LawArticle-1501/1740-Slave-Code-of-South-Carolina-Articles-34-37.aspx.

Southern, Eileen. *The Music of Black Americans: A History*. New York: W. W. Norton, 1971.

Sparks, Nikolas Oscar. "Lost Bodies/Found Objects: Storyville and the Archival Imagination." PhD diss., Duke University, 2017.

Spear, Jennifer M. *Race, Sex, and Social Order in Early New Orleans*. Baltimore: John Hopkins University Press, 2009.

St. Cyr, Johnny. "Interview." Alan Lomax Digital Archive. Association for Cultural Equity, April 2, 1949. https://archive.culturalequity.org/field-work/new-orleans-jazz-interviews-1949/johnny-st-cyr-449/interview-johnny-st-cyr-about-creole.

———. "Jazz as I Remember It: Part 1, Early Days." *Jazz Journal* 19, no. 9 (September 1966): 6–10.

St. John, Rachel. *Line in the Sand: A History of the Western U.S.-Mexico Border*. Princeton, NJ: Princeton University Press, 2012.

Stanyek, Jason. "Transmissions of an Interculture: Pan-African Jazz and Intercultural Improvisation." In *The Other Side of Nowhere: Jazz, Improvisation, and Communities in Dialogue*, edited by Daniel Fischlin and Ajay Heble, 87–130. Middletown, CT: Wesleyan University Press, 2004.

Starr, Frederick. *In Indian Mexico: A Narrative of Travel and Labor*. Chicago: Forbes & Co, 1908.

Stebbins, Robert A. "Role Distance Behaviour and Jazz Musicians." *The British Journal of Sociology* 20, no. 4 (1969): 406–15.

Sterling, Dorothy, ed. *The Trouble They Seen: The Story of Reconstruction in the Words of African Americans*. New York: Da Capo Press, 1994.

Steward, *Twenty-Two Years a Slave, Forty Years a Freeman*. Syracuse: Syracuse University Press, 2002 [1861].

Stewart, D. B., ed. *Gosse's Jamaica 1844-45*. Kingston: Institute of Jamaica Publications, 1984.

Stewart, Jack. "The Mexican Band Legend: Myth, Reality, and Musical Impact; A Preliminary Investigation." *The Jazz Archivist* VI, no. 2 (December 1991): 1–14.

———. "The Mexican Band Legend: Part III." *The Jazz Archivist* XX (2007): 1–10.

Stewart, Jesse. "Freedom Music: Jazz and Human Rights." In *Rebel Musics: Human Rights, Resistant Sounds, and the Politics of Music Making*, edited by Daniel Fischlin and Ajay Heble, 88–107. Montreal: Black Rose Press, 2003.

Stipriaan, Alex van. *Surinaams Contrast: Roofbouw En Overleven in Een Caraïbische Plantagekolonie, 1750–1863*. Leiden: Brill, 1993.

Stoler, Ann Laura. *Along the Archival Grain: Epistemic Anxieties and Colonial Common Sense*. Princeton, NJ: Princeton University Press, 2010.

Stone, Robert L. *Sacred Steel: Inside an African American Steel Guitar Tradition*. Urbana: University of Illinois Press, 2010.

Strongman, Roberto. "Transcorporeality in Vodou." *Journal of Haitian Studies* 14, no. 2 (2008): 4–29.

Struge, Joseph, and Thomas Harvey. *The West Indies in 1837*. London: Hamilton, Adams and Co., 1838.

Stuart, Dave. "Kid Ory." *Jazz Information* 2, no. 9 (1940): 5–8.

Sublette, Ned. *Cuba and Its Music: From the First Drums to the Mambo*. Chicago: Chicago Review Press, 2004.

Sublette, Ned, and Constance Sublette. *The American Slave Coast: A History of the Slave-Breeding Industry*. Chicago: Chicago Review Press, 2015.

Sullivan, Lester. "Composers of Color of Nineteenth-Century New Orleans: The History behind the Music." *Black Music Research Journal* 8, no. 1 (1988): 51–82.

Sutherland, George E. "The Negro and the Great War." In *War Papers*, by Wisconsin Commandery, 170–88. Milwaukee, WI: Burdick, Armtage, and Allen, 1891.

Sweet, James H. "'Brothers Gonna Work It Out': Imagining a Black Planet." *Journal of the Early Republic* 40, no. 2 (2020): 217–22.

Synder, Jared. "'Garde Ici et 'garde Lá-Bas: Creole Accordion in Louisiana." In *The Accordion in the Americas: Klezmer, Polka, Tango, Zydeco, and More!*, edited by Helena Simonett, 66–86. Chicago: University of Illinois Press, 2012.

Szwed, John F., and Morton Marks. "The Afro-American Transformation of European Set Dances and Dance Suites." *Dance Research Journal* 20, no. 1 (1988): 29–36.

Tadman, Michael. "The Demographic Cost of Sugar: Debates on Slave Societies and Natural Increase in the Americas." *The American Historical Review* 105, no. 5 (2000): 1534–75.

Taibo II, Paco Ignacio. *Yaquis: Historia de Una Guerra Popular y de Un Genocidio En México*. México: Planeta, 2013.

Tanner, Lynette Ater, ed. *Chained to the Land: Voices from Cotton & Cane Plantations*. Salem, NC: Blair, 2014. Kindle Edition.

Tarasti, Eero. *Signs of Music: A Guide to Musical Semiotics*. New York: Mouton de Gruyter, 2002.

Tardieu, Jean-Pierre. *Resistencia de Los Negros En El Virreinato de México (Siglos XVI–XVII)*. Madrid: Iberoamericana / Vervuert, 2017.

Tatum, Jim C. "Veracruz En 1816–1817: Fragmento Del Diario de Antonio López Matoso." *Historia Mexicana* 19, no. 1 (1969): 105–24.

Tavares Romero, Octavio Enrique, and Juan Hugo Barreiro Lastra. "La influencia de la danza cubana en compositores latinoamericanos." *Jóvenes en la Ciencia* 3, no. 2 (December 30, 2017): 1840–45.

Taylor, Christin Marie. "'Release Your Wiggle': Big Freedia's Queer Bounce." *Southern Cultures* 24, no. 2 (2018): 60–77.

Teague, Jessica E. *Sound Recording Technology and American Literature: From the Phonograph to the Remix*. Cambridge: Cambridge University Press, 2021.

———. "A Story in Sound: The Unpublished Writings of Sidney Bechet." *MELUS* 47, no. 4 (December 1, 2022): 49–73.

Teish, Luisah. *Jambalaya: The Natural Woman's Book of Personal Charms and Practical Rituals*. San Francisco: Harper & Row, 1988.

Tenorio-Trillo, Mauricio. *Mexico at the World's Fairs: Crafting a Modern Nation*. Berkeley: University of California Press, 1996.

Terreblanche, Christelle. "Ubuntu and the Struggle for an African Eco-Socialist Alternative." In *The Climate Crisis*, edited by Vishwas Satgar, 168–89. Johannesburg: Wits University Press, 2018.

Thierry, Camille. *Les Vagabondes: Poésies Américaines*. Paris: Lemerre, 1874.

Thiong'o, Ngũgĩ wa. *Penpoints, Gunpoints, and Dreams: Towards a Critical Theory of the Arts and the State in Africa*. Oxford: Clarendon Press, 1998.

Thistlethwaite, Frank. "Migration from Europe Overseas in the Nineteenth and Twentieth Centuries." In *XI Congres International Des Sciences Historiques*, 32–60. Rapports: Stockholm, 1960.

Thomas, Deborah A. *Political Life in the Wake of the Plantation: Sovereignty, Witnessing, Repair*. Durham, NC: Duke University Press, 2019.

Thomas, Henry G. "The Colored Troops at Petersburg." *Century Magazine* 12 (September 1887): 777–79.

Thornberry, Jerry John. "The Development of Black Atlanta, 1865–1885." PhD diss., University of Maryland, 1977.

Thompson, Robert Farris. *Flash of the Spirit: African and Afro-American Art and Philosophy*. New York: Random House, 1983.

———. *Tango: The Art History of Love*. New York: Random House, 2010.

Thompson, Shirley. "'Ah Toucoutou, Ye Conin Vous': History and Memory in Creole New Orleans." *American Quarterly* 53, no. 2 (2001): 232–66.

Thompson, Shirley Elizabeth. *Exiles at Home: The Struggle to Become American in Creole New Orleans*. Cambridge, MA: Harvard University Press, 2009.

Thomson, Guy P. C. "Bulwarks of Patriotic Liberalism: The National Guard, Philharmonic Corps and Patriotic Juntas in Mexico, 1847-88." *Journal of Latin American Studies* 22, no. 1 (1990): 31–68.

Tick, Judith, and Melissa J. de Graaf. "Three Slave Lullabies." The Feminist Sexual Ethics Project of Brandeis University, October 26, 2020. https://brandeis.edu/projects/fse/slavery/lullabies/three-lullabies.html.

Timitoc Borrero, Dalia. *Montecafé*. La Habana: Ediciones Extramuros, 2004.

Tinajero, Araceli. *El Lector: A History of the Cigar Factory Reader*. Austin: University of Texas Press, 2010.

Tinker, Edward Larocque. *Les Décrits Des Langue Française En Louisiane*. Paris: Librairie Ancienne Honoré Champion, 1931.

Tirro, Frank. *Jazz: A History*. New York: Norton, 1977.

Tobin, Beth Fowkes. *Colonizing Nature: The Tropics in British Arts and Letters, 1760-1820*. Philadelphia: University of Pennsylvania Press, 2011.

Tobin, Jacqueline L., and Raymond G. Dobard. *Hidden in Plain View: A Secret Story of Quilts and the Underground Railroad*. New York: Knopf Doubleday Publishing Group, 2011.

Tomich, Dale W. *Through the Prism of Slavery: Labor, Capital, and World Economy*. Lanham, MD: Rowman & Littlefield Publishers, 2003.

Tregle, Joseph G., Jr. "Creoles and Americans." In *Creole New Orleans: Race and Americanization*, edited by Arnold R. Hirsch and Joseph Logsdon, 131-85. Baton Rouge: Louisiana State University Press, 1992.

Trotter, James M. *Music and Some Highly Musical People*. Boston: Lee and Shepard, 1878.

Trollope, Frances Milton. *Domestic Manners of the Americans*. Edited by Pamela Neville-Singleton. New York: Penguin Classics, 1832.

Trouillot, Michel-Rolph. *Haiti, State Against Nation: The Origins and Legacy of Duvalierism*. New York: Monthly Review Press, 1990.

———. "The Odd and the Ordinary: Haiti, the Caribbean, and the World." In *Trouillot Remixed: The Michel-Rolph Trouillot Reader*, edited by Yarimar Bonilla, Greg Beckett and Mayanthi L. Fernando, 85-96. Durham, NC: Duke University Press, 2021.

———. *Silencing the Past: Power and the Production of History*. Boston: Beacon Press, 2015.

Troutman, John W. "Steelin' the Slide: Hawai'i and the Birth of the Blues Guitar." *Southern Cultures* 19, no. 1 (2013): 26-52.

Trudeau, Noah Andre. *Like Men of War: Black Troops in the Civil War 1862-1865*. Boston: Back Bay Books, 1999.

Tucker, Sherrie. "A Feminist Perspective on New Orleans Jazzwomen." New Orleans: New Orleans Jazz National Historical Park, 2004.

———. "Jazz History Remix: Black Women from 'Enter' to 'Center.'" In *Issues in African American Music: Power, Gender, Race, Representation*, edited by Portia K. Maultsby and Mellonee V. Burnim, 256-69. London: Taylor & Francis Group, 2016.

Tuiz Torres, Rafael A. "Las Bandas Militares de Música En México y Su Historia." In *Bandas de Viento En México*, edited by Georgina Flores Mercado, 21-44. Mexico City: Instituto Nacional de Antropología e Historia, 2015.

Turino, Thomas. *Music as Social Life: The Politics of Participation*. Chicago: University of Chicago Press, 2008.

Turner, Henry McNeal. *Respect Black: The Writings and Speeches of Henry McNeal Turner*. New York: Arno Press, 1971.

Turner, Richard Brent. *Jazz Religion, the Second Line, and Black New Orleans*. Bloomington: Indiana University Press, 2009.

———. "Mardi Gras Indians and Second Lines/Sequin Artists and Rara Bands: Street Festivals and Performances in New Orleans and Haiti." *Journal of Haitian Studies* 9, no. 1 (2003): 124-56.

Tutino, John. *From Insurrection to Revolution in Mexico: Social Bases of Agrarian Violence, 1750–1940.* Princeton, NJ: Princeton University Press, 1989.

Tyler, Ronnie C., and Lawrence R. Murphy, eds. *The Slave Narratives of Texas.* College Station: State House Press, 2006.

Unsworth, Barry. *Sacred Hunger.* New York: Knopf Doubleday Publishing Group, 2012.

Urofsky, Melvin I. "Dred Scott Decision." In *Encyclopedia Britannica*, February 10, 2023. https://britannica.com/event/Dred-Scott-decision.

Uzee, Philip Davis. "Republican Politics in Louisiana, 1877–1900." PhD diss., Louisiana State University, 1950.

Vance, Robert B. "The Profile of Southern Culture." In *Culture in the South*, edited by W. T. Couch, 30. Chapel Hill: University of North Carolina Press, 1935.

Vance, Rupert B. *Human Geography of the South.* Chapel Hill: University of North Carolina Press, 1932.

Vandal, Gilles. "Black Utopia in Early Reconstruction New Orleans: The People's Bakery as a Case-Study." *Louisiana History: The Journal of the Louisiana Historical Association* 38, no. 4 (1997): 437–52.

Vaughn, Bobby. "México Negro: From the Shadows of Mestizaje to New Possibilities in Afro-Mexican Identity." *Journal of Pan African Studies* 6, no. 1 (2013): 227–40.

Vermeulen, Heather V. "Thomas Thistlewood's Libidinal Linnaean Project: Slavery, Ecology, and Knowledge Production." *Small Axe: A Caribbean Journal of Criticism* 22, no. 1 (March 1, 2018): 18–38.

Vernhettes, Daniel. *Visiting Mexican Bands, 1876–1955.* Rouvary, France: Jazzédit, 2022.

Vernhettes, Dan, and Bo Lindstörm. *Jazz Puzzles: Volume 1.* Saint Etienne, France: Jazz Edit, 2012.

Vernhettes, Dan, and Peter Hanley. "The Desdunes Family." *The Jazz Archivist* XXVII (2014): 25–45.

Vernhettes, Dan, Bo Lindstörm, Peter Hanley, and Karl Gert zur Heide. "The Desdunes Family." In *Jazz Puzzles: Volume 4*, 52–94. Saint Etienne: Jazz Edit, 2021.

Vézina, Caroline. "Jazz à La Creole." *The Jazz Archivist* XXXVIII (2015): 38–45.

———. *Jazz à La Creole: French Creole Music and the Birth of Jazz.* Jackson: University Press of Mississippi, 2022.

Vidacovich, Johnny, Herlin Riley, and Dan Thress. *New Orleans Jazz and Second Line Drumming: Book & CD.* Miami: Manhattan Music, 1995.

Viddal, Grete. "'Sueño de Haiti': Danced Identity in Eastern Cuba." *Journal of Haitian Studies* 12, no. 1 (2006): 50–64.

———. "Vodú Chic: Cuba's Haitian Heritage, the Folkloric Imaginary, and the State." PhD diss, Harvard University, 2014.

———. "Vodú Chic: Haitian Religion and the Folkloric Imaginary in Socialist Cuba." *NWIG: New West Indian Guide / Nieuwe West-Indische Gids* 86, no. 3/4 (2012): 205–35.

Vincent, Charles. *Black Legislators in Louisiana during Reconstruction.* Carbondale: Southern Illinois University Press, 2011.

———. "Black Louisianians during the Civil War and Reconstruction: Aspects of Their Struggles and Achievements." In *Louisiana's Black Heritage*, edited by Robert Macdonald, John Kemp, and Edward Haas, 85–106. Louisiana State Museum, 1979.

Vincent, Ted. "The Blacks Who Freed Mexico." *The Journal of Negro History* 79, no. 3 (1994): 257–76.

Vincent, Theodore G. "The Contributions of Mexico's First Black Indian President, Vicente Guerrero." *The Journal of Negro History* 86, no. 2 (2001): 148–59.

———. *The Legacy of Vicente Guerrero, Mexico's First Black Indian President*. Gainesville: University Press of Florida, 2001.

Vinson, Ben. *Bearing Arms for His Majesty: The Free-Colored Militia in Colonial Mexico*. Stanford, CA: Stanford University Press, 2001.

Vinson III, Ben. *Before Mestizaje: The Frontiers of Race and Caste in Colonial Mexico*. New York: Oxford University Press, 2017.

Volpato, Gabriele, Daimy Godínez, and Angela Beyra. "Migration and Ethnobotanical Practices: The Case of Tifey among Haitian Immigrants in Cuba." *Human Ecology* 37, no. 1 (February 1, 2009): 43–53.

Waddell, Hope Masterton. *Twenty-Nine Years in the West Indies and Central Africa: A Review of Missionary Work and Adventure, 1829–1858*. Edinburgh: T. Nelson and Sons, 1863.

Wagner, Bryan. "Disarmed and Dangerous: The Strange Career of Brás-Coupé." *Representations*, no. 92 (2005): 117–51.

———. *Disturbing the Peace: Black Culture and the Police Power after Slavery*. Cambridge, MA: Harvard University Press, 2009.

———. *The Life and Legend of Bras-Coupé: The Fugitive Slave Who Fought the Law, Ruled the Swamp, Danced at Congo Square, Invented Jazz, and Died for Love*. Baton Rouge: Louisiana State University Press, 2019.

Wald, Elijah. *Escaping the Delta: Robert Johnson and the Invention of the Blues*. New York: Harper Collins, 2004.

———. "Mamie's Blues (219 Blues)." Old Friends: A Songobiography, June 15, 2016. https://elijahwald.com/songblog/mamies-blues/.

———. *The Blues: A Very Short Introduction*. New York: Oxford University Press, 2010.

Walser, Robert, ed. *Keeping Time: Readings in Jazz History*. New York: Oxford University Press, 1994.

Ward, Jerry. "Southern Black Aesthetics: The Case of 'Nkombo' Magazine." *The Mississippi Quarterly* 44, no. 2 (1991): 143–50.

Ward, Martha. "Where Circum-Caribbean Afro-Catholic Creoles Met American Southern Protestant Conjurers: Origins of New Orleans Voodoo." In *Caribbean and Southern: Transnational Perspectives on the U.S. South*, edited by Helen A. Regis, 124–38. Athens: University of Georgia Press, 2006.

Wardi, Anissa J. *Water and African American Memory: An Ecocritical Perspective*. Gainesville: University Press of Florida, 2011.

Warmoth, Henry Clay. *War, Politics, and Reconstruction: Stormy Days in Louisiana*. Columbia, S.C.: Univ of South Carolina Press, 2006.

Washburne, Christopher. "The Clave of Jazz: A Caribbean Contribution to the Rhythmic Foundation of an African-American Music." *Black Music Research Journal* 17, no. 1 (1997): 59–80.

———. *Latin Jazz: The Other Jazz*. New York: Oxford University Press, 2020.

Washington, Grover Jr. "University of Pittsburgh Annual Seminar on Jazz 1990." *International Jazz Archives Journal* (1993): 140–57.

Washington, Salim. "'All the Things You Could Be by Now': Charles Mingus Presents Charles Mingus and the Limits of Avant-Garde Jazz." In *Uptown Conversation: The New Jazz Studies*, edited by Robert O'Meally, Brent Hayes Edwards, and Farah Jasmine Griffin, 27–49. Columbia University Press, 2004.

———. "The Avenging Angel of Creation/Destruction: Black Music and the Afro-Technological in the Science Fiction of Henry Dumas and Samuel R. Delany." *Journal of the Society for American Music* 2, no. 2 (2008): 235–53.

Watts, Lewis, and Eric Porter. *New Orleans Suite: Music and Culture in Transition.* Berkeley, CA: University of California Press, 2013.

Watkins, Mel. *On the Real Side: Laughing, Lying, and Signifying.* New York: Simon & Schuster, 1994.

Webb-Gannon, Camellia, Michael Webb, and Gabriel Solis. "The 'Black Pacific' and Decolonisation in Melanesia: Performing 'Négritude' and 'Indigènitude.'" *The Journal of the Polynesian Society* 127, no. 2 (2018): 177–206.

Wegmann, Andrew N. *An American Color: Race and Identity in New Orleans and the Atlantic World.* Athens: University of Georgia Press, 2022.

Weir, Stan. *Singlejack Solidarity.* Minneapolis: University of Minnesota Press, 2004.

Weiss, Holger. *Framing a Radical African Atlantic: African American Agency, West African Intellectuals and the International Trade Union Committee of Negro Workers.* Leiden: Brill, 2013.

Wells-Barnett, Ida B. *Lynch Laws in Georgia.* Chicago: Self-Published, 1899.

———. *Mob Rule in New Orleans: Robert Charles and His Fight to Death, the Story of His Life, Burning Human Beings Alive, Other Lynching Statistics.* Chicago: Self-Published, 1900.

———. *On Lynchings, Southern Horrors, A Red Record, Mob Rule in New Orleans.* New York: Arno Press, 1969.

Wells-Barnett, Ida B., and Frederick Douglass. *The Reason Why the Colored American Is Not in the World's Columbian Exposition: The Afro-American's Contribution to Columbian Literature.* Edited by Robert W. Rydell. Chicago: University of Illinois Press, 1999.

Wells-Oghoghomeh, Alexis. *The Souls of Womenfolk: The Religious Cultures of Enslaved Women in the Lower South.* Durham, NC: University of North Carolina Press Books, 2021.

West, Michael O., and William G. Martin. "Haiti, I'm Sorry: The Haitian Revolution and the Forging of the Black International." In *From Toussaint to Tupac: The Black International since the Age of Revolution*, edited by Michael O. West, William G. Martin, and Fanon Che Wilkins, 72–104. Chapel Hill: University of North Carolina Press, 2009.

Westwood, Harold C. "The Cause and Consequence of a Union Black Soldier's Mutiny and Execution." *Civil War History* 31 (1985): 222–36.

Wever, Jerry. "Dancing the Habanera Beats (in Country Music) The Creole-Country Two-Step in St. Lucia and Its Diaspora." In *Hidden in the Mix: The African American Presence in Country Music*, edited by Diane Pecknold, 204–33. Durham, NC: Duke University Press, 2013.

White, Michael G. "A Musician's Life in the Second Line." In *Freedom's Dance: Social Aid and Pleasure Clubs in New Orleans*, edited by Karen Celestan and Eric Waters, 120–21. Baton Rouge: Louisiana State University Press, 2018.

White, Shane. "'It Was a Proud Day': African Americans, Festivals, and Parades in the North, 1741-1834." *The Journal of American History* 81, no. 1 (1994): 13–50.

Wideman, John Edgar. "Charles Chesnutt and the WPA Narratives: The Oral and Literate Roots of African-American Literature." In *The Slave's Narrative*, edited by Charles T. Davis and Henry Louis Gates Jr., 59–77. New York: Oxford University Press, 1991.

Wiggins, Sarah Woolfolk. *The Scalawag in Alabama Politics, 1865–1881.* Tuscaloosa: University of Alabama Press, 1977.

Wilcox, Carol. *Sugar Water: Hawaii's Plantation Ditches.* Honolulu: University of Hawai'i Press, 1997.

Wiley, Bell Irvin. *Southern Negros, 1861–1865.* New York: Rinehart & Company, 1938.

Williams, James Gordon. *Crossing Bar Lines: The Politics and Practices of Black Musical Space.* Jackson: University Press of Mississippi, 2021.

Williams, Martin T. *Jazz Masters of New Orleans*. New York: Macmillan, 1967.

Williams, Raymond. *Marxism and Literature*. Oxford: Oxford University Press, 1977.

Williams, T. Harry. "The Louisiana Unification Movement of 1873." *The Journal of Southern History* 11, no. 3 (1945): 349–69.

Williams-Jones, Pearl. "Afro-American Gospel Music: A Crystallization of the Black Aesthetic." *Ethnomusicology* 19, no. 3 (1975): 373–85.

Williamson, Frederick W., and George T. Goodman, eds. *Eastern Louisiana: A History of the Watershed of the Ouachita River and the Florida Parishes*. 3 vols. Monroe: Historical Record Association, 1939.

Williamson, Joel. *After Slavery: The Negro in South Carolina During Reconstruction, 1861–1877*. Chapel Hill: University of North Carolina Press, 1965.

Wilson, Keith. *Campfires of Freedom: The Camp Life of Black Soldiers During the Civil War*. Kent, OH: Kent State University Press, 2002.

Wilson, Olly. "The Heterogeneous Sound Ideal in African American Music." In *New Perspectives on Music: Essays in Honor of Eileen Southern*, edited by Samuel Floyd Jr. and Josephine Wright, 327–40. Sterling Heights, MI: Harmonie Park Press, 1992.

———. "The Significance of the Relationship between Afro-American Music and West African Music." *The Black Perspective in Music* 2, no. 1 (1974): 3–22.

Winberry, John J. "The Mexican Landbridge Project: The Isthmus of Tehuantepec and Inter-Oceanic Transit." *Yearbook. Conference of Latin Americanist Geographers* 13 (1987): 12–18.

Winfield, Arthur Anison, Jr.. "Slave Holidays and Festivities in the United States." PhD diss., Atlanta University, 1941.

Winters, Lisa Ze. *The Mulatta Concubine: Terror, Intimacy, Freedom, and Desire in the Black Transatlantic*. Athens: University of Georgia Press, 2016.

Wiredu, Kwasi. *Cultural Universals and Particulars: An African Perspective*. Bloomington: Indiana University Press, 1996.

Woods, Clyde. *Development Arrested: The Blues and Plantation Power in the Mississippi Delta*. New York: Verso, 1998.

———. *Development Drowned and Reborn: The Blues and Bourbon Restorations in Post-Katrina New Orleans*. Edited by Jordan T. Camp and Laura Pulido. Athens: University of Georgia Press, 2017.

Woodward, C. Vann. *Origins of the New South, 1877–1913*. Baton Rouge: Louisiana State University Press, 1951.

Woodward, Ralph Lee. "Spanish Commercial Policy in Louisiana, 1763–1803." *Louisiana History: The Journal of the Louisiana Historical Association* 44, no. 2 (2003): 133–64.

Work, Henry Clay. "Marching Through Georgia." In *The American Civil War: An Anthology of Essential Writings*, edited by Ian Frederick Finseth, 354. London: Taylor & Francis Group, 2006.

Work, Monroe N. "Some Negro Members of Reconstruction Conventions and Legislatures and of Congress." *The Journal of Negro History* 5, no. 1 (1920): 63–119.

WPA (Works Progress Administration). *WPA Slave Narratives 1936–1938: North Carolina*, vol. XI. Washington, DC, 1941.

WPA (Works Progress Administration) Nebraska Writer's Project. *The Negroes of Nebraska*. Omaha: Urban League Community Center, 1940.

Wright, Laurie. *Mr. Jelly Lord*. Chigwell, Essex: Storyville Publications, 1980.

Wynter, Sylvia. "Novel and History, Plot and Plantation." *Savacou* 5 (June 1971): 95–102.

Yanow, Scott. *Afro-Cuban Jazz: Third Ear*. San Francisco: Backbeat, 2000.

———. "Lizzie Miles: Complete Recorded Works, Volume 1 (1922–1923)." In *All Music Guide to the Blues: The Definitive Guide to the Blues*, edited by Vladimir Bogdanov, Chris Woodstra, and Stephen Thomas Erlewine, 402. Milwaukee: Hal Leonard Corporation, 2003.

Yard, Alexander. "'They Don't Regard My Rights at All': Arkansas Farm Workers, Economic Modernization, and the Southern Tenant Farmers Union." *The Arkansas Historical Quarterly* 47, no. 3 (1988): 201–29.

Yeager, Gene. "Porfirian Commercial Propaganda: Mexico in the World Industrial Expositions." *The Americas* 34, no. 2 (October 1977): 230–43.

Yellin, Eric Steven. *Racism in the Nation's Service: Government Workers and the Color Line in Woodrow Wilson's America*. Chapel Hill: University of North Carolina Press, 2014.

Zacaïr, Philippe. "Haiti on His Mind: Antonio Maceo and Caribbeanness." *Caribbean Studies* 33, no. 1 (2005): 47–78.

Zeuske, Michael. "The Second Slavery in the Americas." In *The Palgrave Handbook of Global Slavery throughout History*, edited by Damian A. Pargas and Juliane Schiel, 429–39. Cham: Springer International Publishing, 2023.

Zimmerman, Andrew. "Africa and the American Civil War: The Geopolitics of Freedom and the Production of Commons." In *The Transnational Significance of the American Civil War*, edited by Jörg Nagler, Don Harrison Doyle, and Marcus Gräser, 127–48. Cham: Palgrave Macmillan, 2016.

Zoellner, Tom. *Island on Fire: The Revolt That Ended Slavery in the British Empire*. Cambridge, MA: Harvard University Press, 2020.

Zolla Márquez, Emiliano. "Territorial Practices: An Anthropology of Geographic Orders and Imaginations in the Sierra Mixe." PhD diss., University College London, 2013.

Zuczek, Richard. *State of Rebellion: Reconstruction in South Carolina*. Columbia: University of South Carolina Press, 1996.

Zúñiga, Raúl Mejía. *Valentín Gómez Farías, hombre de México, 1781-1858*. Mexico City: Fondo de Cultura Económica, 1981.

INDEX

Illustrations indicated by page numbers in *italics*

Abbott, Lynn, 162
abolitionist politics, 127–28, 129–31, 132, 134–35, 168–69. *See also* enslaved people
Abraham, Martin, 157–58
activism: by Afro-Creole radicals, 30–31, 38–42, 44–47, 50; by Black women, 93; brass bands and, 37, 53–55, 254, 273–75; dockworkers' organized labor and protests, 238–40, 241–42, 247–51, 271–72; Freedom Ride (1892 railroad sit-in), 30, 35–37, 54, 55; jazz as revolutionary music, 2–3, 276–78; musical resistance during Civil War, 213–14, 222–24; *New Orleans Tribune* and, 45–46; by sex workers, 94–97, *96*. *See also* Black Reconstruction; racism and violence
"Adam's Apple" (song), 67
Afful, Anthony, 274
African Americans: divisions from Afro-Creoles, 23, 49; Eighth Cavalry Band and, 156–58; Great Migration, 72, 89; and Louis and Lorenzo Tio Sr., 161–62; in Mexico, 123, 127–28, 130–31, 139–40, 192, 306n65; music and, 1–2; in Omaha, 72–73; social order imagined by, 171–72, 192; solidarity with Afro-Creoles, 23–24, 25, 30, 49–55, 257. *See also* activism; Afro-Creoles; Black churches; Civil War; enslaved people; racism and violence
Afro-Creoles (Creoles of color): about, 21; assault on creole identity, 29–30; brassroots democracy and, 28–29; divisions from African Americans, 23, 49; Eurocentric mischaracterizations, 23, 26–28; Freedom Ride (1892 railroad sit-in), 30, 35–37, 54, 55; Haiti and, 29, 38–42, 44–45; identity and radical politics, 25–28, 29, 30–31, 38–42, 44–47, 50; Latin Americans in New Orleans and, 141–42; in Mexico, 118, 129–30, 136–37, 139–40, 142–43, 166, 304n1, 313n276; music (secondary creolization) and, 21–23, 24–25, 26, 28, 30, 47, 68; passing for white (jumping the fence), 47; sex industry and, 98–99; slave trade and, 127, 305n52; social order imagined by, 192; solidarity with African Americans, 23–24, 25, 30, 49–55, 257; Union military attacks on, 48–49. *See also* activism; African Americans; Desdunes, Daniel; Desdunes, Mamie; Desdunes, Rodolphe; enslaved people; racism and violence
Afro-Latin Jazz Orchestra, 131
agrarian socialism, 76–77
agroecology: about, 32–33, 170–71, 174–75; Afro-Louisianan commoning, 195–98; Black church music and, 206–7; festivals and, 187–89; in Haiti, 175, *176*; intercropping practices, 183–84, *185*, 188, 196–97; medicine and, 176–77, 202; mobile commoning, 192–93; musicians and, 202, 209–10; vs. plantations, 171–72, 175–76, 181, 183–84, *185*; watermelon, 187–88, 316n115. *See also* counter-plantation; plantations
Ahmad, Eqbal, 4
"Ah Toucoutou" (song), 47, 291n73
Ake, David, 49

Alabama Labor Union, 227
Albert, A. E. P., 30, 50–51, 54, 62
Alcenat, Westenley, 39
Alexandria Gazette (newspaper), 225
Alexis (enslaved person), 16
Alfredo Brito and His Siboney Orchestra, 163
Alston, James H., 226, 227, 228, 230
Ameringer, Oscar, 77, 239, 241, 242, 249, 271
Anderson, Mother, 264
Anderson, William J., 20
Andrews, Inez, 308n107
Anthony, Arthé Agnes, 49
Anzaldúa, Gloria, 124
archive, colonial, 12–13
Ardouin, Coriolan, 43
Armstrong, Louis: on aural power of brass bands in public spaces, 236–37; on Bunk Johnson, 82; Creoles of color and, 23, 47; as dockworker, 8, 239; encouragement from sex workers, 91; with Fletcher Henderson jazz orchestra, 163; gospel scale and, 148; on herbal remedies, 176–77; improvisational languages of, 153, 154; Labor Day parades and, 268, 269; at Longshoremen's Hall, 264; "Mamie's Blues" and, 114; plantation dance hall scene and, 210
Arnold, George, 211
Attali, Jacques, 31
Austerlitz, Paul, 65
Avery, Byllye, 85
Avilés, Jesus (El Panchón), 168
Ayler, Albert, 278

Bacardí y Moreau, Emilio, 102
Baker, Gregg, 256–57
Baker, Jessica Swanston, 124
Ball, Robert Charles, 60, 61
bamboula (dance), 105, 107
Banda del Octavo Regimiento de Caballería (Eighth Cavalry Band), 62, 121–22, 148, 154–57, 155
banjo, 55, 135, 254
Banks, Joe, 171
Banks, Nathaniel P. (general), 48, 217
Baptist, Edward, 20, 196, 285n46
Baptist churches, 24, 25, 56, 90, 124, 158, 203, 205–6, 264–65. *See also* Black churches
Baquet, Achille, 137
Baquet, George, 137, 162, 232, 312n254, 324n125
Baquet, Theogene, 324n125
Baraka, Amiri, 71, 81, 84
Barbarin, Isidore, 54, 159
Barbarin, Paul, 265
barbershops, 15–16, 286n76
Bardes, John, 277
Barker, Danny, 92–93, 94, 95, 237, 251, 253, 270
Barnes, Harrison, 24, 171, *182*, 199, 202, 205, 207, 209, 246–47
Bassi, Ernesto, 123
Battle, Cullen A., 226, 227
Beaumont, Joseph, 47, 291n74
Bechet, Sidney: in Field Bands, 213; on grandfather Omar, 2, 5, 181, 277–78, 280, 283n7; Haitian identity and, 29; on jazz, racial violence, and collective memory, 2, 181, 276–80; jazz commons and, 5, 71; Lorenzo Tio Jr. and, 159, 163, 166, 312n254; mobile commoning and, 193; on music of plantation migrants, 5–6, 8; on playing Bolden's music, 266, 267; Tio family and, 137
Beckles, Hilary, 26
Behrend, Justin, 206, 218, 229
Bell, Caryn Cossé, 39
benevolent societies, 74, 95–96, 261–62, 263
Benjamin, Walter, 119
Berlin, Ira, 222
Berry, Jason, 264–65
Bethell, Tom, 19
Bigard, Barney, 164, 166
Bigeou, Esther, 252
Big Ike K, 171
Bissett, Jim, 76–77
Black, William, 188
Black Arts movement, 176, 276
"Black Bottom Stomp" (song), 190
Black churches, 24, 56, 203, 205–7, 220, 264–65, 294n140. *See also* Baptist churches
Black ecologies, 284n15. *See also* maroon ecologies
Black internationalism, 23–24, 42, 63, 251
Black people. *See* African Americans; Afro-Creoles; enslaved people

Black Power movement, 276, 318n162
Black Reconstruction: Afro-Creole perspective on, 40–41; brass bands and, 5–6, 217–18, 225–26; brassroots democracy and, 4, 47, 224; Desdunes family and, 39; fire companies and brass bands post-Reconstruction, 232–35; hopes for, 118; improvisational democratic practices, 215–16, 218; music and, 29, 213–14, 227–29, 231; public space as commons, 229–30, 231–32, 236–37; Redemption response to, 50, 109, 121, 234–35; Union Leagues, 226–27; voting, 230–31
Black Southern Theatre, 176
Black Vigilance Fire Company, 232–33, 235
Black women: blues singers, 85, 230; civil rights activism by, 93; dockworkers' strike (1907) and, 238–39; "fever doctors," 141, 176; in Labor Day parades, 270; maroon ecologies and, 193. *See also* Desdunes, Mamie; sex work and sexuality
Blakey, Art, 225, 228
Blanchard, Terence, 1–2
Bloncourt, Melvil, 45
blues: blues for dancing, 262; blues singers, 85, 230; Christianity and, 90; *corridos* and, 134; as demand for freedom, 84, 270–71; female sexuality and, 83, 86–88, 97, 113, 116; jazz and, 82. *See also* Desdunes, Mamie; jazz
blues and gospel scales (pentatonic scales), 113, 114, 148, 163, 164, *165*
Blunt, Rayford, 201
Bocage, Charlie, *165*
Bocage, Peter, 162–63, 164, *165*
Bolden, Buddy: aural power of, 237; Baptist influences, 90, 264, 265; barbershops and, 16; blues for dancing and, 262; "Buddy Bolden's Blues," 93, 266; dockworkers and union halls, 240, 261, 263, 265–66; "Don't Go Way Nobody," 244–46, *246*, *247*, 326n40; in Labor Day parades, 268; in mental institution, 96
Bordenave, Isidore, 166
"Bouncing Around" (song), 150, 151, *151*, *153*
Boyer, Jean-Pierre, 42
Boys Town Orphanage (Omaha): Father Flanagan's Boys' Band, 72, 75–76, 77–78, 79

Brackner, Joey, 234
Bradbury, David, 154
Bras-Coupé (maroon revolutionary), 277, 283n7
brass bands: and activism and intercultural solidarity, 37, 53–55, 273–75; Afro-Creole use of term, 52–53; aural power of in public spaces, 33, 213–14, 217–18, 236–37; Black Civil War soldiers and, 214–15, 217–24; dockworker activism and, 254; emancipation of enslaved people and, 211–13; fire companies and, 232–35; and funerals and mourning, 254–57, 259; Labor Day parades, 268–70; marching traditions, 69–71; in Mexico, 145–47; on plantations, 172–74, 199–202, 207–8, 209, 210; Reconstruction and, 5–6, 217–18, 224, 225–26. *See also* jazz
brassroots democracy, 4–8, 28–29, 31–34, 171, 224, 229, 275–76, 280–82. *See also* agroecology; brass bands; creolization; Desdunes, Daniel; Desdunes, Mamie; dockworkers; Haiti; Mexican borderlands; sex work and sexuality; Tio family
Brass Solidarity, 274
Brathwaite, Kamau: "Circles," 175
Breaux, McNeal, 261
Breaux, Richard, 73
Brickhouse, Anna, 45
Brindis de Salas, Claudio, 307n95
Brito, Alfredo, 163
Brothers, Thomas, 23, 24, 124, 125, 159–60, 205, 265
Brown, Danielle, 273–74
Brown, Elsa Barkley, 20, 216, 231
Brown, Marquis, 273–74
Brown, Raymond, *200*
Brown, Steve, 174
Bruce, Henry Clay, 242–43
"Buddy Bolden's Blues" (song), 93, 266
"Buddy's Habit" (song), 67
Burnard, Trevor, 180
Butler, Benjamin, 44, 203

Cable, George W., 18, 109, *110*
Cahill, Percy: "Don't Go Way Nobody," 244–46, *246*, *247*, 326n40

calenda (dance), 107, 111
Camp, Stephanie, 242
Canario y su Grupo, 163
Cane River (LA), 308n120
Capdeville, Paul, 263
capitalism, 2–3, 21, 68, 91–92, 119, 240, 275–76
Carbajal, Bernardo Galvez, 91
Carby, Hazel, 299n49
Carey, Jack, *182*
Carey, Thomas "Mutt," 171, *182*, 265
Caribbean, 8–12. See also common wind; Haiti
Carney, Judith Ann, 176
"Caroline" ("Pauvre piti Mamselle Zizi," song), 101, 109, *110*
Carpentier, Alejo, 103, 153, 311n200
Carr, James Revell, 253
Carson, P. H., 287n93
Carter, Regina, 131
Carver, George Washington, 170
Casid, Jill, 175
Casimir, Jean, 12, 44, 57, 103–4, 175
Casimir, John, 171, 209
Castañeda, José, 138
Cervantes, Ignacio, 64, 65, 147, 155; "Invitación," 150–51, *152*
Césaire, Aimé, 199
Céspedes, Carlos Manuel de, 106
Chaligny, Louis, 158
Chapman, John Abney, 229
Charles, Robert, 93–94, 266
Chávez, Alex, 124
"Chère, mo lemmé toi" (song), 28, 51–52
Chernoff, John, 295n196
Cherrie, Eddie, 137
Cheung, Floyd, 109
Childress, Samuel, 192
Chodos, Asher, *114*
Christianity. See Baptist churches; Black churches; Sanctified Church
cigar industry, 141–44, *143*
cinquillo complex (*habanera, tresillo*): about, 37–38, 56–57; adaptability and resonance, 106–7; Afro-Creoles and, 28, 37; Cuban immigrants and, 307n95; Daniel Desdunes and, 63–64, *65*, 68; examples, *65*, *66*, 99, *110*, *112*, *114*; intratemporal international

and, 62–68; jazz and, 65–67; political positionality and, 100–101; rhythmic conventions of, 99; sexual critiques and, 97–98, 99–100, 101, 107–8, 111, 113, 115; white demonization of, 67, 295n192
civil rights activism. See activism
Civil War: Black soldiers and activists, 218–19; brass bands and, 212–13, 217–18, 220–21; emancipation, 211–12, 213; improvisational music and, 214–15, 219–20, 221–22; musical resistance, 213–14, 222–24; pro-Union musical culture, 217
clarinet, 124, 145, 146–50, 153–55, 158, 159, 161, 163–64, 166, 169
Clark, Emily, 108
Clavin, Matthew J., 322n52
Clayton, Jimmy "Kid," 171, 209
Colby, Abram, 231
Coleman, Steve, 100
Collins, Harriet, 177
Collins, Lee, 313n261
Colored Knights of Pythias, 74, 77
Colored Veterans Benevolent Association, 91, 234
Coltrane, John, 71, 160
Comité des Citoyens, 36, 50, 135, 144
commoning. See agroecology
commons: brassroots democracy and, 3–4; euphoria as, 69–71; and grassroots democracy and takeover of public spaces, 229–32; jazz commons, 4–5, 71; maroon ecologies, 4–5, 15–17, 71, 122–23, 129–30, 193, 195–96, 206, 284n15; public space as, 229–30, 231–32, 236–37; resistance to expropriation of, 275
common wind: about, 13, 55; abolitionism and, 132; Afro-Creoles as second gale of, 40; barbershops and, 15–16; cinquillo complex (*habanera*) and, 106–7; maritime transport and, 17–18; revolutionary songs and, 13–15, 18–19, 71; taverns and, 16–17; Zeno's song and, 13, 19–20, 30, 38, 43
Comonfort, Ignacio, 136, 142
conch shells, 184–85
Cone, James H., 6
"Conga del Viejo" (song), 131

Congo Square (New Orleans), 31, 107, 111, 175, 277
Coolidge, Calvin, 72, 77
Co-operators Hall, 251–52
Coquet, Bernado, 16
Cordill, Charles C., 241–42, 247–48
Cornelius, Catherine, 203
Cornish, Willie, 82
Coronado, Raúl, 123
Corral, Ramón, 120
corridos, 134–35, 307n102
Cortázar, Julio, 81, 117
cotton, 20, 172, 178–79, 187, 196. *See also* New Orleans Cotton Centennial Exposition; plantations
Cotton Men's Executive Council, 256
Cottrell, Louis, Jr., 137
Cottrell, Louis, Sr., *165*
counter-plantation: about, 12, 175–76; antagonism against, 44–45, 197; Black churches and, 206; dockworkers and, 253–54, 261–62; festivals and, 188–89; gardening and, 176; interiority and, 279; medicine and, 176–77; music and, 25, 71, 97, 106, 123, 153, 220, 228, 235, 275–76; watermelon and, 188
Courtois, Sévère, 126
Couvent, Marie Justine, 38
Cox, George Washington, 227
Cox, Ida: "One Hour Mama," 88
Crasson, Hannah, 212
Crawley, Ashon T., 274
creolization, 21–23, 27–28, 30, 53, 63, 159. *See also* Afro-Creoles
Crumley, Elmer, 79
Crusader (newspaper), 36, 50, 53, 135
Cuba: cinquillo complex and, 153; counter-plantation practices, 172; emigration to Veracruz, 132–34, 307n95; fear of Haitian revolutionary influences, 104, 302n136; Haitian musical influences, 67, 295n191; Santiago de Cuba, 10, 102, 105, 107, 142, 153, 176, 191; "Spanish" as pseudonym for, 295n194; *tumba francesa*, 65, 102–3, 105–6, 107, *112*
cuerpos filarmónicos, 145–46, 147, 173

Cuney Hare, Maud, 100–101, 106; "Dialogue D'Amour" reproduction, 111, *112*, 303n175
Curaçao, 14, 188–89
Cutchey, Wallace, 158

Daily Picayune (newspaper), 256. See also *New Orleans Picayune*; *Times Picayune*
Daily States (newspaper), 255
dance, 55, 107, 131, 189–91, 243–44, 286n69. See also *bamboula*; calenda; *tumba francesa*
Daniels, Douglas Henry, 190–91
Danticat, Edwidge, 70–71
danza, 62, 147, 149, 153–56, *156*, 295n191
danzón, 67, 103, 105, 138, 147–49, 150–51, 153, 163, 295n191, 311n198
Darensbourg, Joe, 202
Davis, Angela, 86, 87, 90, 91, 101
Davis, Thulani, 229–30, 231, 258
Dawdy, Shannon, 6
De Bieuw, Edward, 181
Debord, Guy, 232
Dédé, Edmond, 143–44
Dehesa, Teodoro A., 167
Dejan, Harold, 137
Delany, Martin R., 197
DeLay, Mike, 47
Delisle, "Big Eye" Louis "Nelson," 137
Denning, Michael, 252
Densmore, Daniel, 220
Desdunes, Agnes, 144
Desdunes, Clarence, 72, 79–80
Desdunes, Daniel: about, 29–30, 31–32, 37–38; brassroots democracy and, 37, 54–55; cinquillo complex and, 63–64, *65*, 68; Dan Desdunes Band, *78*; danzón and, 147; death, 79; Dédé and, 144; Father Flanagan's Boys' Band (Omaha) and, 72, 75–76, 77–78, 79; Freedom Ride (1892 railroad sit-in), 30, 35–37, 54, 55; "Happy Feeling Rag," 63, *65*, 76; ideology, 79–80; in Omaha, 72, 73–75, 79; at Straight University, 54, 209; Tios and, 161, 162
Desdunes, Edna, 88
Desdunes, Emile, 43
Desdunes, John, 88
Desdunes, Louis, 88

Desdunes, Mamie: about, 29–30, 32, 80, 83, 85, 116; blues and, 82, 97; Creole of color and, 98–99; death, 83; family background, 49–50, 83; Longshoremen's Hall and, 265; untraditional relationships, 88

Desdunes, "Mamie's Blues" ("219 blues"): about, 32, 81–82, 84, 91, 97, 115–17; Cortázar on, 81; "Dialogue D'Amour" and, 111; *habanera/tresillo* influences, 68, 98, 99, 106, 113; lyrics, 87; Mamie credited for, 83; Morton's rendition, 88, 90, 99, 99, 113, *114*; sacred sensibility, 90; on sex trafficking, 88–89; on sexual liberation, 87–88

Desdunes, Mathilde, 72

Desdunes, Pierre-Aristide, 23, 38, 43, 50, 71, 79, 282, 291n52

Desdunes, Pierre-Jérémie, 42

Desdunes, Rodolphe: about, 31–32, 37; background, 38–39; Comité des Citoyens and, 36, 50; Creole identity, 80; on Creoles attempting to pass as white, 47; death, 79; Dédé and, 144; on emigration to Mexico, 136; on family's Haitian history, 42–43; *A Few Words to Dr. DuBois 'With Malice Toward None'*, 38; Haitian Embassy and, 37; in Omaha, 72, 78; *Our People and Our History*, 42–43; photo, *39*; radical politics and activism, 39–40, 48–49, 55, 113, 135, 257; relationship with Clementine Walker, 49–50, 83, 88; worldview, 40–41

Deslondes, Charles, 11, 285n46

Dessalines, Jean-Jacques, 14, 40

"Dialogue D'Amour" (song), 111, *112*, 186, 303n175

Díaz, Porfirio, 119, 121, 145, 167

Diouf, Sylviane, 16

Dixon, Akua, 131

Dobard, Raymond G., 184

dockworkers: about, 33, 239–41, 259–60, 270–72; Black musicians and, 239, 260; brass bands and, 254; contested time and, 242–47; and cultural and musical exchanges, 251–54; "Don't Go Way Nobody" and, 244–46, *246*, 247, 326n40; funerals and, 255–57, 258–59; interracial solidarity, 240, 241–42, 247–48; organized labor and protests, 238–40, 241–42, 247–51, 271–72; strike (1907), 238–39, 242, 247–48; union halls and Black cooperative society, 260–62, 264, 265–67

Dodd, Madia, 72

Dodds, Baby, 100, 134

Dodds, Johnny, 265

Doheny, John, 59, 295n190

Dominguez, Paul, 49, 312n245

Dominque, Natty, 143, 293n116

"Don't Go Way Nobody" (song), 244–46, *246*, 247, 326n40

Douglass, Frederick, 14–15, 25, 45–46, 171–72, 179, 194, 219, 306n63

Downing, Andrew Jackson, 183

Downs, Gregory, 146, 160

"Dreamy Blues" (song), 164, 313n264

Dred Scott vs. Sanford (1857), 136

Drouet, Nicholas, 129

Dubois, Laurent, 13

Du Bois, W. E. B., 4, 15, 38, 40, 101, 109, 158, 213, 243

Duggan, T. A., 263

Dumas, Alexandre "Alejandro," *140*

Dunn, Oscar J., 46, 47

Duque, George, 88

Duquesne University, 273–74

Dusen, Frankie, 93, 266

Dymond, Florence, 205

Eagle Band, 24, 25, 163, 266, 267

Eagle Brass Band, 53, 293n112

Economy Hall, 25, 53, 95, 159

Eddins, Crystal, 26

education, 15, 207–8

Eighth Cavalry Band (Banda del Octavo Regimiento de Caballería), 62, 121–22, 148, 154–57, *155*

"El Chuchumbé" (dance), 131

Eldridge, Roy, 166

Ellington, Duke, 164, 166

Ellis, A. J., 242, 247, 249–50, 258

Ellis, Bob, 187

Ellison, Ralph, 58, 71; *Invisible Man*, 196

Eltis, David, 57–58

Emancipation Circuit, 229–30, 258

"En Avan' Grenadié" (song), 126
Enríquez, Tito, 254
enslaved people: abolitionist politics, 127–28, 129–31, 132, 134–35, 168–69; Afro-Creole ownership, 127, 305n52; archives, 12–13; bounty ad for Pierre, 15, 17, 286n70; common wind and, 13–14; critiques of capital by, 22–23; cultural heterogeneity, 57–58; emancipation, 211–12, 213; New Orleans auctions, 20, 330n23; runaways in Mexico, 127–28; runaways in New Orleans, 16–17; sexual slavery, 84–85; as true victors of Civil War, 213. *See also* African Americans; Afro-Creoles; plantations
Equal Justice Association (later Equal Rights League), 257–58
euphoria, 69–71
Eureka colony (Mexico), 123, 136–37, 139, *140*, 144, 159
Evans, Freddi Williams, 70
Excelsior Brass Band (Mobile, AL), 234
Excelsior Brass Band (New Orleans), 28, 33, 93, 118, 154, 159, 232–33, 235, 257, 324n125

Failde, Miguel, 149
family, 84
fandangos, 129, 131
Fanon, Frantz, 7
Father Flanagan's Boys' Band (Boys Town orphanage, Omaha), 72, 75–76, 77–78, 79
Ferdinand, Malcom, 192
Fiehrer, Thomas, 6, 28, 47
Field Bands, 213
Fihle, George, 35, 37, 62, 143, 158
fire companies, 232–35
Fischlin, Daniel, 214, 218
Fisk University, 28
Fiz, Santiago, 191
Flanagan, Father Edward J., 75–76
Fletcher, Moses, 187
Fleuriau, François, 18
Flores, Manuel, 128
Flores y Escalante, Jesús, 147
Floyd, Samuel, 57, 307n82
Foner, Eric, 172, 229
food, 176, 177–78, 262. *See also* agroecology

Ford, James W., 250
Forster, Harry, *200*
Fortune, Timothy Thomas, 212
Foster, Abbey "Chinee," 29, 149, 251
Foster, Pops: on Afro-Creoles, 49; on Holiness Church music, 207; hybrid life as dockworker and musician, 239, 260; on Labor Day parades, 269; on Louis Tio, 161; plantation background, 171, *182*, 202; on police, 93, 266; on sex workers, 90; on slow music, 243–44; on union halls, 262
Foucault, Michel, 96, 269
Fouché, Nelson, 136
Fourier, Henri: "Proclamation de Soulouque Aux Haïtiens" (song), 43, *44*
Fox, Austin, 17
Freedmen's Aid Association, 45
Freedmen's Bureau, 196, 197, 201
Freedom Ride (1892 railroad sit-in), 30, 35–37, 54, 55
Friedenthal, Albert, 59
Friedman, Gerald, 248
Friedrich, Paul, 146
frontera sónica. See Mexican borderlands
Fuentes, Marisa, 19, 84
funerals, 254–57, 258–59, 273–74

Gabbard, Krin, 283n7
Gabriel, Joe, 122, 157, 171, *182*
Gantt, Nicole Mitchell, 60
García López, Patricia, 147
gardens. *See* agroecology
Garon, Paul, 270–71
Garvey, Marcus (Garveyism), 252
Gaye, Marvin: "What's Going On," 1–2
Geffrard, Fabre, 9
Gehman, Mary, 304n1
gender, 85, 116, 270. *See also* Black women; sex work and sexuality
Genovese, Eugene, 15
Georgia, 189, 195, 231
Gillam, Albert, 132
Gillespie, Dizzy, 59, 61
Gilroy, Paul, 276, 280
Giorgianni, Eugenio, 70
Girdina, Tony, 137

Glissant, Édouard, 4–5, 21, 22, 177, 186, 189, 247, 273
Goffin, Robert, 56
Gómez Farías, Valentín, 306n65
Gómez Vincent, Celeste, 142
Gompers, Samuel, 267–68
Gonzalez, Johnhenry, 26
gospel and blues scales (pentatonic scales), 113, 114, 148, 163, 164, 165
Gosse, Philip Henry, 183
Gottschalk, Louis, 100
Gould, Jeffrey, 320n241
Grant, Jacqueline, 103
Great Migration, 72, 89
Green, James K., 227
Griego, Antonio García de León, 131
Griffin, Farah Jasmine, 85
Guerrero, Vicente, 130, 306n73
Guesnon, George, 30
Guillard, Charlie, 286n70
Guillén, Nicolás, 133
gumbo, 176
gumbo ya ya, 216
Gushee, Laurence, 65–66, 239, 293n135
Gutiérrez, José Bernardo, 126

habanera. See cinquillo complex
Hahn, Steven, 213, 231
Haiti (Saint-Domingue): Afro-Creoles and, 29, 38–42, 44–45; barbed sexual and musical critiques, 97–98, 99–100, 101–2; as Black liberation symbol, 14–15; cinquillo complex and, 65, 99–100, 105; common wind and, 14; counter-plantation practices, 172, 175–76; cultural exchanges with Louisiana, 9–12, 13, 15, 20–21, 38, 71–72, 107, 277; cultural plasticity and influence, 103–5; dance and, 189, 191; Desdunes family and, 38, 39–40, 42–43; Dessalines vs. Louverture, 40; emigration to Veracruz, 132, 307n90; "Haitian turn" in history and Black studies, 12; Manje Yam festival, 188; name, 193; Quadroon balls, 108; *rara* parades, 69–71, 190, 193; *tumba francesa* and, 65, 102–3, 105–6; Vodou, 23, 40, 43, 65; Vodou Jazz movement, 276

"Haitian Blues" (song), 97–98
Hall, Gwendolyn Midlo, 294n142
Hamilton, Thomas, 179
Handy, Sylvester, 174
Handy, W. C., 148, 162; "Memphis Blues," 134; "St. Louis Blues," 67
Hanley, Peter, 82
"Happy Feeling Rag" (song), 63, *65*, 76
Harker, Brian, *153*
Harper, Frances Ellen Watkins, 54, 224
Harris, Lisa E., 1
Harris, Melanie L., 206, 207
Harrison, Thomas and Isabella, 14
Hart, Junius, 154, *156*
Hartman, Saidiya, 13, 91
Hauzer, Louis, 126, 136
Hauzer, Louise Marguerite Anthenais, 136, 308n116
Havis, Devonya Natasha, 187, 243
Hawaiian (Kānaka Maoli) musicians, 252, 254
Hawkins, James, 54, 255–56
Hayes, Harry, 52
Hayne, Robert Y., 130
Haywood, Felix, 128
healthcare, 261. *See also* medicine
Hearn, Lafcadio, 55, 293n129
Heble, Ajay, 214, 218
Helping Hand Benevolent Association, 95–96, *96*
Henry, Sonny: on Black Baptist church, 205; on brass band parades, 69; on funerals, 255; plantation background, 171, *182*, 199, 202, 209; on plantation brass bands, 200, 201, 208, 229, 230
Hernández, Domingo, 128
Hersch, Charles, 7, 19, 244, 247, 268–69
Hidalgo, Arcadio, 131
Hidalgo y Costilla, Miguel, 126
Higginson, Thomas Wentworth, 221–22
Higman, B. W., 175
Hilliard, Sam Bowers, 178
Hine, Darlene Clark, 84
hip-hop activists, 276
Hite, Elizabeth Ross, 189, 190
Ho, Fred, 2–3, 58
Hodson, Christopher, 40

Hofman, Ana, 281
Hooton, Laura, 123
Horne, Gerald, 7, 168, 250
Hosbey, Justin, 4, 284n15
Hose, Sam, 93, 300n83
Hossein, Caroline Shenaz, 26, 76
Howard, Avery "Kid," 30
Hudson, Marie Rose, 16
Hudson, Sara, 144
Hughes, Langston, 115
Huiswoud, Otto, 250
Humphrey, James, 8, 173, 196, 199–201, 208–9, 232
Humphrey, Willie J., 137
Hunter, Tera, 2, 214
Hurston, Zora Neale, 24, 206

"I'm Going Home to Jamaica" ("West Indian Blues," song), 252
improvisation, 5–6, 22, 71, 98, 214–17, 218, 219–24, 239–40, 284n17
Indigenous peoples, 119–20, 141, 146, 149, 192–93, 250, 254
interiority, 279–80
internationalism: Black, 23–24, 42, 63, 251; cinquillo consciousness and intratemporal international, 62–68; *New Orleans Tribune* and, 45–46; swing and intersubjective international, 55–62
"Invitación" (song), 150–51, *152*
Iyer, Vijay, 8

Jabir, Johari, 13, 54, 222
Jackson, Andrew, 126
Jackson, Shona, 1, 187
Jackson, Thanayi Michelle, 229
Jaegerhuber, Werner, 191
Jamaica, 14, 172, 183, 184–85, 251–52
James, C.L.R., 27, 238, 241
James, James Calhart, 217
James, Louis, 171, 203, 205
James, Neddy, 171, *182*
James, Willie, 171
Jasiri X, 329n1
jazz: approach to, 7–8; Afro-Creole identity and, 30; Baptist influences, 264–65; beginnings of, 35, 37, 262; blues and, 82; cigar industry and, 143; cinquillo complex and, 65–67; clarinet and, 124, 145, 146–50, 153–55, 158, 159, 161, 163–64, 166, 169; communal musical creation and, 237; danzón and, 147–48, 150–51, 163; gender and, 116, 270; improvisation and, 71, 216; Latin American influences, 124–25; Lorenzo Tio Jr. and, 164, 166; in Mexico, 167–68; mischaracterized as apolitical, 7; musicians as hybrid actors, 8; in Omaha, 74; piano and, 86; plantations and, 171, 173–74, 177, 181, *182*, 203, 205, 209; as revolutionary music, 2–3, 276–78; timing and, 243–44; Tio family influence, 137. *See also* blues; brass bands; brassroots democracy; swing
jazz commons, 4–5, 71
Jeantys, O., 66
Jefferson, Thomas, 85
Jenson, Deborah, 102, 108
Jiles, Albert, Jr., 171, *182*, 251
Jiles, Albert, Sr., 171, *182*
Johnson, Blind Willie, 267
Johnson, Bunk, 82–83, 88, 90, 122, 158
Johnson, Fred, 70
Johnson, Gaye Theresa, 122
Johnson, George, 187
Johnson, Hafiz Shabbaz Farel, 295n196
Johnson, Jack, 135, 167, 313n276
Johnson, James W., 229
Johnson, James Weldon, 142
Johnson, Jerah, 109
Johnson, Mark, 226
Johnson, Sara E., 99–100
Johnson, Timothy, 178
Johnson, Zada, 70
Jones, Dalton Anthony, 7
Joplin, Scott, 64, 147; "The Entertainer," 67
Joseph, Papa John, 262
joy, 69–71
Juárez, Benito, 125–26, 137, 139, 140–41, 142, *143*, 309n137
Juba (dance), 60
Juvenile Protective Association, 243

Kānaka Maoli (Hawaiian) musicians, 252, 254
Kaussen, Valerie, 60

Kaye, Anthony, 212, 219, 243
Keelan, James, 231–32
Kelley, Robin D. G., 86, 125, 235, 240–41, 255
Kelley, Sean, 123
Kelly, Ben, 229
Kelly, Chris, 171, 174, *182*, 201, 209
Kennedy, Henry, 225
Keppard, Freddie, 268, 269; "Adam's Apple," 67
Kersands, Billy, 75, 161–62
King, Boston, 177
Kinzer, Charles E., 137, 138, 164
Knights of Labor, 120
Kousser, J. Morgan, 264
Kovel, Joel, 71
Krasner, David, 73
Ku Klux Klan, 72, 227, 231

labor, organized. *See* dockworkers
Labor Day parades, 267–70
Lacarra, Eugenia, 142
Ladies Providence Benevolent Association, 263
Lake, Oliver, 237
Lamanière, Lucien, 42
Lampert, Lucien, *140*
land, 171–72. *See also* agroecology; plantations
Landau, Emily Epstein, 92, 263
Lanusse, Armand, 46; "The Young Lady at the Ball," 109
"La Patti Negra" (song), 147
"Las Altura de Simpson" (song), 149–50, *150*
La Société d'Économie et d'Assistance Mutuelle, 42, 52, 53, 55
Latrobe, Benjamin, 175
Laurent, August, 148–49
Lawless, Alfred, Jr., 78
Lawton, James, 206
LeConte, Emily, 220
Les Cenelles (poetry collection), 109
Lewis, George, 8, *10*, 19, 170, 173–74, 213, 239, 263
Lewis, James, 52
Lewis, Matthew, 183
Lewis, Steve, *165*
Lewis-Hale, Phyllis, 25
Ligon, Richard, 184
Lindsey, John, *165*

Linebaugh, Peter, 47–48
Lipsitz, George, 76, 214, 218
"Lisette" (poem), 102
Liston, Melba, 175
Logsdon, Joseph, 39
Lomax, Alan, 59–60, 100
Longshoremen's Hall, 246, 260, 262, 264, 265
Longshoremen's Protective Union Benevolent Association (LPUBA), 33, 247, 254, 258–59, 261–62, 264
López Matoso, Antonio, 131
Lott, Eric, 37, 161
Louisiana: Constitution (1868), 36, 39, 41; cultural exchanges with Haiti, 9–12, 13, 15, 20–21, 38, 71–72, 107, 277; cultural heterogeneity of enslaved people, 57–58; Southern fascism and, 50, 292n101; trans-Caribbean culture and, 8–10. *See also* Afro-Creoles (Creoles of color); New Orleans
Louisiana Democrat (newspaper), 156, 217
Louisianan (newspaper), 51
Louisiana Tehuantepec Company, 250
Louverture, Toussaint, 10, 40, 175, 287n93
Love, Preston, 72–73
Lumumba, Patrice, 236
Lundy, Benjamin, 129, 306n64

Maceo, Antonio, 134–35, 308n107
Mackandal, François, 277
Mackey, Nathaniel, 58, 275, 298n17
Madrid, Alejandro, 138, 148, 149
Maggio, Antonio, 54, 267
Malcomson, Hettie, 103, 311n198
"Mamie's Blues" (song). *See under* Desdunes, Mamie's Blues"

Manetta, Manuel, 86, 91
Manuel, Peter, 295n191
marching traditions, 69–71, 296n201
Mardi Gras Indians, 193
Mardi Gras parades, 51, 70, 209, 234
maroon ecologies, 4–5, 15–17, 71, 122–23, 129–30, 193, 195–96, 206, 284n15
Marquis, Donald, 16, 24, 263, 266
Martinet, Louis André, 54
Martinique, 14

Marx, Karl, 1, 43, 115, 119, 181
masculinity, 270
Matamoros (Mexican border town), 128, 129–30, 136
Matory, J. Lorand, 30, 57
Matthews, Bill, 264
Matthews, Chif, *200*
Matthews, Stonewall, *200*
McAlister, Elizabeth, 69, 193
McCalla, Leyla, 8
McCusker, John, 265
McEnery, Samuel D., 120
McKittrick, Katherine, 89, 275
Mechanics' Institute, 28, 51–52
medicine, 141, 176–77, 202. *See also* healthcare
"Memphis Blues" (song), 134
Memphis Minnie, 86, 115
Méndez, Justo Sierra, 136
Menes, Theramene, 64
Mercier, Louis, 14
Metoyer, Arnold, 137
Metoyer, Auguste Dorestan, 137, 308n120
Mexican borderlands (*frontera sónica*): about, 32, 122–24, 125–26, 135–36, 138, 166–69; abolitionist politics, 127–28, 129–31, 132, 134–35, 168–69; Afro-Creole communities, 118, 129–30, 136–37, 139–40, 142–43, 166, 304n1, 313n276; anti-Black racism, 168; Black communities, 123, 127–28, 130–31, 139–40, 192, 306n65; brass band culture, 145–47; cigar industry and, 141–44, *143*; clarinet and, 148–49; *corridos*, 134–35, 307n102; Cuban immigrants, 132–34, 307n95; *cuerpos filarmónicos*, 145–46, 147, 173; danzón and, 105, 138, 147–48, 149, 150–51, 153; Eureka colony, 123, 136–37, 139, *140*, 144, 159; *fandangos*, 129, 131; Haitian immigrants, 132, 307n90; independence movement, 126–27, 130; jazz and, 167–68; Mexican Revolution, 41, 167; New Orleans and, 122, 125–26, 157–58; Porfiriato (Díaz government), 119–20, 121, 145, 146, 167; *son jarocho*, 131–32, 307n82; Tinchant and, 41; Tio family in Veracruz and Tampico, 136, 138, 144–45, 149, 158
Mier, Sebastian B. de, 119
Miles, Buddy, 72

Miles, Lizzie, 29, 301n98; "Haitian Blues," 97–98
Miller, Gene, 209
Miller, Punch, 171, 203
Mingus, Charles, 59, 60, 61, 135
Minor, John, 172
minstrelsy, 161–62
Mitchell, Georgette, 26
Mitchell, Nicole, 1
Mitchell, Reagan Patrick, 105
mobile commoning, 192–93
Montelongo, Abel, 168
Montgomery, William E., 24
Moore, Robin, 124–25, 138, 147–48, 149
Morelos, José María, 130
Morgan, Isaiah, *182*, 205
Morgan, Jennifer, 84
Morgan, Philip, 57–58
Morgan, Sam, 171, *182*, 205, 209
Morin, Antoine, 11, 179
Morris, Butch, 56, 58
Morrison, Toni, 157
Morton, Jelly Roll: "Black Bottom Stomp," 190; on Bolden, 237; danzón influences, 147; dock work and, 239, 243, 253; Haitian ancestry, 29; Longshoremen's Hall and, 265; Lorenzo Tio Jr. and, 164, 313n261; on Mamie Desdunes and "Mamie's Blues," 82–83, 98; "Mamie's Blues" rendition, 88, 90, 99, *99*, 113, *114*; "New Orleans Blues," 99; on police, 93, 94; sex workers and, 86, 89, 90, 98–99; on "Spanish tinge," 64, 68, 100; on Tio clarinetists, 137
Moten, Fred, 23–24, 52, 60, 63, 190, 217, 298n17
mourning, public, 254–57, 258–59
mutual aid associations, 208. *See also* union halls

Navarrete Pellicer, Sergio, 146
Nawahi, Bennie, 252
Negra, Toña la, 132
Negro New Orleans beat, 59
Nelder, Alexander, 12, 285n49
Nelson, Louis, 171
New Orleans: brassroots democracy in, 3–4; creolization, 6, 158–59; cultural and musical

exchanges, 251–54; Latin Americans and, 122, 124, 125–26, 141, 157–58; population and demographics, 11, 285n43; pro-Union musical culture, 217; refuge for Black people, 16–17; Storyville (sex industry), 83, 85, 86–87, 89, 90–91, 91–93, 94–97, 108–9, 115–16; swing music, 59. *See also* Afro-Creoles; dockworkers; Louisiana
"New Orleans Blues" (song), 99
New Orleans Cotton Centennial Exposition, 62, 118–19, *120*, 121–22, *123*, 252
New Orleans Daily Delta (newspaper), 136
New Orleans Democrat (newspaper), 52
New Orleans Item (newspaper), 157
New Orleans Orchestra (formerly Society Orchestra), 149, *151*, 160, 163–64, *165*
New Orleans Picayune (newspaper), 83, 93, 172–73, 239, 251, 255, 258–59, 261. See also *Daily Picayune*; *Times Picayune*
New Orleans Tribune (newspaper), 4, 45–46, 48, 192, 197, 223
New York Times (newspaper), 36, 198
Nicholas, Albert, 53
Nicholls, David, 40
Nicholls, Francis T., 234
Nissen, Peter: *Buddy Bolden's Storyville Blues*, 326n40
Nkombo/Echoes from the Gumbo (magazine), 176
Noone, Jimmie, 137
Noret, George, 324n125
North Louisiana Journal, 230
Northup, Solomon, 127–28, 181
Nuñez, Alcide "Yellow," 149

O'Farrill, Arturo, 131
Okiji, Fumi, 7, 27, 56, 58, 202
Oliver, Joe, 8, 53, 95–96, 97, 154, 161, 236–37; "Buddy's Habit," 67
Oliver, King, 164, 260, 265
Olsson, Tore C., 146
Omaha (NE), 72–75, 79. *See also* Father Flanagan's Boys' Band
Onward Brass Band, 53, 159, 236–37, 255
Ortiz, Fernando, 64, 295n192
Ory, Edward "Kid": on Bolden, 265, 329n147; gardening by, 8, 202; on industrialized agriculture, 203; at Longshoremen's Hall, 264; on mother's death, 181; plantation background, 11, 173, *182*, 201; racism experienced by, 263; on sex industry, 92; on swing, 56; in Woodland Band, *200*
Otero, José T., 119
Otto, Jesse, 72, 73

Page, Hot Lips: "Good for Stompin'," 191
Pages, Anthony, 143
Pagés, Ramón, 36, 135, 144, 250
Paquette, Robert, 180
Pardo, Juan, 70
Parham, Angel Adams, 21
Parker, Willie, 8, 24, 209, 232–33, 238, 239, 251, 253, 271
Pascoe, Juan, 131
Passemont, Mateo, 130
"Pauvre piti Mamselle Zizi" ("Caroline," song), 101, 109, *110*
Peerless Orchestra, 72
Pellegrinelli, Lara, 86
Penn, Ojeda, 216
Penn, William H., 30, 33, 257–58, 267
pentatonic scales (blues and gospel scales), 113, *114*, 148, 163, 164, *165*
People's Vindicator (newspaper), 201
Peregrino, Severo, 132
Pérez, Manuel, 53, 56, 65, 143, 163, 293n116
Pershing, John J., 73
Pétion, Alexandre, 42, 50
Peyton, Henry, 173
piano, 55, 86, 97
Pichon, Walter "Fats," 252
Pickett, John T., 132
Picou, Alphonse, 59, 137
Pierre (Haitian-born maroon), 15, 16, 17, *17*, 278
Pike, James S., 215–16, 218, 220
Pinchbeck, P. B. S., 28, 36
Pingret, Edouard: "Músico de Veracruz," *133*
Pinkett, Harrison J., 79
Piron, Armand J.: New Orleans Orchestra (formerly Society Orchestra), 149, *151*, 160, 163–64, *165*
Piron, Myrtil, 52
plantations: about, 22–23; vs. Afro-Louisianan

commoning, 195–98; Black refusal to work, 201; Black schools at, 207–8; brass bands and, 172–74, 199–202, 207–8, 209, 210; contested time, 187–88; cotton, 20, 172, 178–79, 187, 196; vs. counter-plantation practices, 171–72, 175–76, 183–87, *185*; vs. dance, 189–91; improvisational music and, 24–25; jazz and, 171, 173–74, 177, 181, *182*, 203, 205, 209; vs. mobile commoning, 192–93; modernized agriculture (second slavery), 177–81, 203, *204*; music restrictions, 193–94; mutual aid associations and, 208; plantation futures, 275; sugar, 8, 11, 179–81, *182*, 184–86, 194, 198, 199, 201–3, *204*, 315n56. *See also* agroecology; counter-plantation; enslaved people

Plessy, Homer, 37, 74

Plessy v. Ferguson (1896), 37, 54, 72, 113

police, 92–95, 255, 266, 273, 277

political activism. *See* activism

Pope, John A., 234

Porter, James Edward, 265

postcolonial ears, 13

Powell, Henry, 130

Prampin, Laura, 72

Pratt, Mary Louise, 282

Prince, Nancy, 179

"Proclamation de Soulouque Aux Haitiens" (song), 43, *44*

Providence Hall, 263

Pugh, Mary, 120–21

Pulaar, 41, 290n36

Quadroon balls, 108, 109

Queenie Venerable (sex worker), 94, 299n42

Quintero Rivera, A. G., 106, 311n200

race, dockworkers and interracial solidarity, 240, 241–42, 247–48

racism and violence: against Afro-Creoles, 29–30, 48–49; against Black people, 120–21, 227, 228, 232, 234, 254–55, 262–64; and Black self-determination and jazz, 2, 181, 276–80; *Dred Scott vs. Sanford* (1857), 136; against Eighth Cavalry Band, 156–57; in Mexico, 168; *Plessy v. Ferguson* (1896), 37, 54, 72, 113; by police, 92–95, 255, 266, 273, 277; Redemption policy, 50, 109, 121, 234–35; sexual slavery, 84–85; Thibodaux Massacre (1887), 120–21, 201, 208. *See also* activism

Raeburn, Bruce Boyd, 30, 122, 163

Rainey, Ma, 87; "Prove It on Me Blues," 87

Ramos, Florencio, 121, 149, 158

Randolph, J. P., 46, 47

rara parades, 69–71, 190, 193

Reconstruction. *See* Black Reconstruction

Redd, Alec Zander, 329n1

Redemption policy, 50, 109, 121, 234–35

Rediker, Marcus, 47–48, 253–54, 275

"Red Man Blues" (song), 163, *165*

Redmond, Shana, 233

Reed, Alex, 244, 266

Regis, Helen, 254–55

Reid, Whitelaw, 46

Richardson, David, 57–58

Richardson, Jim, 171

Ridgley, William Bébé, 163, 171, *182*, 201, 203

Rivera, Raquel, 19

Roane, J. T., 4, 88, 284n15

"Robert Charles Ballad" (song), 94, 266

Robichaux, John, 121, 148, *182*, 208

Robinson, Edward, *200*

Robinson, Isaiah "Big Ike," 171, *182*

Robinson, Jim, 58, 60, 61, 174, *182*

Rodríguez, Rodolfo, 157

Rodríguez, Simón, 15

Rogers, A. J., 237

Rogers, Hattie, 212

Rojas, Mariano, 146

Rojas, Rafael, 141

Romero, Matías, 139

Romero, Roger, 329n1

The Roots of Music (music school), 274

Rosas, Juventinos, 122, 149

Rose, Al, 164

Rosen, Hannah, 85

Rosenberg, Daniel, 108, 239–40, 261

Rosomoff, Richard Nicholas, 176

Rosseau, Joseph, 27

Roudanez, Louis Charles, 45, 49

Rousseau, Joseph Colastin, 38, 42

Ruffin, Edmund, 178
Russell, Luis, 250
Russell, William (Bill), 9, 19
Russell, William Howard, 179

Saint-Domingue. *See* Haiti
Saintonge, Edmond: *Prélude Méringue*, 66
Saint-Rémy, Joseph: *Pétion et Haïti*, 50
Sakakeeny, Matt, 7, 67, 159, 274
Salaam, Kalamu ya, 2, 176
Salvaggio, Ruth, 109
Sánchez, Cheché, 168
Sanctified Church, 24, 25, 206–7, 269. *See also* Baptist churches; Black churches
Sandke, Randall, 19
San Lorenzo de los Negros, 130–31
Santa Anna, Antonio López de, 126, 132, 141
Santacilia y Palacios, Pedro, 141, 309n137
Santaman, Teofilo, 137
Santiago de Cuba, 10, 102, 105, 107, 142, 153, 176, 191
Savary, Joseph, 126
Saville, Julie, 226
Sayles, Emanuel, 59, 61, 244
Scarry, Elaine, 280
Schwartz, Radam, *114*
Scott, Julius, 13
Scott, Rebecca J., 6, 7, 38, 41, 48, 295n194
Scott-Heron, Gil, 1, 196–97
sea shanties, 253
second-lining, 69–70, 109, 153–54, 237, 270
seis music, 153, 154
Séjour, Victor, 12, *140*; "Le Mulâtre" (The Mulatto), 12
self-rent, 16
Sentmanat y Zayas, Francisco de, 132
Separate Car Act (Louisiana, 1890), 35–36, 289n6
sex work and sexuality, 84–85, 86–87, 88–91, 92, 94–97, *96*, 98–99, 108–13; blues and, 83, 86–88, 97, 113, 116; community among sex workers, 90–91; Creoles of color and sex work, 98–99; enslaved people and, 84–85; "Mamie's Blues" and, 30, 83–84, 85, 87–90, 91, 96, 98, 113; musical critiques, 99–100, 101–3, 107–8, 109, 111, 113, 115; Quadroon balls, 108, 109; resistance by sex workers, 94–97, *96*; sex trafficking, 88–89; sex work in New Orleans (Storyville), 85, 92, 108–9
Shaik, Fatima, 52–53
Sheller, Mimi, 111, 190
Shorter, John, 223
Shugg, Roger, 203
Simeon, Omar, 137
Simpson, James, 183
Sinclair, George, 248
Singleton, Zutty, 58, 301n98
slavery. *See* enslaved peoples
Slidell, John, 250
Smith, Adeline, 94
Smith, Bessie, 86; "Young Woman's Blues," 88
Smith, Charles Edward, 89
Smith, Haskin and Ellen, 228–29
Smith, Jeff, 75
Smith, Laura Alexander, 253
Smith, Willie "The Lion," 286n76
"Sobre las Olas" (song), 122, 149
social aid and pleasure clubs (SAPCs), 208
socialism, agrarian, 76–77
Somers, Robert, 201
son jarocho, 131–32, 307n82
"Sonnambula" (song), 155
Sonthonax, Léger-Félicité, 108
Soriano, Christina, 15
Soulouque, Faustin-Élie, 42–43
Sousa, John Philip, 72, 77
Southwestern Christian Advocate (newspaper), 23, 51, 53
"Spanish Fandango" (song), 134
St. Cyr, Johnny, 49, 67, 270, 292n95, 294n140
Stewart, Anthony, 221
Stewart, Jack, 148, 162
St. Joseph Colored Society, 54, 255
St. Landry Democrat (newspaper), 256
"St. Louis Blues" (song), 67
stomps, 190–91
Storyville (New Orleans), 83, 85, 86–87, 89, 90–91, 91–93, 94–97, 108–9, 115–16
Straight University, 51, 54, 209
Straker, Daniel A., 30, 121, 138
Stubbs, W. C., 252
Sublette, Ned, 57, 142

sugar, 8, 11, 179–81, *182*, 184–86, 194, 198, 199, 201–3, *204*, 315n56. *See also* plantations
Sutherland, George, 228
Sutton, Katie, 183
Swann, E. S., 244, 258, 261
swing, 35, 37–38, 56–57, 58–62, 293n135. *See also* jazz

Tabb, Derrick, 274
Tadman, Michael, 180
Taibo, Paco Ignacio, II, 121
taverns, 16–17
Taylor, Elliot, 137
Teague, Jessica, 283n7
Tennant, Edward "Ned," 228
Terez, Alex, 234
Thibodaux Massacre (1887), 120–21, 201, 208
Thierry, Camille: "Lament of an Aged Mulatta," 107–8, 303n156
Thiong'o, Ngũgĩ wa, 35
Thomas, Henry G., 214–15
Thomas, Walter "Foots," 100, 295n194
Thompson, Robert, 184
time, 187–88, 242–47
Times Democrat (newspaper), 119
Times Picayune (newspaper), 250, 257, 263, 268. See also *Daily Picayune*; *New Orleans Picayune*
Timitoc Borrero, Dalia, 191
Tinchant, Édouard, 29, 41, 46–47, 49, 142, 209
Tinchant, Joseph (José), 142, 143–44
Tio family: about, 32, 135–36, 138; cigar industry and, 138, 144; influence of, 137, 160–61; political evolution, 305n52; in Veracruz and Tampico, 136, 138, 144–45, 149, 158
Tio, Antoinette, 144
Tio, Joseph, 127, 305n52
Tio, Lorenzo, Jr., 137, 149, 162–64, *165*, 166, 312n254, 313n261; "Bouncing Around," 150, 151, *151*, *153*; "Dreamy Blues," 164, 313n264; "Red Man Blues," 163, *165*
Tio, Lorenzo, Sr.: about, 122, 126; and AfBro-Creole and Black musicians, 30, 159–60, 161–62; civil rights activism and, 54; *Crusader* newspaper and, 50; death,
167; desire to return to Mexico, 167; in Excelsior Band, 28, 93, 235, 257; *habanera* influences on, 65–66; influence of, 137, 160–61; Mexican background, 145; mobile commoning and, 193; at New Orleans Cotton Exposition, 118, 121; "Sonnambula," 155; "Trocha: A Cuban Dance," 151
Tio, Louis: about, 122, 126; and Afro-Creole and Black musicians, 30, 159–60, 161–62; birth and Mexican background, 8, 144–45, 149; in Excelsior Band, 28, 93, 235, 257; influence of, 137, 160–61; mobile commoning and, 193; at New Orleans Cotton Exposition, 118, 121
Tio, Louis Marcos, 127, 144
Tio, Louis R., 136, 158, 164, 167
Tio, Thomas, 137, 308n116
Tobin, Jacqueline L., 184
Tregle, Joseph G., Jr., 21
Trejo, Ignacio, 134
tresillo. *See* cinquillo complex
"Trocha: A Cuban Dance" (song), 145, 149, 151, *152*
Trouillot, Michel-Rolph, 19
Tucker, Sherrie, 7, 92, 270
tumba francesa, 65, 102–3, 105–6, 107, *112*
Turner, Henry M., 30, 93, 121
Turner, Josiah, 227
Turner, Richard Brent, 70
Turner, Wallace, 187
Tuxedo Band, 163
Twain, Mark, 203
Tyres, William: "Trocha: A Cuban Dance," 145, 149, 151, *152*

union halls, 260–62, 264, 265–66. *See also* mutual aid associations
Union Leagues, 226–27
unions, 248. *See also* dockworkers
Union Sons Relief Association (Union Sons Hall), 265–66
United Fruit Company, 250

Vanegas Arroyo, Antonio, 134, 147
Vasconcelos, José, 168
Venet Danger, Gaudiosa, 105

Veracruz, 105, 130–35, 136–38, 139–40, 142, 146–47, 167, 192, 307n90. *See also* Mexican borderlands
Vernhettes, Dan, 74
Vézina, Caroline, 28
Vigne, Ratty Jean, 95
Vincent, Theodore, 127
violence. *See* racism and violence
Vodou, 23, 40, 43, 65
Vodou Jazz movement, 276
voting, 230–31

Wagner, Bryan, 90, 283n7, 300n85
Wald, Elijah, 82
Walker, Clementine, 49–50, 83, 88, 113
Walker, William, 223–24
Warmoth, Henry Clay, 44–45, 51, 173, 198, 199, 208
Warnecke, Louis, 165
Washburne, Christopher, 67, 99, 124
Washington, Grover, Jr., 160
Washington, Salim, 205, 276, 288n118
watermelon, 187–88, 316n115
Waters, Ethel: "No Man's Mamma Now," 88
Watkins, Mel, 161
Watt, Sumpter J., 257
Weekly Louisianian (newspaper), 256
Weekly Pelican (newspaper), 121, 235, 257
Wegmann, Andrew, 292n87
Weir, Stan, 239
Wells, Ida B., 119
"West Indian Blues" ("I'm Going Home to Jamaica," song), 252
Wever, Jerry, 64
whalers, 253

White, Lulu: "Mahogany Hall," 108–9
White, Michael G., 70
white, pass as (jumping the fence), 47
White League, 52, 227, 234, 235
Whiteman, Paul, 72, 77
white supremacy. *See* racism and violence
Wilkerson, Norice, 219
Williams, Catherine, 212
Williams, Clarence, 94
Williams, Henry, 93
Williams, John Albert, 78
Williams, Mary Lou: "Messa Stomp," 191
Wilson, Olly, 68
Wilson, Woodrow, 73
Winfield, Arthur Anison, Jr., 187
Winters, Lisa Ze, 98
women. *See* Black women; Desdunes, Mamie; sex work and sexuality
Woodland, Thomas P., 248–49, 254
Woodland Band, 200
Woods, Clyde, 7, 63, 116, 134, 262, 267, 268, 292n101
Woodward, C. Vann, 248
World Saxophone Quartet, 237
Wyatt, Bayley, 192
Wynter, Sylvia, 177

Yanga, Gaspar, 130–31, 139–40
Yaqui people, 119–20
Young, Lester, 280
Ysaguirre, Bob, 165

"Zacamandú" (dance), 131
Zeno, Alice, 9, *10*, 13, 19–20, 30, 38, 43, 170, 284n34

MUSIC / CULTURE

A series from Wesleyan University Press
Edited by Deborah Wong, Sherrie Tucker, and Jeremy Wallach

The Music/Culture series has consistently reshaped and redirected music scholarship. Founded in 1993 by George Lipsitz, Susan McClary, and Robert Walser, the series features outstanding critical work on music. Unconstrained by disciplinary divides, the series addresses music and power through a range of times, places, and approaches. Music/Culture strives to integrate a variety of approaches to the study of music, linking analysis of musical significance to larger issues of power—what is permitted and forbidden, who is included and excluded, who speaks and who gets silenced. From ethnographic classics to cutting-edge studies, Music/Culture zeroes in on how musicians articulate social needs, conflicts, coalitions, and hope. Books in the series investigate the cultural work of music in urgent and sometimes experimental ways, from the radical fringe to the quotidian. Music/Culture asks deep and broad questions about music through the framework of the most restless and rigorous critical theory.

MUSIC/CULTURE FALL 2024

Benjamin Barson
Brassroots Democracy: Maroon Ecologies and the Jazz Commons

Donna Lee Kwon
Stepping in the Madang: Sustaining Expressive Ecologies of Korean Drumming and Dance

Sumarsam
The In-Between in Javanese Performing Arts: History and Myth, Interculturalism and Interreligiosity

A COMPLETE LIST OF SERIES TITLES CAN BE FOUND AT
https://www.weslpress.org/search-results/?series=music-culture

ABOUT THE AUTHOR

Ben Barson's work lives at the intersection of academic, activist, and performing arts worlds. He is a historian and musicologist whose writing explores the sounding of social movements in jazz and Black Atlantic music. He received his PhD from the University of Pittsburgh in 2020, where his dissertation focused on the intersection of early jazz and antiracist social movements in the nineteenth-century Caribbean basin. His research on the Black Power solidarity activism of Asian American jazz musicians has been published in the edited volume *Black Power Afterlives: The Enduring Significance of the Black Panther Party* (2020). He also has contributed pieces to the *Routledge Handbook on Jazz and Gender* and the *Routledge Guide to Ecosocialism*.

In addition to his work as a scholar, Barson is an ASCAP award-winning composer and baritone saxophonist. He has been acknowledged as a "Pittsburgh arts innovator" by the *Pittsburgh Post-Gazette*, and his work has been called "utterly compelling" (*I Care if You Listen*), "fully orchestrated and magnificently realized" (*Vermont Standard*), and "pushing boundaries in a well-conceived way." (*Midwest Review*).